Pro BizTalk 2009

■ ■ ■

George Dunphy, Sergei Moukhnitski,
Stephen Kaufman, Peter Kelcey,
Harold Campos, David Peterson

Apress®

Pro BizTalk 2009

ISBN-13 (pbk): 978-1-4302-1981-1

ISBN-13 (electronic): 978-1-4302-1982-8

Printed and bound in the United States of America 9 8 7 6 5 4 3 2 1

Lead Editor: Jonathan Gennick
Technical Reviewer: Richard Seroter
Editorial Board: Clay Andres, Steve Anglin, Mark Beckner, Ewan Buckingham, Tony Campbell, Gary Cornell, Jonathan Gennick, Jonathan Hassell, Michelle Lowman, Matthew Moodie, Jeffrey Pepper, Frank Pohlmann, Douglas Pundick, Ben Renow-Clarke, Dominic Shakeshaft, Matt Wade, Tom Welsh
Project Managers: Sofia Marchant, Kylie Johnston
Copy Editor: Kim Wimpsett
Associate Production Director: Kari Brooks-Copony
Production Editor: Kelly Gunther
Compositor: Linda Weidemann, Wolf Creek Publishing Services
Proofreader: Nancy Sixsmith
Indexer: John Collin
Artist: April Milne
Cover Designer: Anna Ishchenko
Manufacturing Director: Tom Debolski

Distributed to the book trade worldwide by Springer-Verlag New York, Inc., 233 Spring Street, 6th Floor, New York, NY 10013. Phone 1-800-SPRINGER, fax 201-348-4505, e-mail orders-ny@springer-sbm.com, or visit http://www.springeronline.com.

For information on translations, please contact Apress directly at 233 Spring Street, New York, NY 10013. E-mail info@apress.com, or visit http://www.apress.com.

Apress and friends of ED books may be purchased in bulk for academic, corporate, or promotional use. eBook versions and licenses are also available for most titles. For more information, reference our Special Bulk Sales–eBook Licensing web page at http://www.apress.com/info/bulksales.

The source code for this book is available to readers at http://www.apress.com.

To my daughter, Gillian—thank you for brightening each day with your smile and laughter. To my son, Bennett—congratulations on your new job as a Big Brother and for making us feel so young. And for my wife, Keressa—my eternal gratitude for your love and support after all these years.
—George Dunphy

To my family: Elena, Boris, Alex, and Julia.
—Sergei Moukhnitski

This book is dedicated to my family.
—Stephen Kaufman

To my wife, Susy: For the love and support you have given me as well as for your patience putting up with all of my long nights stuck behind a computer screen.
To my daughter, Isabella: You arrived three weeks later than we expected, which gave me time to finish my work on this book. May your timing continue to be that perfect through the rest of your life.
To my mom: For all those school assignments and reports where you served as editor and proofreader for a very stubborn author.
—Peter Kelcey

To my parents, Amelia Urquiza and Benjamin Campos, and to my siblings, Daniel Campos and Annia Campos, for their love and eternal support.
To my lovely wife and daughter, Claudia Luz and Valeria Valentina, for being the light that shines my life and that makes my heart dance the most beautiful music.
—Harold Campos

Contents at a Glance

Contents

About the Authors

GEORGE DUNPHY is an architect with Microsoft Consulting Services' World Wide Technical Quality Assurance. He has 14 years of experience and focuses on technologies such as the Microsoft .NET Framework, BizTalk Server, Visual Basic and Visual Basic .NET, Active Server Pages, COM, SQL Server, XML, SOAP and WSDL, T-SQL, and web development. In addition to his technical skills, George focuses on managing development teams for large enterprise application development projects. He works with a variety of customers ranging from governments to Fortune 100 companies to start-ups. He lives in Ottawa, Canada, with his wife, Keressa, and their two children.

SERGEI MOUKHNITSKI is a senior software architect with Sanoraya Consulting in Ottawa, Canada. He has 14 years of experience developing software and systems. Currently, Sergei is consulting and managing outsourcing projects.

His area of professional interest is Microsoft business process and integration technologies. His Microsoft certifications include MCAD.NET and MCSD.NET. Sergei has a master's degree from the State Technical University in St. Petersburg, Russia.

STEPHEN KAUFMAN is a delivery architect with Microsoft Consulting Services focusing on middle-tier technologies and has worked with BizTalk since the original BizTalk CTP in 1999. In addition, he is an author, trainer, and speaker. He has written Microsoft Knowledge Base articles, a BizTalk tools white paper, and a number of other articles. He was a contributing author for the BizTalk Certification Exam 74-135. He also writes a blog focused on integration technologies at http://blogs.msdn.com/skaufman. Stephen has also spoken both nationally and internationally at events such as TechEd North America, TechEd EMEA, Microsoft's SOA & BPM Conference, Microsoft's Developer Days, and a number of other conferences and events.

■**PETER KELCEY** is a senior technology specialist with Microsoft Canada who focuses on architectures and technologies related to connected systems and integration. He focuses on concepts such as service-oriented architecture, Enterprise Service Bus, enterprise application integration, business-to-business integration, business process management, modeling, and RFID.

Within his current role, he is responsible for technical presales activities across Microsoft's enterprise clients located in central and eastern Canada. An early adopter of Microsoft's Enterprise Service Bus Toolkit, he developed Microsoft's first ESB "training in a box" course as part of his activities to drive developer readiness for this new technology.

Prior to his current role, he spent more than a decade in the IT consulting world where he architected, developed, and delivered enterprise applications for large organizations across Canada while working for TELUS Business Solutions.

An experienced presenter, Peter has spoken at a wide range of conferences, events, and seminars including Microsoft's SOA Conference, Microsoft's TechReady Conference, Canadian Strategic Architecture Forum, Canadian Financial Architects Summit, and the Aspiring Architect's Webcast Series.

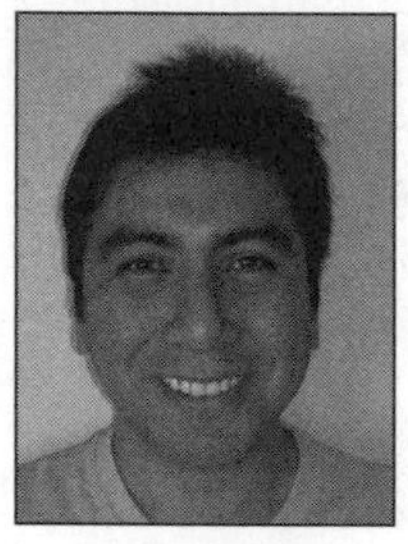

■**HAROLD VALENTIN CAMPOS URQUIZA** is a consultant with Microsoft Consulting Services specializing in SOA, legacy integration, collaboration, and e-commerce. He has more than ten years of experience in IT business around the world. He has managed, architected, and developed solutions in the government, defense, banking, energy, telecommunications, retail, mining, and health-care sectors.

Harold has a bachelor's degree in systems engineering at the prestigious National University of Engineering in Lima, Peru, where he was ranked second in his class. He is also a Microsoft Certified Solutions Developer and Microsoft Certified Technology Specialist in BizTalk and SharePoint technologies.

Currently, Harold lives in Toronto, Canada, spending most of his time working in legacy integration and collaboration solutions for Canadian customers. You can reach him at Harold_campos@hotmail.com.

■**DAVID PETERSON** is a solution architect with Microsoft Consulting Services specializing in enterprise application architecture and development. He has 18 years of experience in software development with both Microsoft and a large Canadian retail organization and has extensive experience is architecting, building, and deploying enterprise-scale applications in mission-critical environments. David is a Microsoft Certificated Solution Developer focusing on technologies such as Microsoft .NET Framework, Commerce Server, SQL Server, Visual C#, Visual Basic, Windows Communication Foundation, Windows Workflow, Smart Client, and ASP.NET web development.

About the Technical Reviewer

RICHARD SEROTER is a solutions architect for an industry-leading biotechnology company, a Microsoft MVP for BizTalk Server, and a Microsoft Connected Technology Advisor. He has spent the majority of his career consulting with customers as they planned and implemented their enterprise software solutions. Richard worked first for two global IT consulting firms, which gave him exposure to a diverse range of industries, technologies, and business challenges. Richard then joined Microsoft as a SOA/BPM technology specialist where his sole objective was to educate and collaborate with customers as they considered, designed, and architected BizTalk solutions. One of those customers liked him enough to bring him onboard full-time as an architect after they committed to using BizTalk Server as their Enterprise Service Bus. Once the BizTalk environment was successfully established, Richard transitioned into a solutions architect role where he now helps identify enterprise best practices and applies good architectural principles to a wide set of IT initiatives.

Richard is the author of the recently released *SOA Patterns for BizTalk Server 2009* book, which covers how to apply good SOA principles to a wide variety of BizTalk scenarios.

Richard maintains a semipopular blog of his exploits, pitfalls, and musings with BizTalk Server and enterprise architecture at http://seroter.wordpress.com.

Acknowledgments

First I have to thank the entire integration community at Microsoft. You are all really a world-class group of individuals, and it has been my pleasure to work with all of you during my career at Microsoft. I also have to thank the other authors in this book, without whom this book would not be possible. They have gone above and beyond what I asked of them, and they each gave this project 110%. I would really like to thank Richard Seroter for agreeing to be our tech reviewer. Richard is absolutely a gem for anything BizTalk related and has helped us so much in the creation of this revision of the book. I would also like to thank Jonathon Gennick at Apress for again being our editor and helping us navigate through the many issues both big and small that we came across while writing this book. Lastly, I have to thank Sergei for all his hard work and dedication to this project. You have made this project a success with your honesty and work ethic.

George Dunphy

I want to thank Richard Seroter, technical reviewer of the book. Richard's expertise, advice, and comments have greatly improved the quality of the book. Richard, thanks!

I also would like to thank the entire Apress team: Jonathan Gennick, Kylie Johnston, Sofia Marchant, and Kelly Gunther. Special thanks to Kim Wimpsett for her tireless copyediting of my work and attention to detail. Kim, I thank you.

Sergei Moukhnitski

Introduction

A Tale of Two Products

In the beginning, when BizTalk was still in its infancy, there were two teams within Microsoft: the Commerce Server Team and the COM+ team. The Commerce Server Team was implementing technology it called Commerce Server Messaging Pipelines, which was essentially software that allowed applications to move messages from one system to another system using the commerce server framework. The goal was to abstract away the sending and receiving of messages from the transports that they used. For example, using this framework, a developer would not care about the physical implementation of how the messages were sent; that information would be abstracted away into another construct called a *port*. The port would talk to an adapter that handled the communication to and from the medium in question, whether it was a file system, an FTP server, or a web server.

At the same time, the COM+ team was implementing a new graphical workflow representation system they called XLang. XLang schedules, as they were called, would compile down to a binary format and run within the XLang engine inside COM+. Each schedule would be *drawn*, not coded, to model a business process that the developer was trying to automate. This schedule could also access existing components that were present within the organization, assuming they used the principles of *n*-tiered architecture and had implemented a well-defined business object library.

The rumor was that when Bill Gates saw these two technologies, he immediately sought to find a way to combine them. His vision was to allow the developer to graphically draw a workflow that modeled a business process and allow the information needed by that process to be received and sent freely within or outside an organization. He envisioned a "next-generation programming language" type of tool that allowed even the most nonprogrammer type to model a business process, interact with already defined business objects, and send and receive messages without having to worry about the details of how to physically implement this transport. With that, BizTalk 2000 was born.

The Platform Today

BizTalk Server has progressed into a world-class application platform capable of supporting the most complicated business requirements and scenarios. BizTalk can do this while providing a rich development experience and allowing for the rapid development of solutions at a much faster pace than was capable even a few years ago.

In its early versions, the tool was powerful but not complete. The first two editions of BizTalk laid the groundwork for implementing real business process automation within many organizations, but it lacked the robustness of a real development environment, proper administration tools, an application release management service, and several other features.

This book is targeted toward the architect. This is the person who, at the end of the day, wears either the success or failure of any software project. My hope is that this book will give that person the tools and know-how to successfully implement a BizTalk solution and feel comfortable that they have designed the best application possible.

Downloading the Code

The source code for this book is available to readers on the book's page at www.apress.com. Please feel free to visit the Apress web site and download all the code there. You can also check for errata and find related titles from Apress.

George Dunphy

PART 1

Readme.1st

The first two chapters of this book are designed to help architects and team leaders perform the most important tasks of any BizTalk project starting in its infancy. In these chapters, we cover the following:

- What BizTalk is and is not designed for
- An overview of BizTalk Server's key features
- Where BizTalk fits in to the Microsoft Application Platform stack
- BizTalk versus service-oriented architectures
- Resource and estimated budget requirements
- Example BizTalk Server configurations
- Answers to the most common questions concerning implementing BizTalk in a new project scenario

CHAPTER 1

BizTalk in the Enterprise

The BizTalk Server 2009 product is a group of application services that facilitate the rapid creation of integration solutions. BizTalk Server is designed specifically to integrate disparate systems in a loosely coupled way. BizTalk Server is a toolkit, and within this toolkit you will find tools to help you build your application. The trick, like the wise Scottish man said, is "using the right tool for the right job."

The art of creating a BizTalk solution is exactly that—using the right tool from the BizTalk toolkit to accomplish the task at hand. If you were to look at two BizTalk projects that address identical problems, designed by two architects, you would most likely see two completely different-looking solutions. Both solutions would probably work; however, generally one solution would be more correct because it would properly use BizTalk's tools as they were intended. This book will attempt to address how to properly use each of the tools within BizTalk in the manner in which they were intended. The other thing the book will do is show how each of the tools can be used to solve integration problems in an efficient way. In reality, though, most of the features within BizTalk are flexible enough that you can generally solve most problems using only one piece of the BizTalk puzzle.

Since BizTalk allows you to address a problem in dozens of different ways, there is no one answer as to how to implement a BizTalk solution. To help address this issue of how best to implement a given solution, Microsoft has released several enterprise application guidelines[1] for BizTalk 2009 that should alleviate some of this confusion; however, this problem will never go away. This book will build upon those patterns as well as provide some advanced concepts, examples, and patterns to allow software architects to properly build complex solutions using BizTalk Server.

What Is in the Toolkit

Inside BizTalk Server, you will find several tools, each of which addresses a specific type of problem. Before learning about those tools, it is important to know what the architecture is for a "typical" BizTalk solution. Figure 1-1 illustrates the typical architecture for a BizTalk-based solution.

1 See http://msdn.microsoft.com/en-ca/biztalk/default.aspx for more information.

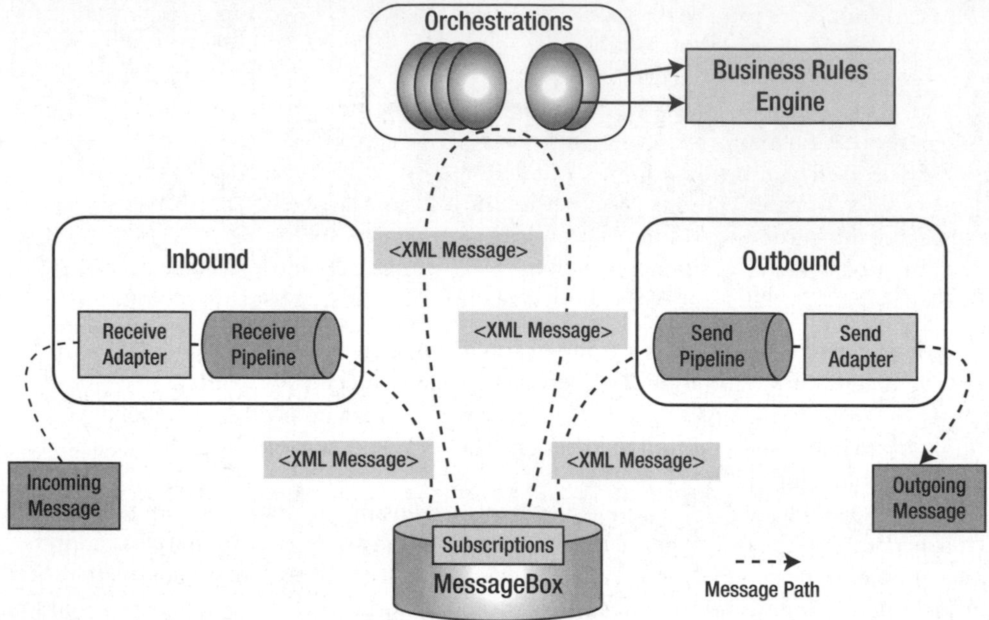

Figure 1-1. *Typical BizTalk scenario*

At its most basic, BizTalk is designed to receive inbound messages, pass them through some form of logical processing, and then deliver the result of that processing to an outbound location or subsystem. The art of architecting a BizTalk project begins with how to solve these three simple yet all-important tasks. Most of the tools in the following list are dissected throughout various sections of the book, but a simple explanation of each is provided after the list:

- Ports and adapters
- Business Activity Monitoring (BAM) Services
- Pipelines
- Pipeline components
- Orchestrations
- Schemas and transformations
- Messaging Engine
- Business Rule Engine
- EDI Services
- Radio Frequency ID (RFID) Services
- Enterprise Service Bus (ESB)
- Host Integration Server (HIS) for legacy application connectivity

Ports and **adapters** provide the logical abstraction for sending and receiving messages to and from BizTalk. They allow you to code your application in a generic fashion and not worry about the implementation details of how these messages will be consumed and delivered. A **port** is a logical construct that can receive and send messages to/from the BizTalk Messagebox. The port must be married to a specific receive location to accept the message. The receive location then is tied to a specific **adapter**, which provides the details of how the message will be transported. These two constructs along with the BizTalk Messagebox provide the basis for the messaging infrastructure within the product.

BizTalk provides several adapters out of the box including those for FTP, file access, SOAP, HTTP, SMTP, POP3, MSMQ, and MQSeries, all examples of transport-specific adapters. Transport adapters are usually tied to a specific wire protocol, providing the means by which to send the message. BizTalk also includes application adapters, which are used to integrate with specific third-party products such as Oracle's Database Server and Enterprise Resource Planning (ERP) packages like SAP and PeopleSoft. You can find the complete list of transport and application adapters included within BizTalk at www.microsoft.com/biztalk. Additional adapters can be purchased from third-party vendors or custom developed within Visual Studio 2008 using the BizTalk Adapter Framework and the WCF Adapter Framework. A chapter within this book is dedicated to creating custom adapters using the WCF Adapter Framework.

Business Activity Monitoring (BAM) provides the infrastructure to perform application instrumentation and metric reporting. BAM provides the ability to instrument your application to provide business-level data that is much more relevant than the default system-level information that is available in the base product. Examples of this would be

- How many purchase orders were processed?
- How many transactions failed last week? Last month?
- What was the total volume of messages received from a supplier?

Pipelines provide a way to examine, verify, and potentially modify messages as they are received from and sent to BizTalk. They allow you to deconstruct messages that contain multiple documents and/or header information into a format that is more logical to the application or business user. Pipelines are applied to ports and are either a **send pipeline** or a **receive pipeline** depending on the directional flow of the message. Pipelines provide the necessary infrastructure for pipeline components (which we'll discuss in more detail a little later) or components that are executed within the various stages of a pipeline. Pipelines and pipeline components are unique constructs that exist only within the context of a BizTalk solution and as such are generally unique to solutions that use BizTalk. Pipelines and pipeline components are created within the Visual Studio development environment using C# or VB .NET.

Pipelines function according to the concept of **assembly and disassembly**. Pipelines, which can assemble or disassemble, contain pipeline components, which are responsible for preparing the message to be sent. These components convert the internal BizTalk XML message to the appropriate XML or non-XML outbound format of the message, based on the type of assembler and properties set in the schema. For example, the assembling component of the pipeline may dictate that the message is to be sent in a flat-file text format and not XML format. BizTalk ships with default assemblers that allow you to assemble XML or flat-file messages by default with the option of writing custom assembling components. In addition, pipelines that contain assembling components assemble and wrap the message in an envelope or add a header or trailer (or both) to the message. During assembly, some properties are moved from the message context to the body of the document or to the envelope. The message context is the internal BizTalk representation of the metadata about the message such as the inbound transport type, the message type, and any special properties to be included that describe the message.

The opposite of assembling components are disassembling components, which execute on the receiving side of a message flow. Disassembling components prepare a message to be broken down into separate message documents according to the envelope and document schemas defined within BizTalk. Like assembling components, disassembling components may convert non-XML messages into their XML representation, to be processed by BizTalk. The message is then disassembled into individual messages that can be consumed by separate orchestrations or send ports. The message is disassembled by stripping the envelope information, breaking the message up into individual documents, and then copying envelope or message body property information to the individual message **contexts**. The message context is metadata about the message that is tied to the message data when it is processed by BizTalk. Exactly which properties are copied to the context is determined by the schema of the document and what properties it has defined for **promotion**, a term used to describe the way BizTalk copies properties from the message body to the message context.

Pipelines have various **stages** in which components can be executed. Stages are much like events in that they have a set order in which they execute and can be used to ensure that pipeline component logic executes in the correct order. Each stage can potentially execute more than one pipeline component depending on where it is located. This is explored in detail in Chapter 4. The pipeline is coded within the Visual Studio 2008 environment, as shown in Figure 1-2. The stages for the two types of pipeline are as follows:

- Send pipeline stages:
  - Pre-Assemble
  - Assemble
  - Encode
- Receive pipeline stages:
  - Decode
  - Disassemble
  - Validate
  - Resolve Party

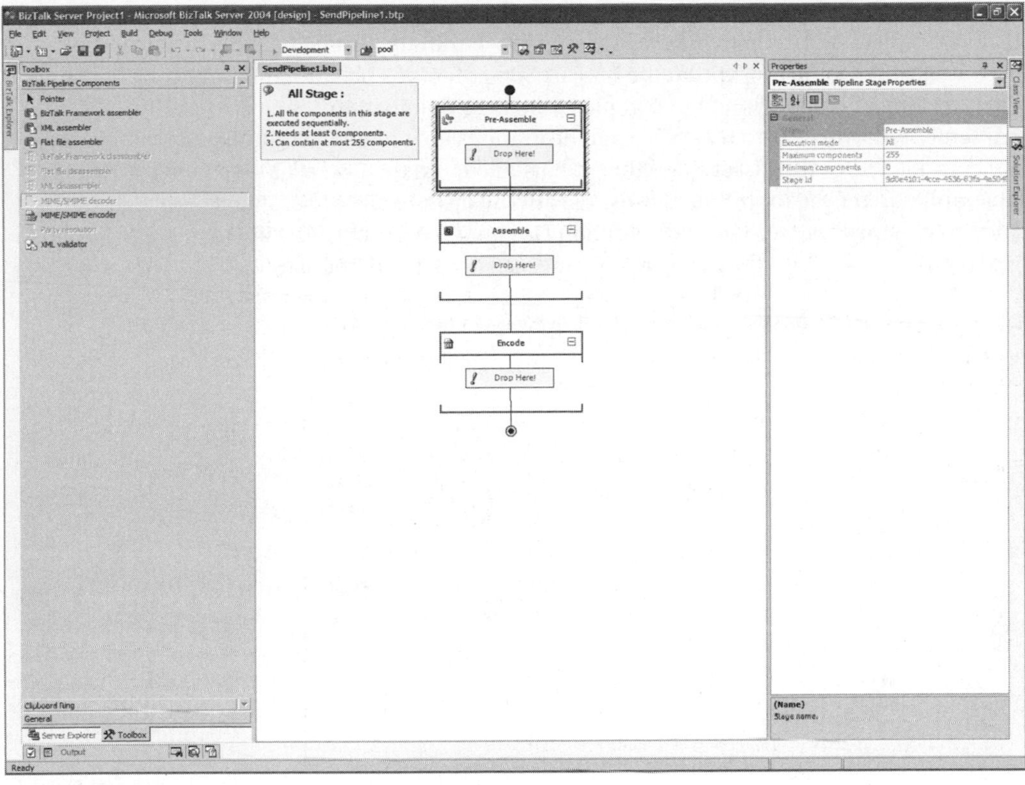

Figure 1-2. *BizTalk Send Pipeline Designer*

Pipeline components are classes that are executed within the various stages of a BizTalk server pipeline. Custom pipeline components implement a specific set of application interfaces required by the BizTalk framework. Several default pipeline components are shipped with the product that provide standard functionality that most pipelines require, examples of which are as follows:

- **Disassemblers and assemblers**: Components that allow a pipeline to examine an inbound document and separate it into logical parts, or likewise take several separate documents and assemble them into one document. In most projects, the inbound or outbound document is a container or an **envelope** document that may contain several other distinct but related document types, each with its own schema.

- **Validators**: These allow for the pipeline to validate the document according to a default specification. The default validators allow the pipeline to verify that the document is valid XML. Custom validators can be written to perform solution-specific validation.

- **Encoders and decoders**: As the name suggests, these allow the pipeline to either decode an inbound message or encode an outbound message. The default BizTalk components allow you to encode or decode S/MIME messages. Most custom encoder/decoder components perform either custom security routines or specialized cryptographic operations. (See Chapter 5 for a pipeline component implementation that performs cryptographic operations.)

Orchestrations are used to graphically model workflow and provide the primary mechanism to implement business process automation within the product. Orchestrations are by far the most powerful tool within the BizTalk Server toolbox because they allow for the rapid development and deployment of complex processes that in many circumstances can be implemented with little to no coding. Orchestrations are created within Visual Studio and are compiled into .NET assemblies that are installed into the BizTalk Management Database. Assemblies deployed to this database must also be installed into the Global Assembly Cache and have a strong name. The Orchestration Designer is a primarily visual tool. It allows you to graphically see the workflow you are creating, as Figure 1-3 demonstrates.

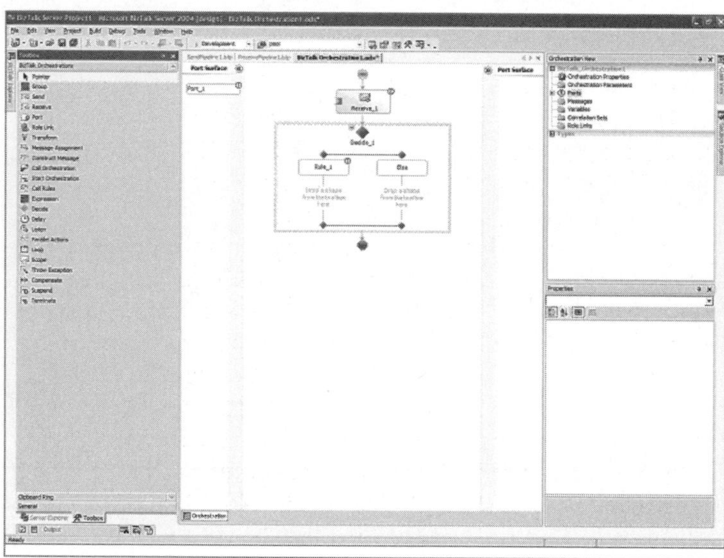

Figure 1-3. *BizTalk Orchestration Designer*

Transformations allow the application to map one message specification to another and transform data as it is processed. BizTalk messages are XML documents within the system, and as such, transformations are created from Extensible Stylesheet Language (XSL) stylesheets. Transformations in BizTalk 2004 used the Microsoft XML Document Object Model (XML DOM) as their primary transformation engine. Starting in BizTalk 2006, the transformation engine is a custom solution developed by the BizTalk Server team, and this functionality is unchanged in BizTalk 2009. This new transformation engine is designed to increase the performance of transforming complex and especially large messages while preserving fault tolerance. Transforming large messages (greater than 10MB) proved to be problematic in BizTalk 2004 because of issues with out-of-memory conditions that occurred within the transformation engine, which was the main reason for this feature's redesign.

Transformations can be applied in two places within a BizTalk solution—on a port when a message is sent or received and from within an orchestration. Each design pattern has its own pros and cons, which are discussed later in Chapter 6.

The **Messaging Engine** is the heart of BizTalk. The engine is responsible for ensuring that messages are received and routed to the proper location, that transaction isolation and consistency occur, and that errors are reported. In reality, the Messaging Engine is the "Server" component of BizTalk Server. The Messaging Engine uses several BizTalk databases to store message information and metadata as well as system-level parameters. The Messaging Engine uses Microsoft SQL Server as its data storage facility. The central database for messages within BizTalk is called the **Messagebox**. SQL Server is not required to be physically installed on the same machine as BizTalk Server, and we recommend it be installed in its own environment for high-transaction and fault-tolerant solutions. A SQL Server license is required for BizTalk and is not included in the price of the product.

Typically, organizations will invest in separate and robust SQL Server development, testing, and production environments. Each BizTalk solution within the organization would use the appropriate SQL Server environment depending on the requirements of the application and its phase of implementation.

The **Business Rule Engine (BRE)** is a facility where business rules can be modeled using a simple GUI and called from within the BizTalk Server environment. The BRE is designed to allow for versioning and modification of implemented business rules without having to change the processes within BizTalk that use them. Most solutions use the BRE to implement things that require frequent updates such as a discount policy percentage or calculations that are updated frequently as a result of legal or government regulations.

The **Enterprise Service Bus Toolkit (ESBT)** is code that has been developed by the Microsoft Patterns & Practices group to enhance the core BizTalk set of tools with traditional ESB functionality. The ESBT has been re-released to specifically support BizTalk 2009 and includes much of the base infrastructure that is necessary to provide dynamic routing, service mediation, endpoint resolution, and other core features of an ESB. The ESBT is covered extensively in Chapter 16.

Host Integration Server (HIS) was a separate product that is now included as part of the core BizTalk solution offering. HIS provides connectivity to legacy mainframe and host-based applications along with a set of data services for interoperating with legacy IDMS, COBOL, and VSAM data sources. For a complete synopsis of HIS, refer to Chapter 15.

Electronic Data Interchange (EDI) Services is a documented and accepted set of standards for exchanging electronic documents between organizations. EDI is traditionally used within legacy applications that have been implemented prior to the XML standard from the W3C. EDI documents are text based in nature and have a variety of document specifications depending on the data to be exchanged and the industry that uses them. BizTalk Server provides mechanisms for parsing these EDI documents into XML and providing interoperability between different EDI document standards. It is important to note that VANs and dial-up connections are not specifically supported in the BizTalk EDI implementation. VAN connectivity is limited to FTP access through the traditional FTP adapter. For more information on BizTalk's EDI features, refer to Chapter 14.

Common Enterprise Usage

Most enterprises are looking for BizTalk to solve a particular problem. In many scenarios, this problem is related to having unrelated and disconnected systems exchange data in a standard, consistent, and reliable way. Often enterprises need to automate and streamline manual or inefficient processes in order to achieve a competitive advantage. Whether you are implementing an integration solution or a workflow automation solution, the tools that BizTalk provides allow an architect to design reliable and robust solutions faster than is often achievable by custom coding a solution from scratch using standard development languages and tools. With this in mind, it is important to understand what BizTalk achieves well and what it does not in order to fully realize any efficiency that a BizTalk solution can bring.

In other scenarios, organizations are using BizTalk orchestrations to connect and route messages to services within SOA environments. Often, the web services within the organization may be managed within different groups or even external parties. In these cases, orchestrations provide an excellent way to expose higher-level business functionality by calling, transforming, and routing messages between decoupled web services.

BizTalk Is Not Dead

Despite the rumors and innuendo, BizTalk is not dead—far from it. BizTalk remains the core of the Microsoft integration product stack. Technologies such as Dublin and Windows Workflow provide many "BizTalk-like" features in the Windows platform, but the core need for BizTalk is still there.

Dublin, WCF, and WF provide the basis for many integration components natively in the .NET platform. Many functionalities such as workflows, transport abstraction, transaction consistency, and so on, that BizTalk provides are now part of the .NET platform—natively. However, and this is a big however, there still is no container to run them in (unless you count IIS 7.0 with your own process).

In much the same way that Windows SharePoint Services (WSS) being made free in Windows did not spell the end of SharePoint, Dublin and WF do not mean that BizTalk is no longer relevant. BizTalk provides the base services to do powerful application integration across disparate systems and even organizations. The features that are available as part of Dublin are meant to be used within a single application. To use them in much the same way as BizTalk would require monumental amounts of application code. OSLO as it is today is focused on the modeling aspects of software development and ensuring that models developed in one tool are usable in another. Code generated with the OSLO modeler can be used as the basis for application development, and eventually model-driven development using OSLO will become a new manner in which developers can code next-generation, feature-rich application integration tools. At this stage, this vision of the platform does not negate the need for the services that BizTalk provides. There are a number of discussions, opinions, talks, and PowerPoint presentations on the subject, and there is no reason to dive into them here. An excellent white paper that Microsoft has published goes into these discussions in detail and is a must-read.[2]

BizTalk Is Not SOA, and SOA Is Not BizTalk

We hear a common complaint among architects that "BizTalk doesn't support SOA." It also takes the form of "BizTalk isn't an SOA engine." To the first point, we usually respond with "That depends on what you mean by SOA," and to the second point we respond with an emphatic "Yes, sir, BizTalk is not an SOA engine."

BizTalk is definitely *not* an SOA engine. It was never designed to be one. SOA is about a software philosophy and a set of governing principles that describe how software should be

2 Additionally, Stephen Thomas' blog on the subject is an excellent read and gives some real-world scenarios for Dublin and BizTalk usages. It is available at www.biztalkgurus.com/blogs/biztalk/archive/2008/11/15/biztalk-vs-dublin-do-not-get-confused.aspx.

built to promote interoperability, open standards, and reuse. BizTalk is a messaging engine—plain and simple. BizTalk can consume services that are exposed via an SOA architecture, but BizTalk is not the be-all and end-all of the SOA stack on the Microsoft platform. There are other tools like the Managed Services Engine[3] that are purpose-built tools designed to promote SOA within organizations.

The Rise and Fall and Rise of SOA

In its infancy, SOA was an idea related to web services. The goal of SOA was basically an extension to traditional software methodologies: promote application reuse inside and outside of application silos. In the beginning, SOA was marketed almost as a "Windows DNA 2.0." Instead of building COM+ objects, we are now building web services to facilitate reuse. The dawn of the web service era brought with it interoperability across platforms that traditionally was unheard of.

As the programming model matured, architects, CIOs and developers alike began to realize that a common set of problems was occurring. These problems manifested in questions like these:

- How do I manage all these services I have built?
- How do I implement security across these services?
- How do I version these things?
- How do I know if my SLAs are being met in terms of response times?
- How do people in my organization find and use these services?

As these questions become more understood, standards, tools, and processes started to emerge to tackle each of these issues. As these matured, the concept of SOA as it is today began to grow as an underlying set of capabilities that a good SOA platform should have.

If you look at the types of issues SOA is trying to address, it is clear to see that BizTalk is not trying to address them by itself. The tools that come within the BizTalk toolkit can address some of these issues and complement other solutions, but it is not the solution alone.

SOA has once again come to the forefront of computing with the advent of cloud computing and distributed data centers. The ability to scale applications seamlessly across datacenters and across the Internet is a revolutionary idea that has real benefits that are easily measured in terms of their economic value to any organization.[4]

BizTalk and the Cloud

Cloud computing is at the forefront of modern SOA architectures. Services within the Windows Azure platform are enabling a vastly different set of architectures than were prevalent even 12 months ago.

BizTalk itself is not part of the cloud in that it doesn't live in the cloud (at least not yet). However, advances such as cloud-based ESBs and BizTalk Cloud services are becoming more

3 www.codeplex.com/servicesengine

4 For a deeper review of using BizTalk within a service-oriented architecture, consider reading Richard Seroter's new book, *SOA Patterns with BizTalk Server 2009* (www.packtpub.com/soa-patternswith-biztalk-server-2009/book).

relevant as cloud computing becomes more mainstream. The BizTalk platform will evolve to support the cloud in much the same way other software will; it will begin to decouple the services that must be hosted "on-site" with those that can be distributed. Recent advances such as Live Mesh and Azure services offer great promise for organizations looking to redistribute computing power to and from the cloud.

New BizTalk Solution Checklist

One of the key decisions that most new BizTalk application architects have to make is whether to use BizTalk or build their solution completely from scratch. The choice can come only from experience and an understanding of what BizTalk does well. The following sections explore some questions that need answering before starting any major BizTalk initiative.

What Are the Team's Current Core Skills? What Skills Will the Team Need to Attain?

BizTalk projects require many skills to varying degrees depending on the size and complexity of the solution being implemented. These skills along with knowledge of the Microsoft Windows Server operating system represent a base of knowledge to start planning a BizTalk development and support team.

.NET Development

BizTalk is designed to be extended in several ways: the most common being through the custom development of .NET code and the second being through the implementation of custom business logic within orchestrations. If your project will require a significant amount of customization and business logic code, it is imperative that your team's core skill set be in .NET development.

Most teams underestimate the amount of custom code that they will need to write. It is extremely rare that a solution will have its entire business logic exclusively written within orchestrations or BizTalk transformations. If custom pipeline or adapter coding is required, a solid understanding of application programming interfaces (APIs) and object inheritance is a necessity.

The native BizTalk APIs are exposed exclusively to Windows applications usually running managed code; however, it is possible to access the BizTalk assemblies using COM but not as efficiently. All samples that are shipped with the product are written in Managed Code.

Windows Communication Foundation

It is amazing to see the strides that a few years has made with web services and transport-level interop. WCF has become the new de facto standard for Service Interop within most SOAs that reside on the Microsoft platform. BizTalk 2009 has included a WCF adapter, which allows BizTalk to send and receive messages from WCF services. Knowledge of WCF has become a new core skill set in today's modern architectures. WCF abstracts much of the wire transport specifics away from the developer in much of same way as a BizTalk adapter does. WCF service development is a much lower-level type of task, and it requires deep .NET development expertise and a good working knowledge of transport protocols such as SOAP, HTTP, and certificates.

Using WCF Exclusively

There has been a new trend in BizTalk architectures over the past year or so to attempt to use WCF exclusively as the adapter of choice for interoperating with external systems. Some architects believe that by choosing WCF as the sole adapter of choice, they can abstract away any dependency the solution may have on the BizTalk Adapter Framework. WCF has a very important place in service automation and modern SOA architectures, but using WCF exclusively as the transport of choice negates much of the value of using BizTalk in the first place. Also, by using WCF, the developer is taking on the responsibility to ensure that much of the base functionality that is exposed by the BizTalk adapter is present in the WCF transport protocol, which almost always isn't the case. Like all things, use WCF as appropriate, and make an educated choice about when to use the native adapter interface and when to use a WCF service interface. Often the benefit of adding another layer of abstraction with WCF is not worth the increased configuration, coding, and administration overhead of simply using a native BizTalk adapter.

XML

People often overlook the fact that BizTalk is built entirely using XML as the data representation mechanism. Everything that passes through BizTalk is represented as an XML document at one point or another. If the solution requires the use of BizTalk schemas, then knowledge of XML Schema Definition (XSD) language and XML document manipulation is a must-have. One of the great features of the product is that it exposes nearly all of its internal data structures and properties and allows you to examine, search, and modify most of the metadata that is stored for a BizTalk artifact, whether it is a message in the system or a system object such as a port. To take advantage of this, however, you must understand how XSD schemas are coded and how to examine and manipulate them using the Microsoft XML Document Object Model.

Windows Management Instrumentation

Windows Management Instrumentation (WMI) is one of the most underused and potentially least understood features of the Windows operating system. WMI is a management technology that allows scripts to monitor and control managed resources throughout the network. Resources include hard drives, file systems, operating system settings, processes, services, shares, registry settings, networking components, event logs, users, and groups. WMI is built into clients with Windows 2000 or newer and can be installed on any other 32-bit Windows client.

Thorough understanding of WMI is not required for a small- to medium-sized BizTalk implementation, but it certainly helps. BizTalk has numerous WMI events that can be subscribed to and monitored to help give detailed information about the overall health of a BizTalk solution. Additionally, custom WMI events can be coded and inserted into your BizTalk application to allow for custom instrumentation code that will be available to most enterprise server monitoring tools such as Microsoft Operations Manager. This is something that is often overlooked. Teams will generally implement instrumentation in the forms of performance logging, text files, debug output, and so on, but this data is rarely available to system administrators who can most benefit from it. Implementing custom application instrumentation using WMI can help facilitate transitions for an application into a production environment scenario.

Microsoft Systems Center Operations Manager (SCOM) is Microsoft's enterprise system management tool and is able to listen to WMI events. SCOM can be used to notify administrators in the case of a system failure and provide information about the overall health of a system. BizTalk 2009 has a management pack for SCOM that is used for this purpose. Additionally, custom management packs can be created to provide additional counters and information to SCOM.

SQL Server

BizTalk uses Microsoft SQL Server as its primary data storage mechanism. SQL Server provides BizTalk with the ability to cluster database installations to achieve fault tolerance and high availability, as well as providing a supported and reliable way to ensure transaction stability and overall performance.

Deep SQL Server knowledge is not required for low-volume application designs; however, for systems that will have large volumes of messages being processed (in the order of greater than 20 messages per second), SQL Server knowledge on the team is a definite must-have. In high-volume scenarios, it becomes increasingly important to understand how to properly distribute the BizTalk Server databases to achieve maximum performance as well as maintain reliability and scalability options. SQL Server also includes several performance-tuning tools such as SQL Profiler, Tracing, and the SQL Server Enterprise Management Console, which allow DBAs to tune and monitor traffic within the database. This performance-tuning knowledge becomes increasingly more important as the volume of transactions a system is designed to accommodate increases.

What Type of Upstream and Downstream Systems Are You Connecting With?

By far, one of the most overlooked areas in BizTalk architecture can be defined by these questions: What type of "upstream and downstream" systems are you connecting with? Do you have skillsets in those technologies? How flexible are those systems to change? BizTalk is a routing engine; it takes data from one source, does something, and sends the output somewhere. Think of it like this:

Stuff goes in. Stuff happens. Stuff comes out.

Many architects are preconsumed with the *Stuff happens* part without really thinking about getting data in or getting data out of BizTalk. As part of integrating disparate systems, you better make sure that you have access to experts and SMEs who understand the systems that BizTalk will be Biz-talking with. Working with enterprise-class solutions such as SAP, PeopleSoft, and MQSeries often requires configuration changes to these systems to optimize their performance within the new architecture. It is not common to spend weeks or months tuning and testing the upstream and downstream systems to ensure that solution service-level agreements are met and that performance is acceptable. Many architectures unwisely assume that because a BizTalk adapter is present, the complexity of the underlying system goes away. In reality, this cannot be further from the truth. Just because an adapter is present does not mean that all of the complexity of integrating with that system is negated. It is still critically important to understand the nuances of what you will be communicating with and how.

Understanding Basic Enterprise Application Interchange/Interop

BizTalk is an excellent EAI tool—it is well suited for moving data from one system to another, even if those systems have completely different architectures. It is common to see one legacy system needing to send data to another within most large IT organizations, and this scenario is where BizTalk really shines.

Issues arise when you don't take into account the impact of this integration on the legacy application. The downstream system[5] must be able to cope with this new source of data, and likewise, the data that is being received from the upstream system must be in a strong format for BizTalk to be able to parse it. In many instances, the downstream system can become "flooded" with messages from the upstream system, and these types of scenarios need to be taken into account when defining the solution architecture.

Working with Legacy Data Sources

BizTalk provides a number of mechanisms for interoperating with mainframe host-based systems, VSAM files, and other legacy sources. For a deep technical dive into legacy connectivity options, refer to Chapter 15.

A common issue is that BizTalk communication can be "bursty" if it is not tuned properly. A typical scenario is that the downstream system can become overwhelmed with requests and become unresponsive. It is important to properly load test any external interfaces before implementing BizTalk into your environment. These load tests are necessary to determine the sustainable throughput of your solution and identify any potential bottlenecks. New architects often assume that BizTalk will be the "slowest" point in any messaging solution, but often this is not the case.

What Are the Project Timelines? Will the Team Be Using BizTalk Exclusively to Decrease Development Time?

If the only reason you are looking at BizTalk is because you hope it will allow you to hit a project milestone or decrease overall project risk, then you need make sure you are using BizTalk for the right reasons. BizTalk is not a cure-all solution. Projects that are running behind schedule do not just have "BizTalk thrown in there" to make the unrealistic deadline go away. Most project managers want to find the "magic bullet" that can solve all their projects' problems. BizTalk has a place in these types of scenarios, but it is a means to an end, and not the end in and of itself.

Implementing BizTalk within any project carries with it a certain level of risk and challenges. In the end, what may happen is that you trade one risk for another. To be successful in this type of scenario, the solution must have features or subsystems on the projects' critical path that can be easily inserted and replaced with the appropriate BizTalk tool while at the same time not increasing the overall project risk.

5 For the purposes of this book, we will refer to the system that is "sending" BizTalk data as the *upstream* system and the recipient of that data as the *downstream* system. This metaphor works if you think about messages within BizTalk "flowing" through the system. Messages that enter BizTalk must be acted upon, or there is an error generated. In that sense, all messages "flow" through BizTalk and are created by the upstream system and sent to the downstream system.

If your project is in danger of not meeting a deadline and you think that BizTalk may be just the tool for implementing some of the project requirements, the easiest way to evaluate whether BizTalk will work is to implement a series of simple proof of concepts. In most situations, software does not need to be purchased for this, and a 120-day demo copy of the product can be downloaded from www.microsoft.com/biztalk/en/us/trial-software.aspx for free. During this proof-of-concept phase, Microsoft field staff can be engaged to help ensure the prototypes are successful and address any technical issues that may arise. Involving Microsoft field staff in these types of situations is generally the easiest way to help alleviate the risk of taking on the creation and success of any proof-of-concept or prototype activities while engaged in an already risky project.

Is There Enough in the Budget to Implement BizTalk?

Whether you have the budget to implement BizTalk will depend on the size and complexity of the solution. Typical implementations cost anywhere from $15,000 on the low end to upward of $500,000+ on the high end for hardware and software costs. These are exclusive of any custom development, support, or hosting costs.

BizTalk Server Editions and Pricing

BizTalk as a solution provides many options for configuring the product to help ensure the right mix of hardware and software is purchased. The product is available in the editions listed in Tables 1-1 and 1-2. Table 1-1 lists standard editions, and Table 1-2 lists specialized editions of BizTalk aimed at certain very specific types of applications.

Table 1-1. *BizTalk Editions and Pricing*[6]

Edition	U.S. Price	Description
Enterprise	$34,999	* Complete EAI, B2B, and Business Process Management functionality * Includes all vertical industry accelerators (RosettaNet, HIPAA, HL7, and SWIFT) * Includes BizTalk Adapter Pack. Includes all current and new application and technology adapters * Includes BizTalk RFID Server and Mobile capabilities with support for unlimited devices * Supports high availability/failover for multiple RFID Servers Includes Host Integration Server * Unlimited "applications" allowed (see the BizTalk Server 2009 Pricing and Licensing FAQ) * Scale out/failover multiple message boxes Remote or local DB * Available for 120-day evaluation at no cost

6 This table is taken from http://www.microsoft.com/biztalk/en/us/pricing-licensing.aspx. For complete licensing costs, consult the Microsoft web site or your local product reseller.

Edition	U.S. Price	Description
Standard	$8,499	* Complete EAI, B2B, and Business Process Management functionality * Includes all vertical industry accelerators (RosettaNet, HIPAA, HL7, and SWIFT) Includes BizTalk Adapter Pack * Includes all current and new application and technology adapters * Includes BizTalk RFID Server and Mobile capabilities with support for unlimited devices Includes Host Integration Server * Limited to two CPUs on a single server * Five "applications" allowed (see the BizTalk Server 2009 Pricing and Licensing FAQ) * Single server solution/single message box Remote or local DB
Branch	$1,800	* Subset of BizTalk Server functionality appropriate for intra-enterprise hub-and-spoke scenarios (see the BizTalk Server 2009 Pricing and Licensing FAQ) * Includes BizTalk RFID Server and Mobile capabilities with support for unlimited devices Includes Host Integration Server * Used in conjunction with a BizTalk Server "hub" that coordinates/aggregates events across multiple Branch Editions * Limited to two CPUs on a single server * One "application" allowed (see the BizTalk Server 2009 Pricing and Licensing FAQ) * Single server solution/single message box Remote or local DB
Developer	$499 per user (free with MSDN Premium Subscription)	* Complete EAI, B2B, and Business Process Management functionality Includes BizTalk Adapter Pack * Includes all current and new application and technology adapters * Includes BizTalk RFID Server and Mobile capabilities with support for unlimited devices * Supports high availability/failover for multiple RFID Servers * Limited solely to designing, developing, and testing solutions * Note: Many customers who deploy BizTalk Server implement separate development, testing, and production environments for their BizTalk Server 2009 solution. For the development and testing environments, you need a user license for each developer and tester, which can be obtained through either BizTalk Server Developer Edition or an MSDN Premium Subscription. * For the production environment, you need a valid processor license of BizTalk Server 2009 Enterprise, Standard, or Branch Edition for each processor on which you install an edition of BizTalk Server 2009.

Table 1-2. *Specialized BizTalk Server Editions*[7]

Edition	U.S. Price	Description
RFID Enterprise	$4,999	Microsoft BizTalk RFID is an innovative device management and event processing platform at the edge of the enterprise. It is designed to provide a scalable, extensible platform for development, deployment, and management of rich RFID and sensor solutions. * Includes BizTalk RFID Server and BizTalk RFID Mobile * Customers can connect to unlimited number for RFID devices * Provide SDK for building RFID-enabled applications * Supports high availability/failover for multiple RFID servers
Adapter Pack (English Only)	$5,000	BizTalk Adapter Pack is a set of adapters based on the Windows Communication Foundation (WCF) programming model. The BizTalk Adapter Pack provides a single solution to easily and securely connect to line-of-business (LOB) data from any custom-developed .NET application, SQL Server–based business intelligence solution, or Office Business Application (OBA). * Includes adapters for SAP, Siebel, and Oracle Database * Includes ADO.NET providers for SAP and Siebel Requires: WCF LOB Adapter SDK

SQL Server Editions

Like BizTalk, SQL Server also has separate editions to meet the varying needs of customer requirements and installation situations. The two main versions of SQL Server are **Standard Edition** and **Enterprise Edition**. The key difference between the two versions in the context of a BizTalk Server environment is their support for database clustering. Only SQL Server Enterprise Edition supports database clustering, and it requires Microsoft Windows Server Enterprise Edition as its installed operating system to install the cluster server software.

Required BizTalk Server and SQL Server Hardware

The minimum hardware requirements for BizTalk Server as published by Microsoft are as follows:

- 900 megahertz (MHz) or higher Intel Pentium–compatible CPU
- 2048 megabytes (MB) of RAM
- 10 gigabyte (GB) hard disk
- CD-ROM or DVD-ROM drive

Please note that this is a minimum configuration to allow the product to run. In actuality, a typical BizTalk Server machine will have some variant of the following hardware. This is a common configuration:

- 2.6 GHz or higher Pentium (Dual or Quad Core)
- 4096MB of RAM

7 This table is taken from www.microsoft.com/biztalk/en/us/pricing-licensing.aspx. For complete licensing costs, consult the Microsoft web site or your local product reseller.

- RAID 5 hard disk array for application data
- RAID 0+1 hard disk array for operating system
- CD-ROM or DVD-ROM drive

As stated earlier, every BizTalk installation needs a SQL Server instance. In low-volume scenarios, it is possible to install both BizTalk Server and SQL Server on the same physical machine. This configuration will work quite well and is fully supported. Issues with this configuration tend to arise when transaction volume increases and additional processing resources are required to service incoming requests.

In high-volume scenarios, it is not realistic to expect to be able to run both BizTalk and SQL Server on the same physical machine. From a performance perspective, SQL Server traditionally is a "RAM-hungry" application. This is mainly because of the memory management system used internally within the product. The upside to this is that query executing time within SQL Server is generally extremely fast, and the server engine is able to cache query results to increase performance. It is possible to configure SQL Server to use less memory, but the performance of the database engine could degrade accordingly.

From a fault-tolerance perspective, it would be disastrous to expect maximum uptime and reliability from a shared BizTalk/SQL Server hardware platform. SQL Server enterprise provides clustering support to allow for failover occurring across separate physical machines in the event of a hardware failure. Database clustering is a key component to ensure that the environment achieves maximum uptime despite failures in hardware or software.

A typical SQL Server Enterprise Edition clustered environment is shown in Figure 1-4 and will have a configuration similar to the following:

- 3.0 GHz or higher Pentium Dual or Quad Core processor
- 8192MB or more of RAM[8]
- RAID 5 hard disk array for application installations
- RAID 0+1 hard disk array for operating system
- CD-ROM or DVD-ROM drive
- Shared Fibre Channel array or storage area network (SAN) for SQL Server database files

---

Note In a clustered environment, two database server machines are required. In most configurations, the first server accepts database requests, while the other is considered a "hot standby." This configuration is referred to as *active/passive clustering*.

---

8 BizTalk Server is now available with full 64-bit support. SQL Server is also fully supported on the 64-bit platform. Unless there is a clear reason not to use 64-bit, you should plan to have all servers installed as 64-bit operating systems; 8192 should be considered as a minimum starting point for any enterprise-grade 64-bit computing platform.

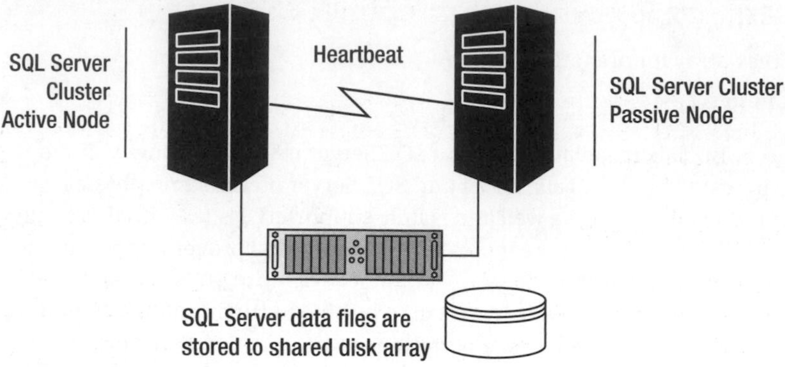

Figure 1-4. *SQL Server clustering configuration*

Software Costs

When estimating costs for a new BizTalk project, it is imperative to consider the total cost of what the software will be. Don't forget, too, that you must consider the cost of both BizTalk *and* SQL Server.

BizTalk Costs

When project managers begin estimating the cost for the solutions hardware environment, many often forget one thing—BizTalk is not freeware. Each edition has its own per-processor cost. The software licensing costs are shown in Table 1-3 from the previous section.

SQL Server Costs

SQL Server can be licensed in two modes: per client access license (CAL) or per processor. Per-CAL licensing requires that you purchase a separate license for each concurrent connection to the SQL Server database, whereas per-processor licensing licenses the software based on the number of processors installed in the machine. Given the complex nature of BizTalk and SQL Server processing, it is generally not advisable to license SQL Server based on the CAL model. Developer and testing servers are permitted to use SQL Server Developer Edition. Like BizTalk Developer Edition, this is a full-featured version of the product licensed for use on development and testing machines only and is available through MSDN subscriptions. Per-processor licensing costs are outlined in Table 1-3.

Table 1-3. *SQL Server Pricing*[9]

Edition	SQL Server 2008
Enterprise Edition	$24,999 USD per processor
Standard Edition	$5,999 USD per processor
Developer Edition	Part of MSDN Universal subscription

9 See www.microsoft.com/sqlserver/2008/en/us/pricing.aspx for more details.

How Many Servers Are Required to Implement a BizTalk Solution?

Low-volume systems can be implemented with one BizTalk server machine and one SQL Server machine. High-volume solutions can use eight or more machines depending on the type and volume of processing required.

Virtualized Environments Using Hyper-V

Virtualization technology has drastically changed how architects view the physical server environment on which their application will be hosted. At one time, having separate servers performing distinct tasks was both cost-prohibitive and time-consuming. With the advent of BizTalk 2009 and Windows Hyper-V virtualization technology, BizTalk and SQL Server are officially supported by Microsoft on Virtual OS environments using Hyper-V. The result is that full virtual environments can now be built with no costs to the actual project.

One of the key issues that project delivery teams often face is the lack of a proper development/test/integration environments. Up until about a year ago, this requirement often meant that teams either went without or went unsupported down this road. Now, there is no reason why proper test environments cannot be created using Hyper-V. Traditionally, test environments were simplified production environments, often with one or maybe two BizTalk Servers and a SQL Server. With Hyper-V, multiple, virtual BizTalk Servers can be used in a test environment to model the physical production environment. Likewise, developer workstations can also have separate virtual BizTalk servers and SQL Servers. Traditionally, these were all installed on a virtual PC image. Now with Hyper-V, the developer tools can be installed on the developer's physical workstation and separate the BizTalk runtime environment from the development environment.

Typical Low-Volume Solution Configuration

Figure 1-5 shows a configuration that will work for a typical low-volume transaction system.

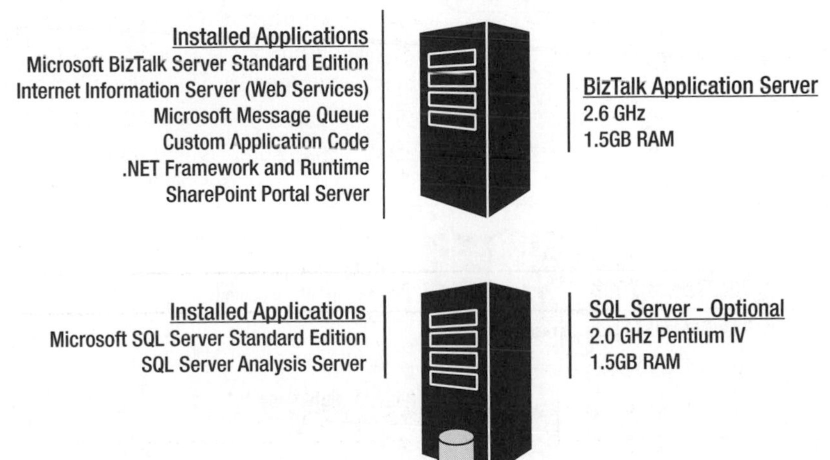

Figure 1-5. *Low-volume BizTalk Server configuration*

Typical High-Volume System Configuration

High-volume transaction systems require a more robust configuration than is shown in Figure 1-5. Figure 1-6 gives one example of how you might configure BizTalk to handle a high volume of transactions.

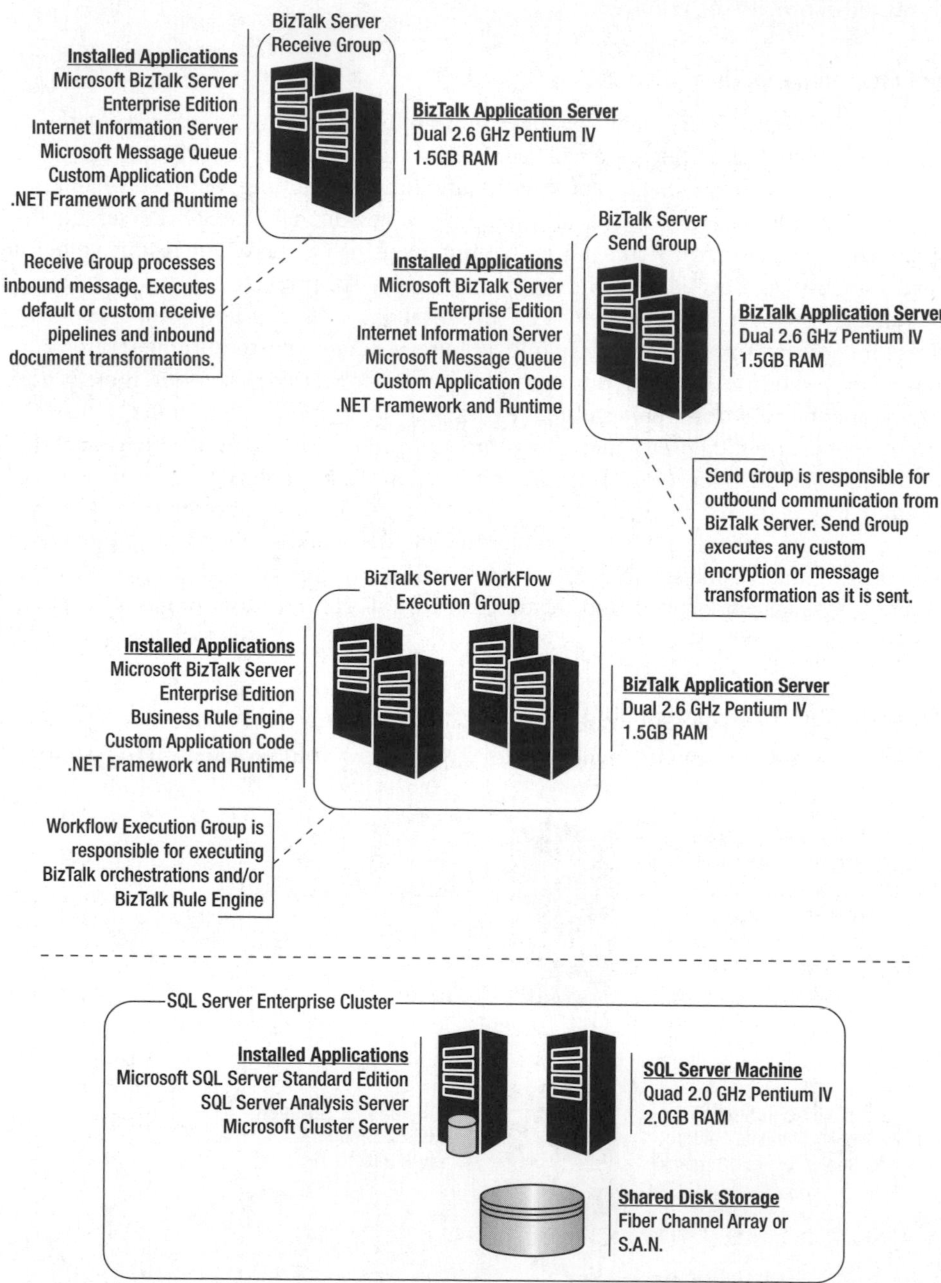

Figure 1-6. *High-volume BizTalk Server implementation*

How Much Custom Code Are You and Your Team Willing to Create? Would You Rather Use Completely Out-of-the-Box Functionality?

Most BizTalk solutions do not require significant amounts (more than 20,000 lines) of code to implement. Simple projects may not require any. The amount of custom code required will depend greatly on the type of system and the complexity of the business logic that is required.

There are several key types of processing that require a BizTalk solution to implement custom code:

- **Custom message processing logic**: This generally refers to custom pipelines and custom pipeline components. If you need to perform custom encryption or decryption, custom digital signature or message verification, compression routines, or custom envelope processing, you will need to write .NET code.
- **Custom transformation logic**: Transformation logic is handled within BizTalk maps. Most transformations can be implemented using the default BizTalk **functoids**. Functoids are pieces of application code that are used to manipulate how values from an incoming message are mapped to the outgoing message within a BizTalk transformation. BizTalk ships with more than 100 default functoids that are able to accommodate most standard tasks. In the case where custom logic needs to be created, most projects will want to code custom functoids to facilitate code reuse. You will want to code custom functoids when you notice that the same scripts or routines are implemented several times across multiple maps.
- **Custom business logic**: .NET components are usually called within orchestrations and contain common business procedures and classes. This is not a BizTalk item per se because the project will need to implement this logic regardless of the platform.
- **Workflow automation**: These are BizTalk orchestrations. In most situations, there is one BizTalk orchestration for each workflow to be automated. In many cases, complicated workflow is broken out into multiple orchestrations so that common pieces can be used in several orchestrations and be coded by multiple developers.
- **Custom adapters**: One of the key selling features of BizTalk is the vibrant adapter partner community that supports it. Adapters allow BizTalk applications to communicate with different transport mechanisms and applications without requiring that the coder understand the details of how this communication will work. Adapters exist for more than 300 platforms, operating systems, and ERP applications. In certain circumstances, either an adapter is not available for a desired platform or it is more cost effective to develop a custom adapter from scratch because of licensing costs. In these cases, you will need to create a custom adapter using the BizTalk Adapter Framework classes. Depending on the transaction volume requirements, transport specifics, and protocols involved, this may be a difficult task for the novice developer.

Is BizTalk Suited for the Application in Question?

Refer to the four main types of BizTalk projects—workflow automation, legacy application integration, trading partner exchange, and organizational message broker scenarios. If your application has any of these types of pieces, BizTalk may be a fit. If not, you need to examine where and why BizTalk is being evaluated.

Synchronous versus Asynchronous

The key thing to remember in this type of situation is to define early in the solution's design phase what data will be exchanged with BizTalk, what the schema definitions are, and how data will be returned to the calling application. Another key decision is to decide whether the main application requires a **synchronous** or an **asynchronous** response from BizTalk and what the threshold values are for an acceptable transaction. If the calling application needs a subsecond synchronous response from BizTalk to process the message, it is imperative that the system be sized properly to ensure that response times are acceptable. If the communication can be asynchronous, it is easier to restrict the flow of messages to an acceptable level by using either a queuing mechanism or some sort of batch processing.

BizTalk and Low Latency

As we've stated, BizTalk is a messaging engine. As a product, it inherently wants to work on "batches" of messages at a time to ensure that transaction volumes are met. This is the concept of *throughput*—how many messages a second can you push through your system and sustain over an extended period of time? In addition, how much time does each of the individual messages take to process? If you publish 1,000 messages in 10-second intervals, you are technical achieving 100 messages per second throughput, which is quite respectable. However, if you have an SLA that states that no message can take more than two seconds to process, then you have a serious problem. This is the fundamental issue with message latency.

Out of the box, BizTalk is tuned for throughput, not latency. It is quite possible to tune BizTalk to support low-latency scenarios, but it often means you are sacrificing throughput to achieve that. You need to be aware of this trade-off when setting expectations around what is achievable. Expecting to achieve a throughput of hundreds of messages a second while at the same time expecting subsecond latency is not wise. This underscores the importance of prototyping and performance testing. Most projects have no idea that they will have a performance problem until they are just about to release (or have released) the product. In an ideal world, prototyping should be performed at various stages of the product's life cycle to ensure that the expectations of the project are reasonable, that sufficient hardware has been purchased, and that the software code performs as expected. Waiting until the 11th hour to do performance testing (or not doing any at all) is a surefire way to have an unpleasant conversation with your project sponsor.

At the same time, the BizTalk low-latency scenario reaffirms the classic EAI problems described earlier about interoperating with legacy systems. If you are interoperating with a mainframe that can accept only two messages per second, then your overall throughput will be only two messages per second, and you will begin to see some awful performance behavior and throttling occurring within BizTalk. BizTalk performance tuning is more about identifying and addressing bottlenecks in the system than it is about fixing code. Generally, any coding issues will be present in either a pipeline, an orchestration, or a map. Most if not all other performance-related issues in BizTalk are caused by either the upstream or downstream systems that BizTalk is integrating.

Will Every Transaction in the System Need Monitoring? Will the Tracked Data Need Saving for Archiving Purposes?

This issue is often overlooked when a new project begins. BizTalk provides a very simplistic user interface to view the message specifics and transaction history within the product. This interface within the BizTalk Management Console is shown in Figures 1-7 and 1-8.

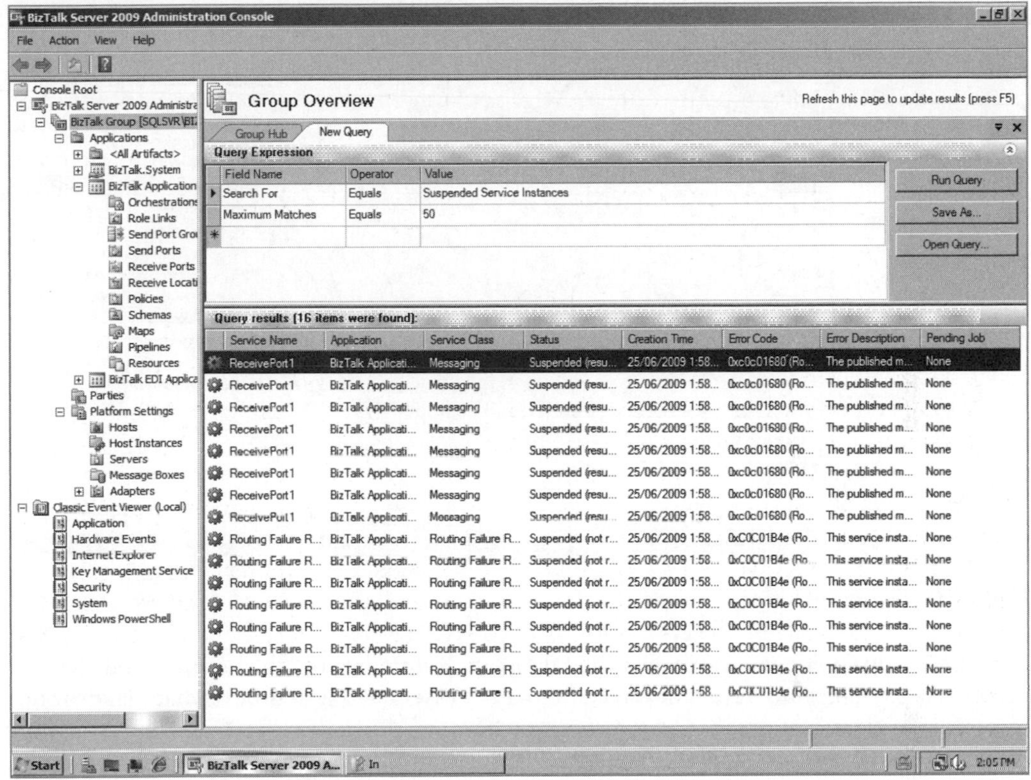

Figure 1-7. *BizTalk Management Console*

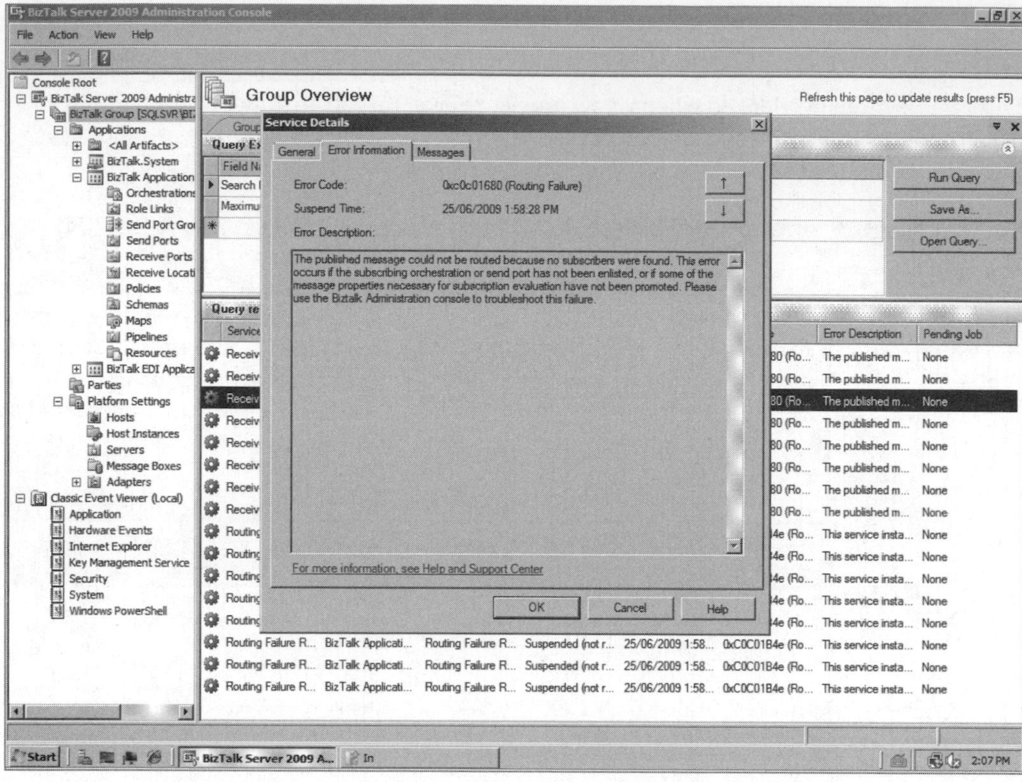

Figure 1-8. *Message details*

The Group Query page can provide the data that is stored within the message and give the message context properties; however, this data is essentially system-level data. There is no "business-relevant" information in the context other than the message type and any exception information. If there is a requirement to see the transaction from an end-user perspective (i.e., the message is received, processed by system XXX, and failed at updating system YYY), the BizTalk Management Console will not be sufficient. Often the type of application that needs to see a transaction from an end-user perspective is integrated into an existing SharePoint portal site. In previous versions of BizTalk, this was done using BAS, but in BizTalk 2009, BAS has been deprecated. At this point, developing a dashboard using the BAM portal is the most effective way to implement this functionality. Developing this application is generally not a trivial task and can add time onto the final product's delivery date. If the type of information is volumetric data (e.g., how many transactions failed, how many were successful, what was the volume at peak processing time), the data can be created using BAM and accessed with Microsoft Excel or another similar tool. Implementing a BAM-based solution is generally less time-consuming than creating a complete customized SharePoint application. Starting in BizTalk 2006, the BAM service ships with a default SharePoint portal application that allows you to view all BAM-related information within the system. This base application is usually then modified or integrated with another main SharePoint site to provide the relevant business-level metrics required. The trade-off may be that all the required functionality for business-level users is not present in the default BAM portal.

CHAPTER 2

Starting a New BizTalk Project

Every BizTalk development team, regardless of the size, will encounter the same types of problems. The two most difficult issues that new BizTalk architects face in organizing the development team are how to structure the project in terms of the development/build/test/deploy process and how to appropriately structure the project source tree so that it is optimal for each developer given the task he is working on.

In most cases, a developer on a BizTalk solution will fall into one of three categories:

- Developers who create BizTalk artifacts exclusively
- Developers who create .NET classes exclusively
- Developers who perform a combination of both

In small teams of five developers or less, it is not uncommon to see most developers performing both BizTalk tasks as well as pure .NET coding tasks. For these types of teams, delineation of work becomes simple and is usually based on functional aspects of the system. Small teams can "carve out" pieces of the solution based on some functional aspect, and these solution divides are generally referred to as **subsystems**. In a perfect world, each subsystem can then be coded and tested independent of the rest, which helps to decrease intersolution dependencies and project schedule critical paths. Small teams will also need a **lead**. The lead is responsible for ensuring that coding standards are met, unit test plans are created and executed, and system integration and code promotion into formal application testing happens smoothly and consistently.

In large teams of 15+ developers, the process of managing developer deliverables, subsystem integration and testing, application versioning, and solution builds start to become a nontrivial task. For these teams, it becomes necessary to implement a formal project structure that scales to accommodate large numbers of subsystems while at the same time provide consistency and uniformity across the entire team as a whole. Figure 2-1 shows a simplified diagram for how a development team is structured. Each of the roles within the team is described in Table 2-1.

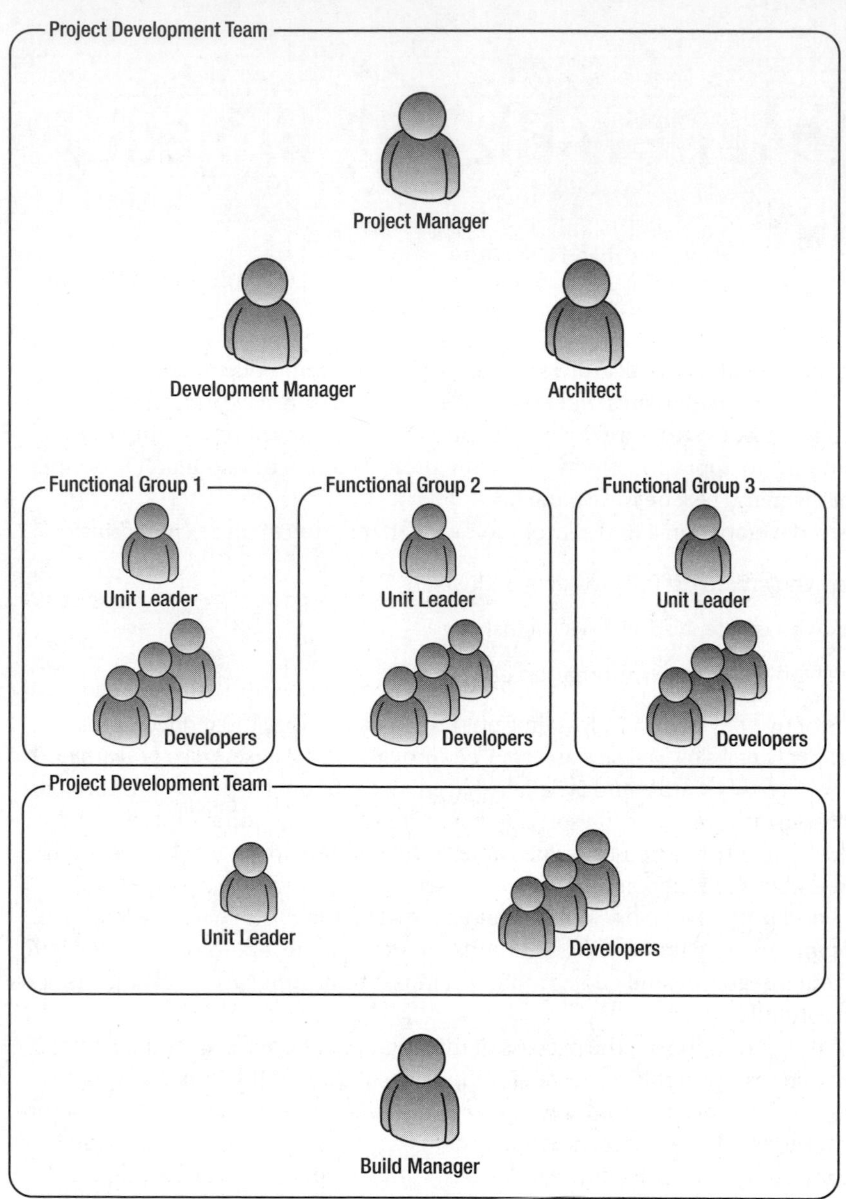

Figure 2-1. *Simplified team structure*

Table 2-1. *Project Roles and Responsibilities*

Role	Key Areas of Responsibility
Project Manager	Ensuring deliverables are to client specifications Ensuring project delivery Creating and managing budget and schedules Managing Change Requests
Development Manager	Integrating features across functional teams Managing Change Requests Working with functional teams to create deliverable lists and ensure timely delivery
Architect	Defining overall system architecture and design Defining development standards and naming conventions Defining source control layout and project solution structure Defining application namespaces Working with Unit Leaders and Development Manager to create developer specifications Defining performance testing metrics Defining subsystem integration points and working with Development Manager to ensure the entire system integrates properly Defining external and internal system interfaces Working with common infrastructure team to define reusable system-level infrastructure components
Build Manager	Ensuring integration between functional teams Performing daily builds into integration and testing environment Creating build scripts/installation packages
Unit Leader	Working with Development Manager to ensure all deliverables within Functional Unit are created Performing code walkthrough and sign-off with Developer Ensuring unit test plans are created and adhered to Depending on nature of team, coding of common subsystem routines
Developer	Producing code according to specification Creating BizTalk artifacts according to development standards Coding .NET classes Creating unit test plans Developing unit tests Executing unit tests

---

■ **Caution** Figure 2-1 is a simplified development team model. It is by no means a complete structure because the functions of quality assurance testing and product releases have not been taken into account. For a complete development methodology, Microsoft Solutions Framework is a great place to start: `http://msdn.microsoft.com/en-us/teamsystem/aa718795.aspx`.

Starting Preliminary Design

The team structure outlined previously gives the basics for forming and managing a large group of developers. It also allows the team to scale outward or inward depending on new requirements being introduced or having features move out of scope. The key take-aways from this model are the following:

- Break the solution down into functional groups or subsystems. Assign and manage deliverables based on these groupings.
- For projects that require common infrastructure, create a separate team that is responsible for creating and managing this. Ensure that the design for any common components is well defined and used by other functional teams.
- Assign developers to either a functional team or to the common infrastructure team. Assigning developers to more than one team is often problematic because it forces them to split time for multiple deliverables.
- Rotate developers across teams when deliverables are complete. This encourages cross-group collaboration and decreases "knowledge silos."
- Encourage a regular build cycle. This will help to keep the project on track and gives the team members regular code check-in dates that must be met.

On a BizTalk development project, these concepts become even more important. Most BizTalk architects do not take the time necessary to determine how to properly structure the application so that it can be coded using a model like the one defined earlier. Likewise, very few map out what common infrastructure will be needed and what types of artifacts are "feature specific" and which are common infrastructure. Following is an exercise that illustrates this.

EXERCISE 2-1. DESIGN THE SOLUTION

List what features are needed for the solution to be implemented in this exercise scenario. Then list what common components will be required for each subsystem.

Scenario

ABC Company, Inc., is creating a new solution using BizTalk Server. The system is an order fulfillment application that will receive order information from the public web site, a retail point-of-sale (POS) system, and a custom bulk order solution that is used by large customers. Only customers in good standing are eligible for automatic fulfillment, and currently the project is only piloting customers in four geographic regions. If a customer does not meet the requirements for automatic fulfillment, the order is rejected and manually fulfilled. For orders that can be auto-fulfilled, the solution must first check the stock availability for each product by an SAP ERP system using a custom API. If stock is not available, it must decide whether the order can be split into multiple shipments and fulfill each separately. If the order cannot be split shipped, it must be rejected and processed manually. If an order can be fulfilled, it must update the billing and shipping systems appropriately. The shipping system is a legacy mainframe-based application that requires custom code to be executed to properly authenticate and send transactions to it.

Note This solution will be the basis for all coding and BizTalk artifact examples given in the book. This is to bring a level of consistency to each example as well as to show how it can be used in a real-world example.

Possible Solution

In this scenario, the most logical approach would be to separate the solution based on the requirements. There are three key features of this solution:

- Order taking from external sources (POS, web site, and bulk orders)
- Stock checking and rules associated with split shipments
- Updating downstream systems

Each subsystem will have its own pieces and artifacts; however, all of them will need to use the following types of core components:

- Access to customer information
    - Common schema to define customer information
    - Standard way to get access to that customer information
    - Executing customer rules associated with automatic fulfillment
- Coordination to ensure that the fulfillment process is handled in the proper order
- Order rejection subsystem
- Standard way to process exceptions and errors

In this scenario, the solution can be implemented using the architecture in Figure 2-2.

Feature 1. External Interfaces

This subsystem is responsible for receiving inbound messages from the three external interfaces. Here, the external interfaces can be XML messages, flat-file messages, or custom inbound API calls.[1] In any case, this subsystem will need to parse the inbound document and transform it to a common schema that represents an "order" within this solution. This order schema will be used by all other subsystems. In the case of the bulk upload, the subsystem will be required to create individual orders based on the entire payload of messages stored within the order file.

This scenario can be implemented using receive ports within BizTalk along with several receive locations. Each receive location will define a custom receive pipeline if the document needs to be examined and/or disassembled before being processed. The port would then have different BizTalk transformations assigned to it to allow it to map the inbound system order schema to the common system order schema that is used by all subsystems.

1 In later chapters, we will explore the scenario of creating a custom Receive Adapter. In many cases, the system that will be sending BizTalk messages is either a proprietary COTS (commercial, off-the-shelf) system or requires special transports such as a custom TCP listener. In these scenarios, it may be preferable to buy an external adapter or create a custom one using the Adapter Wizard. It is recommended that all custom adapters utilize the new WCF adapter framework. The adapter framework and WCF adapters will be covered in a future chapter. Keep in mind that adapters created in the old adapter framework will still continue to function.

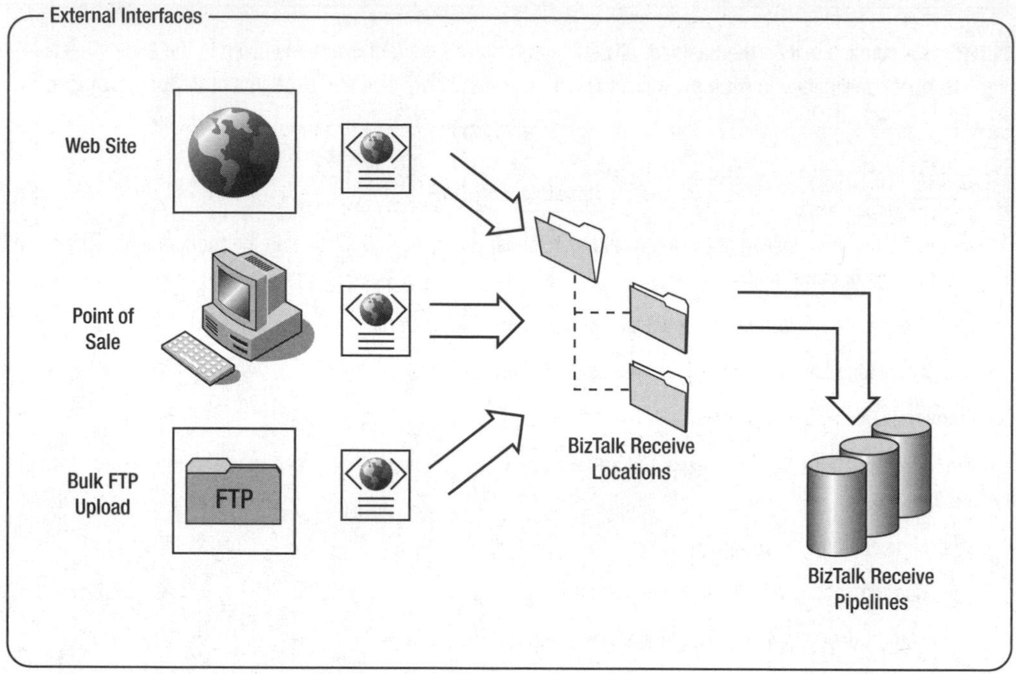

Figure 2-2. *External interfaces design*

Feature 2. Check Stock and Associated Rules

The stock-checking subsystem will be responsible for calling the customer lookup system, as shown in Figure 2-3. This will also check whether or not the order can be fulfilled and return the response. Note that in this scenario, the coordination of calling the order rejection system as well as the coordination of this process into the larger fulfillment process is left to the responsibility of the common infrastructure. This subsystem is responsible for determining whether an order can be fulfilled and is not responsible for how or why this information is needed. This is often referred to as black-boxing a solution. This will allow the subsystem to be built in isolation of any other subsystem. Only integration points are needed to be defined before development is started, in this case, the schemas for an order and a customer as well as the format of the response.

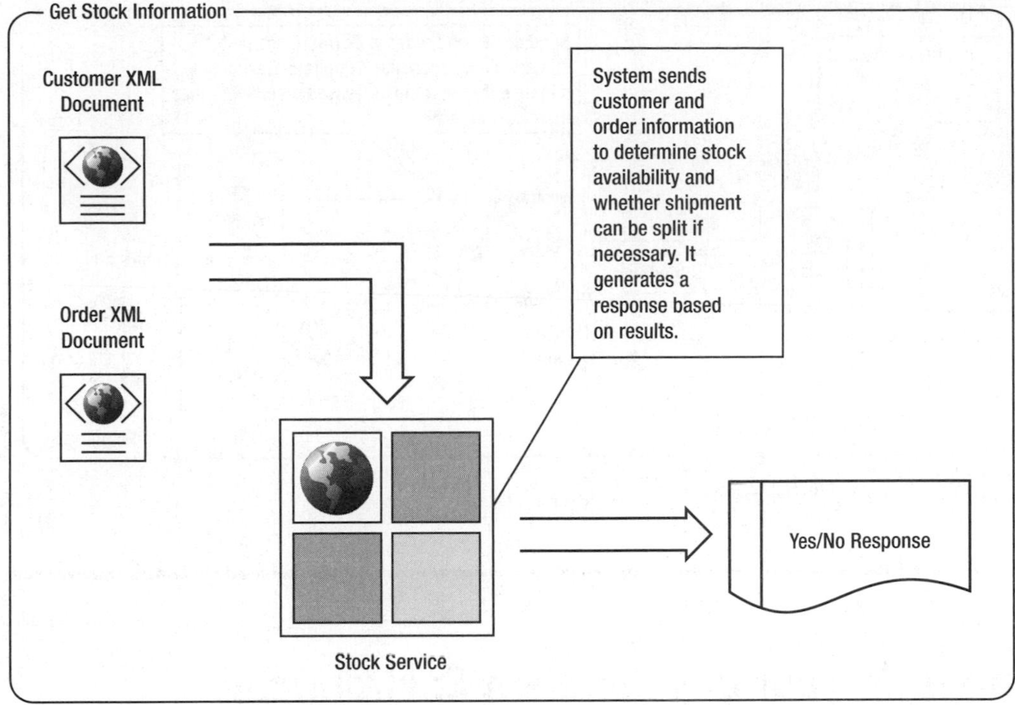

Figure 2-3. *Stock information service design*

Feature 3. Update Downstream Systems

To update the downstream ERP and shipping systems, the validated order will need to be sent via a BizTalk send port via the appropriate adapter. This is demonstrated in Figure 2-4. The adapter to be used depends on what downstream system is going to be updated. In the case of the ERP system, if this were an SAP application, the port would use the SAP adapter. The same would hold true if it were an MQSeries queue—the port would use an MQSeries adapter. For the custom shipping solution, a custom adapter will need to be created if no off-the-shelf adapter is available. Note that in this system, the send pipelines are responsible for packaging the message into its appropriate format, adding any security information such as digital certificates, and encoding it properly so that the downstream system can read the order information. The send ports also return a response message back that indicates whether or not the update was successful. What to do with that response message is the responsibility of the caller, not the pipeline, adapter, or send port.

These common subsystems also need to be built:

- Coordinate fulfillment process.
- Get customer information.
- Handle errors.
- Handle order rejections.

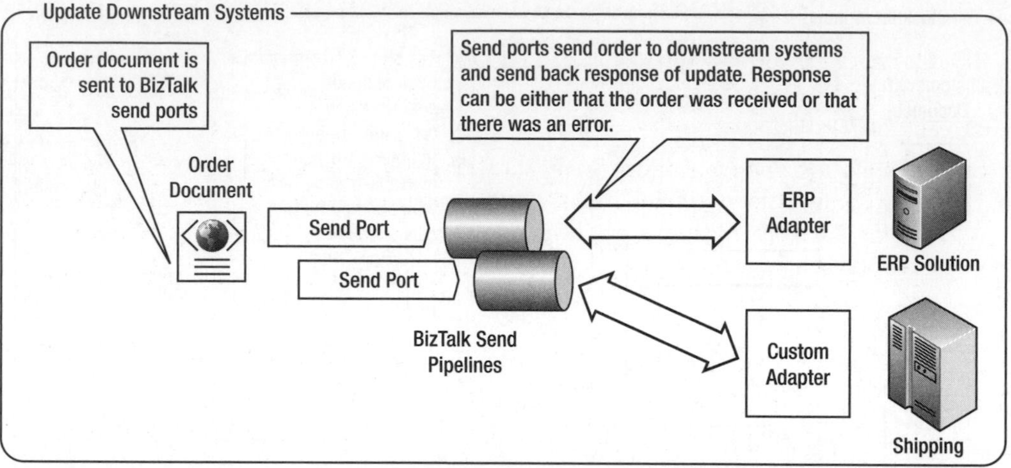

Figure 2-4. *Update Downstream Systems design*

Creating Your Development Environment

Once you have a team established, the next step is to create an environment where you can create, test, and deploy code. Some variables will affect how this is going to be accomplished:

- How are the development servers going to be configured?
- How will source control be configured?
- How are the Visual Studio projects going to be laid out?

The answer to each of these questions can often separate a well-organized and efficient environment from one that can kill a team's productivity. Potential solutions to each of these questions are given in the next sections.

Isolated Development Configuration

BizTalk development is an isolated development model. This model requires each developer to have a stand-alone development environment and not a shared environment such as in web development.

In the isolated model, a developer performs each task independently from other developers on the team. They can code, debug, edit, and restart services without worrying about affecting others on the team. Each developer has a self-contained development workstation with a local BizTalk Server Group. Access to the master source files is controlled via a Visual SourceSafe (VSS) database located on a network file share. Team Foundation Server (TFS) workgroup edition will be good fit in this scenario as well. Figure 2-5 illustrates an isolated development model.

The isolated model of BizTalk Server development provides the following benefits:

- No chance that BizTalk Server shared configuration information will interfere with another developer's work (for example, XML target namespace clashes occurring from multiple installed versions of shared schema)
- No opportunity for any one individual's BizTalk Server deployment and test processes interrupting other users (for example, the starting and stopping of BizTalk Server host instances, receive locations, or dependent services like IIS, SQL Server, and SSO)
- Ability to clear resources like event logs and tracking databases without disrupting other users
- Ability for developers to use different versions of shared resources, for example, helper classes and error-handling processes
- Ability for developers to attach and debug the BTNTSvc.exe process without halting other developers' processes

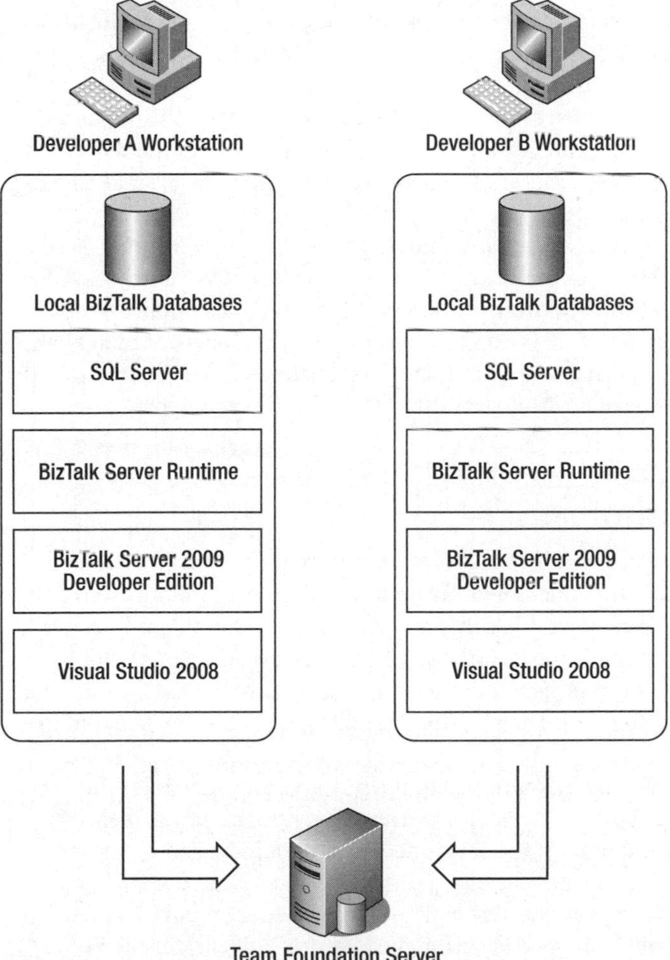

Figure 2-5. *Isolated BizTalk Server development*

Using Virtual Machines

Many organizations use **virtual desktops** for development. In these cases, organizations should look at products such as Virtual PC/Virtual Server or a Hyper-V instance to allow developers to have multiple virtual machines running within the same physical hardware. Virtual desktops provide two things well. The most important thing is that they allow your developer to get a fresh install in a matter of minutes rather than hours. How many times have developers needed to rebuild their PCs because of bad code they had written, too much unsupported code getting installed, or a bad configuration they might have done? Typically this will happen at least two to three times over the run of a year. Having a fresh virtual image that they can load onto a clean host operating system greatly reduces the time for this to occur. All developers need to do is copy over any files they want to save from the virtual machine onto the host operating system before it is removed.

The second thing that virtual desktops allow for is the ability to host multiple configurations inside one physical box. Often developers need to have separate versions of either the operating system or a development environment. This is often the case when a developer is coding both BizTalk and classic .NET objects. When the BizTalk development tools are installed and the environment is configured, there are significant changes made to the underlying operating system. Developers will often have a "BizTalk" image and a ".NET" image just to keep things separated.

The configuration just described is also often required when creating a web application that targets different browser platforms and versions. Anyone who needs to support IE 6.0 or older, IE 7, and IE 8 will need to have something similar to this configuration, since these browsers cannot live on the same host OS.

As you look to utilize virtual machines, keep in mind the ramifications of keeping a completely sandboxed environment. Many times these systems are not part of the domain and not connected to the corporate network. In these cases, shared resources like mail servers or directory accounts aren't available. This will create an environment that does not match what your application will encounter and can cause a number of issues that may not show up until deployment. You will want to create an environment that resembles the deployment environments as closely as possible.

Organizing Source Control

Not implementing a structured source control process is a sure-fire way to derail a project before it gets started. It is important to model the source control directory structure to one that closely simulates the namespaces and assemblies that are actually stored in the project. For example, assuming that your company name is ABC Inc., the easiest place to start would be to create a root directory called ABC. Each project that is being implemented at ABC would then get its own folder, for example, Fulfillment. The structure would look something like that in Figure 2-6.

Notice that the subfolder names are matching up to the proper namespaces for the projects within that TFS project. Once the high-level folder structure is implemented, it easily allows new projects to be added, and organizational namespaces should be self-enforcing. Consider the example of the Fulfillment application; in this scenario you can use subprojects that map to the subsystems you need to create. Each subsystem would then have its own namespace, and the TFS project will be named accordingly. Figure 2-7 illustrates the Fulfillment application, its subsystems, and even some sub-subsystems.

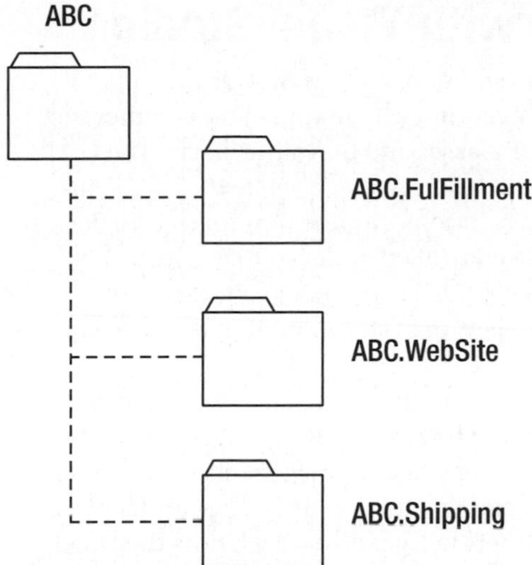

Figure 2-6. *Simple source control project layout*

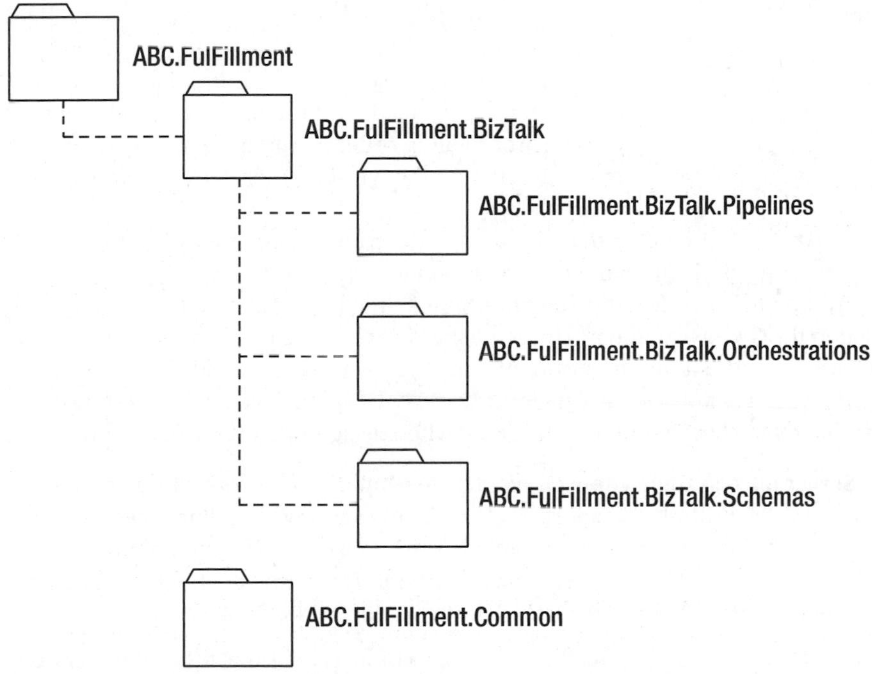

Figure 2-7. *Source control solution layout*

If you do happen to be using Visual SourceSafe, ensure that the binary file types for *.btm, *.btp, *.xsd, and *.odx have been added to VSS. This is required so that SourceSafe does not attempt to version these file types as text.

Structuring and Integrating with Visual Studio

There is no standard way to structure a Visual Studio solution that has BizTalk projects included. Essentially, a properly defined naming convention will be applicable whether the solution is a complete .NET solution or a mix of .NET classes and BizTalk artifacts. The key decision to make is whether the entire application will be created as a single VS .NET solution or whether it will be broken down into multiple solutions. Another approach is to decide whether or not to have the Visual Studio solution file controlled under source control at all. In this scenario, each developer has a local solution file that is not under source control. The individual developer then adds the Visual Studio projects to his local solution that are required to complete the application being created.

How the Visual Studio solutions are structured will have many ramifications on how developers will use the solution, how it will be built, and how it can be packaged and deployed. Additional things to consider are whether each developer will have the BizTalk development tools installed on their workstation. If a group of developers never code BizTalk artifacts and only create standard .NET classes, then these developers will get errors each time they load a BizTalk development project. A configuration like this will not work for a single-solution scenario where every project is included in the solution and is loaded upon startup. In single-solution scenarios, it is necessary to break the solution up into multiple solutions that can be worked on either by BizTalk developers or by .NET-only developers.

In cases where multiple developers are working on isolated pieces of a solution, a separate integration environment should be created. The purpose of this environment is to allow a common area for each build of the application to be placed. Additionally, the deployment process is developed and tested using this environment in order to minimize deployment errors when the solution is moved from the development environment into testing and finally production.

Since the BizTalk development model is isolated as described in the preceding section, it is crucial that the integration environment provide a place where unit testing can occur in a controlled environment. The integration environment configuration should closely match what will be used in the QA environment. The actual hardware that is used is not as important as the software. In many situations, given that most projects have limited resources, the integration environment is often a small, single-CPU server or spare developer workstation. Following are some things that should be considered when designing this environment:

- **BizTalk Server port configuration**: Often on a developer's local workstation, required BizTalk ports will be simple transports such as the file adapter to facilitate easy testing. Also, port filter criteria may be simplified as the entire list of document filters and transformations may not be required. The integration environment should try to give the developer as controlled and realistic a configuration as possible.

  When talking about creating as realistic a configuration as possible, think about adding a spare machine to your BizTalk group. This can be either in the development environment or in the integration environment. The spare machine can be as simple as an older or underutilized machine. The benefit of doing this is that there is a lot of value in having a two-server group environment. Most new BizTalk developers (and sometimes even seasoned developers) can forget about the implications of a multiserver solution and fall back to behavior such as referencing a local machine path (instead of a network share) or using a logging mechanism, such as the event log, that will show up on only one machine.

- **Strong name key storage**: When building BizTalk components that will be deployed to the management database, it is necessary to implement a strategy for how to manage the strong name keys. Since BizTalk assemblies that are deployed need to be stored in the Global Assembly Cache (GAC), and all assemblies in the GAC need a strong name, this means that all BizTalk assemblies will need to use a strong name key. How this is managed often depends on the type of solution. If the solution will be a "for sale" commercial product, it is critically important to ensure that access to the strong name key is limited to key team members to ensure that the integrity of the application is maintained. In this case, developers are often given a **test key file** that is used to facilitate their building, deploying, and testing activities. Once the code is promoted, the build master then replaces the test key with a production key file.
- **Restricting code deployed**: Only build and deploy code to the integration environment if it is included in the formal build that will be sent to QA. This also helps to keep the integration environment a "managed" environment and not an isolated sandbox like the developer's local workstation.
- **BizTalk MSI exports**: Starting in BizTalk 2006, applications could be exported using Windows Installer technology to a Microsoft Installer (MSI) package. This MSI can be customized to include all required BizTalk Server artifacts and referenced assemblies and configuration. The integration environment is the ideal environment for exporting the MSI package to be used for installation in the QA and production environments.
- **BizTalk 2009 MSBuild functionality**: One of the new features in BizTalk Server 2009 is that BizTalk Solutions can be built using MSBuild. The MSBuild-aware solution and project files can be incorporated into larger MSBuild projects that include the build as well as the deployment scripts. The MSBuild functionality provides additional choices for scripted deployment to integration, QA, and production environments. Most often MSBuild scripts will be created and utilized if additional parts of the larger solution need to be included in the deployment. The MSBuild script may include Commerce Server solutions, custom .NET solutions, and other custom solutions that would not get included in the standard BizTalk MSI functionality. The MSBuild scripts will usually be created by the developers creating the BizTalk solution and may be executed by either the developers or the systems administrators.

The following sections discuss the various approaches for integrating with Visual Studio.

Single Visual Studio Solution

For small- to medium-sized applications (less than 12 VS .NET projects), it is quite feasible to contain all the required Visual Studio projects inside one solution. This one solution is then stored within TFS and is used by all developers, as depicted in Figure 2-8.

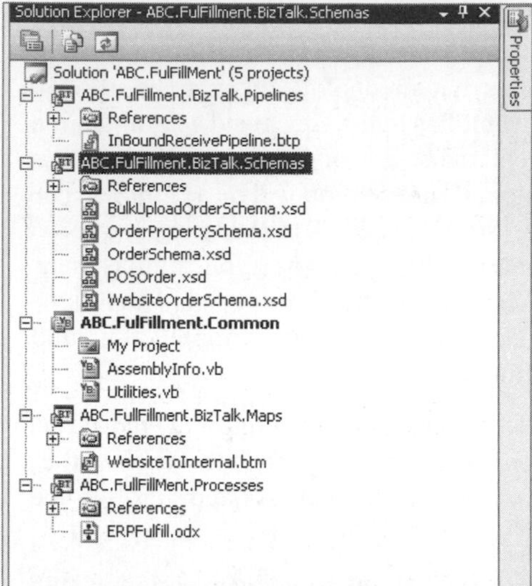

Figure 2-8. *Visual Studio solution layout*

The one solution shared by all developers is often referred to as the **Master solution**, and the solution is bound to the application root in TFS. If the example application were structured as a single-solution configuration, it would most likely be named "ABC.FulFillment.sln" and would be bound to the ABC.FulFillment folder in TFS. This configuration has a number of advantages and disadvantages. First some of the advantages:

- It is simple and easy to manage.
- The entire solution namespace hierarchy is easy to see. Each project will contain only one set of namespaces that will compile to an assembly with the namespace of each class in the assembly equal to the assembly's physical name.
- It allows the entire solution to be built and deployed as a whole without complex build scripts.
- It allows for references between projects to be **project references** and not hard references to a built assembly. This will allow code changes in one project to be automatically reflected in any referenced project and helps to ease version conflict issues.
- Developers will automatically see any checked-in changes from other developer team members. The only action required is to get the latest code check-ins from TFS.

And now some disadvantages:

- It requires the solution file be checked out from TFS if any new projects are added. Each time a project is added to the solution, every developer will be prompted to connect to TFS and get the latest copy of the newly added project.
- Frequent updates to the file cause it to be locked in TFS. Care will need to be taken to ensure that the .sln file in SourceSafe is not checked out for extended periods of time.

- It isn't feasible for teams who don't have BizTalk installed on every development workstation.
- It usually requires that all referenced projects be built along with the main project that is being built. This becomes time consuming as the number of projects increases.
- Solution loading time increases as the number of projects increase. This becomes an issue as the number of BizTalk projects and artifacts within those projects starts to increase.

Multiple Visual Studio Solutions

For larger, more complex projects, it may become necessary to split an application into multiple Visual Studio solutions. In this scenario, there are multiple VS .NET .sln files checked into TFS. Each solution would be logically related to a feature of the application that you are implementing. Each .sln file is bound to a directory in TFS and contains the projects that are required to build the solution. This means that all projects within the solution are part of the solution, and referenced assemblies are referenced in the VS .NET project files as references to assemblies, not references to VS .NET project files.

One of the issues with this approach of carving an application into multiple Visual Studio solutions is how to include common project assemblies within each of the multiple solutions. Consider if there were three VS .NET solutions for each of the three subsystems defined in the earlier example. How would each of these solutions reference the Common Utilities project or the shared BizTalk Schemas project? It is possible to include these common projects within each of the solutions. To have each solution add the project that is needed, you choose the Add Project from Source Control option within the VS .NET solution, as demonstrated in Figure 2-9.

The issue with adding the common VS .NET projects to each of the solutions becomes a matter of controlling who is allowed to edit and modify the shared source control. If a team of developers is specifically assigned to make additions and modifications to shared library assemblies, it is more advisable to have these assemblies included as references to the built DLL, rather than the VS .NET project file. The team responsible for these assemblies will deploy the correct version to the integration server and publish the correct build number. Each project that references the DLL must be updated to include the new assembly version number, or the reference must not include the version information and a new assembly is simply overwritten.

In a multiple solution configuration, a separate build-and-deploy process is necessary. Since the application is divided into separate VS .NET solutions, there are two approaches to building the solution:

- Build and deploy each solution separately.
- Create a **Master VS .NET solution** that includes all VS .NET projects from each solution. Build and deploy this Master solution as a single unit.

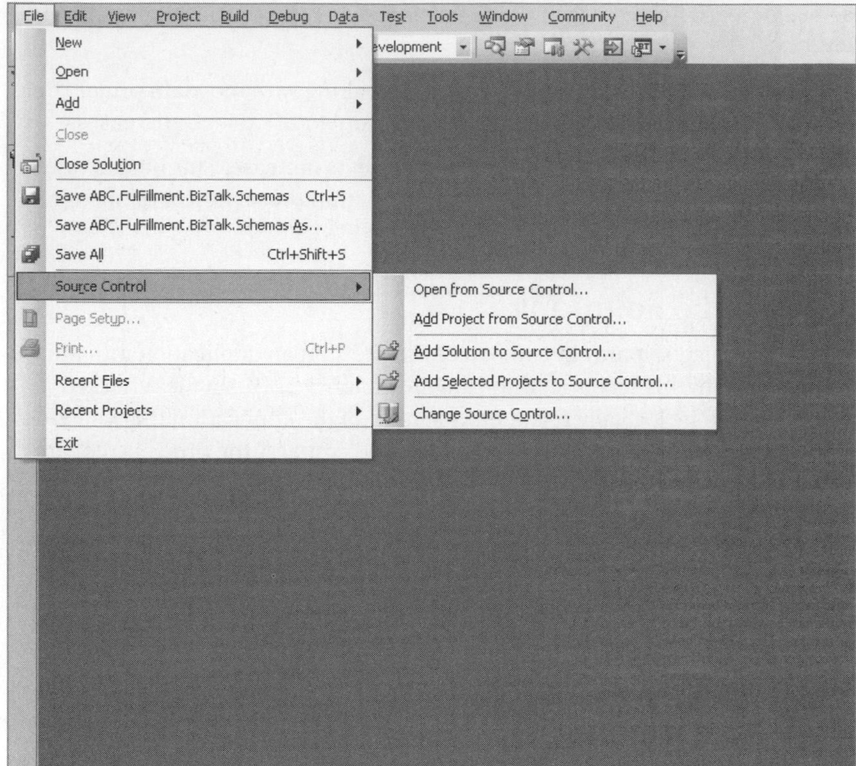

Figure 2-9. *Adding a Visual Studio project from source control*

Advantages of the multiple-solutions approach include the following:

- Only projects that are required to build the solution are loaded when the solution is opened in VS .NET. This can help decrease the amount of time required to load the solution.
- Each solution file is based on a logical application subsystem or feature. The .sln file is then maintained and modified by the group that owns that feature.
- Configuration allows application to be built and deployed as pieces. This allows teams to build and test their feature independent of others.
- It allows the application to incorporate new features without having to dramatically change its layout in TFS.
- Contention for Visual Studio .sln files within TFS will be decreased. Each feature team can add/remove VS .NET projects to their solution without affecting developers from other teams.

The list of advantages is long, but there are also a few disadvantages to the multiple-solutions approach:

- It increases build-and-deploy complexity.
- It increases the chances of versioning issues arising from referencing common components.
- Increased management is needed. A formal build-and-deploy process becomes essential.

Developer-Independent Solutions

In some cases, it is possible to not have the VS .NET solution files checked into TFS. In these situations, each developer has a local .sln file that he uses to add/remove projects as he needs; the .sln file is not used to organize the application into its appropriate features. This configuration works well for teams where the .NET assemblies they support are common to several different applications, and the VS .NET project file can be compiled on its own or with minimal references. The build process will need to take this into account by either creating custom build scripts or creating a master .sln file that is used deploy the solution to the integration environment.

Advantages of developer-independent solutions are as follows:

- It is ideal for small teams or projects with very few independencies.
- It is simple.
- It is flexible and gives developers control over development environment.

As always, there are tradeoffs, this time in the form of the following:

- It causes increased build-and-deploy complexity.
- There is a potential loss of control for development leads.
- It still requires a separate build process or Master solution file.

Application Lifecycle Management with BizTalk Server

Now that we have covered organizing Visual Studio solutions, it is important to make sure that we look at how we integrate into the larger picture. That picture being the larger lifecycle of the application we are about to create. This application may have started before you began your efforts on the project. It will typically continue after you have moved on to your next project. As developers we need to make sure that we are building applications that will be able to serve their purpose long after we are done working on them. In order to do that we need to ensure a sound foundation and architecture, as well as account for governance, manageability, and monitoring. Essentially, we need to plan for the lifecycle of the application as a whole.

This brings us to Application Lifecycle Management (ALM). ALM is broadly defined as the application lifecycle management functions that represent a typical software lifecycle. These functions include requirements, analysis, development, testing, deployment, and operations, and they are categorized into three phases.

We label the three phases of the ALM as follows: Plan, Develop, and Operate/Monitor. Included in the Plan phase are typically the requirements management, analysis, and project management activities, as well as the business vision. In the Develop phase is coding, testing, test case management, build, and deploy. In the Operate/Monitor phase are automated monitoring and alerting functions as well as threshold monitoring and operations improvements. This is not an exhaustive list, but rather just an overview of the types of activities that are found in each phase.

Visual Studio Team System along with Team Foundation Server provides the framework required to deliver what is needed to manage the ALM process including the Microsoft Solutions Framework (MSF) for Agile development and MSF for CMMI process improvement templates to quickly implement software development practices to cover each of the three phases.

In focusing on the Develop phase in this chapter, we will look at how BizTalk Server 2009 has introduced new functionality which enhances its fit into this phase through enhancements in the Visual Studio environment, improvements to the BizTalk project system, TFS integration, Team Test functionality, enhanced debugging support and the inclusion of MSBuild.

Enhancements in the Visual Studio Environment

The enhancements that were introduced in BizTalk Server 2009 included compiler changes, designer changes, MSBuild support and a new project system. The compiler changes affect all of the artifacts. In previous versions, the compiler would take an artifact and compile it directly to an assembly. There was no consistent way to see the code that was generated from the designers.

In previous versions of BizTalk you could modify the GenerateCSFiles registry key to see the intermediate source code but that method is now obsolete. In the current version the compiler works by doing two passes. The first creates a C# file for every artifact and the second pass takes that C# code and creates an assembly. Once you do a build on your project you will see the C# files in your directory. You can also see them in your solution by clicking on the Show All Files toolbar item.

The designer changes are somewhat limited but bring the BizTalk development environment in line with the .NET development environment. What that means is that you have consistency in things like:

Property Dialog Boxes. In previous versions of BizTalk when you would click on the Map or Schema and select Properties from the drop down menu you would be presented with a popup properties dialog box that was different from the regular properties dialog box you get when you hit F4, and that is located in the bottom-right corner of Visual Studio. For developers who were new to BizTalk, this was quite confusing and didn't make sense why this was separated from the rest of the properties. In BizTalk 2009 the data that was contained on this popup properties dialog box has now been integrated with the standard Visual Studio properties dialog box.

Build Types. Build types are consistent with .NET project types and now use the Release and Debug key words instead of the Development and Deployment key words. However, you will continue to see the Development and Deployment configurations for the projects that are migrated from BizTalk Server 2006 R2.

Lastly, it is hard to talk about enhancements without mentioning that BizTalk now takes advantage of the latest versions with support for Visual Studio 2008, the .NET framework 3.5, SQL Server 2008 and Windows Server 2008.

Improvements in the BizTalk Project System

The project system is where some of the largest changes in BizTalk 2009 were introduced. The improvements in the BizTalk project system included the complete overhaul of the .btproj project file. The project file is now a "flavored" version of the baseline C# project file. What this means is that the features found in C# project types will now be available in the BizTalk project types. Flavoring involves creating a project system on top of an existing base project to provide customized functionality that is not available through the base project system. By doing this, BizTalk is able to leverage several important features such as an integrated designer and debugging experience, build & validate error navigation, source control and TFS integration, and exposing project assembly properties through the AssemblyInfo.cs file. Project flavoring provides additional customizations such as deployment, project item properties, MSBuild support, add web reference, BizTalk build install options and additional functionality around errors and error navigation.

In the previous section we mentioned the combined properties dialog box. Property settings from that dialog box are now located in the .btproj.user file. Since the settings are stored in this file in plain text they can be manipulated outside of Visual Studio by unit testing frameworks or continuous integration systems.

One thing to keep in mind is that the .btproj.user file is typically not included when checking code into source code repositories. It will be up to your individual preferences if you want that file checked in and available to all of the developers on your team.

The storing of properties in the .btproj.user file, along with the changes to the .btproj file, provides additional options in the ALM cycle. You now can have custom test tasks and build tasks modify the data in these files to change and automate the way that tests run and the way that builds occur. Continuous integration and build scripts are examples of this type of automation.

Another feature that has changed is that the Embed Tracking Information and Generate Debugging Information output configuration properties have been replaced by the Define TRACE constant and Define DEBUG constant build options on the Build tab of Project Designer. This further brings the development experience in sync with what you get when doing standard, .NET development.

You can't talk about ALM without talking about Unit Testing. Unit Testing is important enough that we've devoted a major section later in the chapter to just to this subject. Look at the section named " Using Test-Driven Development."

Lastly, by using the flavored project type and the features of MSBuild, BizTalk developers can now build projects without Visual Studio. This means that having your BizTalk solution files on a computer that has MSBuild, you will be able to build BizTalk projects without having BizTalk or Visual Studio installed. Using a build server for BizTalk is so much easier and no longer requires anything additional to what we have always used for .NET builds. In addition, the build process is incremental. Each BizTalk artifact is a C# class and therefore when building a project only those classes that have changed will be built thus shortening the time it takes to build BizTalk projects.

TFS Integration

BizTalk Server 2009 provides tighter integration with TFS then any of its predecessors. This integration includes source control, bug tracking, automated unit tests, automated builds, and the ability to perform continuous integration.

When looking at the build and deploy phase of the development process, you probably want to be able to take a BizTalk solution and check in updated files, kick off a build (and have it complete without errors), perform unit tests, perform a deployment, and then run a set of build verification tests (BVTs). All of this is now possible with TFS and BizTalk.

Throughout this chapter and this book, we will cover many of the items just listed. One new concept that we should explore now is that of continuous integration.

Continuous integration refers to the practice of frequently integrating your code with the rest of the codebase that will be released.

To take advantage of continuous integration within TFS, start by creating a new build definition inside of Team Explorer. When the Build Definition dialog box appears, set the Workspace setting to your source control folder, and then click the Project File section. Click Create to make a new build project. When the wizard appears, select your solution, and continue to follow through the wizard pages. Next select your build type in the Configurations section, and click Next to move to the Options page. Next you can select the Run Tests check box and click your unit tests that you created as part of your solution. Click Finish to save the settings in the wizard.

At this point, you are back in the Build Definition dialog box. Move to the Build Defaults section, and select New to create a new build agent. Fill in the values according to your environment, and click OK. Once back in the Build Definition dialog box, fill in the network share location for the builds to be copied. You are now at the last step, the Trigger section. In this section, select the "Build each check-in (more builds)" radio button, and click OK. You now have an automated solution to provide you with a continuous build system.

At a high level, an organization that is looking to take full advantage of their investment in these technologies should look to implement a fully streamlined process, which includes the ability to take a BizTalk solution and move it through the build, unit test, deployment, and BVT tasks in an automated and consistent manner.

Enhanced Debugging

There were a number of enhancements in the area of debugging. The one we will cover here is Map debugging.

Map debugging is now included on the popup menu on the map file. When you select this option Visual Studio will open a debug session with the generated XSLT. You can provide input instance and start stepping through each line of the XSLT. The debugger will also let you debug script code in certain instances.

As you walk through the lines of code you can hover over variables to see their values. There are a couple of things to keep in mind when debugging. The debugger does not support maps with multiple input schemas nor does it support maps that use extension objects.

Now that we have covered the ALM experience and how the development effort fits into the larger effort, we can talk about organizing artifacts in BizTalk.

Organizing Artifacts in BizTalk Server

You're likely to use BizTalk for more than one application. You'll then quickly run into the problem of organizing your application artifacts such as ports, schemas, and so forth. There are two facets to organizing. First you must understand the concept of a **BizTalk application**. Then you can use the Administration Console to do the actual work of sorting your artifacts so that you can easily see which artifacts go with which application.

BizTalk Applications

BizTalk 2009 continues with the application model within the BizTalk administrator. If you remember back to BizTalk 2004, all artifacts such as ports and orchestrations were not organized according to what application used them. Instead each artifact was simply deployed to the management database. In addition, the BizTalk Explorer tool in Visual Studio could also be utilized to create many of the BizTalk artifacts, such as send and receive ports, that we now create using the BizTalk administrator.

With BizTalk 2006 the situation had dramatically improved with the introduction of BizTalk applications. Applications allowed an administrator to logically group artifacts according to the application that used them. At that point the Visual Studio BizTalk explorer was not updated to support that functionality. Figure 2-10 shows the BizTalk Administrator with its applications, as well as the dialog box to set the application in Visual Studio.

In BizTalk 2009 the move to solely use the BizTalk Administration Console is complete. The BizTalk Explorer that was included in Visual Studio has been deprecated and will be removed in future versions. All of the functionality that was provided through BizTalk Explorer is now provided through the BizTalk Administrator.

The application is an important aspect in BizTalk development as it is a container for all of your solutions artifacts including the send and receive ports. In addition, it represents the scope of a deployment. As you look at the design of your solution you need to keep in mind how it will fit into the application container.

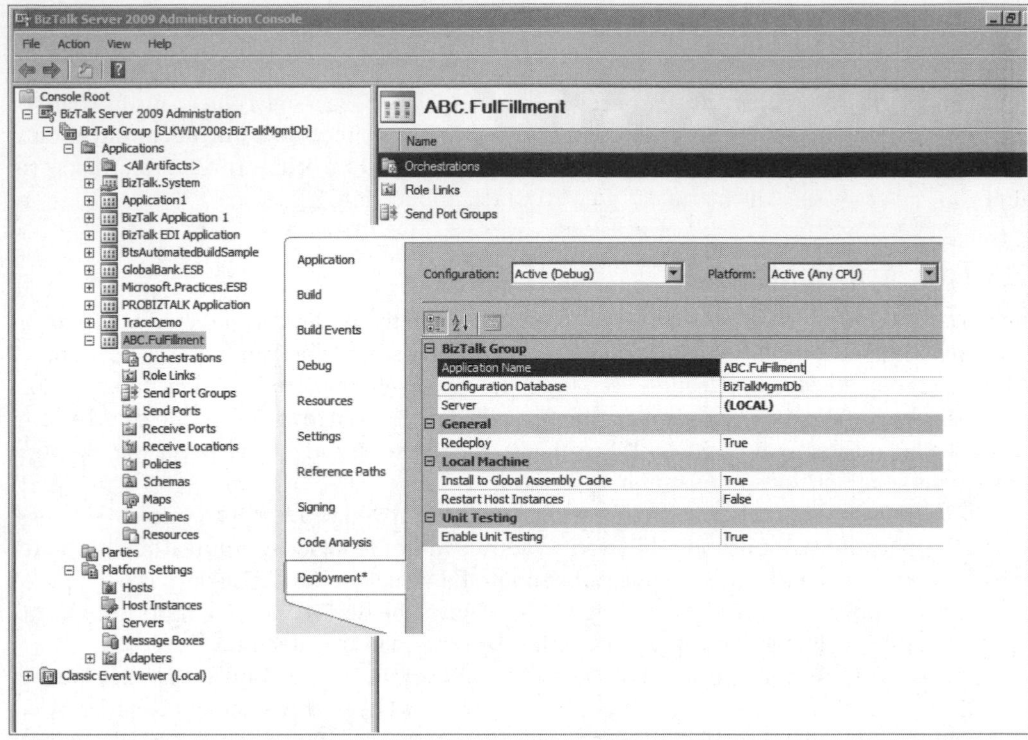

Figure 2-10. *BizTalk 2009 applications in the BizTalk Administrator and the Visual Studio BizTalk project properties dialog box*

BizTalk's Administration Console

BizTalk's **Administration Console** is a Microsoft Management Console (MMC) that allows for the ability to create, configure, and manage one or more applications across multiple servers. Additionally, the MMC includes the ability to import and export applications for installation across multiple servers or to facilitate the moving of applications between staging and production environments. Finally, the console includes the message- and service-monitoring capabilities previously provided by HAT, the Health and Activity Tracking tool introduced in BizTalk Server 2004. The functionality provided by HAT is now folded into the Administration Console and HAT is no longer included.

In Figure 2-11, you can see the organization of BizTalk applications in the Administration Console. Each application is contained within the **applications root** of the server. Fresh installs of BizTalk Server create a system application called **BizTalk.System** that contains all global schemas, assemblies, and artifacts and a default application called **BizTalk Application 1**. If you don't explicitly create a new application and enter that name in the project properties of Visual Studio, each time you deploy, your artifacts will go into the default application.

If you are upgrading from BizTalk Server 2004, your artifacts will also be installed in the BizTalk Application 1 root. After the upgrade is complete, it is advisable to create a new logical application container and move the artifacts to it to avoid confusion. The upgrade from BizTalk 2006 will be smooth transition and BizTalk application settings will be maintained.

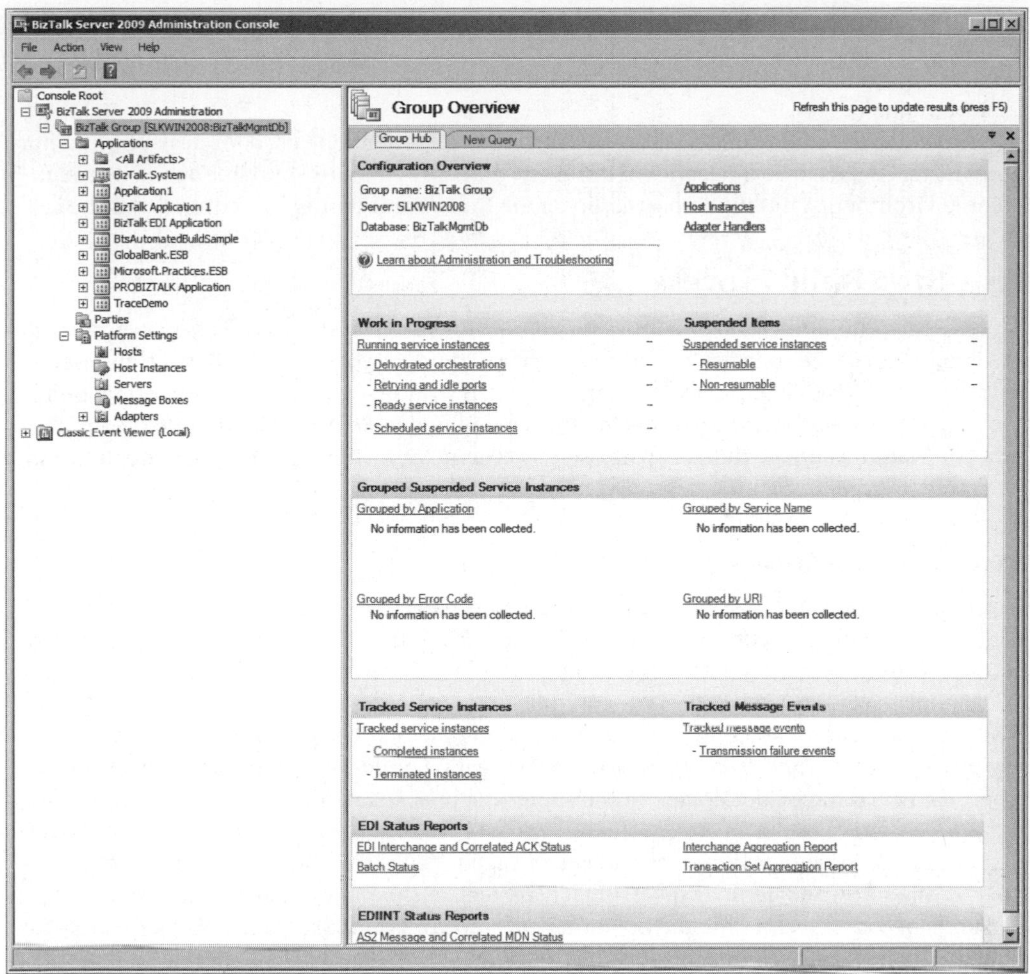

Figure 2-11. *BizTalk 2009 Administration Console*

Creating a Build-and-Integration Environment

As stated in the section "Configuring Your Development Environment," BizTalk development is an isolated model. Because of that, whenever you have a team of people working on a project, you will need to create a build-and-integration environment in which you can deploy and test the unit-tested assemblies and artifacts from each team. You can then use the build-and-integration environment to produce the new version of the installation package through which to update any other environments. It is crucial that this installation package be versioned to allow for bugs/issues to be logged against specific versions of the application to ensure that regression bugs can be tracked down quickly.

The hardware configuration for a build-and-integration environment is usually fairly simple. This usually consists of one machine that is not used for development purposes, generally one small server or developer workstation that is used to get the latest version of the source code from TFS, label the source code, build the code, deploy to the integration environment, and build the MSI deployment package. The environment must be configured as a standalone environment with the BizTalk databases installed and configured separately from other environments.

It is critical that the build-and-integration environment not be used for development purposes as this needs to be a "clean" environment that only contains source code to be used in other environments. It is the responsibility of the Build Manager to ensure that this is the case.

Five-Step Build Process

Every development team needs a process to build and test their software. This is as important as the creation of the code itself. Many different build processes exist, but they are all essentially the same with slight twists or enhancements. If your team does not have a formal build process, you need to get one. For this reason, a simplified build process is included here. This process is simple enough that it can be used by even novice teams, yet flexible enough to allow it to scale to larger development groups.

Step 1: Developer Check-In

Pick a regular time each day when unit-tested code needs to be checked into source control. Ideally, this check-in occurs at the same time each day to help enforce a "rhythm" to the project. The most important rule to enforce in this step is *code checked in for a build must compile.*

If code in source control does not compile, there needs to be a process in place to ensure that only compilable code is in source control. If not, the build is considered "broken." Usually there is a special gift for any developer who breaks a build. One of us was once on a team where we would have a dunce cap for the coder who checked in broken code. It was required that he wear the "I Broke the Build" cap for two days while at work. It only took this particular author once to learn to never check bad code in again. Since this form of negative encouragement is often frowned upon by the politically correct, another trick is to have a "swear" jar. Each line of code checked into the build that doesn't work costs $20. At the project's completion, the money goes towards the party.

Step 2: Build Manager Sets Version and Labels Code

Labeling the code is the process of time-stamping all source files with an identifiable tag so that a specific version can be retrieved. In TFS, a label can be anything, but usually the label contains the build number for that day. For example, if the build number for today were 1.0.3.45, then the label would also be 1.0.3.45. This allows the Build Manager to easily retrieve source code for previous builds if there ever is an issue with regression. It is critical that the version label from TFS match the assembly version information that is included in the build. Each .NET assembly must have its AssemblyInfo file updated with the proper build and version number for each build. By default, Visual Studio sets the version number to 1.0.0.0. This is a change in the latest version of Visual Studio. Previously it would set the version number to 1.0.*. This will cause the version to auto-increment each time the solution is built. There are still companies that use this auto-increment as a standard. As in previous versions of BizTalk it is a recommended best practice to change this number manually or by using a version structure as outlined in the next section.

In this latest version of BizTalk the assembly information, that used to be on the Assembly tab of the project properties dialog box, now appears in the AssemblyInfo.cs file that is in the Properties folder of your project. This is another item that was modified to align with the .NET development environment. An example of one is provided here:

```
using System.Reflection;
using System.Runtime.CompilerServices;
using System.Runtime.InteropServices;
using Microsoft.XLANGs.BaseTypes;
using Microsoft.BizTalk.XLANGs.BTXEngine;

// General Information about an assembly is controlled through the following
// set of attributes. Change these attribute values to modify the information
// associated with an assembly.
[assembly: AssemblyTitle("")]
[assembly: AssemblyDescription("")]
[assembly: AssemblyConfiguration("")]
[assembly: AssemblyCompany("")]
[assembly: AssemblyProduct("")]
[assembly: AssemblyCopyright("Copyright ©  2009")]
[assembly: AssemblyTrademark("")]
[assembly: AssemblyCulture("")]
[assembly: Microsoft.XLANGs.BaseTypes.BizTalkAssemblyAttribute(typeof(BTXService))]

// Setting ComVisible to false makes the types in this assembly not visible
// to COM components.  If you need to access a type in this assembly from
// COM, set the ComVisible attribute to true on that type.
[assembly: ComVisible(false)]

// The following GUID is for the ID of the typelib if this project is exposed to COM
[assembly: Guid("dee3b006-20d8-4cec-b1bf-6552472a5cce")]

// Version information for an assembly consists of the following four values:
//
//      Major Version
//      Minor Version
//      Build Number
//      Revision
//
// You can specify all the values or you can default the Build and Revision Numbers
// by using the '*' as shown below:
// [assembly: AssemblyVersion("1.0.*")]
[assembly: AssemblyVersion("1.0.0.0")]
[assembly: AssemblyFileVersion("1.0.0.0")]
```

Another option besides the standard AssemblyInfo.cs file is that of an Assembly Info Manager.

An assembly info manager is a simple .NET-based structure that can be used to store static properties for assemblies within a solution. This class is then used by all AssemblyInfo files within the solution. This will allow the Build Manager to have to change only one file and have its information reflect in all assemblies within the build. An example implementation is given here:

```
namespace ABC.FulFillment.Common
{
    public class AssemblyInfoManager
    {
        public const string Company = "ABC Company";
        public const string ProductName = "FulFillment Application";
        public const string Copyright = "Copyright(c) 2009 ABC Inc.";
        public const string Trademark = "";
        public const string MajorVersion = "1";
        public const string MinorVersion = "01";
        public const string BuildNumber = "1";
        public const string RevisionNumber = "35";
    }
}
```

In order to use the class a reference to the assembly which contains the class will need to be made. In addition, the AssemblyInfo.cs file will need to be modified to look like the following:

```
using System.Reflection;
using System.Runtime.CompilerServices;
using System.Runtime.InteropServices;
using ABC.FulFillment.Common;

// General Information about an assembly is controlled through the following
// set of attributes. Change these attribute values to modify the information
// associated with an assembly.
[assembly: AssemblyTitle("ABC.BizTalk.PipelineComponents")]
[assembly: AssemblyDescription("ABC Pipeline Components")]
[assembly: AssemblyConfiguration("")]
[assembly: AssemblyCompany(AssemblyInfoManager.Company)]
[assembly: AssemblyProduct(AssemblyInfoManager.ProductName)]
[assembly: AssemblyCopyright(AssemblyInfoManager.Copyright)]
[assembly: AssemblyTrademark(AssemblyInfoManager.Trademark)]
[assembly: AssemblyCulture("")]
```

```
// Setting ComVisible to false makes the types in this assembly not visible
// to COM components.  If you need to access a type in this assembly from
// COM, set the ComVisible attribute to true on that type.
[assembly: ComVisible(false)]

// The following GUID is for the ID of the typelib if this project is exposed to COM
[assembly: Guid("368a756f-fe85-4d16-b522-946ee7fda624")]

// Version information for an assembly consists of the following four values:
//
//      Major Version
//      Minor Version
//      Build Number
//      Revision
//
// You can specify all the values or you can default the Build and Revision Numbers
// by using the '*' as shown below:
// [assembly: AssemblyVersion("1.0.*")]
[assembly: AssemblyVersion(AssemblyInfoManager.MajorVersion + "." + ➥
AssemblyInfoManager.MinorVersion + "." + AssemblyInfoManager.BuildNumber + ➥
"." + AssemblyInfoManager.RevisionNumber)]
```

Step 3: Build the Master Solution

Depending on the configuration (single, multiple, or none) of the Visual Studio solution files, this step can either be a single task or a multistep task. Assuming there is a Master Build Visual Studio .NET solution that contains all VS .NET projects to be included in the build, the Build Manager opens this solution within Visual Studio and builds it. Each Visual Studio project should be configured to output its assembly to the proper folder so that it can be loaded from the proper location.

Step 4: Deploy to the Integration Environment

This is a simple step that can be completed by selecting the Deploy build option within Visual Studio as demonstrated in Figure 2-12. The name of the server to deploy the solution is hard-coded in the .sln file. A way around this is to use the "." (dot) as the server name. This will cause Visual Studio to deploy the solution to the local machine. VS .NET will automatically deploy any BizTalk assemblies to the management database without having to create any additional build scripts.

Table 2-3. *Continued*

Shape	Standard	Notes	Examples
Construct Message (Transform)	Xform_<SourceSchema>To <DestSchema> (for Construct) or X_<SourceSchema>To <DestSchema> (for expression) or Construct_<DestSchema>	If a Construct shape contains a message transform, it should be prefixed with "Xform_" followed by an abbreviated description of the transform (i.e., source schema to destination schema). The actual message transform shape contained should generally be named the same as the containing shape, except with an "X_" prefix to save space.	Xform_LoanRequest ToCreditRequest which contains transform shape X_LoanRequestTo CreditRequest or Construct_Invoice
Construct Message (containing multiple shapes)		If a Construct Message shape uses multiple assignments or transforms, the overall shape should be named to communicate the net effect, using no prefix.	
Call Orchestration Start Orchestration	Call_<OrchestrationName> Start_<OrchestrationName>		
Throw	Throw_<ExceptionType>	The corresponding variable name for the exception type should (often) be the same name as the exception type, only camel cased.	Throw_RuleException, which refers to the ruleException variable.
Parallel	Parallel_<DescriptionOfParallel Work>	Parallel shapes should be named "Parallel_" followed by a description of what work will be done in parallel.	Parallel_CreditVendor Calls
Delay	Delay_<DescriptionOfWhat WaitingFor>	Delay shapes should be named "Delay_" followed by an abbreviated description of what is being waited for.	Delay_POAcknowledge Timeout
Listen	Listen_<DescriptionOfOutcomes>	Listen shapes should be named "Listen_" followed by an abbreviated description that captures (to the degree possible) all the branches of the Listen shape.	Listen_POAckOrTimeout Listen_FirstShippingBid
Loop	Loop_<ExitCondition>	Loop shapes should be named "Loop_" followed by an abbreviated description of what the exit condition is.	Loop_AllMsgsSent
Role Link		See "Roles" in Table 2-2 earlier.	
Suspend	Suspend_<ReasonDescription>	Suspend shapes describe what action an administrator must take to resume the orchestration. More detail can be passed to an error property—and should include what should be done by the administrator before resuming the orchestration.	Suspend_ReEstablish CreditLink
Terminate	Terminate_<ReasonDescription>	Terminate shapes describe why the orchestration terminated. More detail can be passed to an error property.	Terminate_Timeouts Expired
Call Rule	CallRules_<PolicyName>	The policy name may need to be abbreviated.	CallRules_Credit Approval
Compensate	Compensate or Compensate_<TxName>	If the shape compensates nested transactions, names should be suffixed with the name of the nested transaction—otherwise it should simply be "Compensate".	Compensate_ TransferFunds or Comp_TransferFunds

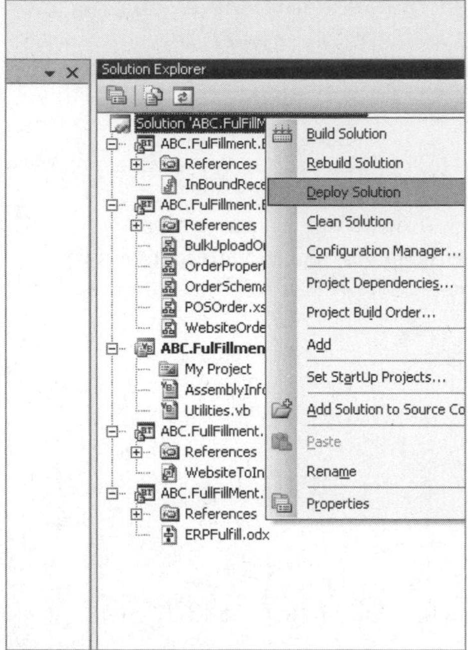

Figure 2-12. *Deploying a BizTalk solution from Visual Studio .NET*

Step 5: Run a Build Verification Test

Once the build is installed in the integration environment, the last task is to perform a test of the build. Generally this is an automated test such as processing a set of test messages and verifying that the output is as expected. This is often called a **build verification test** or **BVT**. An easy way to implement a BVT is to configure a file-based receive location that a set of test messages can be dropped into. These messages would simulate a process that produces a known result such as a set of output messages. Another option would be to automate the BVT test through the use of the BizUnit Automated testing tasks for BizTalk. The BizUnit tasks would provide the means to set up a repeatable set of tests that could be run each and every time a build was done. In either scenario, a series of messages should be created that model several different test scenarios. Once each of the scenarios has been run and the results verified, the build is said to be "good."

Using Test-Driven Development

Test-driven development is a methodology that states developers should first think about how to test their software before they build it. The software tests are written during the design phase and traditionally take the form of a unit test and unit test plans. **Unit tests** are the "sanity check" tests that developers will create for their software to ensure that all the primary features and test points specified in the unit test plan for the feature are covered. For example, a piece of code that adds two numbers A and B and produces the result will most likely have a unit test plan that states that when you pass in 1 and 2 as parameters, you should get 3 as a result. If not, something is wrong with the code. This is probably the simplest form of a unit test. Extending this example further, unit test plans also should cover error conditions. For example, if your code were to display the result of the division of two numbers, an error check should be made to ensure that the divisor is not zero. In this case, there would be a unit test that attempts to divide by a zero value and check to make sure that this is handled.

Enabling Unit Test Support

The previous versions of BizTalk did not offer a straightforward way to unit test BizTalk artifacts. To facilitate the creation of unit tests, BizTalk 2009 introduces a number of new developer productivity features in the form of unit testing support for Schemas, Maps and Pipelines.

To configure your BizTalk project to take advantage of the new unit testing support, open the properties page and click on the Deployment tab. There is a new section at the bottom called Unit Testing. Select 'True' for the Enable Unit Testing property. This will modify the BizTalk artifacts so that they inherit from TestableSchemaBase, TestableMapBase or TestablePipelineBase.

Validating a Schema

Create a new unit test by selecting New Test from the Test menu in Visual Studio. Add the Microsoft.BizTalk.TestTools assembly to the project references. If you are testing pipelines then you will also need to add Microsoft.BizTalk.Pipeline and Microsoft.BizTalk.PipelineOM. These will provide access to these new features for your test project.

The validate schema method signature looks like:

```
Public bool ValidateInstance (string inputInstanceFileName, ➥
OutputInstanceType inputType)
```

And testing a schema is as simple as:

```
[TestMethod]
public void TestSchema()
{
String fileIn = @"c:\dev\testinput.xml";
//The schema we are testing is called POSchema
POSchema schema = new POSchema();
Assert.IsTrue(schema.ValidateInstance(fileIn, OutputInstanceType.XML));
}
```

A test like this will tell you whether the input failed or succeeded. However, if the test fails there is no way to get the details as to why the input failed. In order to obtain the information to help you diagnose the issue you will have to open the schema in Visual Studio, change the setting to use the failed input message and look at the results in the output window.

Testing a Map

The test map method signature looks like:

```
Public void TestMap (string inputInstanceFilename, InputInstanceType inputType, ➥
string outputInstanceFilename, OutputInstanceType outputType)
```

And testing a map can be as simple as:

```
[TestMethod]
public void TestMap()
{
TestableMapBase map = new ExampleProject.SampleMap();
Map.TestMap(@"c:\dev\testinput.xml", Schema.InputInstanceType.Xml, ➥
"MapOutputFile.xml", Schema.OutputInstanceType.XML);

//at this point we have a result from the map. Lets validate it against the schema.

Schema.TestableSchemaBase outputSchema = new ExampleProject.OutputSchema()
Bool result = outputSchema.ValidateInstance("MapOutputFile.xml", ➥
Schema.OutputInstanceType.XML);

Assert.IsTrue(result, "The output does not validate")'
}
```

It is common practice to compare the output of the map to a known good output file.

Testing a Pipeline

And the test pipeline method signature looks like:

```
public void TestPipeline (StringCollection documents, StringCollection parts, ➥
Dictionary<string, string> schemas)
```

And testing a pipeline can be as simple as:

```
[TestMethod]
public void TestReceivePipeline()
{
StringCollection documents = new StringCollection();
Documents.Add(@"c:\dev\testinput.xml");

StringCollection parts = new StringCollection();

Dictionary<string, string> schemas = new Dictionary<string, string>();
Schemas.Add("ExampleProject.InputSchema", @"➥
..\..\..\ExampleProject.InputSchema.xsd");

Microsoft.BizTalk.TestTools.Pipeline.TestableReceivePipeline pipeline➥
  = new ExampleProject.Pipeline();
Pipeline.TestPipeline(documents, parts, schemas);
}
```

Taking Advantage of BizUnit

In addition to the unit testing enhancements to BizTalk it is also helpful to utilize BizUnit to help facilitate the creation of unit test plans. BizUnit, which is a free tool available at `http://bizunit.codeplex.com/`, is an add-on library that can be used with the Visual Studio Team System Testing Tools (MSTest) functionality or with **NUnit**, a community-developed tool that allows developers to create unit test harnesses for their source code. For more information on NUnit, see the release package at www.nunit.org. BizUnit provides additional reusable test steps that allow you to test the entire range of code in your BizTalk applications.

Getting Your Test Process Together

Once you have created the unit test plans and the associated unit tests using BizUnit with either MSTest or NUnit, you need to think about how to get your test process up and running. In traditional software projects, the unit tests will simply reference the DLL and its methods to be tested. Test data will be passed as arguments to each of the functions in question and the result recorded, which will indicate whether the unit test was successful or not. This is not the case in a BizTalk project.

What you will need to do in a BizTalk project is to create a series of test messages that will simulate the various conditions outlined in your unit test plans. For example, in the previous exercise, you defined the interfaces for the fictitious integration project. If you were to create unit test plans, you would need to create XML documents to be used to simulate real-world messages that would be flowing through the system. These documents would be structured so that they will cause conditions in your unit test plans to be executed. A condition might be to check whether items that are not in stock should be rejected. This is an example of a business requirement being tested.

An example of an error condition would be to check that an incoming document conforms to a proper schema. If the document does not, it should be routed to an exception mechanism. Using test-driven development helps you to think about all the potential scenarios that might otherwise go unnoticed. Test-driven development also helps to avoid the "we didn't code for the scenario and it wasn't in your requirements document" argument that often occurs with the end customer of the software. Test-driven development often helps to find these types of issues before coding even begins and allows the customer to decide whether or not the issue is something they want to address.

Creating a BizTalk Installation Package

The primary mechanism within BizTalk to create an installation packet is through the creation of an MSI package by using the BizTalk Administration Console. Since BizTalk solutions are organized according to applications, the console provides the functionality to export an MSI package based on the configuration and artifacts that are included within the BizTalk application. Additional files can be included as referenced assemblies, which is ideal for packaging satellite DLL files or configuration files that are not included as artifacts but are still required for the solution to run properly. If your solution exposes web services, the MSI package will also include the web settings. The MSI file is generated by first right-clicking the BizTalk application in the BizTalk Administration Console and choosing Export MSI to bring up the Export

Wizard. The wizard will guide you through the process of creating your export package by having you select the resource(s), dependencies, and destination location for the MSI. During the process, a progress status window is provided and a final summary page appears with any failures encountered during the export process. The MSI package that is created contains the binaries, resources, configuration, and binding file information to import the application on another BizTalk installation, as shown in Figures 2-13 and 2-14.

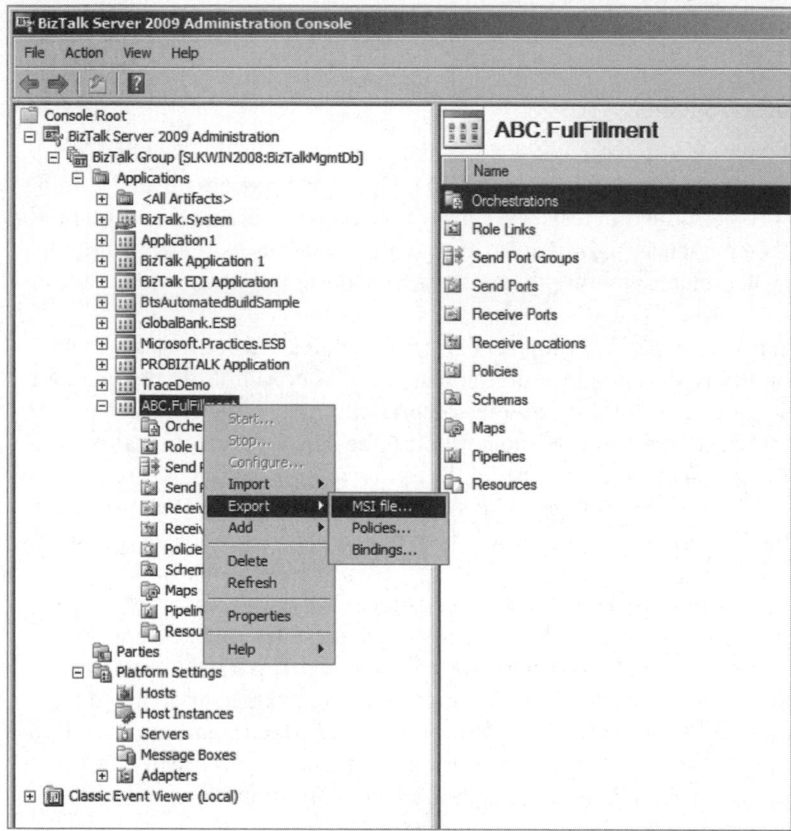

Figure 2-13. *Exporting an MSI using the BizTalk Administration Console*

In order to install the application, you need to first run the MSI package on each machine that will be hosting it. To do this, simply click the MSI package to import all the necessary assemblies and resources and install them into the GAC. This must be done on each BizTalk Server node that will host the application. You then need to import the BizTalk Server artifacts into the system by opening the BizTalk Administration Console, right-clicking the application, and choosing Import as shown in Figure 2-14. For a complete walkthrough of the deployment process within BizTalk 2009, see Chapter 10.

The import process not only imports the BizTalk Server artifacts, but when a binding file is included in the MSI, it also sets the port bindings and port configurations. This needs to be performed only once per install since these settings are deployed to the BizTalk Management DB.

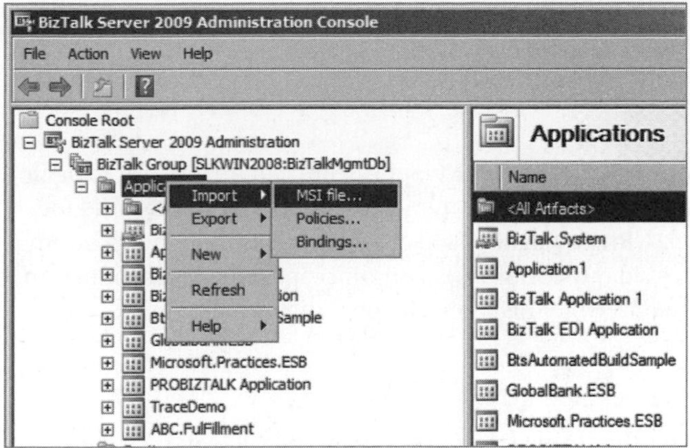

Figure 2-14. *Importing a BizTalk Server MSI*

BizTalk Assembly Naming and Versioning

A BizTalk assembly is created by compiling a BizTalk project using VS .NET.[2] Any artifacts in the project will be included in the compiled assembly that is to be deployed. BizTalk assemblies should match the name of their associated namespace. For example, if your namespace is `Company.Project.Subsystem`, then your assembly should be named Company.Project.Subsystem.dll.

In theory, the formal assembly name and the DLL name can be different, but you can only make them different by creating a custom build script outside of Visual Studio. Generally, it isn't necessary to use a DLL name that doesn't correspond to the namespace, and you're better off avoiding the extra work by keeping the names the same.

Note that a division into assemblies such as the following will often be quite suitable for a small- to medium-sized BizTalk project, as in many cases the BizTalk artifacts are shared across all features and subsystems:

- MyCompany.MyProject.Orchestrations.dll
- MyCompany.MyProject.Schemas.dll
- MyCompany.MyProject.Pipelines.dll
- MyCompany.MyProject.Transforms.dll
- MyCompany.MyProject.PipelineComponents.dll

If these artifacts were not shared and were specific to a feature, the namespace would be `MyCompany.MyProject.MySubsystem`.

2. The material in this section originally appeared in "DotNet, BizTalk, and SQL Team Development," (REED003675).zip. Copyright by Microsoft Corporation. Reprinted with permission from Microsoft Corporation.

■ **Note** The Visual Studio solution name will likely be MyCompany.Project.BizTalk in this case.

Often long names such as MyCompany.MyProject.MySubsystem can be difficult to deal with (especially in Visual SourceSafe 6.0, where the file open dialog boxes do not expand for longer names). The benefits, however, with having the full scoping available when the assemblies and associated artifacts are accessed outside of Visual Studio, especially in a production support and deployment scenario, far outweigh this minor inconvenience.

Side-by-Side Deployments

Within most BizTalk projects, there may be "in-progress" development that can take days, weeks, or even months to complete. In such scenarios, deploying new releases or hot fixes is difficult to achieve. In order to upgrade to a new version of the currently running application, it becomes necessary to allow any in-progress processes to reside **side by side** with the newer releases. When all in-progress processes are complete, then the earlier versions can be safely undeployed without affecting any processes of the newer releases.

In some cases, there may also be a need for multiple versions to reside side by side for an indefinite amount of time. In these scenarios, it becomes vital to ensure the activating logic is unique to guarantee the correct messages are passed on to correct versions. The default versioning process is shown in Figure 2-15.

Following are some unique requirements for side-by-side deployments:

- Provide an ability to deploy new releases.
- Provide an ability to deploy incremental releases (without affecting previous deployments).
- Provide an ability to deploy hot fixes (redeployment of recent deployment installs without affecting previous deployments).
- To ease maintenance, stamp all assemblies with the same version.

Default Versioning

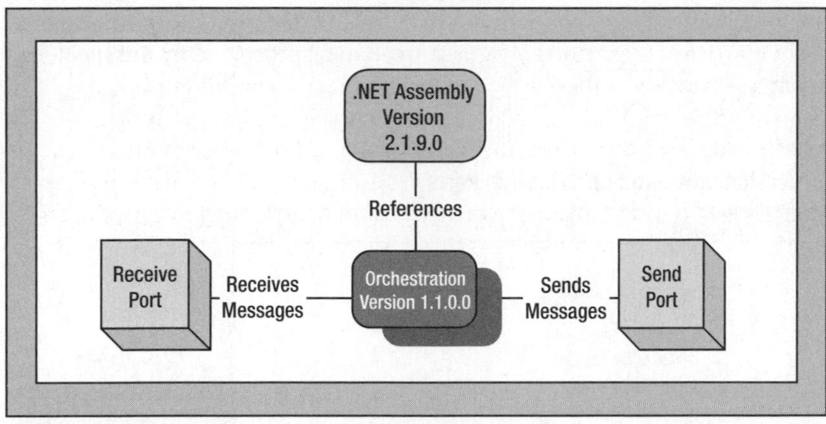

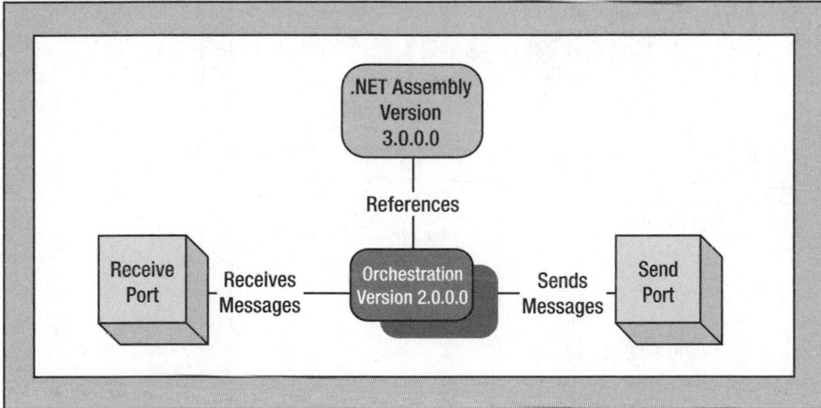

Figure 2-15. *Default versioning*

Side-by-Side Deployment Strategies

To achieve side-by-side deployment, it is necessary to ensure versioning is maintained appropriately between all referenced assemblies. Without a versioning strategy, any side-by-side deployment strategy is prone to errors. Within .NET, any assembly references (either BizTalk or non-BizTalk) need to match the assembly versions defined within referenced objects at compile time.

The default versioning scheme causes a conflict within the BizTalk environment. In a typical BizTalk environment, along with the assemblies, you also have external objects like receive/send ports and schemas that are shared between different versions. Messages meant for one version can be picked up and processed by another version, which may lead to errors or undesired results.

To solve this problem, it becomes necessary to extend .NET's versioning scheme for BizTalk. The following sections describe three common strategies for doing this.

Versioned Deployment Using Versioned Receive/Send Ports

In this strategy, all receive port and send port names are unique across multiple deployments. Hence any messages that arrive at these ports are guaranteed to be processed by the specific versioned modules that are listening to these specific ports. A diagram of this approach is shown in Figure 2-16.

Versioning Using Send/Receive Ports

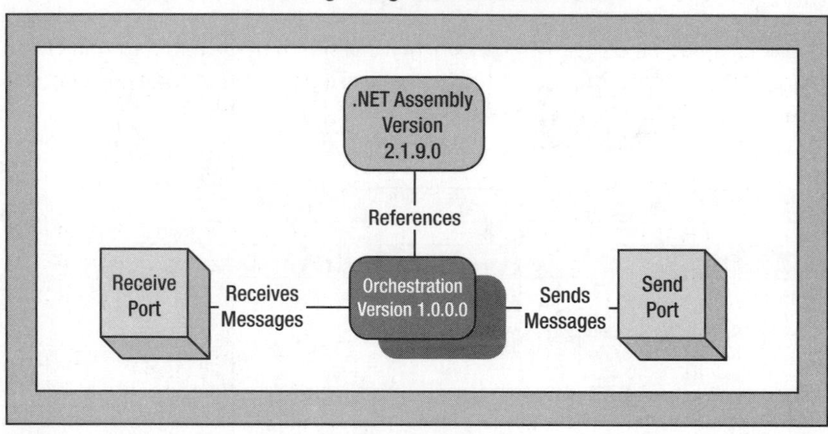

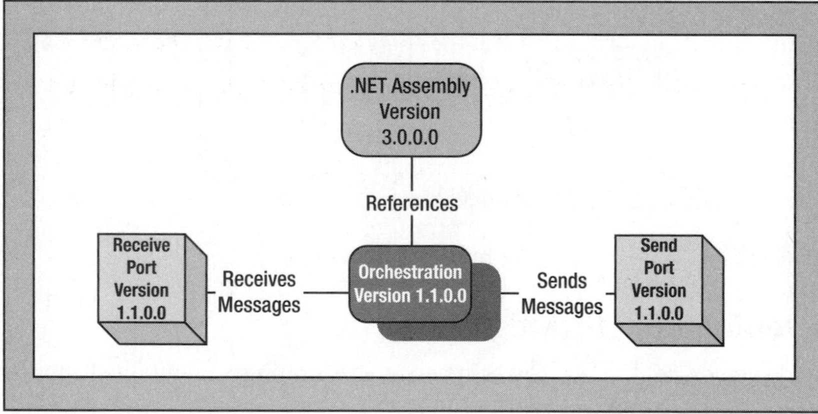

Figure 2-16. *Versioned deployment using ports*

Following are the steps involved:

1. Update the assembly version defined within the specific BizTalk project.
2. Update the assembly version defined within the associated non–BizTalk assemblies.
3. Before compilation, update each binding file associated with the BizTalk modules with appropriate port names (port names will be suffixed with the assembly version). If the binding step is included during deployment, these ports will get created during deployment.

The advantages of this process are as follows:

- The deployment strategy is clean.
- Any number of deployments are guaranteed to process only those messages that arrive at specific binded ports.
- Namespaces of associated schemas do not need to be changed.

The sole disadvantage is this:

- For every release, all associated receive/send ports will need to be updated to reflect the new version. If external partners are submitting messages, new locations will need to be communicated with external partners.

Versioned Deployment Using Versioned Schema Namespaces

This strategy involves changing the namespaces associated with specific schemas. Changing a namespace is easily accomplished by suffixing each schema's namespace with a specific version number before compilation. This strategy solves the correlation error encountered with the preceding approach and is diagrammed in Figure 2-17.

Perform the following procedure to deploy the assemblies in your project using versioned schema namespaces:

1. Update the assembly version defined within the specific BizTalk project.
2. Update the assembly version defined within the associated non–BizTalk assemblies.
3. Update all references for imports and includes within schemas if you have included any.
4. Before compilation, programmatically update namespaces associated with individual schemas to include references to specific versions (e.g., `http://Microsoft.BizTalk/Service/v1.0.0.0`). Also, keep in mind that there are a lot of places where schema namespaces come into play and may impact your solutions. These include orchestrations, maps, and pipeline components as well as rules. Make sure you check for these out before compilation as well.

Following are the advantages of the versioned deployment approach:

- As BizTalk distinguishes schemas based on namespaces and root node, specific messages are processed by specific versioned assemblies.
- This process works in scenarios where correlation sets are initialized.
- Receive/Send port names do not need to be changed. This is beneficial in scenarios where external partners are submitting messages to specific ports. Using this approach, new port locations do not need to be communicated to external partners.

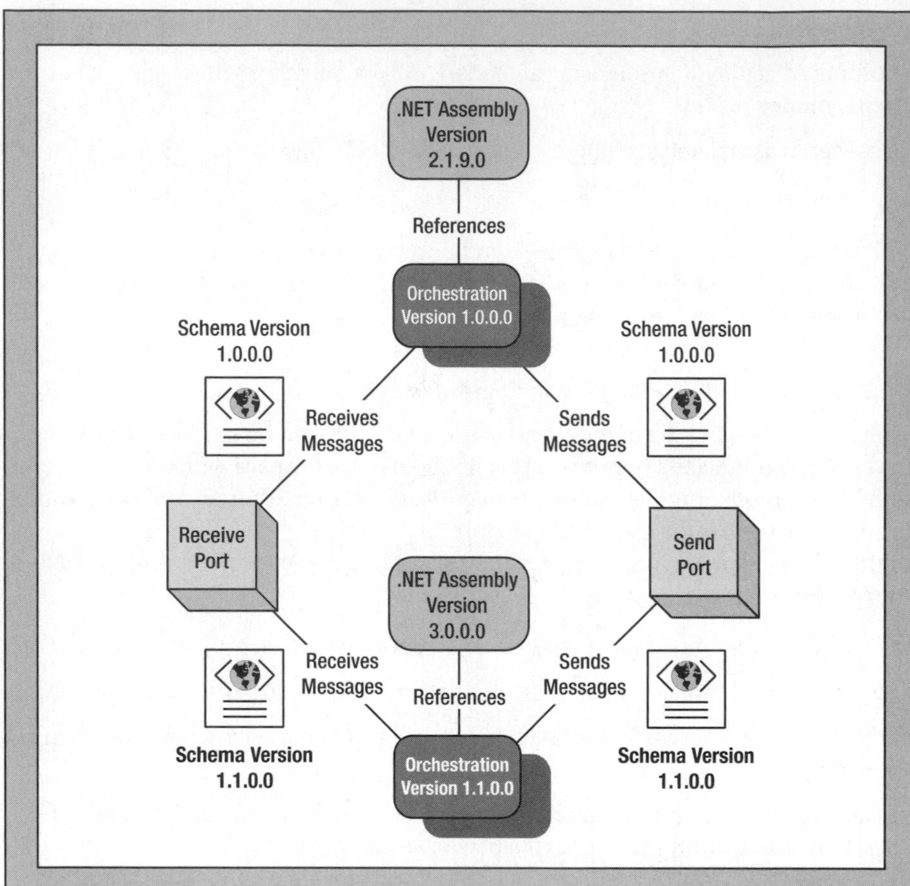

Figure 2-17. *Versioned deployment using namespaces*

Disadvantages of the versioned deployment approach include the following:

- Namespaces of associated schemas should be changed even if there are no structural changes to these specific schemas. This is to ease the management of the schemas once they have been deployed. For instance, it is much easier to examine a DLL and know that all the schemas within it contain the same version. If not, the management of the schemas can become cumbersome.

- For every release, all associated schema namespaces will need to be updated to reflect the new version. This could constitute a significant architectural change.

Combining the Two Approaches

You can combine the previous two approaches using versioned schema namespaces in conjunction with versioned receive/send ports. This approach is shown in Figure 2-18.

Schema Namespace Versioning and Versioned Ports

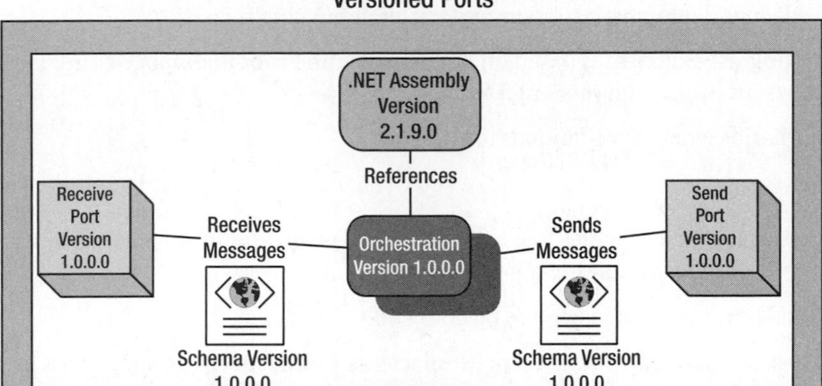

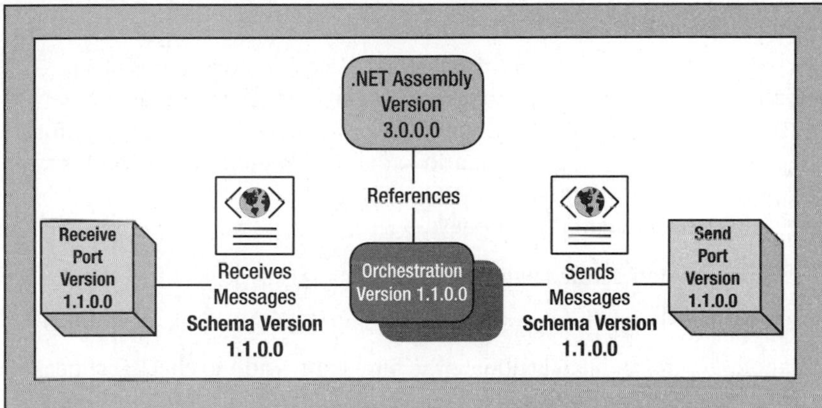

Figure 2-18. *Versioned deployment using ports and namespaces*

The steps involved in the combined approach are as follows:

1. Update the assembly version defined within the specific BizTalk project.
2. Update the assembly version defined within the associated non–BizTalk assemblies.
3. Update all references for imports and includes within schemas if you have included any.
4. Before compilation, programmatically update namespaces associated with each schema to include references to specific versions (e.g., `http://Microsoft.BizTalk/Service/v1.0.0.0`).
5. Before compilation, update each binding file associated with BizTalk modules with appropriate port names (port names will be suffixed with assembly version). These ports will be created if the binding step is included during deployment.

Advantages of the combined approach are as follows:

- It presents a cleaner deployment strategy and easier debugging scenarios.
- As BizTalk distinguishes schemas based on namespaces and root node, specific messages are processed by specific versioned assemblies.
- It works in scenarios where correlation is used.

And the disadvantages:

- Namespaces of associated schemas need to be changed even if there are no structural changes to these specific schemas.
- All receive/send port names also need to be changed.
- For every release, all associated schema namespaces as well as receive/send ports will need to be updated to reflect the new version.

Versioned Deployment Using Filtering

This strategy involves promoting an element within a message (e.g., version) that is used within the filter associated with a Receive shape that gets activated when a message is received by the orchestration. This has the benefit of allowing you to use content-based routing information, which can be changed in a production scenario with no code modification and very little downtime. This approach is shown in Figure 2-19.

Use the following steps to implement this strategy:

1. Update the assembly version defined within the specific BizTalk project.
2. Update the assembly version defined within the associated non–BizTalk assemblies.
3. Before compilation, programmatically update the filter expression to check for specific data that contains version information (e.g., Message1.version = "1.0.0.0"). A version-specific message will get picked up by correct versions and processed.

The advantages of this method are as follows:

- Only filter expressions need to be updated.
- Receive/Send port names do not need to be changed.
- Schema namespaces do not need to be changed.

And the disadvantages:

- It will not work for scenarios where orchestrations are required to initialize a correlation set. If correlation sets are being initialized and schemas of the same version are being referenced between different deployments (different assembly versions), BizTalk does not know which combination of assembly and associated schema to use and generates a runtime error.
- An element within the schema that contains the version number will need to be promoted.
- For every release, this filter will need to be changed to reflect the current version.

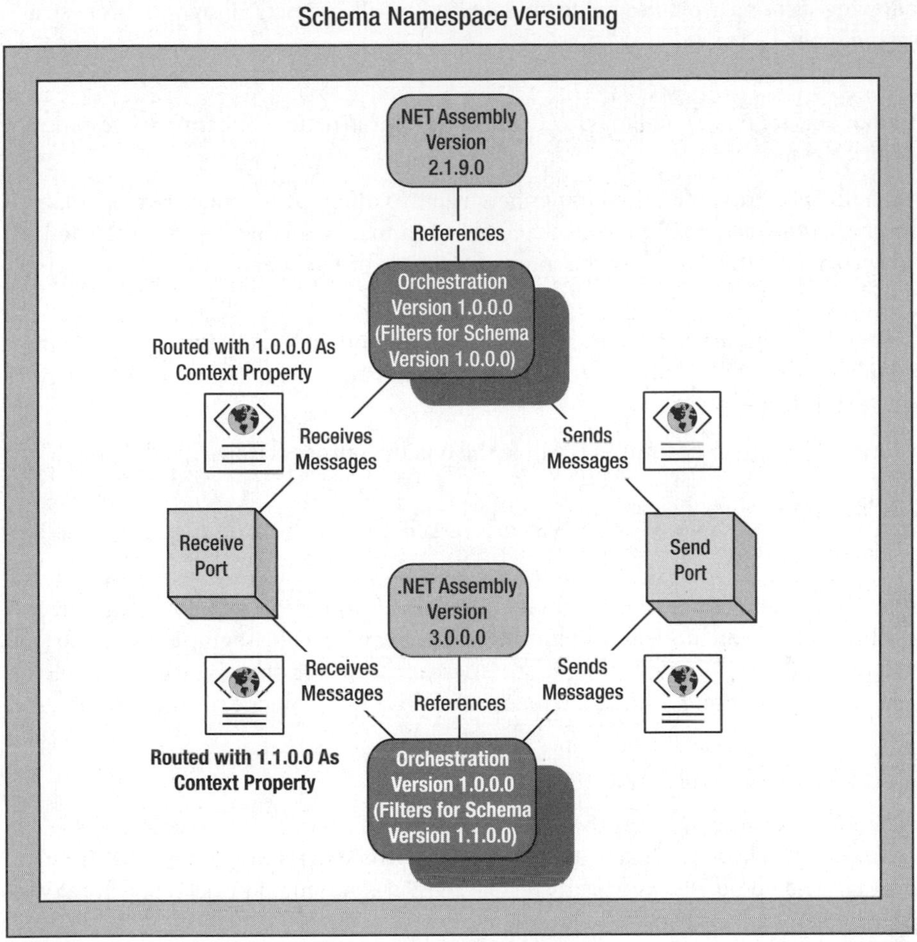

Schema Namespace Versioning

.NET Assembly Version 2.1.9.0

References

Orchestration Version 1.0.0.0 (Filters for Schema Version 1.0.0.0)

Routed with 1.0.0.0 As Context Property

Receives Messages

Sends Messages

Receive Port

Send Port

.NET Assembly Version 3.0.0.0

Receives Messages

References

Sends Messages

Routed with 1.1.0.0 As Context Property

Orchestration Version 1.0.0.0 (Filters for Schema Version 1.1.0.0)

Figure 2-19. *Versioned deployment using filtering*

BizTalk Naming Conventions

One of the key benefits of coding business processes using BizTalk orchestrations is the visual representation of the workflow. When building complex orchestrations, naming conventions are critical for orchestration workflow shapes. Naming conventions are equally important to naming BizTalk artifacts such as maps, ports, and pipelines properly. Using well-defined naming conventions allows both technical and nontechnical persons to view the orchestration and understand the process it is attempting to model. Well-named and commented orchestration shapes enhance the readability and organization of the workflow and allow the reader to follow the flow of messages through the orchestration and understand the source, destination, and content of the message data.

The following sections provide a guide for naming BizTalk artifacts along with orchestration shapes and types.[3]

A BizTalk artifact is any one of the following:

- **Schema**: This is an XSD schema that defines the data structure. Schemas can define XML or a flat file.
- **Map**: A BizTalk map defines mappings between two different schemas. For instance, a purchase order schema has fields that can be mapped to an invoice schema. The map will transfer the data from the source (purchase order) schema to the destination (invoice) schema.
- **Pipeline**: This can be a send or receive pipeline component. Pipelines are used on the send or receive points of BizTalk to do special processing on a message before it is sent out or as it is received.
- **Orchestration**: An orchestration is where the business process is designed and executed.
- **Property schema**: This is a special type of XSD schema used to define properties to be employed in BizTalk.
- **Ports**: Ports can be either send or receive ports as well as receive locations. Naming conventions are even more important when working with a messaging-only scenario. Thought should be put into the naming of these artifacts and should be named well since a large deployment is tough to maintain with a hodge-podge of endpoint names.

BizTalk Artifact Namespaces

The artifacts in BizTalk Server, such as the schemas, maps, orchestrations, and pipelines are compiled into .NET classes. As such, it is generally advisable to follow proper .NET naming conventions as would be followed in any regular .NET development project. Specifically, classes should be named based on the following pattern:

```
Company.Project.Feature
```

In the case of BizTalk projects, most developers want a clear delineation between objects that are only used within BizTalk Server and regular .NET classes. In these cases, the ".BizTalk" part of the namespace is added to give the following pattern:

```
Company.Project.BizTalk.Feature
```

As an example of this pattern, if a Pipeline existed within the FulFillment feature, that pipeline would be under the namespace of `ABC.FulFillment.BizTalk.InBoundReceivePipeline`.

A schema uses a namespace to uniquely qualify elements and attributes within that schema to ensure that conflicts do not occur. Ultimately, uniquely identifying your BizTalk artifacts with target namespaces is important and should not be skipped.

Note that the naming conventions are Pascal cased, and nested namespaces will have dependencies on types in the containing namespace.

3. The remainder of this section originally appeared in "DotNet, BizTalk, and SQL Team Development," (REED003675).zip. Copyright by Microsoft Corporation. Reprinted with permission from Microsoft Corporation.

BizTalk Messaging Artifacts

All names should follow Pascal-case convention unless mentioned otherwise for the specific artifact, although underscores are used to separate logical entities. For schemas, maps, orchestrations, and pipelines, ensure that the .NET type name matches the file name (without file extension). Table 2-2 gives patterns for properly naming BizTalk artifacts.

Table 2-2. *BizTalk Artifact Naming Conventions*

Artifact	Standard	Notes	Examples
Schema file	<RootNode>_<Standard>vn-ma.xsd or <DescriptiveName>vn-ma_ <Standard>.xsd	Standards include XML, X12, flat file (FF), and other custom formats. If root node does not distinguish the schema or if the schema is for a well-known standard, use a descriptive name. vn refers to major version number, m refers to minor number. For unreleased schemas, use a letter suffix to the minor version (like "a"). Include version in the version attribute of the schema element. .NET type name should match, without file extension. .NET namespace will likely match assembly name.	ClaimInvoice.xsd PurchaseOrder Acknowledge_FF.xsd FNMA100330_FF.xsd
Schema target namespaces	Nonshared schemas should have a target namespace corresponding to the .NET namespace of the associated .NET type, prefixed with "http".	.NET type name should match, without file extension. .NET namespace will likely match assembly name.	For a PatientClaim.xsd file, http://<Company>. <Function>.Patient Claim or http://<Contoso>. HealthClaims. PatientClaim. This is a recommendation, but there are times that this can change. One of these times is when you are managing a solution with a single namespace that you want all artifacts to fall under.
Property schema files	<PropSchema>_PropSchema.xsd	Should be named to reflect its common usage across multiple schemas, if needed.	poPropSchema.xsd
Maps	<SourceSchema>_To_ <DestinationSchema>.btm	Name should define/describe what is being mapped.	PurchaseOrder_FF_To_ PurchaseOrder Acknowledge_XML.btm
Orchestrations	A meaningful name that represents the underlying process, likely with a verb-noun pattern.		EvaluateCredit.odx ProcessHealthClaim.odx

Continued

Table 2-2. *Continued*

Artifact	Standard	Notes	Examples
Send/Receive Pipelines	rcv<SchemaName>.btp or rcv<ProjectName>.btp or rcv<Function>.btp snd<SchemaName>.btp or snd<ProjectName>.btp or snd<Function>.btp	A pipeline might be used to ensure reception of particular schema(s) or to perform some other function. A project name might be used when multiple schemas are specified for ASM/DASM.	rcvPOAckPipelineFF.btp rcvCatalogPipeline.btp rcvHealthClaimPipeline EDI.btp rcvInvoiceFromSupplier Pipeline.btp sndPaymentPipeline.btp sndClaimProcess Pipeline.btp sndOrderToWarehouse Pipeline.btp
Receive ports	<BizApp><InputSchema>To <OutputSchema>Port or <BizApp><FunctionalDescription> or rcv<InputSchema>To <OutputSchema>Port or rcv<FunctionalDescription>Port	"BizApp" prefix (corresponding to the name of the app deploying to BizTalk) helps when many applications are deployed to the same BizTalk installation. Use functional description if the input schema (and potentially output schema, if request/response) does not adequately describe the port. One-way ports use functional description form.	ERP_PurchaseOrder_ XML_To_POAck_XML rcvPurchaseOrder ToPOAckPort (for request/response port) ERP_PurchaseOrder_ XML (for one-way port) ERP_CheckOrderStatus rcvPurchaseOrder XMLPort rcvERPStatusPort
Receive locations	<ReceivePortName>_<Transport>		ERPCheckOrderStatus_ MSMQ rcvERPStatus_File
Send Port Groups	<BizApp>_<FunctionalDescription>	"BizApp" prefix—see the receive ports entry.	CRM_CustomerUpdate Notification
Send ports	<BizApp><Schema><Transport> or <BizApp><FuncDescription> <DestApp>_<Transport> or snd<InputSchema>To <OutputSchema>Port or snd<FunctionalDescription>Port sndOrderStatusPort	In some cases, the schema being sent is descriptive enough. In others, a functional description of the action to be taken by a destination app is better suited.	CRM_CustomerUpdate_ ERP_MSMQ sndUpdateToERP SystemPort
Parties	A meaningful name for a trading partner.	If dealing with multiple entities in a trading partner organization, the organization name could be used as a prefix.	INV_MyTradingPartner Name
Roles	A meaningful name for the role that a trading partner plays.		Shipper

Orchestration Naming Conventions—Workflow Shapes

The BizTalk Orchestration Designer allows you to create complex workflow automations quickly and easily. If you are not careful, however, a large orchestration can often become confusing and difficult to debug. One way to help ensure that your orchestration is maintainable is to properly name the orchestration shapes so that they are easily readable and self-explanatory. Microsoft has published some patterns on how to name orchestration shapes,[4] and Table 2-3 expands upon these.

Note To add documentation to a group of related workflow shapes, use a Group shape. These will display as much text as you care to associate with them and can add quite a bit of documentation value to the diagram. (Shape names should always follow upper-camel casing after the prefix that is specified in Table 2-3.)

Table 2-3. *Orchestration Workflow Shape Naming Conventions*

Shape	Standard	Notes	Examples
Scope	Scope_<DescriptionOfContainedWork> or Scope_<DescOfContainedWork>_<TxType>	Info about transaction type may need to be included in some situations where it adds significant documentation value to the diagram.	Scope_CreditServiceCall
Receive	Rcv_<MessageName> or Receive_<MessageName>	Typically, MessageName will be the same as the name of the message variable that is being received.	Rcv_rawCreditReport Receive_CreditReport
Send	Snd_<MessageName> or Send_<MessageName>	Typically, MessageName will be the same as the name of the message variable that is being sent.	Snd_poAcknowledge Send_poAck
Expression	<DescriptionOfEffect>	Expression shapes should be named with upper-camel case convention (no prefix) to simply describe the net effect of the expression, similar to naming a method. The exception to this is the case where the expression is interacting with an external .NET component to perform a function that overlaps with existing BizTalk functionality—use closest BizTalk shape for this case.	GetFindingsReport
Decide	Decide_<DescriptionOfDecision>	Decide shapes should be prefixed with "Decide_" followed by a full description of what will be decided in the "If" branch.	Decide_Approval Required
If Branch	If_<DescriptionOfDecision>	If Branch shapes should be prefixed with "If_" followed by a (perhaps abbreviated) description of what is being decided.	If_ApprovalRequired
Else Branch	Else	Else Branch shapes should always be named "Else".	Else
Construct Message (Message Assignment)	Assign_<Message> (for Construct shape) <ExpressionDescription> (for expression)	If a Construct shape contains a message assignment, it should be prefixed with "Assign_" followed by an abbreviated name of the message being assigned. The actual message assignment shape contained should be named to describe the expression that is contained.	Assign_paymentVoucher which contains the expression CopyPaymentDetails

Continued

4. http://msdn.microsoft.com/library/default.asp?url=/library/en-us/BTS_2004WP/html/ffda72df-5aec-4a1b-b97a-ac98635e81dc.asp

Shape	Standard	Notes	Examples
Multi-Part Message Type	<LogicalDocumentType>	Multipart types encapsulate multiple parts. The WSDL spec indicates "Parts are a flexible mechanism for describing the logical abstract content of a message." The name of the multipart type should correspond to the "logical" document type, i.e., what the sum of the parts describes.	InvoiceReceipt (Might encapsulate an invoice acknowledgement and a payment voucher)
Multi-Part Messsage Part	<SchemaNameOfPart>	This shape should be named (most often) simply for the schema (or simple type) associated with the part.	InvoiceHeader
Message	camelCased	This shape should be named using camel casing, based on the corresponding schema type or multipart message type. If there is more than one variable of a type, name it after its use in the orchestration.	purchaseOrderAck
Variable	camelCased		
Port Type	<function>PortType	Port types should be named to suggest the nature of an endpoint, with upper-camel casing and suffixed with "PortType". If there will be more than one port for a port type, the port type should be named according to the abstract service supplied. The WSDL spec indicates port types are "a named set of abstract operations and the abstract messages involved" that also encapsulates the message pattern (e.g., one-way, request-response, solicit-response) that all operations on the port type adhere to.	ProcessPurchaseOrder PortType which might have operations such as SubmitPO or RequestPOStatus
Port	<function>Port	Ports should be named to suggest a grouping of functionality, with upper-camel casing and suffixed with "Port".	ProcessPurchaseOrder Port
Port Operation	<MethodName>	Port operations should be named according to the "method"—i.e., what subset of the port functionality will be exercised. For a port that has one operation, it can be commonly named "Submit". Note that these operation names appear in WSDL for web-service-published orchestrations.	
Correlation Type	UpperCamelCased	Correlation types should be named with upper-camel case convention, based on the logical name of what is being used to correlate.	PurchaseOrderNumber
Correlation Set	camelCased	Correlation sets should be named with camel-case convention based on the corresponding correlation type. If there is more than one, it should be named to reflect its specific purpose in the orchestration.	purchaseOrderNumber
Orchestration Parameter	camelCased	Orchestration parameters should be named with camel-case convention, and match the caller's names for the corresponding variables where needed.	

PART 2

BizTalk Revealed

Now that you have explored BizTalk at a conceptual level and examined some of the challenges that many teams face in implementing it, let's look at the specifics of the BizTalk toolkit. In Chapters 3 through 8, we discuss the most common tools that you will find within a typical BizTalk solution. Additionally, you get a chance to explore some real-world patterns, examples, and implementations you can use to address specific problems that may be present in your own solutions. Over the course of this part, we will dive into the following topics:

- How BizTalk messaging works
- Specifics of subscriptions and messages
- Pipelines, pipeline components, and example implementations
- Advanced orchestrations and concepts
- Business Rule Engine concepts and examples
- Patterns and practices for solving real-world examples

CHAPTER 3

Thinking Inside the Box

The BizTalk Messagebox is the core of the messaging subsystem. It has the responsibility of storing all in-flight messages that are being processed by the BizTalk server engine. The Message Bus subsystem queries the Messagebox and looks for messages that match a subscription. The BizTalk Message Bus is a **publisher/subscriber** model, or **pub/sub**. Simply stated, every message going into the Messagebox is "published" so that subscribers with matching message subscriptions can receive the message and send it to the appropriate orchestration or send port and finally to the corresponding adapter. Figure 3-1 shows the Message Bus architecture.

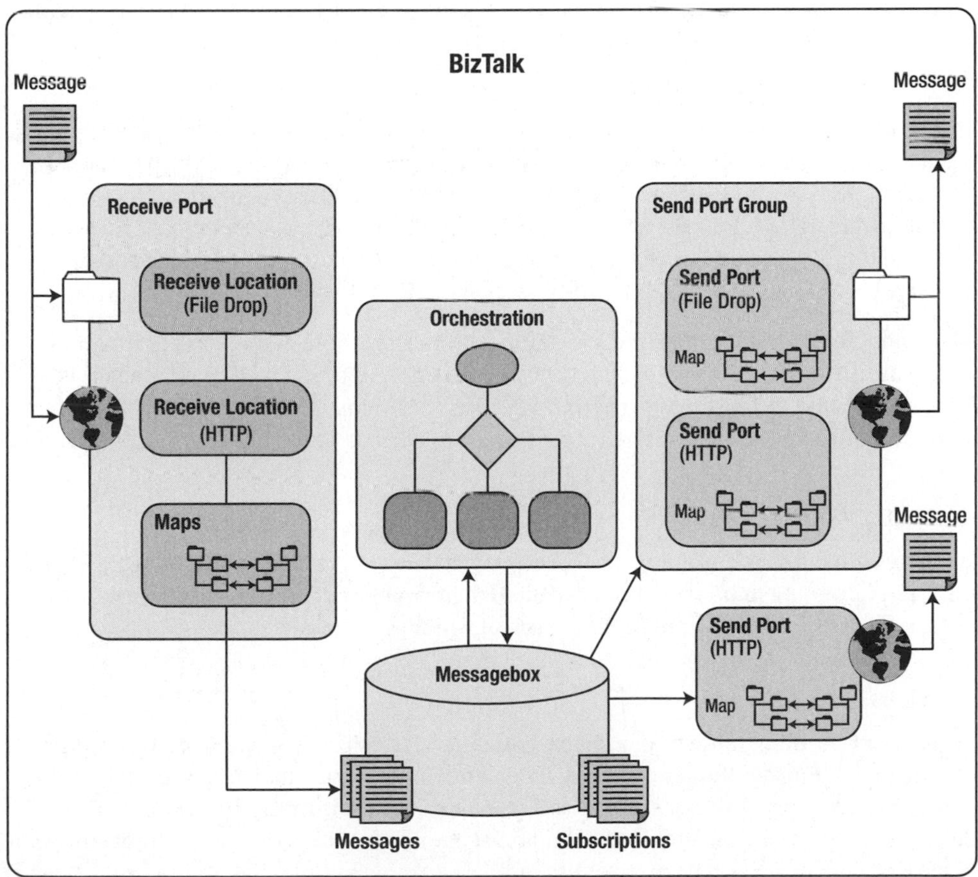

Figure 3-1. *Message Bus architecture in BizTalk Server*

Understanding the Message Bus

The Message Bus is the backbone of the BizTalk Server product. The bus contains unique parts, each of which are explained later in the subsection "Messaging Components." The most obvious of these is the Messagebox, which is explained first. The others include the messages within the Messagebox and the messaging components that move messages to their proper endpoints.

The Messagebox

The Messagebox is simply a database. This database has many tables, several of which are responsible for storing the messages that are received by BizTalk. Each message has metadata associated with it called the **message context**, and the individual metadata items are stored in key/value pairs called **context properties**. There are context properties that describe all the data necessary to identify elements such as the following:

- The inbound port where the message was received from.
- The inbound transport type.
- Transport-specific information such as `ReceivedFileName` in the case of the file adapter, `InboundQueueName` in the case of MSMQ or MQSeries, and so on.
- Autogenerated internal `MessageID` of the message so it can be uniquely identified.
- The schema type and namespace of the message, assuming it is an XML message using namespace#root as the message type. A common misconception is that the message type is always composed of the namespace and the root node name. In fact, this is not necessarily so. Richard Seroter, Microsoft MVP, explains this in his blog in greater detail (`http://seroter.wordpress.com/2009/02/27/not-using-httpnamespaceroot-as-biztalk-message-type/`).

Many people generally equate the Messagebox to be the whole of the BizTalk Server messaging infrastructure. This is absolutely false and is similar to saying that a database is basically a set of data files sitting on a hard drive. The messaging infrastructure, or Message Bus, consists of a dozen or so interrelated components, each of which performs a specific job.

Messaging Components

When new architects start designing BizTalk solutions, few stop to think about how the messages are actually going to be sent and received to their proper endpoints. This job belongs to the messaging components within BizTalk, each of which is explained next.

Host Services

A **BizTalk host** is nothing more than a logical container. Hosts provide you with the ability to arrange the messaging components of your application into groups that can be distributed across multiple memory processes and across machines. A host is most often used to separate adapters, orchestrations, and ports to run on separate machines to aid in load balancing.

A **host instance** is just that, an instance of the host. The instance is actually just a service called BTSNTSvc.exe that runs on the machine. This process provides the BizTalk engine with a place to execute and allows for instances of different hosts to be running on one machine at a given time. Each host instance will end up being a separate instance of the BTSNTSvc.exe service from within the Windows Task Manager. If you examine the Windows Services control panel applet, you will find that each of the hosts that is configured on the machine will show up as a separate service named whatever the host was originally called. The host instance exists simply to allow the BizTalk subservices a place to run. Most people think of the BizTalk service as a single unit, but really it is a container for multiple services, each of which is described in the following text.

The difference between an **Isolated host** and an **In-Process host** is that an Isolated host must run under another process, in most cases IIS, and an In-Process host is a complete BizTalk service alone. Additionally, since Isolated hosts exist outside of the BizTalk environment, the BizTalk Administration Tools are not able to determine the status of these hosts (stopped, started, or starting). Security is also fundamentally different in an Isolated host versus an In-Process host. In-Process hosts must run under an account that is within the In-Process host's Windows group, and they do not maintain security context within the Messagebox. For Isolated hosts, you normally create a separate account with minimum permissions since Isolated hosts in most cases receive messages from untrusted sources such as Internet. Isolated hosts are useful when an external process that will be receiving messages either by some proprietary means or by some other transport protocol such as HTTP already exists. IIS is a good example of such a process. In such cases, the Isolated host runs only one instance of the End Point Manager and is responsible for receiving messages from its transport protocol and sending them to the Messagebox through the EPM. Outside of hosting an IIS process, Isolated hosts could be used to attach to a custom Windows service that is polling a message store looking for new items that it will publish to the Messagebox. Isolated processes provide an architectural advantage for these scenarios. They do not require any interprocess communication (IPC) between the EPM and the Windows service that hosts it. The only real IPC that exists between the Isolated host and the Messagebox database is a database service, hosted most likely on another machine.

In-Process hosts can host all BizTalk subservices depending on how they are configured. They not only can receive messages from the outside world, but they can send them through Send Adapters, poll for messages that match a subscription, and host XLANG engine instances. In the case of a Send Adapter, an In-Process host must be used because of how the security context of the Adapter Framework is built. To use adapters with Isolated hosts, the adapters have to use custom IPC. HTTP and SOAP adapters use this technique to interact with aspnet_wp.exe/w3wp.exe processes. Each Isolated host has the set of subservices running within it shown in Table 3-1. These services can also be viewed from the adm_HostInstance_SubServices table in the Management Database.

Table 3-1. *Host Instance Subservices*

Service	Description
Caching	Service used to cache information that is loaded into the host. Examples of cached information are assemblies that are loaded, adapter configuration information, custom configuration information, and so on.
End Point Manager	Go-between for the Message Agent and the Adapter Framework. The EPM hosts send/receive ports and is responsible for executing pipelines and BizTalk transformations.
Tracking	Service that moves information from the Messagebox to the Tracking Database. See the section "Tracking and Message Management."
XLANG/s	Host engine for BizTalk Server orchestrations.
MSMQT	MSMQT adapter service; serves as a replacement for the MSMQ protocol when interacting with BizTalk Server. The MSMQT protocol has been deprecated in BizTalk Server 2006 and should be used only to resolve backward-compatibility issues.

Subscriptions

To fully understand the Message Bus architecture, it is critical to understand how **subscriptions** work and what **enlisting** is. Subscriptions are the mechanism by which ports and orchestrations are able to receive and send messages within a BizTalk Server solution.

Each BizTalk process that runs on a machine has something called the **Message Agent**, which is responsible for searching for messages that match subscriptions and routing them to the End Point Manager (EPM), which actually handles the message and sends it where it needs to go. The EPM is the broker between the Messagebox and the pipeline/port/adapter combination. Orchestration subscriptions are handled by a different service called XLANG/s. These services are executed within the BTSNTSvc.exe process that runs on the host

Subscribing

According to Microsoft, "A subscription is a collection of comparison statements, known as predicates, involving message context properties and the values specific to the subscription."[1] Following our previous example from Chapter 2 with the ABC Company, the `MessageType` context property would be used to evaluate the subscription criteria. Predicates are inserted into one of the Messagebox's predicate tables, based on what type of operation is specified in the subscription being created. Note the list of predicate tables that follows; these are the same predicates that are used in the filter editor for defining filter criteria on ports. The reason the list of tables is the same as the list of filter predicates is because a filter expression is actually being used to build each subscription. When you are defining a filter expression, what you are actually doing is modifying the underlying subscription within BizTalk to contain the new filter information that is included in your filter expression.

1 Microsoft MSDN: `http://msdn.microsoft.com/en-us/library/ms935116.aspx`

- BitwiseANDPredicates
- EqualsPredicates
- EqualsPredicates2ndPass
- ExistsPredicates
- FirstPassPredicates
- GreaterThanOrEqualsPredicates
- GreaterThanPredicates
- LessThanOrEqualsPredicates
- LessThanPredicates
- NotEqualsPredicates

The BizTalk services create a subscription in the Messagebox by calling two stored procedures. These are `bts_CreateSubscription_{HostName}` and `bts_InsertPredicate_{HostName}`. The subscription is created based on which host will be handling the subscription, which is why these stored procedures are created automatically when the host is created in the Microsoft Management Console.

Enlisting

Most people ask what the difference is between **enlisting** a port and **starting** a port. The difference is simple. Enlisted ports have subscriptions written for them in the Messagebox, while unenlisted ports do not. The same is true for orchestrations. Artifacts that are not enlisted are simply in "deployment limbo" in that they are ready to process messages but no way exists for the Messaging Engine to send them one. The main effect this will have is that ports and orchestrations that are enlisted, but not started, will have any messages with matching subscription information queued within the Messagebox and ready to be processed once the artifact is started. If the port or orchestration is not enlisted, the message routing will fail, since no subscription is available and the message will produce a "No matching subscriptions were found for the incoming message" exception within the Event Log. You have to be aware of a common and potentially risky situation when you have more than one subscriber for a particular message type. In such cases, if the published message routed to at least one of the subscribers, unenlisted offenders would never get the message, and moreover no error would be raised since the message satisfied another subscriber.

When a port is enlisted, the Message Agent will create subscriptions for any message whose context property for `TransportID` matches the port's transport ID. For orchestrations, it also creates the subscription based on the `MessageType` of the message that is being sent to the port within the orchestration. Binding an orchestration port to a physical send port will force the EPM to write information about that binding to the Management Database. Should the orchestration send messages through its logical port to the physical port, it will include the transport ID in the context so that the message is routed to that specific send port.

The next point is related to the pub/sub nature of the Message Bus. Since any endpoint with a matching subscription can process the message once it is sent from an orchestration to the send port, it is possible for multiple endpoints to act upon that message. This is critical to understand. Sending a message through an orchestration port to a bound physical port simply guarantees that a subscription will be created so that the message is routed to that particular endpoint. There is nothing that says no other subscriber may also act on that message. Most developers often overlook this point. Most people assume that since the port is bound, it simply ends up at the correct send port by magic. In reality, all that is happening is that the Message Agent is writing a subscription that hard-codes the context properties of that message so that it will always end up *at least* at that particular send port. Sending the message through the send port simply publishes the message in the Messagebox, and the engine and subscriptions take care of the rest so that you won't have to publish a message over and over again in order to reach multiple targets.

Messages

A message within BizTalk is more than just a direct representation of the document received from the outer world. BizTalk has a model where messages contain both data and context. Understanding how messages are stored internally within the Messagebox is crucial to understanding how to architect systems that take advantage of how the product represents messages internally.

What Is a Message?

A **message** is a finite entity within the BizTalk Messagebox. Messages have context properties and zero-to-many message parts. Subscriptions match particular context properties for a message and determine which endpoints are interested in processing it. As mentioned before, there is one critical rule that will never change:

Messages are immutable once they are published.

Many people who have worked with BizTalk for years do not fully understand this rule. A message cannot be changed once it has reached the Messagebox. At this point most developers would say rather proudly, "But what about a pipeline component? I can write a pipeline component that modifies the message and its payload along with the context properties, right?" The answer to this question is already in the request. Modifying the message can be done only in a pipeline, either sending or receiving. A receive pipeline modifies the message before it gets to the Messagebox. At the end of the pipeline, the message is published. A send pipeline operates on the message after it leaves the Messagebox and before it is sent out. The original message is still unmodified in the Messagebox database regardless of what the send pipeline decides to do with the message.

Messages vs. Message Parts

Messages are composed of zero or more **message parts**. All messages with parts generally have a part that is marked as the **body** part. The body part of the message is considered to contain the data or "meat" of the message. Many adapters will examine only the body part of the message and ignore any other parts in case of multipart messages. These are the messages containing more than one document. A multipart message can have one "body" and any number of additional parts. The closest analogy is an email message with attachments. If you look at the Messagebox database, there are two specific tables, one that holds all messages that flow through BizTalk and one that holds all the message parts. This zero-to-many relationship implies something—message parts can be reused in multiple messages. And that is absolutely true. Each message part has a unique part ID that is stored in the MessageParts table and is associated with the message ID of the main message. The organization of messages and message parts is explored in more detail in Chapter 4 in the discussion on writing custom pipeline components. It is also important to understand that message parts contain message bodies, which are generally XML based. If a message is received on a port that uses a pass-through pipeline, then the message can be anything including binary data. When using a pass-through pipeline, a Receive Adapter stamps its values into message context, but no properties can be promoted from the data of the message. If you think about it, this is obvious. In the case where you are accepting binary data, BizTalk has no mechanism to examine the message body part and determine the message type, so how can it promote it? In this case, the message will contain one message part whose message body is a stream of binary data.

Message Context Properties

Message context properties are defined in what is called a **property schema**. The properties themselves are then stored into **context property bags**. The context property bags are simply containers for the properties, which are stored as key/value pairs.

Context Property Schemas

The schema of the inbound message is used by BizTalk Server to associate it with any corresponding property schemas. There is a global properties schema every message can use by default that contains system-level properties. It is possible to create custom properties schemas that can define application-specific and typically content-based properties that may be required such as an internal organizational key, the customer who submitted the document, and so on.

System-level properties defined within global property schemas are essentially the same as custom context properties defined within a custom property schema. Both types have a root namespace that is used to identify the type of property, and both are stored within the context property bag for a given message. In reality there is no real difference to the runtime in terms of whether a context property is a "system-level" property or a "custom" property.

Context properties, whether they are system or custom properties, define part of the subscription that is used to evaluate which endpoint(s) have a valid subscription to the message. The most common message subscription is based on the message type. BizTalk typically identifies the message type in the message context as a combination of the XML namespace of the message along with the root node name plus the #. For example, say that you had a document with the declaration in Listing 3-1.

Listing 3-1. *XML Order Request Sample Document*

```
<ns0:Request xmlns:ns0="http://schemas.abccompany.com">
<Header>
            <ReqID>4</ReqID>
            <Date>6/6/2005</Date>
            </Header>
```

```
    <Item>
        <Description>Description_0</Description>
        <Quantity>10</Quantity>
        <UnitPrice>2</UnitPrice>
        <TotalPrice>2</TotalPrice>
    </Item>
</ns0:Request>
```

The BizTalk message type in this example would be `http://schemas.abccompany.com#Request`. For message type–based subscriptions, the subscription would then be evaluated by the Message Agent to determine whether any endpoints have subscriptions for the message in question. The list of all subscriptions can be viewed within the BizTalk MMC snap-in tool by viewing all the subscriptions within the solution. Figure 3-2 shows that each of the message properties can be viewed within the BizTalk Administration Console and selected in the message properties drop-down list, which can be used to search for messages within the tool.

■Note The message context properties will only be available if the XML or flat-file pipelines were used. If the pass-through pipeline processed the message, no properties would be available for searching in the BizTalk Administration Console.

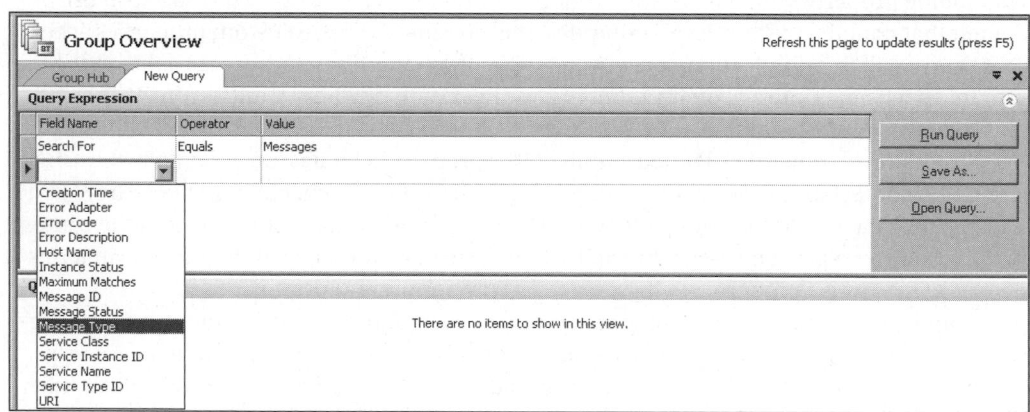

Figure 3-2. *BizTalk Administration Console*

Using subscriptions to route documents to the proper endpoints is called **content-based routing** (**CBR**). Having a thorough understanding of the pub/sub nature of the BizTalk Message Bus is crucial when designing any large messaging-based application, especially in situations where there is going to be significant amounts of routing between organizations and trading partners.

The Context Property Bag

As stated previously, context properties are simply key/value pairs stored in an object that implements the IBasePropertyBag interface. As you can see in the following code and in Table 3-2, the definition of the interface is quite simple:

```
<Guid("fff93009-75a2-450a-8a39-53120ca8d8fa")>
<InterfaceType(ComInterfaceType.InterfaceIsIUnknown)>
Public Interface IBasePropertyBag
```

Table 3-2. *IBasePropertyBag Interface Definition*

Public Properties	--
CountProperties	Gets the number of properties in the property bag
Public Methods	--
Read	Reads the value and type of the given property in the property bag
ReadAt	Reads the property at the specified index value in the property bag
Write	Adds or overwrites a property in the property bag

Given that the context property bag is such a simple structure, it is possible to use the BizTalk API to write any property you want into the property bag. Note that this does not require the property be promoted. Writing a property into the property bag does not mean it is promoted and available for message routing. If a value needs to be visible to the Message Bus for routing purposes, it has to be promoted. By using the property schema to promote a property, either by using a custom property schema or by promoting a value into a property defined in the global property schemas, what you are doing is first writing the value into the property bag and then marking it as promoted. When adding context values from within a pipeline component, you should be aware that there are different API calls for simply writing properties and actually promoting them. This is explored in more detail in Chapter 4.

■ **Caution** It is critical to understand that everything that is written to the property bag is visible within the MMC. Likewise, it is quite easy to view the subscription information for any ports that route on context properties. If you are promoting properties into the message context, make sure that they *do not contain any sensitive data*. For example, if you have a field in a schema that contains credit card numbers, do not promote this value without taking precautions. If you do store the credit card information in a schema, make sure to make it *sensitive* within the schema definition. This will cause the BizTalk runtime to throw an error should that element's value be promoted. If it is absolutely necessary to promote this value, make sure you encrypt it using a third-party tool.

Using XML Namespaces

BizTalk is heavily dependent on XML namespaces. One of the worst possible things that can be done when building BizTalk schemas is to not properly map out what the namespaces are going be for each of the documents. Think of the XML namespaces as the equivalent to .NET namespaces for custom classes. Most architects know to build a proper namespace hierarchy when creating a reusable class library, but most will tend to leave the namespace property of their solution's schemas to the default values. As just stated, the XML namespace is used as part of the values to create the BizTalk `MessageType` context property. This property is the most commonly used property for routing documents, and it makes debugging and maintaining applications much easier if this is a well-thought-out value. As you will see, this becomes even more important when creating and using property schemas.

XML namespaces generally take the following form:

```
http://companyname.com/Project/Subsystem/
```

Defining custom namespaces is crucial for the following reasons:

- They provide unique names for elements and attributes.
- They prevent naming conflicts with other schemas.
- You can use them for code generation. The namespace will be used to generate the type that represents the schema within the assembly once it is compiled.
- The schema's namespace#root combination must be unique unless you are creating a probing pipeline.[2] However, schemas with the same namespace#root combination can be placed in the GAC *without being deployed* and used by some other components.

When creating a BizTalk schema, the following namespaces are automatically included by default:

```
xmlns:b="http://schemas.microsoft.com/BizTalk/2003"
xmlns:xs="http://www.w3.org/2001/XMLSchema"
```

These namespaces are included to allow the schema to reference common elements that are required by the BizTalk runtime.

Understanding Property Promotions

When new BizTalk developers are asked to "promote a property," they all perform the same task: they open up the schema editor, right-click the element, and choose Quick Promotion. Most have no idea about what is actually happening under the covers or how this element will move into the message's context. Property promotion and the message context are keys to the Message Bus architecture within BizTalk and need to be properly understood.

Promoted Properties

Promoted properties are advantageous, because they allow the Messaging Engine to route messages looking only into the message context. If the property that you need to route on does

2 For a complete discussion of this issue, see the last section in the chapter entitled "The BizTalk Management Database."

not exist within one of the default property schemas, you will need to create a custom property schema that is used within your project.

Promoted properties are the most common way to enable content-based routing, because promoted properties are available to pipelines, adapters, the Message Bus, and orchestrations. To promote a property within BizTalk Server, you have two options—**quick promotion** and **manual promotion**.

Quick Promotion

Quick promotion is the simplest way to promote an element's value into the message context. To quick promote, all you do is right-click the element's node and choose Quick Promotion. The BizTalk schema editor will create a new property schema and add an XML reference to the new property schema. By default the new schema is called PropertySchema.xml, although this can be changed by editing the properties of the schema file. Each property you promote using a quick promotion will create a corresponding element in the new property schema with the same name and type as in the source schema. When the pipeline associated with the port parses the inbound message, it will move the value from the message's data payload into the message context and assign the namespace of that property to the name defined in the property schema for that element.

Manual Promotion

Manually promoting a property using a custom property schema involves creating a new property schema and creating elements that will hold the promoted values. Once all the elements are created, the property schema is associated to the main content schema by choosing the Show Promotions function in the schema editor. For an example of how to do this, see Exercise 3-1 later in this chapter. Every element that is defined in the promotions section of the schema will be promoted automatically when the pipeline processes the message. Manual promotions are also useful when you want to store values in the system property namespaces. The pros and cons of doing this are discussed later in the "Considerations When Promoting Properties" section of the chapter.

Promoting vs. Writing

Promoted properties defined in a property schema can have one of two base types: `MessageDataPropertyBase` or `MessageContextPropertyBase`. If a property is inherited from `MessageDataPropertyBase`, then the value of the property comes from the payload of the message. Properties defined in property schemas are derived of this type. Properties derived from `MessageContextPropertyBase` do not have values from the message payload, but they will generally contain data that relates to the transport of the message and can have configuration information necessary for the subscription to be evaluated. Properties with `MessageContextPropertyBase` as their base type are often promoted by adapters and pipelines and generally include values necessary for the adapter to process the message.

When defining property schemas and coding custom pipeline components and adapters, it is crucial to understand the difference between the two base types and how the BizTalk Messaging Engine treats them. Should the property inherit from `MessageDataPropertyBase`, the orchestration design engine (ODX) examines the property and checks to see whether the namespace and property name match a promoted property. If no promoted property exists in the schema and no matching property is found, the ODX design surface does not allow you to see the property. Inheriting a property from `MessageContextPropertyBase` allows you to see the property regardless of its namespace.

As mentioned previously, the API for writing vs. promoting is essentially the same, but there are two separate methods. On the `IBaseMessageContext` object of every message in BizTalk, there is a `Write()` method and a `Promote()` method. Both of these methods take the property name, the namespace, and the value. For the property to be available for routing, when promoting a property, the namespace and property name must be the same as those defined in a referenced property schema. This process is different if you want to dynamically write a distinguished field. **Distinguished fields** are special context properties that can be directly accessed from the expression editor through IntelliSense within an orchestration. If you need to write a distinguished field, you must use the distinguished field namespace of `http://schemas.microsoft.com/BizTalk/2003/btsDistinguishedFields`. The name of the property must be a valid XPath expression to the element being written to the context. The following code sample illustrates how to dynamically promote and write properties to the message context from code:

```
//BizTalk system properties namespace
Private Const BTSSystemPropertiesNamespace As String = _
"http://schemas.microsoft.com/BizTalk/2003/system-properties"

Private Const BTSDistinguishedFieldsPropertiesNamespace As String = " _
http://schemas.microsoft.com/BizTalk/2003/btsDistinguishedFields"

//Promote the MessageType property
messageType = "http://" + "schemas.abc.com/BizTalk/" + "#" + "Request"
message.Context.Promote("MessageType", BTSSystemPropertiesNamespace, messageType);

//Write a transient value to the message context
message.Context.Write("MyVariable", "SomeNameSpace", SomeData);

//Write a distinguished property
message.Context.Write("OdxProperty", BTSDistinguishedFieldsPropertiesNamespace,
myVar);
```

Considerations When Promoting Properties

Blindly promoting properties is not only inefficient, but it can also be costly in terms of both performance and scalability. The following is a short list of items to be considered before promoting a property into the message context:

- **Property size**: To increase routing performance, promoted properties are limited to 255 characters. There is no limit to the size of properties that are simply written to the context. However, writing large properties to the message context will still decrease performance, because the Messaging Engine still needs to process and manage the context regardless of how big it is.
- **Performance**: All promoted fields are explicitly inserted into a database table in order to make them available to the subscription resolution stored procedure. If you promoted more properties than actually necessary "just in case," you would waste the

cycles of inserting those fields and evaluating them against subscriptions. Also note that large message properties cannot be "streamed" and must be entirely loaded into memory by the runtime. This will become an issue if you write large values for message properties into the message context.

- **Overwriting of promoted properties**: If you have promoted a property to the message context and you issue a context write operation, the property is no longer promoted.
- **Dealing with Nulls**: Null properties are not persisted to the context. If you set a property's value to Null, it will no longer exist, and you cannot see a context property in the MMC with a value of Null.

Distinguished Fields

There are two types of property promotion: distinguished fields and property fields. The latter type uses property schemas. In the BizTalk schema editor, you manage both of these types of property promotion by using the Promote Properties dialog box, which you access either by using the Promote Properties property of the Schema node or by right-clicking a node in the tree and selecting the Promote menu item. Distinguished fields are useful only when they are accessed within orchestration. Promoted properties can be accessed either in orchestrations or from custom code, routing, and pipelines.

Distinguished fields, on the other hand, cannot be used for routing and are used only by the orchestration engine. When dealing with large messages, this can save significant server processing, because the engine would need to use XPath expressions to search through the document to find the piece of data that it needs each time the expression is evaluated. This way, the data is loaded once when the document is parsed by the runtime engine. Distinguished fields are used within orchestrations to move required elements into the context and read the context property only within the orchestration without having to load the entire document into memory. Distinguished fields also offer nice IntelliSense capabilities within the orchestration expression editor and message assignment shapes.

Depending on the type of access that is needed, you can choose to create either promoted properties or distinguished fields depending on how the property will be used.

Using Port Filters and Content-Based Routing

As stated in the previous section, subscriptions and context properties are integral to the messaging subsystem. Property schemas are the mechanism by which the context properties or message data values are stored in the message context. Besides the properties promoted by a developer, the BizTalk Message Bus also automatically promotes system-level properties from the system property namespaces, depending on the type of inbound and outbound transports that are being used. Each adapter will stamp its specific values into context properties that then become available to subscribers to act upon.

Most people new to BizTalk don't understand how messages are routed within the product or how to use the property schemas to affect the subscription. Exercise 3-1 will show you how you can use the property promotion to implement routing logic.

EXERCISE 3-1. USING CUSTOM PROMOTED PROPERTIES TO ROUTE MESSAGES

Let's continue our example from Chapter 2 of an organization that takes inbound documents from multiple sources, normalizes them to a canonical input schema, and sends them to different outbound locations. Assume that there are three systems: a web site, a POS application, and an automated FTP upload location. Each of these locations takes a different schema and must map it to internal schema. This mapped message then needs to be sent to the ERP system. However, as an added piece of functionality, documents from the web site need to be sent to a separate location as well, and documents from the POS system need to be sent to a file system directory so they can be batch uploaded at a later time. Figures 3-3 and 3-4 define the schema for the internal messages and a possible solution architecture.

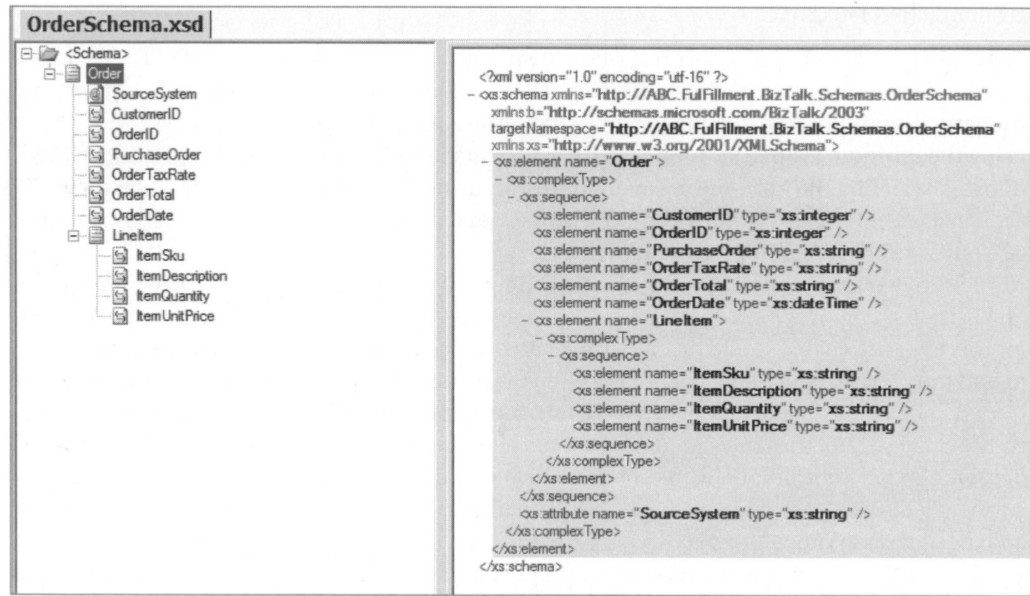

Figure 3-3. *Internal order request schema*

The requirements for this solution are quite common in most BizTalk projects, and most new BizTalk architects design it incorrectly. Generally those unfamiliar with the subscription nature of the Message Bus will tend to build an orchestration that has logical ports directly bound to the physical ports. The orchestration would then use Decide shapes to send the message to the appropriate send port, which will then send the message on its way. An even worse solution is to create three orchestrations, each of which receives the inbound message directly from the receive location, executes the map from within the orchestration, and then has a static bound port that is bound to the send port from within the orchestration. This problem requires only messaging to be solved. No orchestrations should be created here since no business logic is needed. Routing the message to the correct location is not business logic, and as such, an orchestration is not the correct tool to use from the BizTalk Server toolbox.

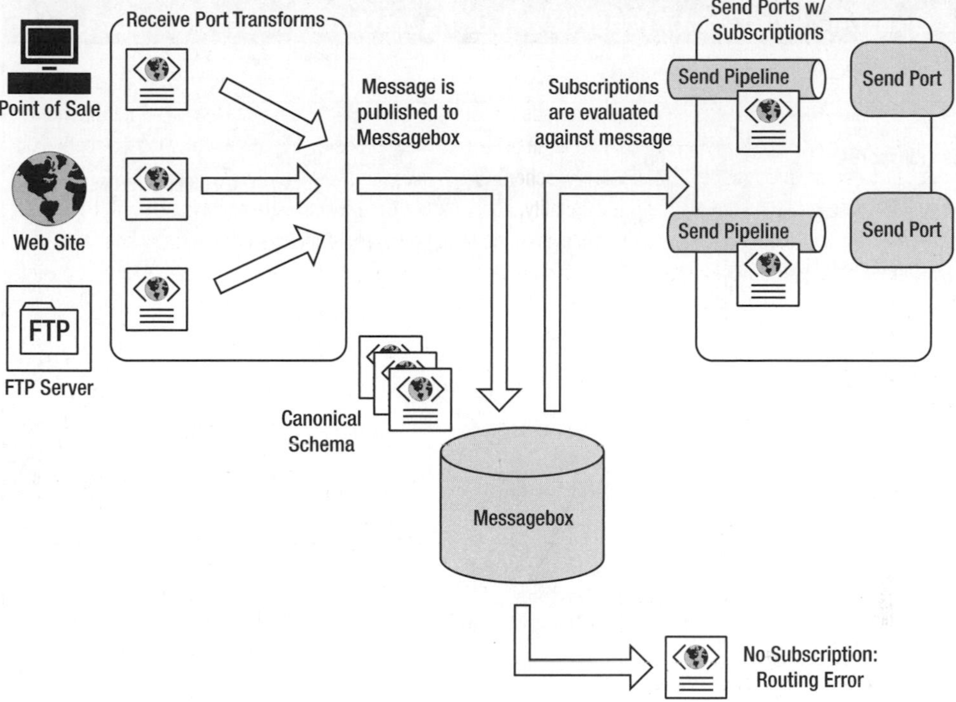

Figure 3-4. *Solution architecture*

To implement the routing logic, subscriptions need to be created that allow the inbound message, once it has been mapped, to be sent to the correct port. Here, you create filters based on the `MessageType` context property that allow the Messaging Engine to automatically forward any messages of type `http://ABC.FulFillment.BizTalk.Schemas.OrderSchema#Order` to the adapter, which communicates with the ERP system. The filter of the port will modify the subscription in the Messagebox accordingly. In the filter properties of the ERPSendPort, the expression shown in Figure 3-5 will be present.

You still have not seen how to solve the problem of differentiating messages that are received from each of the three separate order-producing systems. Notice that the internal schema definition includes an element that will allow you to store that data should it be available, but there are two problems: how you get the value in this element and how you route messages based on it. For adding this value into the data document, you use the inbound map defined on the receive port. All you need to do is create a map from the external schema to the internal schema and assign a constant value for the `SourceSystem` element.

To allow you to route on the `SourceSystem` property, you need to create a property schema to define what properties you want to store in the context and to allow the Messaging Engine to promote the value from the data in your inbound document. To do this, add a new item to the schema project: in the list of BizTalk project items, choose Property Schema. Add an attribute to the schema called `SourceSystem`, as shown in Figure 3-6.

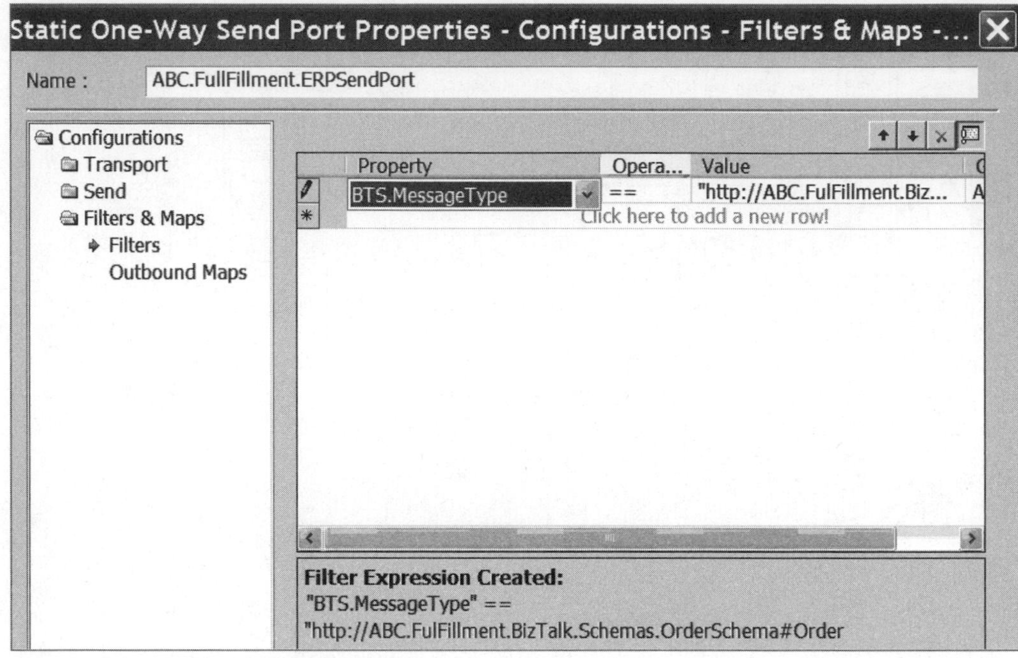

Figure 3-5. *ERPSendPort properties*

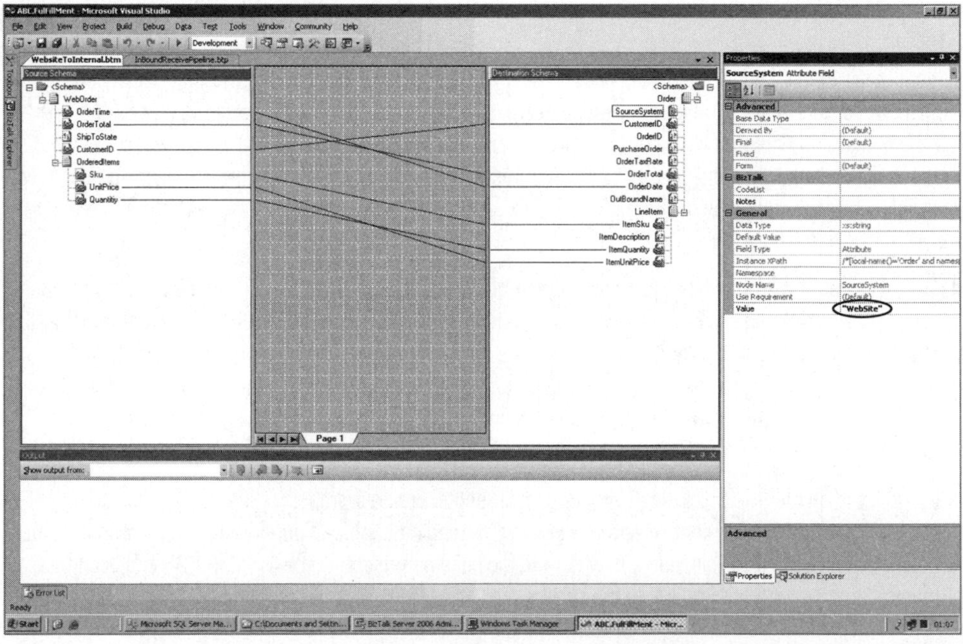

Figure 3-6. *Web site to internal schema map*

Figure 3-7 shows the schema for the internal order property schema as viewed in the BizTalk schema editor.

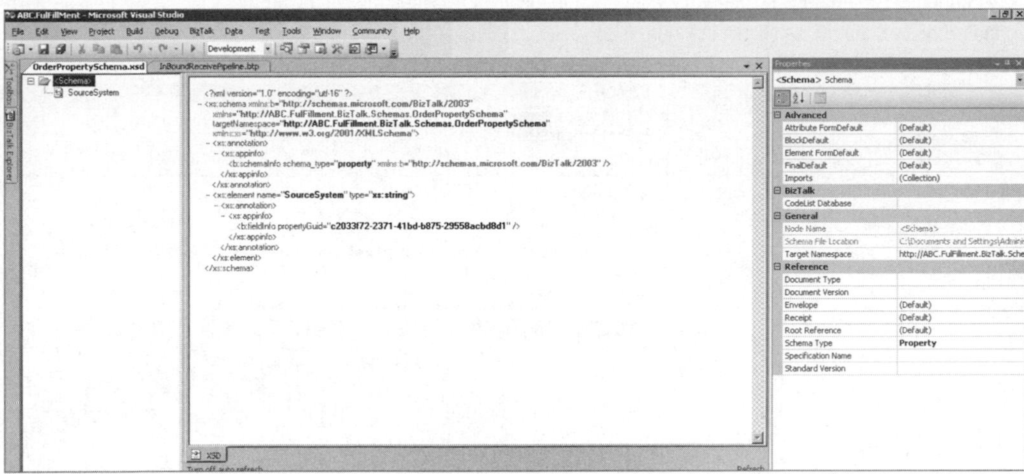

Figure 3-7. *Order property schema*

The next step is to associate the custom property schema to the internal order schema. To do this, right-click the `SourceSystem` element in the internal order property schema, and choose Promotions ➤ Show Promotions, as demonstrated in Figure 3-8. Next, click the Promoted Properties tab, and click the open folder icon.

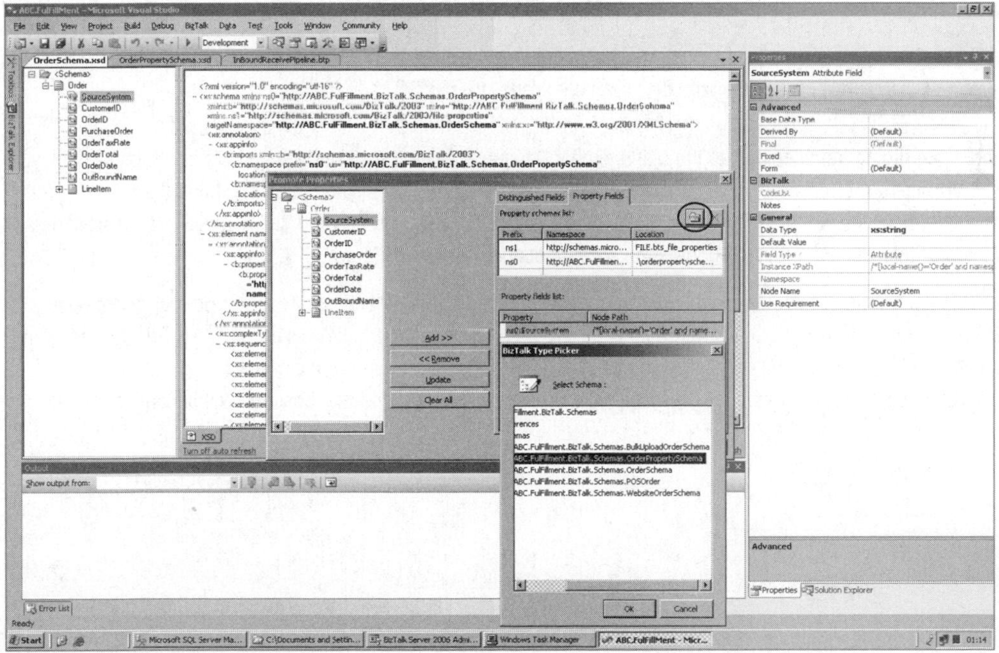

Figure 3-8. *Type Picker dialog box*

Once you have chosen OrderPropertySchema, highlight the `SourceSystem` element on the left, and click the Add>> button. This will add the element to the list of promoted properties. Notice that since there is only one property defined in the property schema, the editor automatically associates this field with the `SourceSystem` property in the property schema, as shown in Figure 3-9.

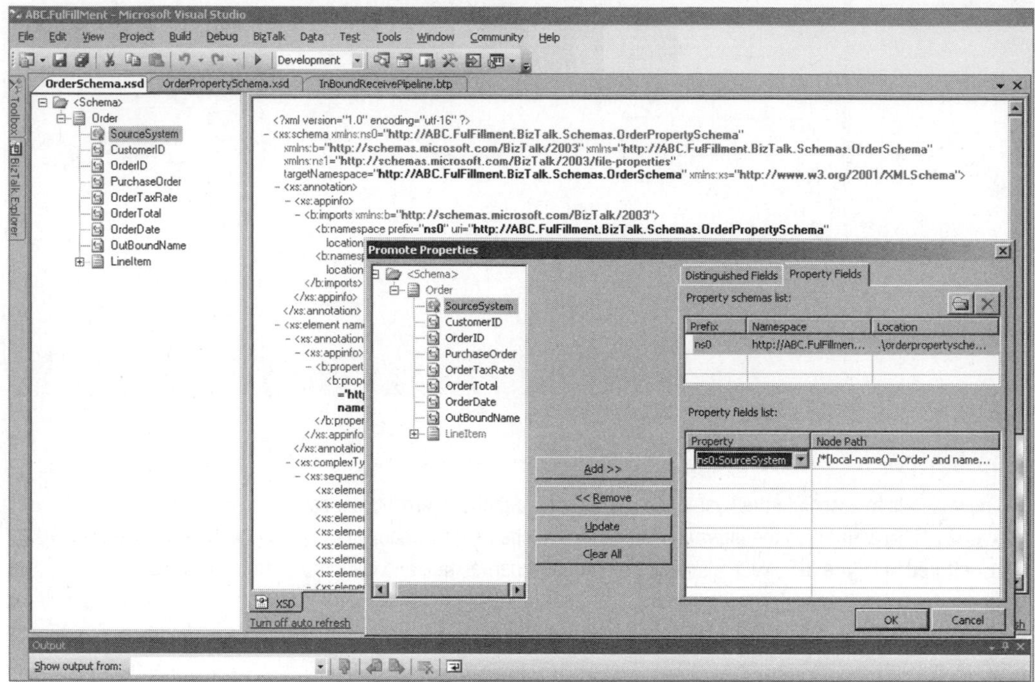

Figure 3-9. *Manually promoting the SourceSystem property*

Compile the project and deploy it to the Management Database. Once the property schema's assembly is deployed to the Management Database, it will automatically be available in the list of properties in a ports filter. If you create a new send port and want to only send documents from the web site, you can add its `SourceSystem` property as a filter, and this will automatically update the subscription, as shown in Figure 3-10.

Another important fact to note is that in this situation, you need to create only one receive port with three receive locations. You also need to create three maps and add them each to the transforms on the port. The pipeline will examine the inbound schema for each map and send the inbound document to the correct map. If no port has a subscription for a matching inbound message type, an error will occur, and the message will become suspended.

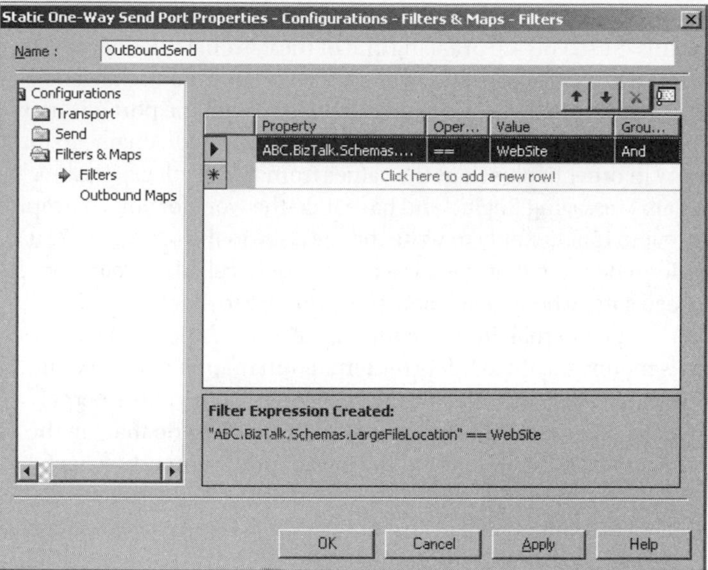

Figure 3-10. *Routing based on a custom promoted property*

Using System Property Schemas

As mentioned previously, a number of system property schemas come with the product. Most of these property schemas contain general BizTalk properties and the properties to support each of the transports and adapters included with the product out of the box. Most of the time, each new transport or application adapter will bring with it a new property schema that is used to define any custom metadata needed to process the message by the adapter. Each of the system property schemas is included in the base assembly Microsoft.BizTalk.GlobalPropertySchemas.dll. Referencing this assembly from a BizTalk project in Visual Studio will allow you to access each of the schemas as you would with any other schema type.

Modifying Values from System Property Schemas: Simple Example

So, at this point, many people ask the question, “Big deal, I can modify values that BizTalk uses, so why would I need this ability?” To fully understand why the creation of property schemas becomes an invaluable tool, let’s look at a simple example. Continuing with the scenario from Exercise 3-1, let’s assume that an order received from the bulk order system needs to be written to a file location on a server within the organization. Let’s also assume that we need to dynamically modify the name of this file depending on some value from the message: the customer ID plus the character # and the total amount of the order.

At first, modifying the file name based on a message value seems like an easy thing to do, but it becomes a little more complicated when you look at it. In reality, there are three solutions to the problem. Solution A would be to use an orchestration with a dynamic port and within the orchestration use some XPath expressions to get the data you need from the message;

dynamically set the address of the file adapter; and send the file to the dynamic port. However, in reality there is a cost to doing this. First, you are breaking one of the cardinal rules of BizTalk—you are using orchestrations to do routing logic. Second, you have an orchestration that is exclusively bound to a port and has to be deployed, enlisted, and started with the port it is bound to.[3] Third, if this were a large message, using XPath would force the orchestration engine to load the entire document into memory in order to parse out the values from the XPath expression.[4]

Solution B is to use the BizTalk Messaging Engine and have it do the work for you. To implement this solution, you use the macro functionality to write the message in the send port. You need to modify your internal order schema so that there is a new element called `OutBoundName` or something similar, and you need somewhere to promote this property to. For this, use the file adapter property schema. In the internal order schema, there is an element called `ReceivedFileName`. What you do is modify the BulkOrderToInternal.btm map so that the value of the `CustomerID`, along with the total, is concatenated into your new element in the internal schema. You still have to promote the `CustomerID` property into the context. To do that, on the Property Promotions tab of the schema, add a reference to the file adapter's property schema.

The next step is to create a send port that subscribes to the correct message type, set the outbound destination in the send port to the desired directory, and set the file name to be %source-filename%. The BizTalk Messaging Engine will use whatever value is stored in the `ReceivedFileName` message context property when writing out this value. Since you have changed it and promoted it, the engine will use your new value instead of the original one, as shown in Figure 3-11.

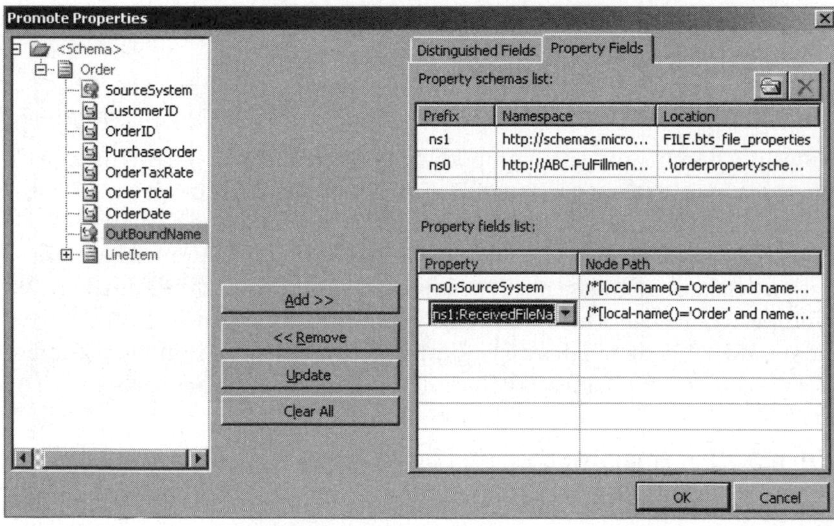

Figure 3-11. *Promoting a value using a system property namespace*

---

3 In later chapters, we will discuss orchestrations with direct-bound ports (i.e., not bound to a physical port, but bound to the Messagebox database) vs. orchestrations with static/dynamic bindings. There are pros and cons to each, but there are more pros than cons to a direct port, and generally they are preferable to static or dynamically bound ports.

4 We could use distinguished properties to get around this. The orchestration engine will not load the entire document if the property were distinguished. As stated previously, these would be written into the context when the message is processed by the Messaging Engine. However, the point is that using XPath in orchestrations is costly, especially on large messages.

Solution C is to create a custom pipeline component, add it to a stage in a custom receive pipeline, and have it promote the value you want into the context using the message API. The code would look something like the following:

```
Private Sub PromoteProperties(ByVal message As IBaseMessage, ByVal CustomerID As _
String, ByVal OrderTotal As Decimal)

Dim BTSFilePropertiesNamespace As String = _
"http://schemas.microsoft.com/BizTalk/2003/file-properties"
Dim FileName As String

'Get the original directory the file was received from by reading the message _
context and creating a FileInfo object
Dim FileInfoObject As new
System.IO.FileInfo(message.Context.Read("ReceivedFileName", _
BTSFileropertiesNamespace))

'Replace the original name with the new one
FileName = FileInfoObject.DirectoryName +  "\\ + CustomerID + "#" + _
OrderTotal.ToString() + ".xml"
message.Context.Promote("ReceivedFileName", BTSFileropertiesNamespace, FileName)

End Sub
```

The send port is configured the same as in solution B. Although solution C uses the Messaging Engine to accomplish the task, it requires you to write a custom pipeline and pipeline component that you would then have to maintain. The benefit of solution C is that it does not require you to modify the internal schema or transformation in any way. Solution C would be ideal if you had a production-emergency type of scenario where you needed to implement the proposed change with as little possible downtime or modification to the deployed solution. All you would need to do is deploy the pipeline assembly to each of the BizTalk servers, along with copying the pipeline component to the %Program Files\Microsoft BizTalk Server 2009\Pipeline Components\ directory and changing the pipeline configuration on the receive port. In this scenario, there would be no server downtime and few configuration changes required. The trade-off is that you would have additional custom logic and custom assemblies that must be maintained and deployed with the solution as a whole.

Modifying Values from System Property Schemas: Extended Example

Now that you see a simplistic usage of modifying a system property, we will show you something a little more interesting. Continuing with the previous example, assume that you need to send information to your ERP system with messages received from the web site. Also assume that there have been performance problems calling the ERP solution. Currently the ERP system uses a custom API written in VB 6.0 and exposed through COM+ objects. You need to track how long these calls are taking, but you want the information included within the Messagebox, and you want it bundled with all the other tracking information that is stored in the database and accessible through MMC for the server administrators. You also want individual tracking information per message so that you can correlate what types of transactions are taking the most time.

Assume that the code to call the API is fixed and cannot be modified. Due to architectural limitations, you also cannot impose a wrapper (i.e., web service or custom adapter), you must call the API directly as you would be normally, and these calls must be synchronous because the API will not support asynchronous calls because of threading issues. Currently, the API is called from an Expression shape inside an orchestration, and depending on a series of return values, different business logic is executed. As an added bonus, the administrators want a copy of all messages that take more than 5 seconds to process to be sent to a drop location where those messages can be viewed offline. The development team does not want any major logic modifications to the existing receive ports/send ports/orchestrations to implement the logging logic (i.e., you can't store the tracking value somewhere and have the orchestration insert a Decide shape that sends a copy to the send port). Also, message tracking is not enabled, since this is a production system, and the administrators do not want to decrease the performance of the system any further.

Now that your hands are a little more tied, the options are becoming a bit limited. Most people at this point will want to modify the orchestration that logs information either to the event log or to a performance counter, but that still doesn't address the problem of how you can associate a message that you processed with its timing values and have them show up somehow in MMC, nor does it address the problem of how to properly route on those timing values. Also, this breaks one of the cardinal rules: you use orchestrations for something other than business logic. Another option would be to create some custom tracking elements in the document and write these from within the orchestration, but that would require a schema change and some new code. Luckily, there is a better way, and it requires only five lines of code be inserted into the orchestration along with two variables.

BizTalk includes a tracking property schema within the product. Although this schema is very poorly documented (as in not at all), it is possible to write values to it. The property schema is used to define context properties that adapters can write to that will aid in the very type of scenario we're discussing now. The fact that we can write values to the tracking property schema really doesn't help since tracking is not enabled. Also, since the performance bottleneck in this scenario is not based on an adapter, the tracking information is not accurate. However, you can still use the property schema to write information to the context from within the orchestration that will help you, as shown in Figure 3-12.

```
InboundDoc(MessageTracking.ActivityIdentity) = "WebSite Order FullFillment";
InboundDoc(MessageTracking.AdapterTransmitBeginTime) = System.DateTime.Now;
ERPAPI.CallERP(InboundDoc);
TotalTime = System.DateTime.Now.Subtract(StartTime);
InboundDoc(MessageTracking.ActivityIdentity) = System.Convert.ToString(TotalTime.Seconds);
```

Figure 3-12. *Orchestration expression*

The system property schema is in the bts-messagetracking-properties.xsd schema file. By default, this schema is populated with values from adapters, but there is nothing that says you can't put your own values in here. Also, since the schema is a property schema, the values will be available for routing. The problem of how you can configure your send port to automatic pickup times that are greater than 5 seconds has now been solved. What you can do is create a little expression in the expression editor that gets the current `Now()` time and subtracts it from the time that the operation finished. The `StartTime` variable is a local variable defined as a System.DateTime that is initialized to the current time within the orchestration. Since the result will be of type System.Timespan, you cannot simply store it in the property `MessageTracking.AdapterTransmitEndTime` since that property is of type System.DateTime. There is another property called `MessageTracking.ActivityIdentity` that is of type string, which will allow you to store anything you want. You simply store your computed time in that property and use it to route your messages, as shown in Figure 3-13.

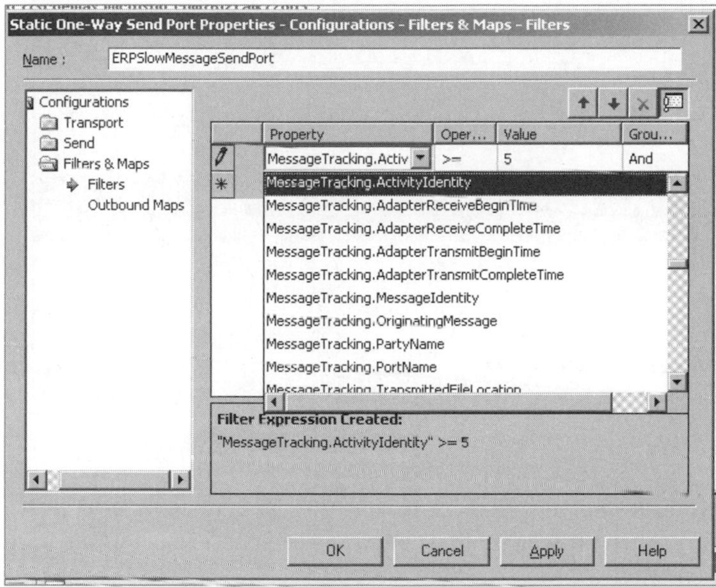

Figure 3-13. *Send port filter expression*

Custom Properties and Orchestration Routing

As demonstrated earlier, custom properties can be very useful in routing scenarios. The previous example showed how to route the message to an orchestration based on a custom property and a subscription created via the filter expression. If you were routing this message to an orchestration based on a filter defined in the Receive shape of the orchestration, you would get the following error:

```
"message data property 'ABCPropertySchema.CustomProperty' does not exist in
messagetype 'myOrchestrationMessage'"
```

What is happening in this case is that the orchestration engine is examining the message within the orchestration and throwing an error stating that the property you want to route on does not exist in the message. Typically the engine is correct; however, in this case, you know that this is okay. The solution is to tell the engine that data for your property will not come from the message and that you will provide it.

To fix this, you need to set the Property Schema Base for the property under the Reference section of the schema editor, as shown in Figure 3-14.

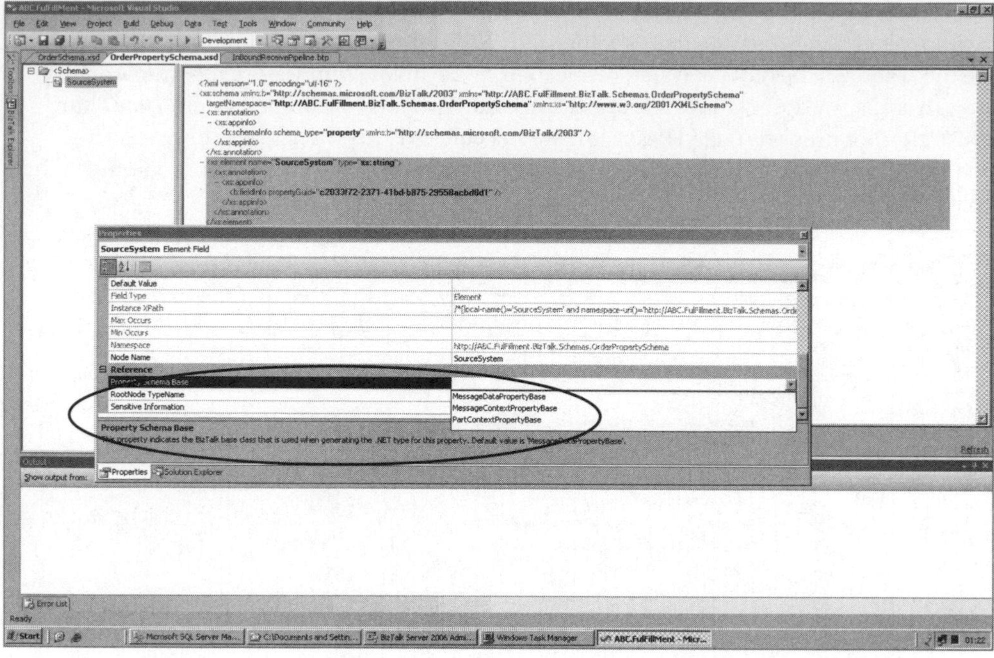

Figure 3-14. *Changing the base type for a property*

To the runtime, this determines what the base type will be used for in the property in question. The base type for the property will be used to determine where the data for the property will come from. The possible values for this are as follows:

- **MessageDataPropertyBase (Default)**: The data in this field will come from a message.
- **MessageContextPropertyBase**: The data in this field may not exist in a message (i.e., it could be prompted inside a custom pipeline). The values will not be inside the message.
- **PartContextPropertyBase**: This tells the runtime that the value for the property will be part of the `MessagePart` context.

The key take-away is that if you are promoting properties that do not exist in the message, be sure to set the proper base type for the property (i.e., MessageContextPropertyBase).

As you can see, using system properties can solve a number of rather complex scenarios with very little effort. This is explored in further detail later in the book.

Tracking and Message Management

Now that you have seen how BizTalk stores, routes, and publishes messages, the next step is to understand how those messages can be tracked and what happens to them once they have been processed. Each subscriber of a particular message references the same single copy of that message. This approach requires that a reference counter be kept for all messages flowing through the system. Although this minimizes storage, it requires that the messages be cleaned up once their reference counters reach 0. To accomplish this, the product includes a set of SQL Agent jobs that perform garbage collection for zero-reference-count messages and message parts. The stored procedures that handle garbage collection are as follows:

- **MessageBox_Message_Cleanup_BizTalkMsgBoxDb**: Deletes all messages that have no references by any subscribers.
- **MessageBox_Parts_Cleanup_BizTalkMsgBoxDb**: Deletes all messages that have no references by any messages. Remember what we stated at the beginning of the chapter—messages consist of one or more message parts that contain the actual message data.
- **PurgeSubscriptionsJob_BizTalkMsgBoxDb**: Deletes unused subscription predicates leftover from system-created subscriptions.
- **MessageBox_DeadProcesses_Cleanup_BizTalkMsgBoxDb**: Executed when the runtime detects that a server has crashed. This frees the work that the server was working on so another machine within the group can process it.
- **TrackedMessages_Copy_BizTalkMsgBoxDb**: Copies tracked message bodies from the Messaging Engine spool tables into the tracking spool tables in the Messagebox database.
- **TrackingSpool_Cleanup_BizTalkMsgBoxDb**: Removes the message body data from the database table to which the TrackedMessages_Copy_BizTalkMsgBoxDb SQL Server Agent job writes.

The first two items from the preceding list are used to keep garbage messages removed from the Messagebox. When executed, they search the messages and message parts within the Messagebox looking for messages with a reference count of zero. The stored procedures also check for parts that are not referenced by any messages and remove those as well. Once messages are ready to be removed, they are moved to the BizTalk Tracking Database. These two jobs are executed from the machine that hosts SQL Server. For these jobs to run, the SQL Server Agent needs to be running. If SQL Server Agent isn't running, tracked message bodies will never be offloaded to the Tracking Database, and hence the Messagebox will grow. As the database grows, performance will suffer, because the number of messages grows unchecked. This is because the Message Agent that is running within each BizTalk host will be calling a stored procedure that searches through each of the messages in the Messagebox looking for messages with matching subscription information.

To keep the Messagebox as empty as possible, the tracking subsystem will move completed messages to the Tracking Database on a periodic basis. This is accomplished by a BizTalk host that has been tagged as a "tracking" host by specifying an option in the Host Properties page. The Tracking Database is also where the MMC queries for data and displays its tracking information.

Handling Failed Messages and Errors

With BizTalk 2009 you have two options to get at suspended messages. The first option is to use MMC and process suspended messages manually. Although this is acceptable when you have to process only a few messages, this option can become very time- and labor-consuming if you have to deal with a large number of suspended messages. The second, and in most cases better, option is to automate the process using a set of context properties available to be subscribed on. Error handling context properties are defined within the `http://schemas.microsoft.com/BizTalk/2005/error-report` property schema. The new context properties are as follows:

- `Description`
- `ErrorType`
- `FailureCategory`
- `FailureCode`
- `InboundTransportLocation`
- `MessageType`
- `OutboundTransportLocation`
- `ReceivePortName`
- `RoutingFailureReportID`
- `SendPortName`

What needs to be done is to ensure that any receive ports that need to have error handling included have the Generate Error Report check box selected, as shown in Figure 3-15. This will signal the runtime engine to generate the routing failure message and publish it to the Messagebox. Since the message is published, there needs to be a subscription available to receive the routing failure message. To that end, you can create an orchestration that is direct-bound[5] to the Messagebox through a receive port. The Receive shape in the orchestration will have a filter criteria specified that sets the subscription information so that it will receive all failed routing messages.

To implement the routing, the filter expression needs to be set to "ErrorReport.ErrorType == Failed Message," as shown in Figure 3-16.

5 *Direct binding* refers to orchestration ports that are not specifically bound to any physical port but will receive messages solely based on the subscription. As you saw in the "Subscriptions" subsection in the chapter, all this means is that there is no receive port or transport ID information written to the subscription.

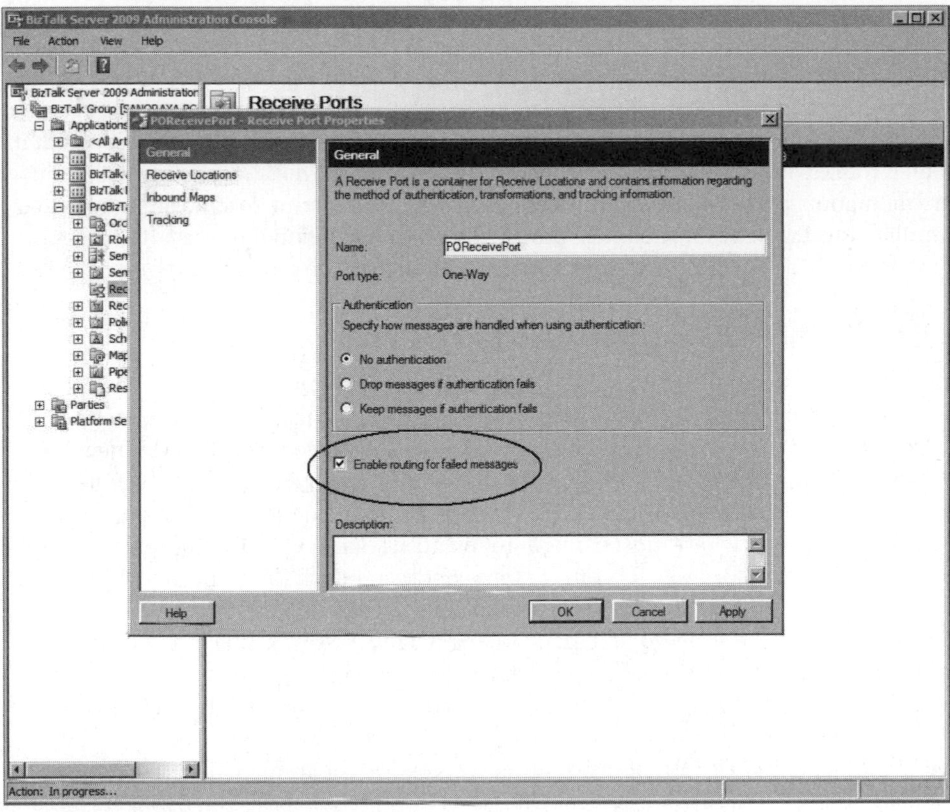

Figure 3-15. *Receive port configuration*

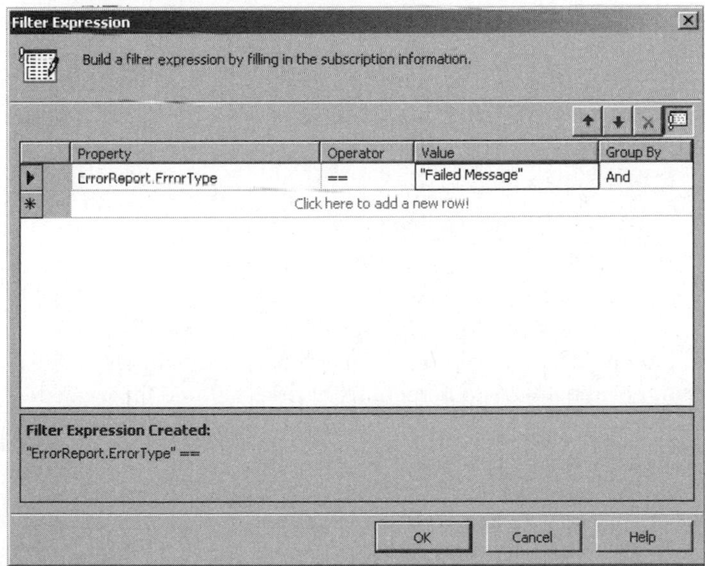

Figure 3-16. *Orchestration Receive shape filter*

This will cause the subscription to be written that will receive all suspended messages. From here, once you have a copy of the failed message within the orchestration, you can send it wherever you need. An example would be to have the orchestration send the message to an e-mail address or to an offline database for examination. All these options will be quite easy to implement since the message has been parsed and routed to the orchestration. Note that if you enabled routing for failed messages, no suspended messages will show up in MMC, and therefore no manual processing options will be available. You have to design your automated error handling routine to be an adequate replacement of the functionality available in MMC.

The BizTalk Management Database

Up until this point, our discussions regarding BizTalk schemas, deployment, and namespaces have been in the practical sense. We have not discussed where schemas are actually stored or what is happening within BizTalk when a new schema is deployed. For that, you need to understand the BizTalk Management Database. Unlike the Messagebox, the Management Database is not used to store messages and is not considered to be "working storage." The Management Database is where most configuration and system-level information is stored and accessed from within BizTalk. It is important to understand what's going on behind the scenes when you perform administrative actions using either UI tools or the ExplorerOM/WMI API,[6] because this will give you a good understanding of how BizTalk artifacts are tied together within the product. Such understanding may save time when dealing with specific issues such as "Why isn't my schema namespace resolving?" or "What version of my schema is this document resolving against?"

The first topic we will cover is how BizTalk Server resolves document/message types and how/where they are stored in Management Database. If you have worked on a BizTalk project previously, you no doubt have seen the following error messages from the BizTalk Messaging Engine:

> *There was an error executing receive pipeline: Finding the document specification by message type {MessageType} failed. Verify the schema deployed properly.*

or

> *There was a failure executing receive pipeline: Cannot locate document specification because multiple schemas matched this message type [MessageType]*

Knowing how BizTalk handles message types will help you address this type of problem. We will also provide you with ExplorerOM[7] code for enumerating deployed document specifications, which you can use in your own helper/supplementary utilities tailored for your specific needs.

---

6 ExplorerOM is the primary API that you will use to work with BizTalk artifacts from within code. WMI is the Windows Management Instrumentation technology we introduced in Chapter 1. For a complete discussion of these techologies as they relate to BizTalk, see Chapter 10.

7 We have included the ExplorerOM code within this chapter for easy reference. For a complete discussion of deploying, managing, and supporting BizTalk using the ExplorerOM API, see Chapter 10.

The second topic we are going to cover is what's going on in the BizTalk Management Database when you deploy a BizTalk assembly. These two discussions should help you troubleshoot any specific issues you may encounter when dealing with schema/version resolution issues.

Let's first create an application containing only one schema file and one orchestration. The document will be received by a receive location, validated against a schema by a pipeline, and routed to the orchestration. Open Visual Studio, and create an empty solution with an appropriate name. Add two BizTalk projects to the solution, and name them Schemas and Orchestrations. In the Visual Studio Explorer, right-click the project name, select the Properties menu item, switch to the Signing tab, and select the Sign the Assembly check box. Specify an existing, or generate a new, strong name key file.

Choose Add a New Project Item, and then choose schema file. Name it SampleSchema. Switch to the Properties window, select the root node, and change the Node Name property to Sample, as shown in Figure 3-17.

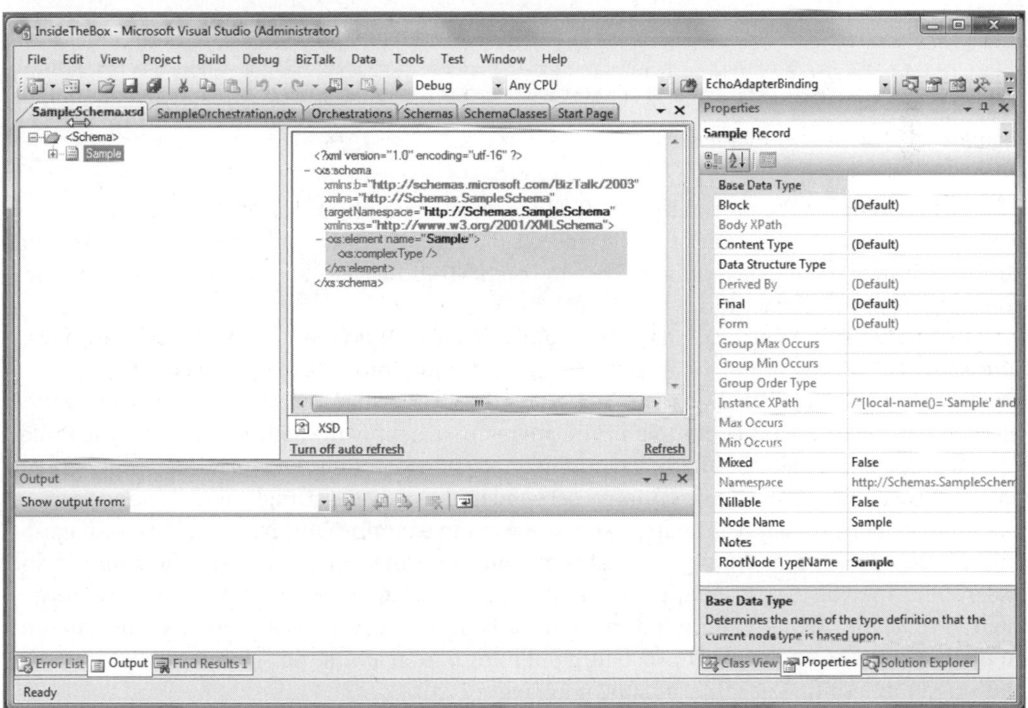

Figure 3-17. *Schemas project within Visual Studio*

Now switch to Solution Explorer, right-click the Schema project, and select Build. BizTalk compiles the XSD schema and places class definitions in its Schemas.dll assembly. You can see it in the project's output directory. If you are curious, you can load the generated assembly Schemas.dll file into a freeware tool such as the .NET Assembly Viewer from Ralf Reiterer[8] to check out the generated .NET class definition matching our SampleSchema.xsd schema, as shown in Figure 3-18.

8 `http://dotnet.jku.at/applications/course03/Reiterer/`

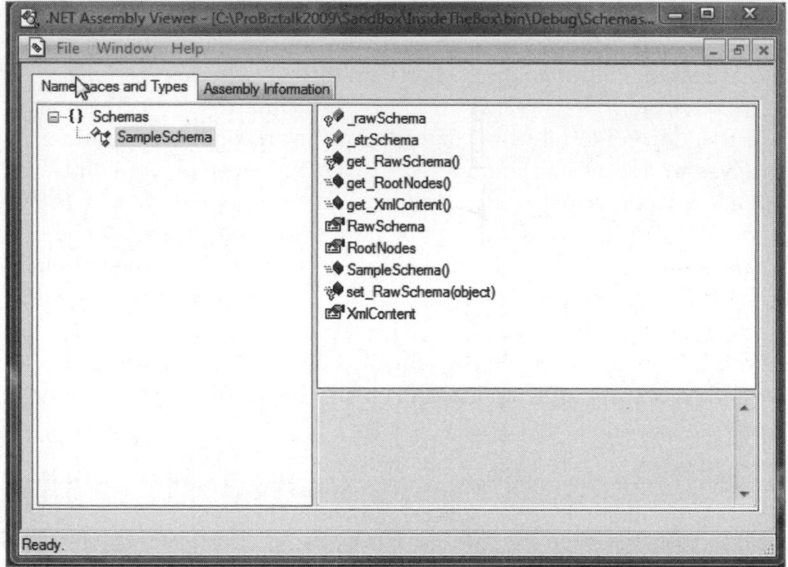

Figure 3-18. *.NET Assembly Viewer*

Switch to the Orchestrations project, add an orchestration, and configure it to pass through any received messages to a file-based send port, as shown in Figure 3-19. Despite that this is definitely not the best practice of using orchestrations, let's accept such a violation for the purpose of this discussion.

Right-click the Orchestrations project, and select the Build menu item. As you may have guessed, the XLANG compiler compiles the orchestration into a C# class and calls the standard csc.exe C# compiler. This in turn generates the Orchestrations.dll assembly. Now that all the preliminary steps are complete, you are ready to deploy the solution. Choose the Build menu, and select Deploy Solution. Executing the Deploy command within Visual Studio puts assemblies into the GAC (if this option is selected in the project settings) and also updates the Management Database. The first table you want to examine within the BizTalk Management Database is bts_Assembly. This table contains information about system assemblies and assemblies specific to custom applications. They are distinguished by an nSystemAssembly field. A value of 1 in this column indicates that assembly is a system assembly. As you can see in the last row, the deployment procedure put information about the Schemas and Orchestrations assemblies into this table, as shown in Figure 3-20.

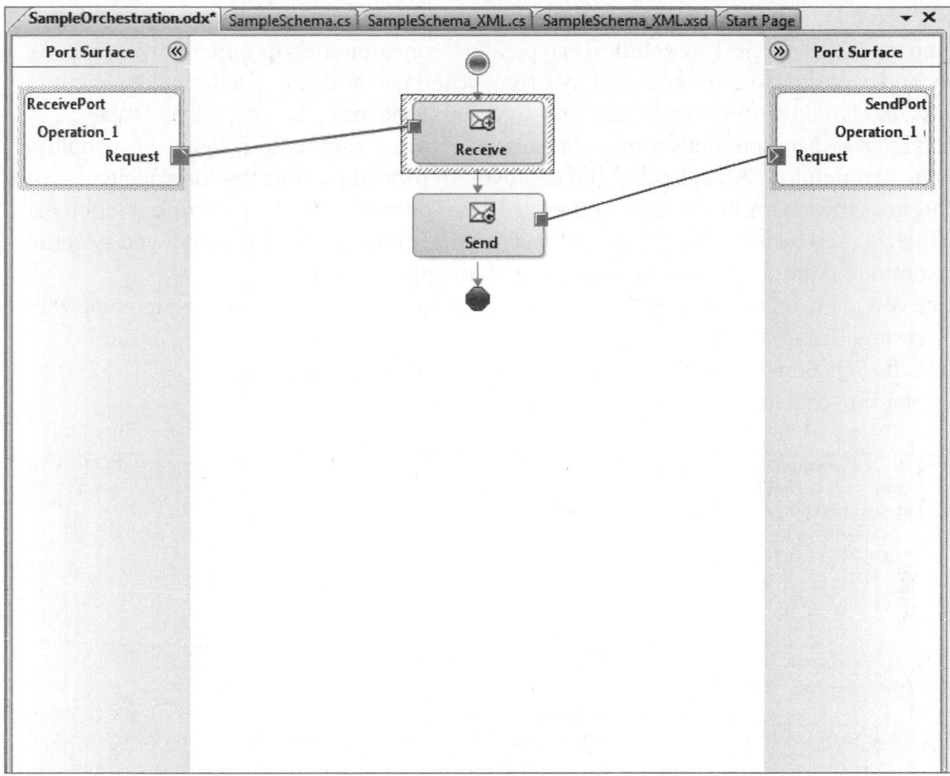

Figure 3-19. *Simple pass-through orchestration*

PROBIZTALK.Bi...assembly.sql* Summary

```
select nID,nvcFullName,nSystemAssembly from bts_assembly
```

Results | Messages

	nID	nvcFullName	nSystemAssembly
1	1	Microsoft.BizTalk.GlobalPropertySchemas, Version=3.0.1.0, Culture=neutral, PublicKe...	1
2	2	Microsoft.BizTalk.DefaultPipelines, Version=3.0.1.0, Culture=neutral, PublicKeyToken...	1
3	3	Microsoft.BizTalk.Adapter.MSMQ.MsmqAdapterProperties, Version=3.0.1.0, Culture=n...	1
4	4	MQSeries, Version=2.0.1.0, Culture=neutral, PublicKeyToken=31bf3856ad364e35	1
5	5	Microsoft.BizTalk.Hws.HwsPromotedProperties, Version=3.0.1.0, Culture=neutral, Pub...	1
6	6	Microsoft.BizTalk.Hws.HwsSchemas, Version=3.0.1.0, Culture=neutral, PublicKeyTok...	1
7	7	Microsoft.BizTalk.KwTpm.StsDefaultPipelines, Version=3.0.1.0, Culture=neutral, Publi...	1
8	8	Microsoft.BizTalk.KwTpm.RoleLinkTypes, Version=3.0.1.0, Culture=neutral, PublicKe...	1
9	9	mscorlib, Version=2.0.0.0, Culture=neutral, PublicKeyToken=b77a5c561934e089	1
10	31	Schemas, Version=1.0.0.0, Culture=neutral, PublicKeyToken=4618e66ff6b403b6	0
11	32	Orchestrations, Version=1.0.0.0, Culture=neutral, PublicKeyToken=4618e66ff6b403b6	0

Figure 3-20. *bts_Assemblies table*

Next, you'll figure out what your message type is. As stated previously in the chapter, a message type within a BizTalk solution is typically a concatenation of target namespace property and root node name separated by # sign. When you add a new schema file to your project, Visual Studio automatically sets the target namespace to `http://[ProjectName].[SchemaFileName]`. The schema's root node name is always preset to Root. When you deploy your project containing XSD schemas, the deployment procedure puts the message types into and references the assembly containing the .NET class definitions in bt_DocumentSchemas table, which is used by BizTalk to store and retrieve the information about deployed system-wide schemas and the schemas pertaining to custom applications.

Since you changed the root node name in your project to Sample, the message type will be `http://Schemas.SampleSchema#Sample`.

Open the SQL Server Management Studio, and run the query against the bt_DocumentSpec table, as shown in Figure 3-21.

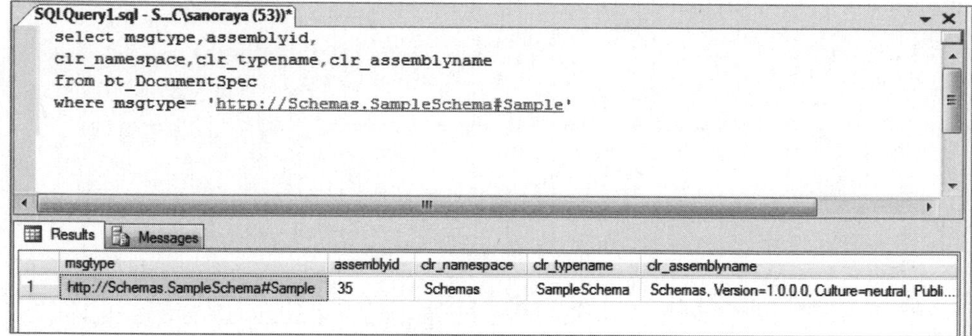

Figure 3-21. *SQL Server Management Studio query*

The output of this query confirms that you defined a new message of type `http://Schemas.SampleSchema#Sample`, and the class `SampleSchema` is representing your schema. Its location is in the assembly Schemas, version 1.0.0.0.

Upon startup, the BizTalk runtime caches this table in memory. When a Receive Adapter passes an inbound message to a disassembling receive pipeline, it first constructs the message type by concatenating the namespace and root node name of the incoming document. It then checks whether the message type is uniquely presented in the bt_DocumentSpec table. If the check is successful, the receive pipeline proceeds with further execution; if not, you will get an error message reporting an inability to resolve the message type. When you use Visual Studio's automatically generated unique namespace for document specification, you won't run into problems. But since you very likely will change the Target Namespace and Root Node Name properties manually, for example, to follow namespace pattern for all artifacts in a solution and to give the root nodes meaningful names, you have to be careful not to create conflicting document specifications. The problem is that deployment procedure doesn't check whether the document specification with the same namespace and root node type name has already been deployed and therefore doesn't produce any warning or error message in case of duplication.

Even if you create and maintain XSD specifications carefully, there is a situation you should be aware of that could potentially lead to problems. While working on different projects, we have seen developers make the same mistake of ending up with duplicate document specifications and then spending hours trying to figure out what's going on and why BizTalk refuses to process the document complaining that multiple schemas are matching the same message type. Here is how this might happen.

As you may already know, the BizTalk programming model is quite flexible, especially when it comes to message type conversion. When you call methods located in external .NET assemblies from your orchestration and pass the BizTalk message to those methods, you most likely pass the message as either a System.Xml.XmlDocument type or a Microsoft.XLANGs.BaseTypes.XLANGMessage type. You can then extract the message in the form of a well-typed .NET class, which is very convenient. The inverse applies to when you need to create a new message inside your .NET code and return it to your orchestration. In your orchestration inside a Construct Message shape, you can call a method that returns a .NET class representing an orchestration message. To generate this typed class, which matches your XSD schema, launch the Visual Studio command prompt, and then run the following command:

```
Xsd.exe /c SampleSchema.xsd
```

This command will generate a file named SampleSchema.cs containing the class named after the root node of the schema, which is Sample. Add a new class library project named SchemaClasses to the solution, and include this file to the project. Now you can extract messages and create new ones as a well-formed type, as in Listing 3-2.

Listing 3-2. *Type Orchestration Message*

```
using System;
using System.Collections.Generic;
using System.Text;
using Microsoft.XLANGs.BaseTypes ;

namespace CustomClasses
{
    public class MyCustomSampleClass
    {

        public Sample  CreateNewMessage(XLANGMessage sourceMessage)
        {
            Sample srcClass = sourceMessage[0].RetrieveAs(typeof(Sample));
            Sample newClass = new Sample();
            newClass = srcClass;
return newClass;

        }
    }
}
```

Surely this is quite a handy technique, but like all conveniences, it can be a source of problems if used indiscriminately. When you declare a message in an orchestration, you are required to specify what type of message it is (not to be confused with the message type routing property). You have four options:

- .NET classes
- Multipart message types
- Schemas
- Web message types

.NET types can be cast to an orchestration message type. So, having both .NET classes produced by the XSD.EXE tool and XSD schemas in the same solution technically allows you to choose either when specifying the type of message or when creating new orchestration message variables.

In your Orchestration project, add a reference to the SchemaClasses project. Then add a new message variable to the orchestration, switch to the Properties View, and select the Message Type combo box. Expand the .NET class branch, and choose Select from Referenced Assembly. This will pop up a Select Artifact Type dialog box, as shown in Figure 3-22.

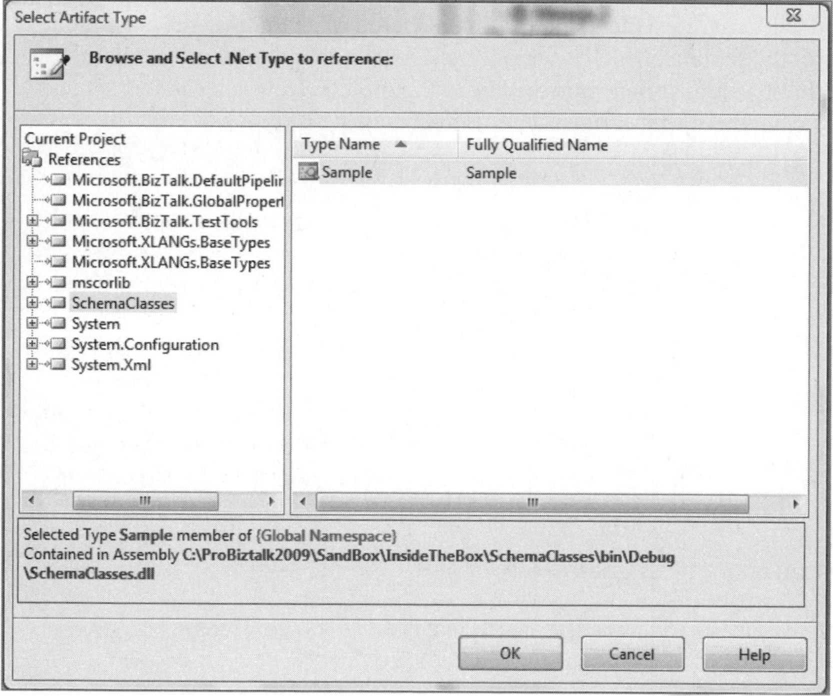

Figure 3-22. *Select Artifact Type dialog box*

Select the Sample item in the right pane, and compile and deploy the orchestration. Now open the SQL Server Management Studio, run the same query as shown in Figure 3-20 against the bt_DocumentSpec table, and check out your results. As you can see in Figure 3-23, the document specification is deployed twice, pointing to different assemblies: one pointing to the assembly created when you deployed XSD schemas and another to the assembly containing classes produced by the XSD.EXE tool.

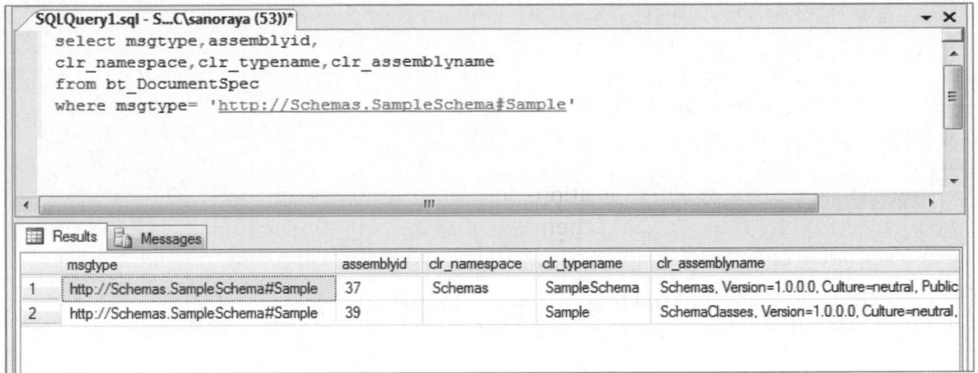

Figure 3-23. *Multiple assemblies, same namespace*

As you see, the deployment procedure makes no attempts to check for possible duplication and simply deploys everything as is. If you now submit a document instance to the receive location, you will get the following error message:

> *There was a failure executing receive pipeline: Cannot locate document specification because multiple schemas matched this message type [MessageType]*

In fact, you can achieve the same result with much less effort, and it is also a real-world scenario. After deploying the Schemas assembly, go to the project's settings, specify a different output assembly name, and redeploy the project. In the Management Database, you will end up having two document specifications with the same message type located in different assemblies. Moreover, as of this writing, the product is still in beta, and the MMC crashes when you attempt to see deployed schemas if there are schemas with duplicate message types. So, familiarity with the major tables in BizTalk Management Database may be quite helpful.

Listing 3-3 shows how you can enumerate deployed assemblies and schemas. The product documentation doesn't mention the important properties of the `Schema` class, namely, `TargetNamespace` and `RootNode`, which together constitute a message type. So, be aware that these properties are available.

Listing 3-3. *Enumerating Deployed Assemblies*

```
using System;
using System.Text;
using Microsoft.BizTalk.ExplorerOM;

namespace Schemas
{
    class Program
    {
```

```
        static void Main(string[] args)
        {
            EnumerateSchemas();
            Console.ReadKey();
        }

        public static void EnumerateSchemas()
        {
            BtsCatalogExplorer catalog = new BtsCatalogExplorer();
            catalog.ConnectionString = "Server=.;Initial
Catalog=BizTalkMgmtDb;Integrated Security=SSPI;";_

            foreach (BtsAssembly assembly in catalog.Assemblies )
            {


                foreach (Schema schema in assembly.Schemas)
                {
                   Console.WriteLine("\t{0}#{1}",
                        schema.TargetNameSpace,schema.RootName    );

                }
            }
        }
    }
}
```

Or you can access deployed schemas directly without enumerating assemblies first, as shown in Listing 3-4.

Listing 3-4. *Accessing Deployed Schemas Directly*

```
using System;
using System.Text;
using Microsoft.BizTalk.ExplorerOM;

namespace Schemas
{
    class Program
    {

        static void Main(string[] args)
        {
            EnumerateSchemas();
            Console.ReadKey();
        }
```

```
        public static void EnumerateSchemas()
        {
            BtsCatalogExplorer catalog = new BtsCatalogExplorer();
           catalog.ConnectionString = "Server=.;Initial
Catalog=BizTalkMgmtDb;Integrated Security=SSPI;";


                foreach (Schema schema in catalog.Schemas)
                {
                   Console.WriteLine("\t{0}#{1}",
                        schema.TargetNameSpace,schema.RootName);

                }
        }
    }
}
```

CHAPTER 4

Pipelining and Components

Pipelines are probably the least properly utilized tools in the BizTalk toolbox. Pipelines are designed to do one thing well:

> *Examine and potentially modify messages or convoys of messages as they are received and sent to/from the Messagebox*

The most important words in the preceding statement are "Examine" and "modify." As stated previously, messages in BizTalk are immutable once they have entered the Messagebox. The only proper way to affect a message is to change it in a pipeline either on the send side or on the receive side. Before starting a new custom pipeline, it is important to understand that a pipeline by itself does nothing. The real work is accomplished by the pipeline components that are attached to the pipeline. If you are building custom pipelines, 99% of your time will be spent coding the custom pipeline components, not building the actual pipeline.

These are some typical out-of-the-box uses of pipelines:

- Breaking up inbound documents into separate individual documents
- Verifying or signing documents with digital signatures
- Processing encoded documents (MIME/SMIME)
- Processing flat text files into XML and back
- Augmenting message data with information from external systems such as a database or mainframe

These scenarios cover about 75% of the typical uses of a BizTalk solution that would need to use a custom pipeline. There are, however, a multitude of other uses that we will dive into later. Pipelines are attached to either a send port or receive location and executed when a message is either received into or sent from the Messagebox. When the port processes a message, the pipeline processing is activated when the message is passed to the start of the pipeline.

■Note If you were to monitor the typical newsgroups relating to BizTalk, you would find that a common question often asked is, "How do I call a pipeline from an orchestration or from custom code?" Although it is possible to do this, try to understand why you need to do this before tackling it. Pipelines are meant to operate on a message or a convoy of messages. A convoy is simply a set of related messages that are logically grouped together by a promoted property called the `InterchangeID`. In BizTalk 2004, calling a pipeline from an orchestration was not a supported scenario. In BizTalk 2006 this has been greatly improved. Unless the application needs to aggregate messages inside the orchestration, there is no real reason to do this. Message aggregation is the primary reason why this feature was improved in BizTalk 2006.

Many new BizTalk architects often ask, "So why not just add all my custom code into the pipeline?" The answer is threefold:

- **Pipeline processing does not occur on multiple machines**: Pipelines execute on only one machine at a time since a message instance is picked up by a host instance. For example, a receive pipeline will execute on the BizTalk machine where the message is processed, not where it is received; if the pipeline has a significant amount of CPU work to accomplish, then this machine can become unavailable while the pipeline is executed. Note that multiple instances of a pipeline can execute simultaneously, but each instance executes on one machine. Likewise, if the messages being processed are quite large, the memory usage on that machine will grow accordingly if the entire document needs to be loaded into memory. This is the primary reason why most BizTalk architectures have receive/send processing servers isolated from orchestration processing servers.
- **Pipelines are stateful**: A pipeline executes in a stateful manner in that once the pipeline starts executing, it doesn't stop until it is completed. Also, if that pipeline instance terminates, that message becomes suspended and does not automatically restart on another machine. This is unlike an orchestration, which can dehydrate itself when the instance is waiting for a task to complete or rehydrate itself on another host if the original machine becomes available. If there are a significant number of messages to process, this can affect how the application will perform.
- **Pipeline exception handling is problematic**: If a pipeline throws an unhandled exception, the pipeline processing stops. This is a major issue for synchronous applications. Synchronous applications that require a notification be sent to the calling application will have issues if the pipeline throws exceptions and no response message is sent back. This issue will be explored later. It is possible in BizTalk 2009 to subscribe to the message failure, but this does not help in a synchronous application scenario.

Getting Started with Pipeline Development

Upon closer inspection, it is clear that a pipeline is simply a container for pipeline components. A pipeline has "stages" as shown in the Pipeline Designer. These stages differ for both send and receive pipelines, but they essentially allow you to do two things: first, they provide a way to logically organize the flow of execution logic within the pipeline, and second, they give the pipeline component developer different APIs to code against depending on what type of pipeline component is needed. If custom pipeline development is something that you haven't tackled before, ask yourself the following questions before you get started:

- What is the end result of my pipeline's execution? What types of message are expected?
- Will my pipeline need to look at the message's data? If it does, how big are the messages? Can I stream them using the XMLReader, or do I need to load them into an XML DOM?
- Is the pipeline schema agnostic, or does it need to validate the incoming message type?
- Does my pipeline need to create multiple messages based on the incoming message or just one?
- How do I handle exceptions within the pipeline? Do I need to log them? Can the pipeline throw an exception and stop processing, or does it need to output an error document?
- Do I have all the necessary context properties in the message context?
- Will I be promoting custom properties?

Pipeline Stages

Custom pipelines are divided into receive and send pipelines. Both types of pipelines have stages unique to either sending or receiving messages. Each stage of the pipeline has the ability to contain multiple pipeline components that are designed to be executed within that particular stage.

Receive Pipeline Stages

Receive pipelines have specific stages that help in processing the message in a logical fashion. The surface of the Pipeline Designer is shown in Figure 4-1. Each of the stages of the pipeline is designed to perform a specific task:

- **Decode**: This stage is used to perform operations that are required to "read" the incoming message. Think of the Decode stage as where you would perform things like decryption, decompression, and any processing logic that will be required as input data for the subsequent stages.
- **Disassemble**: Components tagged as Disassemblers are designed to produce zero or multiple messages based on the input message. Disassemblers often are used to debatch the incoming messages into multiple smaller messages. Each of the messages produced by the Disassembler are then passed to the remaining stages within the pipeline.

- **Validate**: This stage is used to ensure the message that has been decoded and potentially produced by the Disassembler is considered to be "valid" according to the pipeline rules. Often this involves verifying the XML schema of the message to be of a certain type. Custom validators are often created for custom business-level validation logic (i.e., ensuring that the purchase order number of an incoming message is valid and exists within a database).
- **Resolve Party**: This stage is used often in trading partner exchange scenarios. This stage is usually used to examine the digital certificates of a signed message to ensure the validity of the sending party.

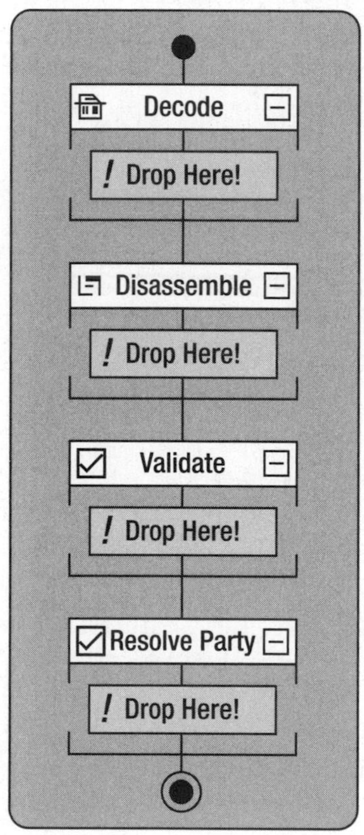

Figure 4-1. *Pipeline Designer stages*

Send Pipeline Stages

Send pipelines have specific stages that are related to preparing the message to be sent out of BizTalk. The surface of the Send Pipeline Designer is shown in Figure 4-2. Each of the stages of the pipeline is designed to perform a specific task:

- **Pre-Assemble**: This stage is often used to gather any specific information that will be needed by an Assembler and add it to the message.
- **Assemble**: Assemblers are responsible for combining multiple smaller messages into one large message. This is often the case when you are aggregating several messages into a batch. Assemblers are also often used in flat-file conversion and EDI scenarios to aggregate the outbound flat file into one large batched file.
- **Encode**: Encoders are responsible for writing the message in a fashion so that it can be read by the downstream system. Often this involves ensuring the proper character set is used, compressing the message, MIME encoding, or attaching a digital certificate.

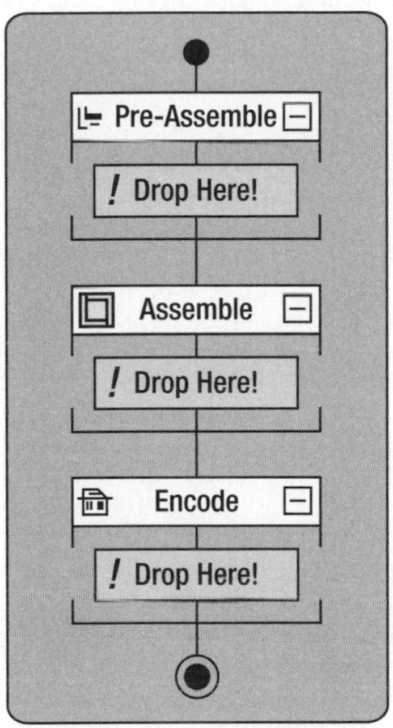

Figure 4-2. *Send Pipeline Designer*

Understanding Pipeline Execution

Pipeline components execute in a sequential order starting from the first stages and working down to the last. The exception to this rule is the Disassembler component, which will execute sequentially within the Disassemble stage of the receive pipeline until a component is found that is able to process the message. The first Disassembler component that accepts the message is executed, and then the resulting messages are passed to the remaining stages of the pipeline. When pipeline components execute sequentially, the output of one pipeline component is used as input to the next one in the sequence. Note the Disassemble stage in Figure 4-3. These components will fire sequentially until one of them determines that they can handle the incoming message. In this scenario, the first component that understands the message will execute.

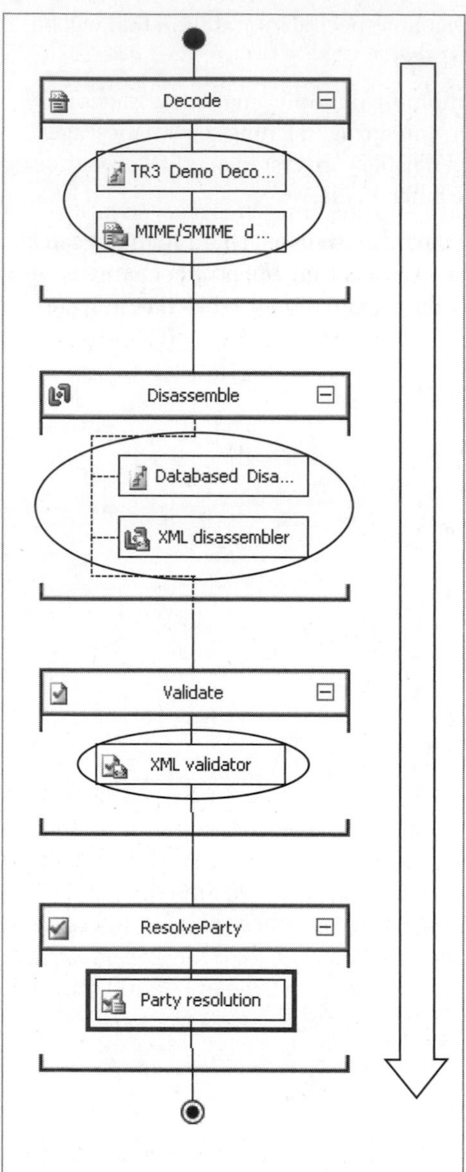

Figure 4-3. *Pipeline execution*

Understanding Interchanges

Most BizTalk developers really do not understand or appreciate fully what an Interchange is. An **Interchange** is a message or series of messages that flow through the Messagebox. Generally, one message = one Interchange. The Interchange is uniquely identified by the `InterchangeID`-promoted property. In many cases, the Interchange contains more than one message. This is often the case when processing flat-file documents or XML documents that contain envelopes. In this case, there will be one Interchange with as many messages as were contained in the original envelope. Each message would have the same `InterchangeID`; however, they would all have unique `MessageIDs`. In pipeline development, only Disassembler and Assembler components need to be concerned about this, since all other components receive one message and return one message. Disassemblers will receive one message and de-batch it into many messages, and the reverse is the case with Assemblers.

In terms of BizTalk processing, an Interchange is the message or series of messages that are received by a receive port and run through a receive pipeline. Interchanges with multiple documents generally relate to batch messages that are de-batched by a Disassembler component within a pipeline. If an envelope message were received with 20 documents inside, the Interchange would contain 20 messages. Each message would contain the same `InterchangeIDs` within the message context and distinct `MessageIDs`, as shown in Figure 4-4.

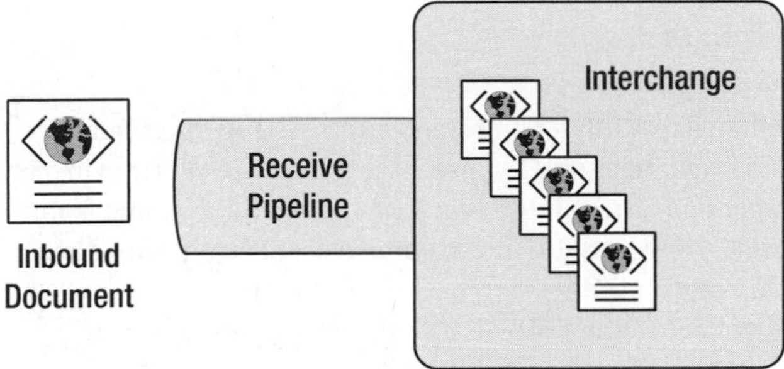

Figure 4-4. *Description of an Interchange*

In BizTalk Server 2004, if a document within the Interchange or "batch" be considered invalid either because of a "subscription not found" error or because the data within the message does not conform to the schema specified, every message within the batch would fail. This had dramatic repercussions for systems that did not want this functionality. Since BizTalk 2006, there is an option on the pipeline to allow it to not fail should one message be bad, continuing processing of the batch and failing only the individual messages that are in error. The remaining messages in the batch would be allowed to proceed. The message that failed can be subscribed to and routed to a generic error handling mechanism such as an orchestration or a port.

Overview of Recoverable Interchange Handling

Recoverable Interchange Processing (RIP) is a mechanism whereby the Messaging Engine will allow you to subscribe to special properties that are promoted by BizTalk when an error condition occurs. Typically, this is used in de-batching scenarios where a pipeline will be creating multiple messages in an Interchange. Should an error occur, the recoverable Interchange setting will allow the pipeline to throw an error only on the documents that failed and permit the remaining documents to be passed through the pipeline.

Message Suspension

If a message is in error and the component processing the message is using recoverable Interchanges, the message in error will be suspended and placed in the suspended queue; other messages will be propagated down the pipeline for further processing.

Once the messages within an Interchange are propagated down the pipeline or placed in the suspended queue, the further processing of those messages is treated transactionally as before. If a message fails at any point during its processing path, except in its routing (for example, no matching subscriber), all of the messages within the Interchange are thrown away, and the originating Interchange is placed in the suspended queue.

Message Failure Points

If you worked with BizTalk Server 2006 you likely know that failure in the message stages defined here result in the entire Interchange being suspended:

- Validate
- Resolve Party
- Map

BizTalk Server 2009 offers significant improvement and extends Recoverable Interchange Processing to Validate and Map stages. Interchanges that fail processing because of errors in the Resolve Party stage will become suspended. These Interchanges can then be resumed from within the BizTalk Administration Console. However, the Interchange will still likely fail unless the underlying cause of the failure is addressed.

Receiving the following errors will not cause the XMLDisassembler component to stop processing messages from an Interchange:

- Schema not found
- Schema ambiguity (more than one schema exists for the same message type)
- XML validation failed
- Flat-file parsing failed

Interchange processing will stop within the XMLDisassembler component if the message data is not well-formed XML. Since the data is read as a stream, a good check is to see whether document properties that would cause `System.Xml.XmlReader` to error are present. If they are, the XMLDisassembler will fail as well.

Messages that are extracted from Interchanges but fail because of a "No matching subscription found" error can be successfully resumed. All that is needed in this case is to ensure the BizTalk port or orchestration that has a subscription for the message is enlisted. The message can then be successfully resumed.

■ **Note** If you've worked with previous versions of BizTalk Server, you likely know that MSMQT adapter didn't support Recoverable Interchange Processing under any circumstances. BizTalk Server 2009 doesn't support MSMQT adapter anymore; instead, you should use the MSMQ adapter, which provides full support for recoverable interchanges.

The two examples that follow illustrate the differences in Interchange processing as affected by RIP.

Example 1: Standard Interchange Processing Behavior for the XMLDisassembler Component

The following XML is for a document that will be submitted to a receive location and then to the XMLReceive pipeline. This XMLDisassembler on the XMLReceive pipeline is configured for Standard Interchange Processing:

```
<MyBatch>
      <SubDoc1>MyDataValue1</SubDoc1>  //No Error
      <SubDoc2>MyDataValue2</SubDoc2> //Routing Error
      <SubDoc3>MyDataValue3</SubDoc3> //No Error
      <SubDoc4>MyDataValue4</SubDoc4> //Pipeline Failure - will be recoverable
      <SubDoc5>MyDataValue5</SubDoc5> //No Error
</MyBatch>
```

This batch of messages contains five messages, all of which will be successfully extracted and put into the Interchange. SubDoc1, SubDoc2, and SubDoc3 are processed through the pipeline and are ready to be published.

SubDoc 4 creates an error at the Disassemble stage in the pipeline. This causes all the messages that have already been processed to roll back and the original Interchange message to be suspended as resumable. The net effect is that no messages are published to the Messagebox. The batch is suspended because in Standard Interchange Processing, any pipeline failures cause the entire Interchange to be discarded, and any messages that may have been successfully disassembled are to be thrown away and suspended.

Example 2: Recoverable Interchange Processing Behavior for the XMLDisassembler Component

Using the same inbound batch document as shown in Example 1, if you set the XMLDisassembler to use RIP, the execution that will occur in the pipeline processing will be dramatically different. SubDoc1, SubDoc2, and SubDoc3 successfully pass through the pipeline and are ready to be published to the Messagebox. SubDoc4 generates an error in the XMLDisassembler and will be suspended. SubDoc5 passes through the pipeline and is able to be published to the Messagebox.

Once the entire Interchange is processed, SubDoc1, SubDoc2, SubDoc3, and SubDoc5 are successfully published to the Messagebox. SubDoc4 is placed in the suspended queue.[1] SubDoc2 is then sent to the suspended queue because of a “no subscriber found” error.

Configuring Recoverable Interchanges

There are two places where you can configure a recoverable Interchange for the Disassemble and Validate stages. The first is in the Receive Pipeline Designer, as shown in Figure 4-5. The ability to configure Recoverable Interchange Processing is available at design time when a custom pipeline that contains either a flat-file Disassembler or an XMLDisassembler or an XML validator is being developed. Recoverable Interchanges is a property of that component.

1 For an example of how to monitor messages that are placed in the suspended queue, see Chapter 6.

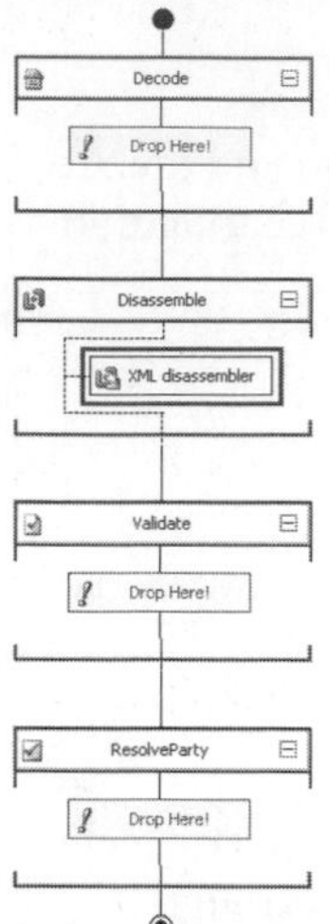

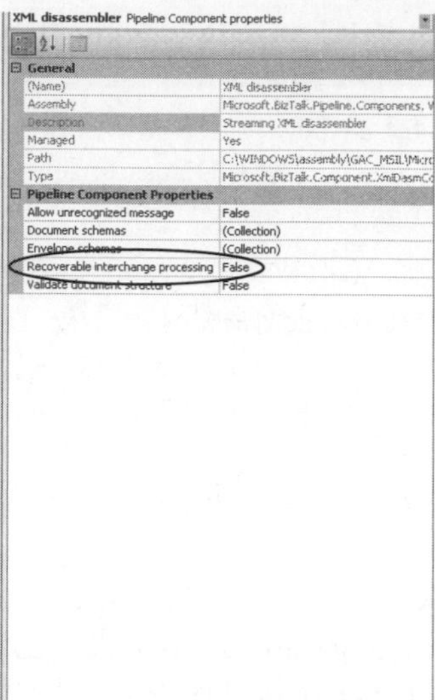

Figure 4-5. *Recoverable Interchanges property*

The second place to configure Recoverable Interchange Processing is on the receive location that will process the inbound Interchange. The property is part of the per-instance pipeline configuration screen, as shown in Figure 4-6.[2]

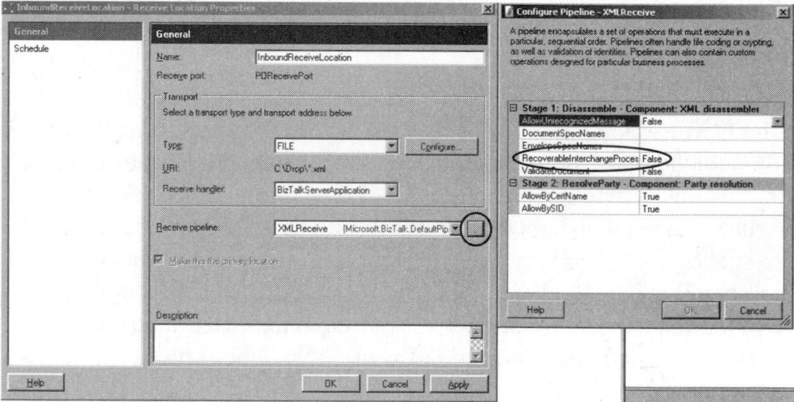

Figure 4-6. *Per-instance pipeline configuration for XMLReceive pipeline*

2 This is a good place to note that the property screen in Figure 4-5 is also where you would set the incoming envelope and document schemas for your receive location, which uses the XMLReceive pipeline. Most people would create a custom pipeline with the default XMLDisassembler and set these properties on the component—but starting in BizTalk 2006, the properties for this are exposed in this new UI. This type of setup was also available in BizTalk 2004 but was configured via the BizTalk object model. Alternatively, Jon Flanders has an excellent blog entry about this subject and a tool that allows you to configure these properties without writing additional code. See `www.masteringbiztalk.com/blogs/jon/PermaLink,guid,2f6500ae-d832-495f-92a3-f7032ef317ca.aspx` for more information.

To enable Recoverable Interchange Processing at the mapping stage you have to add the BTS.SuspendMessageOnMappingFailure property to the message context and set the value of the property to true in a pipeline component as follows:

```
public IBaseMessage Execute(IPipelineContext pc, IBaseMessage msg)
{
    msg.Context.Write("SuspendMessageOnMappingFailure", "http://schemas.microsoft.
com/BizTalk/2003/system-properties",
         true);
    ...
}
```

Unfortunately there is no design-time support for configuring Recoverable Interchange Processing for the Mapping phase.

Using the Default Pipelines

In many circumstances, the default pipelines that ship with BizTalk 2009 are able to handle most common tasks. For example, most developers do not know the default XMLReceive pipeline not only removes envelopes and disassembles but also resolves parties and thumbprint certificates. If you examine the product documentation, the default XMLReceive pipeline already includes the default XMLDisassembler and Party Resolution components. Both of these components can be configured in the per-instance pipeline configuration screen, as shown in Figure 4-6. In short, if your send or receive pipelines look like those shown in Figure 4-7, you don't need to create them. All you need to do is define an envelope schema inside the schema editor and ensure that each of the documents contained in the envelope are included in the schema as `XSD:Includes` in the case of the receive pipeline. The default XMLReceive pipeline will do the rest of the work for you. In general, it is always preferable to use the default pipelines versus building a custom one. The same is true for the default XMLTransmit pipeline. It contains an Assembler component that will assemble all messages passed to it in the Interchange.

In many cases, developers will simply default to using the XMLReceive pipeline in all circumstances regardless of what type of document they are processing and the end target for the message. It is important to note that you *do not* need this pipeline to process XML documents. You need the XMLReceive pipeline to promote properties and validate schemas, but if you know the destinations for the messages without having to route them, you can use the pass-through pipeline. The XMLReceive pipeline adds a fair bit of overhead to the receive-side processes because it is running the Disassembler and promoting properties into the context. There are several circumstances in which you need the XMLReceive pipeline, some of which are as follows:

- **Need to promote properties from the message's data**: The pass-through pipeline does not promote properties, so any custom properties you define in the schema will not be recognized. Note that default properties that were promoted by the adapter will still be available.
- **Need to route messages to an orchestration**: An orchestration needs to have the message properties promoted in order to determine message types. If the end target for the message is an orchestration and the orchestration is expecting a specific schema, you need to use the XMLReceive pipeline since this pipeline has the XMLDisassembler component, which sets the messagetype property.
- **Need to validate the message**: The pass-through pipeline has no concept of message validation. If you need to verify that the inbound message's data is correct, you cannot use the pass-through pipeline. By default, the XMLReceive pipeline also doesn't perform any validation. If you need to turn this feature on, you have two options at your disposal depending on what type of validation you want to perform. If all you need to do is validate incoming messages against specific schemas, you can configure XMLDisassembler by setting the Validate Document Structure property. For other types, such as business-level validation, you will have to write a custom validating component.

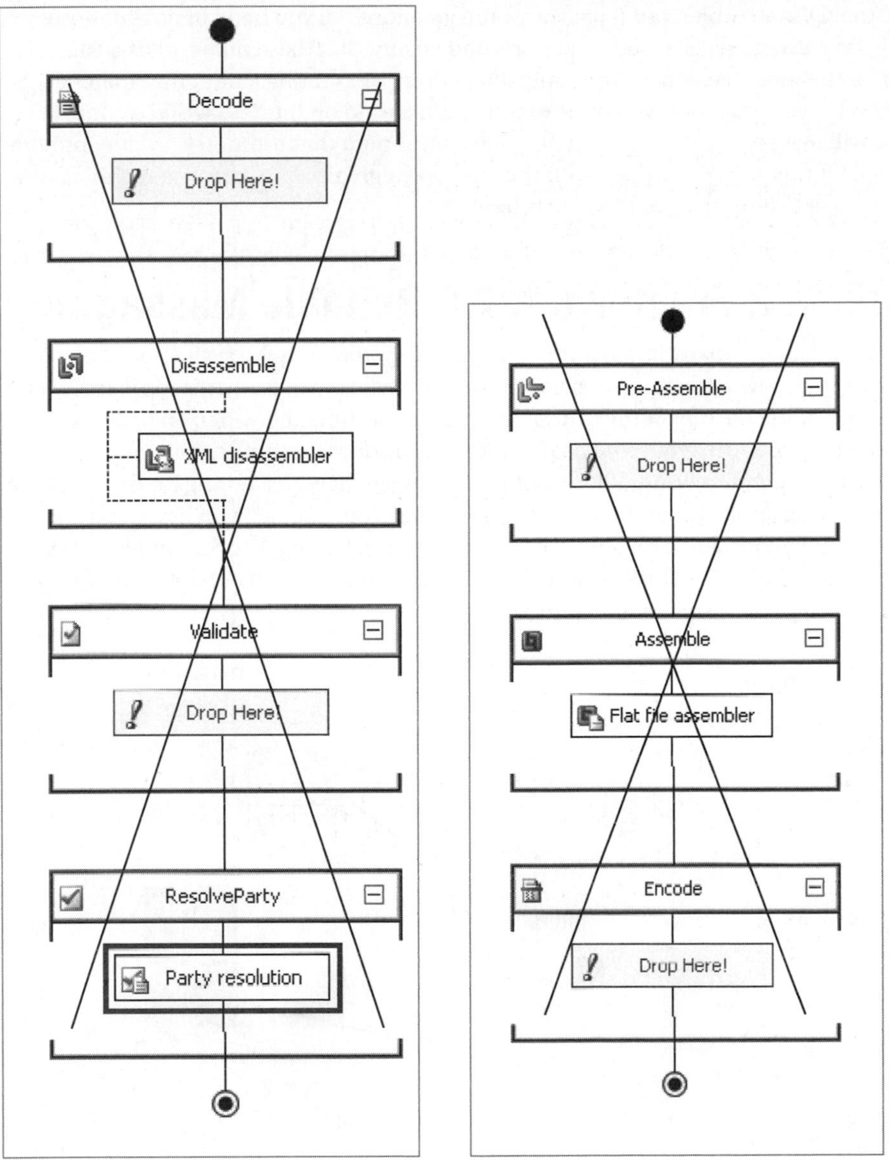

Figure 4-7. *If you have these, you probably don't need them.*

Routing Binary Data

Most people do not think that BizTalk can be used for processing binary data. Since the pass-through pipeline doesn't examine the message data and since the BizTalk Messaging Engine uses streams as its data representation, it is quite easy to move binary data from one source to another. If you need to promote custom properties for an incoming message, you will need to write a custom Disassembler, but if you know the locations, all you need to do is choose pass-through for both the receive and send ports and ensure that the send port has a valid subscription for the message. Most commonly this is done by creating a filter that matches based on `BTS.ReceivePortName`. If you want to route data based on the `MessageType` context property, you will need to create a custom pipeline component that promotes a value into the context. By default this will not happen with the pass-through pipeline, because technically there is no message to look at since the data is binary.

Using BizTalk Framework 2.0 Reliable Messaging

Let's assume that your company has an order processing system and the system not only needs to update your downstream systems, which are internal to your organization, but also needs to notify a trading partner of the transactions.[3] Let's assume that when an order is placed, you need to order the requested product from a supplier to support your zero inventory objectives. This situation brings about a number of challenges. Assuming for now that the sending and receiving applications are both BizTalk Server applications, you first must ensure that the transaction is completed reliably over inherently unreliable protocols and across network boundaries and firewalls. This is where the BizTalk Framework 2.0 Reliable Messaging scenarios come into play, as shown in Figure 4-8.

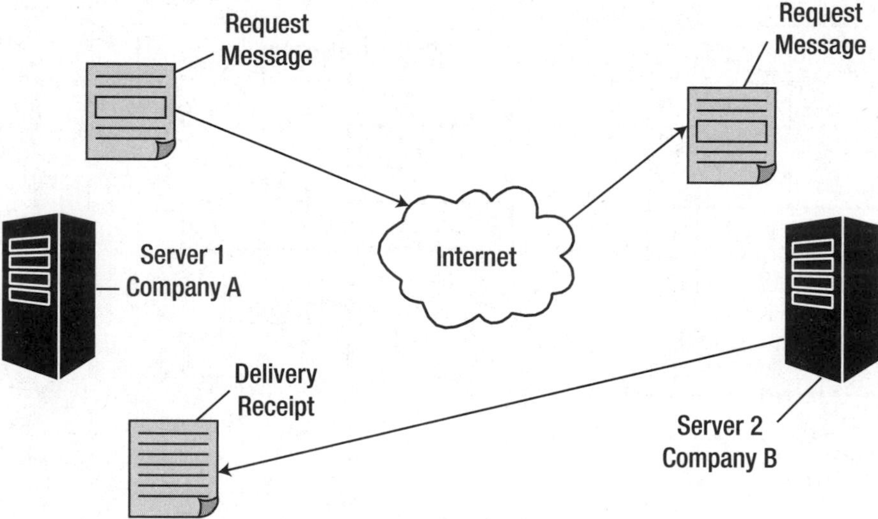

Figure 4-8. *Typical partner exchange scenario*

The BizTalk Framework specification is an XML specification that allows reliable messaging over HTTP and other transports. A BizTalk server according to the definition is a server that implements the BizTalk Framework rules and schemas for processing messages to provide a reliable Interchange mechanism over the wire.

3 This section and its subsections originally appeared in "Configuring BizTalk Framework Reliable Messaging in BizTalk Server 2004," (REED004872).zip. Copyright by Microsoft Corporation. Reprinted with permission from Microsoft Corporation.

In that sense, the product Microsoft BizTalk Server 2009 is a BizTalk server that implements the BizTalk Framework 2.0 specification. Of course, having BizTalk Server 2009 on both sides will allow you to implement reliable messaging Interchanges and processes with relatively small effort.

Microsoft BizTalk Server 2009 provides custom pipeline components for sending and receiving BizTalk Framework envelopes. The BizTalk Framework properties are configured through these pipeline components and can also be updated at runtime within an orchestration.

Figure 4-9 shows the required components (channel/ports and pipelines) to implement an Interchange with BizTalk Framework 2.0. The left side shows the sender configuration, which consists of a static one-way send port to send the business document or message and a static one-way receive port to receive BizTalk Framework 2.0 delivery receipts. The right side shows the receiver configuration, which contains a static one-way receive port to receive the message or business document and a dynamic one-way send port that subscribes (using a **filter expression**) to the Messagebox for messages that have the property `BTS.MessageType` with a value of BTF2DeliveryReceipt.

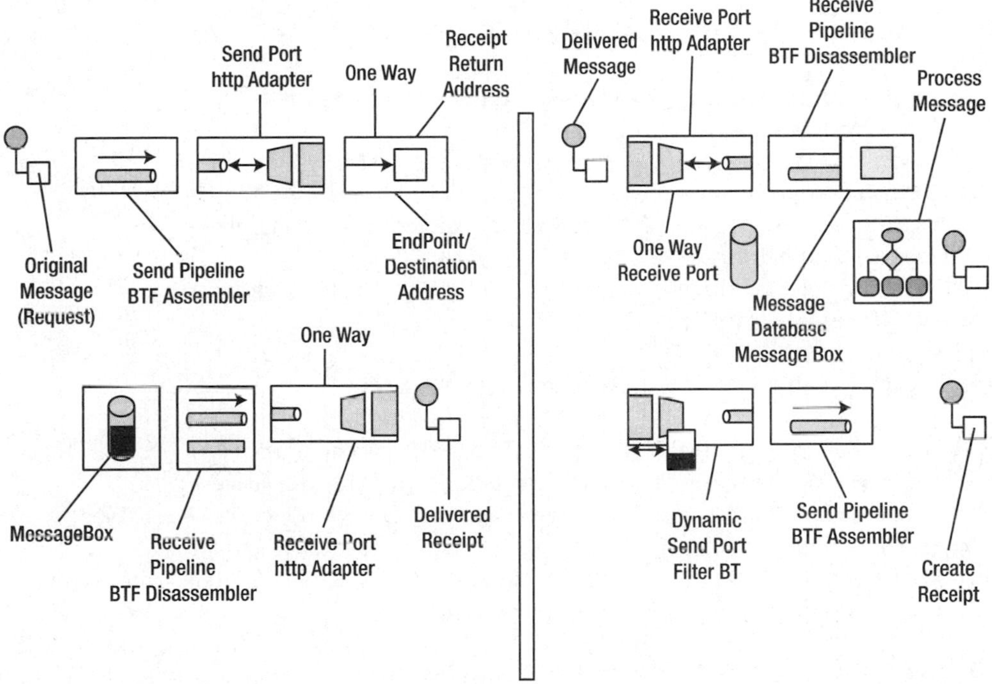

Figure 4-9. *BizTalk reliable messaging configuration*

In all four ports, the BizTalk custom pipeline components are used for receiving (Disassemble) and sending (Assemble) BizTalk Framework envelopes.

BizTalk Framework Assembler and Disassembler Pipeline Components

As mentioned earlier, BizTalk Server 2009 provides custom pipeline components for BizTalk Framework envelopes. The pipeline component that must be configured for messages going out is the Assembler. In our first scenario, only one of the four ports must be configured.

Working with BizTalk Framework Properties Within Orchestrations

In many cases, a business process orchestration will be implemented in either the send or receive side of a business process, and it is more suitable to configure the BizTalk Framework properties there. On top of that, there are properties that are not accessible as design-time pipeline components. The orchestration is a suitable place to modify the values of these properties at runtime.

The following lines of code show how to assign the values to the property field of the outbound message. These values can be written within a message assignment expression and will override any given value set at design time.

```
//Basic settings for BizTalk Framework Reliable Messaging

msgPSB_ReachEnvelope_Outgoing(XMLNORM.AddXMLDeclaration)=false;
msgPSB_ReachEnvelope_Outgoing(BTF2.IsReliable)=true;
msgPSB_ReachEnvelope_Outgoing(BTF2.svc_deliveryRctRqt_sendBy)=_
vBTFDeliveryReceiptSendBy;
msgPSB_ReachEnvelope_Outgoing(BTF2.svc_deliveryRctRqt_sendTo_address)= _
vBTFDeliveryReceiptAddress;
msgPSB_ReachEnvelope_Outgoing(BTF2.svc_deliveryRctRqt_sendTo_address_type)= _
vBTFDeliveryReceiptAddressType;

//Other settings for BizTalk Framework Reliable Messaging

msgPSB_ReachEnvelope_Outgoing(BTF2.prop_topic)=vBTFDocumentTopic;
msgPSB_ReachEnvelope_Outgoing(BTF2.eps_from_address)=vBTFSourceAddress;
msgPSB_ReachEnvelope_Outgoing(BTF2.eps_from_address_type)=vBTFSourceAddressType;
msgPSB_ReachEnvelope_Outgoing(BTF2.eps_to_address)=vBTFDestinationAddress;
msgPSB_ReachEnvelope_Outgoing(BTF2.eps_to_address_type)=vBTFDestinationAddressType;
msgPSB_ReachEnvelope_Outgoing(BTF2.PassAckThrough)=true;
```

Acknowledgment Verification

One of the easiest ways to verify the acknowledgment of the messages is to look at the following SQL tables in the BizTalk Management Database:

- btf_message_sender
- btf_message_receiver

For outgoing messages, look at the sender table, as shown in Figure 4-10. If the message was acknowledged, the acknowledged field will be marked with an *A*.

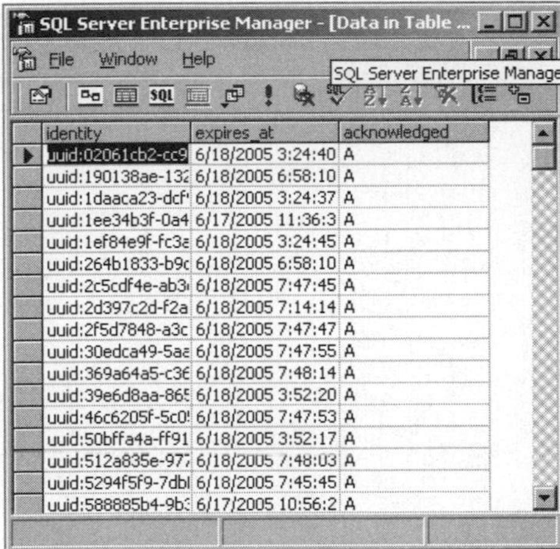

identity	expires_at	acknowledged
uuid:02061cb2-cc9	6/18/2005 3:24:40	A
uuid:190138ae-13:	6/18/2005 6:58:10	A
uuid:1daaca23-dcf	6/18/2005 3:24:37	A
uuid:1ee34b3f-0a4	6/17/2005 11:36:3	A
uuid:1ef84e9f-fc3e	6/18/2005 3:24:45	A
uuid:264b1833-b9c	6/18/2005 6:58:10	A
uuid:2c5cdf4e-ab3	6/18/2005 7:47:45	A
uuid:2d397c2d-f2a	6/18/2005 7:14:14	A
uuid:2f5d7848-a3c	6/18/2005 7:47:47	A
uuid:30edca49-5ae	6/18/2005 7:47:55	A
uuid:369a64a5-c3e	6/18/2005 7:48:14	A
uuid:39e6d8aa-865	6/18/2005 3:52:20	A
uuid:46c6205f-5c0	6/18/2005 7:47:53	A
uuid:50bffa4a-ff91	6/18/2005 3:52:17	A
uuid:512a835e-977	6/18/2005 7:48:03	A
uuid:5294f5f9-7dbl	6/18/2005 7:45:45	A
uuid:588885b4-9b:	6/17/2005 10:56:2	A

Figure 4-10. *btf_message_sender table*

On the receiver side, look at the receive table. In the table will be the records corresponding to the acknowledged documents.

Custom Components

It is critical to understand that each of the different types of pipeline components is designed to do a specific task. Most custom pipelines that we have seen generally include only one custom pipeline component inside a custom pipeline and try to perform all tasks within that one class. Often this becomes problematic and leads to an overly complex class. When starting development, the goal should be to write many small generic components instead of a small number of specialized ones. Pipeline components should be designed to be reused. Additionally, if it makes sense, the components should also accept multiple schema types and allow the user to choose the inbound/outbound schemas. Too often developers will hard-code the schema into the component and assume that the inbound messages will always be of a certain type. The component should, first, be flexible enough to probe the incoming schema and determine that it can handle the document and should, second, provide a user interface for selecting the desired schema in the Pipeline Designer.

Before starting a new project, the most important thing is to understand what type of component you need to build. This will depend on the following:

- Whether the component is executed in a receive pipeline, a send pipeline, or both
- What type of work needs to be done

Too often developers simply "default" to writing what they know instead of what they should. Having a thorough understanding of how pipeline components work, along with a proper design for what work should take place at which pipeline stage, will help you build more reusable and reliable pipeline components.

Component Categories

As you will soon see, the pipeline component development API is quite heavily based on COM Interop. Most of the specifics of how components are defined are based on what COM category they are tagged with along with what interfaces they implement. Component categories, listed here, exist for each of the different types of pipeline components:

CATID_Any

CATID_AssemblingSerializer

CATID_Decoder

CATID_DisassemblingParser

CATID_Encoder

CATID_Parser

CATID_PartyResolver

CATID_PipelineComponent[4]

CATID_Receiver

CATID_Serializer

CATID_Streamer

CATID_Transmitter

CATID_Validate

These are defined by tagged attributes on the pipeline component's class, as shown in the following code:

```
Imports System
Imports System.ComponentModel
Imports Microsoft.BizTalk.Message.Interop
Imports Microsoft.BizTalk.Component.Interop
Imports Microsoft.BizTalk.Component
Imports Microsoft.BizTalk.Messaging

Namespace ABC.BizTalk.FullFillment.PipelineComponents

    <ComponentCategory(CategoryTypes.CATID_PipelineComponent), _
     System.Runtime.InteropServices.Guid("4f1c7d50-e66f-451b-8e94-2f8d599cd013"), _
     ComponentCategory(CategoryTypes.CATID_Encoder)> _
    Public Class MyFirstEncodingComponent
```

Note that it is possible for a component to have more than one category type if it has the proper interface implementation. Also note that the component explicitly defines a GUID for

4 The CATID_PipelineComponent category is basically a generic "catch-all" category that all pipeline components should implement. It doesn't require any specific interface declarations but is used to identify something as a pipeline component.

COM Interop.[5] This can be done by generating a new GUID—using, for example, the VS .NET GUID Generation tool—and adding it here as an attribute of the class.

Component Interfaces

The specific interfaces a pipeline component implements are what differentiate that pipeline component from another. BizTalk Server ships with a number of assemblies that define application interfaces for custom components to implement. Once a component has an interface implementation, it can be called by the BizTalk runtime. The basic interfaces are defined in the following list. All components and component categories live in the `Microsoft.BizTalk.Component.Interop` namespace.

- `IBaseComponent`: Defines properties that provide basic information about the component.

  Public properties:

  - `Description`: Gets the component description
  - `Name`: Gets the component name
  - `Version`: Gets the component version

- `IComponent`: Defines the methods used by all pipeline components except Assemblers and Disassemblers.

  Public method:

  - `Execute`: Executes a pipeline component to process the input message and get the resulting messages

- `IComponentUI`: Defines methods that enable pipeline components to be used within the Pipeline Designer environment.

  Public property:

  - `Icon`: Gets the icon that is associated with this component

  Public method:

  - `Validate`: Verifies that all of the configuration properties are set correctly

Key BizTalk API Objects

All pipeline components, regardless of what they do, will use the interfaces described in the following subsections. Likewise, most of the pipeline component interfaces defined previously accept these interfaces as arguments. That being said, it is important to understand these interfaces first before proceeding. The following is based on material from the BizTalk Server documentation on MSDN.

---

5 Types including interfaces, classes, and assemblies get a unique GUID even if you don't assign one explicitly. However, they can change between builds/assembly versions, so in this case it's best to explicitly assign them so you don't break binary compatibility between builds/versions.

IPipelineContext[6]

IPipelineContext is the main interface that defines the operations and properties for the pipeline instance. Tables 4-1 and 4-2 show the interface's public properties and methods. The key method here is the GetMessageFactory method. This method will return a message factory for the pipeline that can be used to create new messages using the CreateMessage method.

The GetMessageFactory method is the main way to create new messages from within a pipeline component. Also note that you will need to call IPipelineContext.GetMessageFactory.CreateMessagePart to create the message part for the message. As we mentioned in Chapter 3, a message is simply a construct that contains zero to many message parts. Once you create the message part, you can assign it to the IBaseMessage object through the AddPart method.

Table 4-1. *IPipelineContext Public Properties*

Property	Description
ComponentIndex	Gets the index of the current component in the stage.
PipelineID	Gets the ID of the pipeline with which this pipeline context associates.
PipelineName	Gets the name of the pipeline.
ResourceTracker	Gets the IResourceTracker object associated with the pipeline context. This object can be used to track and dispose non-CLR resources.
StageID	Gets the ID of the current stage in the pipeline.
StageIndex	Gets the index of the pipeline stage where the current component is located.

Table 4-2. *IPipelineContext Public Methods*

Method	Description
GetDocumentSpecByName	Gets an IDocumentSpec object for the specified document name
GetDocumentSpecByType	Gets an IDocumentSpec object for the specified document type
GetGroupSigningCertificate	Gets the signing certificate for the group
GetMessageFactory	Get access to the helper interface to work with BizTalk Server message objects

IBaseMessage[7]

IBaseMessage is the base interface that defines a BizTalk Server message. Tables 4-3 and 4-4 show the public properties and methods. Note that messages, created using the IPipelineContext.GetMessageFactory.CreateMessage method, will implement this interface. This will still need an IBaseMessagePart to be assigned through the AddPart method for any data to be included with the message.

6 http://msdn.microsoft.com/en-us/library/microsoft.biztalk.component.interop.ipipelinecontext_members.aspx

7 http://msdn.microsoft.com/en-us/library/microsoft.biztalk.message.interop.ibasemessage_members.aspx

Table 4-3. *IBaseMessage Public Properties*

Property	Description
`BodyPart`	Gets the body part, or main part, of the message
`BodyPartName`	Gets the name of the body part, or main part, of the message
`Context`	Gets or sets the message context
`IsMutable`	Gets a value indicating whether the message can be changed by components during processing
`MessageID`	Gets the unique message ID for the message
`PartCount`	Gets the total number of parts in the message

Table 4-4. *IBaseMessage Public Methods*

Method	Description
`AddPart`	Adds a part to the message.
`GetErrorInfo`	Gets the exception that caused the error.
`GetPart`	Accesses the message part. This is indexed by `PartName`.
`GetPartByIndex`	Retrieves a part and its name by supplying the part index.
`GetSize`	Gets the size of the message.
`RemovePart`	Removes a part from the message.
`SetErrorInfo`	Sets the error information.

IBaseMessagePart[8]

`IBaseMessagePart` is the interface that defines a BizTalk message part. Tables 4-5 and 4-6 show its public properties and methods. The message part is assigned to an `IBaseMessage` through the `AddPart` method. Note the `Data` property. This is the property used to assign a value to the message part. The `Data` property accepts and returns only streams. This is incredibly useful, because it allows any stream to be assigned to the message part. This includes XMLReader streams, MemoryStreams, and raw BinaryStreams.

Another rarely used item is the `PartProperties` property. This is essentially a property bag that can be used to store information and metadata about the part. In reality, the `PartID`, `Charset`, and `ContentType` are actually contained in the `PartProperties IBasePropertyBag` object.

8 http://msdn.microsoft.com/en-us/library/microsoft.biztalk.message.interop.ibasemessagepart_members.aspx

Table 4-5. *IBaseMessagePart Public Properties*

Property	Description
`Charset`	Gets or sets the character set property for the part
`ContentType`	Gets or sets the content type property for the part
`Data`	Gets or sets the part data
`PartID`	Gets the part with a unique ID
`PartProperties`	Gets or sets one or more properties that describe the part data or contain custom information about the part

Table 4-6. *IBaseMessagePart Public Methods*

Method	Description
`GetOriginalDataStream`	Retrieves the original uncloned version of the part data stream
`GetSize`	Retrieves the size of the part

IBaseMessageContext[9]

`IBaseMessageContext` is the interface used to interact with and manipulate the object context accessible through the `IBaseMessage.Context` property. Tables 4-7 and 4-8 show the public properties and methods. The main items of interest here are the `Promote`, `Read`, and `Write` methods. Properties that exist in the context can never have a Null value. A Null value means that the property does not exist. Here's an example:

- Attempting to set (or promote) a property value to Null deletes the property and returns the COM result `S_OK`.
- Attempting to read a nonexistent property returns Null.

Table 4-7. *IBaseMessageContext Public Property*

Property	Description
`CountProperties`	Gets the number of properties in the message context

9 http://msdn.microsoft.com/en-us/library/microsoft.biztalk.message.interop.ibasemessagecontext_members.aspx

Table 4-8. *IBaseMessageContext Public Methods*

Method	Description
`AddPredicate`	Adds a message predicate to the message
`GetPropertyType`	Gets the type of the property
`IsMutable`	Indicates whether the message context can be changed by components during processing
`IsPromoted`	Enables the component to determine whether a property has already been promoted in the message context
`Promote`	Promotes a property into the message context
`Read`	Gets a property value from the message context by the name-namespace pair
`ReadAt`	Gets a property from the message context by index
`Write`	Writes a property into the message context

PipelineUtil

`PipelineUtil` is a helper class that exposes the three methods shown in Table 4-9. These methods are invaluable when you need to create a new message.

Table 4-9. *PipelineUtil Public Methods*

Method	Description
`CloneMessageContext`	Creates a clone of the message context for a given message. This is useful for copying the message context of one message to another.
`CopyPropertyBag`	Creates a clone of the property bag for a given message. This is useful for copying the property bag of one message to another.
`ValidatePropertyValue`	Checks that the object is a valid property value.

■ Caution This class is unsupported and is part of the BizTalk product infrastructure. If you run into trouble using it, Microsoft Product Support may not support you. However, it is common knowledge that it exists and makes pipeline component development much easier.

Writing Your First Pipeline Component

The first component most developers want to write is usually some form of simple encoder or decoder. Basically, they want to be passed a message and take some action. This action usually involves updating a piece of data within the message or creating a new message based on some other factors. Implementing this behavior is simple. The component in question needs to implement IComponent and populate the IComponent.Execute method with code that takes action. The sample function looks much like this:[10]

```
'<summary>
'Implements IComponent.Execute method.
'</summary>
'<param name="pc">Pipeline context</param>
'<param name="inmsg">Input message</param>
'<returns>Original input message</returns>
'<remarks>
'IComponent.Execute method is used to initiate
'the processing of the message in this pipeline component.
'</remarks>
Public Function Execute(ByVal pContext As _
Microsoft.BizTalk.Component.Interop.IPipelineContext, ByVal inmsg _
As Microsoft.BizTalk.Message.Interop.IBaseMessage) As )
Microsoft.BizTalk.Message.Interop.IBaseMessage _
Implements Microsoft.BizTalk.Component.Interop.IComponent.Execute


        'Build the message that is to be sent out
        DoMyMessageWork(pContext, inmsg)
            ...
            ...
        Return inmsg
End Function
```

Creating More Complex Pipeline Components

Once you master the basics of creating a component, looking at the message, and figuring out what you can do with the data, you may ask yourself, “Okay, so what else can these things do?” We usually answer this with “Pipeline components are much like the Matrix in that you cannot be told what they can do; you must see it for yourself.” In this respect, it is much easier to think about components in terms of specific problems they can solve. We’ll show you a few examples so you can see how you use a pipeline component to solve the issue at hand. In the next chapter, we will dive into advanced pipeline component development and show examples of how you can use pipeline components to extend the base functionality of BizTalk well beyond what is included in the product.

10 All of the code snippets in the following sections were generated using the Pipeline Component Wizard, which can be downloaded from http://www.codeplex.com/btsplcw. This is a wonderful tool, and we wanted to specifically reference it here, because the comments and coding styles for the snippets were autogenerated by the tool. The tool dramatically speeds up pipeline component development and generates well-formed and commented code as well. We wanted to specifically not discuss it in detail here because it is more important to understand how the engine uses pipeline components and how to properly write them versus just running the wizard and having it autogenerate the code for you.

Dynamically Promoting Properties and Manipulating the Message Context

The simplest and most common use of a pipeline component is to promote custom properties into the message context for a message. Often the data for the property is not available in the schema or is not easily accessible. For example, you may need to obtain the data at runtime from an external source such as a database; or, in the case of repeating fields, you will need to determine the index of the field to be promoted. In such cases, a simple promotion at design time using the schema editor is not an option. For a simple example, see the Chapter 3 subsection, "Understanding Property Promotions." The code outlined in that subsection demonstrates how to simply write and promote properties to the context.

Dealing with "Out of Order" Message Sequences

When dealing with Interchanges, most often it would be great to know just how many messages are actually in the Interchange and which one is the last one. Preserving order is a major pain for any type of application that needs to do so and potentially resequence messages to an outbound system. Normally selecting ordered delivery is good enough for this task, but two major problems still exist:

- Ordered delivery works only if you receive the messages in the proper order.
- Selecting a port as ordered has a huge performance hit, because messages will essentially be single-threaded as they are dequeued from the Messagebox.

What is needed is a **resequencer pattern** to reorder the messages into the proper order once they are received by an orchestration. The following is a definition and example of a resequencer as given by the Enterprise Integration Patterns site:[11]

A Message Router can route messages from one channel to different channels based on message content or other criteria. Because individual messages may follow different routes, some messages are likely to pass through the processing steps sooner than others, resulting in the messages getting out of order. However, some subsequent processing steps do require in-sequence processing of messages, for example to maintain referential integrity.

How can we get a stream of related but out-of-sequence messages back into the correct order? The figure below logically demonstrates how this concept works.

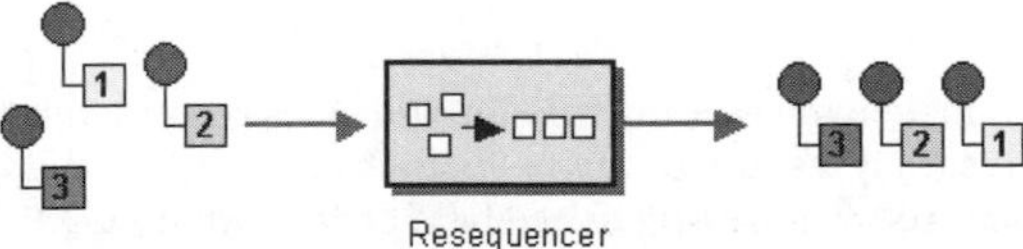

11 Enterprise Integration Patterns site, Resequencer page: `http://www.eaipatterns.com/Resequencer.html`. This site is an excellent resource for all types of patterns that can easily be created using BizTalk Server.

Use a stateful filter, a Resequencer, to collect and re-order messages so that they can be published to the output channel in a specified order.

The Resequencer can receive a stream of messages that may not arrive in order. The Resequencer contains in internal buffer to store out-of-sequence messages until a complete sequence is obtained. The in-sequence messages are then published to the output channel. It is important that the output channel is order-preserving so messages are guaranteed to arrive in order at the next component. Like most other routers, a Resequencer usually does not modify the message contents.

In Chapter 6, we will give a complete example of how to implement custom resequencers using BizTalk orchestrations, convoys, and custom pipeline components. But the most fundamental part of the equation is storing the order. To do that, all you need is a simple pipeline component that can promote what the sequence number is for the current message along with a trigger for determining whether or not it is the last message in the Interchange. Resequencing is most commonly done using a Disassembler component to actually create messages.

Custom Distinguished Fields

When you are writing a custom Disassembler,and you want to have distinguished fields that are accessible from within an orchestration, you will need to ensure that they are written to the context of the message before it is stored in the Messagebox. This is because normally when you use an XMLReceive pipeline, it automatically stores these values for you, but when you are writing a custom component, that storing of values doesn't happen automagically, so you need to deal with it yourself.[12]

■ **Note** In order to access the distinguished field in the orchestration editor, you still need to tag the field as a distinguished field. This is basically to allow the orchestration engine to read the schema and know at design time what the available distinguished fields are. What needs to happen is that you need to manually populate that field with data at runtime. If you don't, the orchestration will fail with an exception when the XLANG class tries to access the distinguished fields data and finds a Null value.

The solution to the problem is simple—just write the value to the message context using code as shown in the following snippet. Note the format of the property name and the

12 People often do not understand what the runtime engine is doing when it processes a distinguished field. Most think that the distinguished field is simply a shortcut to the XPath expression that maps to the field in the document. Actually this is not true. The distinguished field defines what the XPath expression is, but the runtime engine prefetches this data when it processes the message. This is basically done because it is far more performant to do this, and the product team wrote their own XPath navigator component to use streams, making it very efficient to do this as the document is being processed. This is why there is very little performance overhead when you access a distinguished field in an orchestration—it is already loaded and cached. If you used XPath to get the value, the orchestration engine would have to load the entire document and evaluate the XPath expression manually—which is slow and very expensive when dealing with large documents.

namespace. In order to be processed by the orchestration engine, they must be named as follows:

Name: The distinguished field location in XPath: "/*[local-name()='PurchaseOrder' and namespace-uri()='http://ABC.FullFillment']/*[local-name()='UnitPrice' and namespace-uri()='']"

Namespace URI: "http://schemas.microsoft.com/BizTalk/2003/btsDistinguishedFields"

```
//BizTalk System Properties Namespace
Private Const BTSFieldXPathLocation As String =  "/*[local-name()='PurchaseOrder' _
    and namespace-uri()='http://ABC.FullFillment']/*[local-name()='UnitPrice' and _
    namespace-uri()='']"

    Private Const BTSDistinguishedFieldsPropertiesNamespace As String = "_
    http://schemas.microsoft.com/BizTalk/2003/btsDistinguishedFields "

    //Write a distinguished property
    message.Context.Write(BTSFieldXPathLocation, _
    BTSDistinguishedFieldsPropertiesNamespace, 10);
```

Checking for Schema Types in Components

As was stated previously, pipeline components that are expecting incoming documents to conform to a particular schema should do two things:

- They should probe the incoming document and determine whether they can process it based on the schema's namespace and root node.
- They should allow the developer to choose the allowed incoming schemas at design time using the Pipeline Designer.

Probing the message checks the incoming schema and simply indicates to the runtime that the component will be able to handle the schema—essentially a Boolean value. Ensuring that components validate against the schema is critical, because it often allows the same component code to be reused for multiple applications and also allows for per-instance pipeline configuration. This is done using the `IProbeMessage` interface.

IProbeMessage

The `IProbeMessage` interface has only one method—`Probe`. This method checks whether the incoming message is in a recognizable format. The `Probe` method passes in the pipeline context object as an `IPipelineContext` interface along with the message represented as an `IBaseMessage` Interface and returns a Boolean. If the method returns False, the pipeline component cannot process the message, the current component instance stops executing, and the pipeline component execution sequence continues as defined in Figure 4-3. If it returns True, then the pipeline component executes as normal with its primary operation (Encode, Execute, Disassemble, and so on).

The following is an example of a simple IProbeMessage implementation:

```
Public Class MyProber Implements Microsoft.BizTalk.Component.Interop.IProbeMessage
Private _MyDocSpec As Microsoft.BizTalk.Component.Utilities.SchemaWithNone = New_
Microsoft.BizTalk.Component.Utilities.SchemaWithNone("")

'<summary>
'This property is the document specification for the inbound document. Only
'documents of this type will be accepted. The SchemaWithNone allows the developer to
'select the inbound document type from a pick list.
'</summary>
<Description("The inbound request document specification. Only messages of this _
type will be accepted by the component.")> _
Public Property MyDocSpec() As Microsoft.BizTalk.Component.Utilities.SchemaWithNone
            Get
                Return _MyDocSpec
            End Get
            Set(ByVal Value As Microsoft.BizTalk.Component.Utilities.SchemaWithNone)
                _MyDocSpec = Value
          End Set
End Property

Public Function Probe(ByVal pc As _
Microsoft.BizTalk.Component.Interop.IPipelineContext, ByVal inmsg As _
Microsoft.BizTalk.Message.Interop.IBaseMessage) As Boolean Implements _
Microsoft.BizTalk.Component.Interop.IProbeMessage.Probe

            Dim streamReader As New streamReader(inmsg.BodyPart.Data)
            Dim xmlreader As New Xml.XmlTextReader(inmsg.BodyPart.Data)
            xmlreader.MoveToContent()

            If (_MyDocSpec.DocSpecName = xmlreader.NamespaceURI.Replace("http://",
"")) Then
                Return True
            Else
                Return False
            End If
End Function
End Class
```

Schema Selection in VS .NET Designer

The property MyDocSpec in the previous section's MyProber class is actually of type SchemaWithNone. SchemaWithNone is a class that lives in the Microsoft.BizTalk.Component. Utilities.dll assembly. Defining a property of type SchemaWithNone will give the user a drop-down list of all deployed schemas within the current BizTalk Management Database. The class has one public constructor, SchemaWithNone, which initializes a new instance of the SchemaWithNone class. Tables 4-10 and 4-11 list the public properties and methods of the class.

Table 4-10. *SchemaWithNone Public Properties*

Property	Description
AssemblyName (inherited from Schema)	Gets or sets the schema assembly name
DocSpecName (inherited from Schema)	Gets or sets the document spec name for the selected schema
RootName (inherited from Schema)	Gets or sets the root node of the selected schema
SchemaName (inherited from Schema)	Gets or sets the selected schema name
TargetNamespace (inherited from Schema)	Gets or sets the target namespace of the selected schema

Table 4-11. *SchemaWithNone Public Methods*

Method	Description
Equals (inherited from Schema)	Overridden. Determines whether the specified Object is equal to the current Object.
GetHashCode (inherited from Schema)	Overridden. Returns the hash code for this instance.
GetType (inherited from System.Object)	For additional information about the System namespace, see the .NET Framework documentation available from Visual Studio .NET or online at http://go.microsoft.com/fwlink/?LinkID=9677.
ToString (inherited from Schema)	Overridden. Converts the value of this instance to its equivalent string representation using the specified format.

As you can see in Figure 4-11, the properties for the SchemaWithNone class are available in the IDE. If you notice the InboundDocSpec property, it is a list of all the schemas that are currently deployed to the BizTalk solution. The SchemaWithNone property allows you to select one and only one schema from the deployed schemas, and this information will be used to populate the properties of the object as defined previously (AssemblyName, DocSpecName, and so on).

In the example from the preceding section, you want your developer to select only one schema, but what if your developer needs multiple schemas, for example, to handle different message formats in one component? In many cases, your component will be able to handle a variety of schemas; in this case, you need to use the SchemaList property.

In the case where your property needs to select multiple schemas, you need to use the SchemaList object. Such an object will provide developers with an associate window from which they can choose multiple schemas. The selected schemas will be available as a collection of schemas within a main class. The IDE will present the screen shown in Figure 4-12.

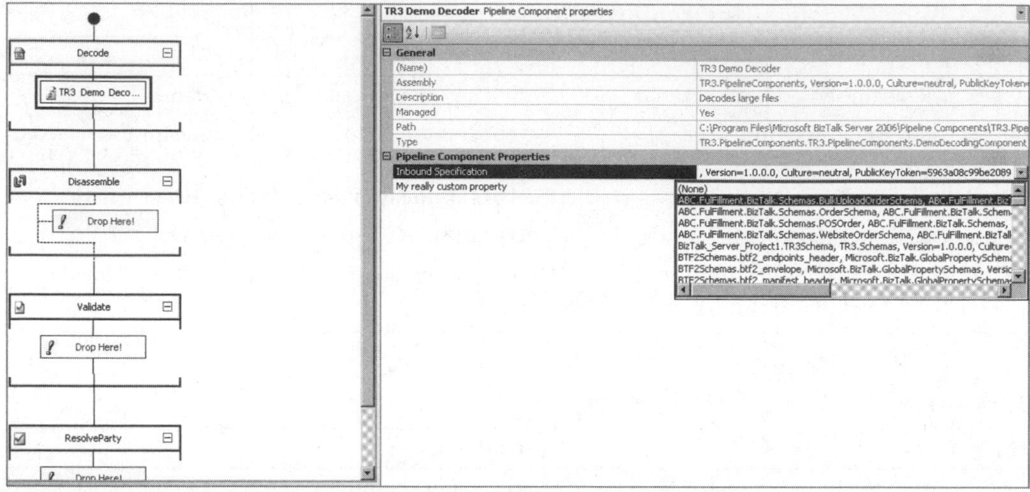

Figure 4-11. *SchemaWithNone example in VS .NET*

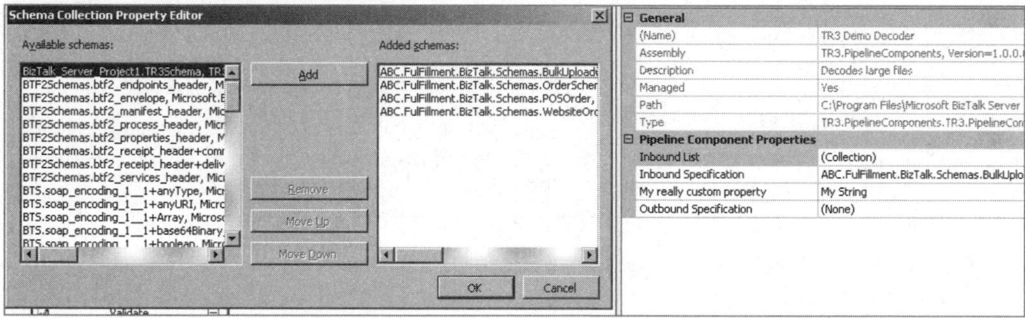

Figure 4-12. *SchemaList example in VS .NET*

Decorating Your Properties

It is important to consider the usability of your components from within the Visual Studio IDE. If you simply expose a public property from within your pipeline component, two things will happen. First, the property name that is displayed in the IDE will be the name of the property (in Figure 4-10 earlier, this would be `InboundDocumentList`, and so on). Second, there is no public description for what the property actually does. In order to make your components usable, you can use custom attributes to decorate your properties with metadata so that the developer experience is improved. The two main attributes you can use to do this are described next.

Using the DisplayName and Description Attributes

The `DisplayName` attribute allows you to set the name for the property that will be displayed in the IDE. The `Description` attribute sets the description box within the VS .NET designer to a friendly description. Figure 4-13 shows the effect of these attributes. The following code snippet demonstrates how these attributes are to be used:

```
'<summary>
   'this property will contain a single schema
'</summary>
<Description("The inbound request document specification. Only   messages of this _
type will be accepted by the component.")> _
<DisplayName("Inbound Specification")> _
 Public Property InboundFileDocumentSpecification() As _
Microsoft.BizTalk.Component.Utilities.SchemaWithNone
    Get
       Return _InboundFileDocumentSpecification
    End Get
    Set(ByVal Value As Microsoft.BizTalk.Component.Utilities.SchemaWithNone)
    _InboundFileDocumentSpecification = Value
    End Set
End Property
```

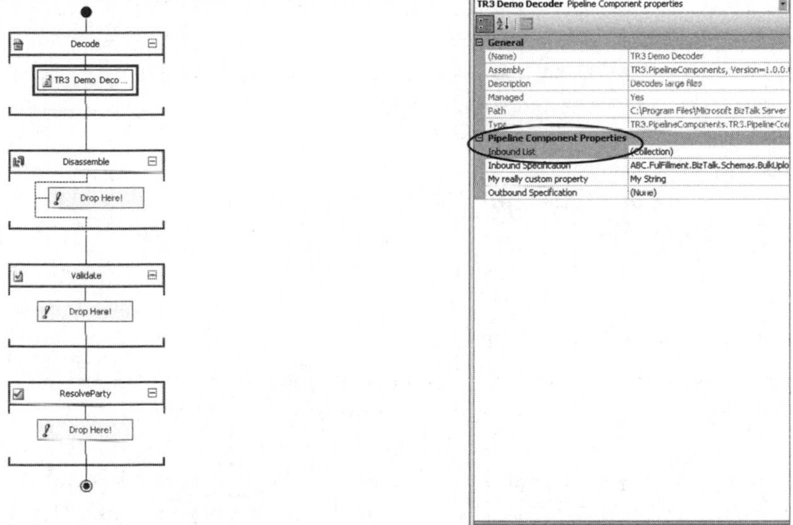

Figure 4-13. *DisplayName and Description attributes set*

Validating and Storing Properties in the Designer

As in any component development model, it is necessary to store properties that a user selects for your component so you can load them at runtime and also validate that the values chosen by the user are appropriate. To perform validation, you need to use the `IComponentUI` interface and implement the `Validate` function. To store and load information for runtime use, you use the `IPersistPropertyBag` interface and implement the `Load` and `Save` functions. Example method implementations are given in the following text.

Validating User Input

IComponentUI.Validate is used to validate any property information and display an error message to the user when the project is compiled if properties are not set up properly or if they're set up inconsistently. Most implementations use either a collection or an ArrayList to store the errors. You then need to return the IEnumerator object from the ArrayList or collection at the end of the method with all the error messages you want displayed populated.

The following example demonstrates how you can validate a developer's input from within the IDE. Any errors are returned to the user as errors in the IDE's error window.

```
'<summary>
'The Validate method is called by the BizTalk Editor during the build
'of a BizTalk project.
'</summary>
'<param name="obj">An Object containing the configuration 'properties.</param>
'<returns>The IEnumerator enables the caller to enumerate through a collection of
'strings containing error messages. These error messages appear as compiler error
'messages. To report successful property validation, the method should return an
'empty enumerator.</returns>
Public Function Validate(ByVal obj As Object) As System.Collections.IEnumerator_
Implements Microsoft.BizTalk.Component.Interop.IComponentUI.Validate
'example implementation:
    Dim errorArray As New ArrayList
    errorArray.Add("This is an error that will be shown...")
    return errorArray.GetEnumerator
    End Function
```

Using the Property Bag to Store Property Information

In order to store property information for pipeline components, you need to implement the IPersistPropertyBag interface and give an implementation to the Save and Load methods. These methods pass in the representative IPropertyBag object that will be used to store the property information. The IPropertyBag is simply a structure that will hold a set of key/value pairs. The key is a string, and the value is of type Object so it can accept any type. You may ask yourself, "Why not store the object itself rather than storing the name of the schema and constructing a New() object in the Load method?" The answer is because the Save function of the component will fail if you do this. When the properties are written to the ContextPropertyBag, they are actually expressed within the BTP file as XML so that they can be used for per-instance pipeline configuration. For more information on this, see the section entitled "Custom Properties and Per-Instance Pipeline Configuration" later in the chapter. Included within the code sample are two helper functions that encapsulate reading/writing the properties to the property bag.[13]

The following code snippet shows how you can use the property bag to read and write custom properties from a pipeline component:

13 As you can see in the sample, there are two helper methods included called ReadPropertyBag and WritePropertyBag. These are generated when using the Pipeline Component Wizard available at http://btsplcw.codeplex.com/.

```
'<summary>
'Loads configuration properties for the component
'</summary>
'<param name="pb">Configuration property bag</param>
'<param name="errlog">Error status</param>
Public Overridable Sub Load(ByVal pb As _
Microsoft.BizTalk.Component.Interop.IPropertyBag, ByVal errlog As Integer) _
Implements Microsoft.BizTalk.Component.Interop.IPersistPropertyBag.Load


    Dim val As Object = Nothing
    val = Me.ReadPropertyBag(pb, "MyDocSpec")
    If (Not (val) Is Nothing) Then
            Me._MyDocSpec = New _
    Microsoft.BizTalk.Component.Utilities.SchemaWithNone(CType(val, String))
    End If
    val = Me.ReadPropertyBag(pb, "OutboundDocumentSpecification")
    If (Not (val) Is Nothing) Then
            Me._OutboundDocumentSpecification = New _
    Microsoft.BizTalk.Component.Utilities.SchemaWithNone(CType(val, String))
    End If
    val = Me.ReadPropertyBag(pb, "FileRootNode")
    If (Not (val) Is Nothing) Then
            Me._FileRootNode = val
    End If
    val = Me.ReadPropertyBag(pb, "DataElementNode")
    If (Not (val) Is Nothing) Then
            Me._DataElementNode = val
    End If
End Sub

'<summary>
'Saves the current component configuration into the property bag
'<summary>
'<param name="pb">Configuration property bag</param>
'<param name="fClearDirty">not used</param>
'<param name="fSaveAllProperties">not used</param>
Public Overridable Sub Save(ByVal pb As _
Microsoft.BizTalk.Component.Interop.IPropertyBag, ByVal fClearDirty As Boolean, _
ByVal fSaveAllProperties As Boolean) Implements _
Microsoft.BizTalk.Component.Interop.IPersistPropertyBag.Save

    Me.WritePropertyBag(pb, "MyDocSpec", Me.MyDocSpec.SchemaName)
    Me.WritePropertyBag(pb, "OutDocSpec", Me.OutboundDocumentSpecification.SchemaName
    Me.WritePropertyBag(pb, "FileRootNode", Me.FileRootNode)
    Me.WritePropertyBag(pb, "DataElementNode", Me.DataElementNode)
End Sub
```

```
'<summary>
'Reads property value from property bag
'</summary>
'<param name="pb">Property bag</param>
'<param name="propName">Name of property</param>
'<returns>Value of the property</returns>
    Private Function ReadPropertyBag(ByVal pb As _
    Microsoft.BizTalk.Component.Interop.IPropertyBag, _
    ByVal propName As String) As Object
        Dim val As Object = Nothing
        Try
            pb.Read(propName, val, 0)
        Catch e As System.ArgumentException
            Return val
        Catch e As System.Exception
            Throw New System.ApplicationException(e.Message)
        End Try
        Return val
    End Function

'<summary>
'Writes property values into a property bag.
'</summary>
'<param name="pb">Property bag.</param>
'<param name="propName">Name of property.</param>
'<param name="val">Value of property.</param>
    Private Sub WritePropertyBag(ByVal pb As _
    Microsoft.BizTalk.Component.Interop.IPropertyBag, _
    ByVal propName As String, ByVal val As Object)
        Try
            pb.Write(propName, Val)
        Catch e As System.Exception
            Throw New System.ApplicationException(e.Message)
        End Try
    End Sub
```

Custom Properties and Per-Instance Pipeline Configuration

As we discussed earlier in the chapter, per-instance pipeline configuration allows you to change the values of custom properties using the BizTalk Administration Tools. The user interface provides you with a mechanism to set the values for pipeline properties dynamically for a receive location without having to create a new custom pipeline for every new receive location. A few points of interest when attempting to use this feature with a custom pipeline and pipeline components are described here.

Custom pipeline component properties for per-instance pipeline configuration are actually stored within the .btp file for the pipeline definition. A sample of the file follows. If you find that your custom properties are not appearing in the per-instance pipeline configuration document, you can manually add them to the XML of the .btp file, and they will appear.

```
<?xml version="1.0" encoding="utf-16"?>
<Document xmlns:xsd="http://www.w3.org/2001/XMLSchema"
xmlns:xsi="http://www.w3.org/2001/XMLSchema-instance"
PolicyFilePath="BTSReceivePolicy.xml" MajorVersion="1" MinorVersion="0">

  <Description />
  <Stages>
    <Stage CategoryId="9d0e4103-4cce-4536-83fa-4a5040674ad6">
      <Components />
    </Stage>
    <Stage CategoryId="9d0e4105-4cce-4536-83fa-4a5040674ad6">
      <Components />
    </Stage>
    <Stage CategoryId="9d0e410d-4cce-4536-83fa-4a5040674ad6">
      <Components>
        <Component>
          <Name>ABC.BizTalk.PipelineComponents.Decoder</Name>
          <Properties>
            <Property Name="MyUnTypedProperty" />
            <Property Name="MyStringProperty">
              <Value xsi:type="xsd:string">My String Value</Value>
            </Property>
          </Properties>
          <CachedDisplayName>Decoding Component</CachedDisplayName>
          <CachedIsManaged>true</CachedIsManaged>
        </Component>
      </Components>
    </Stage>
    <Stage CategoryId="9d0e410e-4cce-4536-83fa-4a5040674ad6">
      <Components />
    </Stage>
  </Stages>
</Document>
```

- In the .btp file for the pipeline definition, you can set the default data of the pipeline component property by inserting a value in the property's <Value> element.
- The <Value> that you insert must be an XSD type. For example, the type must be xsd:string for a string value, or xsd:int for an integer value.

Custom Disassemblers

It's important to call special attention to Disassembler components, because they are often what most developers end up writing. Disassemblers were intended to allow the pipeline to examine the incoming document and break it up into smaller, more manageable documents. The classic example of this is an envelope file. The large document is received that contains an envelope with multiple smaller documents inside it. The envelope is removed, and each of the contained documents is validated against its schema and ends up being a distinct and unique message within BizTalk, as shown in Figure 4-14. The Disassembler component has one key interface, `IDisassemblerComponent`.

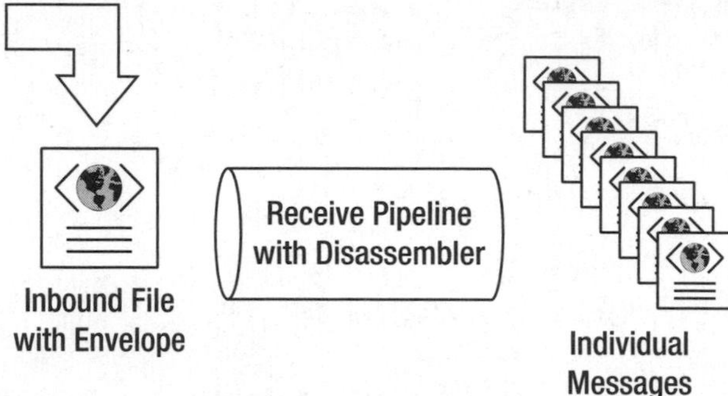

Figure 4-14. *Logical view of a Disassembler*

`IDisassemblerComponent` has two methods, `Disassemble` and `GetNext`, which are listed in Table 4-12. What happens is the BizTalk runtime calls the `Disassemble` method first and passes the original message and the pipeline context. It then calls the `GetNext` method after the `Disassemble` method. The `GetNext` method returns new messages of type IBaseMessage until the component decides that all messages are created and then it returns Null. Returning Null from `GetNext` signals the end of the component's execution and signals the runtime that all messages have been properly created.

Table 4-12. *Public Methods of IDisassemblerComponent*

Method	Description
`Disassemble`	Performs the disassembling of incoming document
`GetNext`	Gets the next message from the message set resulting from the Disassembler execution

A couple of design patterns exist that you can use when creating Disassemblers. One pattern is to use the `Disassemble` method to prime any instance variables, setup, and data, and then return and essentially create no messages. The messages will be created in the `GetNext` method, and new messages will be created each time the method is called. Another pattern is to create all messages in the Disassemble method, enqueue them to a queue structure, and then dequeue the messages from the queue each time `GetNext` is called. Either strategy will work; the second strategy can be more efficient especially if expensive resources need to be instantiated each time a message is created. Using the second method, you need to create these only once at the beginning of the `Disassemble` method, create all the messages, and then dispose of the resource. Using the first method, the resource will either need to be created for each `GetNext()` call or stored as an instance member of the class. An example of the second implementation follows. More detailed implementations will be given in the next chapter, but this example shows the basic structure. Also for this example, assume that this code is cumulative with the previous examples. In this case, a variable named

_InboundDocumentSpecification is used. This is the SchemaWithNone variable we explained in the previous section that allows us to see the developer-requested "new document schema type."

```
'<summary>
'called by the messaging engine until returned null, after Disassemble has been
'called
'</summary>
'<param name="pc">the pipeline context</param>
'<returns>an IBaseMessage instance representing the message created</returns>
    Public Function GetNext(ByVal pc As _
       Microsoft.BizTalk.Component.Interop.IPipelineContext) As _
       Microsoft.BizTalk.Message.Interop.IBaseMessage Implements _
       Microsoft.BizTalk.Component.Interop.IDisassemblerComponent.GetNext
        'get the next message from the Queue and return it
        Dim msg As Microsoft.BizTalk.Message.Interop.IBaseMessage = Nothing
        If (_msgs.Count > 0) Then
            msg = CType(_msgs.Dequeue, _
            Microsoft.BizTalk.Message.Interop.IBaseMessage)
        End If
        Return msg
    End Function

'<summary>
'called by the messaging engine when a new message arrives
'</summary>
'<param name="pc">the pipeline context</param>
'<param name="inmsg">the actual message</param>
    Public Sub Disassemble(ByVal pc As _
        Microsoft.BizTalk.Component.Interop.IPipelineContext, ByVal inmsg As  _
        Microsoft.BizTalk.Message.Interop.IBaseMessage) Implements _
        Microsoft.BizTalk.Component.Interop.IDisassemblerComponent.Disassemble
        'This is an example class which gets a simple list of strings. Each of
        'these numbers will be
        'a unique key in the new messages that we create.
        Dim myArrayList As ArrayList = myHelper.GetArrayofValues
        Dim UniqueCode As String
        'GetDocument is a function we will create in the next chapter.
        'Essentially it is a
        'function that returns an empty XML Document as a
        'string given a fully qualified and
        'deployed BizTalk schema
        For Each UniqueCode In myArrayList
            _msgs.Enqueue(BuildMessage(pc, inmsg.Context, GetDocument _
                               (InboundSchema.DocumentSpec, UniqueCode)))
        Next
    End Sub
```

Note the following function. This is a general function that can be used in any pipeline component where a new message needs to be created. This function takes the pipeline context, the message context (which is available from the original message), and the content for the document as a string. A new message is returned with a cloned copy of the original message context, and a message type as specified by the SchemaWithNone property.

```
'<summary>
'Returns a new message by cloning the pipeline context and original message context.
'The data to be assigned to the message must be a string value.
'</summary>
'<param name="pContext">Pipeline context</param>
'<param name="messageContext">Original Message context to be used in the new
'message</param>
'<param name="messageContent">Data to be put in the message</param>
'<returns>New message</returns>
'<remarks>
'Message Content is assigned to the MessageBody by creating a new MemoryStream
'object
'</remarks>
    Private Function BuildMessage(ByVal pContext As IPipelineContext, ByVal _
     messageContext As IBaseMessageContext, ByVal messageContent As String) As _
     IBaseMessage

        ' Build the message with its context
        Dim message As IBaseMessage
        Dim bodyPart As IBaseMessagePart
        Dim messageStream As MemoryStream
        Dim messageBytes As Byte()
        Dim messageType As String
        ' Prepare and fill the data stream
        messageBytes = Encoding.UTF8.GetBytes(messageContent)
        messageStream = New MemoryStream(messageBytes.Length)
        messageStream.Write(messageBytes, 0, messageBytes.Length)
        messageStream.Position = 0
        bodyPart = pContext.GetMessageFactory().CreateMessagePart()
        bodyPart.Data = messageStream
        message = pContext.GetMessageFactory().CreateMessage()
        message.Context = PipelineUtil.CloneMessageContext(messageContext)
        messageType = "http://" + _InboundDocumentSpecification.DocSpecName + _
        "#" + _FileRootNode
        message.Context.Promote("MessageType", BTSSystemPropertiesNamespace, _
                                messageType)
        message.AddPart("body", bodyPart, True)
        Return message
    End Function
```

CHAPTER 5

Pipeline Component Best Practices and Examples

Chapter 4 outlined the "advanced basics" of creating custom pipelines and pipeline components. You should now have the tools that you will need to create well-structured and professional-looking pipeline components. Now that you have learned the internals of how pipelines and pipeline components work, you'll put your new knowledge into practice. This chapter will explore some of the nuances of pipeline component development as well as give you some best practices for creating and implementing them. We will show you some examples of common problems that pipeline components can solve, along with some advanced implementations of cryptography, compression, and decoding.

Creating Documents

When you look at how a disassembling component is structured, essentially you are building new documents that get submitted to the Messagebox. In our previous examples, we used the `SchemaWithNone` and `SchemaWithList` objects as properties to allow the user to choose what type of document should be accepted through the `IProbeMessage` interface. If you take this one step further, you could build a generic disassembling component that allows the user to select what type of document they want to accept and that provides them with an interface to choose what type of document will be produced. The custom logic will still need to be created to extract the values for the new document, but at least the schema type will be available. But how can you actually create a new message? You will know the schema type of the message, but how do you create a new `XMLDocument` with all the available nodes already inserted but empty?

There are two ways to accomplish this task: the right way and not-so-right way. The not-so-right way is the simplest. What most people do is hard-code the XML for the new empty document in a string and assign it to a new `XMLDocument` object. This approach can be cumbersome for a number of reasons, the most important being that if the structure of the message ever changes, the code will need to be recompiled. Another "wrong," but more correct, way would be to load the XML from a configuration file at runtime or include it as a resource file that is imported when the assembly is loaded. This is still a pain, since you will have to manually keep this in sync with the actual BizTalk schema.

A different way to do this is to use an undocumented API, which allows you to create a new blank `XMLDocument` based on the `DocumentSpec` class. Unfortunately, this class is unsupported and is not made public by the BizTalk product team. It does work well, however, but you need to think about the support implications of using this class in your solution. For most, this isn't an issue, because the other alternative is to create a schema walker class as documented at http://msdn.microsoft.com/en-us/library/aa302296.aspx. Our only issue is that a significant amount of code is required to implement the schema walker. Also, depending on how you create your schema, certain attributes and imports may not be picked up in the new empty document. We have also found a few compatibility issues between the documents that it generates and BizTalk's validation engine. In the end, it is a good solution if you are wary about using an undocumented class, but using the class that exists within the BizTalk Framework guarantees that your documents will match the schema within the engine and will validate properly.

The first thought that comes to many people's minds when they think about creating documents is "Okay, I agree that having an external resource file and keeping it in sync with the actual schema is a pain, but won't my code need to change anyway if I have a schema change?" The answer to this is maybe. In many cases, the code that creates and populates new document instances uses only certain fields. Often schema changes involve adding new elements to the schema, not removing them, or changing element names. In this case, should the BizTalk schema be modified to include new elements, then no code needs modification, and new XML instances will be created with empty elements as you would expect. In the case where fields have been renamed or removed, you will need to determine whether your pipeline component has explicitly added values to those nodes via an XPath expression. If the component has, then you will need a code change.

In order to generate the new empty document in your pipeline component or orchestration, you need to create an instance of the following class:

```
Microsoft.Biztalk.Component.Interop.DocumentSpec.
```

This class is found in the Microsoft.BizTalk.Pipeline assembly.

An example method follows that can be used to create new documents based on the passed schema name.[1] Note that the name can easily be extracted from the SchemaWithNone property used in the previous chapter.

```
Imports Microsoft.BizTalk.Component.Interop
Imports Microsoft.BizTalk.ExplorerOM
Imports System.Xml
Imports System.Text
Imports System.IO

'schemaFullName has to match the value
'in the docspec_name column of the bt_DocumentSpec table in the
'BizTalkMgmtDb database
```

1 One of the authors, George Dunphy, originally used this concept in BizTalk 2004 on an engagement after reading about it on a newsgroup posting. Since then, Martijn Hoogendoorn has blogged about this technique at http://martijnh.blogspot.com/2005/10/schema-instance-generator-for-use.html. The blog entry also discusses how the class is unsupported and offers the MSDN article as an alternative. Martijn has other excellent entries in his blog and is a wealth of knowledge on BizTalk and pipeline components. In actuality, the method he demonstrates in his entry is much more performant and well written than the one we show here, which should be used only as a learning tool to demonstrate how this can be implemented. For a better implementation, see Martijn's blog.

```
Public Function CreateNewBTSDoument(ByVal schemaFullName As String) As XmlDocument

      Dim newDocument As XmlDocument = Nothing

      Dim catExplorer As New BtsCatalogExplorer
      Dim Schemas As SchemaCollection
      Dim myDocSpec As DocumentSpec = Nothing

      Dim mySchema As Schema
      Dim sbuilder As New StringBuilder()

      catExplorer.ConnectionString = "Integrated Security=SSPI; " & _
     " Persist Security_Info=false; Server=(local); Database=BizTalkMgmtDb;"
      Schemas = catExplorer.Schemas
      mySchema = Schemas(schemaFullName)

      If Not (mySchema Is Nothing) Then
          myDocSpec = New DocumentSpec(schemaFullName, _
                   mySchema.BtsAssembly.DisplayName)

          If Not (myDocSpec Is Nothing) Then
              Dim writer As New StringWriter(sbuilder)
              Try
                  newdocument = New XmlDocument()
                  'create and load the new instance into the return value
                  newdocument.Load(myDocSpec.CreateXmlInstance(writer))
              Finally
                  writer.Dispose()
              End Try
          End If
      End If
      Return newDocument
  End Function
```

Using BizTalk Streams

BizTalk Server 2004, 2006, and 2009 have been built to use streams as a key part of the products' architecture. A `stream` as a programming construct is a sequence of bytes with no fixed length. When you begin to read a stream, you have no idea how long it is or when it will end. The only control you have is over the size of the data you will read at any one time. So what does this have to do with good programming? It means that when you are dealing with extremely large amounts of data, if you use a stream, you don't need to load all of this data at once. It is almost like reading a book. You can't just read the entire book at once; you must read the pages one at a time. When reading a book, the amount of data you consume at one time is a page; the letters on the page represent bytes. You also don't know how big the book is until you finish the last page and see "The End" (unless you skip to the back of the book).

In this way, streams make dealing with large amounts of data more manageable. If you have worked with BizTalk 2002 or prior, you know that BizTalk would often produce "out of memory" exceptions when processing large `XMLDocuments`. This was because in BizTalk 2000 and 2002, the XMLDom was used to parse and load XML documents. The DOM is not a streaming-based model. The DOM requires you to load the entire document into memory to use it.

In supporting the streaming paradigm, the BizTalk product team has included three classes that optimize how you can use streams in your pipeline components and orchestrations. These classes allow you to do stream-based XPath queries. Each of these classes is explained in the following sections.

VirtualStream

Included in the BizTalk SDK under the \Program Files\Microsoft BizTalk Server 2009\SDK\Samples\Pipelines\ArbitraryXPathPropertyHandler directory is a class file called VirtualStream.cs. This class is an implementation that holds the data in memory up to a certain threshold (by default 4MB). The remaining data it keeps on disk in temporary files. The ArbitraryXPathPropertyHandler example in the SDK shows you an example of how to use this class.

SeekableReadOnlyStream

`SeekAbleReadOnlyStream` is an implementation of a stream class that provides fast, read-only, seekable access to a stream. It is a wrapper class around a regular stream object and can be used in cases where the base stream object is not seekable, and does not need write access. An example of this class can be found in the \Program Files\Microsoft BizTalk Server 2009\ SDK\Samples\Pipelines\Schema Resolver Component directory.

XPathReader

The XPathReader class lives in the Microsoft.BizTalk.XPathReader.dll assembly. This is a class that provides XPath query access to a stream of XML. This is very advantageous as it allows for very fast, read-only access to a stream of data via an XPath expression. Normally, XPath queries require the entire document to be loaded into memory such as in an XMLDocument. Using the XPathReader, you can load your document via the `SeekAbleReadOnlyStream` class mentioned previously, and then have this stream wrapped by an `XMLTextReader`. The net effect is that you have a stream-based XPath query that does not require the entire XML document to be loaded into memory.[2] The following example shows how this can be implemented in a pipeline component. Note the use of the `SeekAbleReadOnlyStream` variable in the `Execute` method. This is the means by which you can have your stream of data be seekable and read-only, which improves the performance and usability of the pipeline component.

2 Though as always in life nothing comes for free. The XPathReader implementation imposes certain restrictions on what Xath queries you can use. MSDN article at `http://msdn.microsoft.com/en-us/library/ms950778.aspx` discusses this in greater detail

```
Imports System
Imports Microsoft.BizTalk.Component.Interop
Imports Microsoft.BizTalk.Message.Interop
Imports System.Collections
Imports Microsoft.BizTalk.XPath
Imports System.Xml
Imports System.IO
Imports Microsoft.Samples.BizTalk.Pipelines.CustomComponent
Namespace ABC.BizTalk.Pipelines.Components
    <ComponentCategory(CategoryTypes.CATID_PipelineComponent)> _
    <ComponentCategory(CategoryTypes.CATID_Any)> _
    Public Class PropPromoteComponent
        Implements IComponent
        Implements IComponentUI
        Implements IBaseComponent
        Implements IPersistPropertyBag
        Private _PropertyName As String
        Private _Namespace As String
        Private _XPath As String
        Public Property PropertyName() As String
            Get
                Return _PropertyName
            End Get
            Set(ByVal value As String)
                _PropertyName = value
            End Set
        End Property

        Public Property [Namespace]() As String
            Get
                Return _Namespace
            End Get
            Set(ByVal value As String)
                _Namespace = value
            End Set
        End Property

        Public Property XPath() As String
            Get
                Return _XPath
            End Get
            Set(ByVal value As String)
                _XPath = value
            End Set
        End Property
```

```
Public Function Execute(ByVal ctx As IPipelineContext, _
                                  ByVal msg As IBaseMessage)
    Dim xpathValue As Object = Nothing
    Dim outMessage As IBaseMessage = ctx.GetMessageFactory.CreateMessage
    Dim newBodyPart As IBaseMessagePart = _
                       ctx.GetMessageFactory.CreateMessagePart
    newBodyPart.PartProperties = msg.BodyPart.PartProperties
    Dim stream As SeekableReadOnlyStream = New _
   SeekableReadOnlyStream( _
                          msg.BodyPart.GetOriginalDataStream)
    Dim val As Object = msg.Context.Read(PropertyName, [Namespace])
    If val Is Nothing Then
        Throw New ArgumentNullException(PropertyName)
    End If
    msg.Context.Promote(PropertyName, [Namespace], val)
    Dim xpc As XPathCollection = New XPathCollection

    Dim xpr As XPathReader = New XPathReader(New XmlTextReader(stream), xpc)
    xpc.Add(Me.XPath)
    While xpr.ReadUntilMatch = True
        Dim index As Integer = 0
        While index < xpc.Count
            If xpr.Match(index) = True Then
                xpathValue = xpr.ReadString
                ' break
            End If
            System.Math.Min( _
            System.Threading.Interlocked.Increment(index), index - 1)
        End While
    End While
    If xpathValue Is Nothing Then

        Throw New ArgumentNullException("xpathValue")
    End If
    msg.Context.Write("SomeProperty", "http://ABC.BizTalk.Pipelines", _
                             xpathValue)
    stream.Position = 0
    newBodyPart.Data = stream
    outMessage.Context = msg.Context
    CopyMessageParts(msg, outMessage, newBodyPart)
    Return outMessage
End Function
```

```
Public ReadOnly Property Icon() As IntPtr
    Get
        Return IntPtr.Zero
    End Get
End Property

Public Function Validate(ByVal projectSystem As Object) As IEnumerator
    Return Nothing
End Function

Public ReadOnly Property Description() As String
    Get
        Return "Description"
    End Get
End Property

Public ReadOnly Property Name() As String
    Get
        Return "Property Promote"
    End Get
End Property

Public ReadOnly Property Version() As String
    Get
        Return "1"
    End Get
End Property

Public Sub GetClassID(ByRef classID As Guid)
    Dim g As Guid = New Guid("FE537918-327B-4a0c-9ED7-E1B993B7897E")
    classID = g
End Sub

Public Sub InitNew()
    Throw New Exception("The method or operation is not implemented.")
End Sub

Public Sub Load(ByVal propertyBag As IPropertyBag,
                                   ByVal errorLog As Integer)

    Dim prop As Object = Nothing
    Dim nm As Object = Nothing
    Dim xp As Object = Nothing
```

```
            Try
                propertyBag.Read("Namespace", nm, 0)
                propertyBag.Read("PropertyName", prop, 0)
                propertyBag.Read("XPATH", xp, 0)
            Catch
            Finally
                If Not (prop Is Nothing) Then
                    PropertyName = prop.ToString
                End If
                If Not (nm Is Nothing) Then
                    [Namespace] = nm.ToString
                End If
                If Not (xp Is Nothing) Then
                    XPath = xp.ToString
                End If
            End Try
        End Sub

        Public Sub Save(ByVal propertyBag As IPropertyBag, _
                   ByVal clearDirty As Boolean, _
                   ByVal saveAllProperties As Boolean)
            Dim prop As Object = PropertyName
            Dim nm As Object = [Namespace]
            Dim xp As Object = XPath
            propertyBag.Write("PropertyName", prop)
            propertyBag.Write("Namespace", nm)
propertyBag.Write("XPATH", xp)
        End Sub

        Private Sub CopyMessageParts(ByVal sourceMessage As IBaseMessage, _
                                 ByVal destinationMessage As IBaseMessage, _
                                ByVal newBodyPart As IBaseMessagePart)
            Dim bodyPartName As String = sourceMessage.BodyPartName
            Dim c As Integer = 0
            While c < sourceMessage.PartCount
                Dim partName As String = Nothing
                Dim messagePart As IBaseMessagePart = _
                sourceMessage.GetPartByIndex(c, partName)
                If Not (partName = bodyPartName) Then
                    destinationMessage.AddPart(partName, messagePart, False)
                Else
                    destinationMessage.AddPart(bodyPartName, newBodyPart, True)
                End If
                System.Threading.Interlocked.Increment(c)
            End While
        End Sub
    End Class
End Namespace
```

Pipeline Component Examples

Now that you are familiar with the steps and key interfaces that define how pipelines and pipeline components work, we'll show you some clever examples of how pipeline components can be used to solve real problems. Most of the examples in this chapter will be the actual class files included in the samples available for download at www.apress.com. The examples we present here will provide you with working solutions to problems that exist today when developing intricate BizTalk applications. These solutions include

- Dealing with large messages
- Receiving and sending ZIP files
- Using PGP to encrypt and decrypt
- Creating new messages based on a stored procedure

Please note that the code samples provided in this chapter are using two helper classes from the Microsoft.Samples.Utilities namespace: FileStreamReadWrite and PropertyBagReadWrite. Because of space constraints, the source code for these classes is not included; it is available for download at www.apress.com.

Dealing with Extremely Large Messages

A major problem that many have discovered is that accommodating extremely large (200MB+) files can be a major performance bottleneck. The shame is that in many cases the documents that are being retrieved are simply going to be routed to another outbound source. This is typical of the Enterprise Service Bus (ESB) type of architecture scenario.[3] In short, an ESB is software that is used to link internal and partner systems to each other—which basically is what BizTalk is designed to do out of the box. For these types of architectures, large files are generally routed through the ESB from an external party to an internal party or from internal to internal systems. Most times, the only logic that needs to be performed is routing logic. In many cases, this logic can be expressed in a simple filter criteria based on the default message context data, or by examining data elements within the message, promoting them, and then implementing content-based routing. Also in many cases, the actual message body's content is irrelevant beyond extracting properties to promote. The performance bottleneck comes into play when the entire file is received, parsed by the XMLReceive pipeline, and then stored into the Messagebox. If you have ever had to do this on a 200MB file, even though it works, there is a nasty impact to the CPU utilization on your BizTalk and SQL Server machines, where often the machines' CPU usage goes to 100% and the system throughput essentially goes down the drain.

Now imagine having to process 10 or 20 of these per minute. The next problem is going to be sending the file. The system will essentially take this entire performance hit all over again when the large file needs to be read from SQL Server out of BizTalk and sent to the EPM. You can quickly see how this type of scenario, as common as it is, most often requires either significant hardware to implement or a queuing mechanism whereby only a small number of files can be processed at a time.

---

3 We will discuss ESB in greater detail in Chapter 16.

You'll find a simple solution in BizTalk Server's capability to natively understand and use streams.[4] The following examples show a decoding component that will receive the incoming message, store the file to disk in a uniquely named file, and store the path to the file in the `IBaseMessagePart.Data` property. The end result will be a message that only contains the path to the text file in its data, but will have a fully well-formed message context so that it can be routed. The component will also promote a property that stores the fact that this is a "large encoded message." This property will allow you to route all messages encoded using this pipeline component to a particular send port/pipeline that has the corresponding encoding component. The encoding component will read the data element for the path to the file, open up a file stream object that is streaming the file stored to disk, set the stream to the 0 byte position, and set the `IBaseMessagePart.Data` property to the `FileStream`. The end result will be that the file is streamed by the BizTalk runtime from the file stored on the disk and is not required to pass through the Messagebox. Also, performance is greatly improved, and the CPU overhead on both the BizTalk Server host instance that is sending the file and the SQL Server hosting the BizTalk Messagebox is essentially nil.

The partner to this is the sending component. In many scenarios, BizTalk is implemented as a routing engine or an Enterprise Service Bus. This is a fancy way of saying that BizTalk is responsible for moving data from one location within an organization to another. In many cases, what does need to be moved is large amounts of data, either in binary format or in text files. This is often the case with payment or EDI-based systems in which BizTalk is responsible for moving the files to the legacy system where it can process them. In this scenario, the same performance problem (or lack of performance) will occur on the send side as on the receive side. To account for this, the examples also include a send-side pipeline component that is used to actually send the large file to the outbound destination adapter.

Caveats and Gotchas

The solution outlined previously works very well so long as the issues described in the following sections are taken into account. Do not simply copy and paste the code into your project and leave it at that. The solution provided in this section fundamentally alters some of the design principles of the BizTalk Server product. The most important one of these is that the data for the message is no longer stored in the Messagebox. A quick list of the pros and cons of the proposed solution is provided here:

Pros:

- Provides extremely fast access for moving large messages
- Simple to add new features
- Reusable across multiple receive locations
- Message containing context can be routed to orchestration, and data can be accessed from the disk

---

4 If you have never used or dealt with streams before, read through the article "Streams and .NET" at `http://www.codeguru.com/Csharp/Csharp/cs_data/streaming/article.php/c4223/`. Streams essentially allow you to deal with data in a fashion whereby only a piece of the data is read at a time (usually 4KB). They allow you to work with large volumes of data in a very reliable and well-performing manner. They also require you to do a little more work to code against them, but in the end, the performance gains are well worth it in this particular application.

Cons:

- No ability to apply BizTalk Map
- No failover via Messagebox
- Custom solution requiring support by developer
- Need a scheduled task to clean up old data

Redundancy, Failover, and High Availability

As was stated earlier, the data for the large message will no longer be stored in SQL Server. This is fundamentally different from how Microsoft designed the product. If the data within the message is important and the system is a mission-critical one that must properly deal with failovers and errors, you need to make sure that the storage location for the external file is also as robust as your SQL Server environment. Most architects in this situation will simply create a share on the clustered SQL Server shared disk array. This share is available to all BizTalk machines in the BizTalk Server Group, and since it is stored on the shared array or the storage area network (SAN), it should be as reliable as the data files for SQL Server.

Dealing with Message Content and Metadata

A good rule of thumb for this type of solution is to avoid looking at the message data at all costs once the file has been received. Consider the following: assume that you have received your large file into BizTalk and you need to process it through an orchestration for some additional logic. What happens? You will need to write .NET components to read the file and manually parse it to get the data you need. The worst-case scenario is that you need to load the data into an XMLDom or something similar. This will have performance implications and can negate the entire reason for the special large-file handling you are implementing.

If you know you are going to need data either within an orchestration or for CBR, make sure you write the code to gather this data within either the receiving or sending pipeline components. Only open the large data file at the time when it is being processed within the pipeline if you can. The best approach is to promote properties or create custom distinguished fields using code from within the component itself, which you can access from within BizTalk with little performance overhead.

Cleaning Up Old Data

If you read through the code in the section "Large Message Encoding Component (Send Side)," you will notice that there is no code that actually deletes the message from the server. There is a good reason for this. Normally you would think that once the message has flowed through the send pipeline it would be okay to delete it, but this is not true. What about a send-side adapter error? Imagine if you were sending the file to an FTP server and it was down; BizTalk will attempt to resend the message after the retry period has been reached. Because of this, you can't simply delete the file at random. You must employ a managed approach.

The only real solution to this would be to have a scheduled task that executes every few minutes that is responsible for cleaning up the data directory. You will notice that the name of the file is actually the `InterchangeID` GUID for the message flow. The `InterchangeID` provides you with a common key that you can use to query each of the messages that have been created throughout the execution path. The script that executes needs to read the name of the file and use WMI to query the Messagebox and determine whether there are any suspended or active messages for that Interchange. If there are, it doesn't delete the file; otherwise, it will delete the data file. For examples on using WMI to query BizTalk, see Chapter 10.

Looping Through the Message

As stated previously, if you do know you will need the data within the message at runtime, and this data is of an aggregate nature (sums, averages, counts, etc.), only loop through the file once. This seems like a commonsense thing, but it is often overlooked. If you need to loop through the file, try to get all the data you need in one pass rather than several. This can have dramatic effects on how your component will perform.

Large Message Decoding Component (Receive Side)

This component is to be used on the receive side when the large message is first processed by BizTalk. You will need to create a custom receive pipeline and add this pipeline component to the Decode stage. From there, use the `SchemaWithNone` property to select the desired inbound schema type if needed. If the file is a flat file or a binary file, then this step is not necessary, because the message will not contain any namespace or type information. This component relies on a property schema being deployed that will be used to store the location to the file within the message context. This schema can also be used to define any custom information such as counts, sums, and averages that is needed to route the document or may be required later on at runtime.

```
Imports System
Imports System.IO
Imports System.Text
Imports System.Drawing
Imports System.Resources
Imports System.Reflection
Imports System.Diagnostics
Imports System.Collections
Imports System.ComponentModel
Imports Microsoft.BizTalk.Message.Interop
Imports Microsoft.BizTalk.Component.Interop
Imports Microsoft.BizTalk.Component
Imports Microsoft.BizTalk.Messaging
Imports Microsoft.BizTalk.Component.Utilities

Namespace Probiztalk.Samples.PipelinesComponents
    <ComponentCategory(CategoryTypes.CATID_PipelineComponent), _
    System.Runtime.InteropServices.Guid("89dedce4-0525-472f-899c-64dc66f60727"), _
    ComponentCategory(CategoryTypes.CATID_Decoder)> _
    Public Class LargeFileDecodingComponent
        Implements IBaseComponent, IPersistPropertyBag, IComponentUI, _
        Global.Microsoft.BizTalk.Component.Interop.IComponent, IProbeMessage
```

```
Private _OutBoundFileDocumentSpecification As SchemaWithNone = _
    New Global.Microsoft.BizTalk.Component.Utilities.SchemaWithNone("")
Private _InboundFileDocumentSpecification As SchemaWithNone = _
    New Global.Microsoft.BizTalk.Component.Utilities.SchemaWithNone("")
Private _ThresholdSize As Integer = 4096

Private resourceManager As System.Resources.ResourceManager = _
New System.Resources.ResourceManager( _
    "Probiztalk.Samples.PipelineComponents.LargeFileDecodingComponent", _
    [Assembly].GetExecutingAssembly)
Private Const PROPERTY_SCHEMA_NAMESPACE = _
    "http://LargeFileHandler.Schemas.LargeFilePropertySchema"
Private _FileLocation As String

'<summary>
'this property will contain a single schema
'</summary>
<Description("The inbound request document specification. " & _
"Only messages of this type will be accepted by the component.")> _
<DisplayName("Inbound Specification")> _
Public Property InboundFileDocumentSpecification() As _
    Global.Microsoft.BizTalk.Component.Utilities.SchemaWithNone
    Get

        Return _InboundFileDocumentSpecification
    End Get
    Set(ByVal Value As _
        Global.Microsoft.BizTalk.Component.Utilities.SchemaWithNone)
        _InboundFileDocumentSpecification = Value
    End Set
End Property

'<summary>
'this property will contain a single schema
'</summary>
<Description("The Large File Message specification." & _
            "The component will create messages of this type.")> _
<DisplayName("Outbound Specification")> _
Public Property OutBoundFileDocumentSpecification() As _
    Global.Microsoft.BizTalk.Component.Utilities.SchemaWithNone
    Get
```

```
                Return _OutBoundFileDocumentSpecification
            End Get
            Set(ByVal Value As _
           Global.Microsoft.BizTalk.Component.Utilities.SchemaWithNone)
                _OutBoundFileDocumentSpecification = Value
            End Set
        End Property

        <Description("Threshold value in bytes for incoming file to determine" & _
        "whether or not to treat the message as large. Default is 4096 bytes")> _
        <DisplayName("Threshold file size")> <DefaultValue(4096)> _
        Public Property ThresholdSize() As Integer
            Get
                Return Me._ThresholdSize
            End Get
            Set(ByVal value As Integer)
                Me._ThresholdSize = value
            End Set
        End Property

        <Description("Directory for storing decoded large messages." & _
                     "Defaults to C:\Temp.")> _
        <DisplayName("Large File Folder Location")> _
Public Property LargeFileFolder() As String
            Get
                Return Me._FileLocation
            End Get
            Set(ByVal value As String)
                Me._FileLocation = value
            End Set
        End Property
        '<summary>
        'Name of the component
        '</summary>
        <Browsable(False)> _
        Public ReadOnly Property Name() As String Implements _
            Global.Microsoft.BizTalk.Component.Interop.IBaseComponent.Name
            Get
                Return resourceManager.GetString("COMPONENTNAME", _
                            System.Globalization.CultureInfo.InvariantCulture)
            End Get
        End Property
```

```
'<summary>
'Version of the component
'</summary>
<Browsable(False)> _
Public ReadOnly Property Version() As String Implements _
    Global.Microsoft.BizTalk.Component.Interop.IBaseComponent.Version
    Get
        Return resourceManager.GetString("COMPONENTVERSION", _
                    System.Globalization.CultureInfo.InvariantCulture)
    End Get
End Property

'<summary>
'Description of the component
'</summary>
<Browsable(False)> _
Public ReadOnly Property Description() As String Implements _
    Global.Microsoft.BizTalk.Component.Interop.IBaseComponent.Description
    Get
        Return resourceManager.GetString("COMPONENTDESCRIPTION", _
                    System.Globalization.CultureInfo.InvariantCulture)
    End Get
End Property

'<summary>
'Component icon to use in BizTalk Editor
'</summary>
<Browsable(False)> _
Public ReadOnly Property Icon() As IntPtr Implements _
    Global.Microsoft.BizTalk.Component.Interop.IComponentUI.Icon
    Get
        Return CType(Me.resourceManager.GetObject("COMPONENTICON", _
            System.Globalization.CultureInfo.InvariantCulture),  _
            System.Drawing.Bitmap).GetHicon
    End Get
End Property

'<summary>
'Gets class ID of component for usage from unmanaged code.
'</summary>
'<param name="classid">
'Class ID of the component
'</param>
Public Sub GetClassID(ByRef classid As System.Guid) _
Implements _
Global.Microsoft.BizTalk.Component.Interop.IPersistPropertyBag.GetClassID
    classid = New System.Guid("89dedce4-0525-472f-899c-64dc66f60727")
End Sub
```

```
'<summary>
'not implemented
'</summary>
Public Sub InitNew() _
Implements _
Global.Microsoft.BizTalk.Component.Interop.IPersistPropertyBag.InitNew
End Sub

'<summary>
'Loads configuration properties for the component
'</summary>
'<param name="pb">Configuration property bag</param>
'<param name="errlog">Error status</param>
Public Overridable Sub Load( _
    ByVal pb As Global.Microsoft.BizTalk.Component.Interop.IPropertyBag, _
    ByVal errlog As Integer) _
    Implements _
    Global.Microsoft.BizTalk.Component.Interop.IPersistPropertyBag.Load

    Try
        Me._ThresholdSize = ReadPropertyBag(pb, "ThresholdSize")
    Catch
        Me._ThresholdSize = 4096
    End Try

    Try
        Me._FileLocation = ReadPropertyBag(pb, "FileLocation")
    Catch
        Me._FileLocation = "C:\Temp"
    End Try
    Try
        Me.InboundFileDocumentSpecification = New  _
            SchemaWithNone( _
                ReadPropertyBag(pb, "InboundFileDocumentSpecification"))
    Catch
        Me.InboundFileDocumentSpecification = New SchemaWithNone("")
    End Try
    Try
        Me.OutBoundFileDocumentSpecification = New  _
            SchemaWithNone( _
                ReadPropertyBag(pb, "OutboundFileDocumentSpecification"))
    Catch
        Me.OutBoundFileDocumentSpecification = New SchemaWithNone("")
    End Try


End Sub
```

```
'<summary>
'Saves the current component configuration into the property bag
'</summary>
'<param name="pb">Configuration property bag</param>
'<param name="fClearDirty">not used</param>
'<param name="fSaveAllProperties">not used</param>
Public Overridable Sub Save( _
    ByVal pb As Global.Microsoft.BizTalk.Component.Interop.IPropertyBag, _
    ByVal fClearDirty As Boolean, ByVal fSaveAllProperties As Boolean) _
    Implements Global.Microsoft.BizTalk.Component.Interop. _
    IPersistPropertyBag.Save

    WritePropertyBag(pb, "ThresholdSize", Me._ThresholdSize)
    WritePropertyBag(pb, "FileLocation", Me._FileLocation)
    WritePropertyBag(pb, "InboundFileDocumentSpecification", _
                  _InboundFileDocumentSpecification.SchemaName)
    WritePropertyBag(pb, "OutboundFileDocumentSpecification", _
                  _OutBoundFileDocumentSpecification.SchemaName)

End Sub

'<summary>
'Reads property value from property bag
'</summary>
'<param name="pb">Property bag</param>
'<param name="propName">Name of property</param>
'<returns>Value of the property</returns>
Private Function ReadPropertyBag( _
    ByVal pb As Global.Microsoft.BizTalk.Component.Interop.IPropertyBag, _
    ByVal propName As String) As Object

    Dim val As Object = Nothing
    Try
        pb.Read(propName, val, 0)
    Catch e As System.ArgumentException
        Return val
    Catch e As System.Exception
        Throw New System.ApplicationException(e.Message)
    End Try
    Return val
End Function
```

```
'<summary>
'Writes property values into a property bag.
'</summary>
'<param name="pb">Property bag.</param>
'<param name="propName">Name of property.</param>
'<param name="val">Value of property.</param>
Private Sub WritePropertyBag( _
ByVal pb As Global.Microsoft.BizTalk.Component.Interop.IPropertyBag, _
ByVal propName As String, ByVal val As Object)
    Try
        pb.Write(propName, val)
    Catch e As System.Exception
        Throw New System.ApplicationException(e.Message)
    End Try
End Sub

'<summary>
'The Validate method is called by the BizTalk Editor during the build
'of a BizTalk project.
'</summary>
'<param name="obj">An Object containing the
'configuration properties.</param>
'<returns>The IEnumerator enables the caller to enumerate through a
'collection of strings containing error messages. These error messages
'appear as compiler error messages. To report successful property _
'validation, the method should return an empty enumerator.</returns>
Public Function Validate(ByVal obj As Object) As  _
System.Collections.IEnumerator Implements _
Global.Microsoft.BizTalk.Component.Interop.IComponentUI.Validate
    'example implementation:
    'ArrayList errorList = new ArrayList();
    'errorList.Add("This is a compiler error");
    'return errorList.GetEnumerator();
    Return Nothing
End Function
'<summary>
'called by the messaging engine when a new message arrives
'checks if the incoming message is in a recognizable format
'if the message is in a recognizable format, only this component
'within this stage will be execute (FirstMatch equals true)
'</summary>
'<param name="pc">the pipeline context</param>
'<param name="inmsg">the actual message</param>
Public Function Probe(ByVal pc As _
    Global.Microsoft.BizTalk.Component.Interop.IPipelineContext, _
    ByVal inmsg As Global.Microsoft.BizTalk.Message.Interop.IBaseMessage) _
    As Boolean Implements Global.Microsoft.BizTalk.Component. _
    Interop.IProbeMessage.Probe
```

```
    Dim xmlreader As New Xml.XmlTextReader(inmsg.BodyPart.Data)
    xmlreader.MoveToContent()

    If (_InboundFileDocumentSpecification.DocSpecName = _
            xmlreader.NamespaceURI.Replace("http://", "")) Then
        Return True
    Else
        Return False
    End If

End Function
'<summary>
'Implements IComponent.Execute method.
'</summary>
'<param name="pc">Pipeline context</param>
'<param name="inmsg">Input message</param>
'<returns>Original input message</returns>
'<remarks>
'IComponent.Execute method is used to initiate
'the processing of the message in this pipeline component.
'</remarks>
Public Function Execute(ByVal pContext As IPipelineContext, _
ByVal inmsg As IBaseMessage) _
As Global.Microsoft.BizTalk.Message.Interop.IBaseMessage _
Implements Global.Microsoft.BizTalk.Component.Interop.IComponent.Execute
    'Build the message that is to be sent out but only if it is greater
    'than the threshold
    If inmsg.BodyPart.GetOriginalDataStream.Length > Me._ThresholdSize Then
        StoreMessageData(pContext, inmsg)
    End If
    Return inmsg
End Function

'<summary>
'Method used to write the message data to a file and promote the
'location to the MessageContext.
'</summary>
'<param name="pc">Pipeline context</param>
'<param name="inmsg">Input message to be assigned</param>
'<returns>Original input message by reference</returns>
'<remarks>
'Receives the input message ByRef then assigns the file stream to
'the messageBody.Data property
'</remarks>
```

```
Private Sub StoreMessageData(ByVal pContext As IPipelineContext, _
                             ByRef inMsg As IBaseMessage)
    Dim FullFileName As String = _FileLocation + _
                        inMsg.MessageID.ToString + ".msg"
    Dim dataFile As New FileStream(FullFileName, FileMode.CreateNew, _
                        FileAccess.ReadWrite, FileShare.ReadWrite, 4096)
    Dim myMemoryStream As Stream = inMsg.BodyPart.GetOriginalDataStream

    Dim Buffer(4095) As Byte
    Dim byteCount As Integer

    'Not really needed, just want to initialize the data within
    'the message part to something.
    'Proper way to do this would be to create a separate XML
    'schema for messages which have been encoded using the
    'encoder, create a new empty document which has an element
    'named "FilePath" and set the value of the element
    'to FullFileName. But at least this way we can see the value in
    'the document should we need to write it out
    Dim myStream As New MemoryStream(UTF8Encoding.Default. _
                                    GetBytes(FullFileName))

    If myMemoryStream.CanSeek Then
        myMemoryStream.Position = 0
    Else
        'Impossible to occur, but added it anyway
        Throw New Exception("The stream is not seekable")
    End If

    byteCount = myMemoryStream.Read(Buffer, 0, 4096)

    While myMemoryStream.Position < myMemoryStream.Length - 1
        dataFile.Write(Buffer, 0, 4096)
        dataFile.Flush()
        byteCount = myMemoryStream.Read(Buffer, 0, 4096)
    End While
    dataFile.Write(Buffer, 0, byteCount)
    dataFile.Flush()
    dataFile.Close()
    inMsg.BodyPart.Data = myStream
    inMsg.Context.Promote("LargeFileLocation", _
                        PROPERTY_SCHEMA_NAMESPACE, FullFileName)
```

```
            'Useful for CBR operations - i.e. route all messages that are _
            'large to a specific send port.
            inMsg.Context.Promote("IsEncoded", PROPERTY_SCHEMA_NAMESPACE, True)

        End Sub

    End Class
End Namespace
```

Large Message Encoding Component (Send Side)

The large message encoding component is to be used on the send side when the large message is sent by BizTalk. You will need to create a custom send pipeline and add this pipeline component to the Encode stage. This component relies on a property schema being deployed that will be used to store the location to the file within the message context.

```
Imports System
Imports System.IO
Imports System.Text
Imports System.Drawing
Imports System.Resources
Imports System.Reflection
Imports System.Diagnostics
Imports System.Collections
Imports System.ComponentModel
Imports Microsoft.BizTalk.Message.Interop
Imports Microsoft.BizTalk.Component.Interop
Imports Microsoft.BizTalk.Component
Imports Microsoft.BizTalk.Messaging

Namespace Probiztalk.Samples.PipelinesComponents

    <ComponentCategory(CategoryTypes.CATID_PipelineComponent), _
     System.Runtime.InteropServices.Guid("4f1c7d50-e66f-451b-8e94-2f8d599cd013"), _
     ComponentCategory(CategoryTypes.CATID_Encoder)> _
    Public Class LargeFileEncodingComponent

        Implements IBaseComponent, IPersistPropertyBag, IComponentUI, _
         Global.Microsoft.BizTalk.Component.Interop.IComponent

        Private resourceManager As System.Resources.ResourceManager = New  _
         System.Resources.ResourceManager( _
         "Probiztalk.Samples.PipelineComponents.LargeFileEncodingComponent", _
         [Assembly].GetExecutingAssembly)
        Private Const PROPERTY_SCHEMA_NAMESPACE = _
                "http://LargeFileHandler.Schemas.LargeFilePropertySchema"
```

```
'<summary>
'Name of the component
'</summary>
<Browsable(False)> _
Public ReadOnly Property Name() As String Implements _
        Global.Microsoft.BizTalk.Component.Interop.IBaseComponent.Name
    Get
        Return resourceManager.GetString("COMPONENTNAME", _
                            System.Globalization.CultureInfo.InvariantCulture)
    End Get
End Property

'<summary>
'Version of the component
'</summary>
<Browsable(False)> _
Public ReadOnly Property Version() As String Implements _
        Global.Microsoft.BizTalk.Component.Interop.IBaseComponent.Version
    Get
        Return resourceManager.GetString("COMPONENTVERSION", _
                   System.Globalization.CultureInfo.InvariantCulture)
    End Get
End Property

'<summary>
'Description of the component
'</summary>
<Browsable(False)> _
Public ReadOnly Property Description() As String Implements _
    Global.Microsoft.BizTalk.Component.Interop.IBaseComponent.Description
    Get
        Return resourceManager.GetString("COMPONENTDESCRIPTION", _
                            System.Globalization.CultureInfo.InvariantCulture)
    End Get
End Property

'<summary>
'Component icon to use in BizTalk Editor
'</summary>
<Browsable(False)> _
Public ReadOnly Property Icon() As IntPtr Implements _
        Global.Microsoft.BizTalk.Component.Interop.IComponentUI.Icon
    Get
        Return CType(Me.resourceManager.GetObject("COMPONENTICON", _
                  System.Globalization.CultureInfo.InvariantCulture), _
                  System.Drawing.Bitmap).GetHicon
    End Get
End Property
```

```
'<summary>
'Gets class ID of component for usage from unmanaged code.
'</summary>
'<param name="classid">
'Class ID of the component
'</param>
Public Sub GetClassID(ByRef classid As System.Guid) Implements _
Global.Microsoft.BizTalk.Component.Interop.IPersistPropertyBag.GetClassID
    classid = New System.Guid("4f1c7d50-e66f-451b-8e94-2f8d599cd013")
End Sub

'<summary>
'not implemented
'</summary>
Public Sub InitNew() Implements _
    Global.Microsoft.BizTalk.Component.Interop.IPersistPropertyBag.InitNew
End Sub

'<summary>
'Loads configuration properties for the component
'</summary>
'<param name="pb">Configuration property bag</param>
'<param name="errlog">Error status</param>
Public Overridable Sub Load(ByVal pb As _
                Global.Microsoft.BizTalk.Component.Interop.IPropertyBag, _
                ByVal errlog As Integer) _
                Implements Global.Microsoft.BizTalk.Component. _
                Interop.IPersistPropertyBag.Load
End Sub

'<summary>
'Saves the current component configuration into the property bag
'</summary>
'<param name="pb">Configuration property bag</param>
'<param name="fClearDirty">not used</param>
'<param name="fSaveAllProperties">not used</param>
Public Overridable Sub Save _
    (ByVal pb As Global.Microsoft.BizTalk.Component.Interop.IPropertyBag, _
     ByVal fClearDirty As Boolean, ByVal fSaveAllProperties As Boolean) _
     Implements _
     Global.Microsoft.BizTalk.Component.Interop.IPersistPropertyBag.Save
End Sub

'<summary>
'Reads property value from property bag
'</summary>
'<param name="pb">Property bag</param>
```

```
'<param name="propName">Name of property</param>
'<returns>Value of the property</returns>
Private Function ReadPropertyBag( _
    ByVal pb As Global.Microsoft.BizTalk.Component.Interop.IPropertyBag, _
    ByVal propName As String) As Object
    Dim val As Object = Nothing
    Try
        pb.Read(propName, val, 0)
    Catch e As System.ArgumentException
        Return val
    Catch e As System.Exception
        Throw New System.ApplicationException(e.Message)
    End Try
    Return val
End Function

'<summary>
'Writes property values into a property bag.
'</summary>
'<param name="pb">Property bag.</param>
'<param name="propName">Name of property.</param>
'<param name="val">Value of property.</param>
Private Sub WritePropertyBag( _
    ByVal pb As Global.Microsoft.BizTalk.Component.Interop.IPropertyBag, _
    ByVal propName As String, ByVal val As Object)
    Try
        pb.Write(propName, val)
    Catch e As System.Exception
        Throw New System.ApplicationException(e.Message)
    End Try
End Sub

'<summary>
'The Validate method is called by the BizTalk Editor during the build
'of a BizTalk project.
'</summary>
'<param name="obj">An Object containing the
'configuration properties.</param>
'<returns>The IEnumerator enables the caller
'to enumerate through a collection of strings containing error messages.
'These error messages appear as compiler error messages.
'To report successful property validation,
'the method should return an empty enumerator.</returns>
Public Function Validate( _
    ByVal obj As Object) As System.Collections.IEnumerator Implements _
    Global.Microsoft.BizTalk.Component.Interop.IComponentUI.Validate
    'example implementation:
```

```
    'ArrayList errorList = new ArrayList();
    'errorList.Add("This is a compiler error");
    'return errorList.GetEnumerator();
    Return Nothing
End Function

'<summary>
'Implements IComponent.Execute method.
'</summary>
'<param name="pc">Pipeline context</param>
'<param name="inmsg">Input message</param>
'<returns>Original input message</returns>
'<remarks>
'IComponent.Execute method is used to initiate
'the processing of the message in this pipeline component.
'</remarks>
Public Function Execute(ByVal pContext As IPipelineContext, _
                        ByVal inmsg As IBaseMessage) As IBaseMessage _
                        Implements Global.Microsoft.BizTalk.Component. _
                        Interop.IComponent.Execute
    Dim isEncoded As Boolean = False

    Try
        isEncoded = inmsg.Context.Read("IsEncoded", _
            PROPERTY_SCHEMA_NAMESPACE)
    Catch ex As Exception
        isEncoded = False
    End Try

    'Build the message that is to be sent out but only if it is encoded
    If isEncoded Then
        BuildMessageData(pContext, inmsg)
    End If

    Return inmsg
End Function

'<summary>
'Method used to assign the data to a stream.
'Method reads path from promoted property
'</summary>
'<param name="pc">Pipeline context</param>
'<param name="inmsg">Input message to be assigned</param>
'<returns>Original input message by reference</returns>
```

```
        '<remarks>
        'Receives the input message ByRef then assigns the file stream to
        ' the messageBody.Data property
        '</remarks>
        Private Sub BuildMessageData(ByVal pContext As IPipelineContext, _
                                     ByRef inMsg As IBaseMessage)

            Dim messageBody As IBaseMessagePart = pContext.GetMessageFactory(). _
            CreateMessagePart()
            Dim data As New FileStream(inMsg.Context.Read("LargeFileLocation", _
                        PROPERTY_SCHEMA_NAMESPACE), FileMode.Open, _
                        FileAccess.Read, FileShare.Read, 4 * 1024 * 1024)
            messageBody.Data = data
            If data.CanSeek Then
                data.Position = 0
            End If

            inMsg.BodyPart.Data = data
        End Sub
    End Class

End Namespace
```

Dealing with Compressed Files

A common problem that most BizTalk projects encounter is having to either send or receive compressed data in the form of a ZIP file. Often, the incoming ZIP file has multiple entries, each of which need to be submitted to BizTalk. In most cases, these files are XML files, but in some situations, they can be either flat files or binary files instead. The examples in the following sections outline a potential simplified solution for sending and receiving zipped information. Additionally, you'll get a chance to explore ways to augment the solution using new functionality within BizTalk.

Sending Simple Zipped Files

In order to send a ZIP file from BizTalk, you will need to create a custom send pipeline and a custom encoding pipeline component. The pipeline component will be responsible for examining the incoming message, getting access to the message's data, compressing it, and returning it to BizTalk. The simplest scenario is the "single message in/single message out" scenario. Here, a message is sent to the send pipeline, it is compressed, and a single message is sent out. The pipeline component required for this is documented in the following class:[5]

5 This class uses compression routines that are available from www.sharpdevelop.com. The source for the compression library is available from this web site and is distributed under the GNU Public License. The examples shown here did not require the source code from SharpDevelop to be modified, and as such it is not included in the example but is packaged with the entire sample available at www.apress.com.

```
using System;
using System;
using System.ComponentModel;
using System.Collections;
using System.Diagnostics;
using System.Drawing;
using System.IO;
using System.Reflection;
using Microsoft.BizTalk.Component.Interop;
using ICSharpCode.SharpZipLib.Zip;

    namespace Probiztalk.Samples.PipelineComponents
{
    [ComponentCategory(CategoryTypes.CATID_PipelineComponent)]
    [ComponentCategory(CategoryTypes.CATID_Encoder)]
    [System.Runtime.InteropServices.Guid("56C7B68B-F288-4f78-A67F-20043CA4943E")]
    public class ZipEncodeComponent :
        IBaseComponent,
        Microsoft.BizTalk.Component.Interop.IComponent,
        Microsoft.BizTalk.Component.Interop.IPersistPropertyBag,
        IComponentUI
    {

        // Component information
        #region IBaseComponent
        [Browsable(false)] public string Name
        {
            get
            {
                return "ZIP encoder";
            }
        }
        [Browsable(false)] public string Version
        {
            get
            {
                return "1.0";
            }
        }
        [Browsable(false)] public string Description
        {
            get
            {
                return "Zip Encode Pipeline Component";
            }
        }
        [Browsable(false)] public System.IntPtr Icon
```

```
{
    get
    {
        return ((Bitmap)resourceManager.
                        GetObject("IconBitmap")).
                        GetHicon();
    }
}
#endregion

private System.Resources.ResourceManager resourceManager =
    new System.Resources.ResourceManager(
            "Probiztalk.Samples.PipelineComponents.ZipEncodeComponent",
            Assembly.GetExecutingAssembly());

// Property: Password
private string _password;
[
DisplayName("Password"),
Description("Password used to zip messages.")
]
public string Password
{
    get {  return _password; }
    set {  _password = value; }
}

// Property: Filename
private const string DEFAULT_FILENAME = "file";
private string _filename;
[
DisplayName("Filename"),
Description(@"The name of the file that contains the output message.
             This file will be added to the ZIP compressed output archive.
             Default is """ + DEFAULT_FILENAME + @"""".")
]
public string Filename
{
    get {  return _filename; }
    set {  _filename = value; }
}

// Property: CompressionLevel
const string DEFAULT_COMPRESSIONLEVEL_TEXT = "5";
const int DEFAULT_COMPRESSIONLEVEL= 5;
private string _compressionlevel;
```

```
[
DisplayName("CompressionLevel"),
Description(@"Compression level: 0=Store Only, to 9=Best Compression.
        Default is '" + DEFAULT_COMPRESSIONLEVEL_TEXT + "'.")
]
public string CompressionLevel
{
    get {  return _compressionlevel; }
    set {  _compressionlevel = value; }
}

private Stream Encode (Stream inStream)
{
    Stream outStream = inStream;
    string inFile = Path.GetTempFileName();
    string outFile = Path.ChangeExtension(inFile, "zip");

    try
    {
        ZipOutputStream zipStream = new ZipOutputStream(
                                File.Create( outFile )
                                );

        // get password, if supplied
        if ((_password != null) && (_password != ""))
            zipStream.Password = _password;

        // get compression level, if supplied
        int compressionlevel = DEFAULT_COMPRESSIONLEVEL;
        if ((_compressionlevel != null) && (_compressionlevel != ""))
            compressionlevel = Convert.ToInt32( _compressionlevel );
        if ((compressionlevel < 0) || (compressionlevel > 9))
            compressionlevel = DEFAULT_COMPRESSIONLEVEL;
        zipStream.SetLevel( compressionlevel );

        // get message filename, if supplied
        string filename = (((_filename != null) && (_filename != "")) ?
                        _filename : DEFAULT_FILENAME );
        ZipEntry entry = new ZipEntry( filename );
        zipStream.PutNextEntry( entry );

        // copy the input into the compressed output stream
        byte[] buffer = new byte[4096];
        int count = 0;
```

```
            while ((count = inStream.Read(buffer, 0, buffer.Length)) != 0)
                zipStream.Write( buffer, 0, count );
            zipStream.Finish();
            zipStream.Close();

            outStream = Probiztalk.Samples.PipelineUtilities.
                FileStreamReadWrite.ReadFileToMemoryStream(outFile);
        }
        catch (Exception ex)
        {
            System.Diagnostics.Debug.WriteLine(ex);
        }
        finally
        {
            if (File.Exists(inFile))
            {
                File.Delete(inFile);
            }

            if (File.Exists(outFile))
            {
                File.Delete(outFile);
            }
        }

        return outStream;
    }

    #region IPersistPropertyBag Members

    public void InitNew()
    {
    }

    public void GetClassID(out Guid classID)
    {
        classID = new Guid ("0F94CF83-0B04-49a6-B73C-70473E0CF96F");
    }

    public void Load(IPropertyBag propertyBag, int errorLog)
    {
        string text;
        text = (string)ReadPropertyBag( propertyBag, "Password" );
        if (text != null) _password = text;
        text = (string)ReadPropertyBag( propertyBag, "Filename" );
```

```
    if (text != null) _filename = text;
    text = (string)ReadPropertyBag( propertyBag, "CompressionLevel" );
    if (text != null) _compressionlevel = text;
}

public void Save(IPropertyBag propertyBag, bool clearDirty,
             bool saveAllProperties)
{
    object val;
    val = (object)_password;
    WritePropertyBag( propertyBag, "Password", val );
    val = (object)_filename;
    WritePropertyBag( propertyBag, "Filename", val );
    val = (object)_compressionlevel;
    WritePropertyBag( propertyBag, "CompressionLevel", val );
}

#endregion


#region IComponent Members

public Microsoft.BizTalk.Message.Interop.IBaseMessage Execute
                (IPipelineContext pContext,
                Microsoft.BizTalk.Message.Interop.IBaseMessage pInMsg)

{
    try
    {
        if (pInMsg != null)
        {
            Stream originalStream =
                pInMsg.BodyPart.GetOriginalDataStream();
            pInMsg.BodyPart.Data = Encode( originalStream );
            pContext.ResourceTracker.AddResource( pInMsg.BodyPart.Data );
        }
    }
    catch (Exception ex)
    {
        System.Diagnostics.Debug.WriteLine(
            "Exception caught in ZipEncodeComponent::Execute: " +
            ex.Message );
    }
    return pInMsg;
}
```

```
#endregion

#region IComponentUI Members

/// <summary>
/// The Validate method is called by the BizTalk Editor during the build
/// of a BizTalk project.
/// </summary>
/// <param name="obj">An Object containing the configuration
/// properties.</param>
/// <returns>The IEnumerator enables the caller to enumerate
/// through a collection of strings containing error messages.
/// These error messages appear as compiler error messages.
/// To report successful property validation, the method should return
/// an empty enumerator.</returns>
public IEnumerator Validate(object projectSystem)
{
    // example implementation:
    // ArrayList errorList = new ArrayList();
    // errorList.Add("This is a compiler error");
    // return errorList.GetEnumerator();
    return null;
}
#endregion
#region Utility functions
/// <summary>
/// Reads property value from property bag.
/// </summary>
/// <param name="pb">Property bag.</param>
/// <param name="propName">Name of property.</param>
/// <returns>Value of the property.</returns>
public static object
    ReadPropertyBag(Microsoft.BizTalk.Component.Interop.IPropertyBag pb,
                    string propName)
{
    object val = null;

    try
    {
        pb.Read(propName, out val, 0);
    }
    catch (ArgumentException)
    {
        return val;
    }
    catch (Exception ex)
```

```
            {
                throw new ApplicationException(ex.Message);
            }

            return val;
        }

        /// <summary>
        /// Writes property values into a property bag.
        /// </summary>
        /// <param name="pb">Property bag.</param>
        /// <param name="propName">Name of property.</param>
        /// <param name="val">Value of property.</param>
        public static void WritePropertyBag(
                         Microsoft.BizTalk.Component.Interop.IPropertyBag pb,
                         string propName, object val)
        {
            try
            {
                pb.Write(propName, ref val);
            }
            catch (Exception ex)
            {
                throw new ApplicationException(ex.Message);
            }
        }


        #endregion
    }
}
```

Sending Multiple Zipped Files

In order to accommodate the scenario where a single ZIP file will contain multiple ZIP entries, you need to make some modifications to the preceding example. Specifically, you need to pass in multiple documents and have them all included within the outbound ZIP file. For this, you can write a BizTalk Assembler component. The Assembler component will take an array of messages, loop through them, and compress each of them into the final message output. To actually send the messages to the assembler, you can use the ExecuteSendPipeline from an orchestration feature. What you need to do is build an orchestration that will have a subscription for all messages required to be included within the ZIP file. The orchestration listens for these messages, and when it receives them, it adds them to an `ArrayList` object. At some point, the orchestration will need to call the send pipeline and pass it in the `ArrayList` it has built. From here, the send pipeline will call the Assembler component, which will add each of the messages it has received within the `ArrayList` to the outbound message. An example of this pattern is included in the SDK with BizTalk under the \Program Files\Microsoft BizTalk Server 2009\ SDK\Samples\Pipelines\Aggregator\ directory. Chapter 6 in this book also includes a sample of a resequencing aggregator pattern that you can use should the files you receive not be in the correct order in which you want to place them in the ZIP file.

Receiving Zipped Files

The reverse scenario to sending ZIP files is receiving them. When receiving ZIP files, you will need to create a Decoding component, which can extract the files inside and submit them to the pipeline for further processing. This example only addresses the simple example of a ZIP file containing one XML file inside. The following example could be expanded upon to handle ZIP files with multiple files inside and files of binary types.

```
using System;
using System.ComponentModel;
using System.Collections;
using System.Diagnostics;
using System.Drawing;
using System.IO;
using System.Reflection;
using Microsoft.BizTalk.Component.Interop;
using ICSharpCode.SharpZipLib.Zip;
namespace Probiztalk.Samples.PipelineComponents
{
    [ComponentCategory(CategoryTypes.CATID_PipelineComponent)]
    [ComponentCategory(CategoryTypes.CATID_Decoder)]
    [System.Runtime.InteropServices.Guid("67C8CFB9-D89A-4415-A112-76187FC294D1")]
    public class ZipDecodeComponent :
        IBaseComponent,
        Microsoft.BizTalk.Component.Interop.IComponent,
        Microsoft.BizTalk.Component.Interop.IPersistPropertyBag,
        IComponentUI
    {

        // Component information
        #region IBaseComponent
        [Browsable(false)]
        public string Name
        {
            get
            {
                return "ZIP decoder";
            }
        }
```

```
[Browsable(false)]
public string Version
{
    get
    {
        return "1.0";
    }
}
[Browsable(false)]
public string Description
{
    get
    {
        return "Zip Decode Pipeline Component";
    }
}
[Browsable(false)] public System.IntPtr Icon
{
    get
    {
        return ((Bitmap)resourceManager.
            GetObject("IconBitmap")).GetHicon();
    }
}
#endregion

private System.Resources.ResourceManager resourceManager =
    new System.Resources.ResourceManager(
        "Probiztalk.Samples.PipelineComponents.ZipDecodeComponent",
        Assembly.GetExecutingAssembly());

// Property: Password
private string _password;
[
DisplayName("Password"),
Description("Password used to unzip messages.")
]
public string Password
{
    get {  return _password; }
    set {  _password = value; }
}
```

```
        private Stream Decode (Stream inStream)
        {
            Stream outStream = inStream;
            string inFile = Path.GetTempFileName();
            string outFile = Path.ChangeExtension(inFile, "txt");

            try
            {
                ZipInputStream zipStream = new ZipInputStream( inStream );

                // get password, if supplied
                if ((_password != null) && (_password != ""))
                    zipStream.Password = _password;

                // this algorithm demands that the zip
                //archive contain exactly one file
                ZipEntry entry = zipStream.GetNextEntry();
                if (entry == null)
                    throw new ApplicationException(
                        @"Input ZIP archive does not contain any files -
                        expecting exactly one file" );
                if (entry.IsDirectory)
                    throw new ApplicationException(
                        @"Input ZIP contains a directory -
                         expecting exactly one file" );

                // copy the compressed stream into the output stream
                outStream = new MemoryStream();
                byte[] buffer = new byte[4096];
                int count = 0;
                while ((count = zipStream.Read(buffer, 0, buffer.Length)) != 0)
                    outStream.Write( buffer, 0, count );

                // make sure that was the one and only file
                entry = zipStream.GetNextEntry();
                if (entry != null)
                    throw new ApplicationException(
                        @"Input ZIP archive contains multiple files
                          and/or directories - expecting exactly one file" );

                zipStream.Close();

#if DEBUG
                outStream.Seek( 0, SeekOrigin.Begin );
                Probiztalk.Samples.PipelineUtilities.FileStreamReadWrite.
                                DumpStreamToFile( outStream, outFile );
#endif
```

```
        outStream.Seek( 0, SeekOrigin.Begin );
    }
    catch (Exception ex)
    {
        System.Diagnostics.Debug.WriteLine(ex);
        throw;
    }
    finally
    {
        if (File.Exists(inFile))
        {
            File.Delete(inFile);
        }

        if (File.Exists(outFile))
        {
            File.Delete(outFile);
        }
    }

    return outStream;
}

#region IPersistPropertyBag Members

public void InitNew()
{
}

public void GetClassID(out Guid classID)
{
    classID = new Guid ("19800584-283D-44da-B1EE-0968387DA088");
}

public void Load(IPropertyBag propertyBag, int errorLog)
{
    string text;
    text = (string)ReadPropertyBag( propertyBag, "Password" );
    if (text != null) _password = text;
}

public void Save(IPropertyBag propertyBag, bool clearDirty,
                 bool saveAllProperties)
```

```
{
    object val;
    val = (object)_password;
    WritePropertyBag( propertyBag, "Password", val );
}

#endregion


#region IComponent Members

public Microsoft.BizTalk.Message.Interop.IBaseMessage Execute(
                    IPipelineContext pContext,
                    Microsoft.BizTalk.Message.Interop.IBaseMessage pInMsg)
{
    try
    {
        if (pInMsg != null)
        {
            Stream originalStream =
                pInMsg.BodyPart.GetOriginalDataStream();
            pInMsg.BodyPart.Data = Decode( originalStream );
            pContext.ResourceTracker.AddResource( pInMsg.BodyPart.Data );
        }
    }
    catch (Exception ex)
    {
        System.Diagnostics.Debug.WriteLine(
                    @"Exception caught in ZipDecodeComponent::Execute: " +
                    ex.Message );
        throw new ApplicationException(
                    @"ZipDecodeComponent was unable to decompress
                    input stream. This may occur if there is more than one
                    file in the zip archive. See inner exception
                    for more information.", ex );
    }
    return pInMsg;
}

#endregion

#region IComponentUI Members
```

```
/// <summary>
/// The Validate method is called by the BizTalk Editor during the build
/// of a BizTalk project.
/// </summary>
/// <param name="obj">An Object containing the
/// configuration properties.</param>
/// <returns>The IEnumerator enables the caller to enumerate through a
/// collection of strings containing error messages. These error messages
/// appear as compiler error messages. To report successful property
/// validation, the method should return an empty enumerator.</returns>
public IEnumerator Validate(object projectSystem)
{
    // example implementation:
    // ArrayList errorList = new ArrayList();
    // errorList.Add("This is a compiler error");
    // return errorList.GetEnumerator();
    return null;
}


#endregion
#region Utility functions
/// <summary>
/// Reads property value from property bag.
/// </summary>
/// <param name="pb">Property bag.</param>
/// <param name="propName">Name of property.</param>
/// <returns>Value of the property.</returns>
public static object
    ReadPropertyBag(Microsoft.BizTalk.Component.Interop.IPropertyBag pb,
                    string propName)
{
    object val = null;

    try
    {
        pb.Read(propName, out val, 0);
    }
    catch (ArgumentException)
    {
        return val;
    }
    catch (Exception ex)
    {
        throw new ApplicationException(ex.Message);
    }
```

```
            return val;
        }

        /// <summary>
        /// Writes property values into a property bag.
        /// </summary>
        /// <param name="pb">Property bag.</param>
        /// <param name="propName">Name of property.</param>
        /// <param name="val">Value of property.</param>
        public static void WritePropertyBag(
                            Microsoft.BizTalk.Component.Interop.IPropertyBag pb,
                            string propName, object val)
        {
            try
            {
                pb.Write(propName, ref val);
            }
            catch (Exception ex)
            {
                throw new ApplicationException(ex.Message);
            }
        }


        #endregion
    }
}
```

Using PGP

By default, BizTalk ships with no encryption/decryption component. Many organizations need to encrypt the message data as it is sent from BizTalk and decrypt as well once it is received. A fairly standard way to do this is to use PGP (Pretty Good Privacy). Various vendors sell PGP packages; however, nothing really exists to integrate PGP with BizTalk. The following examples show you a potential implementation for this both on the send side and the receive side.[6]

The `using Microsoft.Utilities.Cryptography.GnuPG` directive in the beginning of the `PGPEncodeComponent` permits the use of the `GnuPGWrapper` wrapper class that supports the interaction with the GNU Privacy Guard API. The code for this wrapper class is available for download from www.apress.com should you want a full implementation; it is not included in this example due to space constraints. Also, this wrapper class is the logical point where you would implement your own PGP library wrapper should you not want to use the GNU Privacy Guard implementation of the PGP standard.

6 This example uses the GNU Privacy Guard package available from www.gnupg.org. This is an implementation of the OpenPGP standard as defined by RFC 2440. In theory, any PGP software package could be used for this example.

PGP Encode Component

The solution for implementing PGP within BizTalk comprises two components, a send-side encoding component and a receive-side decoding component. The following code shows the send-side encoding component.

```
using System;
using System.ComponentModel;
using System.Collections;
using System.Diagnostics;
using System.Drawing;
using System.IO;
using System.Reflection;
using Microsoft.BizTalk.Component.Interop;
using Probiztalk.Utilities.Cryptography.GnuPG;
namespace Probiztalk.Samples.PipelineComponents
{
    [ComponentCategory(CategoryTypes.CATID_PipelineComponent)]
    [ComponentCategory(CategoryTypes.CATID_Encoder)]
    [System.Runtime.InteropServices.Guid("C1917FE1-841B-4583-A59E-B57F76871899")]
    public class GnuPGEncodeComponent :
        IBaseComponent,
        Microsoft.BizTalk.Component.Interop.IComponent,
        Microsoft.BizTalk.Component.Interop.IPersistPropertyBag,
        IComponentUI
    {

        // Component information
        #region IBaseComponent
        [Browsable(false)]
        public string Name
        {
            get
            {
                return "Gnu PGP encoder";
            }
        }
        [Browsable(false)]
        public string Version
        {
            get
            {
                return "1.0";
            }
        }
```

```
[Browsable(false)]
public string Description
{
    get
    {
        return "GnuPG Encode Pipeline Component";
    }
}
[Browsable(false)]
public System.IntPtr Icon
{
    get
    {
        return ((Bitmap)resourceManager.
                GetObject("IconBitmap")).GetHicon();
    }
}
#endregion

private System.Resources.ResourceManager resourceManager =
    new System.Resources.ResourceManager(
        "Probiztalk.Samples.PipelineComponents.GnuPGEncodeComponent",
        Assembly.GetExecutingAssembly());

// Property: Recipient
private string _recipient;
[
DisplayName("Recipient"),
Description(@"Recipient identifier used to retreive
                     public key from encryption.")
]
public string Recipient
{
    get {  return _recipient; }
    set {  _recipient = value; }
}

// Property: GnuPGBinDir
private string _gnupgbindir;
[
DisplayName("GnuPGBinDir"),
Description(@"Installation directory of GnuPG, that contains gpg.exe file.
              Default, if not specified, is ""C:\gnupg"". Do not include
              trailing slash.")
]
```

```
public string GnuPGBinDir
{
    get {  return _gnupgbindir; }
    set {  _gnupgbindir = value; }
}

private Stream Encode (Stream inStream)
{
    Stream outStream = inStream;
    string inFile = Path.GetTempFileName();
    string outFile = Path.ChangeExtension(inFile, "gpg");

    try
    {
        DumpStreamToFile( inStream, inFile );

        GnuPGWrapper GPG = new GnuPGWrapper(_gnupgbindir);
        GnuPGCommand GPGCommand = GPG.Command;
        GPGCommand.Command = Commands.Encrypt;
        GPGCommand.Recipient = _recipient;
        GPGCommand.Armor = true;
        GPGCommand.InputFile = inFile;
        GPGCommand.OutputFile = outFile;

        GPG.Execute(null);

        outStream = ReadFileToMemoryStream( outFile );
    }
    catch (Exception ex)
    {
        System.Diagnostics.Debug.WriteLine(ex);
    }
    finally
    {
        if (File.Exists(inFile))
        {
            File.Delete(inFile);
        }

        if (File.Exists(outFile))
        {
            File.Delete(outFile);
        }
    }
```

```
        return outStream;
    }

    #region IPersistPropertyBag Members

    public void InitNew()
    {
    }

    public void GetClassID(out Guid classID)
    {
        classID = new Guid ("A398E8D1-4213-4438-9010-66F366D4BDF4");
    }

    public void Load(IPropertyBag propertyBag, int errorLog)
    {
        string text;
        text = (string)ReadPropertyBag( propertyBag, "Recipient" );
        if (text != null) _recipient = text;
        text = (string)ReadPropertyBag( propertyBag, "GnuPGBinDir" );
        if (text != null) _gnupgbindir = text;
    }

    public void Save(IPropertyBag propertyBag, bool clearDirty,
        bool saveAllProperties)
    {
        object val;
        val = (object)_recipient;
        WritePropertyBag( propertyBag, "Recipient", val );
        val = (object)_gnupgbindir;
        WritePropertyBag( propertyBag, "GnuPGBinDir", val );
    }

    #endregion


    #region IComponent Members

    public Microsoft.BizTalk.Message.Interop.IBaseMessage Execute(
                    IPipelineContext pContext,
                    Microsoft.BizTalk.Message.Interop.IBaseMessage pInMsg)
    {
        try
        {
            if (pInMsg != null)
```

```
        {
            Stream originalStream = pInMsg.BodyPart.
                GetOriginalDataStream();
            pInMsg.BodyPart.Data = Encode( originalStream );
            pContext.ResourceTracker.AddResource( pInMsg.BodyPart.Data );
        }
    }
    catch (Exception ex)
    {
        System.Diagnostics.Debug.WriteLine( @"Exception caught in
            GnuPGDecodeComponent::Execute: " + ex.Message );
    }
    return pInMsg;
}

#endregion

#region IComponentUI Members

/// <summary>
/// The Validate method is called by the BizTalk Editor during the build
/// of a BizTalk project.
/// </summary>
/// <param name="obj">An Object containing the
/// configuration properties.</param>
/// <returns>The IEnumerator enables the caller to enumerate
/// through a collection of strings containing error messages.
/// These error messages appear as compiler error
/// messages. To report successful property validation, the method should
/// return an empty enumerator.</returns>
public IEnumerator Validate(object projectSystem)
{
    // example implementation:
    // ArrayList errorList = new ArrayList();
    // errorList.Add("This is a compiler error");
    // return errorList.GetEnumerator();
    return null;
}


#endregion

#region Utility functions
public static void DumpStreamToFile(Stream fromStream, string toFilename)
```

```
{
    FileStream file = null;
    try
    {
        file = new FileStream(toFilename, System.IO.FileMode.Create);
        byte[] tmpBuff = new byte[4096];
        int bytesRead = 0;

        while ((bytesRead =
                fromStream.Read(tmpBuff, 0, tmpBuff.Length)) != 0)
        {
            file.Write(tmpBuff, 0, bytesRead);
        }

        file.Close();
        file = null;
    }
    finally
    {
        if (file != null) file.Close();
    }
}

public static MemoryStream ReadFileToMemoryStream(string fromFilename)
{
    FileStream file = null;
    try
    {
        file = new FileStream(fromFilename, System.IO.FileMode.Open);
        MemoryStream memStream = new MemoryStream();
        byte[] tmpBuff = new byte[4096];
        int bytesRead = 0;

        while ((bytesRead = file.Read(tmpBuff, 0, tmpBuff.Length)) != 0)
        {
            memStream.Write(tmpBuff, 0, bytesRead);
        }

        file.Close();
        file = null;

        memStream.Position = 0;
        return memStream;
    }
```

```
    finally
    {
        if (file != null) file.Close();
    }
}
/// <summary>
/// Reads property value from property bag.
/// </summary>
/// <param name="pb">Property bag.</param>
/// <param name="propName">Name of property.</param>
/// <returns>Value of the property.</returns>
public static object
    ReadPropertyBag(Microsoft.BizTalk.Component.Interop.IPropertyBag pb,
                    string propName)
{
    object val = null;

    try
    {
        pb.Read(propName, out val, 0);
    }
    catch (ArgumentException)
    {
        return val;
    }
    catch (Exception ex)
    {
        throw new ApplicationException(ex.Message);
    }

    return val;
}

/// <summary>
/// Writes property values into a property bag.
/// </summary>
/// <param name="pb">Property bag.</param>
/// <param name="propName">Name of property.</param>
/// <param name="val">Value of property.</param>
public static void WritePropertyBag(
                    Microsoft.BizTalk.Component.Interop.IPropertyBag pb,
                    string propName, object val)
```

```
        {
            try
            {
                pb.Write(propName, ref val);
            }
            catch (Exception ex)
            {
                throw new ApplicationException(ex.Message);
            }
        }


        #endregion
    }
}
```

PGP Decode Component

The following code example is the counterpart to the encoding component shown in the preceding subsection. The Decoding component is used on the receive side of BizTalk and is used when encrypted messages are received into BizTalk.

```
using System;
using System.ComponentModel;
using System.Collections;
using System.Diagnostics;
using System.Drawing;
using System.IO;
using System.Reflection;
using Microsoft.BizTalk.Component.Interop;
using Probiztalk.Utilities.Cryptography.GnuPG;

namespace Probiztalk.Samples.PipelineComponents
{
    [ComponentCategory(CategoryTypes.CATID_PipelineComponent)]
    [ComponentCategory(CategoryTypes.CATID_Decoder)]
    [System.Runtime.InteropServices.Guid("AEE2E180-8E4F-426d-9E39-C314E09F977E")]
    public class GnuPGDecodeComponent :
        IBaseComponent,
        Microsoft.BizTalk.Component.Interop.IComponent,
        Microsoft.BizTalk.Component.Interop.IPersistPropertyBag,
        IComponentUI
    {
```

```
// Component information
#region IBaseComponent
[Browsable(false)]
public string Name
{
    get
    {
        return "Gnu PGP decoder";
    }
}
[Browsable(false)]
public string Version
{
    get
    {
        return "1.0";
    }
}
[Browsable(false)]
public string Description
{
    get
    {
        return "GnuPG Decode Pipeline Component";
    }
}
[Browsable(false)]
public System.IntPtr Icon
{
    get
    {
        return ((Bitmap)resourceManager.GetObject("IconBitmap")).
                                GetHicon();
    }
}
#endregion

private System.Resources.ResourceManager resourceManager =
    new System.Resources.ResourceManager(
          "Probiztalk.Samples.PipelineComponents.GnuPGDecodeComponent",
          Assembly.GetExecutingAssembly());
```

```
// Property: Passphrase
private string _passphrase;
[
DisplayName("Passphrase"),
Description("Passphrase used to retreive private key.")
]
public string Passphrase
{
    get {  return _passphrase; }
    set {  _passphrase = value; }
}

// Property: GnuPGBinDir
private string _gnupgbindir;
[
DisplayName("GnuPGBinDir"),
Description(@"Installation directory of GnuPG, that contains gpg.exe file.
                Default, if not specified, is ""C:\gnupg"".
                Do not include trailing slash.")
]
public string GnuPGBinDir
{
    get {  return _gnupgbindir; }
    set {  _gnupgbindir = value; }
}

private Stream Decode (System.IO.Stream inStream)
{
    Stream outStream = inStream;
    string inFile = Path.GetTempFileName();
    string outFile = Path.ChangeExtension(inFile, "txt");

    try
    {
        DumpStreamToFile( inStream, inFile );

        GnuPGWrapper GPG = new GnuPGWrapper(_gnupgbindir);
        GnuPGCommand GPGCommand = GPG.Command;
        GPGCommand.Command = Commands.Decrypt;
        GPGCommand.InputFile = inFile;
        GPGCommand.OutputFile = outFile;
        GPGCommand.Passphrase = _passphrase;
        // TODO: support encrypted passphrase,
        //no passphrase is a security risk
```

```
            GPG.Execute(null);

            outStream = ReadFileToMemoryStream( outFile );
        }
        catch (Exception ex)
        {
            System.Diagnostics.Debug.WriteLine(ex);
        }
        finally
        {
            if (File.Exists(inFile))
            {
                File.Delete(inFile);
            }

            if (File.Exists(outFile))
            {
                File.Delete(outFile);
            }
        }

        return outStream;
    }

    #region IPersistPropertyBag Members

    public void InitNew()
    {
    }

    public void GetClassID(out Guid classID)
    {
        classID = new Guid ("4FC12033-D0BD-4298-BB31-FBDBA72F5961");
    }

    public void Load(IPropertyBag propertyBag, int errorLog)
    {
        string text;
        text = (string)ReadPropertyBag( propertyBag, "Passphrase" );
        if (text != null) _passphrase = text;
        text = (string)ReadPropertyBag( propertyBag, "GnuPGBinDir" );
        if (text != null) _gnupgbindir = text;
    }
```

```
public void Save(IPropertyBag propertyBag, bool clearDirty,
                bool saveAllProperties)
{
    object val;
    val = (object)_passphrase;
    WritePropertyBag( propertyBag, "Passphrase", val );
    val = (object)_gnupgbindir;
    WritePropertyBag( propertyBag, "GnuPGBinDir", val );
}

#endregion


#region IComponent Members

public Microsoft.BizTalk.Message.Interop.IBaseMessage
    Execute(IPipelineContext pContext,
    Microsoft.BizTalk.Message.Interop.IBaseMessage pInMsg)
{
    try
    {
        if (pInMsg != null)
        {
            Stream originalStream = pInMsg.BodyPart.
                                    GetOriginalDataStream();
            pInMsg.BodyPart.Data = Decode( originalStream );
            pContext.ResourceTracker.AddResource( pInMsg.BodyPart.Data );
        }
    }
    catch (Exception ex)
    {
        System.Diagnostics.Debug.WriteLine(
            @"Exception caught in GnuPGDecodeComponent::Execute: "
            + ex.Message );
    }
    return pInMsg;
}

#endregion

#region IComponentUI Members
```

```
/// <summary>
/// The Validate method is called by the BizTalk Editor during the build
/// of a BizTalk project.
/// </summary>
/// <param name="obj">An Object containing
/// the configuration properties.</param>
/// <returns>The IEnumerator enables the caller to enumerate through a
/// collection of strings containing error messages. These error messages
/// appear as compiler error messages.
/// To report successful property validation,
/// the method should return an empty enumerator.</returns>
public IEnumerator Validate(object projectSystem)
{
    // example implementation:
    // ArrayList errorList = new ArrayList();
    // errorList.Add("This is a compiler error");
    // return errorList.GetEnumerator();
    return null;
}


#endregion

#region Utility Functions

public static void DumpStreamToFile(Stream fromStream, string toFilename)
{
    FileStream file = null;
    try
    {
        file = new FileStream(toFilename, System.IO.FileMode.Create);
        byte[] tmpBuff = new byte[4096];
        int bytesRead = 0;

        while ((bytesRead =
                fromStream.Read(tmpBuff, 0, tmpBuff.Length)) != 0)
        {
            file.Write(tmpBuff, 0, bytesRead);
        }

        file.Close();
        file = null;
    }
```

```
        finally
        {
            if (file != null) file.Close();
        }
    }

    public static MemoryStream ReadFileToMemoryStream(string fromFilename)
    {
        FileStream file = null;
        try
        {
            file = new FileStream(fromFilename, System.IO.FileMode.Open);
            MemoryStream memStream = new MemoryStream();
            byte[] tmpBuff = new byte[4096];
            int bytesRead = 0;

            while ((bytesRead = file.Read(tmpBuff, 0, tmpBuff.Length)) != 0)
            {
                memStream.Write(tmpBuff, 0, bytesRead);
            }

            file.Close();
            file = null;

            memStream.Position = 0;
            return memStream;
        }
        finally
        {
            if (file != null) file.Close();
        }
    }
    /// <summary>
    /// Reads property value from property bag.
    /// </summary>
    /// <param name="pb">Property bag.</param>
    /// <param name="propName">Name of property.</param>
    /// <returns>Value of the property.</returns>
    public static object
        ReadPropertyBag(Microsoft.BizTalk.Component.Interop.IPropertyBag pb,
                        string propName)
    {
        object val = null;
```

```
            try
            {
                pb.Read(propName, out val, 0);
            }
            catch (ArgumentException)
            {
                return val;
            }
            catch (Exception ex)
            {
                throw new ApplicationException(ex.Message);
            }

            return val;
        }

        /// <summary>
        /// Writes property values into a property bag.
        /// </summary>
        /// <param name="pb">Property bag.</param>
        /// <param name="propName">Name of property.</param>
        /// <param name="val">Value of property.</param>
        public static void WritePropertyBag(
                            Microsoft.BizTalk.Component.Interop.IPropertyBag pb,
                            string propName, object val)
        {
            try
            {
                pb.Write(propName, ref val);
            }
            catch (Exception ex)
            {
                throw new ApplicationException(ex.Message);
            }
        }


        #endregion
    }
}
```

The Databased Disassembler

Often, people need to get information from a database and submit it to BizTalk or have BizTalk send it out to a third-party destination. The usual response for this is to use the appropriate database adapter, generate the schemas for the SQL statement or the stored procedure, and use some combination of an orchestration/port and adapter to generate the data, publish it to the Messagebox, and send it to the appropriate destination. While this solution works, it often is met with a response like "But I just want to call a stored procedure and have each row be sent to BizTalk as an XML document."

Our solution to this scenario is called the Databased Disassembler (yes, it is a pun on words as the data is based on a database). The walkthrough for how this solution works is as follows:

1. A receive pipeline is created that hosts the custom Disassembler component.
2. The Disassembler only accepts a primer message. A **primer message** is a message that contains all the parameters needed for the pipeline component to begin executing. It is a primer because it is a message that gets the process going, or "primes" it. The message itself contains data that is not meaningful to anyone but the Databased Disassembler pipeline component.
3. The pipeline component examines the primer message and retrieves all the parameters needed for execution. These parameters can include
    a. The connection string for the database
    b. The stored procedure name
    c. The parameters needed to call the stored procedure
    d. The resulting schema type for the returned data
    e. The number of rows to include in an output message (The default is usually 1, but it can contain multiple documents wrapped in an envelope if so desired.)
    f. If an envelope is requested, the XPath to the body element in the envelope as well as the schema name for the envelope
4. If no values exist for a given parameter, the pipeline component can have them defaulted to a value when it is placed in the pipeline surface designer.
5. Once all the parameters are gathered, the component calls the stored procedure with the parameters supplied in the primer message.
6. It creates a `DataReader` object from the result of the stored procedure call. If no records were returned, an exception is thrown.
7. If more than one record is requested per created message, then the component generates a new empty instance of the envelope schema that was specified in the primer message. If only one record is requested, then no envelope is used. If more than one document is requested per message but no envelope schema is supplied, then an exception is thrown.
8. For each row that is returned, a new but empty XML document is created based on the requested schema in the primer message. This document is created using the `DocumentSpec` class shown earlier in the chapter.

9. Each element name in the blank XML instance must exist as a named column in the `DataReader` with the same name.[7] This way, the schema instance can change, and all that is required is an update to the stored procedure. In this fashion, you have a logical connection between your XML schema and your database schema.

10. The component continues to create new XML documents in the `GetNext()`method of the Disassembler interface until no more rows exist. When all rows have been processed, the component returns `Nothing`.

The following code shows the schema for the primer message that will be used to signify the start of the processes:

```
<?xml version="1.0" encoding="utf-16"?>
 <xs:schema xmlns:b="http://schemas.microsoft.com/BizTalk/2003"
 xmlns="http://TR3.Schemas.Primer" targetNamespace="http://TR3.Schemas.Primer"
 xmlns:xs="http://www.w3.org/2001/XMLSchema">
<xs:element name="PrimerData">
    <xs:complexType>
      <xs:sequence>
        <xs:element minOccurs="0" maxOccurs="1" name="ConnectionString"
 nillable="true" type="xs:string" />
        <xs:element minOccurs="0" maxOccurs="1" name="StoredProcedureName"
 nillable="true" type="xs:string" />
        <xs:element name="StoredProcParams" nillable="true">
          <xs:complexType>
            <xs:sequence minOccurs="0" maxOccurs="1">
              <xs:element minOccurs="0" maxOccurs="unbounded" name="ParamValue"
 nillable="true" type="xs:string" />
            </xs:sequence>
</xs:complexType>
</xs:element>
<xs:element minOccurs="0" maxOccurs="1" default="1" name="RecordsPerMessage"
 type="xs:integer" />
<xs:element minOccurs="0" maxOccurs="1" name="OutputMessageSchema"
 nillable="true" type="xs:string" />
<xs:element minOccurs="0" maxOccurs="1" name="EnvelopeSchema"
 nillable="true" type="xs:string" />
<xs:element minOccurs="0" maxOccurs="1" name="BodyXPath" nillable="true"
type="xs:string" />
      </xs:sequence>
    </xs:complexType>
  </xs:element> </xs:schema>
```

7 Many other approaches to this problem are available. A second potential solution would be to have a BizTalk transformation that maps the schema created from the component to the requested output schema. A third would be to access the schema and the data columns by index only. This assumes that there is always the same number of elements as the number of columns in the result set and that they are stored in the correct order. Any of these implementations will work; we chose the "named columns" approach because it served the purpose of illustrating this technique the best.

Figure 5-1 gives a pictorial representation of the message flow that will take place for this process to work. Note one key element in Figure 5-1. The data from which the Disassembler gets its rows is not the BizTalk Messagebox. This is a key feature of this pattern. Since the database can be essentially "anything," it becomes trivial to get data from any OLEDB-compliant data source such as Oracle, DB2, and Sybase. This technique only requires writing a stored procedure and getting a connection string to access the data source. There is no need to purchase additional adapters for this solution to be used across different databases. This is a key selling point for many projects that might want to use this approach.

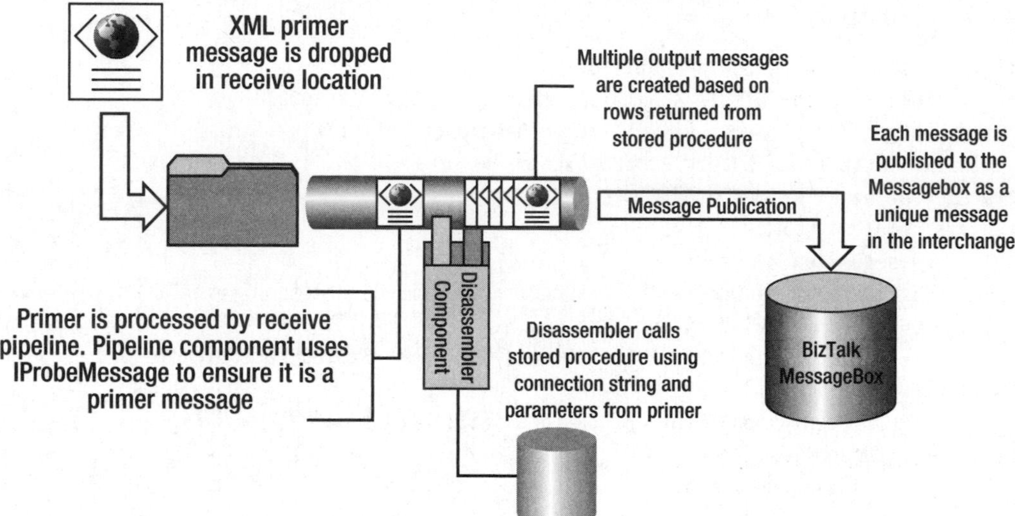

Figure 5-1. *Databased Disassembler execution flow*

Another key architectural component of this solution is that fact that a Disassembler is used to create the messages. Each of the messages that are created from a unique primer message will be tagged as being from the same Interchange. This means that every message that was created from this primer message will have the same `InterchangeID`. This is very useful, as it allows you to easily correlate all the messages in an execution flow within an orchestration using a convoy pattern, because they will all have the same `InterchangeID`. The only issue becomes how to signify that the message received is the last in the sequence. For this, you can use the same pattern that is employed in the resequencing aggregator pattern in Chapter 6. You will need to create a custom property schema that is associated to each of the messages that is created by the Disassembler. Each message will be tagged with a sequence number, and there will be a Boolean flag in the schema that indicates the last message in the sequence. This flag is then used to signal the orchestration that the last message has been received in the convoy.

CHAPTER 6

BizTalk Design Patterns and Practices

The chapters to date have dealt with advanced concepts with regard to pipelines and messaging. Most of the concepts in the previous chapters have involved examining the intricacies of a particular tool within the BizTalk toolkit. Here we'll show you how you can use some of the more advanced concepts within BizTalk to solve some higher-level scenario-based problems.

Implementing Dynamic Parallel Orchestrations

Microsoft BizTalk Server orchestrations allow parallel business execution branches, using the native **Parallel Actions** shape.[1] However, the number of branches is static: to add an execution branch, you need to modify and recompile an orchestration.

When to Use Them

The behavior for Parallel Actions shapes doesn't fit in scenarios where you know only at runtime the number of execution branches that you can spawn. An example is the travel agent service scenario described at `www.w3.org/TR/ws-arch-scenarios/`, where a travel agent requests in parallel a list of flights for each airline included in a customer list. This sample can be generalized to scenarios where a client application sends a request to a broker that splits it into individual requests for similar target systems; then the broker collects the responses from the target systems and aggregates them into a single response for the client (see Figure 6-1).

1 This section originally appeared in "BizTalk Server 2004 Implementing Dynamic Parallel Orchestrations," (REED001965).doc. Copyright by Microsoft Corporation. Reprinted with permission from Microsoft Corporation.

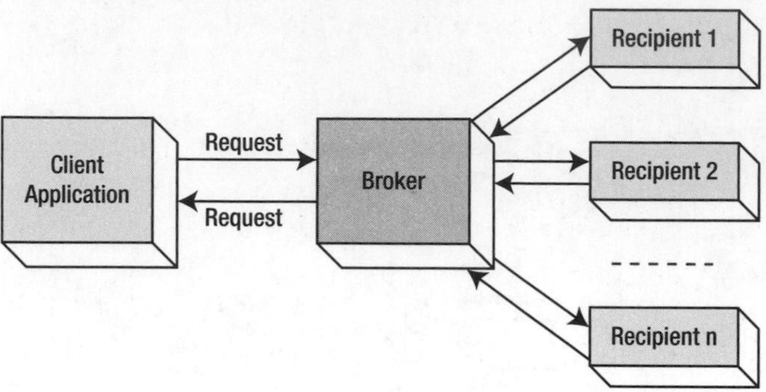

Figure 6-1. *Sample broker implementation*

One approach to solve this problem is to use the **Recipient List** pattern as described by the book *Enterprise Integration Patterns*. The Recipient List pattern is explained by the Enterprise Integration Patterns site as the following:

> *A Content-Based Router allows us to route a message to the correct system based on message content. This process is transparent to the original sender in the sense that the originator simply sends the message to a channel, where the router picks it up and takes care of everything.*
>
> *In some cases, though, we may want to specify one or more recipients for the message. A common analogy are* [sic] *the recipient lists implemented in most e-mail systems. For each e-mail message, the sender can specify a list of recipients. The mail system then ensures transport of the message content to each recipient. An example from the domain of enterprise integration would be a situation where a function can be performed by one or more providers. For example, we may have a contract with multiple credit agencies to assess the credit worthiness of our customers. When a small order comes in we may simply route the credit request message to one credit agency. If a customer places a large order, we may want to route the credit request message to multiple agencies and compare the results before making a decision. In this case, the list of recipients depends on the dollar value of the order.*
>
> *In another situation, we may want to route an order message to a select list of suppliers to obtain a quote for the requested item. Rather than sending the request to all vendors, we may want to control which vendors receive the request, possibly based on user preferences.*

How do we route a message to a list of dynamically specified recipients?

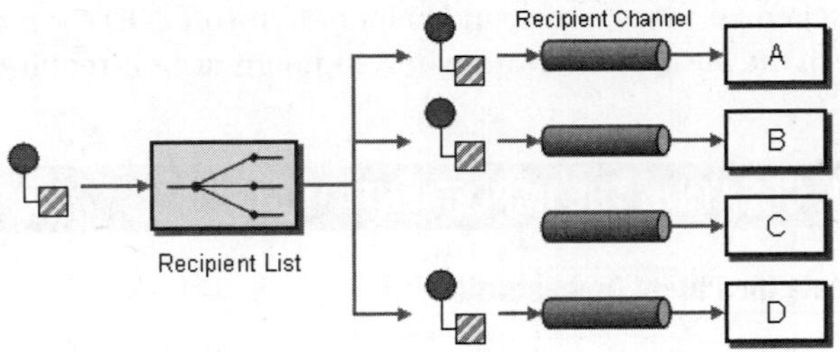

Define a channel for each recipient. Then use a Recipient List to inspect an incoming message, determine the list of desired recipients, and forward the message to all channels associated with the recipients in the list.

The logic embedded in a Recipient List can be pictured as two separate parts even though the implementation is often coupled together. The first part computes a list of recipients. The second part simply traverses the list and sends a copy of the received message to each recipient. Just like a Content-Based Router, the Recipient List usually does not modify the message contents.[2]

This section describes a dynamic parallel implementation of this pattern with a BizTalk orchestration.

An alternative approach would have been using the **Publish-Subscribe** and **Message Filter** patterns. We don't describe here this alternative approach, because this implementation could be more resource consuming in terms of database queries to resolve the filter conditions, and more error prone while setting filter conditions on the channels.

Broker Implementation Overview

Our implementation of the broker requires using two different orchestrations.[3] A parent orchestration builds the list of recipients, based on the received document. The parent orchestration uses the Start Orchestration shape to launch a child orchestration for each recipient. The child orchestration executes the actual flow of messages with the recipient. We assume that all the recipients share a common workflow model and schema documents; otherwise you wouldn't need such a dynamic invocation model, because a manual activity would be needed to introduce each additional recipient! The child orchestration makes use of **dynamic port binding** to send messages to each different recipient.

The parent orchestration collects the results returned by each child and builds an aggregated response document. The parent orchestration makes use of a **self-correlating** binding port to receive the responses from the started child orchestrations.

2 www.enterpriseintegrationpatterns.com/RecipientList.html

3 This subsection and the accompanying exercise originally appeared in "BizTalk Server 2004 Implementing Dynamic Parallel Orchestrations," (REED001965).doc. Copyright by Microsoft Corporation. Reprinted with permission from Microsoft Corporation.

In Exercise 6-1, we concentrate on the general design and on the orchestration mechanisms involved in the dynamic parallelism implementation; we don't give a complete implementation sample including schemas, maps, ports, and helper Microsoft .NET Framework objects. A working knowledge of the basic orchestration development tasks is required.

EXERCISE 6-1. CREATING THE IMPLEMENTATION

Create the Parent Orchestration

The following are the steps required to create the parent orchestration as shown in Figure 6-2 for the solution within Visual Studio.

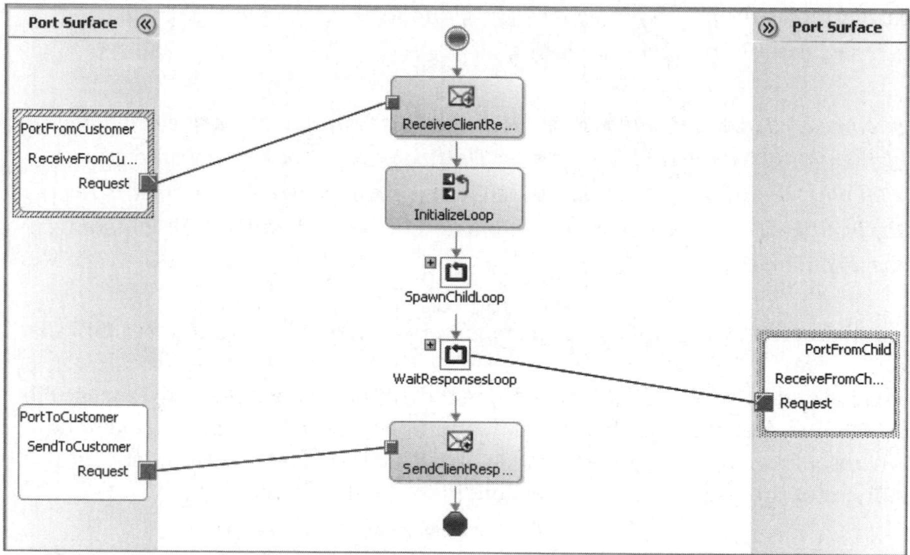

Figure 6-2. *Parent orchestration main blocks*

1. Define the schemas for the Customer Request, Customer Response, Recipient Request, and Recipient Response.
2. Promote a property in the Recipient Request schema that can be used to build the dynamic address of the recipient.
3. Define one message for each of the mentioned schemas, that is, a CustomerRequest, a CustomerResponse, a RecipientRequest, and a RecipientResponse message.
4. Drag a Receive shape to receive a CustomerRequest message from a client application.
5. Define variables to control the two loops of the parent orchestration: the SpawnChild loop and the CollectResponses loop.
6. Drag an Expression shape that you use to calculate the recipient list from the CustomerRequest message and initialize the SpawnChild loop control variable. The customer request message must contain the number of messages to spawn. The SpawnChild variable will contain this number.

7. Drag a Loop shape for the SpawnChild loop and define the Boolean looping control expression.
8. Drag a Loop shape for the CollectResponses loop and define the Boolean looping control expression.
9. Drag a Send shape to return the CustomerResponse message to the client application.
10. Drag two ports to be used as PortFromCustomer and PortToCustomer; their actual properties depend on the particular scenario and are not relevant to the discussion.
11. Drag a port to be used as PortFromChild. In the Port Configuration Wizard, define the following properties:
    a. In the Select a Port Type tab, choose to create a new port type named TypePortFromChild with the communication pattern One-Way.
    b. In the Port Binding tab, choose "I'll always be receiving messages on this port" as port direction of communication.
    c. Choose Direct as port binding and then Self Correlating.[4]

Next, create the SpawnChild loop whose steps are defined here and shown in Figure 6-3.

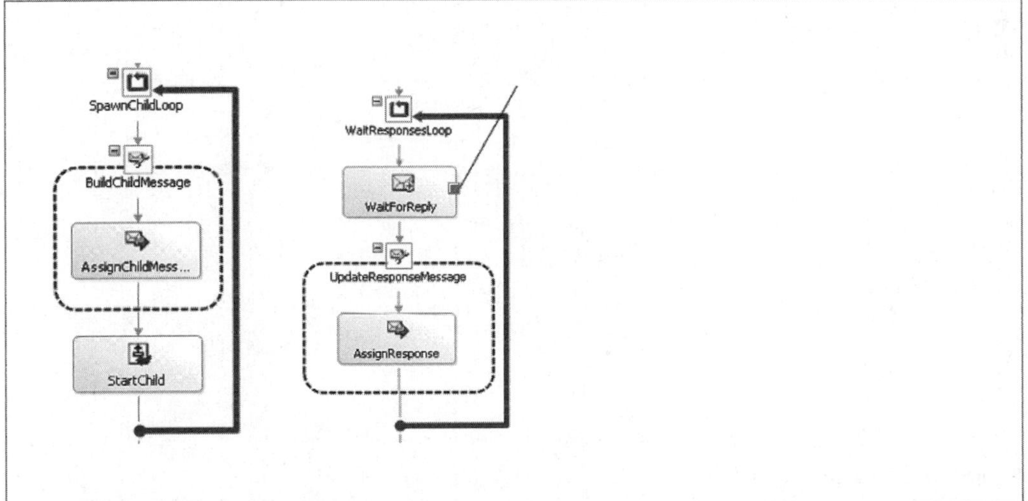

Figure 6-3. *Parent orchestration loops*

1. Drag a Message Assignment shape inside the SpawnChildLoop shape; in the enclosing Construct Message shape, define RecipientRequest as the message to be constructed.
2. In the Message Assignment expression, you will build the RecipientRequest message from the CustomerRequest message according to the current loop cycle; you will probably want to use a helper .NET component to build the message.[5] You will also update an orchestration variable with the number of spawned children.
3. Drag a Start Orchestration shape below the ConstructMessage shape. Leave it unconfigured for the moment.

4 Direct port binding and correlation are advanced orchestration topics covered in Chapter 7.

5 Alternatively you could use a BizTalk map to create the new message—either approach will work.

Once the preceding steps are completed, the final step is to create the wait responses loop as defined here:

1. Drag a Receive shape inside the WaitResponsesLoop shape. Define RecipientResponse as the message that will be received by this shape.
2. Drag a Message Assignment shape below the Receive shape; in the Construct Message shape, define CustomerResponse as the message to be constructed.
3. In the Message Assignment expression, you will build[6] the CustomerResponse message aggregating the RecipientResponse message received in the current loop cycle. You will also update an orchestration variable with the number of received responses that will have to match the number of spawned children to exit the loop.

Create the Child Orchestration

Once the parent orchestration is created, the next step is to create the child orchestration. The steps for this are defined here and the orchestration is shown in Figure 6-4.

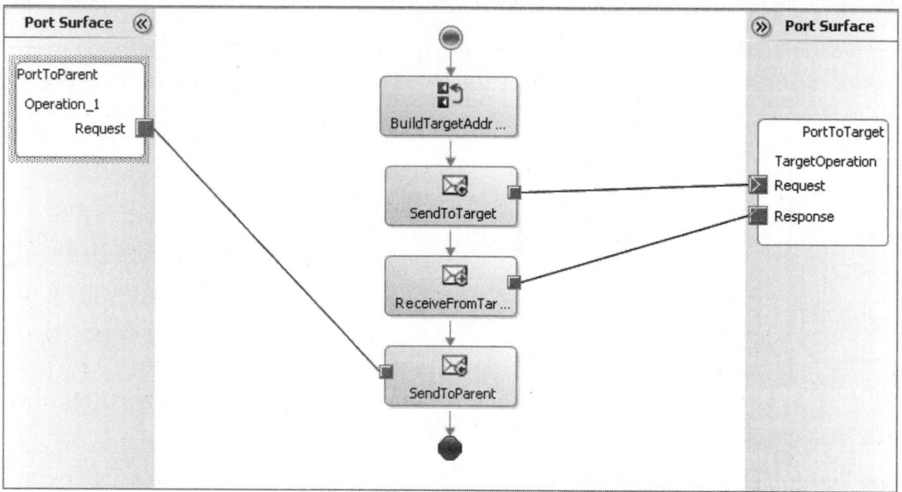

Figure 6-4. *Child orchestration*

You will reuse the Recipient Request and Recipient Response schemas defined before.

1. In the Orchestration View section, right-click Orchestration Parameter and choose New Port Parameter; assign to this port parameter the port type TypePortFromChild, defined previously in the parent orchestration; assign to this port parameter the identifier PortToParent; change the communication direction of this port parameter to Send.
2. Right-click Orchestration Parameter again and choose New Message Parameter; assign to this message parameter the message type RecipientRequest and the identifier MsgFromParent.

---

6 This can be accomplished a number of ways. A potential choice would be to use an aggregating pipeline, collect all the messages to be aggregated, and call the pipeline with the array of messages. An implementation of an aggregating pipeline is given in the BizTalk SDK under the Program Files\ Microsoft BizTalk Server 2009\SDK\Pipelines directory. Another choice would be to create a .NET component to accept the messages as they are received and aggregate them together.

3. Define one TargetResponse message that uses the Recipient Response schema.
4. Drag a port to be used as PortToTarget. In the Port Configuration Wizard, define the following properties:
   a. In the Select a Port Type tab, choose to create a new port type named TypePortToTarget with the communication pattern Request-Response.
   b. In the Port Binding tab, choose "I'll be sending a request and receiving a response" as port direction of communication.
   c. Choose Dynamic as port binding and then choose a receive pipeline and a send pipeline suitable for your Recipient Request and Recipient Response schemas.
5. Drag a Send shape onto the Orchestration Designer surface and name it SendToTarget; configure this shape to send the MsgFromParent message to the PortToTarget port.
6. Drag a Receive shape onto the Orchestration Designer surface that you will name ReceiveFromTarget; configure this shape to receive the TargetResponse message from the PortToTarget port.
7. Drag a Send shape onto the Orchestration Designer surface that you will name SendToParent; configure this shape to send the TargetResponse message to the PortToParent port.
8. Drag an Expression shape at the top of the orchestration that you will name BuildTargetAddress; use this expression to assign the URI to the dynamic port PortToTarget[7] based on the value of a promoted property[8] in the MsgFromParent message.

Bind the Parent Orchestration to the Child Orchestration

To complete the exercise, you need to add the following additional configuration to the parent orchestration:

1. Double-click the Start Orchestration shape to open its configuration box. In the Select the orchestration you want to start combo box, select the child orchestration. The Orchestration Parameters grid is automatically updated with the right matches between the variables in scope of the parent orchestration and the parameter name of the child orchestration: the PortFromChild variable is matched with the PortToParent parameter; the RecipientRequest variable is matched with the MsgFromParent parameter.
2. In the Properties pane of the orchestration, change the transaction type to Long Running and set a value for the timeout; otherwise, in case a child orchestration is terminated abnormally, the parent orchestration would wait indefinitely for a response.

The previous exercise shows you how you can use orchestrations to solve a real-world problem. Let's look at another issue that often arises when processing messages—dealing with order.

7 The code for the Expression shape will look something like `PortToTarget(Microsoft.XLANGs.BaseTypes.Address) = "Http://wsOrders/Interface.asmx"`.

8 This implementation requires that the address of where the messages are to be sent is known ahead of time. In the original message that was received by the parent orchestration, an element must exist that contains this address. This value must be promoted into the context via either the schema definition or a distinguished field.

Handling Ordered Delivery

As anyone who has worked with HL7[9] would know, ensuring the order of a sequence of messages is a major issue. Most know that BizTalk has a mechanism called Ordered Delivery that is available for a port inside an orchestration or within a messaging port. In short, this setting forces the port to deliver the messages out of the Messagebox in the order in which they were received. This ensures that the First In—First Out pattern is followed when dealing with messages arriving on a port. In BizTalk 2004, this mechanism was available only when using the MSMQT transport adapter. Luckily in BizTalk 2009, ordered delivery has become an adapter-agnostic option and even extends to custom adapters.

Building a Resequencer

Ordered delivery guarantees order in and out of the Messagebox. However, before you can consider the order problem solved, there are a couple of show-stopping things that you need to deal with:

- Using ordered delivery is a major performance bottleneck. As great as this option is, when the rubber hits the road, your overall solution throughput will drop drastically when you use the default End Point Manager (EPM) ordered delivery. This is because the BizTalk engine essentially has to "single-thread" each of the messages as they arrive on the port to their appropriate destination. This means that every message that arrives on the port can be dequeued, transformed, and delivered one at a time only. In many high-throughput scenarios, using the default ordered delivery pattern is simply not an option because of this fact.
- Ordered delivery assumes the messages arrive in the correct order. In many situations, this simply isn't the case. In this scenario, the default ordered delivery pattern simply doesn't work.

As described in Chapter 4, what is needed to implement proper ordering is a **Resequencer** pattern. The job of the resequencer is to examine incoming messages, check the order of the messages (i.e., current message is 7 of 9), and reorder the messages as they arrive into the proper order. To implement such resequencing in BizTalk, you need a couple of components as listed in the following subsections, along with some base assumptions.

Resequencer Assumptions

Like most patterns, the Resequencer pattern is based on a number of assumptions:

- Assuming the messages are arriving out of order, there is a way to examine the incoming message and know
  - What number the message is in the sequence to be received
  - A flag exists somewhere in the message payload to indicate whether the current fragment is the last in the sequence, or the total number of messages

9 Health Level 7 (HL7) is a standard for the exchange of medical information via an electronic format. The standard also has strict requirements about the order in which messages are processed in relation to the order in which they were received. An HL7 accelerator is available for BizTalk and is downloadable from www.microsoft.com/biztalk/evaluation/hl7/default.mspx.

- Once the messages are received into your resequencer, you can start sending messages out immediately so long as you can preserve the order. For example, assume the messages are arriving into your orchestration in the following order:

  3, 5, 1, 2, 4, 8, 9, 11, 23

  The following diagram illustrates this concept, because it can get a little confusing. Technically once you receive the third message, which is the first message in the logical sequence, you can send it. You then receive the fourth message, which is logical sequence number 2, which you also can immediately send. The resequencer then looks through the list of previously received messages and finds logical sequence numbers 3 and 5, so it immediately sends sequence number 3, since it is next in the logical sequence, and waits for the message that is number 4 in the logical sequence to arrive, since that is the next message that needs to be sent in the logical sequence, but has not yet been received.

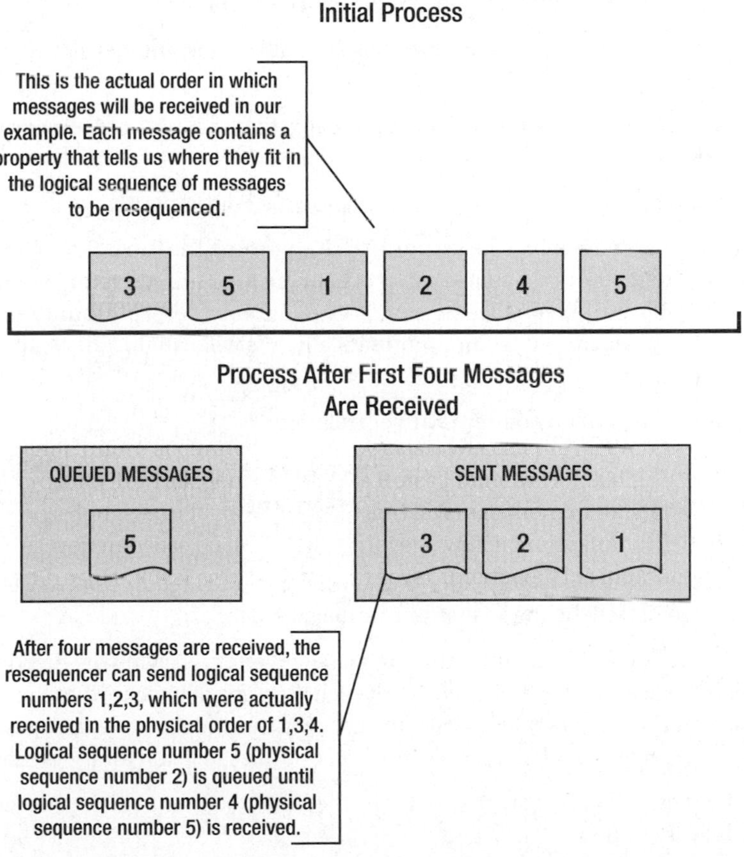

- The resequencer is stateful and exists for the life of the sequence. It terminates itself once the last message in the sequence is received. This is using a Singleton pattern and may potentially have performance issues over time.

- The message sequence is atomic. If a message in the sequence cannot be sent, the sequence stops until the issue is fixed.
- In cases where multiple instances of the resequencer are running (i.e., processing multiple distinct sequences), there exists a way to uniquely identify each sequence based on the data in the message. For example, in cases where messages are arriving in distinct interchanges (not from a disassembler nor from multiple message parts), there is a way to distinguish which sequence the message belongs to.

BizTalk Components Needed

To implement the resequencer, you will need the following BizTalk components:

- Schema to describe the inbound message
- Custom property schema to hold three properties:
  - The `SequenceID` (GUID that uniquely identifies the sequence)
  - The current `SequenceNumber` (identifies that the message is number XXXX of YYYY in the sequence)
  - `LastMessageInSequence` Boolean, which indicates that the current message is the last in the sequence
- Custom inbound receive pipeline with custom pipeline component:
  - The pipeline component will be responsible for probing the incoming schema and validating whether or not it can handle it, checking for a unique sequence ID in the message as well as the sequence number. Upon finding these, it promotes these values to the message context programmatically. We will call this the **Resequencing Decoder**.
- Orchestration using Convoy pattern with correlation:[10]
  - The orchestration will be initiated by the receipt of the first message received in the sequence. (Note: this message doesn't necessarily need to be the logical first message to be sent.)
  - The orchestration will store the inbound message in a `SortedList` object. The key for the sorted list will be the sequence number.
  - The orchestration will listen for incoming messages after receiving the first one and add them to the array. Upon the receipt of each message, it checks what the next sequence number to be sent is against the list of currently received messages. If the required message hasn't been received yet, it continues to listen for more messages.
  - When the required message arrives, it is immediately sent out via the orchestration with a delivery notification.
  - Upon receipt of the delivery notification, the orchestration searches through the `SortedList` of messages to see whether the next sequence number has been received. If it hasn't, it listens for more messages. If it has been received, it is immediately sent, and the loop starts over again.

---

10 Convoys and correlations will be discussed in the next chapter.

- The orchestration uses a correlation set that is initialized by the receipt of the first message. The set is correlated based on the `Promoted` property of `SequenceID`, which was promoted in the custom pipeline component.
- When a message arrives that has the `LastMessageInSequence` property set to True, the orchestration stores this message's sequence number in a private variable. When this sequence number is successfully delivered, the orchestration exits the receive messages loop and finishes normally.

The high-level architecture diagram for this pattern is shown in Figure 6-5.

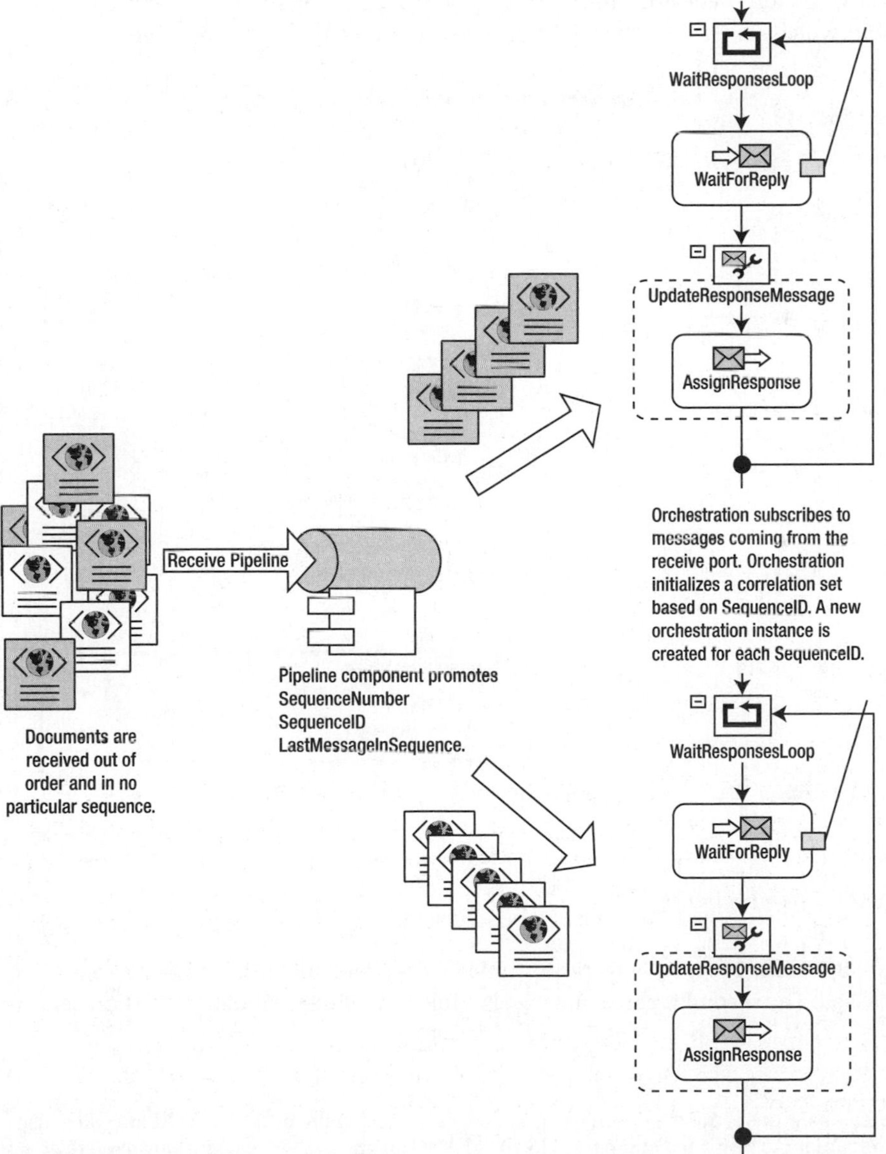

Figure 6-5. *Resequencer implementation*

Building the Solution

As the creation of pipeline components has been well explored in previous chapters and the component implementation is quite simple for this example, let's look at how the orchestration will be implemented. Figures 6-6, 6-7, and 6-8 show how the orchestration will be created.

In the orchestration snippet shown in Figure 6-6, the key areas to observe are at the first Receive shape and the receiving loop. The first Receive shape initializes the correlation set. The correlation set is using the `PropertySchema.SequenceID` that you defined and promoted within your custom pipeline upon receipt of the message. The IsLastFragment Decide shape is checking the Boolean `IsLastMessage` property using an XPath expression.[11] If it is not the last fragment, the Expression shape adds the message to a `SortedList` variable and sets a private integer variable, which stores what the last `SequenceNumber` was for the received message.

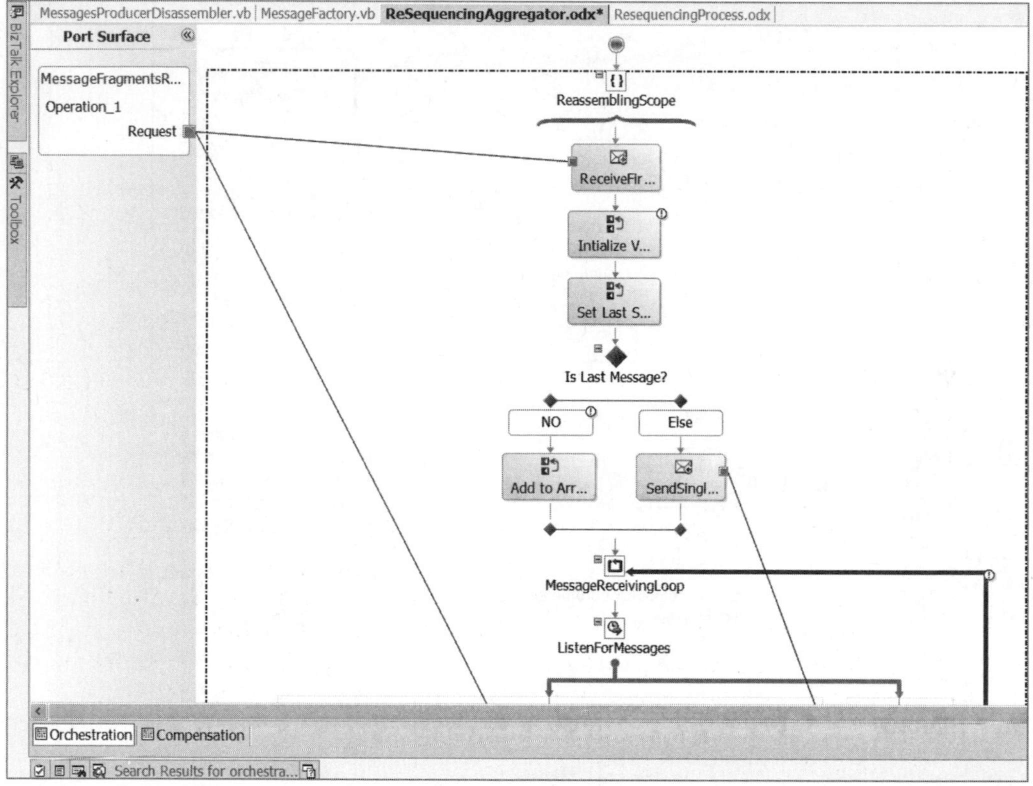

Figure 6-6. *Orchestration beginning*

The loop illustrated in Figure 6-7 is responsible for receiving incoming messages as they are processed. The second receive message is a follower of the original correlation set

11 As stated previously, this is not the optimal way to do this. Checking the property via XPath will cause the whole document to be loaded and parsed by the XLANG engine. A more elegant way to do this would be to change the inbound schema to have an IsLastMessage element and add a custom distinguished field as demonstrated in Chapter 4.

that was initialized by the first receive. From this point on, this is a typical Convoy pattern implementation.[12]

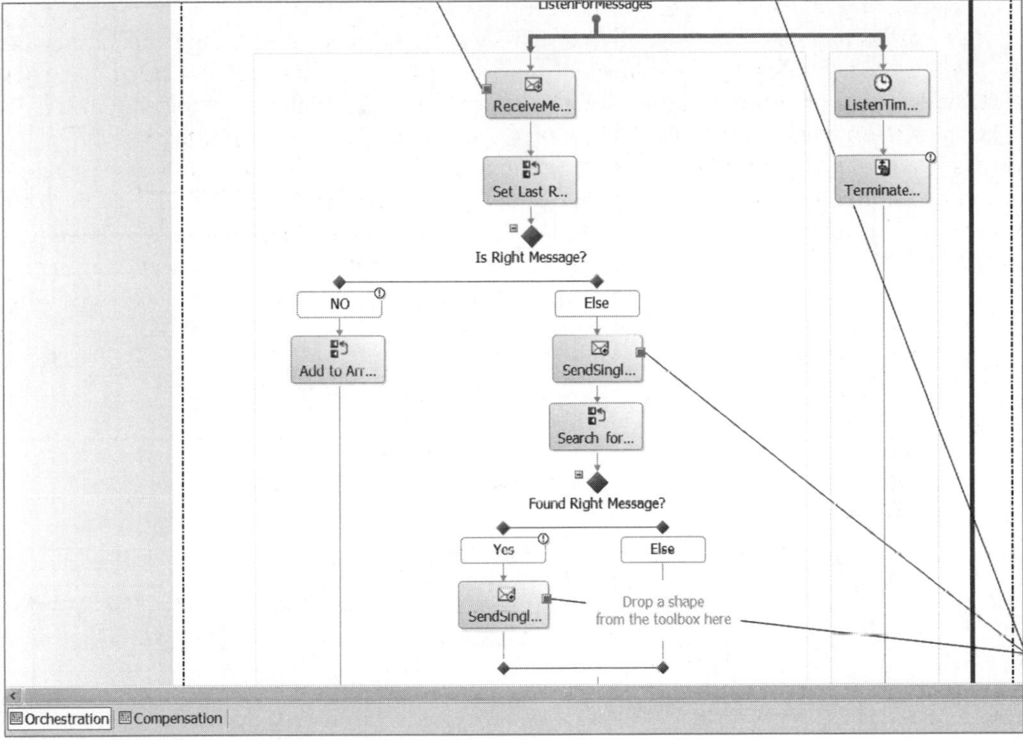

Figure 6-7. *The receiving loop*

What happens next is that when the next message is received, its `SequenceNumber` is checked against the internal variable for the next required `SequenceNumber`. The next required sequence number is simply the last in-order received sequence number incremented by 1. If the received message does not have the required `SequenceNumber`, it is added to the `SortedList` object. If it is, then it is immediately sent and the `SortedList` is checked for the next lowest received sequence number to see whether it should be set as well. This repeats until all messages that could be sent are.

The final step in the process once all the messages have been received and sent in the proper order is to perform cleanup (see Figure 6-8). In this pattern, the received messages were stored to disk in a temporary location as they were received. Cleanup is an optional step and isn't required. It is useful, however, when you want to see how many messages were received and verify that all messages have been sent out in cases where you are debugging. The last step in this orchestration is to delete those messages from the location once the resequencer has finished.

12 See http://msdn.microsoft.com/en-us/library/ms942189.aspx. The concept of a convoy is not new by any means in BizTalk 2006. Convoys are a simple messaging pattern that exist from the previous version of the product and are documented well in the referenced article.

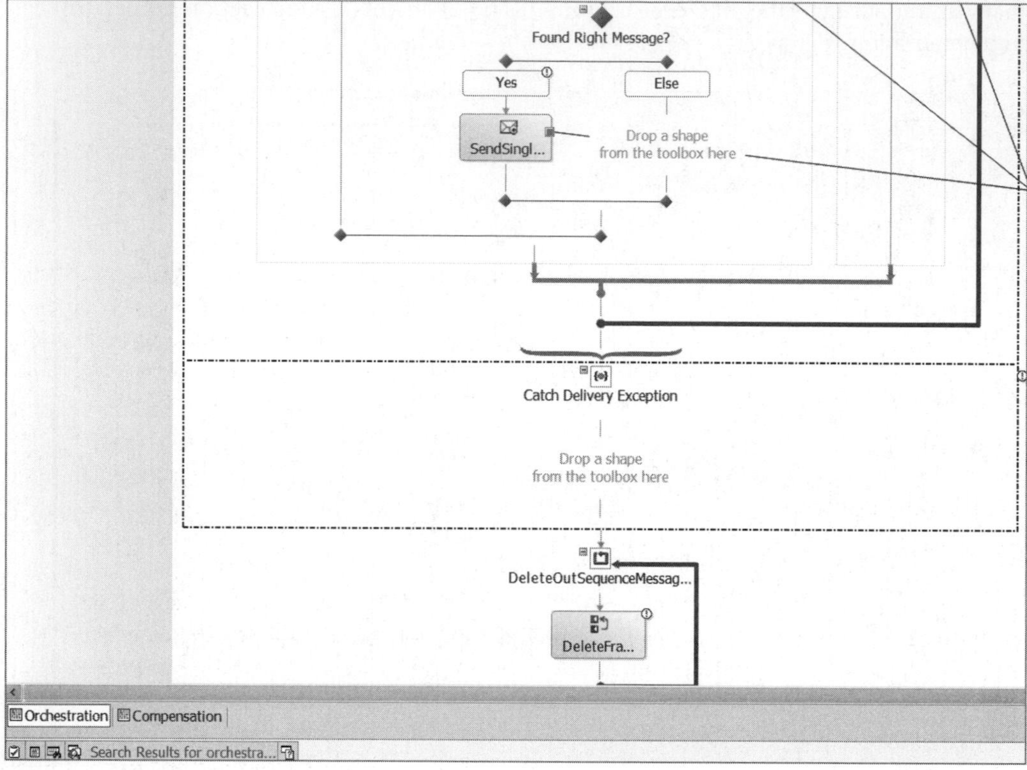

Figure 6-8. *Orchestration finish*

Also note the Catch block illustrated in Figure 6-8. In the described Resequencer pattern, there is no implementation for the scenario where a message in the sequence cannot be delivered. In most cases, the implementation would be a simple Terminate shape or a Throw Exception shape depending on the requirements. In some cases, it may be possible to recover from the scenario in which a message cannot be delivered. If this is the case, you could implement the offline message storage to disk and input a Suspend shape. Logic would be needed to restart the orchestration, remember what messages have already been received and sent, and resend the message that was in error.

Building a Resequencing Aggregator

So now that you know how to solve the problem of receiving messages out of order, you can properly receive messages, resequence them, and send them in the correct order to their destination. But what about batch scenarios—what happens in the case where you need to combine the received messages, order them, and then aggregate them into a batch? This need is quite common in the EDI world where batching has existed for years. Also, in many legacy system integration projects, large aggregated data files are needed to load downstream systems with data. For example, let's look at the company ABC example. Assume that orders received from the FTP bulk upload are compressed and need to be sent as a batch to the fulfillment system, which only understands flat text files. Luckily you have all the pieces you need to solve this except one. To recap, you can

1. Use the Unzip component from Chapter 5 to decompress the files.
2. Use the resequencing pipeline and pipeline component from the resequencing example to add the sequence information.
3. Use the resequencing orchestration to order them properly.

However, you still have no way to a) combine the messages into one message, and b) turn the sorted list of the messages received into a flat file. Luckily, with BizTalk 2009 this becomes a trivial task. There are, however, two possible solutions to this problem depending on how the messages are received. If the messages are not received as described, but are received as independent Interchanges, you need to use the Resequencer pattern described previously. If they are indeed received as a batch, a more elegant solution is available.

Solution 1: Status Quo—Messages Received as Independent Interchanges

If the messages are received independently, a simple change is required to the resequencing orchestration to allow the pattern to work. All you need to do is **not** send the messages as they arrive and wait to receive all messages before sending them. Once all the messages in the batch are received, you can use the new Call Pipeline from Orchestration code that ships with BizTalk 2009 to send the `SortedList` to a send pipeline that contains a flat-file Assembler component. So long as the messages are defined with a schema that uses the flat-file extensions of BizTalk, the pipeline will return a text message with all the messages inside aggregated in their proper order. The orchestration will look something like Figure 6-9.

The code for the Call Send Pipeline Expression shape will look like this:

```
//Initialize pipeline output
AggregatedOutMessage = null;
//Add the messages to the list via a component13
PipelineHelper.AddSortedMessages(SortedList, SendPipeMsg)
Microsoft.XLANGs.Pipeline.XLANGPipelineManager.ExecuteSendPipeline
(typeof(ABC.BizTalk.Pipelines.FlatFileSendPipeline),SendPipeMsg,
AggregatedOutMessage);
```

You will need to use a Construct shape, since the shape is creating new messages via the component. The `SendPipeMsg` is of type Microsoft.XLANGs.Pipeline.SendPipelineInput Messages. The reason why you need to add these messages to the `SendPipeMsg` via a component is because within the component you will need to loop through each of the messages stored in the sorted list, and add them one at a time to the `SendPipeMsg` to ensure that the order is properly maintained. Alternatively, you could use a Loop shape in the orchestration, but this is much easier done in code. Once this is done, the send pipeline is called, the messages are aggregated, and the complete message is sent to the send port.

---

13 This class is an example of what the API would look like. A Pipeline helper class would need to be created that simply assigns the SortedList object to the Array of Messages within the SendPipeMsg object.

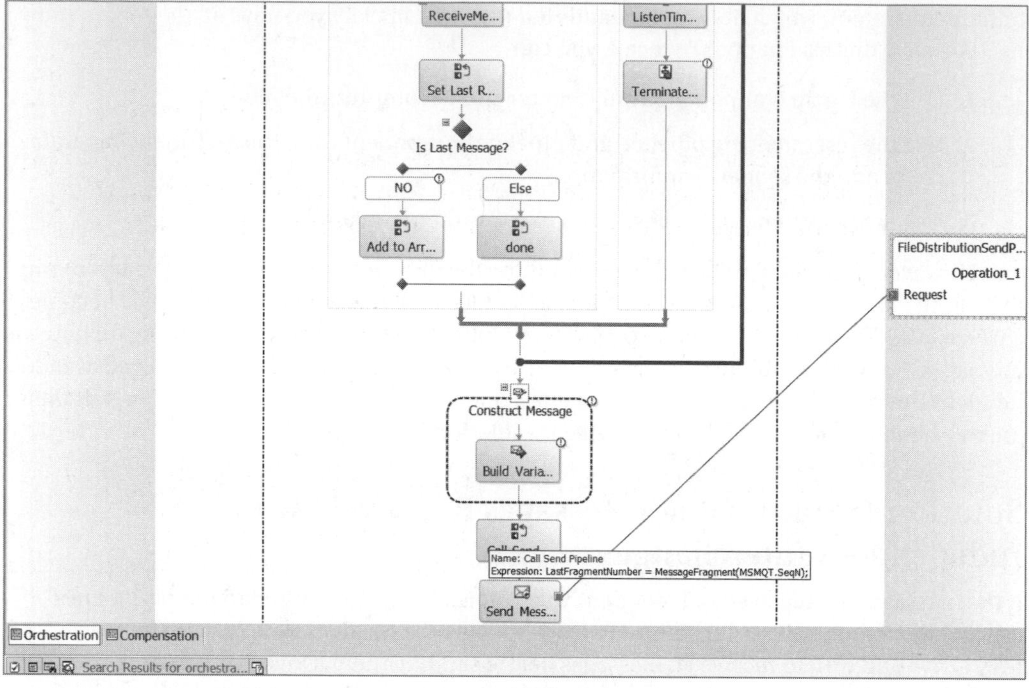

Figure 6-9. *Aggregating resequencing orchestration*

Solution 2: Not So Status Quo—Messages Received as a Batch

In the resequencing aggregator outlined earlier, the messages are received as a complete Interchange. They may be out of order when stored inside the ZIP file, but they are completely batched as a whole. In this case, you actually don't need a resequencing orchestration and can implement this solution entirely within a pipeline and use content-based routing.

Let's reexamine our list of pipeline components from previous examples:

- **Unzip component**: The Unzip component extracts the ZIP file contents and creates a multipart message based on the files included.
- **Resequencing Decoder**: The component examines a message and determines where it fits within a unique sequence.

What if you modified the Resequencing Decoder to handle multipart messages? In this scenario, the component would have additional smarts to know that multipart messages can also be resequenced. In this case, the component would simply loop through each of the message parts, examine its data, determine what number it is in the sequence, and promote that property along with the unique sequence ID and the last message in the sequence property. Also in this case, you need to use another message part feature—they have a property bag. So instead of promoting the values to the message context of the message, you simply write these values as key/value pairs to the parts property bag. Once all the message parts are resequenced properly, the message can flow through BizTalk like any other message. The send port hosting the FlatFileAssembling component would be subscribed for messages of this type, parse the incoming messages, and output one aggregated message, which is sent to the downstream system.

■ **Caution** While the preceding example is technically easier to implement, it has some drawbacks. First, as stated earlier, since pipeline execution is stateful, should the pipeline fail for whatever reason, processing stops. You will manually need to have some error-handling logic and subscribe to the failed message for processing. This is explored in the next section. Also, care should be taken to properly performance test the solution. If the ZIP file is large and contains a high number of individual transactions, the CPU on this machine could be affected. Make sure that you test this scenario properly before implementing it.

Editing and Resubmitting Suspended Messages

Subscribing to an event and pulling messages from BizTalk Server is a fairly straightforward task. A bigger problem is that now that you have the suspended message, how do you fix it and get it back to BizTalk? Ultimately the answer will depend on the roles involved, the technology that is used, and the business process necessary around handling the messages.

For the purpose of this implementation, the suspended messages that are addressed are inbound messages that fail validation. This can often happen when a message is sent into the integration solution that is malformed. Other errors may occur, but this is the most common scenario for resubmitting messages.

Strategy for Edit and Resubmit

Subscribing to the WMI event MSBTS_ServiceInstanceSuspendedEvent and calling the `SaveToFile` method allows access to the suspended message and its context.[14] If it has multiple message parts, each is saved to a separate file. The context file contains the message and message part information. This gives developers all the information they need to handle the message. Chapter 10 provides examples for allowing a user to save the files and get the file names. This implementation will use those concepts. After this point, there are a number of different decisions that you will need to make. The rest of this section briefly addresses a number of those decisions.

Pulling Data from the Suspended Queue

In pulling the data from the suspended queue, you could just pull the data itself and try to process the message, but then you are lacking any context for the origination of the message. Most likely this context will be necessary in order to route the message to the appropriate support personnel, resubmit the message, or take other steps with the message. To handle this problem, the same Windows service that you will create to capture the suspended event will create a new canonical format based off the message context and the message data.

14 These subsections and upcoming exercise originally appeared in "Edit and Resubmit from Suspend Queue" (REED000632).doc. Copyright by Microsoft Corporation. Reprinted with permission from Microsoft Corporation.

Canonical Format

One strategy this implementation is using is a canonical format for the suspended message, SuspendedMessage.xsd. This schema is provided later in this chapter. This contains a context section for the message that can contain any particular contextual information that needs to be passed along. For example, the receive port name may be included. The other part of the message contains the message parts themselves. In the walkthrough described later in Exercise 6-2, the data is stored in an element that is marked as a CDATA tag. CDATA sections are ignored by XML parsers and allow you to include any data you want in them, regardless of format.

Clients for Editing the Message

For editing a document, there are two obvious options. One is to use an ASP.NET page that will take the raw data file and display it in a text box. The other is to use InfoPath, which could consume the canonical XML document and display that in a form. InfoPath is a natural fit for this, except that the data you want to edit is one element in your XML document, but represents your entire message. If the message is a flat file, it could contain invalid XML characters. To get around this problem, you could place the data in a CDATA section. The challenge though is what control to use in InfoPath. There are restrictions on using a rich text-box control such as formatting issues with XML and HTML tags, which would otherwise be a great choice. A text box is possible with XML documents. Also in InfoPath SP1, you can specify the text box to show carriage returns.

Additional Workflow

In this implementation, orchestration is not used to control the flow of the SuspendedMessage XML file. If this example were expanded, it would be advantageous to use an orchestration. With an orchestration, the SuspendedMessage XML document could be sent into the orchestration, do some additional processing, call rules, and then route the document to the appropriate user or group of users who need to fix the message. Once the user fixes the message, it could be routed back to the orchestration, and the orchestration could do further processing. Also, by using an orchestration, you could later leverage BAM to be able to get additional insight into your suspended messages.

Moving Correct Data Back into BizTalk

Once data is corrected, it needs to get back into the Messagebox. One option is to add a web service receive location to the same receive port where the messages were originally sent. This will allow orchestration-bound ports and subscribers to a receive port to still receive the message. The disadvantage is an extra receive location is necessary for each receive port that needs to handle suspended messages.

Another option for moving data back into BizTalk is to have a generic orchestration do a direct binding and send the data directly to the Messagebox. As long as no routing is based on the receive port, you will still be OK. However, if the message is a non-XML file that must first be disassembled, you need to send it back through a receive location for pipeline processing.

Sample Flows for Edit and Resubmit

Figures 6-10 through 6-12 represent possible flows for editing and resubmission of messages to BizTalk Server. These are just possibilities that have their own pros and cons. Hopefully, this will give you some additional ideas on how to best handle suspended messages for your particular solution.

Figure 6-10 illustrates the easiest, although most manual, of the three flows.

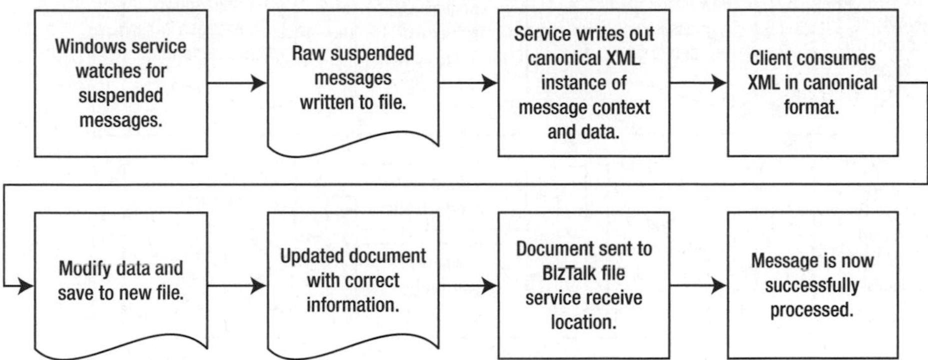

Figure 6-10. *Editing and resubmitting with file receive*

The flow in Figure 6-11 leverages an orchestration to route the message to Windows SharePoint Services. This strategy would allow the solution to be able to route messages to different groups and people based on their roles. The Business Rule Engine could be used to implement the routing logic. The Business Rule Engine could provide the URL and adapter information for message resubmission based upon a given message type. When resubmitting the document back to BizTalk, the client would send the message back to a web service that is specific for that particular message type. A solution could have the flow shown in Figure 6-11.

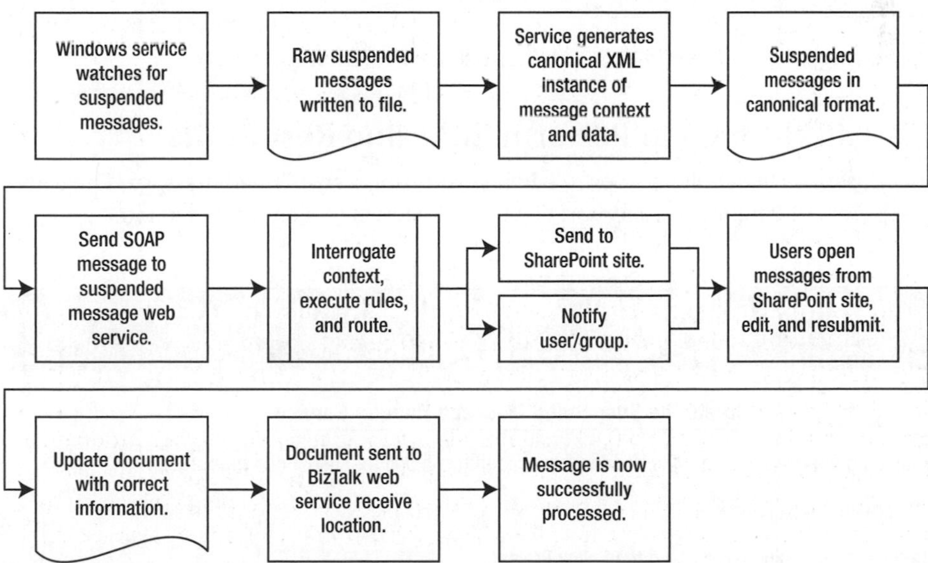

Figure 6-11. *Editing and resubmitting with routing and SharePoint*

Finally, the flow in Figure 6-12 builds off of that in Figure 6-11 and uses a long-running orchestration to keep track of the progress of the message. This allows further processing to be done if desired. The solution also submits directly back to the Messagebox, which may or may not be desired depending on whether the message requires processing in a receive pipeline.

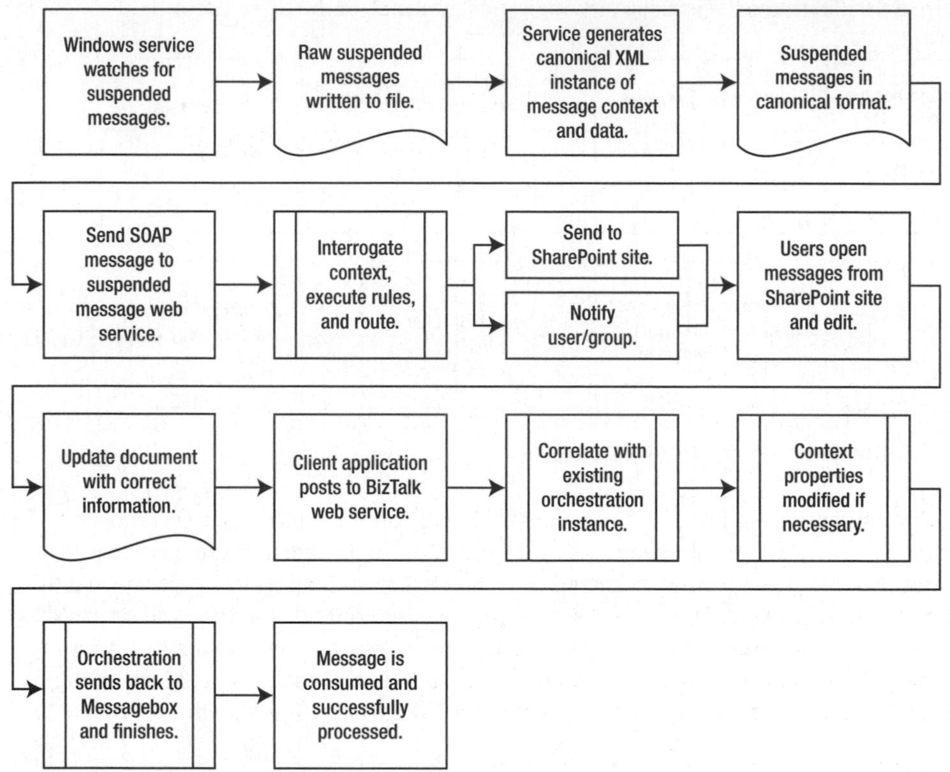

Figure 6-12. *Editing and resubmitting with orchestration correlation*

Pseudo-Walkthrough to Perform Edits and Resubmits

Exercise 6-2 describes in detail the steps to edit and resubmit a suspended message. The walk-through in Exercise 6-2 follows the steps in Figure 6-11, shown earlier in this section.

EXERCISE 6-2. CREATING A NEW WINDOWS SERVICE PROJECT AND APPLYING SETTINGS

Create the Suspended Message Handler Service

The following steps are used to create the Windows service that will poll for suspended messages:

1. Start Microsoft Visual Studio 2008.
2. On the File menu, point to New, and then click Project.

3. Click Visual Basic Projects under Project Types, and then click Windows Service under Templates.
4. Type BizTalkSuspendedMessageHandlerService in the Name text box. Change location if necessary. Click OK.
5. In the Code Editor window, right-click Design View, and then click Properties.
6. In the Properties pane, click the Add Installer link.
7. Change the display name to BizTalk Suspended Message Handler Service.
8. In the Properties pane for serviceInstaller1, change the ServiceName property to Service1.

Note The ServiceName property needs to match the name of the service class.

---

9. Change StartType to Automatic.
10. In the Code Editor window in Design view, click serviceProcessInstaller1.

    Note that the account is set to User. When the service is installed, it will need to be set to an account that has access to the BizTalk resources.

Add a Configuration File

1. Right-click the project and choose Add New Item.
2. Double-click Application Configuration File in the right-hand pane.
3. Between the configuration tags paste the following XML:

```
<appSettings>
    <add key="SuspendedMessagesTempFileLocation" value="MyDrive:\MyFolder" />
    <add key="SuspendedMessagesFileLocation" value="MyDrive:\MyFolder" />
    <add key="ProcessingInstruction" value="MyInfoPathProcessingInstruction"/>
</appSettings>
```

4. Replace `"MyDrive:\MyFolder"` with appropriate paths. SuspendedMessagesTempFileLocation is the location where the message parts and context will get saved. SuspendedMessagesFileLocation is the location for the `SuspendedMessage` instance.
5. Replace processing instructions if desired within the XML file to point to the proper InfoPath form you want to open. An example of one is

```
solutionVersion='1.0.0.1' productVersion='11.0.5531' PIVersion='1.0.0.0'
href='file:///C:\My%20Documents\EditAndResubmit\InfoPathForms\
SuspendedMessage.xsn' language='en-us'
```

Add References and Class Variables

1. Add a reference within the project to System.Management.dll and System.Configuration.dll.
2. In Solution Explorer, right-click Service1.vb, and then click View Code.

3. At the top of the page add the following `Imports` statements:

```
Imports System.Management
Imports System.Xml
Imports System.IOt
Imports System.Configuration
```

4. Within the class declaration, just under

```
private components as System.ComponentModel.Container = nothing
```

add the following:

```
private watcher as ManagementEventWatcher
```

Add Code to OnStart

1. In Solution Explorer, right-click Service1.cs, and then click View Code.
2. In the `OnStart` event handler, replace the comments with the following:

```
'Listen for messages
Dim scope as string = "root\\MicrosoftBizTalkServer"
Dim wqlQuery  as string = "Select * from MSBTS_ServiceInstanceSuspendedEvent"
watcher = new ManagementEventWatcher(scope, wqlQuery)
AddHandler watcher.EventArrived, AddressOf MyEventHandler watcher.Start
```

This will start listening for the `ServiceInstanceSuspended` event.

Add Custom Event Handler

1. Add the following two procedures to the `Service 1` class:

```
Public Shared Sub MyEventHandler(sender As Object, e As EventArrivedEventArgs)
   Try
       ' Read the TempDirectoryName from config file
       Dim TempDirectoryName As String = _
ConfigurationManager.AppSettings("SuspendedMessagesTempFileLocation")
       ' Read WaitingDirectoryName
       ' This folder is the location for the new XML document that this service
       ' creates based on context and message parts.
       Dim WaitingDirectoryName As String = _
ConfigurationSettings.AppSettings("SuspendedMessagesFileLocation")
       ' If you want to add processing instructions for InfoPath
       ' this will get it.
       Dim pi As String = _
ConfigurationSettings.AppSettings("ProcessingInstruction")

       Dim waitingMessageFileName As String
       ' xwriter for suspended message
       Dim xwriter As XmlTextWriter
```

```
      'Look up MSBTS_ServiceInstanceSuspendedEvent
      'in the BTS04/06 documentation for additional properties
      Dim ErrorID As String = e.NewEvent("ErrorID").ToString()
      Dim ErrorCategory As String = e.NewEvent("ErrorCategory").ToString()
      Dim ErrorDescription As String = e.NewEvent("ErrorDescription").ToString()
      Dim ServiceStatus As String = e.NewEvent("ServiceStatus").ToString()
      Dim ServiceInstanceID As String = e.NewEvent("InstanceID").ToString()
      Dim enumOptions As New EnumerationOptions()

      enumOptions.ReturnImmediately = False

      Dim MessageInstancesInServiceInstance As New _
ManagementObjectSearcher("root\MicrosoftBizTalkServer", _
"Select * from MSBTS_MessageInstance where ServiceInstanceID='" + _
ServiceInstanceID + "'", enumOptions)
      'Enumerate through the result set
      Dim MessageInstance As ManagementObject
      For Each MessageInstance In  MessageInstancesInServiceInstance.Get()
         ' The only way to get at the message body is to utilize the ➥
 SaveToFile
         ' method on the BTS_MessageInstance WMI Class.
         ' This saves all of the message information to files.
         ' Each MessagePart making up a message is saved in separate files,
         ' typically you only get a Body, but you must cater to multipart
         ' messages to cover all scenarios.
         ' As well as the MessageParts, a context file is created; you need to
         ' use this to extract the MessagePartIDs and MessagePartNames so you
         ' can then work out the file names to open!
         ' The context file name format is
         ' <MessageInstanceID>_context.xml.
         ' And then the actual message information file name format is
         ' <MessageInstanceID>_<MessagePartID>[_<MessagePartName>].out
         ' MessagePartName is only required if the MessagePart has a name!
         ' You need to build this file name up so you can load it up -
         ' no hacking here!
         ' Save the files
         MessageInstance.InvokeMethod("SaveToFile", New Object() _
{TempDirectoryName})

         ' Get the MessageInstanceID
         Dim MessageInstanceID As String = _
 MessageInstance("MessageInstanceID").ToString()

         ' You now need to load the context file up to get the MessagePart
         ' information
         Dim ContextFileName As String
```

```
        ' Load the context file up
        Dim doc As New XmlDocument()
        doc.Load(ContextFileName)

        ' Pull out context properties that you are interested in
        Dim ReceivedFileName As String = GetContextProperty(doc, _
 "ReceivedFileName")
        Dim InboundTransportLocation As String = GetContextProperty(doc, _
 "InboundTransportLocation")
        Dim InterchangeID As String = GetContextProperty(doc, _
"InterchangeID")
        Dim ReceivePortID As String = GetContextProperty(doc, _
"ReceivePortID")
        Dim ReceivePortName As String = GetContextProperty(doc, _
 "ReceivePortName")

        ' Create an XmlWriter to store the data.
        ' This will get written to a file when complete.
        waitingMessageFileName = [String].Format("")
        xwriter = New XmlTextWriter(waitingMessageFileName, _
 System.Text.Encoding.UTF8)
                xwriter.Formatting = Formatting.Indented
        xwriter.WriteStartDocument()
        'Write the ProcessingInstruction node.
        xwriter.WriteProcessingInstruction("mso-infoPathSolution", pi)
        xwriter.WriteProcessingInstruction("mso-application", _
"progid=""InfoPath.Document""")
        xwriter.WriteComment(String.Format("Created on {0}", _
DateTime.Now.ToString()))
        ' Write the context information
        xwriter.WriteStartElement("ns0", "SuspendedMessage", _
 "http://Microsoft.BizTalk.SuspendQueue.SuspendedMessage")
        xwriter.WriteStartElement("Context")
        xwriter.WriteElementString("ReceivedFileName", ReceivedFileName)
        xwriter.WriteElementString("InboundTransportLocation", _
 InboundTransportLocation)
        xwriter.WriteElementString("InterchangeID", InterchangeID)
        xwriter.WriteElementString("ReceivePortID", ReceivePortID)
        xwriter.WriteElementString("ReceivePortName", ReceivePortName)
        xwriter.WriteEndElement() ' Context
        ' Start the Message Element
        xwriter.WriteStartElement("Message")
```

```
        ' Use XPath to return all of the MessagePart(s) referenced in the
        ' context
        ' You can then load the file up to get the message information
        Dim MessageParts As XmlNodeList = _
doc.SelectNodes("/MessageInfo/PartInfo/MessagePart")
        Dim MessagePart As XmlNode
        For Each MessagePart In  MessageParts
           ' Pull the MessagePart info out that you need
           Dim MessagePartID As String = MessagePart.Attributes("ID").Value
           Dim MessagePartName As String = ➥
 MessagePart.Attributes("Name").Value
           Dim Contents As String
           Dim FileName As String
           ' If you have a MessagePartName, append this to the end of
           ' the file name. It's optional so if you don't have it, don't
           ' worry about it.
           If MessagePartName.Length > 0 Then
              FileName = [String].Format("")
            End If

           ' Load the message, place it in canonical schema, and submit it.
           ' Create an instance of StreamReader to read from a file.
           ' The using statement also closes the StreamReader.
           Dim sr As New StreamReader(FileName)
           Try
              ' Read to end of file
              Contents = sr.ReadToEnd()
           Finally
              sr.Dispose()
           End Try

           ' Write out MessagePart data
           xwriter.WriteStartElement("MessagePart")
           xwriter.WriteElementString("MessagePartId", MessagePartID)
           xwriter.WriteElementString("Name", MessagePartName)
           xwriter.WriteStartElement("Contents")
           ' Write out contents as CDATA.
           xwriter.WriteCData(Contents)
           xwriter.WriteEndElement() ' Contents
           xwriter.WriteEndElement() ' MessagePart
        Next MessagePart
        xwriter.WriteEndElement() ' Message
        xwriter.WriteEndElement() ' SuspendedMessage
        xwriter.Close()
     Next MessageInstance
  End Try
End Sub 'MyEventHandler
```

```
' Helper function to pull out context properties given a property name
Private Shared Function GetContextProperty(doc As XmlDocument, propertyName ➥
 As _
String) As String
   Dim MessageContext As XmlNode = _
doc.SelectSingleNode(("/MessageInfo/ContextInfo/Property[@Name='" + _
propertyName"']"))
   If Not (MessageContext Is Nothing) Then
      If Not (MessageContext.Attributes("Value") Is Nothing) Then
         Return MessageContext.Attributes("Value").Value
      Else
         Return "Value no found"
      End If
   Else
      Return "Property not found"
   End If
End Function 'GetContextProperty
```

Compile Project and Install Windows Service

1. Under the Build menu, select Build Solution.
2. Open a command prompt and change to the project root directory of this project.
3. From the command line type the following:

   "<Drive>:\WINDOWS\Microsoft.NET\Framework\ v2.0.50727\installutil.exe" "bin\Debug\ BizTalkSuspendedMessageHandlerService.exe"

   "<Drive>" is the drive letter where Windows is installed. This will install the EXE as a Windows service.
4. A prompt will come up asking you for credentials. Enter credentials that have access to the BizTalk resources. After entering credentials, a message should be returned indicating success and that the install was completed.
5. From Administrative Tools, open Services.
6. Find the new service, Service1. Right-click and select Start. The service will now start, and the system will write out suspended messages from both the SaveToFile procedure and the canonical SuspendedMessage message that the service creates itself.

Create Client to Edit XML in Canonical Format

The Windows service that you've created generates a new XML document according to the following XSD:

```
<?xml version="1.0" encoding="utf-16"?>
<xs:schema xmlns="http://Microsoft.BizTalk.SuspendQueue.SuspendedMessage"
 xmlns:b=http://schemas.microsoft.com/BizTalk/2003
 targetNamespace=http://Microsoft.BizTalk.SuspendQueue.SuspendedMessage
 xmlns:xs="http://www.w3.org/2001/XMLSchema">
```

```
  <xs:element name="SuspendedMessage">
    <xs:complexType>
      <xs:sequence>
        <xs:element name="Context">
          <xs:complexType>
            <xs:sequence>
              <xs:element name="ReceivedFileName" type="xs:string" />
              <xs:element name="InboundTransportLocation" type="xs:string" />
              <xs:element name="InterchangeID" type="xs:string" />
              <xs:element name="ReceivePortID" type="xs:string" />
              <xs:element name="ReceivePortName" type="xs:string" />
            </xs:sequence>
          </xs:complexType>
        </xs:element>
        <xs:element name="Message">
          <xs:complexType>
            <xs:sequence>
              <xs:element minOccurs="1" maxOccurs="unbounded"
 name="MessagePart">
                <xs:complexType>
                  <xs:sequence>
                    <xs:element name="MessagePartId" type="xs:string" />
                    <xs:element name="Name" type="xs:string" />
                    <xs:element name="Contents" type="xs:string" />
                  </xs:sequence>
                </xs:complexType>
              </xs:element>
            </xs:sequence>
          </xs:complexType>
        </xs:element>
      </xs:sequence>
    </xs:complexType>
  </xs:element>
</xs:schema>
```

In order to consume the XML document generated in accordance with this schema, you need to load the document into some type of editor and modify the contents of the original message contained in the `<Contents>` element. One option for this is InfoPath. Specifically InfoPath 2007 may be more useful because it has a Paragraph Breaks option for text boxes that allows for easier viewing of data. You may also experience problems when trying to perform changes on flat files, since most flat files use CR and LF. Flat files will need to be tested to see whether they work with this scenario.

If you are going to use InfoPath, you can easily create a new form based on the preceding schema, modify the app.config file of the Windows service to point to the processing instruction for the InfoPath form, and then be able to open the SuspendedMessage XML files that get generated. Once modified, you can just save the app.config file.

Send Document to BizTalk File Service Receive Location

The data within the <Contents> element represents the actual data for each suspended message part. Once this data has been repaired, there are two easy options for resubmitting the file:

- Copy and paste the value within the <Contents> element into a new file within Notepad. Place this new file within the receive location drop directory to be processed by BizTalk.
- Create a simple submit button on your InfoPath form that reads the <Contents> element and submits the file to BizTalk based upon the `ReceivedFileName` and `InboundTransportLocation` context property values.

Managing Exceptions in Orchestrations

Designing consistent reusable patterns for exception management within any development project is a fundamental necessity to ensure maintainability and supportability of the application once it's deployed. BizTalk development introduces somewhat new challenges due to the distributed nature of the BizTalk infrastructure. For example, a typical BizTalk application may leverage the BizTalk messaging features, then optionally start an orchestration for processing, call the Business Rule Engine, interact with several lines of business LOB (Line of Business) or ERP systems, and return a response back to another third-party system. This is the typical scenario shown in the previous fictitious examples in the previous chapters. In addition, the execution runtime of these components, including the BizTalk subsystems, may be distributed across one or more servers within the current environment.

The use case just described is not atypical, and would entail catching and reporting on exceptions possibly generated by several decoupled subsystems within BizTalk as well as numerous third-party LOB systems with their own exception-handling constraints. Building on the previous scenario of the fictitious company ABC, what if the mainframe rejected errors while accepting orders from the web site? How does the web site compensate for this, and how should the user be notified? The developer is faced with several exception-reporting options in a BizTalk environment:

- BizTalk Management Console
- BizTalk Administration Console
- Microsoft Event Log
- Custom development options

Given the complexity, the development of a consistent solution for application exception management should embody several common design goals:

- Standardize how application exceptions are detected and caught in the BizTalk environment, i.e., messaging and orchestration subsystems.
- Provide common patterns that allow automated processes to react and manage application exceptions.
- Provide a loosely coupled exception management pattern that facilitates reuse.
- Develop a common reporting paradigm of application exceptions and their available message state that applies to any BizTalk subsystem.

The BizTalk product team considered some of these points during the development of BizTalk Server 2009. For example, BizTalk Server 2006 has the **Failed Message Routing** feature. This essentially allowed users to create orchestration processes or messaging send ports that could be configured to "subscribe" to any exceptions that occurred at the messaging subsystem level.

Consider the following scenario:

A user submits financial records to BizTalk. During the parsing and validation stage, an exception is thrown.

Using BizTalk Server 2004, the message would be moved to a suspended queue where limited options were available. For instance, an operator would first have to independently detect that an exception did in fact occur. Then, the message would have to be manually saved to disk from the HAT user interface. Next, the message would have to be manually corrected and resubmitted to the system.

In BizTalk Server 2009, an operator can simply create either an orchestration or a messaging send port that subscribes to any failed message, thereby solving the issue of automated error detection and routing the original message state for processing. Unfortunately, there was no time to build a similar feature for orchestrations. This leaves you today with two very different ways in which exceptions are processed and managed within a BizTalk system. It's up to the developer to customize the exception handling as necessary.

Failed Message Routing was not the only new feature that shipped with BizTalk Server 2006. A new BizTalk Administration Console provides a set of Group Hub pages that allows the query of suspended instances and exceptions grouped by either application, service name, error code, or URI, as shown in Figure 6-13. Although this provides a common user interface to view exceptions, its views are limited to "live" service instances, and examining state can be a bit cumbersome due to the drill-down required.

Several other factors also limit the BizTalk Administration Console in its application exception reporting role:

- There is no way to mine the data for business intelligence. For instance, how does someone query to see what the worst offending applications are on a monthly basis or examine quarterly trends of application exceptions?
- The business may want to be alerted when certain application exceptions occur or when specific thresholds are reached. How does someone subscribe to such exception events? The MMC as a reporting tool is not the ideal interface, since it's not very convenient to access in production environments. You need at minimum to be in the BizTalk Operator's role, and, in production environments, access to the MMC is usually limited to a terminal server client interface, reducing the audience significantly.
- Only unhandled exceptions, i.e., suspended service instances, are displayed in the Administration Console. If the developer handles the exception within the orchestration, exiting the service, the exception information will never be displayed in the Administration Console.

An obvious suggestion would be to build a custom web portal interface to replace the MMC. However, because of the way data is stored, exposed, and accessed by the BizTalk Administration Console, this is a nearly impossible task. Any unified reporting system would really need to feed off the several sources, including the Microsoft Event Log and WMI events.

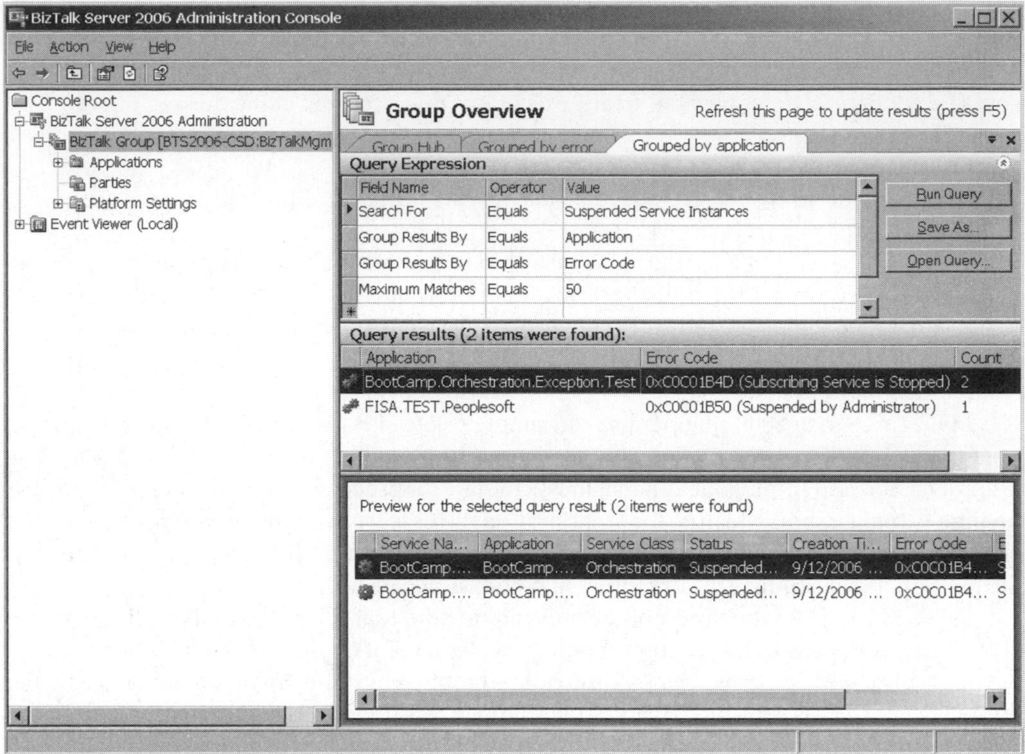

Figure 6-13. *BizTalk Server 2009 Administration Console Group Hub query page showing all suspended services grouped by application*

With BizTalk, you're working in a message-oriented paradigm. Everything in a BizTalk solution is message oriented, and developers think in a message-oriented mindset. Wouldn't it seem natural that exception handling also be done in a message-oriented manner?

Fortunately, BizTalk Server 2006 provides you with a sophisticated infrastructure and object model that will allow you to build a simple API that should address your common goals for application exception management in a message-oriented fashion, for both the BizTalk messaging and orchestration subsystems. The API you build can then be used to take advantage of other features within BizTalk, such as the subscription model and event-based Business Activity Monitoring. Coupled with Windows SharePoint Services, you should be able to provide a fairly robust reporting portal for all application exceptions that occur within BizTalk.

The remainder of this chapter we'll dedicate to examining how current challenges are addressed today, but more importantly we'll drill into building the API that can address these issues for you tomorrow.

The Exception Management Challenge

In BizTalk Server 2004, there was no built-in mechanism to make this an easy accomplishment for the developer. For instance, if an error occurred in the BizTalk messaging subsystem, the message would simply be written to BizTalk's suspended queue. If the developer needed to view, repair, or resubmit the message, it entailed some rather elaborate custom development work. In addition, developers would have to write their own solution, subscribing to WMI events, to detect that the suspension of the message actually took place. The end product would look almost exactly like the example shown previously in this chapter in the "Editing and Resubmitting Suspended Messages" section.

This forced some developers to design their applications not with business considerations in mind, but rather with exception management in mind. For instance, because there was no way to trap the exception that a BizTalk map could generate in the messaging subsystem, many developers opted to put maps in the orchestration, rather than in the receive and send ports where they logically should have been placed. They did so simply because BizTalk offered a graphical mechanism for catching and reacting to application exceptions within an orchestration. Some developers even took this a step further: incorporating more code within the orchestration, code that logically should be placed within a custom pipeline component, for no better reason than to have the ability to catch the exception and react to it.

When using an orchestration, developers could graphically define a Scope shape with one or more exception handlers, similar to the `Try...Catch...Finally` functionality you would incorporate writing any pure .NET application. This gave the developer a way to catch the exceptions, but custom code would still have to be written within the Exception Handler shape to process the exception. By default, just as with a .NET application, BizTalk doesn't do anything with the .NET exception it catches. An example of this is shown in Figure 6-14. It's up to the developer to do something, i.e., write to `Debug.Trace`, incorporate custom logging, write to the Microsoft Event Log.

We've seen some fairly well-thought-out and elaborate exception handling implemented in BizTalk, but usually just at the orchestration level. For example, it wasn't uncommon to see the Exception Management Application Block (posted on the Microsoft Patterns and Practices web site)[15] used as a common way to control exception reporting. Using it was a little challenging, though due to the overhead and configuration files, it was necessary. Other times we've seen custom exception reporting to a database.

However, none of the exception management options we've just described provides a unified pattern for managing and reporting application exceptions in a BizTalk environment that includes both orchestration and messaging subsystems. And neither addresses the issue of managing the state involved in a misbehaving process.

15 See www.microsoft.com/downloads/details.aspx?displaylang=en&FamilyID=8CA8EB6E-6F4A-43DFADEB-8F22CA173E02.

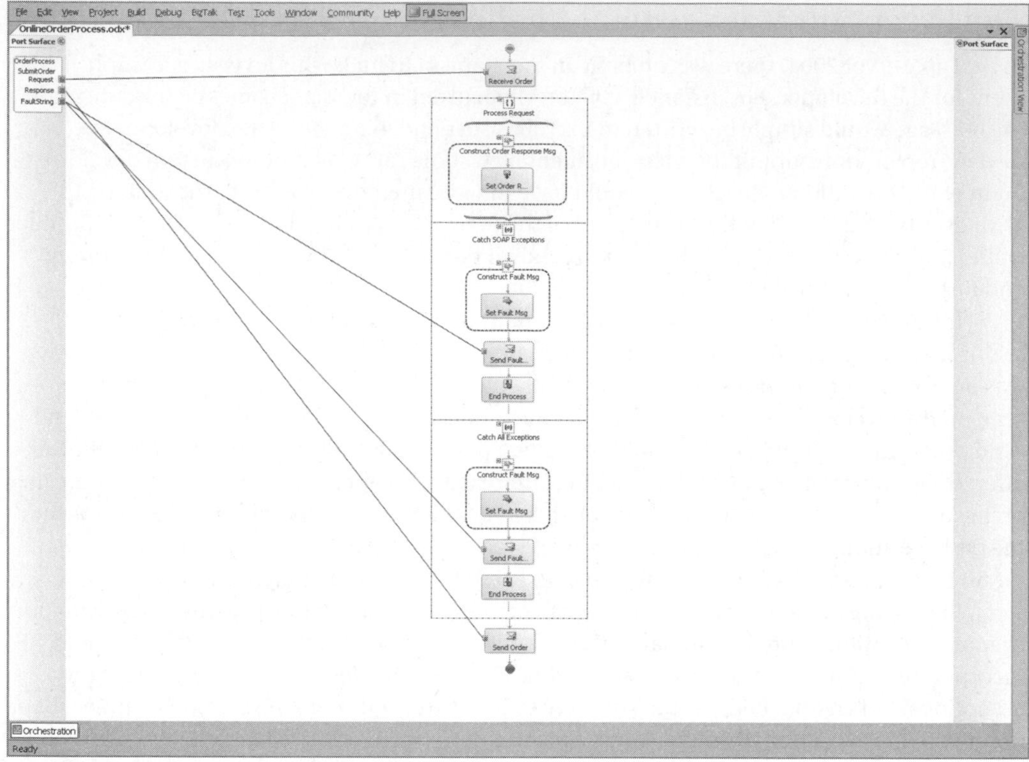

Figure 6-14. *BizTalk Server 2009 Orchestration Designer demonstrating the inclusion of multiple exception handlers*

Managing state, or to be clearer, making the state available as part of the exception management process, is fairly important when you consider scenarios that require the current message state when handling the exception. A common scenario that would require message state availability as well as a robust exception management process would be the following:

A user submits an invoice to the system. During the course of processing the invoice within an orchestration, the Business Rule Engine throws an application exception because a piece of the data is incorrect. The business process should catch the exception and send the offending message to another person or system. That person or system can correct and resubmit the message for processing.

Using existing exception management techniques, the exception management logic could be maintained in the current Exception Handler shape on the existing orchestration. Alternatively, you could tightly couple the current orchestration to a secondary orchestration and pass the message over to it for processing.

The downside to the former approach is that handling more elaborate exception use cases is done within the current Orchestration Exception Handler shapes. This means an orchestration starts to grow in complexity due to exception correction logic being embedded in it. What happens if you have five, ten, or even more Exception Handler shapes that need corrective action or management? This slowly becomes difficult to manage as it limits the development of all exception logic to a single developer (due to the single orchestration handling the exception logic).

The latter approach would move the logic out of the exception handlers and into secondary orchestrations by using either the Start Orchestration or Call Orchestration shapes. This would allow additional developers to work with the exception logic but would maintain a fairly tightly coupled process.

Now consider the following scenario where message state is part of the exception reporting process:

There are several BizTalk applications deployed in the environment. Some are generating application exceptions at the messaging subsystem level, while others are generating application exceptions at the orchestration level. The internal IT Operations department needs to be able view a central portal for all exception messages, their state, and application exception trends by fiscal quarter across applications.

Today, there is no BizTalk feature that provides this functionality, since there is no standard and consistent way of reporting and logging all exceptions generated in a BizTalk environment. The ESB Toolkit will provide this functionality when it is released. For more information on the ESBT, please see Chapter 16.

Clearly, you would want to accomplish several things by developing a unified pattern and API for business exception handling. The goals of this approach would be

- Develop loosely coupled asynchronous orchestration processes that have the ability to subscribe to specific business exceptions generated by either the messaging subsystem or an orchestration.
- Enable identification of common exceptions generated from either orchestration- or messaging-based applications.
- Allow the development of common business exception orchestration handlers that function across multiple orchestration applications.
- Provide the ability to create these business exception orchestration handlers independent of the currently deployed orchestration-based applications.
- Provide a web-based portal that displays application and business exception trends using optional BAM observations models as well as exception messages and application state driven from both orchestration- and messaging-based applications.

BizTalk Server 2009 Failed Message Routing As a Blueprint

In BizTalk 2009, the BizTalk product team tried to alleviate some of the issues that occurred when application exceptions were generated in the messaging subsystem. As mentioned earlier, the team introduced a new feature called Failed Message Routing. For example, if the Enable routing on failed messages check box option was enabled on either the BizTalk send or receive port and a pipeline or routing failure occurred, then the BizTalk EPM would do the following instead of suspending the message:

1. Create a cloned message and de-promote all the promoted properties.
2. Put an error description on the message context (e.g., "The Assembler component cannot load the schema named mySchema.xsd.").
3. Promote the failure-specific properties (e.g., `ReceivePortName == "MyReceivePort"`, `MessageType == "msgtype#mynamespace"`, `FailureCode == "0x1824"`, etc.).

4. Try to publish this message.
5. Discard the original message if publishing succeeds.
6. Suspend the original message and generate NACK as usual if publishing fails because there is no subscription.

If you examine this feature closely, you can see that it touches upon several of the common goals that were previously defined. A similar feature, if created for use in an orchestration, would provide a standard way to trap and report all exceptions in a BizTalk environment.

For instance, consider the following scenario:

A user submits an invoice to the system. During the course of processing the invoice within an orchestration, the Business Rule Engine throws an application exception because some piece of the data is incorrect. The business process should catch the exception, send the offending message to another person or system that can correct the message, and resubmit the message for processing.

If a similar Failed Message Routing feature existed for orchestrations, perhaps it would work something like this:

1. The user creates a Fault message in the exception handler.
2. The system puts an error description on the Fault message context (e.g., "The Business Rule Engine threw a divide/zero error processing the LoanProcessing policy.").
3. The system promotes failure- and application-specific properties such as
   - `Application` (supplied by the developer)
   - `Description` (auto-populated—exception message)
   - `ErrorType` (auto-populated—exception type)
   - `FailureCategory` (supplied by the developer)
   - `FailureCode` (supplied by the developer)
   - `FailureSeverity` (supplied by the developer)
   - `FailureDescription` (supplied by the developer)
   - `Scope` (auto-populated—Scope shape of current exception handler)
   - `ServiceName` (auto-populated—orchestration name)
   - `ServiceInstanceID` (auto-populated—orchestration instance ID [GUID])
4. The system serializes the current `Exception` object into the Fault message.
5. The user optionally adds current orchestration messages to the Fault message, which are serialized and persisted (including their message context properties), for example, `AddMessage(FaultMsg, SomeMessage)`.
6. The user publishes the Fault message.
7. If publishing succeeds, orchestration or send port subscriptions can be deployed to process the Fault, rehydrating the `Exception` object as well as any added messages and message context properties.
8. If publishing succeeds, a global exception handler (send port) publishes the Fault message to a web portal.

Given this description of a proposed Failed Message Routing feature for an orchestration, we'll walk you through how you can provide a simple solution for the scenario we just described.

This approach would look something like the following:

1. A developer is assigned responsibility for the recently deployed Financial Reporting BizTalk application.

2. A new exception message arrives in the SharePoint-based exception management portal indicating a data integrity issue with an orchestration in the Financial Reporting BizTalk application.

3. The developer is notified of the new exception either through his subscription to the SharePoint application list or because the exception exceeded a threshold predefined in BAM.

4. The developer navigates to the SharePoint-based exception management portal and examines the Fault message posted as well as the individual orchestration messages and their context properties that were persisted.

5. The developer determines that this will be a common error that will require manual intervention and correction by the Finance team and resubmission to the system.

6. The developer creates and deploys an independent BizTalk orchestration project that subscribes to the specific exception and application information.

7. The project is designed to retrieve the invalid message from the Fault message, send the message to the Finance team for correction, and correlate the corrected message back to the orchestration and resubmit.

8. A week later, the developer navigates to the SharePoint-based exception management portal to view that the application exception trends for invalid messages have decreased dramatically since the deployment of his solution.

A close examination reveals obvious similarities between this proposed orchestration functionality and the existing Failed Message Routing feature of BizTalk Server 2009. In fact, if you were somehow able to incorporate this feature, you would address the four design goals we discussed earlier in the section, which we list again here for your convenience:

- Standardize how application exceptions are detected and caught in the BizTalk environment, i.e., messaging and orchestration subsystems.
- Provide common patterns that allow automated processes to react and manage application exceptions.
- Provide a loosely coupled exception management pattern that facilitates reuse.
- Develop a common reporting paradigm of application exceptions and their available message state that applies to any BizTalk subsystem.

Additionally, you could use the same mechanism that would feed the exception metrics and portal of your proposed solution to process all failed messages from the messaging subsystem (provided Failed Message Routing is enabled). So given the solution, we'll walk you through what it takes to develop it.

Failed Orchestration Routing API for BizTalk 2009

We'll show you what the Failed Orchestration Routing API looks like when used to catch an exception within an orchestration. First, you need to design a simple orchestration that receives a message, does some processing, and then simulates the generation of an exception within a Scope shape. Figure 6-15 depicts a simple orchestration named EAIProcess. Within this orchestration, you have two messages available, one you receive that is named ApprovedRequest, the other, DeniedRequest, that is created via a map. Following the creation of the second message, you generate an exception by dividing by zero by using the UnitPrice value located in the incoming message. This orchestration would be like the one shown in Figure 6-15.

The orchestration in Figure 6-15 receives the ApprovedRequest message and executes a map to create the DeniedRequest message. It then generates an exception by dividing by zero. The EAIProcess sample resides with three projects within the Msft.Samples.BizTalk.Exception-Management solution. These are listed in Table 6-1.

Table 6-1. *List of Projects Within Exception Management Solution*

Project Name	Description
BootCamp.Orchestration.Exception.Process	Contains the EAIProcess orchestration schedule and references the BootCamp.Orchestration.Exception.Schemas and Msft.Samples.BizTalk.Exception.Schemas projects as well as the Msft.Samples.BizTalk.Exception.dll assembly.
BootCamp.Orchestration.Exception.Schemas	Contains the schemas and maps used by the EAIProcess orchestration.
BootCamp.Orchestration.Exception.FaultHandler	Contains two orchestrations (EAIGenericHandler, EAIProcessHandler) that demonstrate strongly typed and typeless options of using the Failed Orchestration Routing API. References the BootCamp.Orchestration.Exception.Schemas and Msft.Samples.BizTalk.Exception.Schemas project as well as the Msft.Samples.BizTalk.Exception.dll assembly.

Add an exception handler to the Execution Scope shape and configure it to capture all `System.Exceptions`. Once the exception is generated, control will jump to the exception handler.

Within the exception handler, you need to follow a fairly simple methodology:

1. Create a Fault message.
2. Add the ApprovedRequest message to the Fault message.
3. Add the DeniedRequest message to the Fault message.
4. Add the `Exception` object (caught by the exception handler) to the Fault message.
5. Publish the Fault message to the Messagebox.

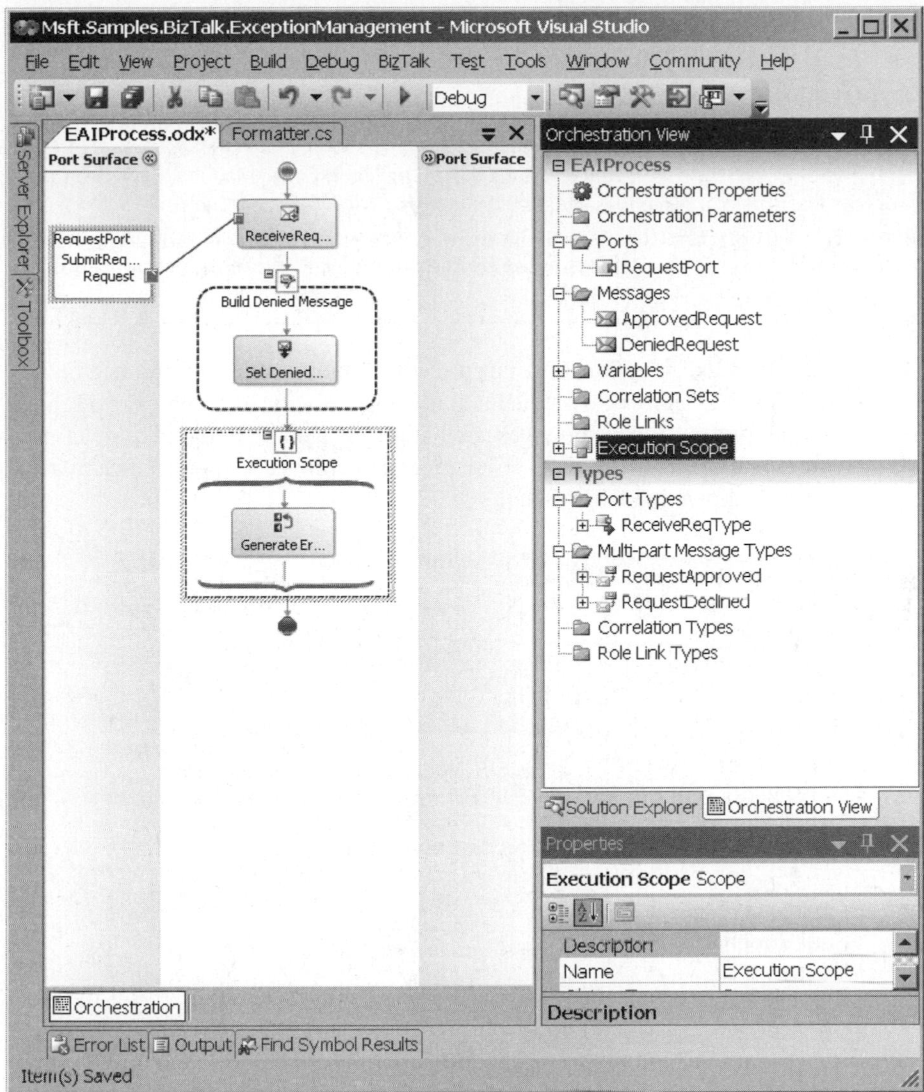

Figure 6-15. *Msft.Samples.BizTalk.ExceptionManagement solution displaying the EAIProcess orchestration*

So, how would you do this? By using an API to enable this functionality, which is embodied within the two projects listed in Table 6-2.

Table 6-2. *Failed Orchestration Routing API Projects*

Project Name	Description
Msft.Samples.BizTalk. Exception	Contains all public methods for handling Fault-message processing within orchestrations. The public methods are `CreateFaultMessage`, `AddMesssage`, `SetException`, `GetException`, `GetMessage`, and `GetMessages`. This assembly must be registered in the local GAC.
Msft.Samples.BizTalk.Exception. Schemas	Contains Fault message schema and system property schema. Deploys to the BizTalk.Sample.ExceptionMgmt application container.

The Msft.Samples.BizTalk.Exception.Schemas project assembly must be referenced by every BizTalk project that references or uses the Fault message schema. It contains two schemas, one that defines an instance of a Fault message (FaultMessage.xsd) and one that defines the property schema (System-Properties.xsd). These must be deployed in the BizTalk environment. The class outline is shown in Figure 6-16.

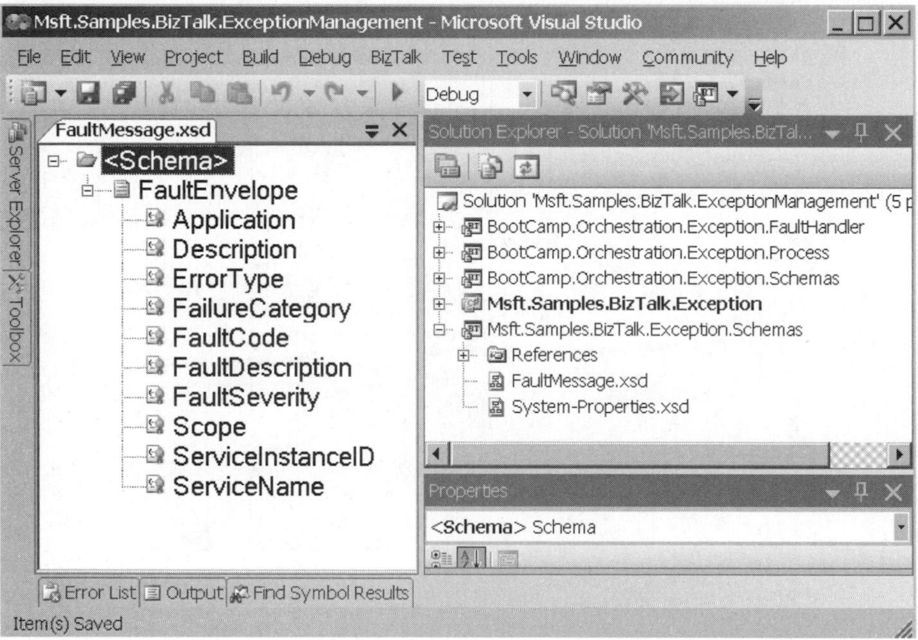

Figure 6-16. *Msft.Samples.BizTalk.Exception.Schemas project displaying the FaultMessage.xsd schema*

The Msft.Samples.BizTalk.Exception.Schemas project must be referenced by all BizTalk projects that need to create an instance of the Fault message for publication. Many of the properties have been promoted or defined as distinguished properties.

For the developer, the next step would be to define a Fault message using the FaultMessage.xsd schema reference. Once the message variable is created (name it `FaultMsg`) within the orchestration view window, an instance of it needs to be created within the Exception Handler shape using the API exposed in the Msft.Samples.BizTalk.Exception project.

Just as in the case of the Msft.Samples.BizTalk.Exception.Schemas project, the Msft.Samples.BizTalk.Exception project assembly must be referenced as well by all BizTalk projects that need to use the API. The API exposes public methods to create Fault messages, and manage and retrieve them for processing, as described in Table 6-3.

Table 6-3. *Public Failed Orchestration Routing API*

Class.Method	Use Case	Description
`ExceptionMgmt.CreateFaultMessage`	Exception handler scope	`public static XmlDocument CreateFaultMessage()` Accepts no arguments.Returns an instance of the Fault message (XmlDocument), populated with the current orchestration name and the orchestration instance ID (GUID).
`ExceptionMgmt.AddMesssage`	Exception handler scope	`public static void AddMessage (XLANGMessage faultMsg, XLANGMessage message)`Accepts the created Fault message as the first argument. Accepts any existing message instance within the orchestration as the second argument. This method will persist the added message instance and its message context properties into the Fault message and make it available for later retrieval via the `GetMessage()` API.Returns void.
`ExceptionMgmt.SetException`	Exception handler scope	`public static void SetException (XLANGMessage faultMsg, Object exception)`Accepts the created Fault message as the first argument. Accepts the existing `Exception` object caught within the exception handler as the second argument. This method will persist the `Exception` object into the Fault message and make it available for later retrieval via the `GetException()` API.Returns void.
`ExceptionMgmt.GetMessage`	Subscriber/processor	`public static XLANGMessage GetMessage (XLANGMessage faultMsg, string msgName)` Accepts the received (via subscription) Fault message as the first argument. Accepts the name of the message previously added to the Fault message from the originating Orchestration Exception Handler shape.Returns the fully typed XLANGMessage that matches the `msgName` argument. The XLANGMessage will contain all original context properties, including custom promoted properties.

Continued

Table 6-3. *Continued*

Class.Method	Use Case	Description
`ExceptionMgmt.GetMessages`	Subscriber/processor	`public static MessageCollection GetMessages (XLANGMessage faultMsg)` Accepts the received (via subscription) Fault message as the argument.Returns a `MessageCollection` class populated with **all** XLANGMessages previously added to the Fault message from the originating Orchestration Exception Handler shape.The XLANGMessages will contain all original context properties, including custom promoted properties.
`ExceptionMgmt.GetException`	Subscriber/processor	`public static System.Exception GetException (XLANGMessage faultMsg)` Accepts the received (via subscription) Fault message as the argument. Returns the `System.Exception` object previously added to the Fault message from the originating Orchestration Exception Handler shape.
`FaultSeverity`	Exception handler scope and subscriber/processor	Exposes public properties simulating the following enumeration:`enum FaultCodes { Information = 0, Warning = 1, Error = 2, Severe = 3, Critical = 4 }`Used to either set or compare against the FaultSeverity value in the Fault message.
`MessageCollection`	Subscriber/processor	Returned by the `ExceptionMgmt.GetMessages` API. This class derives from an `ArrayList` and implements an enumerator allowing `MoveNext()` operations.

Using the APIs listed in Table 6-3, you can add the following shapes to your exception handler and execute the methodology previously discussed. Add the following to the EAIProcess orchestration's exception handler:

- Message Assignment shape enclosed within the Construct shape
- Send shape (for Fault message)
- Outbound Direct Bound Port (one-way) shape
- Terminate shape
- Send shape (for ApprovedRequest message)

Next, set the Construct shape to create a new Fault message. Name the Fault message variable `FaultMsg`.

Within the Message Assignment shape, add the following code:

```
// Create Fault exception message
FaultMsg.Body = Msft.Samples.BizTalk.Exception.ExceptionMgmt.CreateFaultMessage();

// Set Fault message properties
FaultMsg.Body.Application = "EAI Process Application";
FaultMsg.Body.FailureCategory = "MessageBuild";
FaultMsg.Body.FaultCode = "1001";
FaultMsg.Body.FaultDescription = "Some error occurred";
FaultMsg.Body.FaultSeverity = Msft.Samples.BizTalk.Exception.FaultSeverity.Severe;
FaultMsg.Body.Scope = "Execution Scope";

// Add each message you want to process later to the Fault message
Msft.Samples.BizTalk.Exception.ExceptionMgmt.AddMessage(FaultMsg,
ApprovedRequest);
Msft.Samples.BizTalk.Exception.ExceptionMgmt.AddMessage(FaultMsg,
DeniedRequest);

// Add the exception object you may want to inspect later to the Fault message
Msft.Samples.BizTalk.Exception.ExceptionMgmt.SetException(FaultMsg, _
sysExc);
```

Lastly, set the Message property of the Send shape to use the FaultMsg message and connect the Send shape with the Outbound Direct Bound Port. Once complete, the orchestration should look like the one shown in Figure 6-17.

The orchestration described in Figure 6-17 receives the ApprovedRequest message and executes a map to create the DeniedRequest message. Within the execution scope it generates an exception by dividing by zero. An exception handler has been added to the scope to build the Fault message, set the properties on it, and publish it directly to the BizTalk Messagebox.

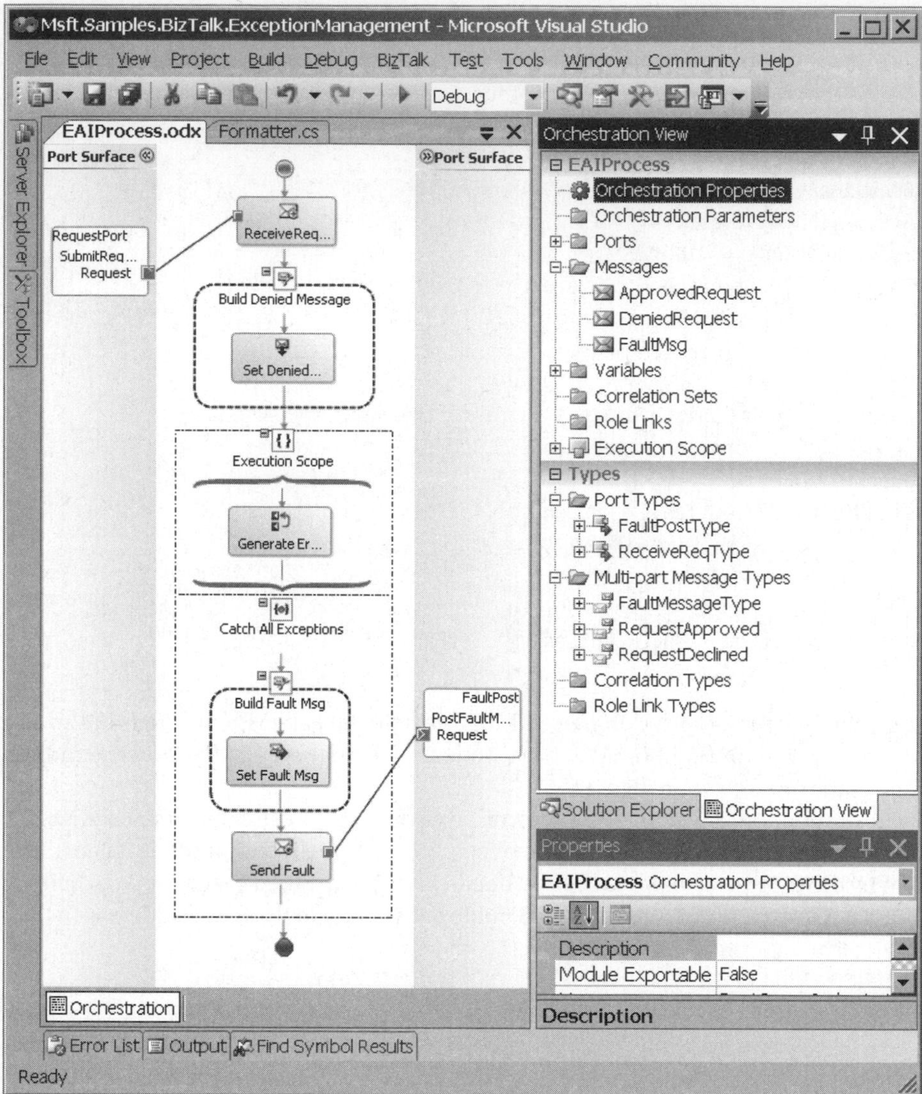

Figure 6-17. *Msft.Samples.BizTalk.ExceptionManagement solution displaying the EAIProcess orchestration*

Running the EAIProcess

The EAIProcess orchestration can be started by binding the logical RequestPort port to a physical port configured to receive files from a folder. Once the project is built and deployed, ensure that there is a subscriber (send port) built for the Fault message and that it is enlisted and stopped; otherwise a persistence exception will be reported. Post a sample file into the folder being monitored, execute the orchestration, and generate the exception, thereby publishing the Fault message. You can inspect the properties of the generated Fault message using the BizTalk Server 2009 Administration Console as displayed in Figure 6-18.

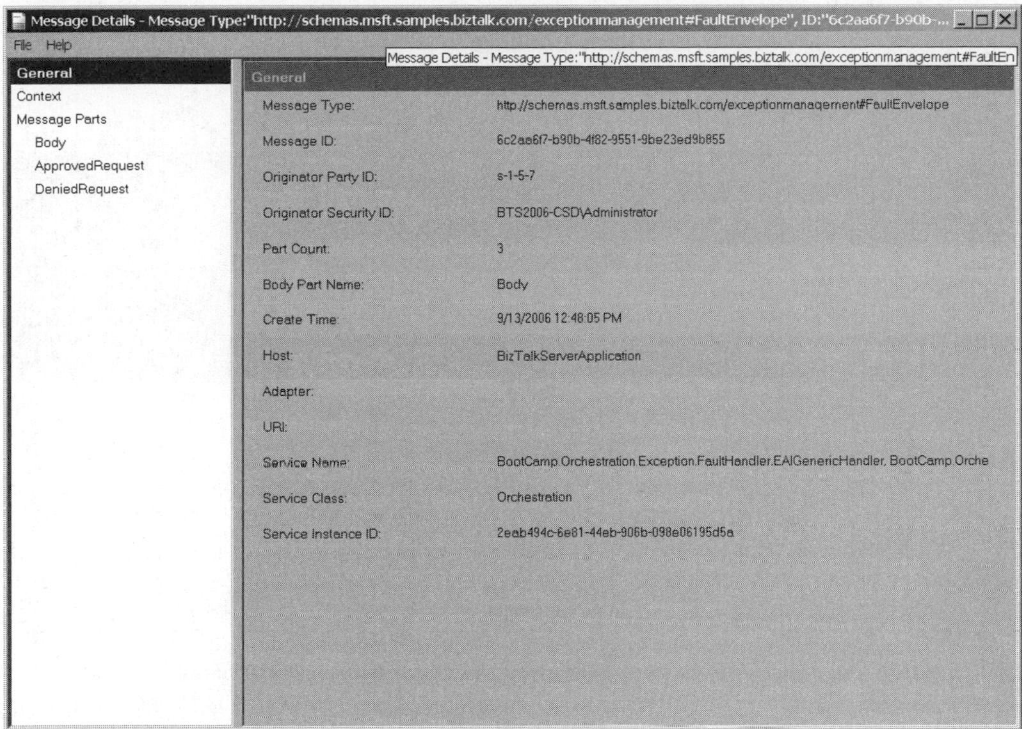

Figure 6-18. *Message Details dialog box displaying properties of the suspended Fault message*

Each message added to the Fault message in the exception handler gets persisted as dynamic message parts to the original Fault message. The Message Details dialog box illustrates some of the niceties resulting from the use of the Failed Orchestration Routing API. First, the message published from the exception handler is still defined as the Fault message derived from your FaultMessage.xsd schema as shown by the message type context property. However, notice two additional message parts listed in the left-hand pane. In the EAIProcess orchestration, the `FaultMsg` message variable was set to a multipart message type of one part, body. The API dynamically adds the individual messages as message parts to the current Fault message.

If you examine the context properties of the Fault message (as shown in Figure 6-19), you can see all of the fault properties you set in the Message Assignment shape, as well as some that the API sets for you (i.e., `ServiceName` and `ServiceInstanceID`).

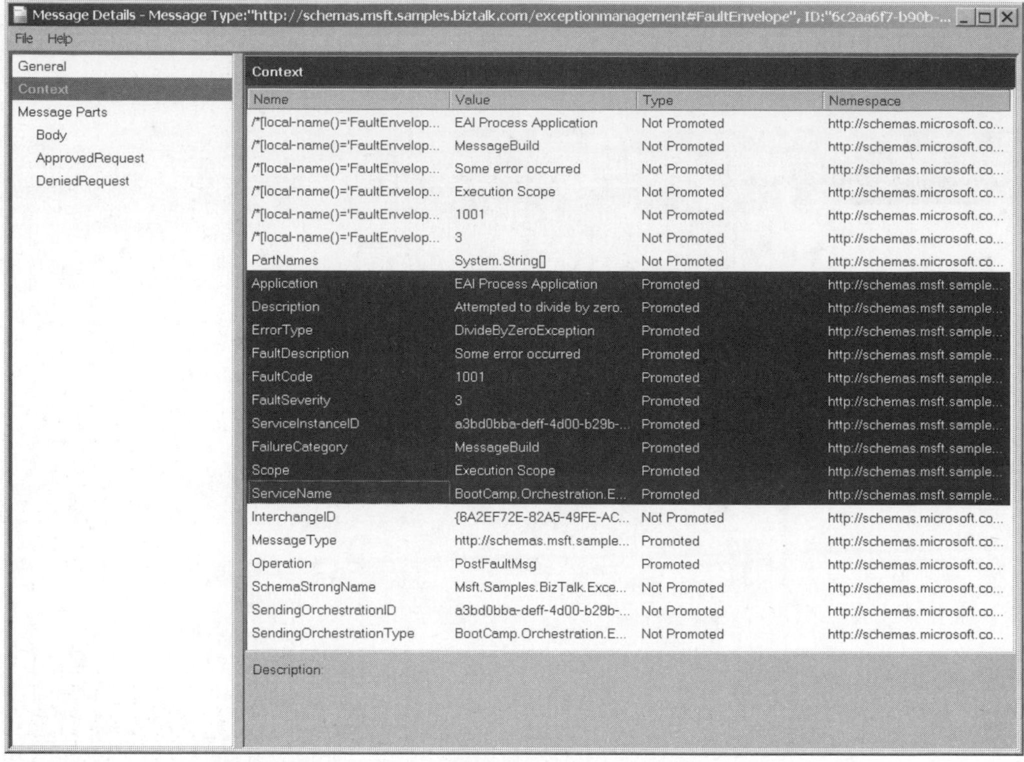

Figure 6-19. *Message Details dialog box displaying the promoted properties of the suspended Fault message. These properties were set in the exception handler as well as within the API.*

Figures 6-20, 6-21, and 6-22 show the Message Details dialog box displaying the content of the original ApprovedRequest and DeniedRequest messages.

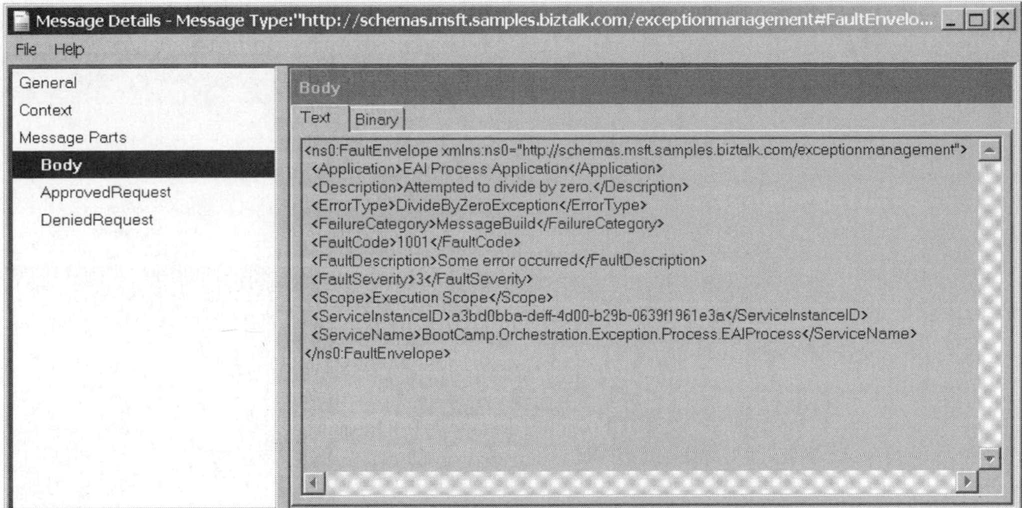

Figure 6-20. *Message Details dialog box displaying the content of the original Fault message published from the EAIProcess exception handler*

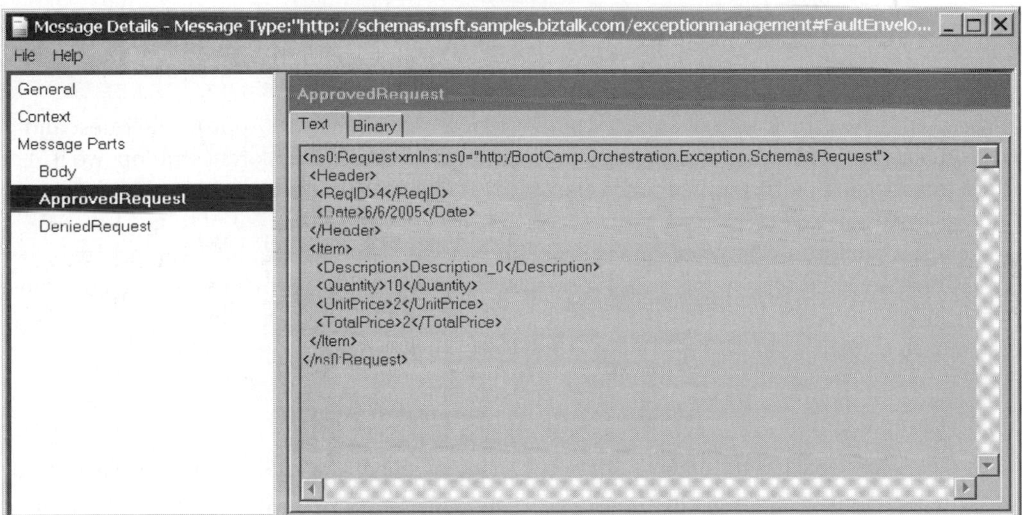

Figure 6-21. *Message Details dialog box displaying the contents of the ApprovedRequest message that was added to the Fault message*

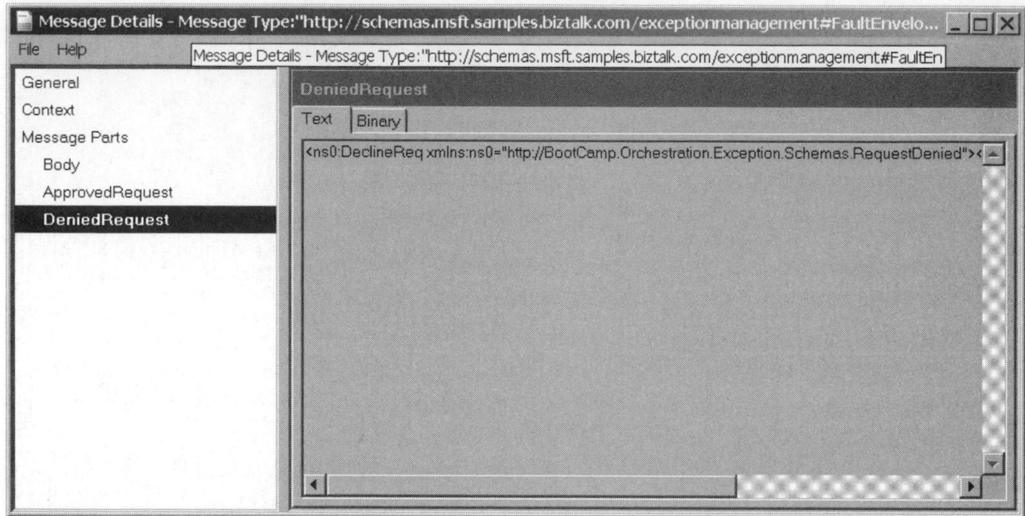

Figure 6-22. *Message Details dialog box displaying the contents of the DeniedRequest message that was added to the Fault message*

Processing and Retrieving Messages and Exceptions from the Fault Message

Having published the Fault message with the two persisted messages (ApprovedRequest and DeniedRequest) and a persisted `Exception` object from the EAIProcess orchestration, we'll move forward and demonstrate how to extract the messages and the `Exception` objects in secondary orchestration schedules.

There is really only one method for extracting an `Exception` object: the `GetException()` API. However, there are two methods for extracting messages. One provides a typeless method to retrieve all messages persisted to the Fault message. The other provides a strongly typed approach.

Typeless Message Retrieval

The typeless approach is useful if you have a general logging need, or you don't have access to the schema assembly used in the originating orchestration that persisted the messages. In this case, a collection of messages can be returned using `MoveNext()` to enumerate through them.

This allows developers to inspect the message context properties and do whatever they want with them, e.g., process them, send them out to a SharePoint site, etc. For example, a generic orchestration exception process may do the following:

- Retrieve array of messages from Fault message.
- Inspect context properties to determine message type or retrieve other context values.
- Based on message type or other criteria, look up processing instructions via Business Rule Engine.
- Process individual messages per business rule evaluation.

This makes for an extremely decoupled exception processing solution. The EAIGenericHandler orchestration, located in the BootCamp.Orchestration.Exception.FaultHandler project, is a good example demonstrating the typeless approach and is shown in Figure 6-23.

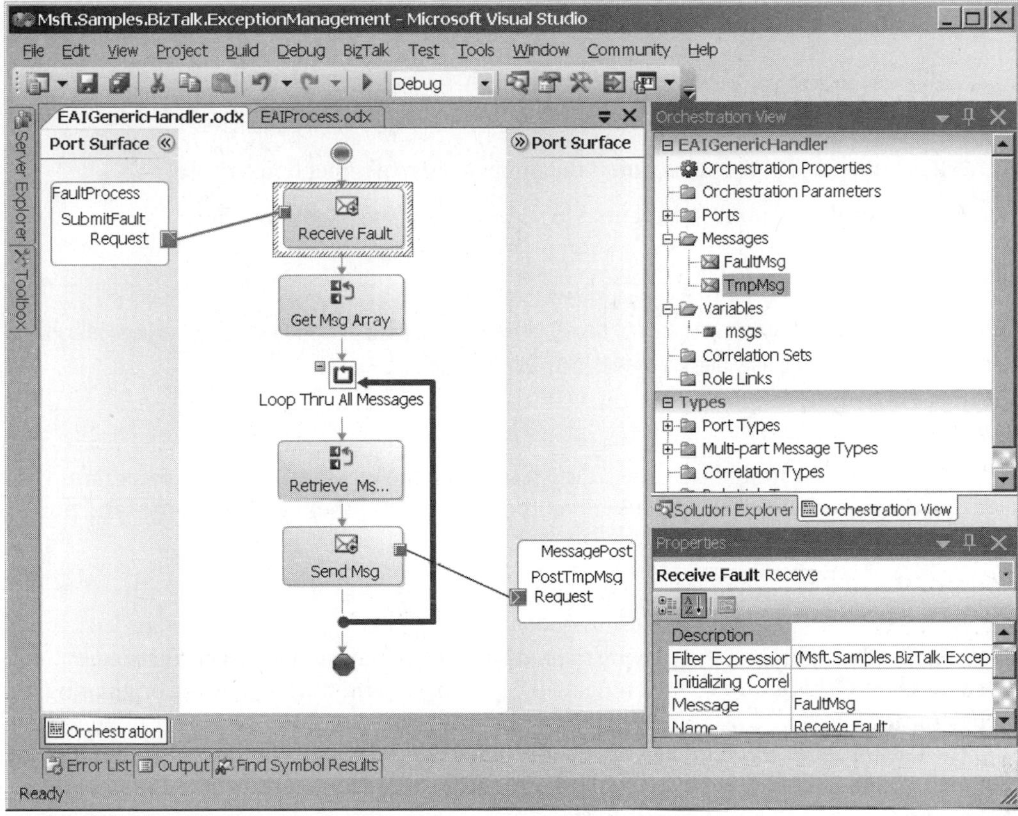

Figure 6-23. *EAIGenericHandler orchestration demonstrating typeless message retrieval and handling using the Failed Orchestration Routing API*

In this example, the orchestration is configured as follows:

1. The Receive shape is configured with a filter expression: (`"Msft.Samples.BizTalk.Exception.Schemas.FaultCode" == "1001"`). This effectively subscribes the orchestration to any Fault messages published where the FaultCode equals 1001.
2. The Receive shape is bound to a direct bound receive port.
3. The Expression shape directly below the Receive shape has the following code snippet that calls the `GetMessages()` API:

```
msgs =  Msft.Samples.BizTalk.Exception.ExceptionMgmt.GetMessages(FaultMsg);
```

The `msgs` variable is declared of type MessageCollection. This returns an array of messages, including their original context properties, from the Fault message.

4. A Loop shape is configured to call

   ```
   msgs.MoveNext()
   ```

5. Within the Loop shape, an Expression shape is configured to retrieve the current message in the collection by calling

   ```
   TmpMsg = msgs.Current;
   ```

   `TmpMsg` is a message variable declared as a `System.Xml.XmlDocument`.

6. Each message in the collection is then published to a direct bound port.

7. A physical send port is configured to serialize each message to a folder.

Note Message Construct shapes are not necessary within the example. The API for the exception handler takes care of constructing new messages within the BizTalk runtime.

When this orchestration executes, it will retrieve all the messages from the Fault message (i.e., ApprovedRequest and DeniedRequest) and serialize them to disk via the send port subscription.

Strongly Typed Message Retrieval

Another effective approach is retrieving the messages from the Fault message as strongly typed messages. This is done by referencing the schema assemblies used by the originating orchestration.

The EAIProcessHandler orchestration, located in the BootCamp.Orchestration.Exception.FaultHandler project, is a good example demonstrating the strongly typed approach. The orchestration flow is shown in Figure 6-24.

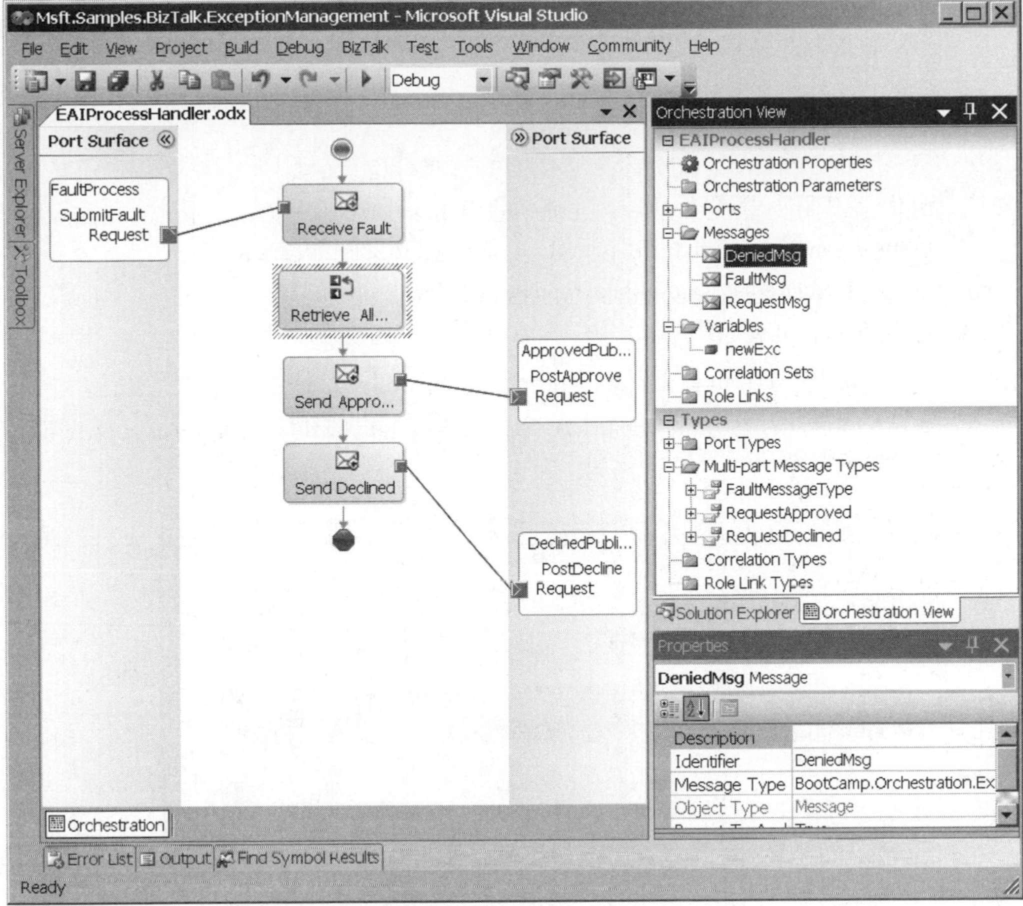

Figure 6-24. *EAIProcessHandler orchestration demonstrating strongly typed message retrieval and handling using the Failed Orchestration Routing API*

In this example, the orchestration is configured as follows:

1. The Receive shape is configured with a filter expression: ("Msft.Samples.BizTalk.Exception.Schemas.FaultCode" == "1001"). This effectively subscribes the orchestration to any Fault messages published where the FaultCode equals 1001.

2. The Receive shape is bound to a direct bound receive port.

3. The Expression shape directly below the Receive shape has the following code snippet, which calls the `GetMessage()` and `GetException()` APIs:

```
//Retrieve the two original messages from the Fault message
RequestMsg = Msft.Samples.BizTalk.Exception.ExceptionMgmt.GetMessage(FaultMsg,
"ApprovedRequest");
DeniedMsg = Msft.Samples.BizTalk.Exception.ExceptionMgmt.GetMessage(FaultMsg,
"DeniedRequest");
```

```
//Retrieve the System.Exception from the original service
newExc = Msft.Samples.BizTalk.Exception.ExceptionMgmt.GetException(FaultMsg);

// Write the error value to event log (need admin rights)
System.Diagnostics.EventLog.WriteEntry _
("EAIProcessHandler",newExc.Message.ToString());
```

Both `RequestMsg` and `DeniedMsg` are strongly typed using the schemas in the originating orchestration.

`newExc` is declared as a variable of type System.Exception.

4. If repair is needed:

   a. `RequestMsg` is sent to the folder drop via a port.

   b. An InfoPath processing instruction is added to it to facilitate editing as shown in Figure 6-25.

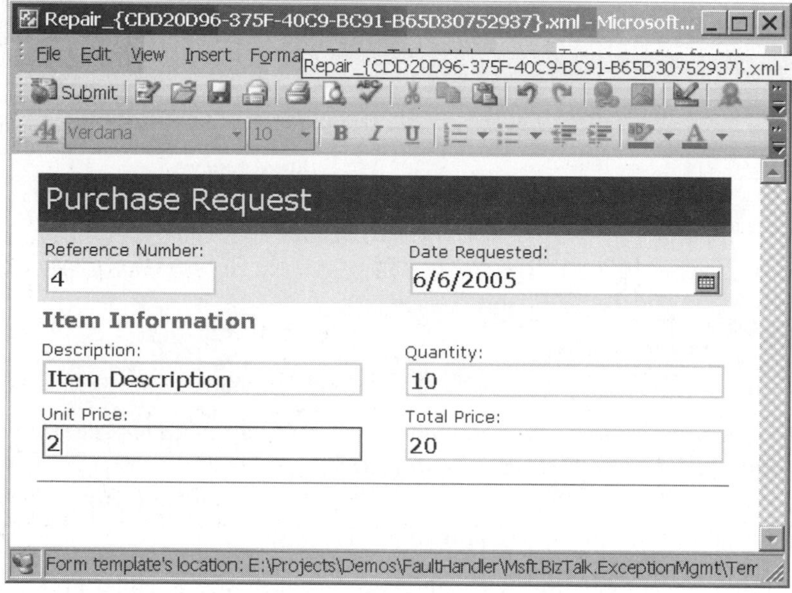

Figure 6-25. *RepairReSubmitForm.xsn Infopath form*

   c. The InfoPath form is designed to submit repaired data to a BizTalk HTTP receive location configured under the receive port for the EAIProcess orchestration.

   d. `DeniedMsg` is published to a direct bound port.

   e. A physical send port is configured to serialize the message to a folder.

5. If repair is **not** needed:

   a. Each message is then published to a direct bound port.

   b. A physical send port is configured to serialize each message to a folder.

Note Message Construct shapes are not necessary within the example. The API for the exception handler takes care of constructing new messages within the BizTalk runtime.

The form in Figure 6-25 is configured to use a BizTalk HTTP receive location URL as its submit data source. Once submitted, it will activate a new instance of the EAIProcess orchestration.

When this orchestration executes, it will retrieve all the messages from the Fault message (i.e., ApprovedRequest and DeniedRequest) and set them into strongly typed message variables. In fact, if you stop the send port subscriptions and run the orchestration, you can see the original context property values on the messages; the context properties were set from the originating orchestration (see Figure 6-26).

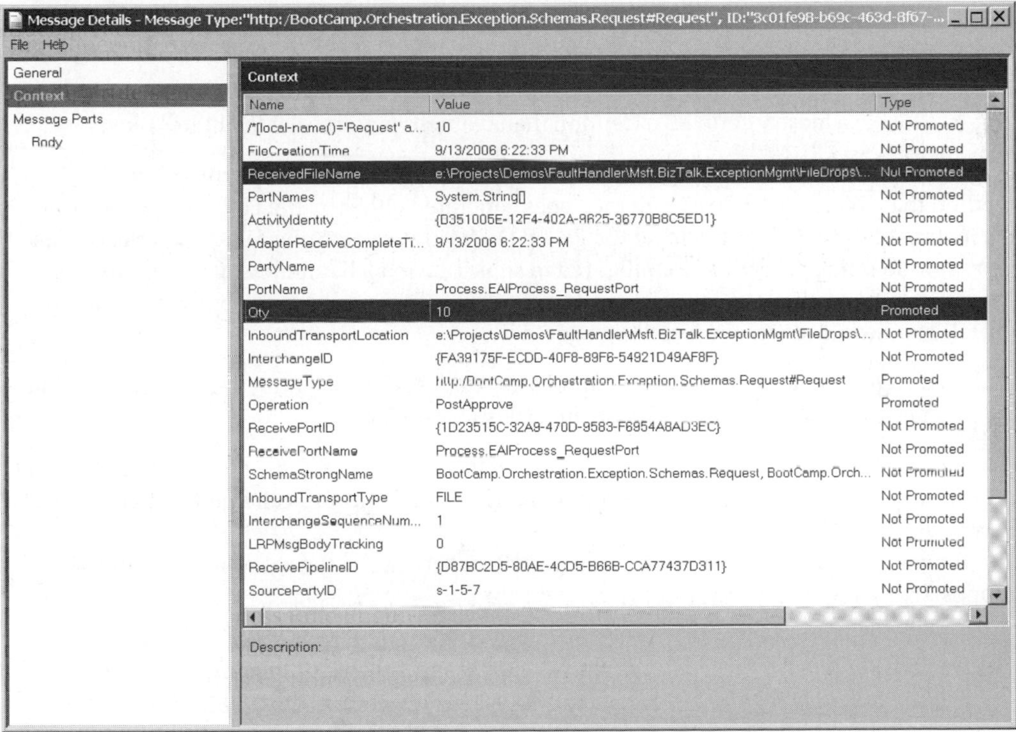

Figure 6-26. *Message Details dialog box displaying the properties of the ApprovedRequest message retrieved from the Fault message using the GetMessage() API*

Note In Figure 6-26, the `ReceivedFileName` property that was set before the originating orchestration processed the message and threw the exception. Also, the API persists all custom `Promoted` properties as noted by the `Qty` property. This is an incredibly handy feature to have.

Beyond the Next Horizon

As can be seen from the previous sections, the Failed Orchestration Routing API is powerful enough to allow developers to handle orchestration-generated exceptions. With a little work and a good design, you can handle orchestration exceptions the same way you would handle messaging subsystem exceptions using the Failed Message Routing feature of BizTalk Server 2009.

The samples provided online,[16] specifically the EAIGenericHandler and EAIProcessHandler orchestrations, demonstrate simple patterns for accessing both the exception messages as well as the state from the original processing orchestration. This state, in the form of the original messages, can be accessed as strongly typed or typeless XLANG messages. This satisfies at least three of the four original common design goals we listed earlier in the chapter, specifically

- Standardize how application exceptions are detected and caught in the BizTalk environment, i.e., messaging and orchestration subsystems.
- Provide common patterns that allow automated processes to react and manage application exceptions.
- Provide a loosely coupled exception management pattern that facilitates reuse.

If you take this pattern a step further and extend the API, you could provide another method that creates canonical Fault messages generated either by the Failed Message Routing feature of BizTalk Server 2009 or the Failed Orchestration Routing API. A generic, BizTalk Group–wide send port could be configured to subscribe to all Fault messages, regardless of source, call the method, and then post all canonical Fault messages to a central web-based portal. That would satisfy the last design goal:

- Develop a common reporting paradigm of application exceptions and their available message state that applies to any BizTalk subsystem.

The final step would be to dynamically generate business intelligence data from the Fault messages going through the BizTalk environment. That's right; you call that BAM in BizTalk Server 2009.

Remember the following scenario we described earlier and the solution walkthrough we proposed:

> *A user submits an invoice to the system. During the course of processing the invoice within an orchestration, the Business Rule Engine throws an application exception because some piece of the data is incorrect. The business process should catch the exception, send the offending message to another person or system that can correct the message, and resubmit the message for processing.*

To implement the use case, we envisioned a sequence of events would need to happen, as presented earlier in the subsection "BizTalk Server 2009 Failed Message Routing As a Blueprint" and repeated here for your convenience:

16 Samples and compiled API to be provided for download at www.apress.com.

1. A developer is assigned responsibility for the recently deployed Financial Reporting BizTalk application.
2. A new exception message arrives in the SharePoint-based exception management portal indicating a data integrity issue with an orchestration in the Financial Reporting BizTalk application.
3. The developer is notified of the new exception either through his subscription to the SharePoint application list or because the exception exceeded a threshold predefined in BAM.
4. The developer navigates to the SharePoint-based exception management portal and examines the Fault message posted as well as the individual orchestration messages and their context properties that were persisted.
5. The developer determines that this will be a common error that will require manual intervention and correction by the Finance team and resubmission to the system.
6. The developer creates and deploys an independent BizTalk orchestration project that subscribes to the specific exception and application information.
7. The project is designed to retrieve the invalid message from the Fault message, send the message to the Finance team for correction, and correlate the corrected message back to orchestration and resubmit.
8. A week later the developer navigates to the SharePoint-based exception management portal to view that the application exception trends for invalid messages have decreased dramatically since the deployment of his solution.

If you extend the Failed Orchestration Routing API, you could make the solution walk-through a reality with very little effort. This need is not unique to a specific BizTalk application; it tends to be ubiquitous in BizTalk environments to provide operational visibility into the health of the applications deployed. This becomes a vital function in Enterprise Service Bus (ESB)[17] type deployments.

In the upcoming release of the Microsoft ESB Toolkit, this API will be extended to accommodate the scenarios we described previously. This should prove invaluable for anyone deploying applications in the future.

Implementing a Scatter/Gather Pattern

One of BizTalk's many powerful features is its ability to loosely couple messages, which allows for the subscription-based processing of messages. The ability to route messages based upon content filters makes BizTalk a natural fit for the Scatter/Gather pattern.

The Scatter/Gather pattern is a method for broadcasting and processing messages in parallel. The "scatter" portion distributes a series messages all at the same time, and then an aggregator "gathers" the messages back into the main response before continuing. Figure 6-27 shows an example.

17 http://en.wikipedia.org/wiki/Enterprise_Service_Bus

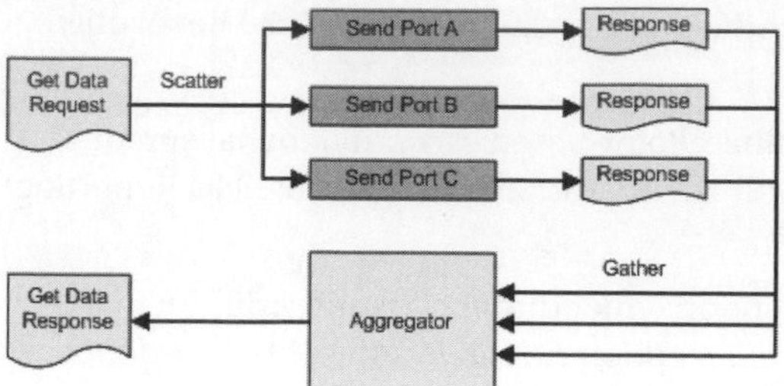

Figure 6-27. *Example of data flow within a Scatter/Gather pattern*

Figure 6-27 shows a Get Data Request being received. An orchestration "scatters" the request to multiple solicit-response send ports in parallel. The orchestration waits for all responses to be received and aggregates them back into a single Get Data Response message, which is sent back to the requestor.

The key to having BizTalk scatter the requests to multiple backend systems is its ability for send ports to be bound by subscription filters. This allows an orchestration to send one message to the Messagebox via direct binding and have one or more send ports process the request in parallel. With BizTalk's ability to scale across multiple hosts, this pattern can also provide significant performance benefits.

This type of pattern is especially useful for executing identical requests to multiple backend systems. For example, say a customer calls into a call center to retrieve information about all their loans at a bank. The following scenario shows how this pattern could be leveraged:

1. A customer calls the bank's call center.
2. The interactive voice response (IVR) system prompts the caller for their account number.
3. An orchestration is started and simultaneously scatters requests to each of the mortgage, line of credit, and loan backend systems.
4. Each system responds with their respective data, and the orchestration gathers the responses into a single response.
5. The customer service representative sees an aggregated view of all systems on their screen.

Figure 6-28 shows a collapsed view of the orchestration that implements the pattern to support this scenario.

The orchestration shown in Figure 6-28 has the following major sections:

- A request shape to receive the request from the calling IVR application
- A Scatter scope that submits a direct "GetLoanInfo" message to the Messagebox where three send ports, one for each backend system, are subscribed to this message schema
- A construct message shape to create the initial response message
- A Gather scope that receives the responses from the backend systems and aggregates them into the response template message
- A send shape to send the aggregated content back to the IVR system

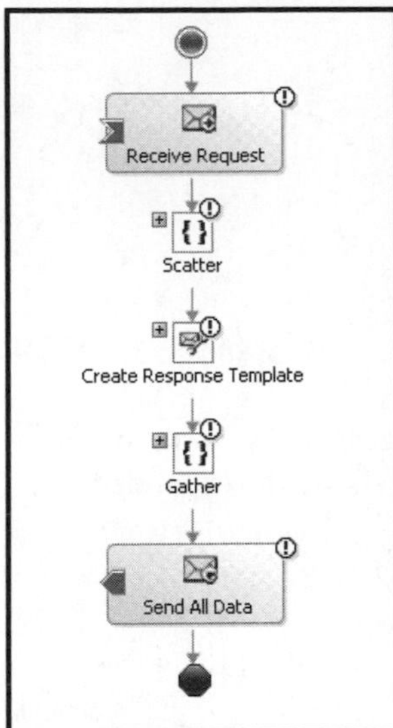

Figure 6-28. *Example collapsed Scatter/Gather orchestration*

Figure 6-29 shows the expanded Scatter scope.

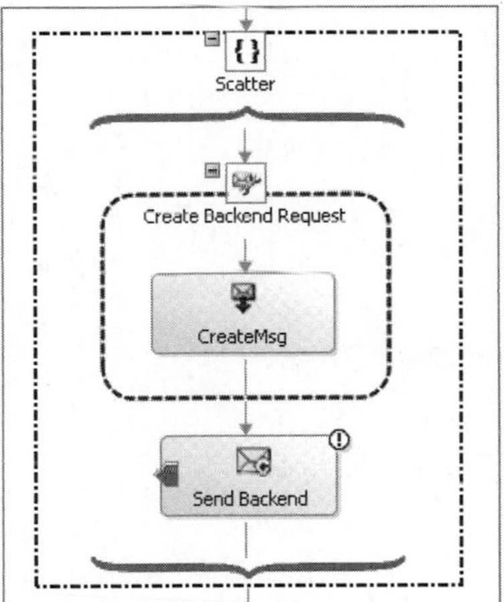

Figure 6-29. *Scatter scope*

The Scatter scope is quite simple. It creates a new backend message type and sends the message to a send port via direct binding to the Messagebox. Then, based upon send port subscriptions, there are many recipients of the message, therefore causing multiple messages to be processed. In addition, each send port could have a map associated with it to further transform the message to a schema format required by the backend application.

Once the message has been sent, an empty response message is created, shown in Figure 6-30, that will ultimately be used to hold all the aggregated result data.

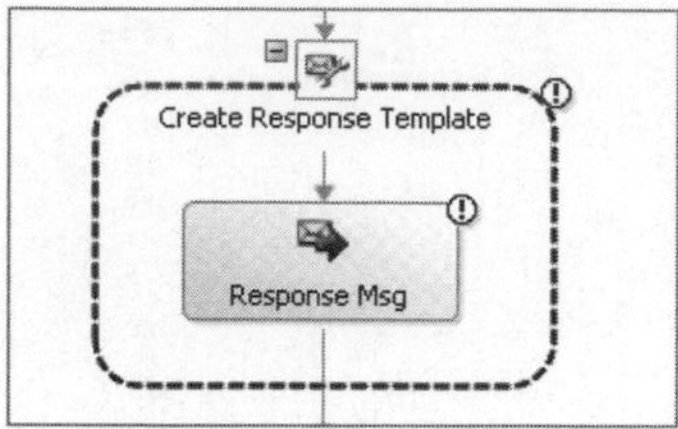

Figure 6-30. *Response message creation*

Now that the messages have been sent and the response message is ready, you can start gathering the responses and aggregating them together. Figure 6-31 shows the expanded Gather scope.

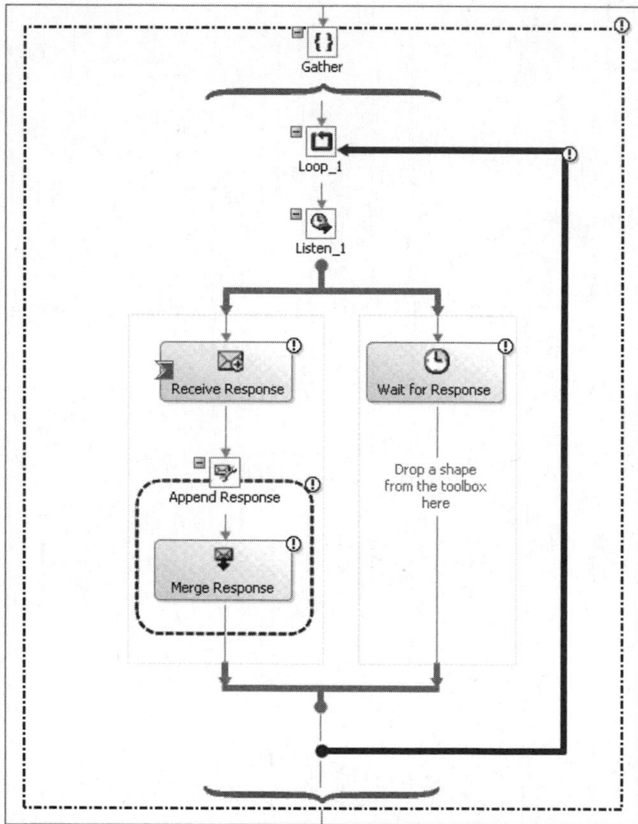

Figure 6-31. *Gather scope*

The Gather scope performs the following functions:

- Loops until all messages are received.
- Listens for a correlated message to be received.
- Appends the received message to the response message.
- If all messages aren't received by the time the delay time occurs, the listen shape is exited.

Once the Gather scope has completed, a send shape is used to send the aggregated messages back to the calling application to complete the pattern.

As you can see from the sample orchestration, the pattern's concept fits seamlessly with one of BizTalk's core features: content-based routing. By using content-based routing, the orchestration's implementation of the pattern is kept quite simple and straightforward.

CHAPTER 7

What the Maestro Needs to Know: Advanced Orchestration Concepts

Orchestrations are series of ordered operations or transactions that implement a business process. To interact with entities outside the boundaries of this business process, orchestrations can use **send** or **receive ports**. You can perform transactions in parallel, execute business rules from within orchestrations, call complex logic in managed .NET assemblies, or call and start other orchestrations. They are by far the most powerful tool in a BizTalk architect's tool belt. To perform complex routing in BizTalk or do any process automation work, you need to use orchestrations.

What an Orchestration Is

BizTalk orchestrations are used to visually model workflows and provide the primary mechanism to implement business process automation within a solution. They are the equivalent of the good-old flowcharts programmers used to detail algorithms in functional specifications before sequence diagrams and object-centric design. Orchestrations are the most powerful tool within the BizTalk Server toolbox, as they allow for the rapid development and deployment of complex processes that in many circumstances can be implemented with little to no coding. They are created within Visual Studio and are compiled into .NET assemblies that are deployed to the Global Assembly Cache and registered in the BizTalk Management Database.

Just like in any subroutine, you can declare and use variables within an orchestration. Orchestrations started or called programmatically or through a caller orchestration may also be passed parameters. In those aspects, an orchestration is no different from a procedure or function. Orchestrations may also receive and send messages, due to the integration of the orchestration engine, known as the **XLANG engine**, and the BizTalk messaging subservice. The orchestration engine's constructs in the Orchestration toolbox allow developers to construct, modify, and transform messages that an orchestration sends and receives. Developers can add C#-like expressions[1]—**XLANG expressions**—to an orchestration flow to perform complex logic or call external assemblies. Orchestration developers may declare transaction scopes within

1 XLANG expressions constitute the subset of C# expressions that can be used within the orchestration. The XLANG engine performs a fair amount of housecleaning and state management after each expression statement. A simple C#-like statement in an Expression shape results in several other operations performed by the XLANG engine.

an orchestration and define compensation blocks that will be implicitly called to roll back the transaction if an exception occurs.

What the Orchestration Engine Provides

The BizTalk orchestration engine, the XLANG engine, consists of a set of SQL Server stored procedures, jobs that run on the BizTalk Messagebox database—msgbox DB—and Management Database as well as a set of managed assemblies that run within BizTalk host instances. The XLANG engine is the maestro that schedules, manages, and monitors orchestration execution across host instances. It manages orchestration instantiation, execution, termination, and migration across host instances using a predefined amount of system resources, like memory and threads. For the engine to be able to perform its functions, it needs to be able to interrupt the executions of orchestration instances regularly. Instead of resorting to a language that gets interpreted at runtime to run on top of the engine, visual orchestration constructs (shapes) that form the flow of an orchestration are compiled into a set of calls to the XLANG APIs in a managed assembly. This allows the engine to control the scheduling and execution of orchestration instances without the performance hit associated with interpreted languages. In essence, the XLANG engine and orchestration instances are running side by side in the BizTalk host instance.

The integration of the XLANG engine and the rest of the BizTalk Server components, as illustrated in Figure 7-1, helps provide the basic services required for building and running reliable enterprise-grade orchestrations:

- The ability to scope transaction and designate compensation blocks and exception handlers.
- Support for atomic or long-running transactional scopes. **Atomic scopes** mean that the engine will cease to dehydrate[2] the running orchestration instance until it exits the atomic scope. Long-running scopes mean that the execution time of each step in the scope is undetermined or very long. The engine persists the instance's state on each operation that crosses the instance boundary, like sending messages, and eventually dehydrates the orchestration instance if it is idle and meeting the dehydration thresholds.[3]
- Fault tolerance. Leveraging state persistence of orchestration instances, the BizTalk orchestration engine can recover from a failure by recycling or restarting a failed host and resuming execution of previously running instances from the last persisted state. If the orchestration is deployed on a BizTalk Server Group running multiple host instances on different servers, the engine may also resume such instances on a different host instance running on a different server. This ensures absolute resilience in the case of a catastrophic failure of a server.

---

2 The dehydration of a running orchestration instance is the act of persisting the current orchestration instance state to the BizTalk Messagebox database and releasing all transient system resources, memory, and threads back to the resource pools. Rehydration of a dehydrated orchestration instance is the act of loading the persisted orchestration instance state into memory and consuming resources from the pools to continue execution of that instance at its last persisted state.

3 A more detailed explanation of dehydration thresholds will follow in this chapter in the section "The Dehydration Algorithm and Thresholds."

- Scalability and load balancing. The power of orchestration instance state persistence allows the engine to dehydrate an orchestration instance on one host instance and resume its execution on another host instance on a different server if the original host instance it was running on is overloaded. It can also balance the load across the running host instances on multiple servers.
- Activity tracking and monitoring. If designed by the Orchestration Designer, an orchestration can log and track activity execution that later can be monitored and reviewed through the Business Activity Monitor.
- Integration with the Business Rule Engine and firing business policies from within orchestrations.
- Integration with the BizTalk Messaging Engine and sending and receiving messages from within orchestrations.
- Leveraging XSLT maps and performing message transformation from within orchestrations.
- Leveraging the BizTalk Messaging Engine to allow for correlation of sent and received messages to ensure their delivery to the proper orchestration instance for the implementation of complex execution flows that span multiple requests.

In short, the BizTalk orchestration engine allows for the implementation and deployment of resilient transactional business processes that are scalable, fault tolerant, and able to send and receive messages or execute business rules.

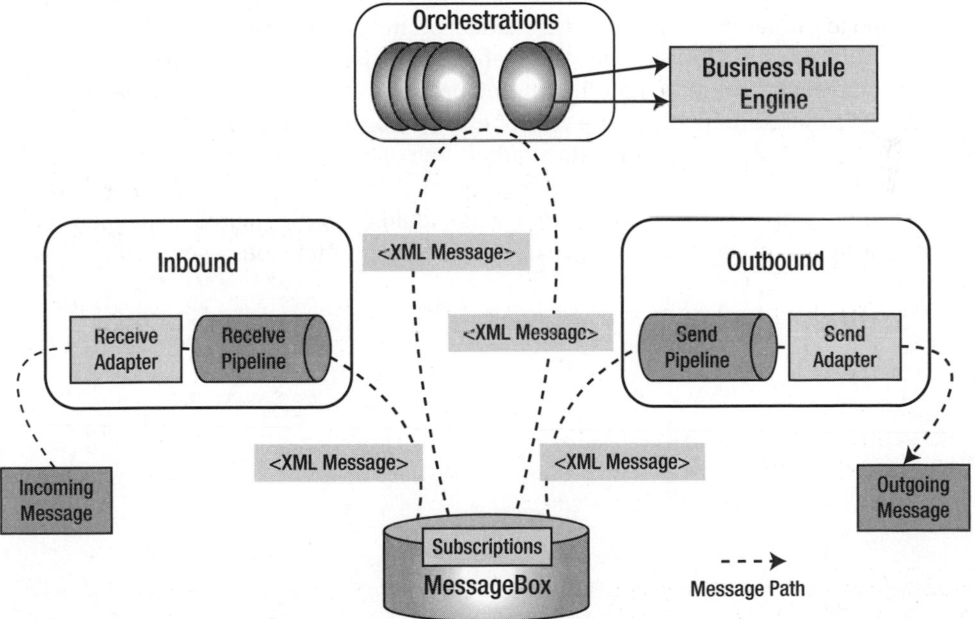

Figure 7-1. *Where the orchestration engine fits in BizTalk Server*

Do You Really Need an Orchestration?

Like all eager developers, you probably want to know the answer to this question right away. After all, an orchestration often seems like the best tool for you to use, as it is simply a procedural algorithm in a visual form. Before identifying when you should and should not use an orchestration, however, we need to explain the rationale behind some of the wrong decisions that some new BizTalk developers make, as well as the reason they are wrong.

The Orchestration Designer is the tool that new BizTalk developers are most comfortable with, as it is simply a visual procedural language. It provides a natural transition from VB .NET or C# to BizTalk development. Almost every new BizTalk developer or architect tends to think of a BizTalk solution as a set of orchestrations with defined external entry and exit points—ports—glued together to perform a business function. Although this visual development approach is the natural transition from procedural or object-oriented development, to leverage BizTalk to its full potential, solutions have to be architected differently. Unfortunately, designing a BizTalk solution is not as simple as abiding by object-oriented design guidelines, applying service-oriented architecture, or defining data structures and schemas. It is a combination of all of the foregoing, but couched in terms of message processing patterns. For the unfamiliar, the combination of these design approaches is a new paradigm shift in solution design.

Fortunately, this combination lends itself easily to business analysis. The mapping from a defined business process or collection of processes including cross-platform transactions to a BizTalk solution is usually a one-to-one mapping. It is a matter of finding the proper set of BizTalk tools—**messaging patterns**—to perform the defined function.[4]

Orchestrations are a powerful tool. However, they come at a high cost. For the orchestration engine to properly manage and maintain an orchestration instance, the engine has to perform multiple round-trips to the Messagebox to persist its state. Message subscription resolution is mostly implemented through stored procedures running on the Messagebox directly. We therefore highly advise you to resort to content-based routing (CBR), as illustrated in Figure 7-2, whenever possible rather than using orchestrations to implement message-routing logic. Simple message routing can be done using content filtering on ports. Unless it is unavoidable, message transformations should be implemented using maps on the ports as well. Use orchestrations if you must correlate multiple messages to fulfill business needs.

4 Enterprise Application Integration patterns and Process Automation patterns were discussed in detail in Chapter 6.

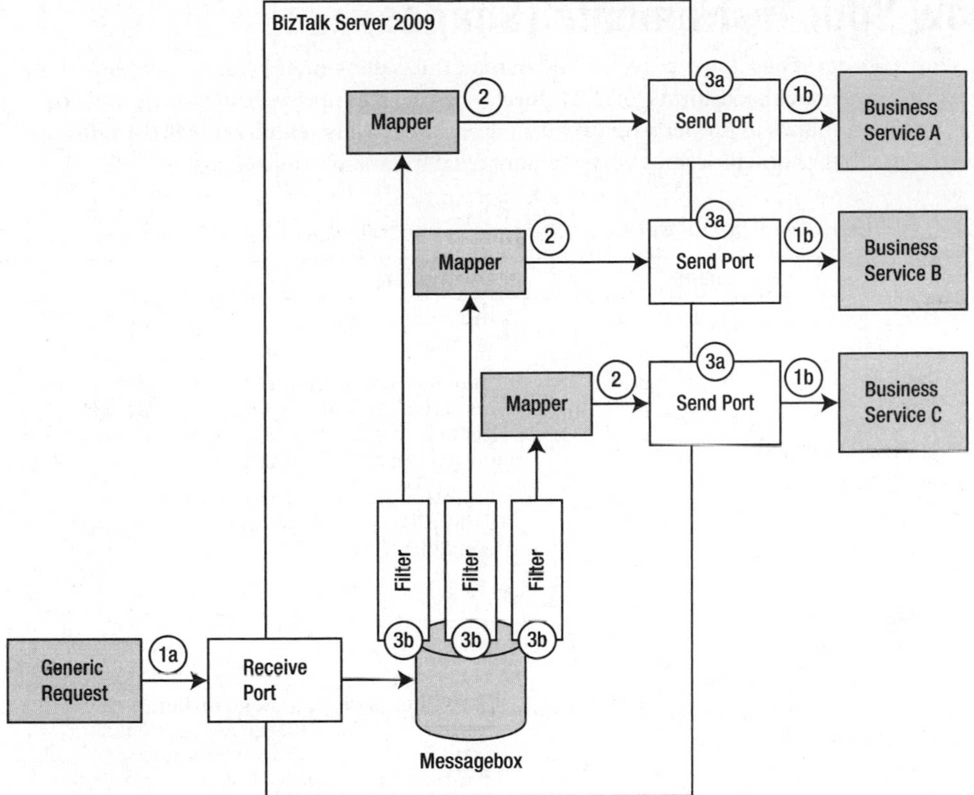

Figure 7-2. *The power of CBR*

In short, orchestrations should **not** be used to

- Simply route messages between ports.
- Perform simple or conditional transformations on messages.
- Simply call remote systems through expressions and managed code.
- Define complex business rules and policies.

Orchestrations **should** be used to

- Correlate multiple messages to fulfill the required business needs.
- Fire business rules in the Business Rule Engine.
- Manage and scope business transactions.

Know Your Instruments (Shapes)

Just as any C++ or C# developer needs to understand the cost of an API call or a statement to properly optimize their algorithms, BizTalk developers need to understand the use and cost of orchestration shapes to properly optimize their orchestrations. Table 7-1 lists the different orchestration shapes and describes what they are used for and what their cost is.

Table 7-1. *Orchestration Shapes (Microsoft, "BizTalk Server 2009 Documentation," 2009)*[5]

Icon	Shape	Description
	Implicit Start	Indicates the beginning of an orchestration instance.
	Implicit End	Indicates the termination of an orchestration instance. The engine persists the orchestration instance's state for the last time as it reaches the end of the orchestration.
	Group	Enables you to group operations into a single collapsible and expandable unit for visual convenience.
	Construct Message	Constructs a new message instance. It must contain either a Message Assignment shape or a Transform shape, and can contain any number of either, but no other shapes. You specify the message variable that you want to construct and make assignments to the message or its parts. Messages are immutable. Once created and persisted to the Messagebox database, they cannot be changed. All assignments to any given message must take place within the same Construct Message shape. If you want to modify a property on a message that has already been constructed—such as a message that has been received—you must construct a new message instance by assigning the first to the second and then modifying the property on the new message instance; both the construction and modification occur within the same Construct Message shape.

5 Copyright © 2009 by Microsoft Corporation. Reprinted with permission from Microsoft Corporation.

Icon	Shape	Description
Transform_Pro	Transform	Moves data from one message into another. The Transform shape is the only way to map one-to-many or many-to-one messages in BizTalk. You need to define one or more input messages, one or more output messages, and an XSLT map for the transform. All messages identified for the transform need to comply with a defined schema. The map assigns message parts from the input messages to message parts in the output messages. Transforms are usable only in the construction of messages, so the Transform shape always appears inside a Construct Message shape.
MessageAssi...	Message Assignment	Constructs messages by assigning one message to another, assigning individual message parts, or calling a .NET class to construct the message. The Message Assignment shape must be enclosed within a Construct Message shape.
CallOrchestra...	Call Orchestration	Synchronously instantiates and runs another orchestration. The caller is blocked until the called orchestration terminates. The called orchestration as well as the caller can only consume a maximum of one thread from the engine's thread pool.
StartOrchestr...	Start Orchestration	Asynchronously instantiates and invokes another orchestration. The invoked orchestration is running on its separate thread and the calling orchestration continues execution. The calling orchestration instance's state is persisted at this point.
	Orchestration Parameters	Port, Message, Variable, Correlation Set, Role Link
RoleLink_Pro Provider PortType_BizTa... Op_BTSPro Request Consumer Insert Send Ports	Role Link	Contains placeholders for an implements role and a uses role. It can include one of either or one of each. You can add port types directly to a Role Link shape using either existing roles or new roles, and existing or new port types.
Correlation_Pro	Correlation Set	Indicates a set of properties with specific values. This is different from a correlation type, which is simply a list of properties. Correlation sets are used to match an incoming message with the appropriate instance of an orchestration. You can create any number of instances of a given orchestration, and while each of them will perform the same actions, they will do so on different data. If an incoming message does not have all of the properties listed in the correlation set, with matching values for each, correlation will fail and the message will not be received by the orchestration instance.

Continued

Table 7-1. *Continued*

Icon	Shape	Description
Variable_Pro	Variable*	Indicates a scoped orchestration variable. Scoped orchestration variables are used the same way as in conventional programming languages. (Variables can be of any .NET class type. The assembly that the class is part of has to be deployed to the GAC and referenced by the BizTalk project. The class has to be serializable unless the variable is being declared within an atomic scope.)
Port_BizTalkPro Op_BTSPro Request	Port	Indicates an instance of a definition of a set of message interaction patterns called operations that are permitted at that endpoint (port). An operation can be one-way, in which case one message is sent or received; or it could be two-way, in which case a message is sent (or received) and a response is received (or sent).
Receive_1	Receive Message	Receives a message from a port. It may be used to start an orchestration by setting the `Activate` property to true so that a message-matching criteria specified in a filter expression will be received and the orchestration instance will execute. Correlation sets may be applied to a Receive shape to ensure that messages corresponding to a given orchestration instance are correctly received by that instance.
Send_1	Send Message	Sends a given message to a specified port. If an indirect response (not using a request-response port) to the sent message is expected to be received, the message has to be correlated with the currently running instance of the orchestration, so that the respondent can get the response to the correct instance. A following correlation set for a previously initialized correlation or an initializing correlation set may be applied to the Send shape. A persistence point is performed after the execution of a send, except within an atomic scope.
Listen_1	Listen	Makes an orchestration instance wait for any one of several possible events before proceeding. The first branch with a condition that evaluates to true (a delay is reached or a message is received) is followed, and none of the other branches will run. The first shape within a Listen branch must be either a Delay shape or a Receive shape. No other shape may be placed below the initial Receive or Delay shape. An activation receive may be used in a Listen shape, but if one branch contains an activation receive, all branches must contain activation receives, and no timeout can be used. The activation receive must be the first action in each branch.

Icon	Shape	Description
Delay_Pro	Delay	Enables you to control the timing of the orchestration progress. A timeout may be set on the Delay shape so that an orchestration instance pauses before resuming execution. The timeout is specified using `System.DateTime` (refer to the definition of DateTime Structure in Microsoft Visual Studio's online help), which causes the orchestration instance to pause until the specified date or time is reached. The timeout may also be specified using `System.TimeSpan`, which causes the orchestration instance to pause for the specified length of time (refer to the definition of TimeSpan Structure in Microsoft Visual Studio's online help). Delay shapes are regularly used within Listen shapes to implement a timeout.
ParallelActions_Pro	Parallel Actions	Contains branches. Any shape may be placed in a parallel branch. Each branch of a parallel runs concurrently but independently. It is possible that more than one branch of a Parallel Actions shape will attempt to access the same data. To avoid errors, shapes that access the data should be placed inside synchronized scopes. You can specify in the properties of a Scope shape whether it be synchronized or not.(If a Terminate shape is placed inside a Parallel Actions shape, and the branch with the Terminate on it is run, the instance completes immediately, regardless of whether other branches have finished running. Depending on the orchestration design, results might be unpredictable in this case.)
Decide_Pro	Decide	Represents a decision based on if/else logic. The shape always has a branch for the "if" statement and a branch for the "else" statement; you can add additional branches for "else if" statements as needed. You may use the Expression editor to add a rule to each branch except the "else" branch. If the rule evaluates to true, the branch will be taken. Below the rule or "else" clause, a branch of a Decide shape can contain additional shapes, just like any other part of the orchestration.
Loop_Pro	Loop	Enables your orchestration to loop until a condition is met.
Scope_Pro	Scope	Provides a contextual framework for its contents. The first block of a Scope shape is the context block, or body, in that the basic actions of the scope take place; it is analogous to the `try` block in a `try/catch` statement. Following the body, the Scope shape may also include one or more exception-handler blocks and a compensation block (refer to the "Scopes" sidebar later in this chapter for more details).

Continued

Table 7-1. *Continued*

Icon	Shape	Description
Compensation_1	Compensation	Enables you to call code to undo or compensate for operations already performed by the orchestration when an error occurs.
CatchException_Pro	Catch Exception	Represents an exception handler and is attached to the end of a Scope shape. You can attach as many Catch Exception blocks as you need. If an exception is thrown that matches the type specified, the exception handler will be called. If some other exception is thrown, it will be handled by the default exception handler. To add a Catch Exception block to a Scope shape, the `Transaction Type` property of the Scope shape must be set to None or Long Running.
ThrowExcepti...	Throw Exception	You can explicitly throw exceptions in an orchestration with the Throw Exception shape. The runtime engine searches for the nearest exception handler that can handle the exception type. It first searches the current orchestration for an enclosing scope, and then considers in order the associated exception handlers of the scope. If the engine does not find an appropriate handler, it searches any orchestration that called the current orchestration for a scope that encloses the point of the call to the current orchestration.(Do not select `GeneralException` in the Throw Exception shape. This type should only be used for rethrowing exceptions in a Catch Exception block.)
Expression_T...	Expression	Enables you to enter any expression you choose in your orchestration. For example, you can make a .NET-based call to run an external library or manipulate the values of your orchestration variables. It is generally not good practice to use it to perform high-level orchestration logic that preferably would be visible in the orchestration flow itself. Your orchestration is easier to understand and maintain if your Expression shapes contain simple and modular expressions.

Icon	Shape	Description
Suspend_My...	Suspend	Makes an orchestration instance stop running until an administrator explicitly intervenes—you do so by setting it to a suspended resumable state,** perhaps to reflect an error condition that requires attention beyond the scope of the orchestration. All of the state information for the orchestration instance is saved, and it will be reinstated when the administrator resumes the orchestration instance. When an orchestration instance is suspended, an error is raised. You can specify a message string to accompany the error to help the administrator diagnose the situation. All of the state information for the orchestration instance is saved, and it is reinstated when the administrator resumes the orchestration instance. If a Suspend shape exists in an orchestration that has been called synchronously (as with the Call Orchestration shape) by another orchestration, the nested instance and all enclosing orchestration instances will be suspended.
Terminate_M...	Terminate	The Terminate shape is used to end an orchestration instance instantly. You can specify a message string to accompany the shape when viewed in MMC. If a Terminate shape is encountered in an orchestration that has been called synchronously (as with the Call Orchestration shape) by another orchestration, the nested instance and all enclosing orchestration instances will be terminated.

** *If the developer wants to process a binary object in an orchestration, the message type should be set to* `System.XMLDocument`. *The orchestration engine treats it as an agnostic type, and it does not care what it is, so it does not have to be valid XML. Cool, huh?*

** *If the engine encounters an error or unhandled exception while executing an orchestration, it will set the orchestration to a suspended nonresumable state. This will maintain the orchestration information in the BizTalk Messagebox database for an administrator to review using MMC and clean up once the information has been examined by the administrator.*

■ **Tip** You can pass a gigantic message to an orchestration, and as long as XPath statements are not called, the orchestration will never load the document. Use distinguished and promoted properties to access a message within an orchestration, and the message in use will never be put in memory.

What Transactions Mean and Cost

Transactions guarantee that any partial updates are rolled back automatically[6] in the event of a failure during a transactional update and that the effects of the transaction are erased. Transactions in BizTalk may be **atomic** or **long running**.

6 Non–long-running transactions will only persist their state to store when the transaction completes, thus achieving auto-rollback. Long-running transactions require the explicit declaration of a compensation block by the Orchestration Designer.

Atomic Transactions

In BizTalk, orchestrations are similar to distributed transaction coordinator (DTC) transactions in that they are generally short-lived and have the four **ACID** attributes—(atomicity, consistency, isolation, and durability). The BizTalk Server 2009 documentation (Microsoft, 2009) describes these as follows:[7]

- **Atomicity**: A transaction represents an atomic unit of work. Either all modifications within a transaction are performed or none.
- **Consistency**: When committed, a transaction must preserve the integrity of the data within the system. If a transaction performs a data modification on a database that was internally consistent before the transaction started, the database must still be internally consistent when the transaction is committed. Ensuring this property is largely the responsibility of the application developer.
- **Isolation:** Modifications made by concurrent transactions must be isolated from the modifications made by other concurrent transactions. Isolated transactions that run concurrently perform modifications that preserve internal database consistency exactly as they would if the transactions were run serially.
- **Durability:** After a transaction is committed, all modifications are permanently in place in the system by default. The modifications persist even if a system failure occurs.

According to the BizTalk Server 2009 documentation (Microsoft, 2009), "Atomic transactions guarantee that any partial updates are rolled back automatically in the event of a failure during the transactional update, and that the effects of the transaction are erased (except for the effects of any .NET calls that are made in the transaction)." Atomic transactions dictate to the engine that their scope should be fully executed before the resources allocated to the orchestration instance are released and reused by another instance. Therefore, the XLANG engine does not persist the orchestration instance state until the transaction is fully committed.[8] This allows for the isolation and consistency of the transaction. This also implies that, in the case of a server failure or a manual host instance recycle while the transaction is executing, the orchestration instance will resume execution at the beginning of the atomic transaction scope. An atomic transaction cannot contain any other transaction within it nor can it contain an exception handler.

Crossing the process boundary within an atomic transaction scope is highly undesirable. For example, a call to a receive port within the atomic scope will not allow the engine to dehydrate if there are no messages to receive.[9] Such a design decision might lead to the quick depletion of processing threads in the host instance's thread pool and the inability of the

8 "BizTalk Server ensures that state changes within an atomic transaction—such as modifications to variables, messages, and objects—are visible outside the scope of the atomic transaction only upon commitment of the transaction. The intermediate state changes are isolated from other parts of an orchestration" (Microsoft, "BizTalk Server 2009 Documentation"). Copyright © 2009 by Microsoft Corporation. Reprinted with permission from Microsoft Corporation.

9 An atomic transaction cannot contain matching send and receive actions—that is, a request-response pair or a send and receive that use the same correlation set.

host instance to instantiate new orchestrations. On the other hand, if an atomic transaction contains a Receive shape, a Send shape, or a Start Orchestration shape, the corresponding action will not be performed until the transaction is committed. Therefore, scoping multiple consecutive sends within an atomic scope is very useful. The XLANG engine will not persist the orchestration instance's state on every send, instead batching the round-trips to the Messagebox database to be performed once at the end of the atomic transaction. Atomic transaction scopes are also handy for wrapping nonserializable managed variables; although such wrapping is poor design, sometimes it is inevitable, especially when leveraging third-party managed assemblies or legacy components.

Note DTC transactions, mentioned early in this section, are atomic transactions using COM+ objects derived from `System.Enterprise Services.ServicedComponents` and agreeing isolation levels between transaction components.

Long-Running Transactions

Long-running transactions provide you with great flexibility in designing robust transaction architecture through custom scope-based compensation, custom scope-based exception handling, and the ability to nest transactions. Long-running transactions are the right candidate if transactions might run for an extended time and full ACID properties are not required (that is, you do not need to guarantee isolation of data from other transactions). A long-running transaction might have long periods of inactivity, often due to waiting for external messages to arrive. The XLANG engine might dehydrate the running orchestration instance at this point and release its resources back to the pool. Long-running transactions impose consistency and durability, but not atomicity and isolation. The data within a long-running transaction is not locked; other processes or applications can modify it. The isolation property for state updates is not maintained because holding locks for a long duration is impractical.

By declaring variables, messages, and .NET components, a scope can define its own state. A long-running transaction has access to the state information of its own scope, any scope that encloses it, and any state information globally defined within the orchestration. It does not have access to the state information of any scopes that do not enclose it.

The following sidebar, based on material from the BizTalk Server 2009 documentation (Microsoft, 2009), discusses scopes in detail.[10]

---

10 Copyright © 2009 by Microsoft Corporation. Reprinted with permission from Microsoft Corporation.

SCOPES

A *scope* is a framework for grouping actions. It is primarily used for transactional execution and exception handling. A scope contains one or more blocks. It has a body and can optionally have appended to it any number of exception handling blocks. It may have an optional compensation block as well, depending on the nature of the scope. Some scopes will be purely for exception handling and will not require compensation. Other scopes will be explicitly transactional and will always have a default compensation handler, along with an optional compensation handler that you create for it. A transactional scope will also have a default exception handler and any number of additional exception handlers that you create for it.

BizTalk developers can specify that scopes are synchronized or not synchronized. By synchronizing a scope, developers will ensure that any shared data that is accessed within it will not be written to by one or more parallel actions in your orchestration, nor will it be written to while another action is reading it. Atomic transaction scopes are always synchronized. All actions within a synchronized scope are considered synchronized, as are all actions in any of its exception handlers. Actions in the compensation handler for a transactional scope are not synchronized.

You can nest Scope shapes inside other Scope shapes. The rules for nesting scopes are as follows:

- Transactional and/or synchronized scopes cannot be nested inside synchronized scopes, including the exception handlers of synchronized scopes.
- Atomic transaction scopes cannot have any other transactional scopes nested inside them.
- Transactional scopes cannot be nested inside nontransactional scopes or orchestrations.
- You can nest scopes up to 44 levels deep.

Call Orchestration shapes can be included inside scopes, but the called orchestrations are treated the same as any other nested transaction, and the same rules apply.

Start Orchestration shapes can be included inside scopes. Nesting limitations do not apply to started orchestrations.

You can declare variables such as messages and correlation sets at the scope level. You cannot use the same name for a scope variable as for an orchestration variable, however; name hiding is not allowed.

Caution You can still run into a deadlock condition if you do not design your processes carefully. Example: two branches of a parallel action in orchestration A access the same message, one to send it and one to receive it, so both must have a synchronized scope. A second orchestration receives the message and sends it back. It is possible that the sending branch in orchestration A will receive its locks before the receiving branch, and you will end up with a deadlock.

Threading and Persistence

Threads are a limited resource in BizTalk hosts and persisting a running instance state to the Messagebox is an expensive operation. The orchestration engine balances the use of threads and orchestration persistence and dehydration delicately to ensure the continued execution of the maximum number of instances possible with the minimum overhead required.

Dehydration

The XLANG engine saves to persistent storage the entire state of a running orchestration instance at various points so that the instance can later be completely restored in memory. The state includes

- The internal state of the engine, including its current progress
- The state of any .NET components—variables—that maintain state information and are being used by the orchestration
- Message and variable values

The XLANG engine saves the state of a running orchestration instance at various points. If it needs to rehydrate the orchestration instance, start up from a controlled shutdown, or recover from an unexpected shutdown, it will run the orchestration instance from the last persistence point as though nothing else occurred. For example, if a message is received but an unexpected shutdown occurs before state can be saved, the engine will not record that it has received the message and will receive it again upon restarting.

According to the BizTalk Server 2009 documentation (Microsoft, 2009), the orchestration state is persisted under the following circumstances:[11]

- The end of a transactional scope. The engine saves state at the end of a transactional scope to ensure transactional integrity and to ensure that the point at which the orchestration should resume is defined unambiguously, and that compensation can be carried out correctly if necessary. The orchestration will continue to run from the end of the scope if persistence was successful; otherwise, the appropriate exception handler will be invoked. If the scope is transactional and atomic, the engine will save state within that scope. If the scope is transactional and long running, the engine will generate a new transaction and save the complete state of the runtime.
- A debugging breakpoint is reached.
- A message is sent. The only exception to this is when a message is sent from within an atomic transaction scope.
- The orchestration starts another orchestration asynchronously, as with the Start Orchestration shape.
- The orchestration instance is suspended.

11 Copyright © 2009 by Microsoft Corporation. Reprinted with permission from Microsoft Corporation.

- The system shuts down under controlled conditions.[12] Note that this does not include abnormal termination; in that case, when the engine next runs, it will resume the orchestration instance from the last persistence point that occurred before the shutdown.
- The orchestration instance is finished.
- The engine determines that the instance should be dehydrated.

Transactions have an impact on the number of persistence points within an orchestration and the overall performance of the BizTalk Messagebox, SQL Server, and BizTalk server. An increasing number of persistence points may impede the performance of the BizTalk solution, due to the contention on access to the Messagebox database while storing orchestration instances' state. When using atomic and long-running transactions, the BizTalk developer needs to understand the performance impact of each. Although atomic transactions hold limited system resources, like threads and memory, during the lifetime of the transaction scope, they could be used to minimize the number of persistence points in an orchestration and to minimize the contention and round-trips to the database. Long-running transactions, on the other hand, may be used to optimize the use of limited system resources—threads and memory, as the XLANG engine can dehydrate an orchestration instance within the scope of a long-running transaction and reclaim its memory and threads if it meets the dehydration criteria. For this to be achieved, the XLANG engine needs to persist the orchestration instance's state at various points throughout the long-running transaction scope. Proper solution load testing and load modeling can give you indications of the number of persistence points over time, and contention over the database may be predicted and proper sizing of the servers implemented to mitigate the risk of these contentions.[13]

The Dehydration Algorithm and Thresholds

So, how does the engine determine that an orchestration should be dehydrated? If an orchestration instance is idle, waiting at Receive, Listen, or Delay shapes, and the engine predicted that it will be idle for a longer period than the dehydration threshold, it will get dehydrated. The decision that an orchestration instance needs to be dehydrated and the prediction that it might become idle for a long period at the current shape is made based on the configurable maximum, minimum, and static thresholds. Those settings may be configured in the BTSNTSvc.exe.config file.[14] The estimated service idle time,[15] used to predict whether an orchestration instance should be dehydrated or not, is averaged out over time. As more instances of the same orchestration get instantiated, the more realistic that average becomes.

---

12 During a controlled shutdown, the engine saves control information as well as the current state of all running orchestration instances so that it can resume running them when it is started again. The engine will continue to run the instance until it reaches the next persistence point, when it will save the orchestration state and shut down the instance before shutting itself down.

13 For proper scalability and sizing techniques, refer to the BizTalk Performance and Stress Team's white paper on scalability and performance tuning.

14 The section "Orchestration Engine Configuration" covers the different thresholds and their syntax.

15 The estimated service idle time is calculated for instances of the same orchestration type. If a host instance is recycled or the server is rebooted, that value is reset and is averaged out again from scratch.

If a constant dehydration threshold or a memory threshold is used, the check whether an orchestration instance should be dehydrated or not is simple, it is simply

Dehydrate = (Estimated instance idle time > `StaticThreshold`)

or

Dehydrated = (Used host memory > `MemoryThreshold`)

If constant dehydration thresholds are not used, the engine checks whether the estimated instance idle time is greater than `MinThreshold` + `Stress_scaling_factor`[16] * (`MaxThreshold` – `MinThreshold`).

In BizTalk 2006 and 2009, other than the check when an orchestration instance hits Receive, Listen, or Delay shapes, the engine checks periodically for instances that are passed the dehydration threshold by replacing the estimated instance idle time with the actual instance idle time in the preceding checks. Orchestration instances with actual instance idle time past the dehydration threshold are dehydrated immediately.

■ **Caution** The checks for constant dehydration thresholds do not use the `Stress_scaling_factor`. This means that the thresholds do not decrease as the server is under increasing stress!

The Cost of Parallel Shapes

If you were to ask seasoned developers whether to use a multithreaded approach to respond to a set of requests, each resulting in a series of calculations followed by the formatting of a response, or simply resorting to using a limited number of threads to respond to these requests, they would likely say that a single threaded approach would be their method of choice. An alternative would be using a limited pool of prespawned threads to perform these transactions, and they would warn against the use of a single worker thread per request. This is because the act of spawning threads and allocating their proper resources and soft context switching is somewhat expensive, but mostly because of the complexity associated with multi-threaded design and the uncertainty of the order of execution.

You should also be wary of using Parallel Actions shapes for the same reasons. There are hidden costs associated with using Parallel Actions shapes. The engine decides whether new threads need to be allocated to perform the parallel branches and implements a persistence point before the parallel action, then one at the ending synchronization point. Figures 7-3, 7-4, and 7-5 illustrate three different ways to perform the same action and highlight that using parallel actions would result in the worst performance. There is also the risk of corrupting data, as interleaved data access from multiple parallel branches might lead to unexpected behavior and undesirable values. To avoid data corruption, the logic accessing data should be encapsulated within synchronized scopes. Synchronized scopes will ensure that the data is being accessed by one thread or branch at a time. Using synchronized scopes

---

16 Stress_scaling_factor is a number between 0 and 1 that converges to zero with stress. This will ensure that orchestration instances get dehydrated at a much lower estimated idle time if the system is under stress.

will result in parallel branches being blocked on each other to ensure data integrity. This will slow down execution to ensure the predictability of the outcome. Depending on how complex and interdependent the logic is, it might be simpler to serially perform the data access instead of using parallel actions.

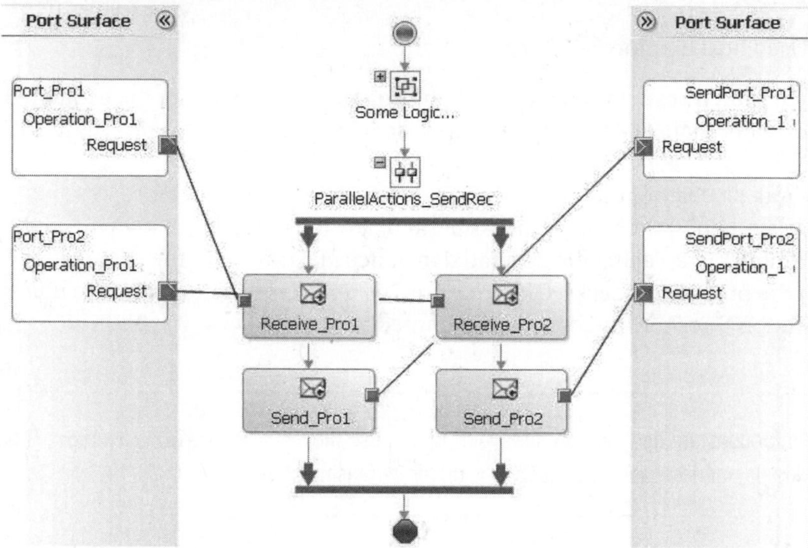

Figure 7-3. *Parallel actions—slowest solution*

Caution The use of parallel branches in orchestrations does not mean that these branches will run on parallel threads. It is simply an indication to the XLANG engine that operations in these branches may be interleaved if necessary! The engine then makes the decision to run them on separate threads or interleave them. For example, if you place a Terminate shape inside a Parallel Actions shape, and the branch with the Terminate shape on it is run, the instance completes immediately, regardless of whether other branches have finished running. Depending on your design, results might be unpredictable in this case.

One of the authors of *Pro BizTalk 2006*, our fellow architect Ahmed Metwally, once got a call from a developer who was seeing his BizTalk host instance recycle every time he sent more than five concurrent messages to his solution. The problem was reproducible and easy to diagnose, as the error message in the event log was “not enough threads” to create new orchestration instances. Although BizTalk dehydrates orchestration instances to manage its resources and the number of active threads versus the number of available threads in the thread pool, if all current running instances are active, BizTalk may not be able to dehydrate them to free up some resources.

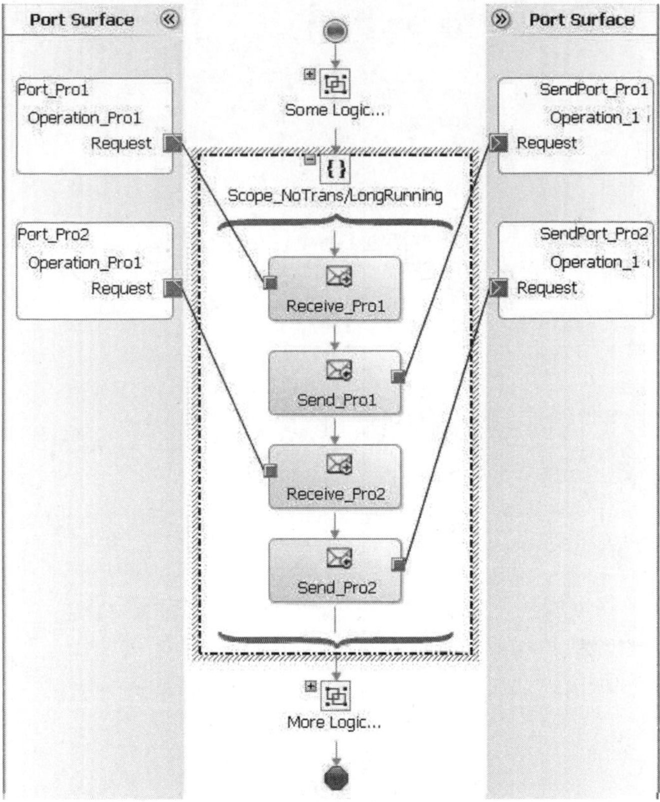

Figure 7-4. *Single long-running transaction or scope with no transaction—second slowest solution*

In the scenario we're talking about, the developer had an orchestration subscribed to a receive port and upon activating a receive would issue five calls to an external managed .NET assembly on five parallel branches in a Parallel Actions shape. The external assembly performed a set of calculations and eventually called a web service to perform a transaction.[17] The test was being implemented on the developer's machine that luckily was set to have a pool of 25 threads max per CPU.[18] Had the settings been higher, it would have taken longer for the developer to find the problem.

17 Calling external logic that might take a considerable amount of time to perform its task before returning should be implemented through the messaging subsystem. A call to an external assembly from within an expression means that the call is executing on the XLANG engine's thread currently assigned to that particular orchestration instance. Making such calls from within expressions means that the engine threads will not be able to manage its threads and dehydrate them as required.

18 Using the BizTalk 2009 Server Administration Console, you can set the thresholds for the number of threads per CPU through the throttling thresholds settings on the Advanced tab of the host property pages.

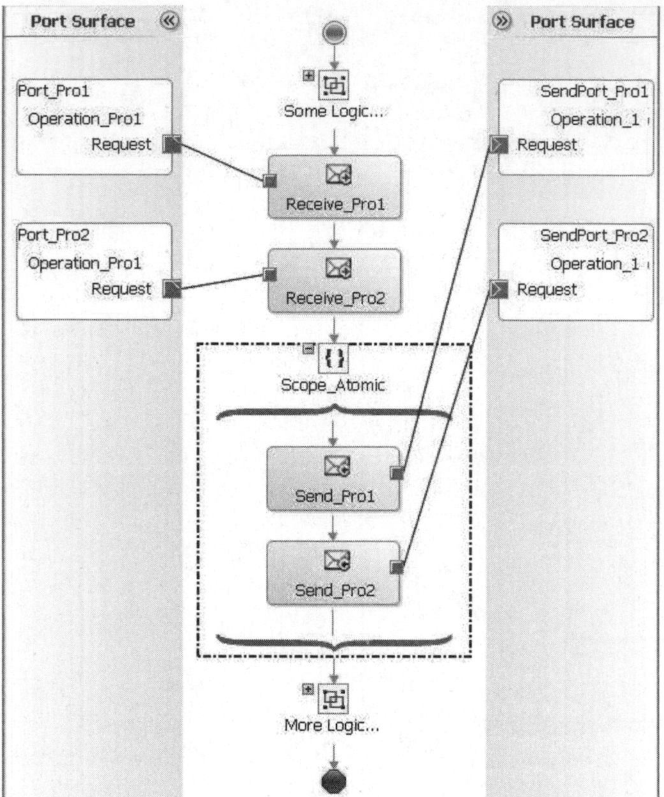

Figure 7-5. *Sends in atomic scope—fastest solution*

We are sure that by now you are aware of the point we are trying to make. Although calling a web service from within an expression instead of using the messaging subsystem would not be considered wise, making the calls in parallel from within Parallel Actions shapes results in the exhaustion of available threads in the thread pool and prevents the host from handling new instances. BizTalk uses the default thread pool provided by the .NET common language runtime (CLR); tuning the thread pool is simply a matter of setting the proper values in the BizTalk Server 2009 Administration Console for the particular BizTalk host. With automatic throttling in BizTalk 2009, you will not have to worry as much about their servers recycling, but tuning the server with the proper values for the thread pool based on the projected and modeled loads will lead to an optimal application performance.

In short, BizTalk application performance can be easily optimized by monitoring and tuning the minimum and maximum number of threads in the thread pool and the number of in-flight messages; monitoring the number of persistence points and their effect on the overall performance; and tweaking orchestrations to minimize the number of persistence points.

Correlation

Automating a business process tends to require associating multiple messages together to achieve the necessary business transaction. **Correlations** are used whenever an orchestration does not have an explicit way of associating a message with an instance, such as an activating receive, a request-response, or a self-correlating port.

What Is Correlation?

Correlation is the process of matching an incoming message with the appropriate instance of an orchestration. You can create any number of instances of a given orchestration, and while each of them will perform the same actions, they will do so on different data. To have the same **orchestration instance** perform a set of actions on different incoming messages to complete a complex transaction, you will need to leverage **correlation sets** and correlate those incoming messages. If, for example, an orchestration developed to automate a purchase from a partner is designed to issue a purchase order, receive an invoice, and send payment, you need to be sure that the invoice is received by the same orchestration instance that the corresponding purchase order was sent from. Imagine ordering a single item and getting back an invoice for 1,000 items, or vice versa, and you will understand the value of correlation.

This sort of correlation of messages with orchestration instances may be achieved by defining correlation sets. A **correlation set** is a set of properties with specific values. If an incoming message does not have all of these properties, with matching values for each, correlation will fail, and the message will not be received by the orchestration instance. Correlation sets are initialized in a receive action or a send action.

Each correlation set is based on a **correlation type**, which is simply a list of properties. These properties might be data properties, which are found in the message itself, or context properties, which describe details of the system or messages that are unrelated to the data being conveyed in the message.

A correlation type may be used in more than one correlation set. If you need to correlate on different values for the properties in a correlation type, you must create a new correlation set—each correlation set can be initialized only once.[19]

Caution Do not set the system-defined property `BTS.CorrelationToken` associated with each message. This is used by the engine in correlating messages, and setting it could result in your orchestration losing messages.

The properties of a message sent from an orchestration may be validated by the engine to ensure that it reflects the properties in its correlation set. By default, this validation is disabled.[20]

19 Correlation sets may be passed as in parameters to other orchestrations.

20 Refer to the "Orchestration Engine Configuration" section near the end of this chapter for more information on how to enable and disable correlation validation.

Convoys: Serial vs. Parallel

Convoys are groups of related messages that are intended by a partner business process to be handled in a specific order within an orchestration. For example, an orchestration might need to receive five different messages before any processing can begin.

When a group of correlated messages could potentially be received at the same time, a race condition could occur in that a correlation set in a particular orchestration instance must be initialized by one of the messages before the other messages can be correlated to that orchestration instance. To ensure that all of the correlated messages will be received by the same orchestration instance, BizTalk detects the potential for such a race condition and treats these messages as a convoy.

There are two main types of convoys: **concurrent correlated receives** and **sequential correlated receives**. A convoy set is a group of correlation sets that are used in a convoy.

Note the following general restrictions on convoys:

- A convoy set can contain no more than three properties.
- Concurrent and sequential convoys can coexist in an orchestration, but they cannot use any shared correlation sets.
- Correlation sets passed into started orchestrations do not receive convoy processing in the started orchestration.
- You cannot initialize two or more correlation sets with one receive to be used in separate convoys. For example, if receive r1 initializes correlation sets c1 and c2, receive r2 follows c1, and receive r3 follows c2, then the orchestration engine will not treat these as convoys. It is a valid convoy scenario if both r2 and r3 follow both c1 and c2, both follow c1 only, or both follow c2 only.

Concurrent correlated receives are correlated receive statements in two or more branches of a Parallel Actions shape. If a correlation is initialized in more than one parallel task, each correlated receive must initialize exactly the same set of correlations. The first such task that receives a correlated message will do the actual initialization, and validation will be done on the others.

Sequential correlated receives are receives that are correlated to previous receives. Convoy processing takes place for cases in which the correlation sets for a receive are initialized by another receive.

■ **Note** Any correlation set that is being followed by a send statement (chronologically) prior to the particular receive statement is not considered a part of the convoy set.

For receives that require convoy processing, the following restrictions apply:

- The correlation sets that constitute a sequential convoy set for a particular receive must be initialized by one preceding receive.
- The port for a receive that requires sequential convoy processing must be the same as the port for the receive initializing the convoy set. Cross-port convoys are not supported.

- Message types for a particular receive that require convoy processing must match the message type for the receive initializing the convoy set, unless the receive statement is operating on an ordered delivery port.
- All receives participating in a sequential convoy must follow all the correlation sets that are initialized (or followed) by the initializing receive, unless operating on an ordered delivery port.
- If a sequential convoy is initialized by an Activating Receive statement, then the Activating Receive cannot have a filter expression unless operating on an ordered delivery port.
- If a sequential convoy is initialized by an Activating Receive, the following receives cannot be inside a nested orchestration. Otherwise the preceding rules apply for nested orchestrations.

Dynamic Message Transformations

Dynamic message transformations are an important technique often overlooked by developers. This feature allows you to choose from a series of maps based on a parameter of the incoming message and perform transformations inside orchestrations. A good example of when this feature may come in handy is automating business processes between a company and its partners located in different countries. The documents arriving from the partners—for example, purchase orders—may have a slightly different structure or different field format depending on the standards of the country of origin. Obviously, such documents have to be transformed to a generic form before being submitted for further processing in the orchestration that handles purchase orders. A straightforward solution would be to create a separate port for each trading partner and configure each port to apply a map performing country-specific transformations. Although this approach is technically absolutely valid, it is not always an optimal solution. If the number of trading partners keeps growing, adding more and more identical ports for the only purpose of applying different maps is not practical. Another compelling reason to transform messages inside orchestrations is that orchestrations offer much greater flexibility than pipelines to handle exceptions from failed maps.

Low-Volume Transformations

If the volume of messages requiring transformations is relatively low, then all you have to do is to perform a few simple steps as follows:

1. Build and deploy the project containing your maps.
2. Add code into Expression shape to determine which map you have to apply. Your source message schema should promote a field that you will pass to the code. For the trading partners mentioned earlier, it can be, for example, the CountryId. The code has to return a string in the following format:

```
mapAssemblyName = "NameSpace.MapClassName,
AssemblyName,Version=..., Culture=...,PublicKeyToken=..."
```

Now add the following line of code to get the map type:

```
MyMapType = System.Type.GetType(mapAssemblyName);
```

where `MyMapType` is a variable of the `System.Type` type.

3. Add the following XLANG code into the Message Assignment shape:

```
transform(MyOutputMsg) = MyMapType(MyInputMsg);
```

where `MyInputMessage` is the source message and `MyOutputMessage` is the destination message. This code performs the transformation and generates the destination message ready for further processing.

4. Proceed with the rest of the business logic.

High-Volume Transformations

Sustaining a high volume of message transformations requires an extra effort. Microsoft recommends writing a cache in user code and then using the cache to retrieve maps before performing the transformations. As the BizTalk Server 2009 documentation[21] states, "If you are not caching the maps, it is possible to see Common Language Runtime (CLR) memory grow significantly. Dynamic mapping requires that the .NET Runtime perform code access check which results in a .NET Evidence object being placed in the Large Object Heap for each transformation and this object is not disposed of until the orchestration completes. Therefore, when there are a lot of these types of transforms occurring simultaneously, you may see the memory usage increase substantially which can also lead to the out of memory exception." Unfortunately, the product documentation doesn't go further than recommendations. Until Microsoft provides a solution that you can reuse in your code, your choice is limited to writing a custom code and using not officially supported internal infrastructure classes.

Listing 7-1 provides a helper class that addresses the memory issue by caching the maps as the product documentation suggests. You can use this class to perform message transformations in high-volume scenarios. Please note the use of the `TransformBase` class from the `Microsoft.XLANGs.BaseTypes` namespace. The `TransformBase` is the base class from which all map classes inherit. You should be aware that since this class supports internal BizTalk infrastructure and is not intended for use in your code, you are not guaranteed that implementation of the class will not change in the future.

Listing 7-1. *DynamicTransformsHelper Class*

```
using System;
using System.Xml;
using System.Xml.Xsl;
using System.Xml.XPath;
using System.Reflection;
using System.IO;
using Microsoft.XLANGs.BaseTypes;
using System.Collections.Generic;
```

21 Copyright Microsoft Corporation, 2009.

```
namespace ProBiztalk.Samples.Utilities
{
    [Serializable()]
    public class DynamicTransforms
    {

        private static Dictionary<string, TransformBase> m_mapCache = null;
        static DynamicTransforms()
        {
            m_mapCache = new Dictionary<string, TransformBase>();
        }

        public static XmlDocument Transform(XmlDocument xmlInputMessage,
                                           string mapAssemblyName)
        {
            XmlDocument xmlOutputMessage = new XmlDocument();

            // TransforBase is a base class
            //which all BizTalk map classes inherit from
            TransformBase mapClass = null;
            //check if we already cached map class
            if (m_mapCache.ContainsKey(mapAssemblyName) == false)
            {
                Type mapType = System.Type.GetType(mapAssemblyName);
                mapClass = (TransformBase)System.Activator.CreateInstance(mapType);
                m_mapCache.Add(mapAssemblyName, mapClass);
            }
            else
            {
                m_mapCache.TryGetValue(mapAssemblyName, out mapClass);
            }

            XslTransform transform = mapClass.Transform;
            XsltArgumentList argList = mapClass.TransformArgs;

            //perform transformation
            xmlOutputMessage = InternalTransform(transform, argList,
                               xmlInputMessage);
            return xmlOutputMessage;
        }
        /// <summary>
        /// Performs XSL transformation
        /// </summary>
        /// <param name="xslt"></param>
        /// <param name="args"></param>
```

```
        /// <param name="inputMessage"></param>
        /// <returns></returns>
        private static XmlDocument InternalTransform(XslTransform xslt,
                                                   XsltArgumentList args,
                                                   XmlDocument inputMessage)
        {
            XmlNodeReader inputMessageRoot = new XmlNodeReader(inputMessage);
            XPathDocument inputMessageXPath = new XPathDocument(inputMessageRoot);
            MemoryStream stream = new MemoryStream();
            XmlTextWriter writer = new XmlTextWriter(stream,
                                                System.Text.Encoding.Unicode);

            xslt.Transform(inputMessageXPath, args, writer, null);

            stream.Flush();
            stream.Seek(0, SeekOrigin.Begin);

            //convert memory stream into XML document
            XmlTextReader outputReader;
            XmlDocument outputMessage;
            outputReader = new XmlTextReader(stream);
            outputMessage = new XmlDocument();
            outputMessage.Load(outputReader);
            return outputMessage;
        }
    }
}
```

Put this class into a separate project, build and GAC the assembly. Once it's done, the `DynamicTransformsHelper` class is ready for consumption. To transform messages using this class, you have to perform the following steps:

1. In your orchestrations project, add a reference to the assembly containing the `DynamicTransformsHelper` class.
2. Add code into an Expression shape to determine which map you have to apply. The code has to return a string in the following form:

   ```
   mapAssemblyName = "NameSpace.MapClassName,
   AssemblyName,Version=..., Culture=...,PublicKeyToken=..."
   ```

3. Into a Message Assignment shape add the following code to perform the transformation:

   ```
   MyOutputMsg = ProBiztalk.Samples.Utilities.➥
   DynamicTransforms.Transform (MyInputMsg,mapAssemblyName)
   ```

   where `MyOutputMsg` is the destination message, `MyInputMsg` is the source message, and `mapAssmeblyName` is the map name that you determined in step 2.
4. Proceed with the rest of the business logic.

Pitfalls of Orchestration Development

Some BizTalk artifacts lend themselves nicely to particular patterns of solutions, while their use could be devastating to the performance of a different solution. The following sections describe some of these solution patterns and the pitfalls that you as a BizTalk developer need to watch out for.

Batch Processing and Legacy Systems

Legacy mainframe systems excel in what they were designed to do best, batch processing. With the emergence of online applications and progressive automation of internal processes, the load onto these legacy systems is exponentially increasing. Instead of handling a handful of requests concurrently, they are now expected to handle hundreds and thousands of concurrent requests as business goes online and customers perform actions resulting in transactions executing on these back-end legacy systems. EAI platforms such as BizTalk facilitate the integration of newly developed interactive systems with legacy back ends such as those batch-processing mainframes. Third-party or custom adapters could be used to communicate with the mainframes, and transformation maps could be used to translate data back and forth. BizTalk-based solutions developed to integrate with the mainframe will leverage the Messagebox as a queue to throttle and batch transaction requests to the mainframes to ensure their ability to handle the incoming load of requests.

Such a solution works perfectly fine, but should be stress and load tested to ensure that the queuing and throttling does not affect the overall performance of the solution. With BizTalk 2006 and 2009 auto-throttling, queuing is not a big problem, but with previous versions of BizTalk, queuing leads to the growth of the spool table in the Messagebox, which affects the overall performance of the Messagebox and consequently the BizTalk server.

Interactive Orchestrations (the Request/Response Approach)

The response time in interactive orchestrations such as workflows exposed as web services could be critical to the correctness of the complete solutions. For example, a call from an ASP.NET web app to an orchestration exposed as a web service might be expected to return within 2 seconds or less so that the web application can complete its response to the client within the required timeout period. To ensure that BizTalk is not holding incoming web service requests from being submitted to the proper orchestration instance as soon as they arrive, the batch size should be set to 1 in the adm_serviceclass table in the Management Database for the web service receive host. To minimize the time spent by the engine performing its plumbing functions, you should use atomic transaction scopes whenever possible to minimize the number of persistence points in the orchestration.

If tuning is not enough to improve the response time, you should consider redesigning the interaction with the orchestration to support polling. For example, the web application will call a one-way web method as soon as the data needed to pass to the orchestration is available to that web application, passing in a parameter that the orchestration will use for correlation. The web application would then call a two-way request-response web method, right before the web application really needs the response from the orchestration instance, passing in the same parameter used for correlation and receiving the expected response from the orchestration. This request/poll method allows the orchestration instance extra time to execute and formulate the response while the web application is still executing and promptly responding to client requests.

Calling an Assembly or Sending a Message to a Web Service

Complex logic in a process is usually wrapped in an external assembly called by the orchestration at different points in its execution. The called logic in those external assemblies will execute on the same thread assigned to the orchestration instance by the engine. The engine cannot dehydrate the thread while it is executing within the external assembly. Also, if a failure occurs and the server is restarted, the orchestration instance will continue execution from the last persistence point, meaning that it will issue the same call to the external assembly again, resulting in the execution of the same logic twice. Logic in those external assemblies should not be affecting state in permanent data stores.

In the rare circumstances that logic in those external assemblies does affect state in permanent data stores, those assemblies should be wrapped in protective transactions that prevent those permanent data stores from being altered until the transaction fully executes successfully. Those assemblies should then be exposed as web services and called through the messaging infrastructure to ensure that they are called once and only once.

For complex logic in external assemblies called by orchestrations that are expected to take a considerable amount of time to execute or pause in idle state for an event to occur and complete, execution should also be isolated and exposed as a web service. This ensures that the orchestration instance calling that logic can dehydrate while waiting for a response to come back from the web service and relinquish its resources instead of holding them while waiting for the response.

Error Handling and Suspended Instances

It's Murphy's Law that in a production environment errors are bound to occur. BizTalk solutions not designed to handle and recover from errors are going to suffer a performance degradation that might lead to an eventual catastrophic failure. You might be thinking, "Impossible, I have fault tolerance built into every part of the solution," but consider the following scenario. A BizTalk orchestration running within your application is issuing solicit/response calls to an external web service. One of the services that you are calling happens to fail intermittently and throws an exception. What will happen to your orchestration? If you are not properly handling exceptions in your orchestration, it is going to fail with an unhandled exception, and you will end with a suspended-unresumable instance on your hands. What is worse is that you just had a business transaction fail, and the only way to retry it is to have the logic to recover from it and retry it all from the beginning. So, lesson number 1: handle exceptions, including those raised by external assemblies, expressions, or the messaging subsystem caused by external systems.

OK, so now you have learned your lesson and are handling exceptions throughout the orchestration. What about those suspended-resumable message instances being accumulated in the queue every time the called web service throws an exception? If not handled, those are going to keep on piling up in the queues and spool and eventually negatively affect the overall system performance. So, lesson number 2: configure and handle error reports.[22] As the BizTalk Server 2009 documentation (Microsoft, 2009) states, "At each point along the pathway that a message follows through the BizTalk Server messaging subsystem, failures can occur in the BizTalk Server infrastructure and in custom pipeline components, orchestrations, and so forth. If you have specified error reporting for the port through which a message is entering or will leave, BizTalk Server publishes an error report message derived from the failing message. The error report message is routed to the subscribing routing destination, such as a send port or orchestration; all previously promoted properties are demoted and selected properties related to the specific messaging failure are promoted to the message context."[23]

BizTalk Server does not suspend the message when failed message routing is enabled, it routes the message instead. Failed message routing can be enabled on both receive and send ports. Any failure that occurs in adapter processing, pipeline processing, mapping, or message routing results in an error message if routing for failed messages is enabled. Also, when a messaging error occurs while an orchestration is receiving from a receive port or sending to a send port, the resulting error message is associated with the messaging ports to which the orchestration is bound. The error message is a clone of the original message. When a failed message is generated, BizTalk Server promotes error-report–related message context properties and demotes regular message context properties before publishing the failed message. If failed message routing is not enabled, messages that fail are simply suspended.

"Error messages are delivered to orchestrations or send ports that have subscribed to receive them. A subscription typically selects an error message based on the name of the port in which the messaging error occurred (either a send or a receive port). A subscription might also filter on other properties promoted to the error's message context (for example, InboundTransportLocation or FailureCode)" (Microsoft, "BizTalk Server 2009 Documentation," 2009).

In short, to ensure the sanity of your business transactions and healthy operation of the system, handle exceptions and configure your application to handle error reports to recover from errors and prevent suspended message instances.

Orchestration Engine Configuration

The orchestration engine uses an XML file called BTSNTSvc.exe.config to determine certain behaviors. A service reads this configuration information once, when it is started. Any changes to it will not be picked up unless the service is stopped and restarted.

See the examples that follow for different nodes and potential values.

22 In BizTalk 2004, the messaging subsystem publishes negative acknowledgments (NACKs) whenever a message fails and its instance is suspended. Orchestrations should be able to subscribe to those NACKs and perform the required recovery and consequent cleanup of those suspended instances. The handling of those NACKs and cleanup of suspended messages is essential to ensure the system's overall healthy operation as well as the sanity of the business transaction.

23 "An error message is a clone of the original failed message, with all previously promoted properties demoted and with a set of error-specific properties promoted to the message context. . . . Previously promoted properties are demoted to avoid unintended delivery to subscribers not designated to receive the error message. The error message is published for distribution to subscribers (orchestrations, send ports, and send port groups)" (Microsoft, "BizTalk Server 2009 Documentation"). Copyright 2009 by Microsoft Corporation. Reprinted with permission from Microsoft Corporation.

Example: All Validations On

The following configuration example illustrates how to enable assembly, schema, correlation, and logging validation.

```
<?xml version="1.0" ?>
<configuration>
       <configSections>
              <section
                     name="xlangs" type="Microsoft.XLANGs ➥
.BizTalk.CrossProcess.XmlSerializationConfigurationSectionHandler, ➥
Microsoft.XLANGs.BizTalk.CrossProcess" />
       </configSections>
       <runtime>
              <assemblyBinding xmlns="urn:schemas-microsoft-com:asm.v1">
                     <probing privatePath="BizTalk Assemblies;Developer Tools; ➥
Tracking" />
              </assemblyBinding>
       </runtime>

       <xlangs>
              <Configuration>
                     <Debugging
                            ValidateAssemblies="true"
                            ValidateSchemas="true"
                            ValidateCorrelations="true"
                            ExtendedLogging="true"
                     />
              </Configuration>
       </xlangs>
</configuration>
```

Example: Assembly Validation Only

The following configuration example illustrates how to enable assembly validation only.

```
<?xml version="1.0" ?>
<configuration>
       <configSections>
              <section
                     name="xlangs"
                     type="Microsoft.XLANGs.BizTalk ➥
.CrossProcess.XmlSerializationConfiguration ➥
SectionHandler, Microsoft.XLANGs.BizTalk.CrossProcess"
              />
       </configSections>
```

```
    <runtime>
        <assemblyBinding xmlns="urn:schemas-microsoft-com:asm.v1">
            <probing privatePath="BizTalk Assemblies;Developer Tools; ➥
Tracking" />
        </assemblyBinding>
    </runtime>

    <xlangs>
        <Configuration>
            <Debugging
                ValidateAssemblies="true"
                ExtendedLogging="false"
            />
        </Configuration>
    </xlangs>
</configuration>
```

Example: Dehydration

The following configuration example illustrates how to configure dehydration settings.

```
<?xml version="1.0" ?>
<configuration>
    <configSections>
        <section name="xlangs" type= "Microsoft.XLANGs ➥
.BizTalk.CrossProcess.XmlSerializationConfigurationSectionHandler, ➥
Microsoft.XLANGs.BizTalk.CrossProcess" />
    </configSections>
    <runtime>
        <assemblyBinding xmlns="urn:schemas-microsoft-com:asm.v1">
            <probing privatePath="BizTalk Assemblies;Developer Tools; ➥
Tracking" />
        </assemblyBinding>
    </runtime>
    <xlangs>
        <Configuration>
            <!--
            MaxThreshold: the maximal time, in seconds,
            that a dehydratable orchestration
            is retained in memory before being dehydrated.
            MinThreshold: the minimum time, in seconds, that a
            dehydratable orchestration is retained in memory before
            it is considered for dehydration.
            ConstantThreshold: the dynamic threshold usually
            fluctuates between the min and max values specified.
```

```
                    However, you can make the threshold
                    a fixed value by setting this. A value of -1
                    tells the engine not to use a constant threshold.
                    -->
                    <Dehydration MaxThreshold="1800" MinThreshold="1"
                      ConstantThreshold="-1">
                           <!--
                           Currently, virtual memory can become a bottleneck
                           on 32-bit machines due to unmanaged heap fragmentation,
                           so you should throttle by this resource as well.
                           You should reconfigure if /3GB is set.
                           Optimal and maximal usage are in MB.
                           -->
                           <VirtualMemoryThrottlingCriteria OptimalUsage="900"
                             MaximalUsage="1300" IsActive="true" />
                          <!--
                           This is a useful criterion for throttling, but
                           appropriate values depend on whether the box is being
                           shared among servers. If the machine has a lot of RAM
                           and is not being shared with other functions,
                           then these values can be significantly increased.
                           Optimal and maximal usage are in MB.
                           -->
                           <PrivateMemoryThrottlingCriteria OptimalUsage="50"
                             MaximalUsage="350" IsActive="true" />
                    </Dehydration>
             </Configuration>
      </xlangs>
</configuration>
```

Example: AppDomain Configuration

Assemblies are assigned to named domains using assignment rules (more about which appears in the comments within the code). If no rule is specified for some assembly, the assembly will be assigned to an ad hoc domain. The number of such assigned assemblies per ad hoc domain is determined by the value of AssembliesPerDomain.

```
<?xml version="1.0" ?>
<configuration>
    <configSections>
        <section name="xlangs"
          type="Microsoft.XLANGs.BizTalk.CrossProcess.XmlSerialization ➥
ConfigurationSectionHandler, Microsoft.XLANGs.BizTalk.CrossProcess" />
    </configSections>
```

```
    <runtime>
        <assemblyBinding xmlns="urn:schemas-microsoft-com:asm.v1">
            <probing privatePath="BizTalk Assemblies;Developer Tools;Tracking" />
        </assemblyBinding>
    </runtime>
    <xlangs>
        <Configuration>
            <!--
                <!--
AppDomain configuration.
               Assemblies are assigned to named domains using assignment. If no ➥
rule is specified for some assembly, the assembly will be
assigned to an ad hoc domain. The number of such assigned assemblies per ad hoc
domain is determined by the value of AssembliesPerDomain.
            -->-->
            <AppDomains AssembliesPerDomain="10">
                <!--
                    <!--
                      In this section, the user may specify default configuration
                      for any app domain created that does not have a named
                      configuration associated with it (see AppDomainSpecs later in
                      this example). SecondsEmptyBeforeShutdown is the number of
                      seconds that an app domain is empty (that is, it does not
                      contain any orchestrations) before being unloaded. Specify -1
                      to signal that an app domain should never unload, even when
                      empty. Similarly, SecondsIdleBeforeShutdown is the number of
                      seconds that an app domain is idle (that is, it contains only
                      dehydratable orchestrations) before being unloaded. Specify -1
                      to signal that an app domain should never unload when idle but
                      not empty. When an idle but nonempty domain is shut down, all
                      of the contained instances are dehydrated first.
                -->
                -->
<DefaultSpec SecondsIdleBeforeShutdown="1200" SecondsEmptyBeforeShutdown="1800">
                    <!--
                        <!--
                        BaseSetup is a serialized System.AppDomainSetup object.
                        This is passed as is to AppDomain.CreateAppDomain()
                        and can be used to influence assembly
                        search path, etc.
                    -->
                    -->
```

```
<BaseSetup>
 <ApplicationBase>c:\myAppBase</ApplicationBase>
 <ConfigurationFile>c:\myAppBase\myConfig.config</ConfigurationFile>
 <DynamicBase>DynamicBase_0</DynamicBase>
 <DisallowPublisherPolicy>true</DisallowPublisherPolicy>
 <ApplicationName>ApplicationName_0</ApplicationName>
 <PrivateBinPath>PrivateBinPath_0</PrivateBinPath>
 <PrivateBinPathProbe>PrivateBinPathProbe_0</PrivateBinPathProbe>
 <ShadowCopyDirectories>ShadowCopyDirectories_0</ShadowCopyDirectories>
 <ShadowCopyFiles>ShadowCopyFiles_0</ShadowCopyFiles>
 <CachePath>CachePath_0</CachePath>
 <LicenseFile>LicenseFile_0</LicenseFile>
 <LoaderOptimization>NotSpecified</LoaderOptimization>
</BaseSetup>
</DefaultSpec>
                <!--
                    - <!--
In this section the user may specify named configurations for specific app domains,
identified by their "friendly name". The format of any app-domain spec is identical
to that of the default app-domain spec.
                -->-->
                <AppDomainSpecs>
                    <AppDomainSpec Name="MyDomain1" SecondsIdleBeforeShutdown= ➥
"-1" SecondsEmptyBeforeShutdown="12000">
                        <BaseSetup>
                            <PrivateBinPath>c:\PathForAppDomain1</PrivateBinPath>
                        <PrivateBinPath>PrivateBinPath_0</PrivateBinPath>
<PrivateBinPathProbe>PrivateBinPathProbe_0</PrivateBinPathProbe>
</BaseSetup>
                    </AppDomainSpec>
                    <AppDomainSpec Name="MyFrequentlyUnloadingDomainMyTrashyDomain"
                     SecondsIdleBeforeShutdown="60" SecondsEmptyBeforeShutdown=
"60" />
                </AppDomainSpecs>
                <!-- The PatternAssignmentRules and ExactAssignmentRules control
                    assignment of assemblies to app domains. When a message
                    arrives, the name of its corresponding orchestration's assembly
                    is determined. Then, the assembly is assigned an app domain
                    name. The rules guide this assignment. Exact rules are
                    consulted first, in their order of definition, and then the
                    pattern rules. The first match is used. If no match is found,
                    the assembly will be assigned to an ad hoc domain. The
                    configuration and number of assemblies per ad hoc domain is
                    controlled by the AssembliesPerDomain attribute and the
                    DefaultSpec section. -->
```

```
<ExactAssignmentRules>

<!-- An exact assembly rule specifies a strong assembly name and an app domain name.
 If the strong assembly name equals the rule's assembly name, it is assigned to
 the corresponding app domain.-->
                    <ExactAssignmentRule AssemblyName="BTSAssembly1, ➥
 Version=1.0.0.0, Culture=neutral, PublicKeyToken=9c7731c5584592ad ➥
                       AssemblyName_0" AppDomainName="MyDomain1" />
AppDomainName_1" />
                    <ExactAssignmentRule AssemblyName=
                      "BTSAssembly2, Version=1.0.0.0, Culture=neutral, ➥
PublicKeyToken=9c7731c5584592ad AssemblyName_0"
 AppDomainName="AppDomainName_1" />
                <ExactAssignmentRule AssemblyName=
"AssemblyName_0" AppDomainName="AppDomainName_1" />
</ExactAssignmentRules>
                <PatternAssignmentRules>
                    <!-- A pattern assignment rule specifies a regular expression
                    and an app domain name. If the strong assembly name matches the
                    expression, it is assigned to the corresponding app domain.
                    This allows version-independent assignment, assignment by
                    public key token, or assignment by the custom assembly key.
                    -->
                    <!--
                        Assign all assemblies with name BTSAssembly3,
                        regardless of version and public key,
                        to the MyDomain1 app domain.
                    -->
                    <PatternAssignmentRule AssemblyNamePattern= ➥
" BTSAssembly3, Version=\d.\d.\d.\d, Culture=neutral, ➥
 PublicKeyToken=.{16}"AssemblyNamePattern_0"
                       AppDomainName="AppDomainName_1" />
                        AppDomainName="MyDomain1" />
                <PatternAssignmentRule
                  AssemblyNamePattern="AssemblyNamePattern_0"
                  AppDomainName="AppDomainName_1" />
</PatternAssignmentRules>
            </AppDomains>
        </Configuration>
    </xlangs>
</configuration>
```

In addition to BizTalk-specific configuration information, the BTSNTSvc.exe.config file is also the place where .NET application components that run in the context of an orchestration, an adapter, or a pipeline obtain their configuration information at runtime using the standard

.NET `<appSettings>` tag under the `<configuration>` tag. Because BizTalk already provides a mechanism for custom adapters and pipeline components to obtain configuration information, the `<appSettings>` tag in the BTSNTSvc.exe.config file would most likely be used by custom .NET components called from within an orchestration.[24] For example:

```
<appSettings>
<add key="configParamName" value="configParamValue" />
</appSettings>
```

24 A separate custom config file may be specified per app domain using the <ConfigurationFile/> key to hold the required configuration and app settings for custom application components.

CHAPTER 8

Playing By the Rules? Use the Business Rule Engine

The Business Rule Engine (BRE) enables you to encapsulate the creation and management of complex rules to be used from within your applications. These rules can be modified and updated in real time without having to update any assemblies in the solution, thereby providing a great deal of flexibility.

What Is a Business Rule Engine?

An organization's most strategic assets are the products/services it provides to its customers as well as the business model and internal processes it uses to differentiate itself from its competition. An organization's IT department's most valuable assets are the data on products/services and customers of the organization as well as the workflows and business rules that drive the internal processes and business model. It is the IT department's main responsibility to ensure the agility of those assets.

Although data management and portability is being addressed by database management systems such as SQL Server and although workflow management and portability is usually addressed by business process management services such as the BizTalk orchestration engine, business rules are usually neglected. Most business rules today are implemented in procedural languages and code that is maintained by application developers and programmers. This ties up one of the most critical organizational assets and limits its agility. The cost and time required to update the business rules and underlying IT services within an organization that implements its business rules in procedural languages is too high for such an organization to react quickly to its business units' needs. Moreover, the business rules might be improperly translated from the design documents (written in a human language) to the procedural code, which contributes to problems and leads to inconsistency.

The BRE addresses these pains. It allows IT departments to properly isolate, consolidate, and manage their business rules and policies in a simple manner so that they can react to their organization's business process changes swiftly at low cost points. The Business Rule Engine allows business analysts to describe business policies and rules in a simple graphical or textual form without the need to use a typical procedural programming language. Those rules are then stored away from the rest of the enterprise applications in a separate business rule store managed by the Business Rule Engine. Isolating business rules from the invoking applications in such a manner allows business analysts and business rule authors to update the business rules dynamically to meet the changes required by their business units. Updating those business rules does not require any changes to enterprise applications or business orchestrations that invoke them, unless changes to those rules require new data input or alter the output in a way that requires updates to the calling application. Running applications will seamlessly fire the latest version of the updated business rules the next time they invoke them. Applications leveraging the BRE invoke business rules through the **Business Rules Framework**.

As stated in the BizTalk Server 2009 documentation (Microsoft, 2009),[1]

> *The Business Rules Framework is a Microsoft .NET-compliant class library. It provides an efficient inference engine that can link highly readable, declarative, semantically rich rules to any business objects (.NET components), XML documents, or database tables. Application developers can build business rules by constructing rules from small building blocks of business logic (small rule sets) that operate on information (facts) contained in .NET objects, database tables, and XML documents. This design pattern promotes code reuse, design simplicity, and modularity of business logic. In addition, the rule engine does not impose on the architecture or design of business applications. In fact, you can add rule technology to a business application by directly invoking the rule engine, or you can have external logic that invokes your business objects without modifying them. In short, the technology enables developers to create and maintain applications with minimal effort.*

Rule engines optimize rule resolution performance. They can evaluate rules within the same policy in parallel and cache their results until the facts involved in their evaluation change. **Business policies**, or **rule sets**, are composed of multiple business rules. Figure 8-1 illustrates this composition. The order of the evaluation of the different rules within a policy may be controlled by setting priorities to these different rules. **Rules** are composed of a **condition** followed by a set of **actions** that are executed if the condition in question is evaluated to be true. Conditions are composed of **operations**—predicates—that can be performed on **facts** to result in a Boolean value. Facts may be part of an XML document, an entry in a relational database, a basic .NET type, or a .NET component. To retrieve the values of complex facts, **fact retrievers**, which are .NET components that implement a particular interface, may be used.

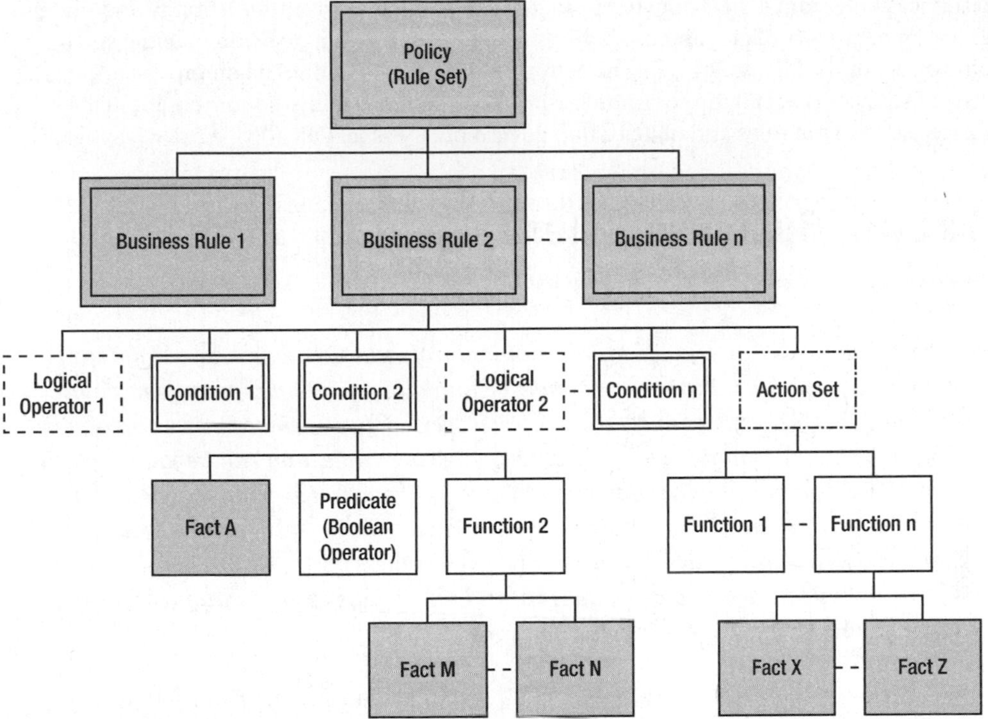

Figure 8-1. *The composition of a business policy*

The Business Rule Engine is composed of multiple components:

- The Business Rule Composer allows business rule authors to identify the sources for the different facts used within their business rules as well as define and version their business policies and business rules.
- The Business Rule Store holds the definition of those business policies and facts.
- The in-memory cache holds the results of the evaluation of the different business rule conditions.
- The Business Rules Framework is used by application developers or orchestration developers to call business policies and execute different business rules from within their applications or orchestrations.
- The Business Rules Update Service monitors the Business Rule Store for published updates of policies and rules to deprecate older versions from the cache and reevaluate conditions as needed.

Studies show that 15% to 50% of annual IT budgets are spent on compiling, testing, and implementing rule changes in applications. Rule engines allow the separation of business rules from the applications that use them and enable the maintenance of business logic without having to resort to code changes and software modification. This reduces application development time and significantly reduces maintenance and enhancement cost by 15% to 50%. IT organizations leveraging rule engines can increase the flexibility of their applications and services and reduce their time to production. Rule engines promote visibility and understanding of business policies and procedures as well as consistent decision making, since a business rule update in a rule engine directly updates the behavior of all enterprise applications and services that call the common business rules managed by the rule engine. This enforces order to the rules and policies that govern business (eFORCE).

What Are Business Rules?

As explained in "Implementation Guide of BizTalk's Business Rules" (Xi, 2005),

> *Business rules (or business policies) define and control the structure, operation, and strategy of an organization. Business rules may be formally defined in procedure manuals, contracts, or agreements, or may exist as knowledge or expertise embodied in employees. Business rules are dynamic and subject to change over time, and can be found in all types of applications. Finance and insurance, e-business, transportation, telecommunications, Web-based services, and personalization are just a few of the many business domains that are governed by business rules. Each of these business domains shares the need to convey business strategies, policies, and regulations to information technology (IT) personnel for inclusion into software applications.*

As mentioned previously, a rule consists of a condition and a set of actions. If the condition is evaluated to true by the BRE, the actions defined in the rule are executed.

Traditional procedural and object-oriented programming languages, such as C, C++, and Microsoft Visual Basic, are oriented toward programmers, thus limiting the ability of nonprogrammers to participate in the maintenance of automated business policies. Even advanced object-oriented languages, such as Java and C#, are still primarily programmers' languages. The Business Rule Engine and the Business Rules Framework address this problem by providing a development environment that enables rapid application creation without the lengthy cycle of traditional application programming. For example, business policies constructed by using this framework can be updated without recompiling and redeploying the associated orchestrations (Xi, 2005).[2,3]

When to Use the BRE?

Traditionally, rule engines have been used for such things as credit scoring and underwriting in financial organizations because of the volume and complexity of business rules that these applications require. Using a procedural programming language to code such rules

2 Copyright © 2005 by Microsoft Corporation. Reprinted with permission from Microsoft Corporation.

3 Despite the simplicity of creating and updating business rules, you should not be tempted to do so in your product environment directly. You should never short-circuit your testing cycle. Proper product testing is required with every change including business rule updates before they are implemented in production.

directly into an application makes application maintenance difficult and expensive, as these rules change often. The difficulty in maintaining these rules is encountered even in the initial release of the application, since such rules often change between the time the code is written and the time it's deployed. Hence, rule engines were devised to separate business rules from application logic (Moran).[4]

Virtually every application includes some logic that needs to change often or needs to change in ways not anticipated in the original design. The real question then is not whether you need a rule engine, but how much time and money the rule engine will save you. Even if only a small subset of your rules is subject to change, your project can benefit greatly by separating these rules from the rest of the program logic. This is particularly true during user acceptance testing when missed requirements and incorrect assumptions become evident. A rule engine enables you to make dramatic changes in system behavior without dramatic changes in your code, and it enables you to make changes at runtime.

Although simple runtime rule customization can be implemented by using database tables or configuration files to store values for facts used in business rules, a rule engine offers much greater flexibility than simple database tables or configuration files. A rule engine allows you to isolate the condition as well as the action from the application flow. You can simply update a rule's condition, change values associated with facts, or change actions in a rule altogether without the need to recompile and redeploy the application.

So when do you use the BRE and when do you keep your rules outside the BRE? A rule engine is suitable when your application involves significant decision making; the rules are complex or change frequently; the rules need to be shared across multiple applications and organizations; or you are in a volatile industry sector where change is the norm or regulation is extensive and complex. Maintaining your rules in custom code that may be configured through database value lookups or configuration files is suitable when the rules are mostly static and computational, or are simple, even if numerous; speed and throughput are more important than flexibility and maintenance cost; or your business rules are never expected to change in the future (eFORCE).

What Are the Artifacts That Constitute a Business Rule?

In the "What Is a Business Rule Engine?" section, we touched briefly on the structure of a business rule and the fact that it is composed of facts (no pun intended), conditions, and actions (see Figure 8-2). In this section, we give you a detailed look at these artifacts.

4 Copyright by Microsoft Corporation. Reprinted with permission from Microsoft Corporation.

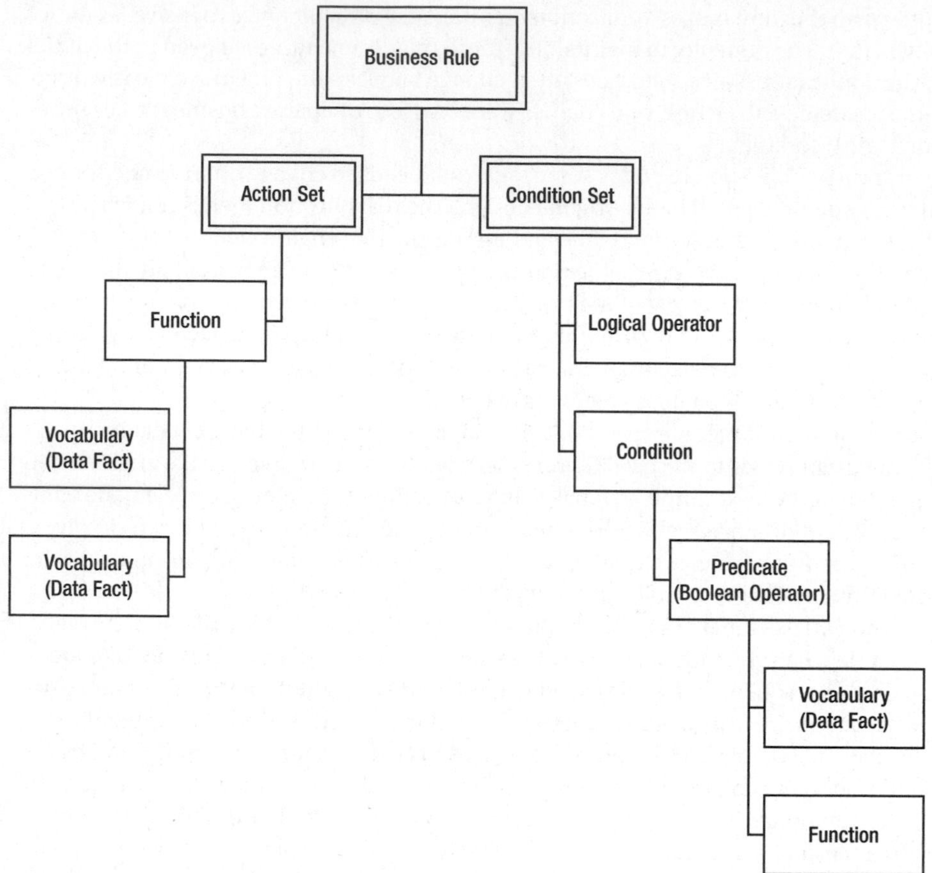

Figure 8-2. *Business rule structure*

Facts and Vocabularies

Before embarking on the creation of business rules, the business analyst should identify the different data facts involved in the evaluation or execution of a particular rule. Those facts are usually aliased using a domain-specific nomenclature understood by peers in that domain. Such domain-specific definitions are referred to in the Business Rule Composer as a *vocabulary*,[5] as in the vocabulary specific to the problem domain for which you are creating the business rules.[6]

5 A vocabulary is a collection of definitions consisting of friendly names for the facts used in rule conditions and actions. These definitions make the rules easier to read, understand, and share by people in a particular business domain (Microsoft, "BizTalk Server 2009 Documentation"). Copyright © 2009 by Microsoft Corporation. Reprinted with permission from Microsoft Corporation.

6 Business rule creators may decide to skip vocabulary definition and embed the facts in their business rules directly. They can reference constants, data in a SQL database, or an XML message directly from within the business rules without resorting to a vocabulary definition. Although this is doable, it is not advisable, as it might render the rules unreadable by future resources maintaining the business rules.

Vocabularies are a wonderful way to abstract facts from their implementation. Although a vocabulary set can be composed of different types of facts, the business analyst and business rule creator can deal with them all in the same fashion while creating or updating their business rules.

These types of facts can be included when composing a vocabulary:

- Constant values, ranges of values, or value sets used to validate and constrain rule parameters.
- .NET classes or class members, which may be used to wrap other vocabularies and/or define bindings and binding parameters. "For example, a vocabulary definition might refer to a .NET method that takes two parameters. As part of the definition, one parameter may be bound to the value in an XML document and the other may be defined by the user at design-time but limited to the valid values defined in another definition that defines a 'set'" (Microsoft, "BizTalk Server Business Rules Framework," 2003).[7]
- XML document elements or attributes.
- Data tables or columns in a database.
- Custom managed facts to be retrieved through a .NET object that implements the fact retriever interface.

Using the Business Rule Composer, you may define vocabularies and store them in the shared rule store. Vocabularies can also be consumed by tool developers responsible for integrating rule authoring into new or existing applications.

■ Note The requirement to define vocabularies and facts before the definition of the business rules within a policy can be cumbersome and annoying for most business analysts, and usually results in them creating and publishing multiple versions of their vocabularies as they are developing the business rules. Hopefully in the future, the Business Rule Composer will allow the composition of business rules based on unpublished vocabularies that business analysts can create and edit while creating their rules, and restrict users from publishing policies until the vocabulary they use is published.

Before being used in business rules, vocabularies must be stamped with a version number and published in the rule store. Once published, a vocabulary version is immutable. This guarantees that the definitions in the vocabulary will not change. It preserves the referential integrity between policies and the vocabulary. This prevents any policies that use a particular version of the vocabulary from failing unexpectedly due to changes in the underlying vocabulary (Microsoft, "BizTalk Server 2009 Documentation," 2009).

Users can define two types of vocabulary items or facts, **short-term** and **long-term** facts. A short-term fact is specific to a single execution cycle of the Business Rule Engine and does not need to exist beyond that execution cycle. A long-term fact is loaded into memory for use over an arbitrary number of execution cycles. Long-term facts are used to represent static datasets or data that changes infrequently, such as a list of U.S. states or daily interest rates.

7 Copyright © 2003 by Microsoft Corporation. Reprinted with permission from Microsoft Corporation.

In the BizTalk BRE, the only real distinction between the two is in implementation (Microsoft, "BizTalk Server 2009 Documentation," 2009).[8] Long-term facts improve performance by limiting queries to source repositories and should be considered for high-performing applications.

To use long-term facts, you must configure your policy to know where to find them and implement a fact retriever object that can fetch those facts from an external store and present them to the policy. According to the BizTalk Server 2009 documentation (Microsoft, 2009), there are three ways to supply fact instances to the rule engine:[9]

- The simplest way to submit fact instances to the rule engine is with short-term, application-specific facts that you pass in to the policy object as an array of objects or as XML messages from an orchestration at the beginning of every execution cycle.
- You can use your rule actions to assert additional facts into the engine during execution when those rules evaluate to true.
- You can write a fact retriever—an object that implements a standard interface and typically uses them to supply long-term and slowly changing facts to the rule engine before the policy is executed. The fact retriever may cache these facts and use them over multiple rule execution cycles.

■ **Note** If your data changes frequently between execution cycles and must be reinstantiated and asserted again, you likely want to represent this data as short-term facts.

XML Fact Strategies

As we mentioned previously, facts asserted into the rule engine's working memory can be .NET objects, XML documents, or data tables. These facts contain fields called **slots** in the world of rule engines. If a business rule requires access to a slot in a fact to evaluate a condition and that slot is not defined—for example, an optional XML element that is not defined in the XML input message—the BRE will throw an exception. The engine will attempt to perform this evaluation because the relevant fact has been asserted. However, when it looks for the slot, it will not find it.

In this situation, why does the engine throw an exception?

When you create a vocabulary definition for a node in your schema or when you use an XML fact directly in the rule, two properties are set: **XPath Selector** and **XPath Field**. These properties are the way the engine can refer to data fields or slots in a given fact. The vocabulary definition maps these to business-friendly terms defined by the **Name** and **Display Name** properties.

The XPath Selector defines and selects a fact. If a vocabulary definition is referring to a fact rather than a slot, the XPath Field property will be empty. However, there will be an additional XPath expression in the XPath Field property if the vocabulary definition is referring to a slot. This XPath expression is used to select a descendant node of the fact. The engine will throw an exception if a fact exists and it tries to evaluate a business rule condition depending on

---

8 Copyright © 2009 by Microsoft Corporation. Reprinted with permission from Microsoft Corporation.

9 Copyright © 2009 by Microsoft Corporation. Reprinted with permission from Microsoft Corporation.

this fact, but the vocabulary in the condition refers to a slot that does not exist in the message instance asserted into the engine's working memory.

If the fact does not exist, no error would occur in the first place. Very simply, the engine would not be able to assert the fact and would therefore realize that it cannot evaluate any rule conditions that depend on this fact. If the fact exists, the engine assumes that the child element exists and throws an error when it tries to access the nonexistent element.

To ensure that you do not run into such situations, you can edit the XPath Selector so that it only selects fact instances with the required slots defined. XPath supports filters that you can use to amend the XPath Selector to ensure those required slots exist.

For example, if you had a message like this one:

```
<MyMessage>
   <Fields>
      <Field1/>
      <Field2> MyField2 value </Field2>
</Fields>
</MyMessage>
```

a vocabulary named MyDataField defined to reference `Field2` will have an XPath Selector value of

```
/*[local-name()='My_Message' and namespace
uri()='http://schemas.test.com/20090307/MyMessageSchema']/*
[local-name()='MyMessage' and namespace
uri()='']/*[local-name()='Fields' and namespace-uri ()='']
```

and an XPath Field value of

```
*[local-name()='Field2' and namespace-uri()='']
```

To avoid exceptions if an asserted `My_Message` instance does not have a `Field2` element defined, you can modify the XPath Selector to the following:

```
/*[local-name()='My_Message' and namespace-
uri()='http://schemas.test.com/20090307/MyMessageSchema']/*
[local-name()='MyMessage' and namespace-
uri()='']/*[local-name()='Fields' and namespace-uri()=''][Field2]
```

You can improve this filtering process further by modifying the XPath Selector to select `My_Message` nodes with a `Field2` child element, which has a nonempty text node only:

```
/*[local-name()='My_Message' and namespace-
uri()='http://schemas.test.com/20090307/MyMessageSchema']/*
[local-name()='MyMessage' and namespace-
uri()='']/*[local-name()='Fields' and namespace-uri()=''][Field2!=""]
```

The key to effectively using the BRE and using XML facts is to understand XPath and the difference between facts and slots, and to edit your XPath Selectors and XPath Fields accordingly to meet your needs. A good example is a business rule that should perform an action only if a certain number of fields have the same value. For instance, an institute that wants to automate the selection of courses it offers to its students would use a business rule that looks at a feedback summary report for a class and adds the class to the offered courses roster only if ten students or more responded that the course was “Very Good”. This could be implemented through a set of complex business rules or custom code. A better alternative is to leverage XPath to define a vocabulary item that represents the count of “Very Good” responses.

Assuming the feedback summary is as follows:

```
<CourseFeedback>
  <Course title="Introduction to BizTalk 2009" />
  <Instructor>John Smith</Instructor>
  <WasThisCourseUseful>
    <answer value="Good"/>
    <answer value="Bad"/>
    <answer value="Very Good"/>
    <answer value="Good"/>
    <answer value="Very Good"/>
    <answer value="Very Good"/>
    <answer value="Very Good"/>
    <answer value="Very Good"/>
    <answer value="Very Good"/>
    <answer value="Very Good"/>
    <answer value="Very Good"/>
    <answer value="Very Good"/>
    <answer value="Very Good"/>
  </WasThisCourseUseful>
  <WouldYouRecommendThisCourseToAFriend>
    <answer value="Good"/>
    <answer value="Bad"/>
    <answer value="Very Good"/>
    <answer value="Good"/>
    <answer value="Very Good"/>
    <answer value="Very Good"/>
    <answer value="Very Good"/>
    <answer value="Very Good"/>
    <answer value="Very Good"/>
    <answer value="Very Good"/>
    <answer value="Very Good"/>
    <answer value="Very Good"/>
    <answer value="Very Good"/>
   </WouldYouRecommendThisCourseToAFriend>
  <CourseOnRoster>Yes</CourseOnRoster>
</CourseFeedback>
```

you could define a vocabulary item named `GoodCount` that counts the number of “Very Good” answers as follows:

```
XPath Selector: /*[local-name()='CourseFeedback' and namespace-
uri()='http://schemas.test.com/20090307"/
CourseFeedbackSchema']/*[local-name()='WasThisCourseUseful'
and namespace-uri()='']/*[local-
name()='WouldYouRecommendThisCourseToAFriend' and namespace-uri()='']

XPath Field: Count(//answer[@value="Very Good"])
```

You can then define a business rule as part of the policy that checks whether the count is greater than ten, and if so sets the course to be OnRoster.

```
XPath Selector: /*[local-name()='CourseFeedback' and namespace-uri()=
'http://schemas.test.com/20090307']

XPath Field: *[local-namc()='CourseOnRoster' and namespace-uri()='']

SetCourseOnRoster (priority = 0)
IF GoodCount
     is greater than or equal to 10
THEN CourseOnRoster = "Yes"
ELSE CourseOnRoster = "No"
```

Leveraging XPath queries in the definition of XPath Field properties is a great way to minimize custom code and optimize the execution of the BRE to evaluate complex rules.

Custom Fact Retrievers

Fact retrievers are used to manage long-term facts used by business policies. "If a fact changes infrequently, rule processing efficiency can be obtained by saving it as a long-term fact and loading it into memory to reuse. By referencing this fact retriever in a policy, the user ensures that the engine (more accurately the policy class) will call the fact retriever to get long-term facts" (Microsoft, "BizTalk Server Business Rules Framework," 2003).[10]

To expose long-term facts to the BRE and leverage them in the definition of business rules and policies, you may use custom fact retrievers, which are custom .NET classes that implement the `Microsoft.RuleEngine.IFactRetriever` interface. This interface has a single public method, `UpdateFacts`. A particular fact retriever may be associated with a particular policy version through the policy property settings. This indicates to the BRE that an instance of that fact retriever object should be instantiated and the method `UpdateFacts` called to update all custom facts associated with that particular policy. It is the responsibility of the fact retriever to determine when the fact base has changed.

10 Copyright © 2003 by Microsoft Corporation. Reprinted with permission from Microsoft Corporation.

■ **Note** A long-term fact only needs to be asserted once for the same rule engine instance. For example, when you use the Call Rules shape in an orchestration, the policy instance is moved into an internal cache. At this time, all short-term facts are retracted and long-term facts are kept. If the same policy is called again, either by the same orchestration instance or by a different orchestration instance in the same host, this policy instance is fetched from the cache and reused. In some batch processing scenarios, several policy instances of the same policy could be created. If a new policy instance is created, you must ensure that the correct long-term facts are asserted.

The following custom fact retriever, DbFactRetriever, selects a set of rows from a database table, adds them to a typed data table, and asserts it as a fact. You can also add your own code to determine whether cached data is obsolete and should be updated.

```
...
public class DbFactRetriever:IFactRetriever
{
      public object UpdateFacts(RuleSetInfo rulesetInfo,
 Microsoft.RuleEngine.RuleEngine engine, object factsHandleIn)
      {
         object factsHandleOut;

         // The following logic asserts the required DB rows only once and always
         // uses the same values (cached) during the first retrieval in
         // subsequent execution cycles
         if (factsHandleIn == null)
         {
            string strCmdSqlCon = "Persist Security Info=False;"+
             "Integrated Security=SSPI;database=mydatabasename;server=myservername";
            SqlConnection conSql = new SqlConnection(strCmdSqlCon);

            // Using data connection binding
            // DataConnection dcSqlCon = new DataConnection("Northwind", "CustInfo",
            // conSql);

            // Using data table binding
            SqlDataAdapter dAdaptSql = new SqlDataAdapter();
            dAdaptSql.TableMappings.Add("Table", "CustInfo");
            conSql.Open();
            SqlCommand myCommand = new SqlCommand("SELECT * FROM CustInfo", conSql);
            myCommand.CommandType = CommandType.Text;
            dAdaptSql.SelectCommand = myCommand;
            DataSet ds = new DataSet("Northwind");
            dAdaptSql.Fill(ds);
            TypedDataTable tdtCustInfo = new TypedDataTable(ds.Tables["CustInfo"]);
```

```
            engine.Assert(tdtCustInfo);
            factsHandleOut = tdtCustInfo;
        }
        else
        {
            factsHandleOut = factsHandleIn;
        }
        return factsHandleOut;
    }
}
...
```

Conditions

After creating the vocabulary and publishing it to the rule store, the business rule creator can now create the business rules constituting the business policies. The creation of the business rules constitutes creating a set of conditions and actions for each rule.

A condition is simply a Boolean expression that consists of one or more **predicates** applied to **facts**. "Predicates can be combined with the logical connectives AND, OR, and NOT to form a logical expression that can be potentially quite large, but will always evaluate to either true or false" (Microsoft, "BizTalk Server Business Rules Framework," 2003).[11]

A set of predefined predicates are available in the Business Rules Framework:

- `After`: Tests whether a date/time fact happens after another date/time fact
- `Before`: Tests whether a date/time fact happens before another date/time fact
- `Between`: Tests whether a date/time fact is in the range between two other date/time facts
- `Exists`: Tests for the existence of an XML node within an XML document[12]
- `Match`: Tests whether the specified text fact contains a substring that matches a specified regular expression or another fact
- `Range`: Tests whether a value is within a range defined by the lower-bound value (inclusive) and upper-bound value (inclusive)
- `Equal`: The equality relational operator
- `GreaterThan`: The greater than relational operator
- `GreaterThanEqual`: The greater than or equal relational operator
- `LessThan`: The less than relational operator
- `LessThanEqual`: The less than or equal relational operator
- `NotEqual`: The not equal to relational operator

---

11 Copyright © 2003 by Microsoft Corporation. Reprinted with permission from Microsoft Corporation.

12 Although the predicate is called Exists, it will only check whether a given node is empty. If the node does not exist in the XML document, an exception will be thrown and the processing will stop.

Actions

Actions are the functional consequences of condition evaluation. If a rule condition is met, a corresponding action or multiple actions will be initiated. Actions can result in more rules being evaluated and trigger a chain effect. They are represented in the Business Rules Framework by invoking methods or setting properties on objects, or by performing set operations on XML documents or database tables. The Business Rules Framework provides a set of predefined functions that can be used in actions:

- `Assert`: Adds a new fact to the current rule engine instance.

■ **Note** To assert a .NET object from within a rule, you can add the built-in `Assert` function as a rule action. The rule engine has a `CreateObject` function, but it is not displayed explicitly with the rest of the functions in the Facts Explorer window in the Business Rule Composer. By simply dragging the constructor method of the object you wish to create from the .NET Class view of the Facts Explorer to the action pane, the Business Rule Composer will translate the constructor method into a `CreateObject` call in the rule definition (Moons, 2005).[13]

- `Update`: Refreshes the specified fact in the current rule engine instance. If this fact is used in business rule conditions in the current policy, this will result in those rules being reevaluated. Rules that use the fact being updated in their actions will not be reevaluated and their actions will remain on the agenda.[14]

■ **Caution** A rule with an action that updates the value of a fact being used in its condition evaluation might result in a cyclical valuation loop, if the value used to update the fact always results in the condition being evaluated to true. By default, the Business Rule Engine will cycle through 2^32 loops before it exits the match–conflict resolution–action cycle (more about which you'll find in the "How Does the BRE Work?" section). This value is a configurable property per policy version.

- `Retract`: Removes the specified fact from the current rule engine instance.
- `RetractByType`: Removes all existing facts of the specified fact type from the current rule engine instance.
- `Clear`: Clears all facts and rule firings from the current rule engine instance.

13 Copyright © 2005 by Microsoft Corporation. Reprinted with permission from Microsoft Corporation.

14 To force the engine to reevaluate rules with an XML element in their condition, you have to update its immediate parent; if you update the element itself or its grandparent, the engine will not pick up on the fact that the element got updated and the rule needs to be reevaluated. We are not sure if this is a bug or a feature by design, as the Update function is inherently efficient in modifying facts and invalidating the agenda. A description of the agenda and how the engine uses it will be provided in the "Rules and Priorities" section.

- `Halt`: Halts the current rule engine execution and optionally clears all rule firings. The facts remain unaffected so that values are returned.
- `Executor`: Returns a reference to the current rule engine instance of type `IRuleSetExecutor`.
- `FindAll`: Returns a string containing all substrings that match a specified regular expression in the specified text.
- `FindFirst`: Returns a string containing the first substring that matches a specified regular expression in the specified text.
- `Add`: Adds two numeric values.
- `Subtract`: Subtracts two numeric values.
- `Multiply`: Multiplies two numeric values.
- `Divide`: Divides two numeric values.
- `Power`: Returns the result of a number raised to a power.
- `Remainder`: Returns the remainder after a number is divided by a divisor.
- `Year`: Returns the year component of the specified date/time fact, a value in the range 1 to 9999.
- `Month`: Returns the month component from the specified date/time fact, a number from 1 to 12.
- `Day`: Returns the day of the month component from the specified date/time fact, a number from 1 to 31.
- `Hour`: Returns the hour component from the specified date/time fact, a number from 0 (12:00 a.m.) to 23 (11:00 p.m.).
- `Minute`: Returns the minute component from the specified date/time fact, a number from 0 to 59.
- `Second`: Returns the second component from the specified date/time fact, a number from 0 to 59.
- `TimeOfDay`: Returns the time component from the specified date/time fact.
- `DayOfWeek`: Returns the day of the week from the specified date/time fact, a number from 0 (Sunday) to 6 (Saturday).

Rules and Priorities

The BRE implements the RETE algorithm.[15] By default the execution of rule actions is nondeterministic. The engine evaluates all rules in the policy and creates an agenda of actions for rules with valid conditions to be executed. The execution of actions on the agenda might result in condition reevaluation or more conditions being evaluated, if those actions update or assert

15 The RETE algorithm, designed by Dr. Charles L. Forgy of Carnegie Mellon University in 1979, is an efficient pattern-matching algorithm for implementing Business Rule Engines. For more information on the RETE algorithm, please refer to the Wikipedia article at `http://en.wikipedia.org/wiki/Rete_algorithm`.

new facts. With all rules having the same priority, there is no guaranteed order of execution for the actions on the agenda. To guarantee an order of execution, you need to resort to using **rule priorities**.

The default priority for all rules is zero. Priority for execution is set on each individual rule. The priority is a positive or negative integer value, with larger numbers having higher priority. Actions added to the agenda for rules with valid conditions are executed in order from highest priority to lowest priority.

To see how priority affects the execution order of rules, take a look at the following example from the BizTalk Server 2009 documentation (Microsoft, 2009):[16]

```
Rule1 (priority = 0)
IF Fact1 == 1
THEN Discount = 10%


Rule2 (priority = 10)
IF Fact1 > 0
THEN Discount = 15%
```

Although the conditions for both rules have been met, Rule2, having the higher priority, is executed first. The action for Rule1 is executed last, and so the final discount is 10%, as demonstrated here:

Working Memory	Agenda
Fact1 (value=1)	**Rule2** Discount = 15%
	Rule1 Discount = 10%

The Business Rule Composer

The Business Rule Composer, illustrated in Figure 8-3, is the environment used by business rule authors to create, update, version, publish, and deploy vocabularies and policies. Policy authors may also test their policies using the testing tool in the Business Rule Composer and review the execution output as well as error messages in the Output window. As mentioned earlier, creating the required vocabularies is necessary before the rule creation, as the vocabulary needs to be published before it can be used in a rule. However, if you like to create your rules top down, you can get around this by simply creating all the business rules with fake arguments using the taxonomy of your domain, then start creating the vocabulary following that nomenclature. The drawback here of course is that you will not be able to save your policy unless you add and publish the vocabulary and update the rules with the right facts.

16 Copyright © 2009 by Microsoft Corporation. Reprinted with permission from Microsoft Corporation.

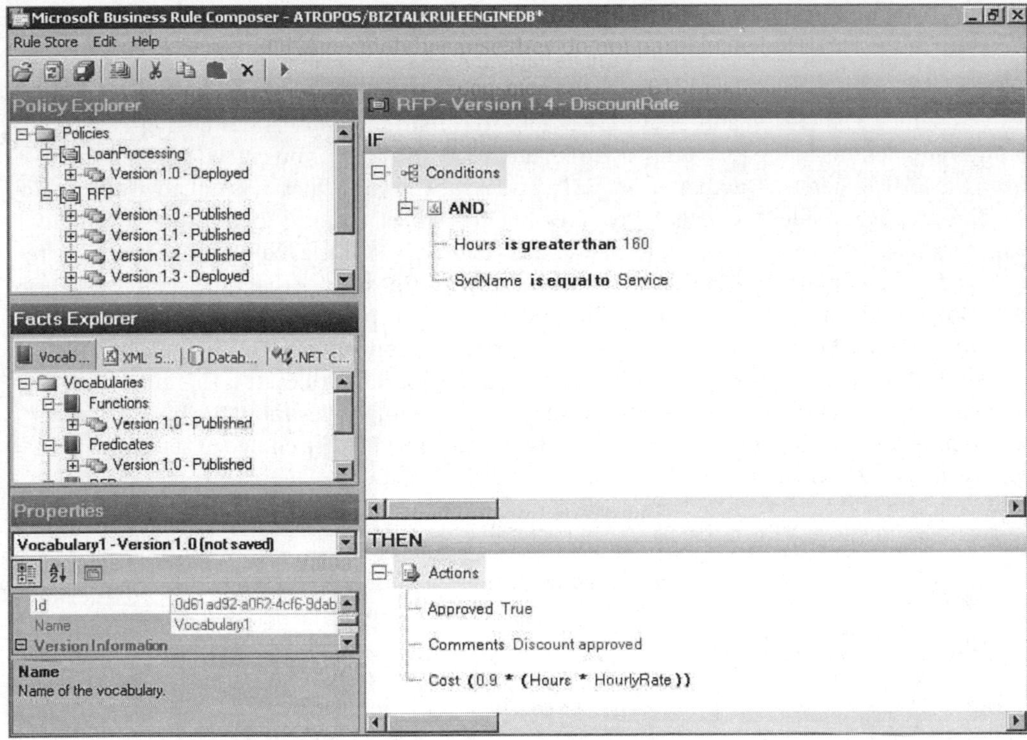

Figure 8-3. *The Business Rule Composer*

We will not discuss the mechanics of creating vocabularies, policies, and rules in this chapter, since the Business Rule Engine and the Business Rule Composer did not change in BizTalk 2009.[17] However, we will go over some of the hazards of rule development that business rule authors go through.

Caution Multiple users of the Business Rule Composer can connect to the shared rule store at the same time. However, the Business Rule Composer does not prevent users from overwriting each other's work. Potentially, a user could see a policy or a vocabulary that is out of sync because another user may have modified the policy or vocabulary.

---

17 If you are interested in learning more on your own, this is well covered in the BizTalk Server 2009 product documentation and in *Microsoft BizTalk 2004 Unleashed* by Scott Woodgate, Stephen Mohr, and Brian Loesgen (SAMS, 2004).

Creating Vocabularies

Even if building a vocabulary is not your immediate concern, you should know how to work with the Facts Explorer, as most of the tasks there apply to rule development. You can use the XML Schemas, Databases, and .NET Classes tabs to construct names and drag them into conditions and actions in the Rule Editor (Woodgate, 2005). Although you can add facts directly from the XML Schemas, Databases, or .NET Classes tabs to your rules, it is not advisable to do so. This greatly impedes the readability of the business rules and thus their future portability. As explained in the section "When to Use a BRE?" earlier, one of the main advantages of using a Business Rule Engine is to abstract and package the business rules that are valuable assets to the IT organization in a highly manageable and portable format. Introducing facts from different data sources directly into the business rules creates a dependency between the business rules and those data sources and hinders the readability of those rules. It is therefore advisable to create a vocabulary to represent the facts in a nomenclature relevant to the business rules' domain. While defining different vocabulary items, the user has the choice to select the item type as illustrated in Figure 8-4.

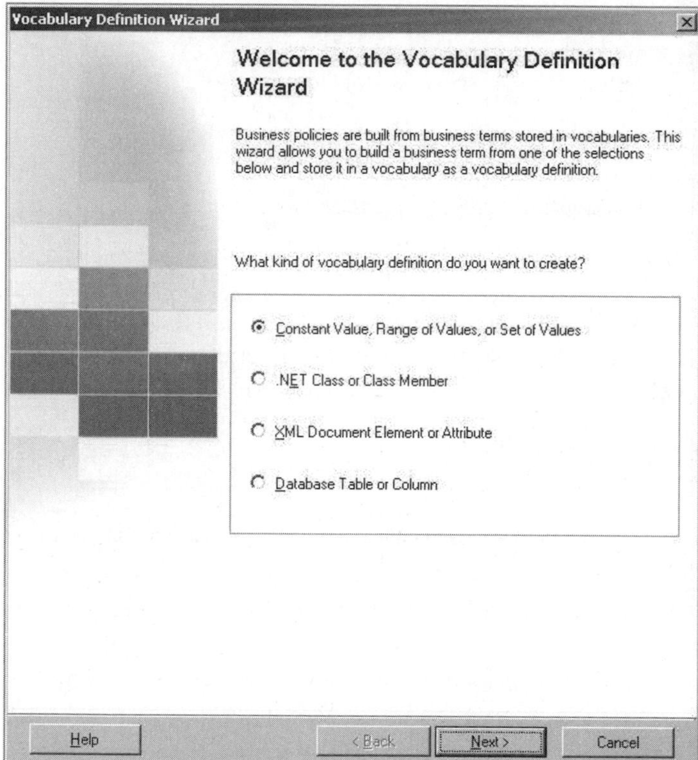

Figure 8-4. *Vocabulary Definition Wizard*

To create a vocabulary item based on a .NET class member, the .NET assembly containing that class has to be deployed to the Global Assembly Cache (GAC). The assembly needs to be deployed to the GAC to ensure that the rule engine can always get to the class definition at runtime.

■ **Tip** If you are not able to pass the required messages to a business policy execution from within an orchestration, ensure that the XML document type specified while creating the vocabulary item is valid. The Business Rule Composer is in the habit of simply adding the document type instead of the fully qualified type name prefixed with all the namespaces if any.

Creating Rules

Creating a policy to encapsulate related rules is the first task in rule creation. If you are updating the rules in the policy or adding onto the existing rules of an already published version of the policy instead of simply creating a new version and starting from scratch, copy the latest version of the policy you need to update and paste it as a new policy version. To create policy rules, you can drag and drop predicates and vocabulary items from the Facts Explorer into the IF pane to create conditions and drag and drop functions and vocabulary items into the THEN pane to create actions. If required, different priorities can be assigned to different rules to affect the order of their actions' execution upon their successful evaluation. Applications executing deployed policies will execute the latest version of the policy by default. However, they may explicitly execute a particular version of the policy instead.

■ **Caution** If you redefine a particular vocabulary item in a new version of a policy, the rules will not pick up the latest version. Rules are explicitly bound to the vocabulary item that was dragged and dropped on the action or condition. This means that if you update your vocabulary, you need to manually update the rules to use the new version of the vocabulary.

How Does the BRE Work?

The main activities of the Business Rule Engine fall into one of two main user experience categories, the design-time experience and the runtime experience. At design time, business rule creators can use the business policy authoring tool, namely the Business Rule Composer in BizTalk, to create and update the business rules and policies. As mentioned previously, business rule authors use the Business Rule Composer to first create the vocabulary required to define the different business rules and then proceed to define their business rules grouped in the form of policies. The different artifacts created by the business rule creator are then compiled and persisted in the Business Rule Store. A service, the Rule Engine Update Service, periodically checks the Business Rule Store for changes to update the rule engine runtime.[18] Applications and orchestrations calling the rule engine to execute policies use the interfaces

---

18 To configure how often the Rule Engine Update Service polls the Rule Store for changes to update the engine, define the registry value PollingInterval under the registry key HKEY_LOCAL_MACHINE\SOFTWARE\Microsoft\BusinessRules\3.0. The PollingInterval value defines the number of seconds that the Rule Engine Update Service waits between Rule Store polls for changes. The default value for this setting is 1 minute.

exposed by the Business Rules Framework to do so. Figure 8-5 shows the separation between the two experiences and how the different components interact together to allow for the auto-update of business rules at runtime.

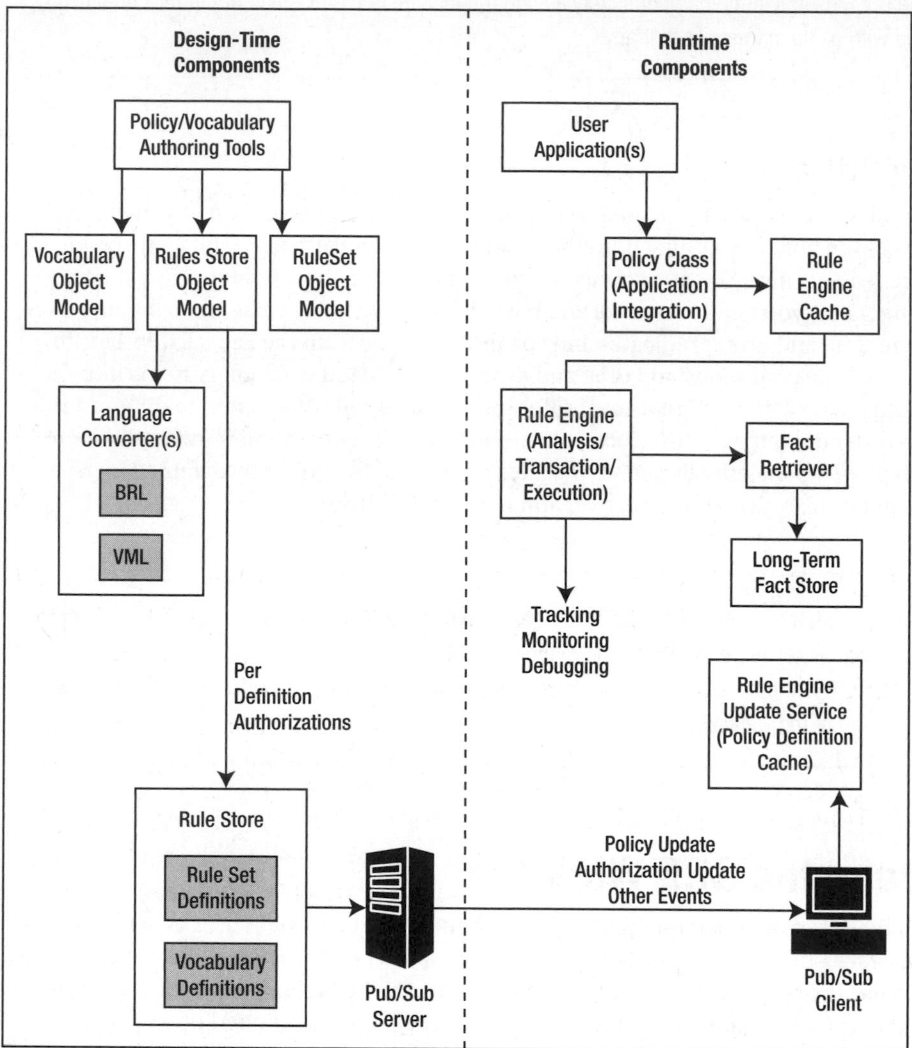

Figure 8-5. *The interaction between the different Business Rules Framework components (Microsoft, "BizTalk Server 2009 Documentation," 2009)*[19]

As we mentioned earlier, a highly efficient rule inference engine serves as the core component of the Business Rules Framework, and it provides the execution context for a policy. The rule engine is primarily composed of three main components:

19 Copyright © 2009 by Microsoft Corporation. Reprinted with permission from Microsoft Corporation.

- An **inference engine**, also called the **rule set executor**, is responsible for the evaluation of rule conditions and action execution. The default rule set executor, implemented as part of the Business Rules Framework, is a "discrimination network-based forward-chaining inference engine designed to optimize in-memory operation" (Microsoft, "BizTalk Server 2009 Documentation," 2009). The inference engine uses forward chaining[20] of rules and conditions to evaluate and action the rules in a rule set. Weighted priorities assigned to the different rules will affect the engine's processing and reorder the execution of their actions.
- A **rule set translator** takes as input a rule set definition—a RuleSet object—and "produces an executable representation of the rule set. The default in-memory translator creates a compiled discrimination network from the rule set definition" (Microsoft, "BizTalk Server 2009 Documentation," 2009). A custom translator can be assigned to a particular policy version through the policy translator property. To assign a custom translator, the policy author needs to identify the .NET assembly containing the rule translator as well as the class implementing the `IRuleSetTranslator` interface in that assembly.
- A **rule set tracking interceptor** receives output from the inference engine—rule set executor—and forwards it to the rule set tracking and monitoring tools that facilitate the tracking and debugging of business rules' execution (Microsoft, "BizTalk Server 2009 Documentation", 2009).[21]

The discrimination network-based forward-chaining logic of the inference engine consists of a three-stage algorithm for policy execution. The stages are as follows (Microsoft, "BizTalk Server 2009 Documentation," 2009):[22]

1. *Match*. In the match stage, facts are matched against the predicates that use the fact type[23] using the predicates defined in the rule conditions. To improve efficiency, pattern matching occurs over all the rules in the policy, and conditions that are shared across rules are matched only once. Partial condition matches may be stored in working memory to accelerate subsequent pattern-matching operations. The output of the pattern-matching phase consists of updates to the rule engine agenda. An agenda is completed when all facts that are simultaneously present in working memory are matched to all active policy rules. The agenda is used by the engine to queue rules and schedule them for execution.
2. *Conflict resolution*. In the conflict resolution stage, the rules that are candidates for execution are examined to determine the next set of rule actions to execute based on a predetermined resolution scheme. All candidate rules found during the matching stage

20 Forward chaining, often called data driven, is one of the two main methods of reasoning when using inference rules in artificial intelligence. The other is backward chaining. For more information on forward chaining, please refer to the Wikipedia article at `http://en.wikipedia.org/wiki/Forward_chaining.2`.

21 Copyright © 2009 by Microsoft Corporation. Reprinted with permission from Microsoft Corporation.

22 Copyright © 2009 by Microsoft Corporation. Reprinted with permission from Microsoft Corporation.

23 The fact type is an object reference maintained in the rule engine's working memory.

are added to the rule engine's agenda. The default conflict resolution scheme is based on rule priorities within a policy.... Therefore if multiple rules are triggered, the higher-priority actions are executed first.

3. *Action*. In the action stage, the actions in the resolved rule are executed. Note that rule actions can assert new facts into the rule engine, which causes the engine to cycle again and start at the matching stage. This is also known as forward chaining. It is important to note that the algorithm never preempts the currently executing rule. All actions for the rule that is currently firing will be executed before the match phase is repeated. However, other rules on the agenda will not be fired before the match phase begins again. The match phase may cause those rules on the agenda to be removed from the agenda before they ever fire.

   An agenda exists per engine instance, and acts on a single policy only. A rule's actions are placed on the agenda and executed according to their priority, when facts are asserted and the rule's conditions are satisfied. A rule's actions are executed as a block and in order from top to bottom, before the execution of the actions of the next rule on the agenda.

The example shown next illustrates the Business Rule Engine's three-stage logic of match–conflict resolution–action:[24]

A policy is defined with two rules. The rules and their facts are detailed in Tables 8-1 and 8-2, respectively.

Table 8-1. *Rules Definition*

Declarative Representation	IF—THEN Representation Using Business Objects
Rule 1: Evaluate Income	
An applicant's credit rating should be obtained only if the applicant's income-to-loan ratio is less than 0.2.	`IF Application.Income / Property.Price < 0.2` `THEN Assert new CreditRating(Application)`
Rule 2: Evaluate Credit Rating	

An applicant should be approved only if the applicant's credit rating is more than 725.	`IF Application.SSN = CreditRating.SSN AND`
	`CreditRating.Value > 725`
	`THEN SendApprovalLetter(Application)`

Table 8-2. *Facts Definition*

Fact	Field
Application: An XML document representing a home loan application	Income = \$65,000 SSN = XXX-XX-XXXX
Property: An XML document representing the property being purchased	Price = \$225,000
CreditRating: An XML document containing the loan applicant's credit rating	Value = 0 – 800 SSN = XXX-XX-XXXX

24 This example is extracted from the BizTalk Server 2009 online documentation available at http://msdn.microsoft.com/en-us/library/aa561430.aspx

Initially, the rule engine working memory and agenda are empty. After the application asserts the Application and Property facts with the values detailed in Table 8-2 to the rule engine, the engine's working memory and agenda are updated, as shown in Table 8-3. Rule 1 is added to the agenda because its condition (Application.Income / Property.Price < 0.2) evaluated to true during the match phase. There is no CreditRating fact in working memory, so the condition for Rule 2 was not evaluated.

Table 8-3. *Engine's Working Memory and Agenda Before Execution*

Working Memory	Agenda
Application Property	Rule 1 `Assert new CreditRating(Application)`

Because the only rule in the agenda is Rule 1, the rule is executed and then disappears from the agenda. The single action defined for Rule 1 results in a new fact (CreditRating document for the applicant) being added to working memory. After the execution of Rule 1 completes, control returns to the match phase. Because the only new object to match is the CreditRating fact, the results of the match phase are as shown in Table 8-4.

Table 8-4. *Engine's Working Memory and Agenda After the Execution of Rule 1*

Working Memory	Agenda
Application Property CreditRating	Rule 2 `SendApprovalLetter(Application)`

At this point Rule 2 is executed, resulting in the invocation of a function that sends an approval letter to the applicant. After Rule 2 has completed, execution of the forward-chaining algorithm returns to the match phase. Because there are no longer new facts to match and the agenda is empty, forward chaining terminates, and policy execution is complete (Microsoft, "BizTalk Server 2009 Documentation," 2009).[25]

Testing Business Rules

Once all business policies and their required vocabularies are defined, you need to test and debug them before deploying them in production.

Because of the nonsequential nature of business processes, the Business Rules Composer doesn't provide the same testing, tracing, and debugging functionality as procedural development environments such as Visual Studio. Nonetheless, it does provide a testing tool, shown in Figure 8-6.

25 Copyright © 2009 by Microsoft Corporation. Reprinted with permission from Microsoft Corporation.

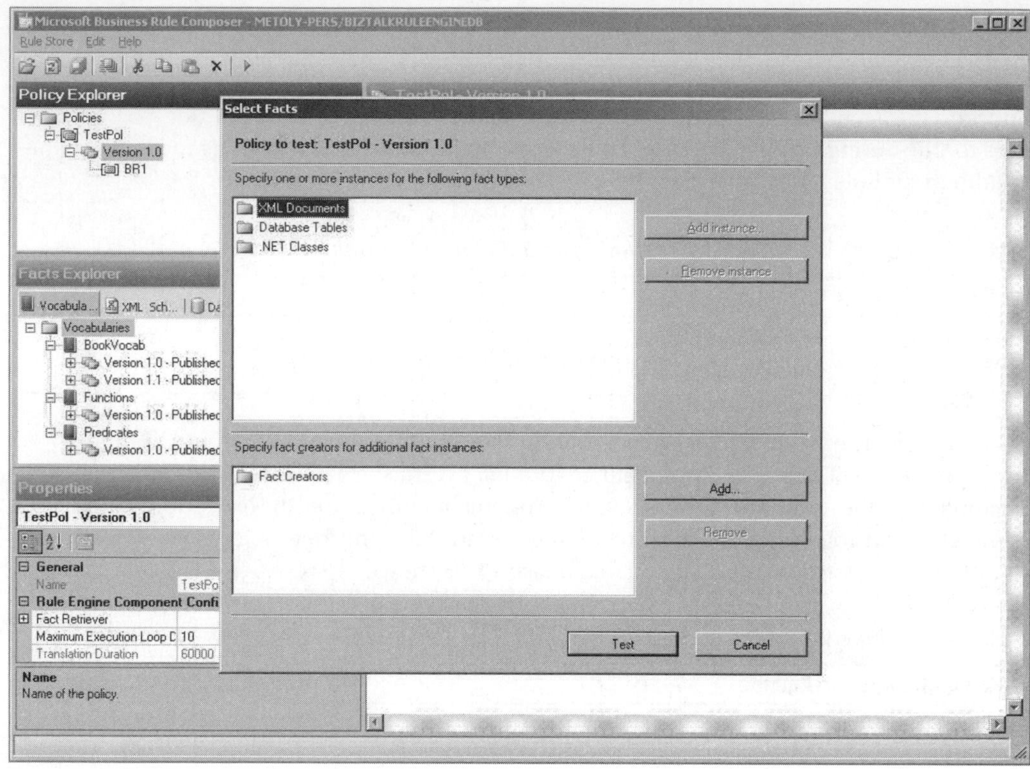

Figure 8-6. *The Business Rule Composer testing tool interface*

You can simply select fact instances for the testing tool to assert into the engine for your policy or select a *FactCreator*[26] that the testing tool will instantiate and call to create the facts required for the policy execution. The testing tool then uses the *DebugTrackingInterceptor*[27] to track the execution of the Business Rule Engine and display it in the output window.

The following extract of output was produced by the Business Rule Composer testing tool when testing the Loans Processing policy from the Loans Sample in the SDK. It shows the details of the tracked information by the *DebugTrackingInterceptor*.

```
RULE ENGINE TRACE for RULESET: LoanProcessing 5/19/2009 12:46:13 PM

FACT ACTIVITY 5/19/2009 12:46:13 PM
Rule Engine Instance Identifier: fb330399-15f0-4dc7-9137-4463a32f580e
Ruleset Name: LoanProcessing
Operation: Assert
```

26 A fact creator, used to generate facts for policy testing, implements the `Microsoft.RuleEngine.IFactCreator` interface. The fact creator needs to implement the `GetFactTypes` and `CreateFacts` methods, which return an array of object types and objects respectively for a given rule set.

27 The Business Rule Engine allows for the registration of tracking interceptors that implement the `Microsoft.RuleEngine.IRuleSetTrackingInterceptor` interface to be notified along with the execution of the engine and track its progress.

```
Object Type: DataConnection:Northwind:CustInfo
Object Instance Identifier: 782

FACT ACTIVITY 5/19/2009 12:46:13 PM
Rule Engine Instance Identifier: fb330399-15f0-4dc7-9137-4463a32f580e
Ruleset Name: LoanProcessing
Operation: Assert
Object Type: TypedXmlDocument:Microsoft.Samples.BizTalk.LoansProcessor.Case
Object Instance Identifier: 778

FACT ACTIVITY 5/19/2009 12:46:13 PM
Rule Engine Instance Identifier: fb330399-15f0-4dc7-9137-4463a32f580e
Ruleset Name: LoanProcessing
Operation: Assert
Object Type: TypedXmlDocument:Microsoft.Samples.BizTalk.LoansProcessor.Case:Root
Object Instance Identifier: 777

CONDITION EVALUATION TEST (MATCH) 5/19/2009 12:46:13 PM
Rule Engine Instance Identifier: fb330399-15f0-4dc7-9137-4463a32f580e
Ruleset Name: LoanProcessing
Test Expression: NOT(TypedXmlDocument:Microsoft.Samples.BizTalk.LoansProcessor.Case:
                                                Root.Income/BasicSalary > 0)
Left Operand Value: 12
Right Operand Value: 0
Test Result: False

CONDITION EVALUATION TEST (MATCH) 5/19/2009 12:46:13 PM
Rule Engine Instance Identifier: fb330399-15f0-4dc7-9137-4463a32f580e
Ruleset Name: LoanProcessing
Test Expression: NOT(TypedXmlDocument:Microsoft.Samples.BizTalk.LoansProcessor.Case:
                                                Root.Income/OtherIncome > 0)
Left Operand Value: 10
Right Operand Value: 0
Test Result: False

CONDITION EVALUATION TEST (MATCH) 5/19/2009 12:46:13 PM
Rule Engine Instance Identifier: fb330399-15f0-4dc7-9137-4463a32f580e
Ruleset Name: LoanProcessing
Test Expression: TypedXmlDocument:Microsoft.Samples.BizTalk.LoansProcessor.Case:
                                          Root.PlaceOfResidence/TimeInMonths >= 3
Left Operand Value: 15
Right Operand Value: 3
Test Result: True
[.. cut for brevity ..]
```

If you are testing or executing policies outside of BizTalk or in a component consumed within BizTalk, you can specify an alternative custom interceptor that implements the

IRuleSetTrackingInterceptor interface.[28] Creating your custom interceptor allows you to track and log as much information as your application requires. It allows you to step through the rule processing and view fact details through the facts you pass to the policy. The following code snippet demonstrates how to invoke your custom interceptor—MyInterceptorClass.

```
...
xmlDocument = IncomingXMLMessage.XMLCase;
typedXmlDocument = new
Microsoft.RuleEngine.TypedXmlDocument("Microsoft.Samples.BizTalk.LoansProcessor.
                                                            Case",xmlDocument);
policy = new Microsoft.RuleEngine.Policy("LoanProcessing");
policy.Execute(typedXmlDocument,new MyInterceptorClass());
OutgoingXMLMessage.XMLCase = xmlDocument;
policy.Dispose();
...
```

The RuleTesterApp project accompanying this book implements a simple rule testing tool. The tool's user interface allows the user to load XML policy definitions, specify the destination trace output file, and then execute those policies. To experiment with your own custom tracking interceptor, instantiate your interceptor in the method FireRule RulesTesterFrm class on line 267 instead of the current instantiation of the DebugTrackingInterceptor.

```
...
// Change the following line to instantiate your own custom Tracking Interceptor
DebugTrackingInterceptor dti = new DebugTrackingInterceptor(traceFileName);
try
{
   for( int i = 0 ; i < policies.Length; i++ )
   {
      string PolicyName = policies[i].Trim();
      lblProcessing.Text = PolicyName;
      ProcessingTxtBx.Text = ProcessingTxtBx.Text +  "Processing ... " + policies[i]
                             + " " +  DateTime.Now + "\r\n";
      Application.DoEvents();
      Microsoft.RuleEngine.Policy tstPolicy = new
                                         Microsoft.RuleEngine.Policy(PolicyName);
      ArrayList shortTermFacts = null;
      shortTermFacts =GetFacts(PolicyName);
      shortTermFacts.Add(doc1);
      // Change the following line to pass in your own custom Tracking Interceptor
      // to the rule set Execute method
      tstPolicy.Execute(shortTermFacts.ToArray(), dti );
      tstPolicy = null;
   }
}
...
```

28 A custom tracking interceptor that implements the Microsoft.RuleEngine.IRuleSetTrackingInterceptor interface needs to implement the SetTrackingConfig, TrackAgendaUpdate, TrackConditionEvaluation, TrackFactActivity, TrackRuleFiring, and TrackRuleSetEngineAssociation methods, which allow it to intercept the execution sequence, agenda, and facts updates for a specified rule set.

Going to Production

Once all business policies and their required vocabularies are defined and well tested, you can deploy them to your production environment. You have a few deployment options. The first is to use the BizTalk Administration Console, which lets you add policies to applications. Thus, you can export rules, dependent .NET classes, and other artifacts used by policies into isolated MSI packages for environment deployment. In many cases, it is the easiest solution.

You can also use the Business Rule Deployment Wizard to package the policies and/or vocabulary for deployment. The Business Rule Deployment Wizard will allow you to export a particular version of a vocabulary definition or policy definition to an XML file. After exporting all the required policies and vocabulary definitions, remember to package all fact retrievers and custom .NET classes used as facts in the solution. You will need to deploy those to the Global Assembly Cache on your production server running the BRE. You will also need to copy the XML schema definitions used by facts in your policies and vocabulary to the same directory path in your production environment as your development and testing environments.

■ **Note** Remember to modify your database facts to point to your production database before deploying the business policies and vocabulary in production. If not, your rules will either fail or read and write to your test database environment.

For more complicated scenarios, application developers might like to package the rules as well as all other collateral material in an interactive setup for the system administrator to use while deploying the application to production. Such a setup package should also contain schema files, .NET assemblies referenced by the business policies, as well as fact retrievers or policy translators used by the policies meant to be deployed. Using an interactive setup, the application developer can prompt the system administrator for the directory location in which he would like to deploy schemas and other collateral files used by the business policies as well as the production database server and database to be used for different database facts.

POLICY DEFINITION IN XML

The following is a dump of a business policy exported to XML. Note the references to the fact retriever assembly and fully qualified class name, the database server information and table names, as well as the schema file location in the fact definitions.

```
<brl xmlns="http://schemas.microsoft.com/businessruleslanguage/2002">
  <ruleset name="RFP">
    <version major="1" minor="4" description=""
         modifiedby="myserver\user"
         date="2004-02-15T00:29:02.6381024-05:00" />
```

```
<configuration>
  <factretriever>
    <assembly>DbFactRetriever, Version=1.0.1505.34508,
     Culture=neutral, PublicKeyToken=d4e488d64aff1da4</assembly>
    <class>
      Que.BizTalk.RFP.myFactRetriever.RFPDbFactRetriever
    </class>
  </factretriever>
</configuration>
<bindings>
  <xmldocument ref="xml_0" doctype="RFPEstimateXML.RulesRFP"
       instances="16" selectivity="1" instance="0">
    <selector>/*[local-name()='RFP' and namespace-uri()=
     'http://RFPEstimateXML.RulesRFP"] </selector>
    <schema>C:\RulesRFP.xsd</schema>
  </xmldocument>
  <datarow ref="db_1" server="myserver\Consulting"
          dataset="Consulting" table="Rates" instances="16"
          selectivity="1" isdataconnection="true"
          instance="0" />
</bindings>
```

EXPORTING/IMPORTING A POLICY TO/FROM AN XML FILE

The following code snippet uses the Business Rules Framework to export a policy version to an XML file.

```
using System;
using Microsoft.RuleEngine;
using Microsoft.BizTalk.RuleEngineExtensions;
namespace SimpleExport
{
   class ExportPolicy
   {
      [STAThread]
      static void Main(string[] args)
      {
         if (args.Length != 3)
            Console.WriteLine("Format: PolicyName MajorVersion MinorVersion");
         else
```

```
            {
                string policyName = args[0];
                int majorRev = Convert.ToInt16(args[1]);
                int minorRev = Convert.ToInt16(args[2]);
                RuleSetInfo rsi = new RuleSetInfo(policyName,majorRev,minorRev);
                Microsoft.BizTalk.RuleEngineExtensions.RuleSetDeploymentDriver dd;
                dd = new
                Microsoft.BizTalk.RuleEngineExtensions.RuleSetDeploymentDriver();
                string fileName = (rsi.Name + "-" + rsi.MajorRevision +
                                          "." + rsi.MinorRevision + ".xml");
                dd.ExportRuleSetToFileRuleStore(rsi,fileName);
            }
        }
    }
}
```

The following code snippet uses the Business Rule Engine Framework to import a policy version from an XML file into the Rule Store and deploy it.

```
using System;
using Microsoft.RuleEngine;
using Microsoft.BizTalk.RuleEngineExtensions;
namespace SimpleImport
{
    class ImportPolicy
    {
        [STAThread]
        static void Main(string[] args)
        {
            if (args.Length != 1)
            {
                Console.WriteLine("Format: ""XML File Name""");
                return;
            }
            String filename = args[0];
            Microsoft.BizTalk.RuleEngineExtensions.RuleSetDeploymentDriver
            dd = new
            Microsoft.BizTalk.RuleEngineExtensions.RuleSetDeploymentDriver();
            SqlRuleStore sqlRuleStore = (SqlRuleStore) dd.GetRuleStore();
            FileRuleStore fileRuleStore = new FileRuleStore(filename);
            RuleSetInfoCollection rsic =
                    fileRuleStore.GetRuleSets(RuleStore.Filter.All);
            foreach (RuleSetInfo rsi in rsic)
```

```
                {
                    RuleSet ruleSet = fileRuleStore.GetRuleSet(rsi);
                    bool publishRuleSets = true;
                    sqlRuleStore.Add(ruleSet,publishRuleSets);
                    dd.Deploy(rsi);
                }
            }
        }
    }
```

Executing Business Rules

Application developers can call upon the BRE to execute business policies from within their .NET code or through the Call Rules shape in their BizTalk orchestrations. At runtime, the Business Rules Framework provides a caching mechanism for RuleEngine instances. Each RuleEngine instance contains an in-memory representation of a specific policy version.

According to the BizTalk Server 2009 documentation (Microsoft, 2009), when a new policy instance is instantiated, either through a direct call from a .NET application through the API or the execution of the Call Rules shape in an orchestration, the following happens:[29]

1. The Policy object requests a RuleEngine instance from the rule engine cache.
2. If a RuleEngine instance for the policy version exists in the cache, the RuleEngine instance is returned to the Policy object. If a RuleEngine instance is not available, the cache creates a new instance. When a RuleEngine instance is instantiated, it does, in turn, create a new fact retriever instance if one is configured for the policy version.

Likewise, when the `Execute` method is called on the `Policy` object, the following steps occur:

1. The Policy object calls the `UpdateFacts` method on the fact retriever instance if a fact retriever exists. The fact retriever's implementation of the method may assert long-term facts into the working memory of the RuleEngine.
2. The Policy object asserts the short term facts contained in the Array that was passed in the Execute call.
3. The Policy object calls Execute on the RuleEngine.
4. The RuleEngine completes execution and returns control to the Policy object.
5. The Policy object retracts the short term facts from the RuleEngine. The long term facts asserted by the fact retriever will remain in the working memory of the rule engine.

29 Copyright © 2009 by Microsoft Corporation. Reprinted with permission from Microsoft Corporation.

After the Dispose method is called on the Policy object, the RuleEngine instance is released back to the rule engine cache.

The rule engine cache will have multiple rule engine instances for a given policy version if the load requires it, and each rule engine instance has its own fact retriever instance.

Calling the Engine from Within an Orchestration

Orchestration developers can use the Call Rules shape to call upon the Business Rule Engine to execute a business rule policy. They can assert facts to the policy that they wish to execute by passing them as parameters to the Call Rules shape. This is done by double-clicking the Call Rules shape, which brings up the parameters dialog depicted in Figure 8-7.

Caution Some logic might require an Orchestration Designer to use the Call Rules shape in a loop. If the loop executes quickly—i.e., it takes only seconds or minutes—then this is fine. If the loop spans days and the logic is hanging on to a specific policy instance, then "policy version updates will not be picked up by the rule engine instance executing the policy…" and "the overall application performance may suffer as the rule engine instance held onto by the policy will be tied up and not returned to the pool to be reused by other orchestrations".

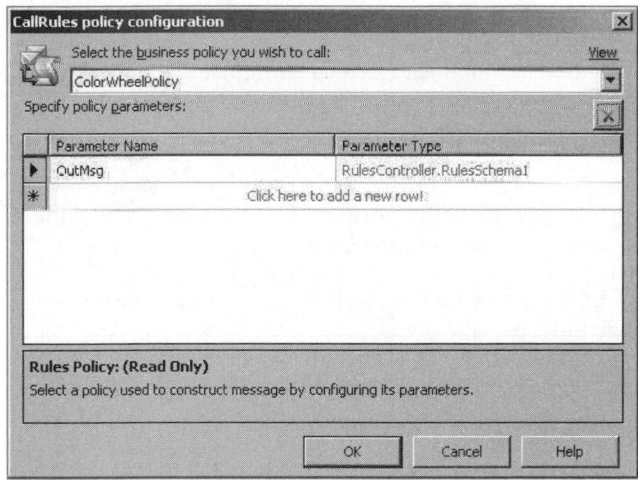

Figure 8-7. *CallRules policy configuration dialog in the Orchestration Designer*

Parameters to an orchestration's Call Rules shape are implicitly defined in the policy. These facts can be XML schema instances, .NET classes, or database elements. If a schema is referenced in a policy's rule, the Orchestration Designer is required to pass in an instance of that schema as a parameter as a fact that will be evaluated.

In their orchestrations, the developers will have to select a message that matches the same type from the drop-down list in the Call Rules shape. Oftentimes developers run into the issue where they are not allowed to add any parameters in the Call Rules shape. This means there are no messages defined in the orchestration with the same type as the schema used in the policy. The problem is that the document type in the Business Rule Engine and the message type in the schema do not match, so the designer cannot find any messages with the appropriate type to populate the drop-down lists in the parameter selection dialog.

■Note We mentioned this before, but so many developers run into the issue that it is worth mentioning again. If you expect to be able to assign messages as parameters to a Call Rules shape in an orchestration and the Orchestration Designer is not allowing you to do so, then most probably the document type defined in the Facts Explorer is not fully qualified; you need to fix that before you add the fields to your rules.

Referencing a .NET Class from a Policy That Is Being Called from an Orchestration

A developer might want to reference and use a .NET class in the business policies. The class could provide helper functions to add nodes to an XML document, the ability to store rule results in an array or a hash table, or make calls to another set of libraries (Moons, 2005).

If the policies are using a .NET class member as a fact in the business rules, and you need to call these policies from within an orchestration using a Call Rules shape, you need to do two things:

- At design time, reference the assembly in the Business Rule Composer to use the methods and/or properties in the policy rules, so that you can create vocabulary items based on that class, or simply use properties and member functions of that class in your rule's conditions and actions.
- Pass an object instance of that class into the policy at runtime. This needs to be done even if you are just referencing static members of the class.

  a. Add a reference to your .NET class in the BizTalk project that contains the orchestration making the call to the business rule policy.

  b. Add a variable to the orchestration of that .NET class type.

  c. Create an instance object of the class in an Expression shape.

  d. Select the policy in the Call Rules shape and select the variable you defined previously in the orchestration as a parameter to that policy. "The messages or variables that are available to you in the rules shape parameter list are determined by the XML Schemas or classes referenced in the policy. When you select the .NET class variable you will be asserting the class instance into the rules engine at runtime" (Moons, 2005).[30]

---

30 Copyright © 2005 by Microsoft Corporation. Reprinted with permission from Microsoft Corporation.

Returning a Value from the BRE to the Calling Orchestration

Sometimes a developer needs a return value from the business rules policy for his code to execute a different piece of logic depending on the policy's results.[31] Despite the fact that the BRE doesn't support return values, it still can "share" a common object with a calling orchestration. The shared object could be an XML document; in this case an orchestration simply passes through a message of that document type to be modified and returned[32] by the Business Rule Engine. Or, it could be either a complex structure or a simple single value, for example, a Boolean value. In either case, it is not efficient to use an XML document—a BizTalk message—to pass those values back and forth; using an object instance of a .NET class would be the right approach. The following example of using a .NET class in a policy will illustrate how an object instance of a .NET class can be used to act as a return value from a policy. A policy will be executed and an action fired that sets a Boolean public property on a class.

You start off by writing a simple class that has a public Boolean property:

```
public class MyReturn
{
  private bool approved;
  public bool Approved
  {
    get{ return approved; }
    set{ approved = value; }
  }
}
```

After compiling this class into a .NET library and deploying its assembly to the GAC, reference that assembly from the Business Rule Composer and set the property of this class in an action to true or false, either by dragging the property from the .NET Class Facts Explorer or by creating and using a vocabulary definition. Your rule should look something like Figure 8-8.

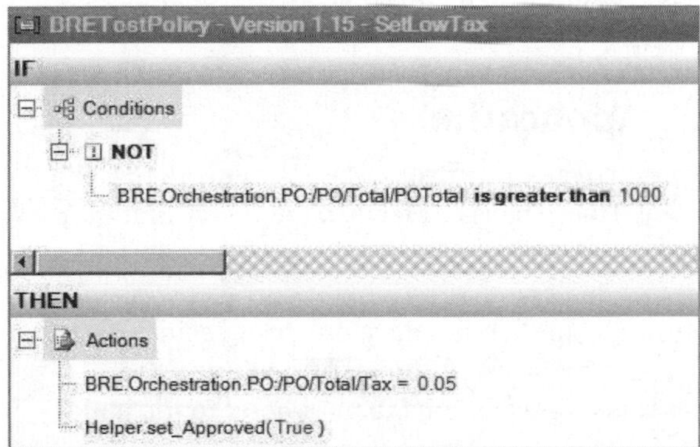

Figure 8-8. *Setting a Boolean value*

31 This discussion is based on material presented in "BizTalk Business Rules Engine Quick Tips" by Jonathan Moons (Microsoft Corporation). Copyright © 2005 by Microsoft Corporation. Reprinted with permission from Microsoft Corporation.

32 BizTalk messages are immutable. The document being returned is a new instance and needs to be assigned to a new document.

Reference that assembly in the BizTalk project hosting the orchestration that will call the policy and create a variable of type MyReturn. Assign a reference of a new object instance of this class to the variable in an Expression shape and pass it as a parameter to the policy in the Call Rules shape as in Figure 8-9.

```
hlpr = new RulesHelper.Helper();
```

The orchestration can access the class's Boolean property in a Decision shape to find out what value it was set to in the Business Rule Engine.

```
hlpr.Approved == true
```

To test the policy from the Business Rule Composer, you can write a fact creator[33] to create an object instance of the `MyReturn` class.

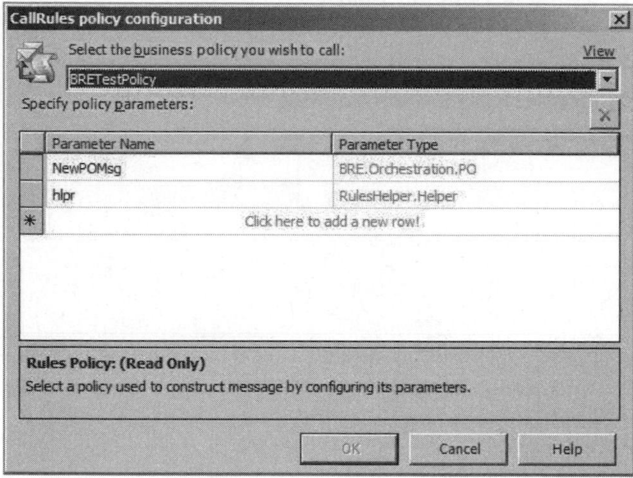

Figure 8-9. *Call Rules shape*

Calling the Engine from a .NET Application

Application developers can use the APIs exposed by the Business Rules Framework to call upon the BRE to execute a business rule policy. They can assert facts to the policy that they wish to execute. This is simply done by passing the engine an array of objects and/or XML document as parameters.

The following code snippet illustrates how the application developer can call the Business Rule Engine to execute the latest version of a particular policy simply by creating a `Microsoft.RuleEngine.Policy` object with the particular rule name passed as a parameter to the policy's constructor.

33 For a detailed description of how to create a fact creator implementing the `IFactCreator` interface, refer to the product documentation.

■Note Calling an older version of a policy is possible only through the Business Rules Framework APIs. The Call Rules shape in the Orchestration Designer calls only the latest version of the policy. To call an older version from within an orchestration, the orchestration developer needs to use the Business Rules Framework APIs from within an expression or an external assembly.

```
using Microsoft.RuleEngine;
using BTSSampleLibrary;
...
// create an instance of the policy (gets the latest version by default)
Microsoft.RuleEngine.Policy policy = null;
policy = new Microsoft.RuleEngine.Policy("Contoso Policy");
```

The developer can then pass the short-term facts as well as objects that will contain return values required for the policy's execution by packaging them in an array and passing it as a parameter to the `Policy.Execute` method.

```
// Create an Employee fact as an example of setting up a fact
StaffMember staff = new Employee();
staff.PersonnelNumber = "123456";
staff.PrimaryRole = "Engineer";
SupportTicket  orderTicket = new SupportTicket();

// create the array of short-term facts
object[] shortTermFacts = new object[3];
shortTermFacts[0] = staff;
shortTermFacts[1] = new SupportTransaction();
shortTermFacts[2] = orderTicket;

//Execute Policy
policy.Execute( shortTermFacts );
```

Once the rule engine instance executing the policy returns, the developer can check for return values from the policy by inspecting the objects whose references were passed in the array.

```
// Process outcome by checking the modified fact, i.e., the authorization ticket
if (orderTicket.IsAuthorized)
{
      MessageBox.Show("Order approved");
}
else if ( orderTicket.RequiresSupervisor)
{
      MessageBox.Show("Support Supivisor Approval is Required");
}
else
{
      MessageBox.Show("Order Rejected: " + orderTicket.FailureReason);
}
```

Policy Chaining

Policy chaining is the ability to call one policy from another. Policy chaining is not natively supported through the Business Rule Engine, but can still be accomplished through additional coding. Essentially, a policy can call .NET code that executes another policy.

The following steps walk through calling one policy from another policy using a console application. It modifies the Loan Processing Sample in the BizTalk SDK. This same sample could be used to call the rule from an orchestration.[34]

1. Create an `Executer` class with the following code snippet. When its `Execute` method is called, the class will use the policy name that is passed to it to assert the facts that were previously passed in via its constructor. In this case it is passing an array to allow multiple objects to be asserted into the engine.

```
using System;
using Microsoft.RuleEngine;
namespace PolicyExecutor
{
        public class Executor
        {
                public Executor(Array passedFacts)
                {
                        facts = passedFacts;
                }
                public void Execute(string policyName)
                {
                        Policy policy = new Policy(policyName);
                        policy.Execute(facts);
                        policy.Dispose();
                }
                private Array facts;
                public Array Facts
                {
                        get{return facts;} set{facts = value;}
                }
        }
}
```

2. Create a console application with the following code snippet:

```
using System;
using System.Xml;
using Microsoft.RuleEngine;
using System.Collections;
using PolicyExecutor;
namespace PolicyChaining
```

34 This example is based on material presented in "BizTalk Business Rules Engine Quick Tips" by Jonathan Moons (Microsoft Corporation). Copyright© 2005 by Microsoft Corporation. Reprinted with permission from Microsoft Corporation.

```
{
 class Class1
 {
  [STAThread]
  static void Main(string[] args)
  {
      string filename = "sampleLoan.xml";
      string policyName = "LoanProcessing";
      // Build TXD
      XmlDocument xd1 = new XmlDocument();
      xd1.Load(filename);
      TypedXmlDocument doc1 = new
        TypedXmlDocument("Microsoft.Samples.BizTalk.LoansProcessor.Case",xd1);
      // Build short term fact array and provide to Executor object
      object[] facts = new object[2];
      PolicyExecutor.Executor executor = new PolicyExecutor.Executor(facts);
      facts[0] = doc1;
      facts[1] =executor;
      // Call parent policy
      Policy policy = new Policy(policyName);
      policy.Execute(facts);
      policy.Dispose();
      // Write out updated XML
      XmlTextWriter writer1 = new XmlTextWriter("sampleLoan_Out.xml",null);
      writer1.Formatting = Formatting.Indented;
      doc1.Document.WriteTo( writer1 );
      writer1.Flush();
  }
 }
}
```

3. Set up and modify the Loan Policy SDK sample.
4. Run the Setup.bat file to set up the Loan Processing SDK sample.
5. Open the Business Rule Composer and create a new policy called LoanPolicyChained.
6. Copy and paste the “Income Status Rule” and the “Negation of Income Status Rule” from LoanPolicy to LoanPolicyChained.
7. Add a new rule to the LoanPolicy called Chain to Income Rules. Set the condition to always be true and in the action call the `Execute` method of the `Executor` class. Set the parameter to the same name as the chained policy, LoanPolicyChained. The new policies will look something like Figure 8-10.
8. Compile and run the console application to have it call the two policies.

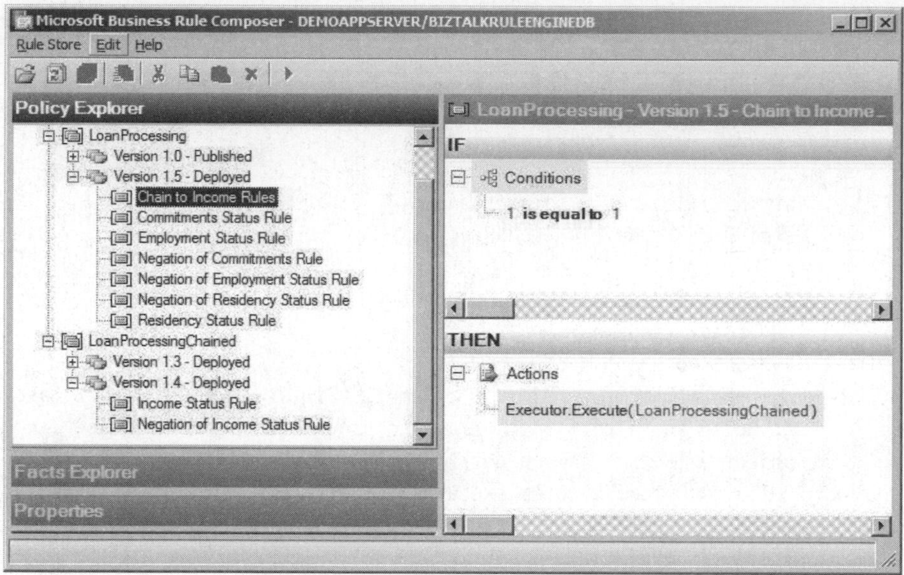

Figure 8-10. *Policy chaining*

■ Note If the policy caller is an orchestration and not an application, the same `Executor` class and policies can still be used. Just replace the console app with an orchestration. One way to do this is to set up the `Executor` class in an Expression shape and then call the Loan policy normally through a Call Rules shape, while passing in the XML message and the `Executor` class instance. The Expression shape would include the following code:

```
facts = new System.Collections.ArrayList();

// Build TXD
xmlDoc = LoanMsg;
typedXmlDoc = new
Microsoft.RuleEngine.TypedXmlDocument("Microsoft.Samples.BizTalk.LoansProcessor
                                                        .Case",xmlDoc);

// Build short term fact array and provide to Executor object
facts.Add(typedXmlDoc);
executor = new PolicyExecutor.Executor(facts.ToArray());
```

The code also depends on four variables that can be defined within the Scope shape that is required for the Call Rules shape: `executor` of type PolicyExecutor.Executor, `facts` of type ArrayList, `xmlDoc` of type XmlDocument, and `typeXmlDoc` of type TypedXmlDocument.

PART 3

You Mean You Aren't a Developer?

Chapters 1 through 8 were primarily targeted toward the developer. As you no doubt have come to realize, BizTalk is a developer-centric product. The tools within BizTalk are built for developers to use. This is a major source of pain for system administrators who are ultimately responsible for ensuring that a BizTalk solution is supported and managed properly once it is commissioned into production. "Productionalizing" a BizTalk Server–based solution is a task that is often overlooked, but it's one we are going to address. In Part 3, we will dive into these anti-developer topics:

- Performance tuning
- BizTalk Server scripting through WMI and ExplorerOM
- Deploying BizTalk Server applications
- Backup and disaster recovery options
- High-availability configurations

CHAPTER 9

BizTalk Server 2009 Operations

In this chapter, we cover BizTalk Server 2009 operations, which include configuration, management, scalability, high availability, backup, restore, and disaster recovery. A well-designed and developed BizTalk system can realize its full potential only when married with a well-architected and managed BizTalk operations environment. BizTalk Server 2009 provides a number of features and tools to improve the operations experience for IT staff. This chapter covers the critical management tasks necessary to ensure a BizTalk system is operating at a high level of performance and availability. In this chapter, you will find discussions of the following topics:

- **Configuration and management**: We discuss the administrative features in BizTalk Server 2009 involving configuration and management. We detail the features of the BizTalk Server Administration Console such as the management of groups, applications, parties, and platform settings. The administration tools and artifacts that accompany BizTalk Server have matured to provide both developers and IT staff with intuitive means to manage, deploy, monitor, and secure production BizTalk systems.
- **Scalability and high availability**: We present the various features of BizTalk Server 2009 and options to consider when designing and implementing a BizTalk system to be both performant and robust in support of a productive and profitable business. We also present the options for scaling out to additional servers for performance and redundancy or scaling up the power of existing hardware to improve throughput. BizTalk Server 2009 provides features such as support for native 64-bit execution on x64 and Windows clustering that can improve performance and uptime.
- **Backup/restore**: We show you how to back up and restore BizTalk Server databases as well as other databases that are part of the overall solution. We also cover how to maintain, archive, and purge data from the BizTalk Tracking database. Plan to test backup and restore procedures before entering production and on a recurring basis.
- **Disaster recovery**: We provide the specific steps and procedures for developing a disaster recovery plan for a BizTalk Server 2009 application, covering both the BizTalk runtime servers and the BizTalk Group hosted in SQL Server. You should plan to test application-specific disaster recovery procedures to ensure the procedures have been successfully tailored to meet application requirements before entering production. Our discussion does not cover procedures for disaster recovery for the following related topics:

- Non-BizTalk applications
- Application source code
- Certificates
- Personnel

There may be additional areas that require documentation in a specific application's disaster recovery plan not listed here that must be addressed on an application-by-application basis.

Configuration and Management

BizTalk Server 2009 builds on improvements that were brought about in BizTalk Server 2006 to simplify administrative tasks. Many of the administration features that were present in BizTalk 2006 have been further refined or improved upon. Most significantly, the Health and Activity Tracker has been removed and integrated into the BizTalk Administration Console. There are key administrative improvements to the console, including the ability to search for completed messages (in other words, search for messages that were processed in the past), improved artifact import and export abilities, and several new features that are discussed later in the chapter.

Administration Tools

The following list defines the tools used to configure and manage BizTalk Server groups, deploy BizTalk Server applications, troubleshoot errors, control security settings, define trading partners, monitor business activities, and administer workflows:

- **BizTalk Server Administration Console**: This is the Microsoft Management Console (MMC) snap-in that has been significantly enhanced to serve as the primary management tool for BizTalk Server. The BizTalk Administration MMC provides a graphical user interface for performing all of the deployment operations for a BizTalk application. It also provides BizTalk group management, message and orchestration troubleshooting such as resume/retry messages and terminate suspended messages/instances, and party definition and platform settings.
- **BTSTask command-line tool**: This is the new command-line administration and deployment tool in BizTalk Server 2009 that supersedes BTSDeploy, which has been removed in this release.
- **Scripting and Programmability APIs**: These are exposed as Microsoft Windows Management Instrumentation (WMI) or BizTalk Explorer Object Model objects. Along with the BTSTask command-line tool, these APIs facilitate creation and execution of scripts to automate very detailed administrative tasks.

■ **Note** The WMI object model exposes and simplifies administrative APIs. All administration APIs expose some form of the following operations on every object they manage: create, enumerate, modify, and delete. WMI exposes this functionality in a consistent manner for all WMI objects.

- **BizTalk Explorer toolbar**: This is used in Microsoft Visual Studio to allow developers to perform common administrative tasks from a single integrated development environment (IDE).
- **BizTalk Server Configuration tool**: This allows each installed BizTalk Server feature to be fully configured, exported, imported, and unconfigured. Configuration of a feature typically involves defining a SQL database to hold setting information, NT service accounts and groups for runtime access permissions, and other feature-specific settings.
- **Business Activity Monitoring (BAM)**: This is set up and configured through the Visio-based Orchestration Designer for Business Analysts (ODBA), the Microsoft Office Excel workbook (BAM.xls), the Tracking Profile Editor (TPE), the BM.exe command-line deployment tool, and the BAM portal web site. BAM provides business users with a way to see a real-time or aggregated holistic view of their business processes.

■ **Tip** Some features previously in BizTalk Server 2004 HAT such as retry/resume messages have been moved to the Group Hub and Query pages in the improved BizTalk Server 2009 Administration Console.

- **Enterprise Single Sign-On (SSO) Administration**: This is a Microsoft Management Console snap-in that enables SSO Administrators, SSO Affiliate Administrators, and Application Administrators to update the SSO database; to add, delete, and manage applications; to administer user mappings; and to set credentials for the affiliate application users. Some operations can be performed only by the SSO Administrators and others by the SSO Affiliate Administrators. All operations that can be performed by the BizTalk Application Administrators can also be performed by the SSO Administrators and SSO Affiliate Administrators.
- **Enterprise SSO Client Utility**: This enables end users to manage their own mappings and set their credentials using this UI tool.
- **Enterprise SSO command-line tools**: These are three different command-line utilities to perform Enterprise Single Sign-On tasks:
  - **SSOConfig**: Enables an SSO Administrator to configure the SSO database and to manage the master secret.

■ **Note** The Configuration Wizard creates the SSO database and the master secret server.

    - **SSOManage**: Enables SSO Administrators, SSO Affiliate Administrators, and Application Administrators to update the SSO database to add, delete, and manage applications; administer user mappings; and set credentials for the affiliate application users. The SSOManage command-line tool contains similar functionality to the SSO Administration MMC snap-in.
    - **SSOClient**: Enables SSO users to manage their own user mappings and set their credentials.
- **BizTalk Web Services Publishing Wizard**: This is a wizard for generating an IIS virtual directory and web service for publishing BizTalk orchestrations and schemas via SOAP. This functionality is scheduled to be deprecated in a future release of the product.
- **BizTalk WCF Services Publishing Wizard**: This is the new companion wizard to the Web Services Publishing Wizard that allows you publish BizTalk orchestrations and schemas as WCF service endpoints.
- **Business Rule Engine Deployment Wizard**: This is a wizard for importing/exporting policies and vocabularies. This tool can also deploy or undeploy a policy in a Rule Engine database.

Application Concept

Formalized in BizTalk Server 2006, the concept of a BizTalk **application** provides a logical container for housing all the artifacts for a given solution. This BizTalk application container can hold design-time artifacts (schemas, maps, pipelines, and orchestrations), messaging components (receive ports, receive locations, and send ports), and other related items (rules policies, pre-processing or post-processing scripts and assemblies) that comprise an integrated business process. By leveraging this concept, the effort to deploy and manage applications is significantly reduced compared to previous versions of BizTalk.

Even as the number of artifacts and components within several complex applications increases, each application can still be managed separately in a simple and intuitive manner. The effect is a streamlining of many everyday tasks, because developers and IT professionals are now able to deploy, manage, start/stop, and troubleshoot at the application level. This results in less confusion and fewer errors. In order to take advantage of the application concept, use the new deployment features in BizTalk Server 2009 or update WMI deployment scripts as necessary. You can explicitly define an application name to group logically related artifacts together; otherwise, artifacts will deploy to the default application for the BizTalk Group.

BizTalk Server Administration Console

The BizTalk Server Administration Console is application-centric. It provides a complete view of one or more BizTalk Server environments. The BizTalk Administration Console is an MMC snap-in that allows the ability to create, configure, and manage one or more applications across multiple servers. Additionally, the MMC includes the ability to import and export applications for installation across multiple servers or for facilitating moving between staging and production environments.

The console also includes monitoring on the message and the service capability previously provided by HAT, the Health and Activity Tracking tool introduced in BizTalk Server 2004. While the Administration Console provides the runtime monitoring, the enhanced BizTalk Server Administration Console is used to manage the following artifacts:

- **BizTalk Group**: The BizTalk Group node in the console tree contains additional nodes that represent the artifacts (applications, parties, and platform settings) for that BizTalk Group (see Figure 9-1). BizTalk groups are units of organization that usually represent enterprises, departments, hubs, or other business units that require a contained BizTalk Server implementation. A BizTalk Group has a one-to-one relationship with a BizTalk Management Database.

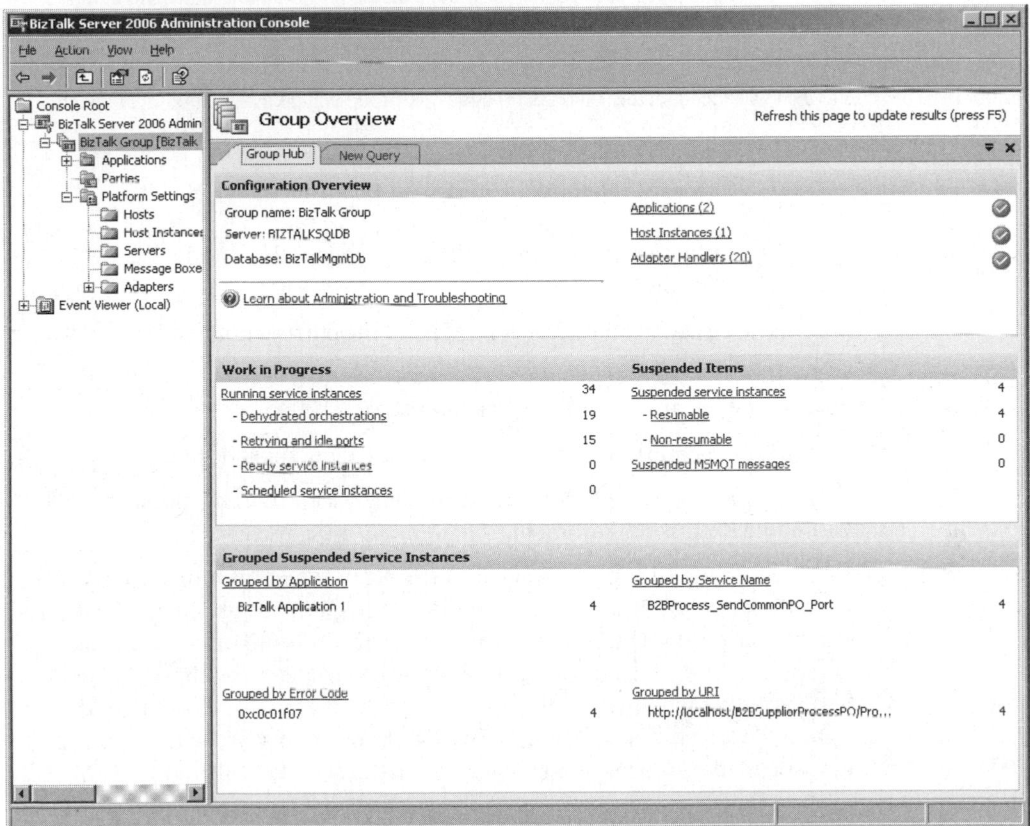

Figure 9-1. *BizTalk Group Hub page in the BizTalk Server Administration Console*

When you select the BizTalk Group node in the BizTalk Server Administration Console, the BizTalk Server Group Hub page is displayed in the details pane. The BizTalk Server Group Hub page, shown in Figure 9-1, provides an overall view of the health of your BizTalk Server system.

Use the Group Hub page in the BizTalk Server Administration Console to investigate orchestration, port, and message failures. The Group Hub page provides access to the current real-time state of the system, accessing data in the Messagebox database to view all service instances such as orchestrations, ports, and messaging, along with their associated messages.

Tip The BizTalk Server Administration Console in BizTalk Server 2009 allows management of multiple BizTalk Groups from a single console. To connect to an additional existing group in an environment, right-click the BizTalk Server 2009 Administration node below Console Root. Choose Connect to Existing Group from the pop-up menu. In the dialog box that appears, enter the SQL Server name and database name for the additional BizTalk Management Database to connect to. The connection will use Windows Authentication. If the account under which the Administration Console is run is part of the added BizTalk Server Administrators group, then the connection will succeed, and an additional BizTalk Group will be available to manage.

Use the Group Hub page to

- See currently running service instances such as orchestrations and messaging, and their associated messages.
- Look into the Messagebox database for a view of the current data and the real-time state of the system.
- Suspend, terminate, and resume service instances.
- Troubleshoot application configuration errors and view subscriptions.
- Search for messages that have completed. This allows for searching of historical data within the BizTalk environment.

Use the Query tab on the Group Hub page in the BizTalk Server Administration Console shown in Figure 9-1 to find specific running and suspended service instances, messages, or subscriptions. Queries performed using the Administration Console search through active items, which are stored in the Messagebox database. A new Query tab will appear each time you run a new query. One key feature of the new console is the ability to save queries so that you can save common searches. This is useful for finding suspended instances or messages from a particular application.

- **Applications**: Applications are managed through the BizTalk Server 2009 Administration Console under the Applications node. BizTalk applications provide a way to view and manage the items, or *artifacts*, that make up a BizTalk business solution. For a new BizTalk Server 2009 installation, a default application named BizTalk Application 1 is created. When upgrading to BizTalk Server 2009 from BizTalk Server 2004, all existing artifacts are placed into BizTalk Application 1. Upgrading to BizTalk Server 2009 from 2006 preserves the application structures that were present before the upgrade. Examples of artifacts are BizTalk assemblies, .NET assemblies, schemas, maps, bindings, and certificates. Artifacts are organized for each application in folders described in the following list:

- **Orchestration**: Orchestrations are designed using the Orchestration Designer in Visual Studio and are deployed to the BizTalk application designated at design time.
- **Role links**: A role link defines the relationship between roles defined by the message and port types used in the interactions in both directions.
- **Send port groups**: A send port group is a named collection of send ports used to send the same message to multiple destinations in a single binding configuration.
- **Send ports**: A send port is a BizTalk object that sends outbound messages to a specific address combined with a BizTalk Server send pipeline.
- **Receive ports**: A receive port is a logical grouping of similar receive locations.
- **Receive locations**: A receive location is defined as a specific address at which inbound messages arrive combined with a BizTalk Server receive pipeline that processes the messages received at that address.
- **Policies**: A policy is a versioned collection of business rules.
- **Schemas**: A schema is the structure for a message. A schema can contain multiple subschemas.
- **Maps**: A map is an XML file that defines the corresponding transformations between the records and fields in one or more source schema and the records and fields in one or more destination schema. A map contains an Extensible Stylesheet Language (XSL) stylesheet that is used by BizTalk Server to perform the transformation.
- **Pipelines**: A pipeline is a software infrastructure component that defines and links one or more processing stages, running them in prescribed order to complete a specific task such as decode, disassemble validate, and so on. Pipelines divide processing into stages, abstractions that describe a category of work. They also determine the sequence in which each category of work is performed.
- **Resources**: A resource is a pre-processing or post-processing script, deployed assembly, or other file associated with a BizTalk application.

- **Parties**: A party is an entity outside of BizTalk Server that interacts with a BizTalk application. All of the partners an organization deals with are considered parties. An organization may have tens to thousands of partners.

- **Platform settings**: The Platform Settings node contains subnodes that represent globally configurable settings that apply across the farm of BizTalk servers in the Group. Those subnodes are as follows:

  - **Hosts**: The Hosts node contains all of the in-process and isolated hosts in the BizTalk Server environment. A BizTalk host is a logical container for items such as adapter handlers, receive locations (including pipelines), and orchestrations. Additional hosts can be created by right-clicking the Hosts node and choosing New ➤ Host.

- **Host Instances**: The Host Instances node contains all of the host instances in the current BizTalk Server group. Host instances are the actual processes that are running within Windows that are the physical containers for logical hosts. Host instances are physically manifested as one or more copies of the BizTalk Server runtime process (i.e., NT service instance) that executes application components. New host instances can be created by right-clicking the Host Instances node and choosing New ➤ Host Instance.
- **Servers**: The Servers node lists all servers that are joined to the selected BizTalk Server group. These are the computers where BizTalk Server is installed and configured, and where host instances are running. Host instances are created by associating a server with a particular host.
- **Message Boxes**: The Message Boxes node contains all Messagebox databases used by the current BizTalk Server Group. Right-clicking the Message Boxes node and choosing New ➤ Message Box allows for creation of additional Messagebox databases. The Messagebox database is the basis for work item load balancing across servers that do cooperative processing. A work item can pass through a Messagebox database more than once during its processing life. The name of the Messagebox database cannot exceed 100 characters.
- **Adapters**: The Adapters node contains subnodes for all the Send and Receive Adapters configured for the BizTalk Server Group and the associated adapter handlers. Adapters are the messaging middleware used to send and receive messages between endpoints. Right-clicking the Adapters node and choosing New ➤ Adapter allows for configuration of additional adapters that have been installed on the BizTalk Server.

Scalability and High Availability

Although BizTalk Server 2009 has fundamentally the same underlying architecture as BizTalk Server 2004 and BizTalk Server 2006, it takes advantage of the latest Microsoft platform technologies, namely, Windows Server 2008, SQL Server 2008, and the .NET Framework 3.5 SP1. BizTalk Server 2009 includes new and improved features in the areas of scalability and high availability:

- New Hyper-V virtualization support
- Improved failover clustering

Windows Server 2008 64-bit Support

64-bit native execution allows BizTalk Server 2009 to take advantage of the benefits of the x64 Windows platform such as a larger memory address space, support for larger RAM, and faster I/O. The white paper "Benefits of Microsoft Windows x64 Editions" located at the following link covers the benefits of the Windows x64 platform in detail: `www.microsoft.com/windowsserver2003/techinfo/overview/x64benefits.mspx`.

We highly recommend implementing BizTalk on Windows x64 editions to take advantage of these benefits where appropriate. With x64, even 32-bit Windows applications can benefit from running on x64 Windows; however, note that BizTalk Server 2009 host instances can run x64 natively.

64-bit Caveats

There are some caveats to BizTalk's 64-bit support, however. Some of the native BizTalk features are available only as 32-bit and must be run in a 32-bit host on a 64-bit Windows Server. Additionally, BizTalk Server Standard does not support 64-bit execution. The product will install fine on a 64-bit Windows Server but will be limited to 32-bit process execution. The product documentation provides good coverage on the native 64-bit support for each particular feature of the product. A few highlights are as follows:

- **ExplorerOM**: Supported only in 32-bit mode. If you have custom code that calls ExplorerOM, it has to be run in a 32-bit process.
- **EDI AS/2**: The EDI AS/2 components must be run in a 32-bit host process.

Hyper-V Support

The formal support of Hyper-V virtualization technology represents a huge step forward for the BizTalk platform. Starting in 2008, Microsoft announced a comprehensive list of server-based products that are officially supported for use within Hyper-V virtual OSs. Fortunately, BizTalk was one of them.

While it is unlikely that many organizations will run BizTalk applications that have a strict performance requirement or where throughput and latency may be a concern, Hyper-V does simplify the creation of virtual images for test, integration, and development environments. Often organizations are reluctant to spend significant hardware budget for functional, acceptance, and integration environments. Hyper-V now allows for these separate environments to be created with no additional hardware costs.

■ **Tip** There are no additional licensing costs from either a BizTalk or Windows perspective to take advantage of the x64 platform.

Scalability

Even after tuning an application, bottlenecks in performance can develop, especially if load increases, which may require upgrading or adding hardware to the existing BizTalk solution architecture. Thankfully, BizTalk Server 2009 provides options to easily scale up or scale out the solution architecture.

Depending on where a bottleneck exists, it might be necessary to scale out or scale up either the BizTalk tier or the SQL Server tier. This is why it is extremely important to monitor a BizTalk solution to help identify trends in hardware resource utilization such as memory, CPU, or disk before the problem occurs. System Center Operation Manager (SCOM) 2007 with the SCOM 2007 management pack for BizTalk Server 2009 can greatly assist with this task.

The white paper "BizTalk Server 2004 Performance Characteristics" is a great document to review in order to get a feel for how application design can affect resource utilization/performance. This white paper can be found here: `http://msdn.microsoft.com/library/default.asp?url=/library/en-us/bts_2004wp/html/04d20926-20d2-4098-b701-52238a267eba.asp?frame=true`.

While the preceding white paper is for BizTalk Server 2004, the scalability concepts still apply in BizTalk Server 2009. A more recent white paper on BizTalk Server 2009 adapter performance, "BizTalk Server 2009 Comparative Adapter Study," is available at this link: `www.microsoft.com/downloads/details.aspx?FamilyID=fdae55db-184b-4d93-ad79-a113b5268ee2&DisplayLang=en`.

In addition to the details on adapter performance, this white paper provides detail on how to determine Maximum Sustainable Throughput (MST), which is a critical step for understanding the performance characteristics of any BizTalk application.

The next subsections cover when to choose an option and the steps involved.

Scaling Out the BizTalk Tier

Scaling out the BizTalk tier is a good option when BizTalk Server is the bottleneck in terms of high CPU, memory, or heavy disk I/O and adding servers makes economic sense and can solve the issue. High CPU can result from intensive pipeline processing, message maps converting between complex schemas, or large/complex orchestrations. High memory or disk I/O can occur under high load and can generally be addressed through scale-out, but not always. See the "Scaling Up the BizTalk Tier" subsection later for more information. In many cases, scaling out by adding another BizTalk Server is more cost effective than replacing an existing machine with a more powerful one as long as it can solve the issue.

Scaling out the BizTalk tier does not help when the Messagebox database is the bottleneck, which again highlights how important it is to monitor resource utilization on both the BizTalk tier and the SQL tier. Another scenario of when scaling out the BizTalk tier may not help is when an adapter is a bottleneck. For example, if the FTP adapter is the bottleneck, adding more BizTalk servers does not help if the limit exists on the other end of the FTP communication.

Scaling out the BizTalk tier is achieved through managing BizTalk hosts and host instances. BizTalk hosts are logical groupings where artifacts such as receive locations, send ports, and orchestrations execute. Hosts are physically implemented as host instances, which are .NET Windows Services. A typical way to organize a BizTalk application is to create a receive host, a send host, a tracking host, and an orchestration host. This type of organization can isolate processing so that if a receive problem is occurring, troubleshooting and debugging can be focused on the receive host instance(s), and it is a good idea even when there is just a single BizTalk server.

■ **Note** Hosts can be configured to run host instances under separate service accounts/Windows groups as a security boundary to provide security isolation between host processing, if needed to meet business requirements.

The way scale-out works is that when a receive adapter (or a send port or orchestration) is configured to run in a host such as a receive host, the adapter physically runs on every BizTalk server where an instance of the receive host is deployed. So, to scale out the host where the receive adapter executes, a new BizTalk server is configured to join the BizTalk Group, and a host instance of the receive host is deployed to the new server. Deploying a new instance of a host takes a few clicks in the BizTalk Server 2009 Administration Console. For information on managing hosts and host instances, please refer to the BizTalk Server 2009 documentation.

Most adapters will scale out as the number of number of BizTalk Servers increases. There are exceptions, however, such as the FTP and POP3 adapters. These adapters are not able to run multiple receive endpoints because of limitations in the underlying protocols (you can't have more than one BizTalk server receiving a file via FTP, for example). In these cases, you will need to introduce Windows clustering to cluster the FTP Receive adapter for purely failover and recovery reasons. There are no performance-based reasons to do this. The same situation may also occur with third-party adapters. Check with the vendor of the adapter for how they implement scale-up and scale-out within their products.

Scaling Out the SQL Tier

Scale-out of the SQL tier is primarily focused on the Messagebox database. The Messagebox database is where BizTalk application processing occurs from a database perspective. The first Messagebox database is created during initial BizTalk configuration and is the master Messagebox database. The master Messagebox contains the master subscription information and routes messages to the appropriate Messagebox database if there is more than one Messagebox.

When it is determined that scaling out the Messagebox database is required, Microsoft recommends dedicating the master Messagebox to do routing only by selecting "Disable new message publication for the master Messagebox database" in the BizTalk Server 2009 Administration Console, and then having the other Messagebox databases perform application processing. Microsoft also recommends going from one Messagebox to three Messagebox databases to benefit from scaling out the SQL tier and to overcome the additional processing overhead that occurs when there is more than one Messagebox database. For more information on scaling out the Messagebox, please refer to the BizTalk Server 2009 documentation.

Scaling the Messagebox

BizTalk Server provides the ability to scale the Messagebox into multiple Messageboxes for load balancing and performance reasons. Creating multiple Messageboxes has no benefit for disaster recovery scenarios and is useful only for spreading load across multiple databases and/or database servers.

The process of creating a multi-Messagebox installation is quite architecturally simple. One Messagebox will always act as the "master Messagebox," and it will have several child Messageboxes. The job of the master Messagebox is to do subscription matching and routing, and it stores all subscription information used by the message agent to match and route messages to the appropriate child Messagebox. If the subscription is an activation subscription, the message is routed to a child Messagebox in a round-robin fashion. If the subscription is an instance subscription, the message is routed to the child Messagebox that holds the dehydrated instance orchestration or the send port, which is waiting for a response from an adapter (e.g., SOAP or HTTP).

Adding multiple Messageboxes adds a fair degree of complexity to a BizTalk solution and should be done only in the cases of extreme load and to distribute instance subscriptions across multiple databases and potentially multiple SQL Servers. Depending on the type of application and the type of work it is doing, implementing a multi-Messagebox architecture will not help performance and may decrease overall throughput.

Scaling Up the BizTalk Tier

Scaling up the BizTalk tier is a good option when BizTalk Server is the bottleneck, if it can solve the issue and is a good alternative economically. Scaling up the BizTalk tier makes sense in the following scenarios:

- Large message transforms
- Large number of messages per Interchange
- High memory utilization by some BTS components such as pipelines or adapters
- A transport-related issue, such as EDI

Scaling up includes adding CPUs, adding memory or faster disk I/O to an existing BizTalk server, or replacing an existing BizTalk server with a more powerful machine. If you are using a 64-bit OS and BizTalk Server Enterprise, you can more easily scale up your available memory because of the OS's ability to address larger processes. This will help if you are constantly bumping up against throttling within the Message Agent because of memory pressure.

Next, we cover scale-up of the SQL tier.

Scaling Up the SQL Tier

Scaling up the database tier avoids the overhead of adding Messagebox databases that results from message routing and can be a good option if it makes economic sense and addresses the issue. In general, scale-up should be considered before scale-out for the SQL tier.

Scaling up the database tier can include adding CPUs, memory, or a faster disk as well as replacing the existing server with a more powerful server. One scenario that scale-up cannot address is when there is SQL lock contention on the SQL tier. In this case, scaling out of the SQL tier should be considered.

High Availability

Most BizTalk Server solutions are mission critical to a company and require high availability to meet business requirements. Therefore, BizTalk Server 2009 provides features for high availability as well as takes advantage of high-availability capabilities in the underlying operating system such as clustering to provide a robust architecture.

Both BizTalk and SQL Server must be highly available in order for the solution to function, and we cover this in the next two subsections. In addition, the master secret server must also be highly available for a BizTalk solution to function. Clustering the master secret server is covered in the following text as well.

BizTalk Tier High Availability

As with scalability, BizTalk hosts are the key feature to provide high availability for the BizTalk tier. As mentioned previously, BizTalk artifacts such as receive locations, send ports, and orchestrations are configured to run in a logical host but actually execute in host instance Windows Services that can be deployed to multiple BizTalk servers in the BizTalk Group.

If there are two BizTalk servers with an instance of a particular host but one server becomes unavailable, processing will continue on the other BizTalk server with the instance of the host, providing processing redundancy or availability.

BizTalk Server 2009 introduces Windows clustering for host instances. Host clustering is necessary for integrated BizTalk adapters that should not be run in multiple host instances simultaneously such as the FTP receive handler or potentially the POP3 receive handler. The FTP does not have file locking, so if there were two FTP host instances running, both could potentially receive the same file, resulting in duplicate processing. Therefore, only one FTP receive host instance should be configured, which is why it should be clustered because it is a single instance. For POP3, the scenario is similar to FTP's. If the POP3 server allows multiple simultaneous connections to the same mailbox such that duplicate messages may be received, the POP3 adapter should be run as a single host instance and should therefore be clustered for high availability. Another scenario where host clustering is necessary for high availability is when a single host instance is required to maintain ordered delivery for the MSMQ or the WebSphere MQ–integrated adapters. For these adapters, the single host instance can be clustered to provide high availability. For more information on implementing high availability for the BizTalk tier, please refer to the BizTalk Server 2009 documentation.

The next subsection covers SQL tier high availability.

SQL Tier High Availability

The BizTalk Group exists in the SQL tier in SQL Server database instances, which can be clustered for high availability. From a BizTalk standpoint, it is transparent whether the SQL Server instance is clustered or not, so SQL tier high availability is a matter of implementing SQL Server in a highly available manner by configuring the BizTalk Group databases on a SQL Server instance that is clustered. For more information on SQL Server high availability, please refer to the SQL Server documentation installed as part of the product or available online here:

- **SQL Server 2005 Books Online**: See `www.microsoft.com/technet/prodtechnol/sql/2005/downloads/books.mspx`.
- **SQL Server 2008 Books Online**: See `www.microsoft.com/downloads/details.aspx?familyid=765433F7-0983-4D7A-B628-0A98145BCB97&displaylang=en`.

Next, we cover how to implement the master secret server for high availability.

Master Secret Server High Availability

If the master secret server becomes unavailable, all runtime operations already running will continue to run, but SSO servers will not be able to encrypt new credentials. Since there can be only one master secret server in the SSO system, Microsoft recommends clustering the master secret server, and the BizTalk Server 2009 documentation covers the steps in detail.

■ **Tip** Though many organizations implement Enterprise SSO with a master secret server on a per–BizTalk Group basis, a single master secret server can be shared between multiple BizTalk Groups as well as with Microsoft Host Integration Server. Another not well-known fact is that Enterprise SSO is backward compatible. If you find yourself with multiple products and/or versions of BizTalk Server running in a single environment, you can configure all applications to use the most recent version of Enterprise SSO and maintain only one ESSO installation and not have to worry about clustering separate ESSO installations.

Clustering the master secret consists of installing Enterprise Single Sign-On on a Windows cluster. Quite often, customers choose to cluster the master secret server on the same Windows cluster that hosts the BizTalk Group databases to avoid the cost of having a separate Windows cluster just for Enterprise SSO. Where you install Enterprise SSO depends on the business requirements of the solution as well as economic considerations. Just ensure that the master secret is installed in a Windows cluster to ensure high availability whether on a standalone Windows cluster or in the same Windows cluster where the BizTalk Group SQL Server database instances are clustered.

■ **Note** You must not cluster the master secret server on any machine that is running BizTalk Server. To use clustering, Enterprise SSO must be clustered on the SQL Server cluster or a separate Windows Server cluster.

Maintaining the BizTalk Group

A BizTalk Group consists of the set of databases hosted in SQL Server. SQL Server provides high availability for BizTalk Server 2009 applications through Windows cluster installations hosting the BizTalk configuration and operation databases. For BizTalk applications, the servers with BizTalk installed provide the runtime environment with SQL Server as the persistent store. Therefore, BizTalk Server 2009 backup, restore, and disaster recovery procedures are heavily focused on procedures related to SQL Server.

A BizTalk Server solution's availability and performance are highly dependent on maintaining the SQL Server–based back end where the BizTalk Group is located. Every message that is received by a BizTalk host instance enters the SQL Server Messagebox database, tracked to some degree, retrieved from SQL Server by the host instance where the subscribing orchestration is executed with the results put back into SQL Server for transmission on a host instance send port. As you can see, overall BizTalk performance is highly dependent on the underlying SQL Server performance.

■ **Caution** Changes to the BizTalk Group SQL Server schema are not supported. Do not modify the SQL Server schema for any tables or stored procedures that are part of the BizTalk Group.

Luckily, the BizTalk product team provides several SQL Agent jobs to assist with keeping the BizTalk Group running in top form. SQL Server Agent makes message bodies available to BizTalk and WMI and enables you to run jobs to clean up the Messagebox databases.

The SQL Agent jobs are created when the BizTalk Group is configured using Configuration.exe. The user who runs Configuration.exe is also designated as the SQL Agent job owner. The account designated as the job owner is the security context that the SQL Agent job executes under. If any SQL Agent jobs are failing, consider changing the job owner to a different account that has the required privileges to folders or UNC shares, and so on, so that the job can complete successfully.

Table 9-1 describes the SQL Agent jobs. Do not alter the schedule for any jobs except possibly for the Backup BizTalk Server SQL Agent job. Details configuring the Backup BizTalk Server SQL Agent job are covered in the subsection titled "Configuring the Backup BizTalk Server SQL Agent Job."

Table 9-1. *BizTalk Group SQL Agent Jobs*

SQL Agent Job	Remarks
Backup BizTalk Server (BizTalkMgmtDb)	This SQL Agent job performs backup operations on BizTalk databases that participate in Distributed Transaction Coordinator (DTC) transactions. Not all BizTalk databases are part of this job. Also, additional databases can be added to this job. This job is disabled by default and must be configured in order to run. Scheduled to perform full backup daily and log backup every 15 minutes by default.
CleanupBTFExpiredEntriesJob_<BizTalkMgmtDb>	This SQL Agent job cleans up expired BizTalk Framework (BTF) entries in the BizTalk Management Database. Scheduled to run every 12 hours and enabled by default.
DTA Purge and Archive (BizTalkMsgBoxDb)	This SQL Agent job automatically archives data in the BizTalk Tracking (BizTalkDTADb) database and purges obsolete data. This job is disabled by default and must be configured in order to run. Scheduled to run every minute by default.
MessageBox_DeadProcesses_Cleanup_<BizTalkMsgBoxDb>	This SQL Agent job detects when a running BizTalk host instance has stopped. This SQL Agent job releases all in-progress work for that host instance so that it can be picked up by another host instance. Scheduled to run every minute and enabled by default.
MessageBox_Message_ Cleanup_<BizTalkMsgBoxDb>	This SQL Agent job removes messages that are no longer referenced by any subscribers in the Messagebox database tables. This job is disabled by default, but it should **not** be manually run. This job is started when needed by the MessageBox_Message_ManageRefCountLog_<BiztalkMsgBoxDb> job.
MessageBox_Message_ManageRefCountLog_<BizTalkMsgBoxDb>	This SQL Agent job manages the reference count logs for messages. It determines when a message is no longer referenced by a subscriber. Scheduled to run every minute and enabled by default.
MessageBox_Parts_Cleanup_<BizTalkMsgBoxDb>	This SQL Agent job removes message parts that are no longer referenced by any messages in the Messagebox database tables. Scheduled to run every minute and enabled by default.

Continued

Table 9-1. *Continued*

SQL Agent Job	Remarks
MessageBox_UpdateStats_ <BizTalkMsgBoxDb>	This SQL Agent job manually updates database statistics for the BizTalk Messagebox database. Scheduled to run every 5 minutes and enabled by default.
Operations_OperateOnInstances_ OnMaster_<BizTalkMsgBoxDb>	This SQL Agent job is required for multiple Messagebox database deployments. It performs operational tasks on Messagebox databases. Scheduled to run every minute and enabled by default.
PurgeSubscriptionsJob_ <BizTalkMsgBoxDb>	This SQL Agent job purges unused subscription predicates from the Messagebox database. Scheduled to run every minute and enabled by default.
Rules_Database_Cleanup <BizTalkRuleEngineDb>	New in BizTalk Server 2006, this SQL Agent job purges old audit data from the Rule Engine database every 90 days. It also purges old history data from the Rule Engine database every 3 days. Scheduled to run every hour and enabled by default.
TrackedMessages_Copy_ <BizTalkMsgBoxDb>	This SQL Agent job copies message bodies of tracked messages from the Messagebox database to the Tracking database. Scheduled to run every minute and enabled by default.

Microsoft strongly recommends monitoring the SQL Agent service and the individual jobs using a monitoring tool such as MOM or similar enterprise monitoring product. If any of these jobs starts failing, it is a strong indication that there are performance issues with the application. It is also a good idea to monitor how long it takes for the SQL Agent jobs to run, perhaps on a weekly basis. If the jobs are taking longer and longer to run over time, it is another indication that there may be performance issues.

For completeness, the BizTalk Server 2004 SQL Agent job TrackingSpool_ Cleanup_<BizTalkMsgBox was removed in BizTalk Server 2006.

The next step is to configure the necessary SQL Agent jobs to perform backups and to maintain the BizTalk Group.

SQL Agent Job Configuration

The following jobs from Table 9-1 require configuration before they can be enabled and can run successfully:

- Backup BizTalk Server (BizTalkMgmtDb)
- DTA Purge and Archive (BizTalkMsgBoxDb)

■ **Note** The SQL Agent job MessageBox_Message_Cleanup_<BizTalkMsgBoxDb> is disabled by default. It is not supported to enable this job or run it manually. This SQL Agent job is managed by the MessageBox_ Message_ManageRefCountLog_<BiztalkMsgBoxDb> SQL Agent job.

The following two subsections cover how to configure these SQL Agent jobs.

Configuring the Backup BizTalk Server SQL Agent Job

The Backup BizTalk Server SQL Agent job is a critical job that must be configured in order to be able to successfully back up the BizTalk Server 2009 databases that participate in Distributed Transaction Coordinator transactions. Databases that participate in DTC transactions such as with BizTalk must be backed up and restored as a set to ensure consistency.

Note Not all BizTalk databases are backed up as part of the Backup BizTalk Server job. Backing up these databases is covered in the next subsection.

The following databases are backed up as part of the Backup BizTalk Server SQL Agent job:

- BizTalk Configuration (BizTalkMgmtDb)
- BizTalk Messagebox (BizTalkMsgBoxDb)
- BizTalk Tracking (BizTalkDTADb)
- Rule Engine (BizTalkRuleEngineDb)
- BAM Primary Import (BAMPrimaryImport)
- Trading Partner Management (TPM)

These databases *must* be backed up by the Backup BizTalk Server SQL Agent job and cannot be backed up using the normal SQL Server backup procedures. The reason is because BizTalk uses SQL Server log marks to keep the set of databases consistent as part of DTC transactions. The Backup BizTalk Server job creates a log mark and then backs up the database log for each database that is part of the Backup BizTalk Server SQL Agent job. This log mark is used when restoring the last log file for each database so that transactional consistency is maintained. Here are the steps to configure the Backup BizTalk Server SQL Agent job:

1. In SQL Server 2005/2008 Management Studio, navigate to the SQL Agent jobs list.
2. Right-click Backup BizTalk Server (BizTalkMqmtDb), and select Properties.
3. In the Job Properties dialog box under "Select a page," click Steps to view the job steps.
4. In the "Job step" list, click BackupFull, and then click Edit.
5. On the General page, in the Command box, replace '<destination path>' with the full path (the path must include the single quotes) to the computer and folder where you want to back up the BizTalk Server databases. Also add a new parameter by typing a comma and then a number one (,1) at the end of the parameter list for the stored procedure `sp_BackupAllFull`. Adding this parameter enables an automatic full backup after a backup failure. Click OK when finished.

■**Note** The default frequency for the BackupFull job is d for daily. Other values are hourly (h/H), weekly (w/W), monthly (m/M), and yearly (y/Y). The first time the job is run during a new period, a full backup is performed. Also, the default name is BTS, which will be part of the backup file name. Change this to reflect a better name for the application such as OrdSys for an application named Order System.

---

6. In the Job step list, click MarkAndBackupLog, and then click Edit.
7. On the General page, in the Command box, replace '<destination path>' with the full path (including single quotes) to the computer and folder where you want to store the BizTalk Server database logs, and then click OK. The <destination path> may be local or a UNC path to another server.

■**Note** We recommend a UNC share to store the backup files on a different file system than where the databases reside for production environments. For a dev or test environment, if you are not concerned with maintaining offsite backup sets or multiple backup sets, you can consider using a local path instead of a UNC path.

Also, for the job step MarkAndBackupLog, Log Mark Name is part of the naming convention for backup files:

```
<Server Name>_<Database Name>_Log_< Log Mark Name >_<Timestamp>
Replace "BTS' with a more appropriate name for the solution.
```

8. In the Job step list, click Clear Backup History, and then click Edit.
9. On the General page, in the Command box, change DaysToKeep=<number> to the number of days (default is 14) you want to keep the backup history, and then click OK twice to close the Job Properties dialog box.

■**Note** The DaysToKeep setting is not related to how many sets of backup files are maintained. Backup file sets must be handled manually by copying to another system for long-term archival.

Change the backup schedule for MarkAndBackupLogSched if desired, and then right-click the Backup BizTalk Server SQL Agent job and select Enable. The default schedule is to perform a log backup every 15 minutes.

Once the Backup BizTalk Server job is configured and enabled, right-click, and select Start Job to test. Click F5 to refresh the status on the Jobs node. If the result is not successful, check the following:

- Verify that the destination folder exists and is reachable if a UNC share.
- Check that the job owner has permissions on the destination folder.
- Ensure that linked servers are configured properly if BizTalk databases are present in multiple SQL Server database instances.

■ **Tip** For SQL Server 2005 and 2008, there are additional security settings for linked servers. When configuring linked servers in SQL Server 2005 or 2008 as part of the Backup BizTalk Server SQL Agent job, click the Security tab, and select the "Be made using the login's current security context" option. Next click Server Options, set RPC Out to True, and then click OK.

Be aware that the file name includes the date/time from when the backup file was created. This date/time is GMT time, not local time. If you look at the Date Modified field in Windows Explorer, you will see the local time.

Also, the Backup BizTalk Server SQL Agent job does not manage disk space, meaning it will continue to copy files into the same directory until the drive runs out of space. This allows the administrator to decide how many backup sets to keep on disk as well as how many to archive to an offsite location, deleting the files from disk after archival.

The next subsection covers how to configure the DTA Purge and Archive SQL Agent job.

Configuring the DTA Purge and Archive SQL Agent Job

With companies having to comply with IRS, general accounting, and legislative requirements for business reporting, BizTalk Server provides extensive tracking capabilities to help with complying with these mandates. This data must be kept for various periods of time to meet reporting requirements. BizTalk Server 2009 has the DTA Purge and Archive job to help automate the backup of tracking data including the ability to perform on-the-fly validation of tracking data backups using another instance of SQL Server to ensure that a complete record of activity is maintained and available.

In addition to providing data archival, the DTA Purge and Archive SQL Agent job performs data pruning to help keep the system running smoothly. As with any database system, unchecked growth in table size will eventually push the limits of the hardware. In general, there are two solutions to this problem: buy more disks or a faster disk or have a purge and archival policy to "prune" the databases where it makes sense. While all database-based systems benefit from more and faster disks, BizTalk has a process to keep the BizTalk Tracking and Messagebox databases performing optimally by automating purging and archival tasks through the DTA Purge and Archive SQL Agent job.

The DTA Purge and Archive job purges various tracking information such as service instance and message information, orchestration event information, and rule engine tracking data. The purge process is based on the age of the tracking data, which is maintained by having a time stamp added when tracking information is inserted into the database. The DTA Purge and Archive job has a **soft purge** and **hard purge** process. The soft purge processes completed instances, while the hard purge processes incomplete instances. Note that both soft purge and hard purge process just the tracking data, not the actual running instances, so they have no effect on actual data processing data. The purge process helps to optimize tracking processes and HAT operations when looking at historical data. Here are the steps to configure the DTA Purge and Archive SQL Agent job:

1. Depending on where you are, navigate to the Management node and view the SQL Agent jobs.
2. In the details pane, right-click DTA Purge and Archive (BizTalkDTADb), and then click Properties.
3. In the Job Properties dialog box, click the Steps tab, click Archive and Purge, and then click Edit.
4. On the General tab, in the Command box, edit the following parameters as appropriate, and then click OK.

■Note For the soft purge, the sum of LiveHours and LiveDays is the live window of data that will be maintained for the BizTalk Tracking database. All tracking data associated with completed instances older than the live window will be deleted and archived.

- `@nLiveHours tinyint`: Default is 0 hours.
- `@nLiveDays tinyint`: Default is 1 day.
- `@nHardDeleteDays tinyint`: Default is 30 days.
- `@nvcFolder nvarchar(1024)`: Specify the folder or UNC share to put the tracking data backup files.
- `@nvcValidatingServer`: SQL Server instance where validation is performed. Default is null.
- `@fForceBackup int`: Default is 0. This is not currently implemented.

Here is an example command that specifies that soft purge occurs every 12 hours and hard purge occurs every 7 days:

```
exec dtasp_BackupAndPurgeTrackingDatabase 12, 0, 7, '\\BizTalkBackupServer\data',
null, 0
```

In the preceding example, we left the validation server value as null; however, we recommend that you set up a validation server for the tracking data to ensure that the backup files of the tracking data for reporting and compliance purposes are valid. Also, the data can be queried on the validation server, offloading potentially long-running queries from the production BizTalk databases. To configure a validation server for the DTA Purge and Archive SQL Agent job, you must have a separate instance of SQL Server available. Having a validation server requires that the `@nvcFolder` variable in the DTA Purge and Archive job points to a UNC share reachable by the validation server. The SQL Server instance where the BizTalk databases are configured cannot also act as the validating server. On the server designated as the validation server, perform these steps:

1. In the SQL Management Studio in SQL Server 2005/2008, open a file to execute a SQL file. Connect to the SQL instance that is the validation server.
2. Select File ➤ Open, and then browse to this SQL script on the server/drive where BizTalk Server 2009 is installed: \Program Files\Microsoft BizTalk Server 2009\Schema\BTS_Tracking_ValidateArchive.sql.
3. Execute the query to create a SQL Agent job called ValidateArchive on the validating server.
4. Open the SQL Management Studio for SQL Server 2005/2008 to set up the required linked servers. Linked servers must be created between the following:
   - Each of the BizTalk Messagebox (BizTalkMsgBoxDB) SQL Server instances and the BizTalk Tracking (BizTalkDTADb) SQL Server instances. The SQL instance hosting the DTA database requires a linked server to each SQL instance hosting a BizTalk Messagebox, and vice versa.
   - The BizTalk Tracking (BizTalkDTADb) SQL Server instance and the validating server SQL Server instance. Create a linked server on each SQL instance to the other SQL instance so that the SQL instance hosting the DTA database has a linked server to the validating server, and vice versa.

Next, we turn our attention to monitoring best practices for the SQL Agent jobs.

Monitoring the BizTalk Group SQL Agent Jobs

Because the SQL Agent jobs are critical to maintaining BizTalk performance, the jobs must be monitored so that operations personnel can be alerted if a job fails. The Microsoft SQL Server Management Pack contains MOM rules for monitoring SQL databases, SQL Server Agent jobs, and so on, for comprehensive monitoring of SQL Server items. The BizTalk Server 2009 Management Pack for Microsoft Operations Manager 2005 includes two rules, disabled by default, for monitoring the health of two of the most important BizTalk SQL Server Agent jobs. The rule names as defined in the Management Pack are as follows:

- Critical Error: A BizTalk SQL Server Agent job failed—Backup BizTalk Server
- Critical Error: A BizTalk SQL Server Agent job failed—Tracked Message Copy

To monitor all BizTalk Server SQL Server Agent jobs from within the BizTalk Server 2009 Management Pack, enable these rules and create additional rules for other jobs that you want to monitor. To enable these rules, perform the following steps in the MOM Administrator Console:

1. Create a copy of the two rules just listed in the BizTalk Server Core Rule group, and rename each rule appropriately.
2. In the criteria section for the MOM rule, change the wildcard comparison for Parameter 1 because the job names are specific to the BizTalk Group configuration.

You need to add the SQL Server computers into the BizTalk Server 2009 Computer Group in MOM. This is because the MOM rule needs to be evaluated on the SQL Server computer and the SQL Server computer will not be recognized as a BizTalk Server computer unless BizTalk and SQL Server happen to be installed on the same machine.

Backup Procedures

This subsection covers the backup procedures for BizTalk applications; however, a BizTalk application is usually just one part of an overall solution that includes other applications, servers, and databases. In general, backing up an application solution that includes BizTalk requires the following general procedures:

- Backing up application code, artifacts, and documentation
- Backing up server configuration documentation
- Backing up BizTalk servers and BizTalk Group databases
- Backing up related non-BizTalk databases

Steps and procedures for backing up the first two items listed are outside the scope of this chapter; however, in general, application code, artifacts, code documentation, and server configuration documentation should be kept in a source code control system that is backed up automatically with rotating backup sets maintained at an offsite location.

The following subsections focus on the last two items listed including backup procedures for BizTalk runtime servers and for the BizTalk Group.

BizTalk Servers

The servers where BizTalk is installed and configured should be backed up using your corporate standards for server backup. In addition, the config.xml file used to configure each server should be backed up along with documentation on what host instances, receive ports, and send ports are installed on the server. This information can be stored in your source code control system as solution artifacts. Essentially, the procedures used to perform the following steps must be in a format that administrators can use to perform a restore or disaster recovery event:

- **BizTalk installation**: Document what features/service pack/hotfixes are installed on the BizTalk runtime server. Document what other products such as SharePoint, IIS, or third-party adapters are installed.
- **BizTalk configuration**: Back up the config.xml file that was used to configure the server. This file can be reused to configure the server with minor edits depending on whether the BizTalk Windows server name changed or the SQL instance location of the databases has changed.

- **Master secret**: This is an extremely important backup item that is covered later in this chapter. Without the master secret, a BizTalk Group cannot be restored. The master secret is encrypted and stored in the registry of the master secret server. It is required in order to access the credential (SSOdb) database.
- **BizTalk application configuration**: Document host instances, receive ports, send ports, and of course versions of BizTalk application binaries.

Maintaining the preceding documentation is the minimum requirement necessary to restore the BizTalk runtime servers. It is recommended to automate installation, configuration, and application deployment as much as possible to support normal operations as well as to provide an automated method to restore the BizTalk runtime servers.

The next subsection covers procedures for backing up the master secret.

The Master Secret

BizTalk Server 2009 uses the Microsoft Management Console snap-in for managing Enterprise SSO and the master secret, as shown in Figure 9-2. To launch the SSO Administration tool, go to Start ➤ All Programs ➤ Microsoft Enterprise Single Sign-On ➤ SSO Administration. To back up the master secret, right-click the System node, and select Backup Secret within the GUI.

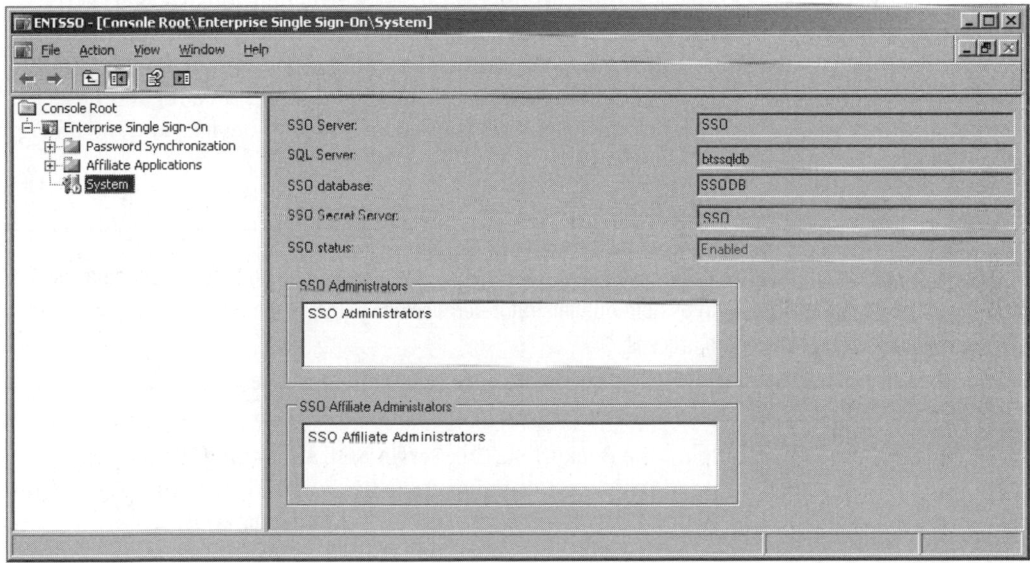

Figure 9-2. *SSO Administration MMC console*

Clicking Backup Secret displays the dialog box shown in Figure 9-3, where you enter a location for the backup file, a password, and optionally a password reminder. This file should be removed from the server and stored in a safe place such as a source control system locally as well as at an offsite location.

Backup Secret

Backup file: * Browse...

File password: *

Confirm password:

Password reminder:

* Indicates required fields OK Cancel

Figure 9-3. *Backup Secret dialog box*

The Enterprise SSO tools SSOManage.exe and SSOConfig.exe are still available in the C:\Program Files\Common Files\Enterprise Single Sign-On directory to support scripting, so the master secret can be backed up using the command-line tool SSOConfig.exe with the `-backupSecret` switch as well.

Next, we cover procedures for backing up the BizTalk Group.

BizTalk Group

This subsection covers backup procedures for the BizTalk Group, which consists of a set of databases created by BizTalk Server 2009 during configuration. All of the normal requirements when performing SQL backups apply: allocating sufficient storage space where backup files are stored, copying backup files to an offsite location, testing restore files on a regular basis such as monthly, and so on. Another consideration is to ensure backup devices and media are secure to protect business-sensitive data.

Note BizTalk Server includes a SQL Server role named BTS_BACKUP_USERS so that BizTalk databases can be backed up without requiring System Administrator permissions within SQL Server, except for the primary server controlling the backup process.

If not done already, configure the Backup BizTalk Server SQL Agent job following the instructions in the earlier subsection titled "Configuring the Backup BizTalk Server SQL Agent Job." The Backup BizTalk Server SQL Agent job backs up the following databases:

- BizTalk Configuration (BizTalkMgmtDb)
- BizTalk Messagebox (BizTalkMsgBoxDb)
- BizTalk Tracking (BizTalkDTADb)
- Rule Engine (BizTalkRuleEngineDb)
- BAM Primary Import (BAMPrimaryImport)
- Trading Partner Management (TPM)
- Credential Database (SSOdb)

You must also back up the following BizTalk Group databases, which are not part of the Backup BizTalk Server SQL Agent job because they do not participate in DTC transactions:

- BAM Archive (BAMArchive)
- BAM Star Schema (BAMStarSchema)

These databases can be backed up using normal SQL Server backup procedures because they do not participate in distributed transactions; however, these databases require special consideration, described in the next subsection, if BAM is configured with BM.exe and used as part of a BizTalk solution.

BizTalk Server 2009 includes a table named adm_OtherBackupDatabases in the BizTalk Management database (BizTalkMgmtDb). Other application databases that participate in DTC transactions (i.e., accessed within an atomic scope in an orchestration) should be added to adm_OtherBackupDatabases to remain transactionally consistent with the BizTalk databases. Table 9-2 lists the column names.

Table 9-2. *Columns in the adm_OtherBackupDatabases Table*

Field Name	Value
DefaultDatabaseName	The alias for the database. Can be the same as the database name or the application name.
DatabaseName	The actual name of the database.
ServerName	The name of the SQL Server instance hosting the database.
BTSServerName	Name of a BizTalk server. Not used, but required.

Databases added to the adm_OtherBackupDatabases table will automatically be backed up by the Backup BizTalk Server SQL Agent job.

■ **Caution** You *must* add any non-BizTalk custom database that performs distributed transactions with BizTalk to this table so that the table can be restored to the same log mark and remain transactionally consistent. For example, if you have an orchestration that updates a database named App1 within an atomic scope in BizTalk, the database App1 must be added to the adm_OtherBackupDatabases table.

The next step is to add the necessary schema changes to the databases added to the adm_OtherBackupDatabases table. Otherwise, the Backup BizTalk Server SQL Agent job will fail. Browse to the <installation directory>\Program Files\Microsoft BizTalk Server 2009\Schema directory, and then run Backup_Setup_All_Procs.sql and Backup_Setup_All_Tables.sql in the destination database. This creates the necessary procedures, tables, and roles to participate in the Backup BizTalk Server SQL Agent job and assigns permissions to the stored procedures.

Now let's take a look at backup procedures for the SQL Server Analysis Services databases.

BAM Analysis Services and Supporting Databases

BizTalk leverages SQL Server Analysis Services for reporting and analysis functionality as part of the Business Activity Monitoring features. In BizTalk Server 2009, the Tracking Analysis Server OLAP database is available in BizTalk installations as part of the BizTalk Group to support the service metrics and message metrics functionality for SQL Server 2000 Analysis Services only. The Tracking Analysis Server database is not supported on SQL Server 2005 Analysis Services and is not available as an option when configuring the BizTalk Group with a SQL Server 2005 database back end.

A BizTalk Group configured with BAM enabled in the BizTalk Configuration Wizard results in two additional SQL Analysis Services OLAP databases if the Tracking Analysis Server database is present:

- BAM Analysis (BAMAnalysis)
- Tracking Analysis Server (BizTalkAnalysisdb)

These Analysis Services databases must be backed up following the procedures for backing up SQL Analysis Services databases.

There are two scenarios for backing up BAM SQL Server databases when BAM is enabled through the BizTalk Configuration Wizard:

- BAM enabled for the BizTalk Group but not configured
- BAM enabled and configured with BM.exe (i.e., the BizTalk solution includes BAM features)

The next two subsections cover these scenarios.

BAM Enabled but Not Configured in a BizTalk Group

Since BAM is not configured with BM.exe, there are not any BAM-related SSIS packages present in the solution. Therefore, the BAM SQL databases can be backed up using regular SQL Server backup procedures or can be added to the Backup BizTalk Server SQL Agent job by adding the table to the adm_OtherBackupDatabases table for convenience. Here is a list of the BAM SQL databases that must be backed up:

- BAM Archive (BAMArchive)
- BAM Star Schema (BAMStarSchema)

This will ensure that a full set of databases for the BizTalk Group is maintained. The next subsection covers backup procedures when BAM is enabled and configured with BM.exe.

BAM Enabled and Configured in a BizTalk Group

When BAM is enabled and configured for a BizTalk Group using BM.exe, it results in the creation of one or more SSIS packages that must be backed up in case they are accidentally deleted as well as duplicated on the disaster recovery site. (Disaster recovery is covered in its own section later in this chapter.) Backup procedures for DTS packages are documented in SQL Server Books Online.

Before backing up the BAM databases, ensure that neither the BAM cube process nor the data maintenance DTS packages are running when the backup package is scheduled to run.

Ensure consistent schema across all BAM databases by backing up the BAM databases and DTS packages each time a BAM activity is deployed and not deployed.

The BAM Analysis and BAM Star Schema databases should be backed up each time a BAM view is deployed and undeployed. Follow these procedures when backing up BAM databases:

1. Run the Backup BizTalk Server job to back up the BAM Primary Import database as well as the other BizTalk Server databases.
2. Run the BAM data maintenance SSIS package for all activities.

Tip Incorporate these steps into an SSIS package, scheduling it to run on a regular basis. To guarantee data integrity, ensure no other BAM cubing or SSIS packages run when this DTS package is scheduled.

Back up the BAM Archive database after the partition is copied into the BAM Archive database but before the partition is deleted from the BAM Primary Import database so that a complete set of archived data is maintained. This can be achieved by modifying the data maintenance SSIS package for each activity to add a step to back up the BAM Archive database before the last step in the SSIS package called End Archiving.

3. Back up the BAM Archive database and then the BAM Star Schema database.

Next, we cover backup procedures for Business Activity Services.

SSIS Packages

All SSIS packages that are part of the solution must be duplicated at the disaster recovery site. The BizTalk Configuration Wizard does not create any DTS packages. However, if Business Activity Monitoring is part of the solution and is configured with the BAM monitoring tool (BM.exe), there will be DTS packages created that generate/update the OLAP cubes. The DTS packages have names like the following:

- BAM_AN_<ViewName>
- BAM_DM_<activity name>

Note There are no DTS packages that require backing up if BAM is not configured using the BM.exe tool.

To back up SSIS packages with SQL Server 2005/2008, follow these steps:

1. Open SQL Server Management Studio, and connect to Integration Services.
2. Expand the Stored Packages folder in Object Explorer.
3. Expand the subfolders to locate the package that needs to be exported.
4. Right-click the package, click Export, select File System, and then browse to a location to save the package.

To back up SQL Server Integration Services packages with SQL Server 2005/2008, follow these steps:

1. Open SQL Server Management Studio, and connect to Integration Services.
2. Expand the Stored Packages folder in Object Explorer.
3. Expand the subfolders to locate the package that needs to be exported.
4. Right-click the package, click Export, select File System, and then browse to a location to save the package.

There may be additional non-BizTalk DTS packages related to the solution. These DTS packages must also be duplicated at the disaster recovery site as well.

Backing Up SQL Agent Jobs

BizTalk Server 2009 Log Shipping will re-create the SQL Agent jobs running in production on the disaster recovery site; however, it is still a best practice to maintain backups of the SQL Agent jobs in case they need to be restored outside of a disaster recovery event.

For SQL Server 2005/2008, the steps are similar:

1. Connect to the database instance using SQL Server Management Studio.
2. Expand SQL Server Agent, and click Jobs.
3. Right-click each job, and select Script Job as ➤ Create To ➤ File.
4. Enter a file name, and click Save.
5. Go through the preceding steps for each job.

The next subsection covers backup procedures for related non-BizTalk applications and databases.

Related Non-BizTalk Applications and Databases

How related non-BizTalk application databases are backed up depends on the BizTalk solution. As mentioned earlier, if an orchestration updates another database from within an atomic scope that results in a distributed transaction, the other database must be added to the adm_OtherBackupDatabases so that it is backed up by the Backup BizTalk Server SQL Agent job and can be restored to the same log mark as all other databases that participate in distributed transactions as part of the solution.

For applications and databases that do not participate in distributed transactions with BizTalk but are still part of the overall application solution, these applications and databases should be backed up following your corporate standards/guidance. Essentially, the same requirements apply in that the source code, code documentation, runtime environment, and so on, must be backed up such that the application and database can be restored successfully. Always practice a restore in a lab environment to confirm that enough information is available to be successful as well as automate as much of the process as possible.

Next, we cover restore procedures for a BizTalk solution.

Restore Procedures

Restoring a BizTalk-based solution, or any large application environment, is a challenging process if not well documented, tested, and periodically rehearsed from an operations training standpoint. BizTalk Server 2009 has its own set of unique steps required for successful restore. This subsection covers steps for recovering from various failure scenarios that do not require transitioning to the disaster recovery site. In some scenarios, this discussion leverages the destination system databases and the SQL Agent automation available in order to safely perform restore procedures minimizing manual steps. This discussion covers restore steps for the following scenarios:

- Restore procedures when refreshing the BizTalk databases in a development or test environment
- Restore procedures when migrating the production BizTalk databases to a more powerful production database server without switching to the disaster recovery site
- Restore procedures when recovering the production database environment from a hardware failure such as a SAN failure without switching to the disaster recovery site (destination system)
- Restore procedures for SQL Agent jobs and DTS packages
- Restore procedures for the master secret
- Restore procedures for the BizTalk runtime environment

The next subsection covers how to stop and start BizTalk processing while performing any of the restore scenarios listed previously.

Stopping and Starting BizTalk Application Processing

This subsection lists the steps to stop, start, pause, or resume BizTalk processing using either the Services administration tool or the command line. Depending on the features configured on a BizTalk runtime server, there are up to six services or more that must be managed:

- BizTalk Service BizTalk Group: <BizTalkServerApplication> (btssvc$BizTalkServerApplication)
- Enterprise Single Sign-On Service (Entsso)
- Rule Engine Update Service (ruleengineupdateservice)
- BAM Event Notification Service (NS$BamAlerts)
- World Wide Web Publishing Service (W3SVC)

Using the Services administration tool in the Control Panel, simply click Start, Stop, Pause, or Resume as needed for the scenario. From a command prompt, enter the following commands (where *ServiceName* corresponds to the values in parentheses in the preceding list):

- Start a service: **net start *ServiceName***
- Stop a service: **net stop *ServiceName***

- Pause a service: **net pause** *ServiceName*
- Resume a service: **net continue** *ServiceName*

These commands can of course be scripted by placing the commands in a batch file or using WMI so that all services can be controlled by a single step. For example, a Stop.cmd file could contain the following:

```
Net stop "edi subsystem"
Net stop Entsso
Net stop ruleengineupdatservice
Net stop btssvc$BizTalkServerApplication
Net stop NS$BamAlerts
Net stop w3svc
```

When writing scripts such as this, you may need multiple `Net stop btssvc$BizTalkServerApplication` lines depending on how many host instances are running on the BizTalk runtime server. Also, the services that are actually present on a BizTalk runtime server depend on the BizTalk configuration. For more information on the BizTalk services, go to the BizTalk Server 2009 core documentation and search for the topic titled "How to Start, Stop, Pause, Resume, or Restart BizTalk Server Services."

The next subsection covers restore procedures for refreshing a development or test environment.

Refreshing a Development or Test Environment

Here we cover the steps to restore a development environment or test environment back to a "known" or "initial state." These procedures can be used to help ensure that a testing environment remains consistent between test runs or as new functionality is added to the application. This scenario requires a consistent full backup set of the following items:

- BizTalk databases
- Related non-BizTalk application databases
- Analysis Services databases for BAM or for Tracking Analysis Server
- DocumentsHome directory for EDI
- Windows SharePoint Services site customizations such as configuration files, site templates, client-side scripts, and so on

---

■ **Note** To create the "initial state" full backup files, configure the development or test BizTalk Group as needed, ensure no processing is occurring by following the procedures to stop processing listed in the preceding subsection, and then perform a full backup on all databases, Analysis Services databases, and the DocumentsHome directory if using EDI by following the guidance detailed in the earlier subsection titled "Backup Procedures."

This procedure is based on "Moving BizTalk Server Databases" and related documentation in the BizTalk Server 2009 core documentation. Please be sure to review this section of the BizTalk documentation before proceeding. This is actually a simpler scenario than described in the documentation, because the BizTalk runtime servers and SQL Server database instance server names remain the same, so the steps to update database names and database locations via script are not required.

1. Stop all processing using the guidance listed in the earlier subsection titled "Stopping and Starting BizTalk Application Processing."
2. Obtain a copy of the "initial state" backup set, and restore each BizTalk database and related non-BizTalk application database (if applicable) using SQL Server database restore procedures.
3. Restore the applicable Analysis Services databases if using BAM or the Tracking Analysis Server database.
4. Restore the DocumentsHome directory using the full backup that is part of the "initial state" backup set if using EDI.
5. Enable application processing by following the steps in the earlier subsection titled "Stopping and Starting BizTalk Application Processing." The development or test environment is now restored to the "initial state."

Migrating Production Databases to More Powerful Servers

Migration is probably the most common scenario that a BizTalk application operations team will encounter with respect to having to move a database. In this scenario, application processing is stopped using the procedure listed in the subsection titled "Stopping and Starting BizTalk Application Processing" earlier. The next step is to perform a full backup on the applicable database that is being migrated. Then perform the steps necessary to update references to the new database location for the BizTalk Group. The specific steps are covered in the BizTalk Server 2009 core documentation in the section titled "Moving BizTalk Server Databases" for the following databases:

- BAM Primary Import database
- BAM Archive database
- BAM Star Schema database
- BAM Analysis database
- BAM Notification Services database
- Messsagebox database

Please refer to the BizTalk Server 2009 core documentation for the specific steps to move these databases.

Recovering Production Database Environment from Hardware Failure

This scenario covers restoring the BizTalk Group databases that are backed up by the Backup BizTalk Server SQL Agent job. There are two options for this scenario. The first is to perform a full disaster recovery event by following the procedures listed in the section titled "Disaster Recovery" later in this chapter. This is the option available when reviewing the BizTalk Server 2009 core documentation.

Another option that leverages the disaster recovery infrastructure without actually performing a full disaster recovery is to obtain a copy of the databases from the disaster recovery destination system database instances and perform a restore of the databases at the production site. The second option is available if the BizTalk application operations team is able to correct the hardware failure in a timely manner in accordance with availability and corporate requirements and those server and database instance names do not change. Since this scenario requires that BizTalk Log Shipping is configured, before proceeding with either option, review the section that follows titled "Disaster Recovery."

■ Caution The second option is not documented in the BizTalk Server 2009 documentation and therefore is not supported by Microsoft. However, choosing the second option does not remove the first option. When performing the second option, a copy of the databases is maintained at the destination system so that if that procedure fails, a full disaster recovery can be performed by completing the steps in the first option to bring the destination system online.

The second option assumes that the BizTalk runtime servers, database servers, and all related servers and sites are back to fully operational, but the most up-to-date version of the application databases are required in order to restart processing. The disaster recovery site (destination system) will generally have the latest copy of the database available, so this scenario leverages the availability of those databases to quickly restore processing at the production site.

■ Note Performing the second option will require that BizTalk Log Shipping be removed and then reconfigured at the destination system once the production system is back online. Otherwise, an error will be received in the destination system that states "The databases have already been restored to a mark," and the destination system SQL Agent job "BTS Log Shipping—Restore Databases" will fail.

In order to obtain the latest version of the databases from the destination system, the operations team must ensure that all of the log backup sets (except for the latest set available) have been successfully restored to the databases. To determine the last successful backup set restored, review the contents of the Master.dbo.bts_LogShippingHistory table on each database instance in the destination system. This table is populated by the Get Backup History job and updated by the Restore Databases job. When a backup is successfully restored, the Restored column is set to 1, and the RestoredDateTime is set to the current date and time.

When all of the databases being restored to the server from a particular backup set have been successfully restored, that backup set ID is written to the Master.dbo.bts_LogShippingLastRestoreSet table. Once all of the log backup sets except for the last available have been confirmed to have been successfully restored, follow these steps:

1. Stop application processing by following the procedures in the subsection titled "Stopping and Starting BizTalk Application Processing" to prevent any database activity from occurring until the production database environment is fully configured.
2. Navigate to the SQL Agent Jobs view on the destination system SQL Server database instances.
3. Right-click and select Disable Job to disable the following SQL Agent jobs on the destination system disaster recovery SQL Server database instances:
   - BTS Log Shipping—Get Backup History
   - BTS Log Shipping—Restore Databases
4. Right-click BTS Log Shipping—Restore To Mark and select Start Job on the destination system SQL Server database instances.
5. Once you have verified that the job BTS Log Shipping—Restore To Mark has completed, detach each database from the destination system SQL Server database instance, and copy each database file over to the appropriate storage area on the source system (production) so the databases can be attached to the correct production SQL Server database instance in order to bring the production database instances online.

Caution Ensure that a copy of the database files remains at the destination system in case it is needed in the event of an unsuccessful attempt to restore production processing, and the destination system must be brought online by completing the steps in the first option.

---

6. Disable the following SQL Server Agent jobs on the source system SQL Server database instances (this step assumes that the Backup BizTalk Server and DTA Purge and Archive jobs have been configured and enabled):
   - Backup BizTalk Server (BizTalkMgmtDb)
   - CleanupBTFExpiredEntriesJob_<BizTalkMgmtDb>
   - DTA Purge and Archive (BizTalkMsgBoxDb)
   - MessageBox_DeadProcesses_Cleanup_<BizTalkMsgBoxDb>
   - MessageBox_Message_ManageRefCountLog_<BizTalkMsgBoxDb>
   - MessageBox_Parts_Cleanup_<BizTalkMsgBoxDb>
   - MessageBox_UpdateStats_<BizTalkMsgBoxDb>
   - Operations_OperateOnInstances_OnMaster_<BizTalkMsgBoxDb>

- PurgeSubscriptionsJob_<BizTalkMsgBoxDb>
- Rules_Database_Cleanup<BizTalkRuleEngineDb>
- TrackedMessages_Copy_<BizTalkMsgBoxDb>

7. Attach the databases copied from the destination system disaster recovery SQL Server database instances to the correct source system production SQL Server database instances.

Note If the BAM Archive, BAM Star Schema, or BAM Analysis databases were affected by the hardware failure as well, then these databases should be restored by using a backup older than the BAM Primary Import database backup.

---

8. Enable the following SQL Agent jobs on the source system production SQL Server database instances:

Note Do not enable the SQL Agent job MessageBox_Message_Cleanup_<BizTalkMsgBoxDb> by mistake. It is always disabled by default.

- Backup BizTalk Server (BizTalkMgmtDb)
- CleanupBTFExpiredEntriesJob_<BizTalkMgmtDb>
- DTA Purge and Archive (BizTalkMsgBoxDb)
- MessageBox_DeadProcesses_Cleanup_<BizTalkMsgBoxDb>
- MessageBox_Message_ManageRefCountLog_<BizTalkMsgBoxDb>
- MessageBox_Parts_Cleanup_<BizTalkMsgBoxDb>
- MessageBox_UpdateStats_<BizTalkMsgBoxDb>
- Operations_OperateOnInstances_OnMaster_<BizTalkMsgBoxDb>
- PurgeSubscriptionsJob_<BizTalkMsgBoxDb>
- Rules_Database_Cleanup<BizTalkRuleEngineDb>
- TrackedMessages_Copy_<BizTalkMsgBoxDb>

9. After confirming that the SQL Agent jobs are running successfully in the source system, enable application processing by following the steps in the subsection titled "Stopping and Starting BizTalk Application Processing."
10. Remove and then reconfigure BizTalk Log Shipping at the destination system.

SQL Agent Jobs

The SQL Agent jobs are a critical tool for maintaining the BizTalk Group. If one of these jobs is accidentally deleted or needs to be restored as part of restoring the BizTalk Group, obtain the backed-up script file for the SQL Agent job, and execute the script for the SQL Agent job in a query window. Check the status of the SQL Agent jobs in SQL Server. Ensure the correct account is configured to run each job.

DTS Packages

If the BizTalk solution has BAM configured with BM.exe, BM.exe will create a set of SSIS packages to produce the OLAP cubes. For each SSIS package, import the package using SQL Server 2005 Integration Services. Check the status of the DTS package in Enterprise Manager.

The Master Secret

The master secret is a critical item that must be backed up and stored in a safe place. It is not possible for BizTalk Server to function or to be restored without the master secret. There are two scenarios where the master secret server must be restored:

- Failure of the master secret server for an existing BizTalk Group
- Restoration of the master secret server as part of restoring a BizTalk Group to another set of servers

This subsection covers the procedures to restore the master secret server for the BizTalk Group. If the original master secret server fails and cannot be recovered but the BizTalk Group is still available and functioning except for the master secret server, another server can be promoted as the master secret server. To promote a Single Sign-On Server in the BizTalk Group to master secret server, follow these steps:

1. Create an XML file that includes the name of the SSO server that will be promoted to master secret server. For example:

```
<sso>
  <globalInfo>
    <secretServer>SSO Server name</secretServer>
  </globalInfo>
</sso>
```

2. On the Start menu, click Run, and then type **cmd**.
3. At the command-line prompt, go to the Enterprise Single Sign-On installation directory. The default installation directory is <*drive*>:\Program Files\Common Files\Enterprise Single Sign-On.
4. Type **ssomanage -updatedb <*update file*>**, where <*update file*> is the name of the XML file created in step 1.
5. Type **ssoconfig -restoresecret** <*restore file*>, where <*restore file*> is the path and name of the file where the master secret backup is stored.

Now let's move on to the procedures for restoring the BizTalk runtime environment.

BizTalk Runtime Environment

If the BizTalk runtime environment is intact, then restoring the BizTalk runtime environment is a matter of verifying connectivity by opening the BizTalk Administration Console and then restarting processing by starting the items stopped in the subsection titled "Stopping and Starting BizTalk Application Processing" earlier.

■ **Caution** If the BizTalk applications are dependent on related non-BizTalk applications and databases, then these related applications and databases must be available before restarting processing.

If the BizTalk runtime environment must also be rebuilt and the server names will be the same, first install BizTalk following the same procedures originally used to install BizTalk. Once BizTalk is installed, run Configuration.exe and join the BizTalk Group that has been previously restored.

■ **Note** Do not create a new BizTalk Group. This will result in a new set of databases, whereas the goal is to use the existing BizTalk Group that was restored.

Restore the master secret on the server with the same server name as the original master secret server. Or, restore the master secret to a new server and then perform the steps to designate the new server as the master secret server. Redeploy the BizTalk applications and bindings into the environment as needed.

Next, you'll learn the restore procedures for non-BizTalk, but related, applications and databases.

Related Non-BizTalk Applications and Databases

A BizTalk solution may update or receive data from non-BizTalk applications as part of the overall solution. If the related non-BizTalk applications include a database that participates in distributed transactions with BizTalk, this database should be added to the Backup BizTalk Server SQL Agent job and restored to the same log mark as the BizTalk databases. Otherwise, restore the non-BizTalk application and databases following the documentation for that application.

This wraps up our discussion on maintaining the BizTalk Group. Next we discuss disaster recovery procedures for BizTalk applications.

Disaster Recovery

Business-critical software solutions must have a disaster recovery plan in order to protect against major system disruptions. A disaster recovery plan must include steps to bring the backup site online as well as steps to deal with potential data loss as a result of the major system disruption. BizTalk Server 2009–based solutions require a comprehensive disaster recovery plan that covers both the BizTalk servers and the BizTalk Group running in SQL Server. BizTalk Server 2009 disaster recovery requirements include the following:

- BizTalk Server 2009 Log Shipping configuration for disaster recovery
- BizTalk Server 2009 Log Shipping procedures for restoring the BizTalk Group as part of disaster recovery
- BizTalk runtime environment disaster recovery procedures

These items make up the core disaster recovery requirements for BizTalk Server 2009. Additional disaster recovery procedures are required for any additional application databases, application code, other middleware products, and so on.

Note Application teams must plan to test disaster recovery procedures before entering production and on a recurring basis to ensure current operations personnel understand the process and can implement it successfully.

There is better automation of the required tasks to configure and implement disaster recovery for a BizTalk Server 2009 solution that helps to simplify the process. Also, the BizTalk Server 2009 core documentation greatly increases the amount of documentation regarding BizTalk Server Log Shipping and disaster recovery. The procedures in this section are based on the product documentation and should be reviewed along with this chapter. In addition, this section details additional configure steps encountered while testing the procedures not found in the BizTalk Server 2009 core documentation.

Caution The steps to manually update the required database fields in order to move a BizTalk Group to a new set of database server instances without using BizTalk Log Shipping are not documented for BizTalk Server 2009. Therefore, we strongly recommend configuring BizTalk Log Shipping as part of any BizTalk Server 2009 production environment.

Next, let's take a look at how BizTalk Log Shipping works.

How Does BizTalk Log Shipping Work?

Because BizTalk Server 2009 implements distributed transactions between BizTalk databases in the BizTalk Group through log marks, typical SQL Server disaster recovery technology such as SQL Server Log Shipping and Database Mirroring cannot be used for BizTalk databases that participate in DTC transactions. Therefore, BizTalk Server 2009 provides BizTalk Log Shipping.

■ **Tip** When referring to BizTalk Log Shipping, the source system is the production SQL Server database instances, and the destination system is the disaster recovery SQL Server database instances.

BizTalk Log Shipping uses capabilities within SQL Server that takes into account log marks and DTC transactions while providing very similar functionality to SQL Server Log Shipping. As with SQL Server Log Shipping, BizTalk Log Shipping performs log backups at the specified interval in the Backup BizTalk Server SQL Agent job. The log backups are then continuously applied to a SQL Server instance that is the disaster recovery server.

The primary difference between SQL Log Shipping and BizTalk Log Shipping is that when performing a disaster recovery event with BizTalk Group databases, the last log is applied with the `STOPATMARK` SQL Server `RESTORE` command option to restore all databases to the same point by the SQL Agent job named BTS Log Shipping—Restore To Mark for each database instance in the destination system. Figure 9-4 describes how BizTalk Log Shipping works.

When the disaster recovery SQL Server instances in the destination system are configured for BizTalk Log Shipping, the backup files created by the Backup BizTalk SQL Agent job are restored at the disaster recovery site every 15 minutes. The backup files are copied over the network by a SQL `RESTORE` command. Full backup files are copied only in the following situations:

- When BizTalk Log Shipping is first configured
- When a new database is added to the BizTalk Log Shipping SQL Agent job
- When a `RESTORE` failure occurs

Each SQL instance at the disaster recovery site is configured individually as part of BizTalk Log Shipping. When a SQL instance is configured for BizTalk Log Shipping and the SQL Agent job is enabled, the SQL Agent job will connect to the management database on the production BizTalk Group, find the most recent full backup set at the UNC share, and attempt to restore the database.

■ **Note** If you move the full or log backups for a source database from the location in which the Backup BizTalk Server job put them, the associated row for that database in the bts_LogShippingDatabases table on the destination system must be updated by setting LogFileLocation or DBFileLocation to the new location where the destination system should retrieve them. By default these values are Null, which tells the destination system to read the backup files from the location stored in the adm_BackupHistory table.

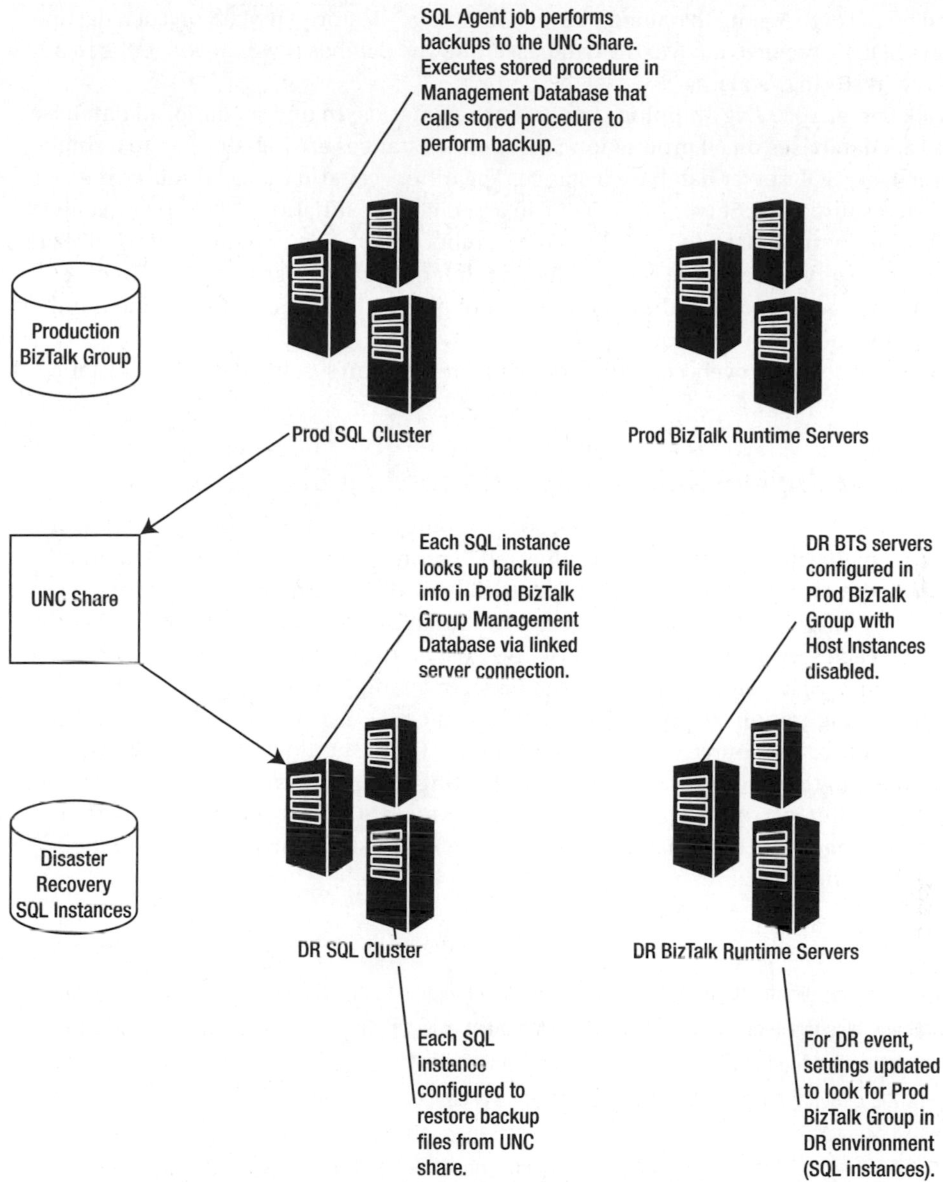

Figure 9-4. *BizTalk Log Shipping process*

On the disaster recovery SQL instances configured for BizTalk Log Shipping, the databases will be displayed in a "restoring" state in SQL Server 2005. This is because the last log in a backup set is never restored automatically. Once a new log is available, BizTalk Log Shipping restores the next-to-last log. When a disaster recovery event occurs and the disaster recovery site must be brought online, the last log is restored automatically using the `STOPATMARK` command by the SQL Agent job named BTS Log Shipping—Restore To Mark on each destination system SQL instance to recover the databases, and the databases will no longer be in a "loading" or "restoring" state.

BizTalk Server 2009 Log Shipping supports two scenarios: In one scenario, all databases on all BizTalk databases on all production SQL server instances are log-shipped to a single disaster recovery SQL server database instance. The other scenario maps all source databases on each source SQL Server instance to an associated destination SQL Server instance. Note that it is fully supported to have the same number of SQL Server database instances in the disaster recovery site as there is in production, but on fewer physical servers. In other words, it is not required to have the same number of physical servers, just the same number of database instances for the second option.

The next subsection covers configuration of the destination system SQL Server instance for BizTalk Log Shipping.

Configuring the Destination System for Log Shipping

Here we cover the steps to configure BizTalk Log Shipping. As mentioned previously, ensure that the same path where database files are located in production exists on the destination system. So, in the earlier example where there are three SQL Server database instances in production, all three database instances must store the database files (MDF and LDF files) in the same path on each server, and this path must also exist on the destination system SQL Server database instances. The database file path can be set or changed within SQL Server.

Another configuration step on the destination system SQL instances is to create a linked server that points to the source system SQL instances. There should be a linked server created that points to the production SQL instance hosting the management database. This will allow the SQL Agent job running on the destination system SQL Server instances to access the BizTalk Management Database to retrieve the backup history and database and log backup file location.

■ **Caution** A key requirement for BizTalk Log Shipping to function is that the same file path where the BizTalk database files (MDF and LDF files) are installed must exist on the destination system. Therefore, if a database in the production BizTalk Group is stored at F:\Data, the drive/path F:\Data must exist on the server where the destination system SQL Server instance is configured. Otherwise, an error message similar to this one will occur: "File 'DBFileName' cannot be restored to 'drive\path'. Use WITH MOVE to identify a valid location for the file." BizTalk Log Shipping does not support `WITH MOVE`, so the path must be present on the destination system for BizTalk Log Shipping to work.

■ **Note** Path references to Microsoft BizTalk Server 2009 will be located in the Microsoft BizTalk Server installation directory if an in-place upgrade was performed when BizTalk Server 2009 was installed. For example, if you upgrade BTS 2006 to BTS 2009, your installation directory will be {Program Files}\Microsoft BizTalk Server 2006\.

Follow these steps to configure BizTalk Log Shipping:

1. In Management Studio on SQL Server 2005/2008, open a query window to execute a SQL file. Connect to the SQL instance on the destination system that must be configured for Log Shipping.
2. Select File ➤ Open, and then browse to the location of the script LogShipping_Destination_Schema.sql. This script is located on the drive where BizTalk Server 2009 is installed in the following default directory location: \Program Files\Microsoft BizTalk Server 2009\Schema\LogShipping_Destination_Schema.sql.
3. Execute the query.
4. Select File ➤ Open, and then browse to the following SQL script: LogShipping_Destination_Logic.sql. This script is located on the drive where BizTalk Server 2009 is installed in the following directory: \Program Files\Microsoft BizTalk Server 2009\Schema\LogShipping_Destination_Logic.sql.

■Note This script is located on the server where BizTalk Server 2009 is installed in the directory \Program Files\Microsoft BizTalk Server 2009\Schema\ by default, so you may need to copy it to the SQL Server machine.

---

5. Execute the query.
6. In SQL Server 2005/2008, the Ad Hoc Distributed Queries option is disabled by default. This must be enabled on the destination system or disaster recovery SQL Server database instances in order to allow the disaster recovery SQL Server database instances to perform the necessary steps. To enable this option, execute the following SQL command in the master database on each production SQL Server database instance:

   ```
   sp_configure 'show advanced options', 1;
   GO
   RECONFIGURE;
   GO
   sp_configure 'Ad Hoc Distributed Queries',1;
   GO
   RECONFIGURE
   GO
   ```

   To confirm the change, run this query to view the configured value:

   ```
   SELECT * FROM sys.configurations ORDER BY name
   ```

   Ad Hoc Distributed Queries should now be set to a value of 1.
7. Open a new query window, and enter the following command:

```
exec bts_ConfigureBizTalkLogShipping @nvcDescription =
'<MyLogShippingSolution>',
@nvcMgmtDatabaseName = '<BizTalkServerManagementDatabaseName>',
@nvcMgmtServerName = '<BizTalkServerManagementDatabaseServer>',
@SourceServerName = null,
-- null indicates that this destination server restores all databases
@fLinkServers = 1
-- 1 automatically links the server to the management database
```

8. Replace `<MyLogShippingSolution>` in the preceding command with a description of the solution, surrounded by single quotes. Also, replace `<BizTalkServerManagementDatabaseName>` and `<BizTalkServerManagementDatabaseServer>` with the name and location of your source BizTalk Management Database, surrounded by single quotes.
9. If there are multiple SQL Server instances in the source system, each source SQL instance can be restored to its own destination SQL instance. On each SQL instance in the destination system, run the preceding scripts and command, but in the `@SourceServerName = null` parameter, replace `null` with the name of the appropriate source server, surrounded by single quotes: `@SourceServerName = 'SQLSvrInstance1'`.
10. Execute the preceding command in the query window. The BizTalk Server 2009 documentation has this information: If the command fails, after you fix the problem with the query, you must start over from step 1 of this procedure to reconfigure the destination system.

Note When you execute the preceding command, this warning will occur, which can be ignored: "Warning: The table '#Servers' has been created but its maximum row size (25059) exceeds the maximum number of bytes per row (8060). INSERT or UPDATE of a row in this table will fail if the resulting row length exceeds 8060 bytes."

---

11. View the Jobs node in the SQL Management Studio depending on which version of SQL you are running. There will be three new jobs:
    - **BTS Log Shipping Get Backup History**: This SQL Agent job copies backup history records from the source system to the destination every minute, and it is enabled by default.
    - **BTS Log Shipping Restore Databases**: This SQL Agent job restores backup files for the specified databases from the source system SQL Server instance on to the destination system SQL Server instance. It is enabled by default and runs continuously.
    - **BTS Log Shipping Restore To Mark**: This SQL Agent job restores all of the databases to a log mark in the last log backup. It ensures that all databases are transitionally consistent. It also re-creates the SQL Server SQL Agent jobs on the destination system, saving the administrator from having to manually re-create the SQL Agent jobs running on the source system.

12. Create SQL Server security logins for the disaster recovery site that correspond to the production site so that in the event that a failover to the disaster recovery site is required, all required security logins are present on the destination system.
13. Once everything is configured, check the status of the newly created SQL Agent jobs to make sure that they are running successfully. Here are a couple of items to check in the event a SQL Agent job is failing:
    - Ensure that the system time and time zone are consistent between all servers.
    - Ensure that the job has the correct account as the owner.
    - Ensure that NETWORK COM+ and NETWORK DTC are enabled in Add/Remove Windows Components.
    - Ensure that the MSDTC security configuration in Control Panel ➤ Administrative Tools ➤ Component Services is configured correctly for your environment. Try checking Network DTC Access, Allow Remote Clients, and Transaction Manager Communication Allow Inbound and Allow Outbound to see if doing so resolves connectivity issues.
14. The last step is to edit the update scripts and XML files to prepare for a disaster recovery event by following these steps:
    a. On a computer running BizTalk Server 2009, browse to the following folder: \Program Files\Microsoft BizTalk Server 2009\Schema\Restore.
    b. Right-click SampleUpdateInfo.xml, and then click Edit.
    c. For each database listed, replace "SourceServer" with the name of the source system SQL Server database instance, and then replace "DestinationServer" with the name of the destination system SQL Server instance.

Caution Do not perform a blanket search and replace, since databases may be present on different SQL Server instances in the source system and may be restored to different SQL Server instances in the destination system. Be sure to include the quotation marks around the name of the source and destination SQL Server instances. Also, if you renamed any of the BizTalk Server databases, you must also update the database names as appropriate.

---

    d. If you have more than one Messagebox database in the source system, add another MessageBoxDB line to the list, and then set `IsMaster="0"` for the non-master databases.
    e. If the source system is using BAM, SSO, the Rules Engine, or EDI, uncomment these lines as appropriate.
    f. If custom databases have been added to the Backup BizTalk Server SQL Agent job, add the custom databases as appropriate under the <OtherDatabases> section.
    g. When finished editing the file, save it and exit.

This completes the configuration of BizTalk Log Shipping. The next two subsections cover disaster recovery procedures for the BizTalk Group and for BizTalk servers, respectively.

BizTalk Group Disaster Recovery Procedures

This discussion assumes that BizTalk Log Shipping is configured and working correctly by following the guidance in the earlier subsection titled "Configuring the Backup BizTalk Server SQL Agent Job" as well as the guidance in the earlier subsection titled "Configuring the Destination System for Log Shipping." Once that is verified, the next step is to prepare for performing a disaster recovery event. A disaster recovery event for the BizTalk Group consists of restoring the BizTalk Group databases as well as related non-BizTalk databases on the destination system SQL Server instances. This also includes any DTS packages as well as SQL Agent jobs that exist in the source system (production).

The first step is to ensure that the last backup set has been restored to all SQL Server instances that are part of the destination system. This can be confirmed by reviewing the Master.dbo.bts_LogShippingHistory table that is populated by the Get Backup History SQL Agent job. When a backup is successfully restored, the Restored column is set to 1, and the RestoreDateTime is set to the date/time the restore was completed. When all of the databases that are part of a backup set have been successfully restored, the backup set ID is written to the Master.dbo.bts_LogShippingLastRestoreSet table. Once you have confirmed that available backup files have been applied, follow these steps on each SQL Server instance in the destination system:

1. Navigate to the SQL Agent Jobs view.
2. Right-click and select Disable Job to disable the following SQL Agent jobs:
    - BTS Log Shipping—Get Backup History
    - BTS Log Shipping—Restore Databases
3. Right-click BTS Log Shipping—Restore To Mark and select Start Job.
4. Once you have verified that the job BTS Log Shipping—Restore To Mark has completed, copy the script and XML files UpdateDatabase.vbs and SampleUpdateInfo.xml to the server where the SQL Server instance is running and execute the following command:

    ```
    cscript UpdateDatabase.vbs SampleUpdateInfo.xml
    ```

Note On 64-bit servers, run the UpdateDatabase.vbs script from a 64-bit command prompt.

As promised, we next cover the disaster recovery procedures for the BizTalk runtime servers. Later subsections cover disaster recovery procedures for BAM and EDI functionality.

BizTalk Runtime Server Disaster Recovery Procedures

The BizTalk runtime servers in the destination system should have BizTalk Server 2009 as well as any required third-party adapters or software installed using the same guidelines for the production BizTalk runtime servers. There are generally two methods for setting up the BizTalk runtime servers:

- **Method 1**: Restore BizTalk Group, configure BizTalk servers in BizTalk Group, and deploy applications.
- **Method 2**: Configure disaster recovery BizTalk servers in production BizTalk Group, disable services, keep the server up to date, and run an update script to update locations of databases in the destination system.

Both methods have advantages and disadvantages, which you'll find out more about in our detailed discussion of these methods next.

Method 1

To proceed with method 1, first verify that procedures to restore the BizTalk Group databases and related application databases have been completed. Once completed, proceed with restoring the BizTalk runtime servers using method 1. Method 1 has all software preinstalled, but not configured, and without any applications deployed on the BizTalk servers in the destination system. When the BizTalk Group is restored in the destination system and the BizTalk severs are configured using Configuration.exe, select Join for the BizTalk Group, not Create. The first server configured should have the master secret restored on it and then designated as the master secret server for the BizTalk Group using the Enterprise SSO management tools. Once all of the BizTalk servers are configured in the BizTalk Group at the destination system, deploy the BizTalk applications (assemblies and bindings).

While many of the steps can be scripted, this method essentially brings online a new environment when recovering from a disaster. At the same time, it reduces the amount of ongoing maintenance work for the destination system to a degree, since just the latest version of the application is deployed.

Method 2

Method 2 also has all software preinstalled, but takes it a step further and actually configures the BizTalk servers in the destination system to be member servers in the production BizTalk Group. Applications (assemblies and bindings) are deployed to the destination system BizTalk servers just like in production, except that the BizTalk host instances and all other BizTalk-related Windows Services are disabled and do not perform any processing in the destination system. During a disaster recovery event, a script is run on the destination system BizTalk servers to update the new location of the BizTalk Group in the destination system SQL instances. Once updated, processing can be enabled. Method 2 is recommended because it results in a faster recovery and less change overall. To proceed with method 2, first verify that procedures to restore the BizTalk Group databases and related application databases have been completed.

Note Path references to Microsoft BizTalk Server 2009 will be located in the Microsoft BizTalk Server installation directory if an in-place upgrade was performed when BizTalk Server 2009 was installed. For example, if you upgrade BTS 2006 to BTS 2009, your installation directory will be {Program Files}\Microsoft BizTalk Server 2006\.

Once verification is completed, perform these steps:

1. Copy the edited SampleUpdateInfo.xml file to the \Program Files\Microsoft BizTalk Server 2009\Schema\Restore directory on every BizTalk server in the destination system.
2. On each BizTalk Server, open a command prompt (must be 64-bit if on a 64-bit OS) by selecting Start ➤ Run, typing **cmd**, and then clicking OK.
3. At the command prompt, navigate to the location of the edited SampleUpdateInfo.xml file and the script (\Program Files\Microsoft BizTalk Server 2009\Schema\Restore is the default), and enter this command:

```
cscript UpdateRegistry.vbs SampleUpdateInfo.xml
```

4. Enable and restart all BizTalk host instances and all other BizTalk services on the BizTalk servers in the destination system.
5. Restart WMI on each BizTalk server in the destination system by selecting Start ➤ Run, typing **services.msc**, and clicking OK. Then right-click Windows Management Instrumentation and select Restart.
6. On each BizTalk server, open the BizTalk Server Administration Console, right-click BizTalk Group, and select Remove.
7. Right-click BizTalk Server 2009 Administration, select Connect to Existing Group, select the SQL Server database instance and database name that corresponds to the BizTalk Management database for the BizTalk Group, and click OK.
8. Restore the master secret on the master secret server in the destination system if not already completed by following the steps detailed in the subsection titled "The Master Secret Restore Procedures" earlier.

Restore Procedures for BAM

The BizTalk Server 2009 documentation covers these procedures extensively, so we won't repeat them here. BAM consists of SQL Server databases, SQL Analysis databases, and DTS packages. Refer to the section titled "Backing Up and Restoring BAM" in the BizTalk Server 2009 documentation for the details. It is also available online here: `http://msdn.microsoft.com/library/default.asp?url=/library/en-us/BTS06CoreDocs/html/5d477492-fdb7-4866-92a8-2720fea15839.asp?frame=true`.

Other Disaster Recovery Tasks

This subsection covers other tasks and recommendations related to disaster recovery. As mentioned in the subsection titled "Configuring the DTA Purge and Archive SQL Agent Job" earlier in the chapter, tracking data is an important part of a BizTalk solution, since that data can be used for reporting and as part of recordkeeping regulations compliance. It can also be used to help recover from a disaster, because it is a record of data processing activity. For this reason, we recommend separating your tracking databases from the runtime databases that generate tracking data by configuring your databases in separate SQL Server instances on different disks in production. Data in the tracking databases can be used to help determine the state of the system up to the point of failure for the runtime databases. Tracked messages and events can indicate what processes may have already happened and what messages have been received or sent.

■Note Tracking data is not written directly to the tracking databases. Instead, it is cached on the Messageboxes and moved to the Tracking database. Therefore, in the event of a Messagebox data loss, some tracking data may be lost as well.

The next subsection covers steps to evaluate data loss for the BizTalk Group with tips on how to recover data.

Evaluating Data Loss for the BizTalk Group

After data loss has occurred, recovering it is often difficult or impossible. For these reasons, using a fault-tolerant system to prevent data loss is extremely important. In any case, a disaster may occur, and even the most fault-tolerant system has some chance of failure. This subsection covers methods to help determine the state of the system when the failure occurred and how to evaluate corrective action.

Managing In-Flight Orchestrations

The Messagebox databases contain the state of orchestrations that are currently in progress. When data is lost from the Messagebox databases, it is not possible to tell exactly what data has been lost. Therefore, it will be necessary to examine external systems to see what activities have occurred in relation to the in-progress orchestrations.

Once it is determined what has occurred, steps can be taken to restore processes. For example, if upon looking at external systems or logs it is determined that an orchestration was activated but didn't perform any work, the message can be resubmitted to complete the operation.

It is important to consider what information will be available to compare with in-flight orchestrations in order to decide whether to terminate or resume particular in-flight orchestrations. Available information is largely determined by the architecture and design of the system such as what logging is performed "out-of-band" so as to not impact performance but at the same time provide an audit of events for comparison purposes.

Viewing After the Log Mark in Tracking Databases

While all databases need to be restored to the same mark for operational reasons in order to restore a consistent BizTalk Group, administrators can use a Tracking database that was not lost in Archive mode to see what happened after the mark. The process of evaluating the data begins by comparing services that are in flight in the BizTalk Administration Console Operations views against their state in BizTalk Group hub reporting. If the Group Hub Reporting shows it as having completed, the instances can be terminated.

BizTalk Message Tracking Reporting may show instances that started after the point of recovery. If so, any actions these instances took must be compensated, and then the initial activation messages can be submitted.

Reporting may also show that instances have progressed beyond the point at which the Operations view indicates. In this case, use the Orchestration Debugger in Reporting to see the last shapes that were executed, and then use Message Flow to see what message should have been sent or received. If they do not match the state in the Operations view, corrective action is required. Options are to terminate, compensate and restart, or resubmit any lost messages.

■ **Note** If the BizTalk Tracking database is lost, all discovery of what happened past the point of recovery will need to be done using the external system's reporting mechanisms.

Marking In-Flight Transactions as Complete in BAM

BAM maintains data for incomplete trace instances in a special active instance table. If some instance records were started before the last backup but completed after the backup, those records will remain in the active instance table because the completion records for the instance will have been lost. Although this does not prevent the system from functioning, it may be desirable to mark these records as completed so that they can be moved out of the active instance table. To accomplish this, manual intervention is necessary.

A list of incomplete ActivityIDs for a given activity can be determined by issuing the following query against the BAM Primary Import database:

```
Select ActivityID from bam_<ActivityName> where IsComplete = 0
```

If data from external systems indicates that the activity instance is in fact completed, use the following query to manually complete the instance:

```
exec bam_<ActivityName>_PrimaryImport @ActivityID=N'<ActivityID>', @IsStartNew=0,
@IsComplete=1
```

Related Non-BizTalk Application Disaster Recovery Procedures

There may be additional non-BizTalk applications that must be restored as part of the overall application solution. If these application databases participate in distributed transactions with the BizTalk Group databases, the databases should be part of the Backup BizTalk Server SQL Agent job and restored to the same mark as the other BizTalk Group databases. In general, each individual application should have a disaster recovery plan tailored to the application that should be part of the overall solution disaster recovery plan.

CHAPTER 10

Deploying and Managing BizTalk Applications

In the previous chapters, you have seen how to create schemas to define the different messages that your BizTalk applications send and receive, how to create orchestrations for the implementation of business workflows, how to create custom pipelines to customize the different stages of message processing, and finally how to create and maintain ports to receive and send messages. In a nutshell, you have seen how to develop each of the major artifacts present in a BizTalk solution.

Now that you are able to develop BizTalk solutions in a development environment, it is time to look at how to build your application and how to deploy your solution onto other environments such as a testing or production environment.

In this chapter, you will first learn how a BizTalk solution is organized. We will also cover the new functionality in BizTalk 2009 regarding build options. Then we will talk about different deployment methods to install your BizTalk applications on other target environments. Finally, you will learn about the different tools available to manage or deploy a BizTalk application.

BizTalk Applications

Up to this point, all of your efforts have been to create the artifacts that will make up a BizTalk application. The BizTalk application becomes the primary scope when dealing with deployment. Remember, the purpose of a BizTalk application is to group BizTalk artifacts. Figure 10-1 depicts a BizTalk application along with the artifacts associated with it.

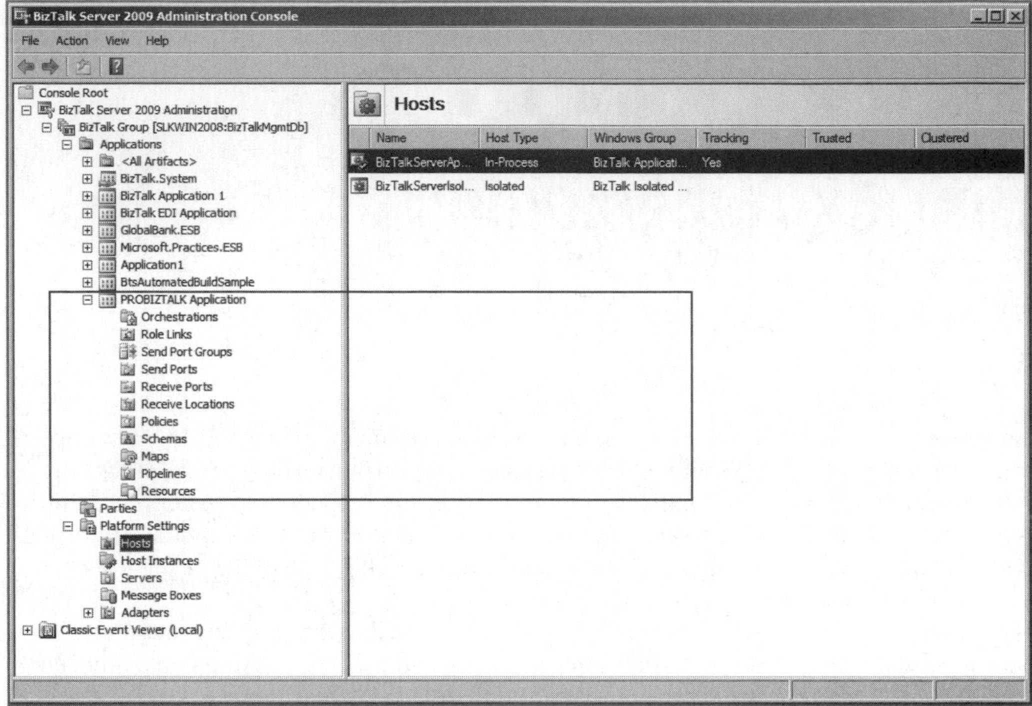

Figure 10-1. *BizTalk application and associated artifacts*

You can perform the following actions on a BizTalk application:

- Enumerate, add, and remove BizTalk artifacts from a BizTalk application. Table 10-1 shows BizTalk resource artifacts that can be associated with a BizTalk application.
- Export or import all the BizTalk artifacts related to a single business solution encompassed in a BizTalk application to an MSI file.
- Start or stop all the BizTalk artifacts that can be enlisted, started, unenlisted, and stopped within a BizTalk application.
- Create or remove dependencies between BizTalk applications by adding or removing references from one application to another.

Table 10-1. *BizTalk Application Resource Artifacts*

Artifact	Fully Qualified Resource Type	Description
.NET assembly	System.BizTalk:Assembly	All .NET assemblies that are used within the BizTalk application.
BAM definition	System.BizTalk:Bam	All BAM definition files used within the BizTalk application.
BizTalk assembly	System.BizTalk:BizTalkAssembly	Assembly that contains BizTalk schemas, maps, orchestrations, or pipelines.

Artifact	Fully Qualified Resource Type	Description
BizTalk binding file	System.BizTalk:BizTalkBinding	XML files that contain a snapshot of the binding as seen at that instant. It does not contain details about the completeness of the binding with respect to the orchestration.
Security certificate	System.BizTalk:Certificate	BizTalk artifact used to verify the identities and to establish secure communications. Certificates are associated to ports.
COM component	System.BizTalk:Com	COM components that are used by the BizTalk application.
Ad hoc file	System.BizTalk:File	Any file that is used by the BizTalk application or that provides information about the BizTalk application.
Post-processing script	System.BizTalk: PostProcessingScript	Scripts that are executed after a BizTalk application has been installed on a host instance.
Pre-processing script	System.BizTalk: PreProcessingScript	Scripts that are executed before a BizTalk application has been installed on a host instance.
Policy or rule	System.BizTalk:Rules	XML files that contain all the different policies and rules contained in the BizTalk rule engine.
Virtual directory	System.BizTalk:WebDirectory	Any IIS virtual directories that must deploy on the target machine to allow the BizTalk application to function properly.

BizTalk 2009 requires all BizTalk artifacts (outside of policies and dependent assemblies) to belong to a BizTalk application. When configuring a BizTalk Server Group, a default BizTalk application named BizTalk Application 1 is created. BizTalk artifacts are deployed to this default BizTalk application in the following situations:

- When upgrading a BizTalk Server 2004 to BizTalk Server 2009. All the BizTalk 2004 artifacts will be found under the default application.
- When deploying BizTalk artifacts using the deprecated BTSDeploy command-line tool.
- When deploying BizTalk assemblies using Visual Studio 2008 without specifying an application name in the deployment configuration properties.
- When creating ports using the deprecated BizTalk Explorer in Visual Studio.
- When adding BizTalk artifacts using the BTSTask command-line application without specifying a BizTalk application name.
- When importing an MSI file using the BTSTask command-line application without specifying a BizTalk application name.

Important Deployment Artifacts

In this section, you will learn about binding files and processing scripts. These two artifacts play a vital role in deploying and managing BizTalk applications. After reading this section, you may still wonder when these artifacts come into play upon deploying applications. We will cover this in more detail when we discuss deployment scenarios. For now, the most important thing is for you to understand what binding files and processing scripts are.

Binding Files

Binding files are XML files describing the different BizTalk artifacts stored in the BizTalk Management Database and the relationship between these artifacts. Binding files are useful because they provide a way for an administrator to export the settings from a BizTalk Server Group, modify them if necessary for the next environment, and import them to another BizTalk Server Group. You can choose to export all the information related to a BizTalk Server Group, or a BizTalk application, or a specific BizTalk assembly.

The easiest way to understand what binding files are and what they look like is to export one from an existing BizTalk application and to look at its content. One of the ways to export a binding file is to open the BizTalk Server Administration Console, right-click a BizTalk application, and select the Export ➤ Bindings context menu item. When the Export Bindings window appears, simply select where you want to export the binding file and that you want to export the bindings for the currently selected application only. Open the exported file in a text editor. You should see an XML document similar to the partial binding file shown in Listing 10-1.

Listing 10-1. *Partial Binding File*

```
<?xml version="1.0" encoding="utf-8"?>
<BindingInfo
   xmlns:xsi="http://www.w3.org/2001/XMLSchema-instance"
   xmlns:xsd="http://www.w3.org/2001/XMLSchema"
   Assembly="Microsoft.BizTalk.Deployment, Version=3.0.1.0, Culture=neutral,
PublicKeyToken=31bf3856ad364e35"
   Version="3.5.1.0"
   BindingStatus="FullyBound"
   BoundEndpoints="2"
   TotalEndpoints="2">
  <Timestamp>2009-04-15T17:44:04.9787774-07:00</Timestamp>
  <ModuleRefCollection>
    ...
  </ModuleRefCollection>
  <SendPortCollection>
    ...
  </SendPortCollection>
  <DistributionListCollection>
    ...
  </DistributionListCollection>
  <ReceivePortCollection>
    ...
```

```
  </ReceivePortCollection>
  <PartyCollection>
    ...
  </PartyCollection>
</BindingInfo>
```

There are five important XML elements under the `BindingInfo` document element:

- `ModuleRefCollection`: Declares all the BizTalk assemblies and orchestrations used within the application. It also specifies which physical ports are used for each orchestration.
- `SendPortCollection`: Contains all the information necessary to create or update all the send port groups.
- `DistributionListCollection`: Contains all the information necessary to create or update all the send port groups.
- `ReceivePortCollection`: Contains all the information necessary to create or update all the receive ports and receive locations.
- `PartyCollection`: Contains all the information necessary to create or update all the parties.

Please refer to the product documentation for the full list of attributes and elements available in a binding file. If you need to validate binding files, you can generate the XML schema for binding files by running the following command in the Visual Studio 2008 command prompt:

```
xsd.exe "C:\Program Files\Microsoft BizTalk Server 2009\
Microsoft.BizTalk.Deployment.dll" /type:BindingInfo
```

The XML schema will be generated in the directory where the command was run, and then the validation can be performed (including through the BizTalk Editor).

Processing Scripts

Processing scripts are scripts or executables that are run when installing, importing, or removing a BizTalk application. Table 10-2 displays the different types of files that can be used as processing scripts. **Pre-processing scripts** run at the beginning of an import or installation process. **Post-processing scripts** run at the end of an import or installation process.

Table 10-2. *Valid Processing Script Files*

Scripts or Executables	Extension
MS-DOS application	.com
Application	.exe
MS-DOS batch file	.bat
Windows NT command script	.cmd
VBScript script file	.vbs, .vbe
JScript script file	.js, .jse
Windows Script Host setting and Script file	.wsh, .wsf

Processing scripts are useful to perform simple or complex operations to reduce the number of manual operations that must occur when installing or removing a BizTalk application. Here are a few examples showing what you can do with processing scripts:

- Create a directory structure.
- Create a database.
- Register COM components.
- GAC .NET components.
- Start or stop BizTalk applications.
- Enlist, start, stop, or unenlist ports and orchestrations.

Listing 10-2 shows the content of a pre-processing script used to create and remove a directory structure when installing and removing a BizTalk application.

Listing 10-2. *Directories Preprocessing Script*

```
REM Creates and Removes Directories to receive or
REM send files

@setlocal
REM ### For verifying BTAD_* environment variables when script is called.
set LogFile=C:\PROBIZTALK\Log.txt

echo Script Log %DATE% %TIME% > "%LogFile%"
echo Install Directory: %BTAD_InstallDir% > "%LogFile%"
echo Install Mode: %BTAD_InstallMode% > "%LogFile%"
echo Change request action: % BTAD_ChangeRequestAction% > "%LogFile%"

REM ### Create directories prior to BizTalk assembly deployment
if "%BTAD_InstallMode%"=="Install" AND "%BTAD_ChangeRequestAction%"=="Update" (
          REM ### Create the folders which will drop messages
          mkdir %BTAD_InstallDir%\TestDocuments\In\
          mkdir %BTAD_InstallDir%\TestDocuments\Out\
)

REM ### Remove directories after undeploying at the end of uninstallation process
if "%BTAD_InstallMode%"=="Uninstall" AND "%BTAD_ChangeRequestAction%"=="Delete" (
    del %BTAD_InstallDir%\TestDocuments\ /s /q
)

REM ### Return exit code of 0 to indicate a success.
echo Script Executed sucessfully > "%LogFile%"
exit /B 0
@endlocal
```

As you can see, Listing 10-2 uses several environment variables containing a context for a script developer. Some variables can be set by a developer, and others are set by the BizTalk Server Installer. Refer to Table 10-3 for the complete list of the environment variables accessible through processing scripts and their description. Table 10-4 displays the values for the environment variables set by the BizTalk Server Installer at different stages of the installation or uninstallation process.

Table 10-3. *Processing Script Environment Variables*

Environment Variable	Description
`BTAD_ChangeRequestAction`	Specifies whether the installer is creating, updating, or removing BizTalk artifacts. The possible values are Create: Imports or installs artifacts without overwriting previous ones Update: Imports or installs artifacts overwriting previous ones Delete: Deletes artifacts
`BTAD_HostClass`	Specifies whether the operation is being applied on the BizTalk Management Database or on the BizTalk host instance. The possible values are ConfigurationDb BizTalkHostInstance
`BTAD_InstallMode`	Specifies whether a BizTalk application is being imported, installed, or uninstalled. The possible values are Import Install Uninstall
`BTAD_InstallDir`	Specifies the installation directory of a BizTalk application.
`BTAD_ApplicationName`	Specifies the name of a BizTalk application. If the name was not provided when launching the BizTalk Server Installer, it will contain the default BizTalk application name.
`BTAD_SilentMode`	Specifies options for running the script in silent mode. The most commonly used values are 0: Does not change the user interface (UI) level. 1: Uses the default UI level. 2: Performs a silent installation (the default). 3: Provides simple progress and error handling. 4: Provides authored UI; suppresses wizards.
`BTAD_Server`	Specifies the name of a SQL Server instance hosting the BizTalk Management Database for a group.
`BTAD_Database`	Specifies the name of the BizTalk Management Database for a group.

Table 10-4. *Environment Variable Values at Different Deployment States*

Deployment State	BTAD_Change RequestAction Values	BTAD_InstallMode Values	BTAD_HostClass Values
Import without flag	Create	Import	ConfigurationDboverwrite
Import with flag	Update	Import	ConfigurationDboverwrite
Install	Update	Install	BizTalkHostInstance
Uninstall	Delete	Uninstall	BizTalkHostInstance
Import rollback	Delete	Import	ConfigurationDb
Install rollback	Delete	Install	BizTalkHostInstance

Deploying a BizTalk Solution

In this section, you will learn the different methods of deploying BizTalk applications. First, you will discover how to deploy a BizTalk application manually. Then, you will see how to export, import, or install a BizTalk application using an MSI package. You'll also learn how you can utilize MSBuild as an alternative to the MSI package. In addition, we will show how you can incorporate PowerShell to deploy and manage your BizTalk applications. Finally, you will investigate a BizTalk application deployment process that allows you to move your BizTalk solution from your development environment all the way to your production environment.

Steps in Deploying a BizTalk Application

There are two major steps in order to deploy an application. First, you must import the BizTalk application to a BizTalk Server Group. Importing a BizTalk application registers all the BizTalk artifacts for a BizTalk application in the Management Database. Once a BizTalk application has been imported into the Management Database, all other BizTalk servers in the BizTalk Server Group are now aware of the new BizTalk application and its artifacts. However, before they can run the application themselves, they must have a physical copy of all the BizTalk artifacts that are referenced in the Management Database. Consequently, the second step is to install all artifacts on each of the BizTalk servers in a BizTalk Server Group. This step includes copying all artifacts to the target servers, registration of COM libraries, registration of .NET assemblies in the Global Assembly Cache, installing certificates in servers' certificate store, and the configuration of virtual directories if needed.

Exercise 10-1 demonstrates how to perform some of the steps just mentioned.

EXERCISE 10-1. DEPLOYING A BIZTALK APPLICATION MANUALLY

The purpose of this exercise is to illustrate how to deploy a BizTalk application manually using the BizTalk Administration Console. You will learn how to

- Create a BizTalk application.
- Deploy a BizTalk assembly manually.
- Create ports manually.
- Start a BizTalk application.

1. Copy all the files located in the Chapter10\DeploymentSampleApplication sample application provided as part of the download files for this book to C:\DeploymentSampleApplication.
2. Open the BizTalk Administration Console:
   a. Select Start ➤ All Programs ➤ Microsoft BizTalk Server 2009 ➤ BizTalk Server, and then click the Administration icon.
   b. In the BizTalk Server 2009 Administration Console, expand BizTalk Server 2009 ➤ BizTalk Group ➤ Applications.
3. Create a new application:
   a. Right-click Applications, point to New, and then click Application.
   b. In the Applications Properties window shown in Figure 10-2, type **PROBIZTALK Deploy Sample Application** in the Name field.
   c. In the Applications Properties window, type **PROBIZTALK's Deployment Sample Application** in the Description field.
   d. In the Applications Properties window, click OK.

■ **Note** You can add references to other BizTalk applications by clicking the reference section. You would do this when you have shared artifacts that are used by more than one application.

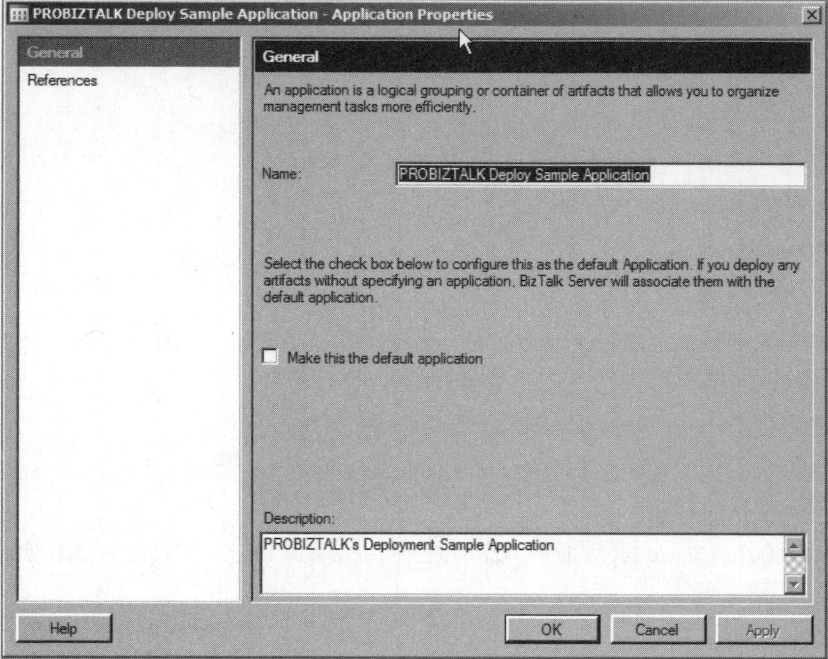

Figure 10-2. *Application Properties dialog box*

4. Add the BizTalk assembly:

   a. In the BizTalk Server 2009 Administration Console, expand BizTalk Server 2009 ➤ BizTalk Group ➤ Applications ➤ PROBIZTALK Deploy Sample Application.

   b. Right-click Resources, point to Add, and click BizTalk Assemblies.

   c. In the Add Resources window, click the Add button.

   d. Browse to the C:\DeploymentSampleApplication\DeploymentSampleApplication.dll, and then click Open.

   e. In the Add Resources window, click the OK button.

   f. Notice in the right pane of the BizTalk Server 2009 Administration Console the newly added assembly.

5. Create a receive port:

   a. In the BizTalk Server 2009 Administration Console, expand BizTalk Server 2009 ➤ BizTalk Group ➤ Applications ➤ PROBIZTALK Deploy Sample Application.

   b. Right-click Receive Ports, point to New, and click One-way Receive Port.

   c. In the Receive Port Properties window shown in Figure 10-3, and type **ReceiveGreetingsPort** in the Name field.

   d. Click Receive Locations on the left pane, then click the New button on the right pane.

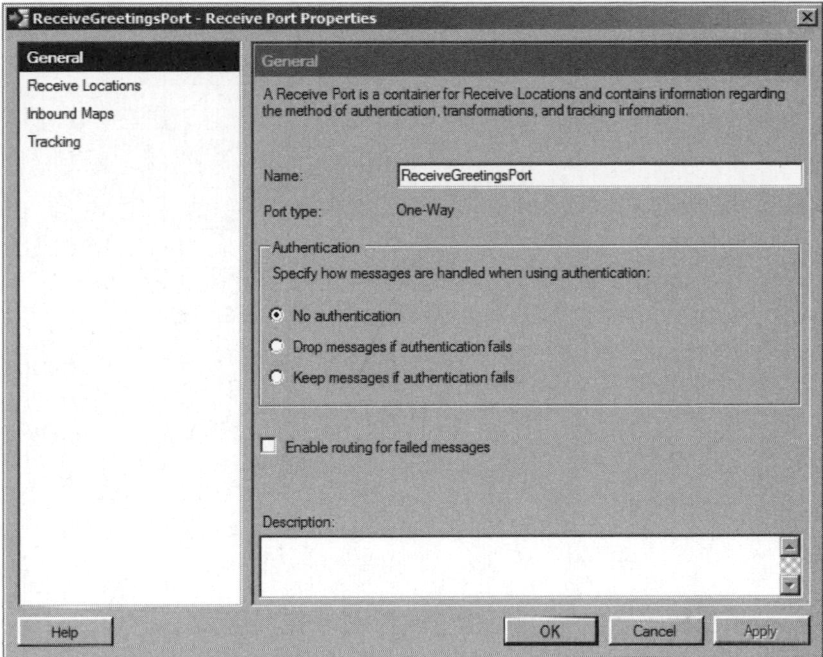

Figure 10-3. *Receive Port Properties dialog box*

   e. In the Receive Location window shown in Figure 10-4, type **ReceiveGreetingsPortFILE** in the Name field.

   f. Select FILE in the Type field.

   g. Click the Configure button.

   h. Type **C:\DeploymentSampleApplication\Documents\In** in the "Receive folder" field.

   i. Click the OK button.

   j. Select BizTalk Server Application from the Receive Handler drop-down menu.

   k. Select XMLReceive in the Receive Pipeline field, and click the OK button.

   l. Click the OK button one more time to close the Receive Properties window.

6. Create a send port:

   a. In the BizTalk Server 2009 Administration Console, expand BizTalk Server 2009 ➤ BizTalk Group ➤ Applications ➤ PROBIZTALK Deploy Sample Application.

   b. Right-click Send Ports, point to New, and click Static One-way Send Port.

   c. In the Send Port Properties window shown in Figure 10-5, type **SendGreetingsResponsePort** in the Name field.

   d. Select FILE in the Type field.

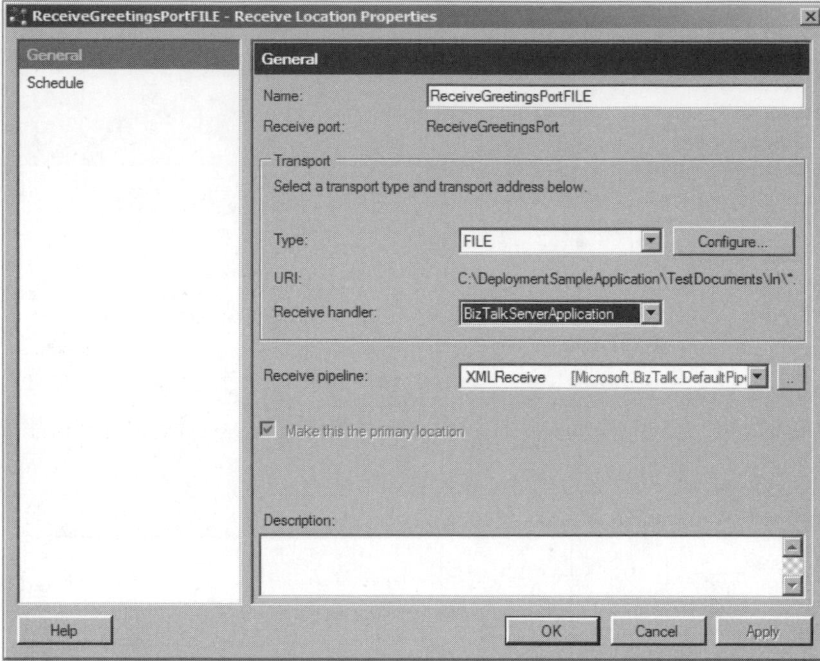

Figure 10-4. *Receive Location Properties dialog box*

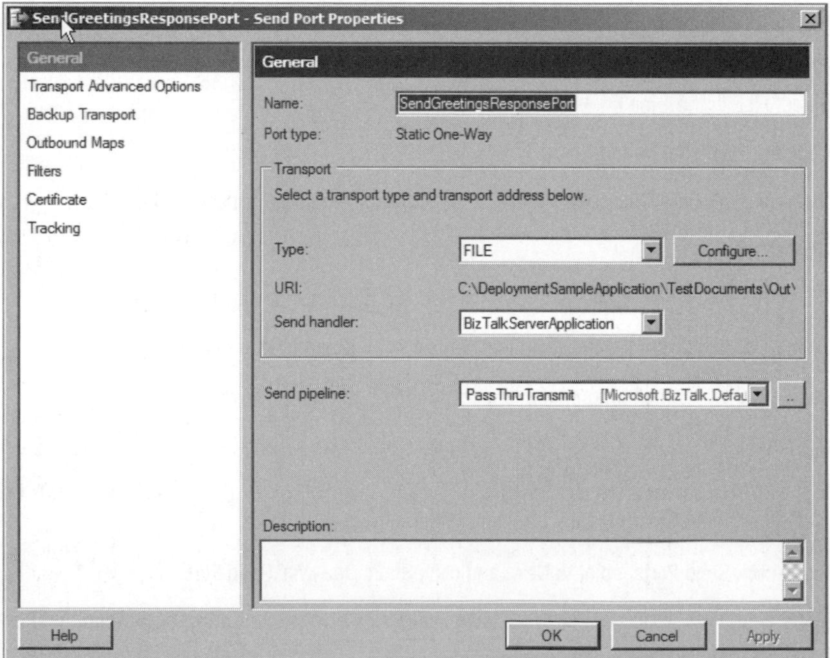

Figure 10-5. *Send Port Properties dialog box*

e. Click the Configure button.

f. Type **C:\DeploymentSampleApplication\Documents\Out** in the "Destination folder" field.

g. Click the OK button.

h. Select PassThruTransimit in the Send Pipeline field.

i. Select BizTalk Server Application in the Send Handler drop-down menu

j. Click the OK button.

7. Configure the PROBIZTALK Deploy Sample Application:

a. In the BizTalk Server 2009 Administration Console, right-click PROBIZTALK Deploy Sample Application, and click Configure.

b. In the Configure Application window, click the ProcessGreetingsOrchestration orchestration.

c. Select BizTalkApplication in the Host drop-down menu.

d. In the Inbound Logical Ports section, select the ReceiveGreetingsPort port in the Port drop-down menu.

e. In the Outbound Logical Ports section, select the SendGreetingsResponsePort port in the Port drop-down menu.

f. In the Configure Application window, click the OK button.

8. Start the PROBIZTALK Deploy Sample Application:

a. In the BizTalk Server 2009 Administration Console, right-click PROBIZTALK Deploy Sample Application, and click Start.

b. In the Start 'PROBIZTALK Deploy Sample Application' window, click Start.

c. Copy C:\DeploymentSampleApplication\Documents\GreetingsSchemaInstance.xml to the C:\DeploymentSampleApplication\Documents\In folder. The file will be picked up by a BizTalk Server for processing, and shortly an output document will be created in the C:\DeploymentSample Application\Documents\Out folder.

MSI Export/Import/Install

You have seen in the previous section how to import and install a BizTalk application manually. Soon you will realize, if you have not already, that deploying an application manually is a long and error-prone process. In order to simplify the process of exporting, importing, and installing a BizTalk application, Microsoft provides BizTalk 2009 with a way to do all the preceding using MSI packages.

Exporting a BizTalk application consists of taking all BizTalk artifacts for a particular application and packaging them into an MSI file. Exercise 10-2 walks you through the process. You do not have to export all the different BizTalk artifacts into a single MSI. You can also decide to split your BizTalk artifacts into multiple MSI packages. This is convenient for BizTalk applications that contain too many artifacts.

EXERCISE 10-2. EXPORTING A BIZTALK APPLICATION

This exercise shows how to export an MSI application. To perform this exercise, please ensure that you completed Exercise 10-1 successfully. Then follow these steps:

1. Open the BizTalk Administration Console:

   a. Select Start ➤ All Programs ➤ Microsoft BizTalk Server 2009 ➤ BizTalk Server, and then click the Administration icon.

   b. In the BizTalk Server 2009 Administration Console, expand BizTalk Server 2009 ➤ BizTalk Group ➤ Applications ➤ PROBIZTALK Deploy Sample Application.

2. Add the testing binding file to the PROBIZTALK Deploy Sample Application:

   a. Right-click PROBIZTALK Deploy Sample Application, point to Export, and then click Bindings.

   b. In the Export Bindings window shown in Figure 10-6, type **C:\DeploymentSampleApplication\TestingBindings.xml** in the Export to file field, and select "Export all bindings from the current application."

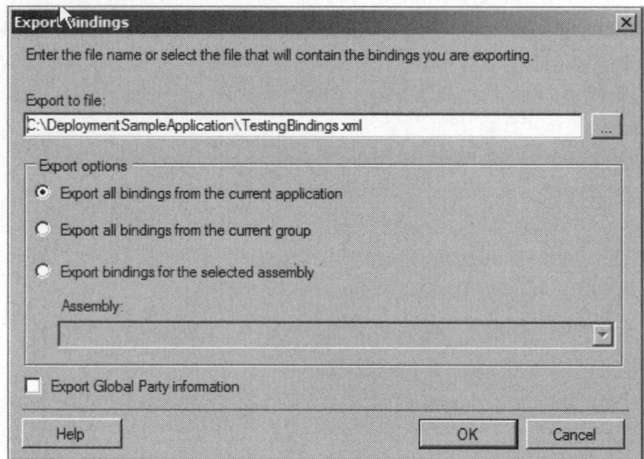

Figure 10-6. *Export Bindings dialog box*

   c. Click the OK button.

   d. Open C:\PROBIZTALK\DeploymentSampleApplication\TestingBindings.xml with Notepad.

   e. Replace all occurrences of the text "\Documents\" with "\TestDocuments\".

   f. Save the file, and close Notepad.

   g. In the BizTalk Server 2009 Administration Console, expand BizTalk Server 2009 ➤ BizTalk Group ➤ Applications ➤ PROBIZTALK Deploy Sample Application.

   h. Right-click the PROBIZTALK Deploy Sample Application, point to Add, and then click Resources.

i. In the Add Resources window, click the Add button, and select the C:\PROBIZTALK\Deployment SampleApplication\TestingBindings.xml file.

j. In the Add Resources window, type **Testing** in the Target Environment text box. This text box allows you to specify which environment a binding file is applied to upon installation of the BizTalk MSI application.

k. In the Add Resources window, click the OK button.

3. Add a pre-processing script to the PROBIZTALK Deploy Sample Application:

a. In Notepad, create a new file, and insert content of the command file presented in Listing 10-2.

b. Save the file as C:\PROBIZTALK\DeploymentSampleApplication\TestingDirs.cmd.

c. In the BizTalk Server 2009 Administration Console, expand BizTalk Server 2009 ➤ BizTalk Group ➤ Applications ➤ PROBIZTALK Deploy Sample Application.

d. Right-click the PROBIZTALK Deploy Sample Application, point to Add, and then click Pre-processing scripts.

e. In the Add Resources window shown in Figure 10-7, click the Add button, and select the C:\PROBIZTALK\DeploymentSampleApplication\TestingDirs.cmd file.

f. In the Add Resources window, click the OK button.

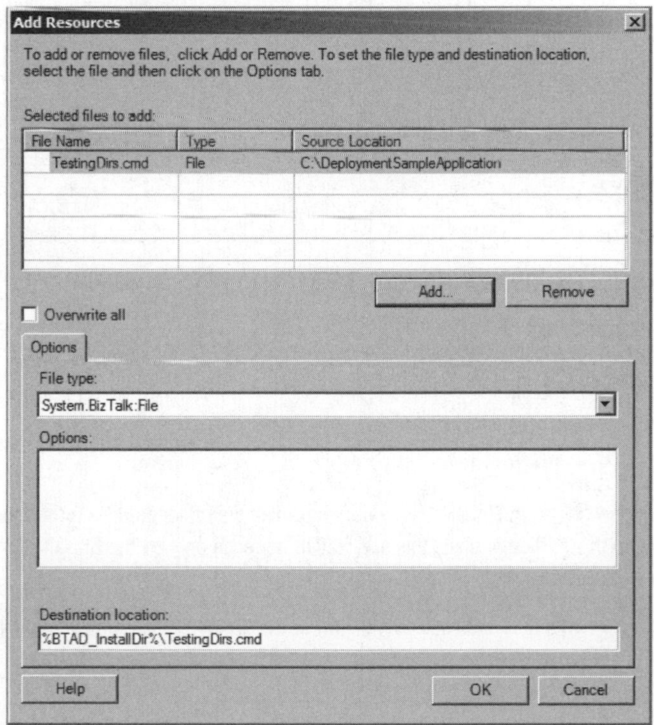

Figure 10-7. *Add Resources dialog box*

4. Export the PROBIZTALK Deploy Sample Application to an MSI file:

   a. In the BizTalk Server 2006 Administration Console, expand BizTalk Server 2009 ➤ BizTalk Group ➤ Applications ➤ PROBIZTALK Deploy Sample Application.

   b. Right-click the PROBIZTALK Deploy Sample Application, point to Export, and then click MSI.

   c. When the Welcome window appears as shown on Figure 10-8, click the Next button.

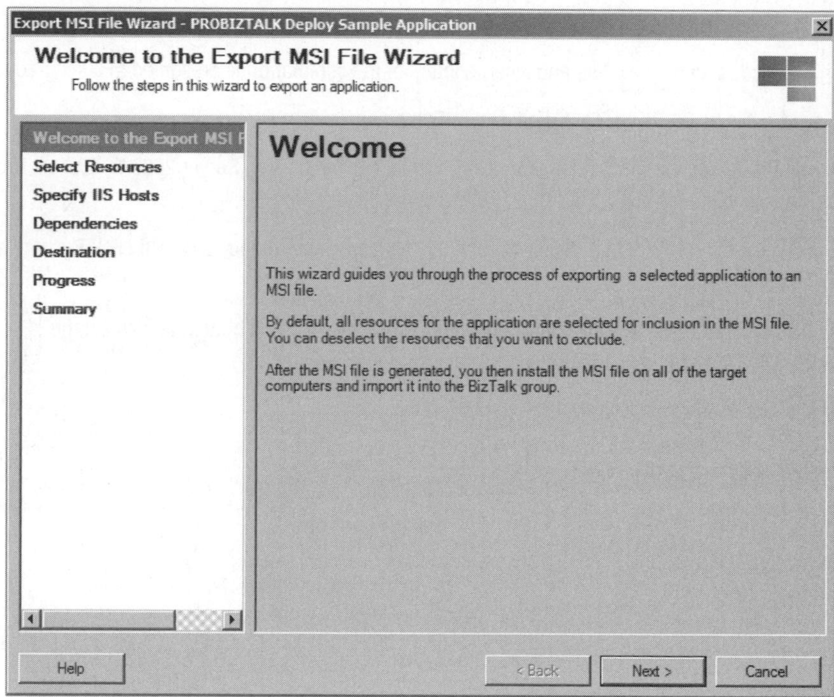

Figure 10-8. *Export MSI File Wizard Welcome screen*

   d. In the Select Resources window shown on Figure 10-9, ensure that all BizTalk artifacts are checked, and then click the Next button.

   e. Since the application does not have any virtual directories, click the Next button in the Specify IIS Hosts window, as shown in Figure 10-10.

   f. The Dependencies window shown in Figure 10-11 enumerates all the dependencies for the application. As you can see in this particular case, this application depends only on the BizTalk.System application. Click the Next button.

   g. Type **C:\ProBizTalkSample.msi**, and then click the Export button in the Destination window, as shown in Figure 10-12.

   h. In the Summary window shown in the Figure 10-13, click the Finish button.

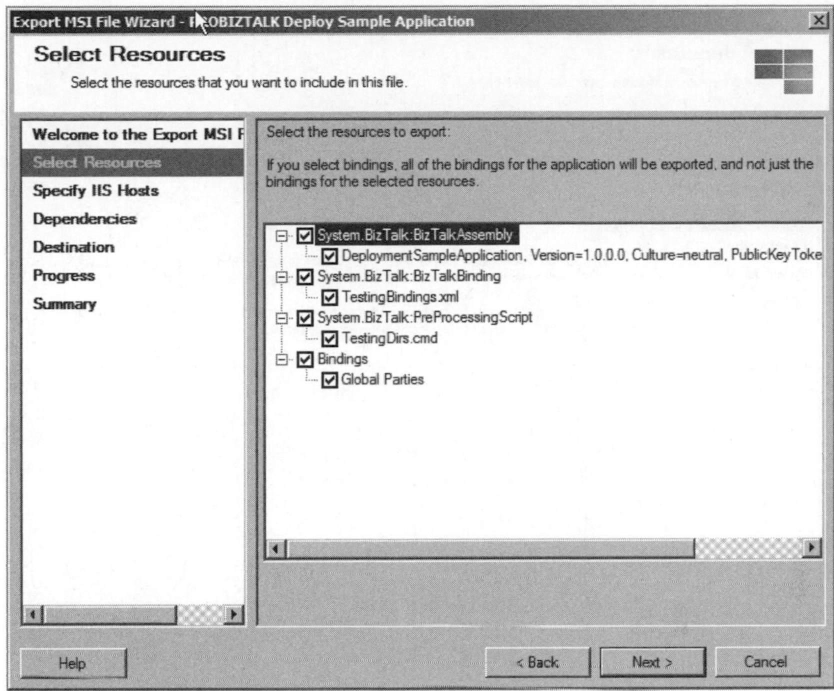

Figure 10-9. *Export MSI File Wizard Resources screen*

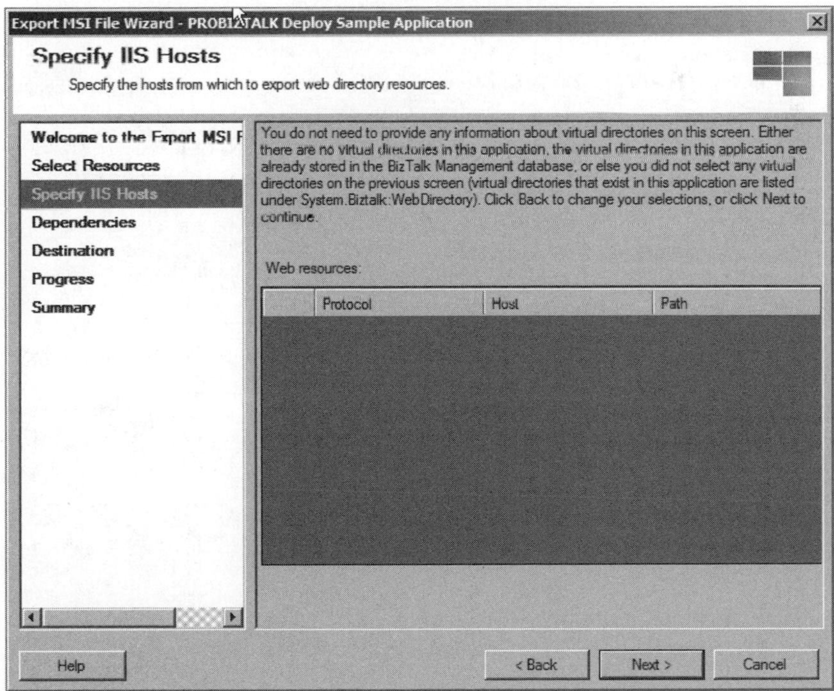

Figure 10-10. *Export MSI File Wizard—Specify IIS Hosts screen*

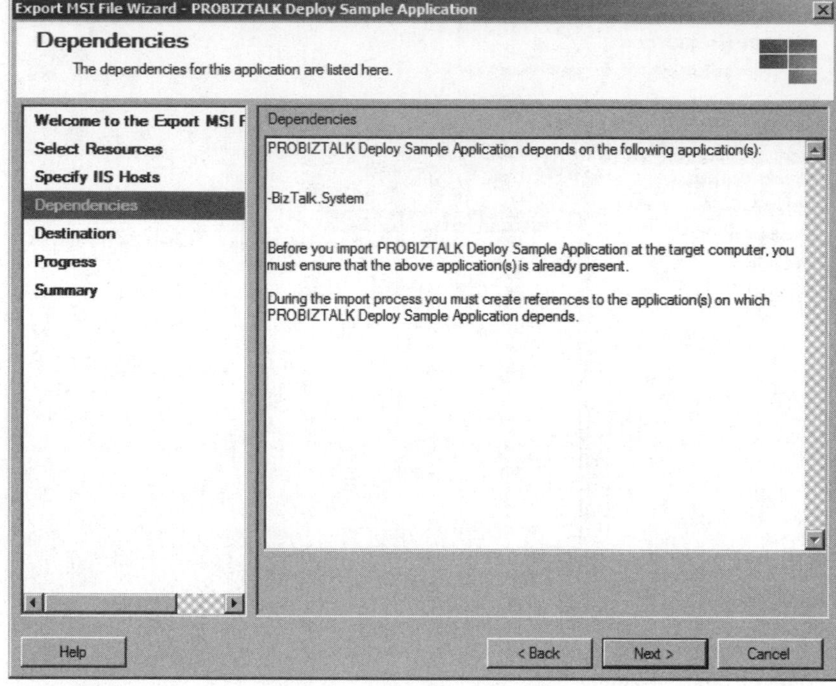

Figure 10-11. *Export MSI File Wizard—Dependencies screen*

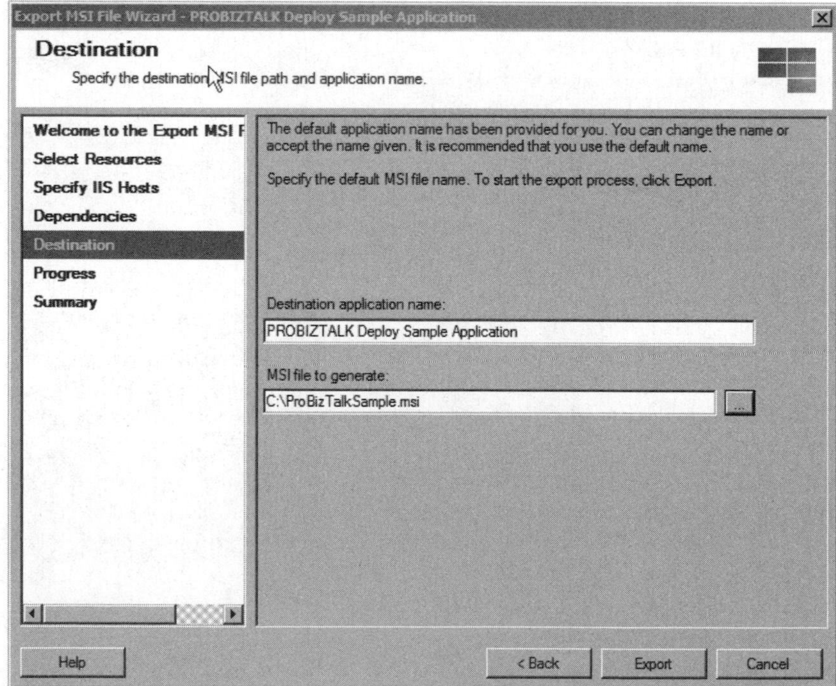

Figure 10-12. *Export MSI File Wizard—Destination screen*

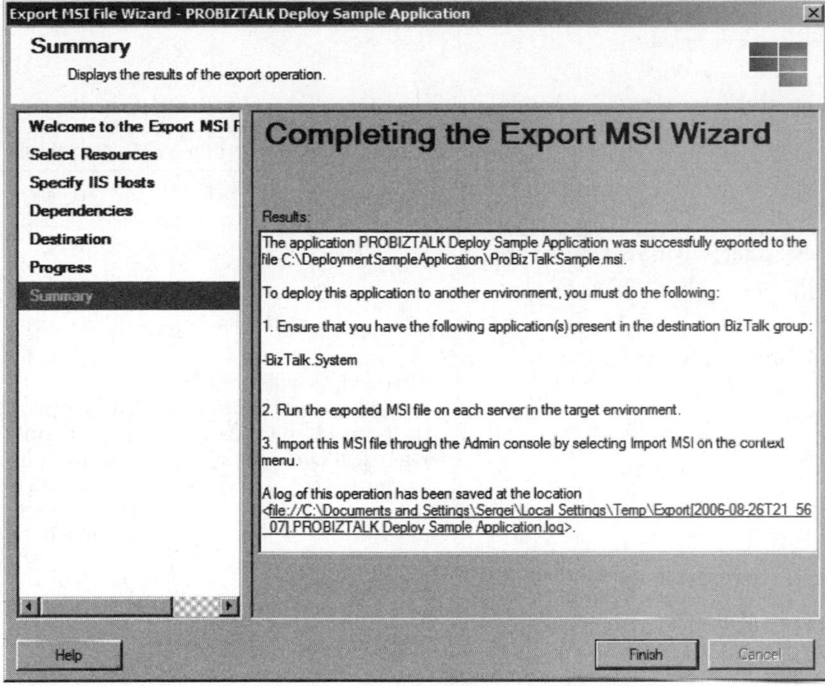

Figure 10-13. *Export MSI File Wizard—Summary screen*

Once you have exported your BizTalk application to an MSI package, you can import or install it onto a new BizTalk Server Group. When importing or installing an MSI BizTalk application, you can specify the following parameters:

- **Application name**: The name of the application used to import or install the MSI package. If the application name is not provided, the default BizTalk application name will be used. If this happens, remember that you can move the artifacts to the application manually.
- **Environment**: The target environment where the MSI package is being imported or installed. This parameter allows all binding files for the specified environment to be applied to the BizTalk server. If the environment parameter is not specified, all the binding files that do not specify a target environment will be applied. The benefit of this is that you can create a bindings file for your receive ports and another bindings file for your send ports. By having the environment setting the same, they will both be applied, which gives you the ability to segment your binding files. This will allow you to create a bindings file that can contain information that needs to be deployed in each and every environment. This is done by keeping the port binding target empty, which sets the default to `ENV:ALL`. This becomes important when you want to do incremental updates in that you don't need to worry about unnecessarily overwriting unchanged items.
- **Overwrite**: This flag specifies whether to overwrite the existing artifacts.

Table 10-5 displays what operations are executed when a BizTalk application is imported or installed.

Table 10-5. *Operations Executed When Importing or Installing a BizTalk Application*

Operation	Occurs While Importing	Occurs While Installing
Add references in the BizTalk Management Database.	X	
Copy BizTalk artifacts to the BizTalk server.	X	X
Apply binding files for the specified target environment.	X	X
Execute pre- or post-processing scripts.	X The scripts will perform only those actions that will run when the `BTAD_InstallMode` is equal to Import.	X The scripts will perform only those actions that will run when the `BTAD_InstallMode` is equal to Install.
Store file-based artifact (assemblies, virtual directories, files, scripts, certificates, BAM artifacts, and BAS artifacts) data in the BizTalk Management Database.	X	
Store policies in the Rule Engine database.	X	
Store BAM artifacts in the BAM.	Primary Import database. Deploy BAM definitions.	X
Add BizTalk assemblies to the Global Assembly Cache.	Only if BizTalk assemblies were added to the BizTalk application with the "Add to global assembly cache on MSI import" option.	Only if BizTalk assemblies were added to the BizTalk application with the "Add to global assembly cache on MSI install" option.

The BizTalk Administration Console and BTSTask command-line application are the two applications that allow a user to export, import, and install a BizTalk MSI file. Please note that the BTSDeploy tool from BizTalk Server 2004 has been deprecated and is no longer included; therefore, scripts should be migrated to the BTSTask tool. Exercise 10-3 walks you through the process of importing a BizTalk application using the BTSTask tool.

EXERCISE 10-3. IMPORTING A BIZTALK APPLICATION

To perform this exercise, please ensure that you completed Exercise 10-2 successfully. Then follow these steps:

1. Remove the PROBIZTALK Deploy Sample Application:

    a. In the BizTalk Server 2009 Administration Console, expand BizTalk Server 2009 ➤ BizTalk Group ➤ Applications ➤ PROBIZTALK Deploy Sample Application.

    b. Right-click the PROBIZTALK Deploy Sample Application, and then select Stop.

    c. In the Stop 'PROBIZTALK Deploy Sample Application' window shown in Figure 10-14, select the Full Stop – Terminate instances radio button, and then click Stop.

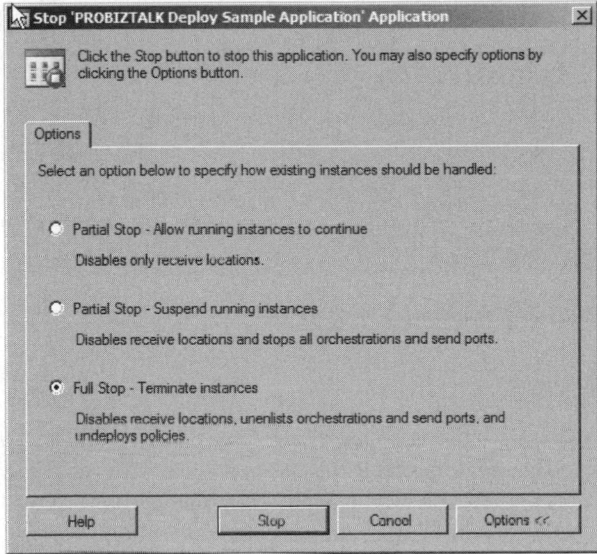

Figure 10-14. *Stop Application dialog box*

    d. In the BizTalk Server 2009 Administration Console, right-click the PROBIZTALK Deploy Sample Application, and then select Delete.

    e. In the confirmation message box, click the OK button. Then, close the BizTalk Server 2009 Administration Console.

2. Import the PROBIZTALK Deploy Sample Application:

   a. Open the Visual Studio 2008 Command Prompt.

   b. In the Visual Studio 2008 Command Prompt, execute the following command: `BTSTask ImportApp /Package:C:\ProBizTalkSample.msi /Environment:Testing /ApplicationName: "PROBIZTALK Deploy Sample Application" /Overwrite`.

   c. If the script was executed successfully, the content of the command prompt will resemble Figure 10-15.

```
Information: Updating binding information.
ConnectionString="Data Source=PROBIZTALK;Initial Catalog=BizTalkMgmtDb;Integrate
d Security=True;Enlist=True;Application Name=Microsoft.BizTalk.ApplicationDeploy
ment.Engine"
Information: Updating send ports, send port groups, and receive ports...
Information: Updated "[Send port "SendGreetingsResponsePort"]"
Information: Updated "[Receive location "ReceiveGreetingsPortFILE"]"
Information: Updated "[Receive port "ReceiveGreetingsPort"]"
Information: Updating parties and enlistments...
Information: Updating orchestration bindings...
Information: Successfully updated binding information.
Information: Commit the change requests...
* Performing EndTypeChangeRequest for resource type "System.BizTalk:PreProcessin
gScript".
* Performing EndTypeChangeRequest for resource type "System.BizTalk:BizTalkAssem
bly".
* Performing EndTypeChangeRequest for resource type "System.BizTalk:BizTalkBindi
ng".
Information: Imported package into application "PROBIZTALK DeploySample Applicat
ion".

Command succeeded with 0 errors, 0 warnings.
```

Figure 10-15. *BizTalk Server MSI import using the BTSTask console application*

Typical Deployment Cycle

In the previous sections, you learned how to deploy a BizTalk solution manually and using the MSI export and import method. In this section, you will learn how to move a BizTalk application from the development environment all the way to production using the steps outlined in the preceding two sections. There are five main steps to move an application from one environment to another:

1. **Deploy assemblies from BizTalk solutions using Visual Studio 2008**: In this step, the BizTalk developers deploy a BizTalk solution on their development environment. This means to both GAC the files locally as well as to deploy the bits to the Configuration database. Once the developers have tested their BizTalk application adequately, they proceed to the next step.

2. **Add BizTalk artifacts to the deployed BizTalk application**: In this step, the BizTalk developers or the integrators add artifacts to the BizTalk application in order to deploy their solution to another environment or BizTalk Server Group. Typically, this step involves creating new binding files specific to the next target environment, adding processing scripts to automate as much as possible the installation of the BizTalk MSI application to the next target environment, and adding any other BizTalk artifacts (like certificates and readme files) necessary on the target environment.

3. **Export the BizTalk application to an MSI file**: In this step, the developers or the integrators proceed to export the complete BizTalk application to an MSI file using the BizTalk Administration Console or the BTSTask command-line tool. They will have to decide whether or not they want to create one or more MSI packages and what BizTalk artifact they want to include in them.
4. **Import and install the MSI file**: Once the MSI package or packages are ready, it is time to import and install them on the target environment. The MSI file will register all BizTalk artifacts in the target environment's BizTalk Management Database. It will also copy and register in the GAC or in the Windows' registry all .NET assemblies and COM libraries on the BizTalk servers where the packages are installed. Please keep in mind that you must install the MSI file on each BizTalk server in a BizTalk Server Group.
5. **Start the application and verify that it is functioning correctly**: At this point, the BizTalk developer or integrator starts and tests the newly installed BizTalk application. Once that person is satisfied with the results, he can repeat steps 2 through 5 to deploy the BizTalk application to other staging environments until he eventually releases the BizTalk application to production.

Administrative Tools

BizTalk 2009 provides different tools to manage BizTalk Server applications:

- BizTalk Administration Console MMC
- BTSTask command-line tool
- WMI and the ExplorerOM APIs

Each of these tools allows you to deploy and manage your solutions. While BizTalk Administration Console has been changed and improved significantly in BizTalk Server 2009, it is, as most UI tools, not intended to automate administration tasks. The BTSTask command-line tool can be used in batch files to perform automation tasks, but batch files are still not as flexible as full-featured programming languages like C# or VB .NET. If you are an experienced developer, you know that real-world projects can easily contain hundreds and even thousands of artifacts. Managing them manually is a daunting and error-prone task and in many cases simply hardly possible. To address these kinds of problems, Microsoft provides two APIs—Windows Management Instrumentation (WMI) and ExplorerOM, which allow you to write your own custom utilities to address all aspects of managing and configuring a BizTalk Server and a BizTalk Server Group. BTSTask can also be utilized from MSBuild and PowerShell. We'll show examples of this later in this chapter.

As shown in Tables 10-6 to 10-15, the tools have an overlapping functionality, and for the most common BizTalk tasks you can use any of them. However, for some tasks you will have a more limited set of tools to choose from. Tables 10-6 through 10-15 list common management tasks and indicate what tools are available to perform each of them.

Table 10-6. *Application Tasks*

Task	Administration Console	BTSTask Tool	WMI	ExplorerOM
Creating a new application	X	X		X
Modifying application properties	X	X		X (but you can't modify the `Default Application` property)
Deleting an application	X	X		X

Table 10-7. *Assembly Tasks*

Task	Administration Console	BTSTask Tool	WMI	ExplorerOM
Deploying an assembly	X	X	X	
Undeploying an assembly	X	X		

Table 10-8. *Host Tasks*

Task	Administration Console	BTSTask Tool	WMI	ExplorerOM
Creating a new host	X		X	
Modifying a host	X		X	
Deleting a host	X		X	
Starting/stopping/modifying	X		X	Host instances

Table 10-9. *Orchestration Tasks*

Task	Administration Console	BTSTask Tool	WMI	ExplorerOM
Browsing orchestration artifacts	X	X	X	X
Finding roles used or implemented by orchestration				X
Binding/enlisting/starting orchestrations	X	Only if BTSTask makes use of processing scripts that internally use WMI or ExplorerOM	X	X
Stopping/unenlisting/unbinding orchestrations	X	Only if BTSTask makes use of processing scripts that internally use WMI or ExplorerOM	X	X

Table 10-10. *Send Port Tasks*

Task	Administration Console	BTSTask Tool	WMI	ExplorerOM
Adding/enlisting/starting a send port	X		X	X
Stopping/unenlisting/deleting a send port	X		X	X
Modifying port properties	X	Only if BTSTask applies binding files	X	X
Managing send port certificates	X	Only if BTSTask applies binding files	X	X
Adding/editing filtering expressions	X	Only if BTSTask applies binding files	X	X
Adding/removing maps for inbound/outbound transformation	X	Only if BTSTask applies binding files	X	X

Table 10-11. *Send Port Group Tasks*

Task	Administration Console	BTSTask Tool	WMI	ExplorerOM
Adding/enlisting/starting a send port group	X		X	X
Stopping/unenlisting/deleting a send port	X		X	X
Adding/deleting port to/from send port group	X	Only if BTSTask applies binding files	X	X
Adding a filter to a send port group	X	Only if BTSTask applies binding files	X	X

Table 10-12. *Receive Port Tasks*

Task	Administration Console	BTSTask Tool	WMI	ExplorerOM
Adding/modifying/deleting a receive port	X	Only if BTSTask applies binding files	X	X
Adding a map to inbound/outbound transformations	X	Only if BTSTask applies binding files	X	X

Table 10-13. *Receive Location Tasks*

Task	Administration Console	BTSTask Tool	WMI	ExplorerOM
Adding/editing/deleting a receive location	X	Only if BTSTask applies binding files	X	X
Enabling/disabling a receive location	X	Only if BTSTask applies binding files	X	X

Table 10-14. *Party Tasks*

Task	Administration Console	BTSTask Tool	WMI	ExplorerOM
Adding/deleting a party	X	X		X
Enlisting/unenlisting a party	X	X		X
Adding/deleting a send port to/from a party		Only if BTSTask applies binding files		X
Adding an alias to a party		Only if BTSTask applies binding files		X
Adding a certificate for a party		Only if BTSTask applies binding files		X

Table 10-15. *Messagebox Tasks*

Task	Administration Console	BTSTask Tool	WMI	ExplorerOM
Adding/deleting a Messagebox	X		X	
Editing Messagebox properties	X		X	

BizTalk Administration Console

The BizTalk Administration Console, shown in Figure 10-16, is a Microsoft Management Console (MMC). This tool is the only administration tool that comes with a Windows graphical UI. It is also the easiest one for novices to use.

If you have used the Administration Console with previous versions of BizTalk Server, you will be pleased to know that once again the Administration Console has been updated with new features. Some of these new features include the remaining functionality that used to be part of HAT. With the Administration Console you can do the following:

- Add, configure, remove, and uninstall a BizTalk application.
- Import and export a BizTalk application as an MSI.
- Import and export binding files.
- Create, configure, and delete ports and receive locations.
- Configure, start, stop, enlist, and unenlist ports and orchestrations.
- Create, configure, delete, and install hosts and host instances.
- Manage and configure parties.
- Run queries from the Group Hub page.
- Debug orchestrations.
- Monitor the work in progress as well as any errors, suspended messages, tracked service instances, and EDI status reports.

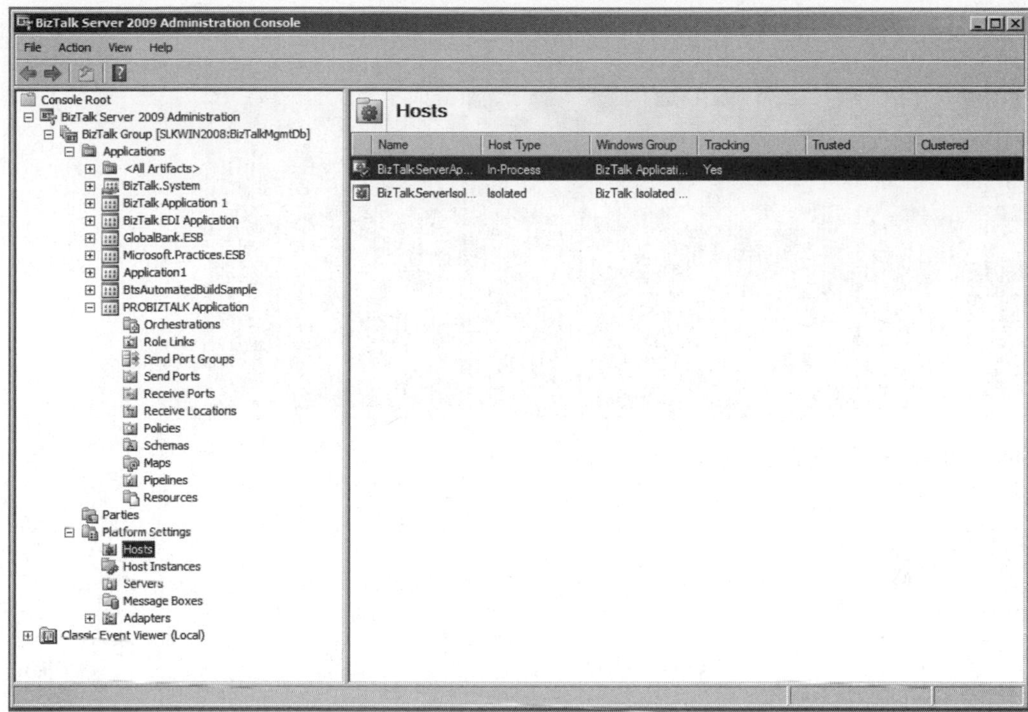

Figure 10-16. *BizTalk Server 2009 Administration Console*

BTSTask

BTSTask is a command-prompt application that replaces BizTalk 2004's BTSDeploy command-prompt application. Unlike BTSDeploy, BTSTask does not come with a wizard. If developers or administrators want to use a GUI, they must use the BizTalk Administration Console.

This application allows you to

- Add, enumerate, remove, and uninstall BizTalk applications.
- Add, list, and remove artifacts (assemblies, bindings, pre-processing scripts, and post-processing scripts) from a BizTalk application.
- Export and import BizTalk applications from an MSI file.
- Export and import binding information from BizTalk binding files.
- List all BizTalk applications in the BizTalk Management Database for the BizTalk Group.
- List the resources in an MSI file.

The sample shown in Figure 10-17 creates an application named PROBIZTALK Application using the BTSTask command-line application. If you open the BizTalk Administration Console, you will see the newly created application. For the full list of the command options, please refer to the product documentation.

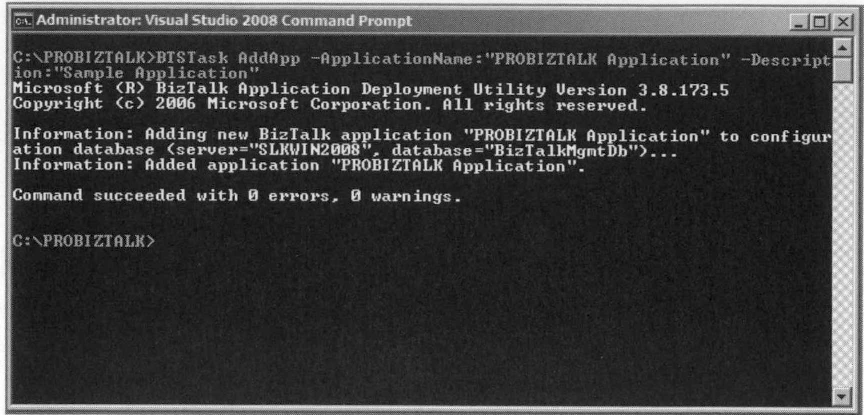

Figure 10-17. *BTSTask add application example*

WMI

Windows Management Instrumentation provides a standard way of managing a computer system. WMI allows you to

- Gather information about systems.
- Configure systems.
- Fire or consume specific WMI events occurring on c = omputers or servers.

Tables 10-16 and 10-17 describe the different BizTalk WMI classes and events. To utilize these classes, you must use the WMI COM API or the System.Management assembly, which is a .NET COM Interop assembly. Listing 10-3 demonstrates how to create a host using WMI API from managed code.

Table 10-16. *BizTalk WMI Classes*

WMI Class Name	Specific Methods	Purpose
`MSBTS_AdapterSetting`	None	Registers new adapters.
`MSBTS_DeploymentService`	`Deploy`, `Export`, `Import`, `Remove`	Deploys/undeploys assemblies and imports/exports binding files.
`MSBTS_GroupSetting`	`RegisterLocalServer`, `UnRegisterLocalServer`	Represents information about BTS Groups.
`MSBTS_Host`	`Start`, `Stop`	Represents a host. Used to start/stop all host instances in a given BizTalk host. It is also used to get/set host properties.
`MSBTS_HostInstance`	`GetState`, `Install`, `Start`, `Stop`, `Uninstall`	Represents a host instance. Used to install/uninstall and start/stop a specific host instance in a given BizTalk host.
`MSBTS_HostInstanceSetting`	None	Represents host settings.

WMI Class Name	Specific Methods	Purpose
MSBTS_HostQueue	ResumeServiceInstancesByID, SuspendServiceInstancesByID, TerminateServiceInstancesByID	Resumes, suspends, or terminates service instances.
MSBTS_HostSetting	None	Sets host settings.
MSBTS_MessageInstance	SaveToFile	Represents a message instance.
MSBTS_MsgBoxSetting	ForceDelete	Represents a single Messagebox setting in the BizTalk Server Group.
MSBTS_Orchestration	Enlist, QueryDependencyInfo, QueryInstanceInfo, Start, Stop, Unenlist	Represents an orchestration. Used to start/stop and enlist/unenlist orchestrations.
MSBTS_ReceiveHandler	None	Represents a receive handler. Used to configure receive handlers.
MSBTS_ReceiveLocation	Disable, Enable	Represents a receive location. Used to enable and disable the receive location.
MSBTS_ReceiveLocationOrchestration	None	Represents all possible combinations of orchestrations and receive locations.
MSBTS_ReceivePort	None	Represents a receive port. Used to configure receive ports.
MSBTS_SendHandler	None	Represents a send handler. Used to configure send handlers.
MSBTS_SendPort	Enlist, Start, Stop, Unenlist	Represents a send port. Used to configure send ports.
MSBTS_SendPortGroup	Enlist, Start, Stop, UnEnlist	Represents a send port group. Used to start/stop and enlist/unenlist send port groups.
MSBTS_SendPortGroup2SendPort	None	Represents a many-to-many relationship between send port groups and send ports.
MSBTS_Server	CheckIfCanInstallHostInstances, Start, Stop	Represents a computer within a BizTalk Server Group. Used to start services on a given server.
MSBTS_ServerHost	ForceUnmap, Map, Unmap	Represents a mapping between BizTalk hosts and host instances. Used to map and unmap relationships.
MSBTS_ServiceInstance	Resume, Suspend, Terminate	Represents an instance of a service. Used to resume, suspend, and terminate services.
MSBTS_TrackedMessageInstance	SaveToFile	Represents a tracked message instance saved in the Messagebox or Archive databases. Used to save a message to a file.

Table 10-17. *BizTalk WMI Events*

WMI Event Name	Specific Properties	Purpose
MSTBS_MessageInstance SuspendentEvent	ErrorCategory, ErrorDescription, ErrorId, HostName, Message InstanceID, MessageType, ReferenceType, ServiceClass, ServiceClassID, Service InstanceID, ServiceTypeID	Represents a suspended event for a BizTalk Message Queuing (MSMQT) message instance
MSTBS_ServiceInstance SuspendentEvent	ErrorCategory, ErrorDescription, ErrorId, HostName, InstanceID, ServiceClass, ServiceClassID, ServiceStatus, ServiceTypeID	Represents a suspended event for a service instance

Listing 10-3. *Create Host Example Using Managed Code*

```
[C#]
using System.Management;

      // Basic WMI operation - Create
      // sample to show MSBTS_HostSetting instance creation
      public void CreateHost(string ServerName, string HostName, int HostType,
string NTGroupName, bool AuthTrusted)
      {
         try
         {
            PutOptions options = new PutOptions();
            options.Type = PutType.CreateOnly;

            // Create a ManagementClass object and spawn a ManagementObject instance
            ManagementClass objHostSettingClass = new ManagementClass("\\\\" +
ServerName + "\\root\\MicrosoftBizTalkServer", "MSBTS_HostSetting", null);
            ManagementObject objHostSetting  = objHostSettingClass.CreateInstance();

            // Set the properties for the Host
            objHostSetting["Name"] = HostName;
            objHostSetting["HostType"] = HostType;
            objHostSetting["NTGroupName"] = NTGroupName;
            objHostSetting["AuthTrusted"] = AuthTrusted;

            // Creating the host
            objHostSetting.Put(options);
            System.Console.WriteLine(string.Format("The Host '{0}'has been
created successfully", HostName ));
         }
         catch(Exception ex)
```

```
        {
            System.Console.WriteLine("CreateHost - " + HostName +
" - failed: " + ex.Message);
        }
    }
```

The same example using VBScript instead of managed code is shown in Listing 10-4.

Listing 10-4. *Create Host Example Using VBScript*

```
[VBScript]
Option Explicit
' wbemChangeFlagEnum Setting
const UpdateOnly = 1
const CreateOnly = 2
Sub CreateHost (ServerName, HostName, HostType, NTGroupName, AuthTrusted)
   On Error Resume Next
   Dim objLocator, objService, objHostSetting, objHS

   ' Connects to local server WMI Provider BizTalk namespace
   Set objLocator = Createobject ("wbemScripting.SwbemLocator")
   Set objService = objLocator.ConnectServer(ServerName,
"root/MicrosoftBizTalkServer")

   ' Get WMI class MSBTS_HostSetting
   Set objHostSetting = objService.Get ("MSBTS_HostSetting")

   Set objHS = objHostSetting.SpawnInstance_

   objHS.Name = HostName
   objHS.HostType = HostType
   objHS.NTGroupName = NTGroupName
   objHS.AuthTrusted = AuthTrusted

   ' Create Host
   objHS.Put_(CreateOnly)

   CheckWMIError
   wscript.echo "Host - " & HostName & " - has been created successfully"
end Sub
```

Another interesting task you can accomplish with WMI is to subscribe to `MSTBS_MessageInstanceSuspendentEvent` and `MSTBS_ServiceInstanceSuspendentEvent`. Consuming these events will allow you to handle certain situations gracefully in your BizTalk solution. For instance, when a mapping error occurs on a send or receive port, you could decide to send an e-mail to an administrator and automatically terminate the service instance. Listing 10-5 shows how to subscribe to a WMI event.

Listing 10-5. *Subscribing to a BizTalk WMI Event*

```
using System.Management;

static public void ListenForSvcInstSuspendEvent()
 {
     try
     {
        // Set up an event watcher and a handler for the
MSBTS_ServiceInstanceSuspendedEvent event
        ManagementEventWatcher watcher =
new ManagementEventWatcher( new ManagementScope("root\\MicrosoftBizTalkServer"),
new EventQuery("SELECT * FROM MSBTS_ServiceInstanceSuspendedEvent") );

        watcher.EventArrived += new EventArrivedEventHandler(MyEventHandler);

        // Start watching for MSBTS_ServiceInstanceSuspendedEvent events
        watcher.Start();

        Console.WriteLine("Press enter to quit");
        Console.ReadLine();
        watcher.Stop();
     }
     catch (Exception ex)
     {
        Console.WriteLine("Error: " + ex.Message);
     }
  }

  static public void MyEventHandler(object sender, EventArrivedEventArgs e)
  {
     // Print out the service instance ID and error description upon receiving
     // of the suspend event
     Console.WriteLine("A MSBTS_ServiceInstanceSuspendEvent has occurred!");
     Console.WriteLine(string.Format("ServiceInstanceID: {0}",
e.NewEvent["InstanceID"]));
     Console.WriteLine(string.Format("ErrorDescription: {0}",
e.NewEvent["ErrorDescription"]));
     Console.WriteLine("");
  }
```

ExplorerOM

The ExplorerOM object model is a set of classes and interfaces from the ExplorerOM namespace used by BizTalk Explorer to configure applications. You can consider ExplorerOM as an API to the Management Database that allows you to perform application management and configuration tasks. To use it in your .NET applications, you have to add a reference to the

[BizTalk Installation directory]\Developer Tools\Microsoft.Biztalk.ExplorerOM.dll assembly. All artifacts in ExplorerOM are stored in collections, and there are three classes hosting collections of artifacts, as listed in Table 10-18.

Table 10-18. *ExplorerOM Container Classes*

Class	Description
`BtsCatalogExplorer`	Provides methods and properties to manipulate artifacts at the BizTalk Server Group level
`BtsApplication`	Provides methods and properties to manipulate artifacts at the BizTalk application level
`Assembly`	Provides properties to access artifacts at the assembly level

BtsCatalogExplorer Class

This class provides access to all artifacts in the Management Database, regardless of their association with a specific BizTalk application or assembly. You can also use this class to add or remove artifacts from the different collections and then commit changes to the Management Database. This class is the most fundamental, since all ExplorerOM code you write will have one thing in common: instantiating the `BtsCatalogExplorer` class and setting the `ConnectionString` property to access the Management Database.

Table 10-19 lists the properties of the `BtsCatalogExplorer` class. As you can guess, all these properties except the `ConnectionString` property are collections of different BizTalk artifacts stored in the Management Database.

Table 10-19. *BtsCatalogExplorer Properties*

Property Name	Description
`ConnectionString`	Connection string to the Management Database.
`Applications`	Read-only. Returns a collection of applications in the Management Database.
`Assemblies`	Read-only. Returns a collection of deployed assemblies.
`Certificates`	Read-only. Returns a collection of certificates installed on the computer.
`Hosts`	Read-only. Returns a collection of hosts in the Management Database.
`Parties`	Read-only. Returns a collection of parties in the Management Database.
`Pipelines`	Read-only. Returns a collection of pipelines in the Management Database.
`ProtocolTypes`	Read-only. Returns a collection of protocol types in the Management Database.
`ReceiveHandlers`	Read-only. Returns a collection of receive handlers in the Management Database.
`ReceivePorts`	Read-only. Returns a collection of receive ports in the Management Database.
`Schemas`	Read-only. Returns a collection of schemas in the Management Database.
`SendPortGroups`	Read-only. Returns a collection of send port groups in the Management Database.

Continued

Table 10-19. *Continued*

Property Name	Description
`SendPorts`	Read-only. Returns a collection of send ports in the Management Database.
`StandardAliases`	Read-only. Returns a collection of standard aliases.
`Transforms`	Read-only. Returns a collection of transforms.

Let's put everything mentioned previously in practice and write a utility that enumerates all send ports in the Management Database and prints out the port name and status, as shown in Listing 10-6.

Listing 10-6. *Enumeration of Send Ports*

```
using System;
using System.Text;
using Microsoft.BizTalk.ExplorerOM;

namespace SendPorts
{
    class Program
    {

        static void Main(string[] args)
        {
            EnumerateSendPorts();
            Console.ReadKey();
        }

        public static void EnumerateSendPorts()
        {
            BtsCatalogExplorer catalog = new BtsCatalogExplorer();
            catalog.ConnectionString = "Server=.;Initial Catalog=BizTalkMgmtDb;
Integrated Security=SSPI;";


            foreach (SendPort sendPort in catalog.SendPorts )
            {
                Console.WriteLine("\tPortName:{0},Status:{1}",
                     sendPort.Name ,sendPort.Status);

            }
        }
    }
}
```

Alternatively, you can get access to the collections of artifacts exposed by the BtsCatalogExplorer class by calling the GetCollection method and passing as a parameter values from the CollectionType enumeration. The member names of this enumeration are exactly the same as the names of the properties of the BtsCatalogExplorer class. Listing 10-7 shows how to print out port names and status using the GetCollection method.

Listing 10-7. *Enumeration of Send Ports Using the GetCollection Method*

```
using System;
using System.Text;
using Microsoft.BizTalk.ExplorerOM;

namespace SendPorts
{
    class Program
    {

        static void Main(string[] args)
        {
            EnumerateSendPorts();
            Console.ReadKey();
        }

        public static void EnumerateSendPorts()
        {
            BtsCatalogExplorer catalog = new BtsCatalogExplorer();
            catalog.ConnectionString = "Server=.;Initial Catalog=BizTalkMgmtDb;
Integrated Security=SSPI;";
            SendPortCollection spCollection =
(SendPortCollection)catalog.GetCollection(CollectionType.SendPort);

            foreach (SendPort sendPort in spCollection)
            {
                Console.WriteLine("\tPortName:{0},Status:{1}",
                     sendPort.Name, sendPort.Status);

            }
        }
    }
}
```

The BtsCatalogExplorer class not only allows you to walk through existing artifacts but also provides methods to add, delete, and configure them and commit changes to the Management Database. Table 10-20 lists such methods.

Table 10-20. *BtsCatalogExplorer Methods*

Method Name	Description
AddNewApplication	Creates and adds a new Application object to the Application collection. Specific to BizTalk Server 2006.
RemoveApplication	Removes the specified application from the Application collection. Specific to BizTalk 2006.
AddNewParty	Creates and adds a new Party object to the Parties collection.
RemoveParty	Removes the specified party from the Parties collection.
AddNewReceivePort	Creates and adds a new ReceivePort object to the ReceivePorts collection.
RemoveReceivePort	Removes the specified receive port from the ReceivePorts collection.
AddNewSendPort	Creates and adds a new SendPort object to the SendPorts collection.
RemoveSendPort	Removes the specified send port from the SendPorts collection.
AddNewSendPortGroup	Creates and adds a new SendPortGroup object to the SendPortGroups collection.
RemoveSendPortGroup	Removes the specified send port group.
SaveChanges	Commits all BtsCatalogExplorer object changes to the Management Database.
SaveChangesWithTransaction	Commits all BtsCatalogExplorer object changes to the Management Database in a specified transaction.
DiscardChanges	Discards all BtsCatalogExplorer object changes.

The code in Listing 10-8 shows how to create a send port using the AddNewSendPort method of the BtsCatalogExplorer class.

Listing 10-8. *Creating a New Send Port Using the AddNewSendPort Method*

```
using System;
using Microsoft.BizTalk.ExplorerOM

namespace AddSendPort
{
    class Program
    {
        static void Main(string[] args)
        {
            CreateSendPort();

        }
```

```
        private static void CreateSendPort()
        {
            // Connect to the BizTalk configuration database
           BtsCatalogExplorer catalog = new BtsCatalogExplorer();
            catalog.ConnectionString = "Server=PROBIZTALK;Initial Catalog=
BizTalkMgmtDb;Integrated Security=SSPI;";

            try
            {
               // Create static one-way send port
                SendPort myStaticOnewaySendPort =
catalog.AddNewSendPort(false, false);
                myStaticOnewaySendPort.Name = "PROBiztalkSendPort";
                myStaticOnewaySendPort.PrimaryTransport.TransportType =
catalog.ProtocolTypes["HTTP"];
                myStaticOnewaySendPort.PrimaryTransport.Address =
"http://DestinationUrl";
                myStaticOnewaySendPort.SendPipeline =
catalog.Pipelines["Microsoft.BizTalk.DefaultPipelines.XMLTransmit"];

                // Commit changes to BizTalk configuration database
                catalog.SaveChanges();
            }
            catch (Exception ex)
            {
                catalog.DiscardChanges();
            }
        }

    }
}
```

In the beginning of this chapter, we mentioned that in BizTalk Server 2009 all artifacts must be associated with a BizTalk application. It is important to note that the code in Listing 10-8 adds a new port and associates it automatically with the current default application. How to associate artifacts with a specific application will be discussed in the next section, which we devote to the `Application` class.

Application Class

The second class hosting collections of BizTalk artifacts is the `Application` class. As you can guess, this class provides similar methods and properties as the `BtsCatalogExplorer` class. The main difference is that the `Application` class deals with the artifacts belonging to a specific application.

If you want to perform actions on the artifacts belonging to a specific BizTalk application, you have to obtain a reference on the desired application and then use the methods and properties of the `Application` class listed in Tables 10-21 and 10-22.

Table 10-21. *Application Class Properties*

Property Name	Description
Assemblies	Read-only. Returns a collection of assemblies associated with the application.
BackReferences	Read-only. Returns a collection of applications referencing the application.
BtsCatalogExplorer	Read-only. Returns the BtsCatalogExplorer object containing the Application object.
Description	Gets or sets the application description.
IsConfigured	Read-only. Returns a Boolean value indicating that all orchestrations' ports in the application are bound.
IsDefaultApplication	Read-only. Returns a Boolean value indicating whether the application is the default application.
IsSystem	Read-only. Returns a Boolean value indicating whether or not the application is the system application.
Name	Gets or sets the name of the application.
Orchestrations	Read-only. Returns a collection of the orchestrations associated with the application.
Pipelines	Read-only. Returns a collection of the pipelines associated with the application.
Policies	Read-only. Returns a collection of the policies associated with the application.
ReceivePorts	Read-only. Returns a collection of the receive ports associated with the application.
References	Read-only. Returns a collection of the applications referenced by the application.
Roles	Read-only. Returns a collection of the roles associated with the application.
Schemas	Read-only. Returns a collection of the schemas associated with the application.
SendPortGroups	Read-only. Returns a collection of send port groups associated with the application.
SendPorts	Read-only. Returns a collection of the send ports associated with the application.
Status	Read-only. Returns the status of the application.
Transforms	Read-only. Returns a collection of the maps associated with the application.

Table 10-22. *Application Class Public Methods*

Method Name	Description
AddNewReceivePort	Adds a new receive port to the ReceivePorts collection
AddNewSendPort	Adds a new send port to the SendPorts collection
AddNewSendPortGroup	Adds a new send port group to the SendPortGroups collection
AddReference	Adds a BizTalk application to the References collection
RemoveReference	Removes a BizTalk application from the References collection
Start	Starts all orchestrations, send ports, and send port groups, and enables all receive locations belonging to this and referenced applications
Stop	Stops all orchestrations, send ports, and send port groups, and disables all receive locations belonging to this and referenced applications

Assuming you have an application named PROBIZTALK Application, the code in Listing 10-9 shows how you can obtain a reference to this application and to add a send port to it.

Listing 10-9. *Adding a New Send Port to a Specific BizTalk Application*

```
using System;
using Microsoft.BizTalk.ExplorerOM

namespace AddSendPort
{
    class Program
    {
        static void Main(string[] args)
        {
            CreateSendPort();

        }


        private static void CreateSendPort()
        {
            // Connect to the BizTalk configuration database
           BtsCatalogExplorer catalog = new BtsCatalogExplorer();
            catalog.ConnectionString = "Server=PROBIZTALK;Initial Catalog=
BizTalkMgmtDb;Integrated Security=SSPI;";

            try
            {
               // Get a reference on existing BizTalk Application
               Application app = catalog.Applications["PROBIZTALK Application"]
```

```
                // Create static one-way send port
                SendPort myStaticOnewaySendPort = app.AddNewSendPort(false, false);
                myStaticOnewaySendPort.Name = "PROBiztalkSendPort";
                myStaticOnewaySendPort.PrimaryTransport.TransportType =
catalog.ProtocolTypes["HTTP"];
                myStaticOnewaySendPort.PrimaryTransport.Address =
"http://DestinationUrl";
                myStaticOnewaySendPort.SendPipeline =
catalog.Pipelines["Microsoft.BizTalk.DefaultPipelines.XMLTransmit"];

                // Commit changes to BizTalk configuration database
                catalog.SaveChanges();
            }
            catch (Exception ex)
            {
                catalog.DiscardChanges();
            }
        }
    }
}
```

If you happened to work with previous versions of BizTalk Server, you are no doubt aware that starting BizTalk solutions was not easy. For example, if one orchestration called another, they had to be started and stopped in the following strict order: called orchestrations first, calling orchestrations last in case of starting, and in reverse order in case of stopping. That's not a problem if you had only a few orchestrations, but what if there were dozens of them and they were interdependent? And how about starting dozens or even hundreds of ports one by one manually? Fortunately, BizTalk Server 2009 provides an easy solution. Simply use the `Start` and `Stop` methods of the `Application` class, taking values from the `ApplicationStartOption` and `ApplicationStopOption` enumerations as parameters. Available values are listed in Tables 10-23 and 10-24.

Table 10-23. *ApplicationStartOption Enumeration*

Enumeration Value	Description
DeployAllPolicies	Specifies all policies to be deployed
EnableAllReceiveLocations	Specifies all receive locations to be enabled
StartAllOrchestrations	Specifies all orchestrations to be started
StartAllSendPortGroups	Specifies all send port groups to be started
StartAllSendPorts	Specifies all send ports to be started
StartReferencedApplications	Specifies all referenced applications to be started
StartAll	Specifies all of the preceding to be enabled and started

Table 10-24. *ApplicationStopOption Enumeration*

Enumeration Value	Description
UndeployAllPolicies	Specifies all policies to be undeployed
DisableAllReceiveLocations	Specifies all receive locations to be disabled
UnenlistAllOrchestrations	Specifies all orchestrations to be unenlisted and stopped
UnenlistAllSendPortGroups	Specifies all send port groups to be unenlisted and stopped
UnenlistAllSendPorts	Specifies all send ports to be unenlisted and stopped
StopReferencedApplications	Specifies referenced applications to be stopped
StopAll	Specifies all of the preceding options

In order to start your application, you can use the code shown in Listing 10-10.

Listing 10-10. *Starting Biztalk Application*

```
using System;
using Microsoft.BizTalk.ExplorerOM;

namespace BTSApplication
{
    class Program
    {

        static void Main(string[] args)
        {
            BtsCatalogExplorer catalog = new BtsCatalogExplorer();
            catalog.ConnectionString = "Server=.;Initial Catalog=BizTalkMgmtDb;
Integrated Security=SSPI;";
            Application app = catalog.Applications["PROBIZTALK Application"]
            app.Start(StartApplicationOptions.StartAll);

        }

    }
}
```

BtsAssembly

The last class we are going to consider is BtsAssembly. Using the properties of this class listed in Table 10-25, you can get access to the collections of compiled artifacts contained in the assembly.

Table 10-25. *BtsAssembly Class Properties*

Property Name	Description
`Application`	Read-only. Returns the application this assembly is associated with.
`BtsCatalogExplorer`	Read-only. Returns the `IBtsCatalogExplorer` interface, which represents the database hosting the assembly.
`Culture`	Read-only. Returns the culture of the assembly.
`DisplayName`	Read-only. Returns the display name of the assembly.
`IsSystem`	Read-only. Indicates whether or not the assembly is system (deployed during Biztalk installation).
`Name`	Read-only. Returns the name of the assembly.
`Orchestrations`	Read-only. Returns the collection of orchestrations in the assembly.
`Pipelines`	Read-only. Returns the collection of pipelines in the assembly.
`PortTypes`	Read-only. Returns the collection of port types in the assembly.
`PublicToken`	Read-only. Returns the public token of the assembly.
`Roles`	Read-only. Returns the collection of roles in the assembly.
`Schemas`	Read-only. Returns the collection of schemas in the assembly.
`Transforms`	Read-only. Returns the collection of maps in the assembly.
`Version`	Read-only. Returns the version of the assembly.

Assuming you have a deployed assembly named BTSOrchestrations, Listing 10-11 shows how you can print out orchestration names contained in this assembly using properties of the `BtsAssembly` class.

Listing 10-11. *Enumerating Orchestrations*

```
using System;
using System.Text;
using Microsoft.BizTalk.ExplorerOM;

namespace EnumerateOrchestrations
{
    class Program
    {

        static void Main(string[] args)
        {
            EnumerateOrchestrations();
            Console.ReadKey();
        }
```

```
        public static void EnumerateOrchestrations()
        {
            BtsCatalogExplorer catalog = new BtsCatalogExplorer();
            catalog.ConnectionString = "Server=.;Initial Catalog=BizTalkMgmtDb;
Integrated Security=SSPI;";
            BtsAssembly assembly = catalog.Assemblies["BTSOrchestrations"];

            foreach (BtsOrchestration orch in assembly.Orchestrations )
            {
                Console.WriteLine("\tOrchestrationName:{0}",
                     orch.FullName);

            }
        }
    }
}
```

As you see, programming using ExplorerOM is not very complicated. Once you get a fundamental idea how classes representing BizTalk artifacts are related to each other, the rest is quite straightforward. For the full list of classes and interfaces, please refer to the product documentation.

MSBuild

MSBuild is Microsoft's build platform and is the technology used by Visual Studio. MSBuild is also included in the .NET Framework and can be used to build Visual Studio projects without requiring Visual Studio to be installed.

The ability to take advantage of MSBuild represents one of the major new features in BizTalk Server 2009. In previous chapters, we talked about the changes that took place in the BizTalk project format. BizTalk has changed its project type to be built on the standard C# project type. The BizTalk project type then adds other flavorings to incorporate the additional functionality that is required by BizTalk on top of the standard C# project type. One of the capabilities that surfaces through the use of this new project type is the use of MSBuild.

Evidence that things have changed is that you can now open a command prompt, navigate to any of your BizTalk Server 2009 projects, type **MSBuild <your project name>.btproj**, and your project will be compiled.

Additionally, you can now have a build environment that no longer requires Visual Studio be installed. This is a huge step forward in being able to integrate with the way that all other .NET projects are built and in being able to take advantage of build automation.

Installing MSBuild

When you install BizTalk Server 2009, you'll see a new check box at the bottom of the available components list, as shown in Figure 10-18. This check box allows you to install just the deployment components.

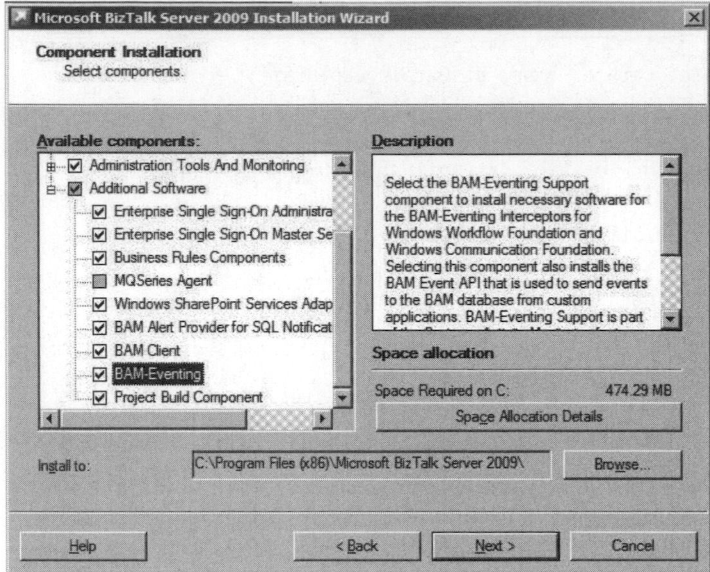

Figure 10-18. *Installation Wizard: Component Installation page*

When setting up your build server, you will install just the deployment components, as shown in Figure 10-18, and doing so will install the MSBuild target files. There are two MSBuild target files that will be installed. They are BizTalkC.Targets and BizTalkCommon.Targets.

Incorporating Team Foundation Build

Although build automation is an important step toward process maturity, a company can take a more encompassing step into the Application Lifecycle Management role by incorporating the tools and functionality found in the Team Foundation Build (also called Team Build) in TFS. Team Foundation Build provides the functionality of the build server while also being part of, and integrating with the components of, the Visual Studio Team Foundation Server. With Team Foundation Build, build managers can synchronize source code, compile an application, run unit tests, perform code analysis, release builds to the file server, and publish build reports showing success or failure of the build and tests. By incorporating Team Foundation Build in your environment, you can take advantage of the whole build lifecycle. BizTalk Server 2009 can now fully participate in this part of the ALM cycle.

Automating Deployment

So far we have talked about the ability to automate the build process with MSBuild. You can also use MSBuild to automate the deployment process.

A number of extension libraries are available. The two most widely known and used are SDC Tasks, found at `http://www.codeplex.com/sdctasks`, and MSBuildTasks, found at `http://msbuildtasks.tigris.org/`. The components in these libraries provide the functionality to create web sites, create application pools, configure virtual servers, create Active Directory users, create folder shares, install into the GAC, configure SQL Server, and configure BizTalk Server.

Together these tools provide the custom tasks to allow you to create a complete automated deployment script.

If you find that you need additional functionality that is not supplied with MSBuild or through any of the available community libraries, you can extend MSBuild through the use of .NET code by creating components that implement the Microsoft.Build.Framework.ITask interface.

Looking at an Example

Earlier in the chapter we looked at deploying the solution you created through the MSI functionality. Now, let's take a look at a simple, fully functional MSBuild script, including the command-line arguments to call the build. This script will deploy the sample solution that is included in the download for this chapter. Here's the script:

```
<!  Command line arguments to call this script:
msbuild BtsAutomatedBuildSample.build /p:Configuration=Debug
/logger:FileLogger,Microsoft.Build.Engine;logfile=MyLog.log;
append=true;verbosity=diagnostic;encoding=utf-8

We are using the latest version of the sdc tasks and the
names are still prefixed with BizTalk 2006 but they still apply to BizTalk 2009.
  >

<Project DefaultTargets="GetBizTalkInstallLocation;BuildBTSSolution" xmlns=➥
"http://schemas.microsoft.com/developer/msbuild/2003">
  <Import Project="..\Sdc_Tasks_2.1.2688.0\Microsoft.Sdc.Common.tasks"/>
  <Import Project="$(MSBuildExtensionsPath)\MSBuildCommunityTasks\MSBuild. ➥
Community.Tasks.Targets"/>

<PropertyGroup Condition="'$(Configuration)'=='Debug'">
<BinPath>.\bin</BinPath>
<BtsInstallLocation>C:\Program Files\Microsoft BizTalk Server 2009➥
</BtsInstallLocation>
<BtsApplicationName>BtsAutomatedBuildSample</BtsApplicationName>
<ApplicationExists>False</ApplicationExists>
    <SchemasAssemblyPath>$(MSBuildProjectDirectory)\
➥BtsAutomatedBuildSampleSchemas\bin\Development\➥
BtsAutomatedBuildSampleSchemas.dll</SchemasAssemblyPath>
    <MapsAssemblyPath>$(MSBuildProjectDirectory)\BtsAutomatedBuildSampleMaps
➥\bin\Development\BtsAutomatedBuildSampleMaps.dll</MapsAssemblyPath>
    <PipelineComponentsAssemblyPath>$(MSBuildProjectDirectory)\➥
BtsAutomatedBuildSamplePipelineComponents\bin\Debug\➥
BtsAutomatedBuildSamplePipelineComponents.dll</PipelineComponentsAssemblyPath>
    <PipelinesAssemblyPath>$(MSBuildProjectDirectory)\➥
BtsAutomatedBuildSamplePipelines\bin\Development\➥
BtsAutomatedBuildSamplePipelines.dll</PipelinesAssemblyPath>
```

```
    <OrchestrationsAssemblyPath>$(MSBuildProjectDirectory)\➥
BtsAutomatedBuildSampleOrchestrations\bin\Development\➥
BtsAutomatedBuildSampleOrchestrations.dll</OrchestrationsAssemblyPath>
    <BindingFilePath>$(MSBuildProjectDirectory)\➥
BtsAutomatedBuildSample.BindingInfo.xml</BindingFilePath>
  </PropertyGroup>

  <Target Name="BuildBTSSolution" DependsOnTargets="ApplicationExists;MakeBinDir">
<MSBuild Projects="$(MSBuildProjectDirectory)\BtsAutomatedBuildSample.sln" ➥
Properties="Configuration=Debug" />
<CallTarget Targets="MoveAssembliesToBin" />
<CallTarget Targets="CreateBizTalkApplication" />
<CallTarget Targets="DeployPipelineComponents" />
<CallTarget Targets="DeployBtsResources" />
<CallTarget Targets="DeployBindings" />
<CallTarget Targets="ExportMsi" />
  </Target>

  <Target Name="MakeBinDir" Condition="!Exists('$(BinPath)')">
<Message Text="Creating bin directory... $(BinPath)" />
<MakeDir Directories= "$(BinPath)"/>
  </Target>

  <Target Name="MoveAssembliesToBin" DependsOnTargets="MakeBinDir">
<Message Text="Move assemblies to common bin directory" />
<Copy SourceFiles="$(SchemasAssemblyPath);$(MapsAssemblyPath);➥
$(PipelinesAssemblyPath);$(OrchestrationsAssemblyPath)"➥
 DestinationFolder="$(BinPath)" />
  </Target>

  <Target Name="CreateBizTalkApplication" Condition="$(ApplicationExists)=='False'">
<Message Text="Creating $(BtsApplicationName) Application..." />
<CallTarget Targets="RemoveApplication" />
<BizTalk2006.Application.Create Application="$(BtsApplicationName)" />
<!  <Exec Command ='"$(BtsInstallLocation)\BTSTask" AddApp ➥
/ApplicationName:$(BtsApplicationName)' />  >
  </Target>

  <Target Name="DeployBtsResources">
<Message Text="Adding Resources (deploying) assemblies to ➥
$(BtsApplicationName)Application" />
<!  <Exec Command ='"$(BtsInstallLocation)\BTSTask" AddResource ➥
/ApplicationName:$(BtsApplicationName) /Type:System.BizTalk:BizTalkAssembly ➥
/Source:"$(SchemasAssemblyPath)"' />  >
<BizTalk2006.Assembly.Deploy Application="$(BtsApplicationName)" AssemblyPath=➥
"$(SchemasAssemblyPath)" InstallInGac="true" />
```

```
<BizTalk2006.Assembly.Deploy Application="$(BtsApplicationName)" AssemblyPath=➥
"$(MapsAssemblyPath)" InstallInGac="true" />
<BizTalk2006.Assembly.Deploy Application="$(BtsApplicationName)" AssemblyPath=➥
"$(PipelinesAssemblyPath)" InstallInGac="true" />
<BizTalk2006.Assembly.Deploy Application="$(BtsApplicationName)" AssemblyPath=➥
"$(OrchestrationsAssemblyPath)" InstallInGac="true" />
  </Target>

  <Target Name="ApplicationExists">
<BizTalk2006.Application.Exists Application="$(BtsApplicationName)">
      <Output TaskParameter="DoesExist" PropertyName="ApplicationExists" />
</BizTalk2006.Application.Exists>
<Message text="Application Exists: $(ApplicationExists)" />
  </Target>

  <Target Name="RemoveApplication" Condition="$(ApplicationExists)=='True'">
<Message Text="Removing $(BtsApplicationName) Application..." />
<BizTalk2006.Application.Stop Application="$(BtsApplicationName)" />
<BizTalk2006.Application.Delete Application="$(BtsApplicationName)" />
  </Target>

  <Target Name="DeployBindings">
<Message Text="Deploying bindings" />
<Exec Command ='"$(BtsInstallLocation)\BTSTask" ImportBindings /Source:➥
"$(BindingFilePath)" /ApplicationName:$(BtsApplicationName)' />
  </Target>

  <Target Name="ExportMsi">
<Exec Command ='"$(BtsInstallLocation)\BTSTask" ExportApp /ApplicationName:➥
$(BtsApplicationName) /Package:"$(MSBuildProjectDirectory)\➥
$(BinPath)\$(BtsApplicationName).msi"' />
  </Target>

  <Target Name="DeployPipelineComponents">
<Message Text="Moving pipeline components to BTS dir" />
<Copy SourceFiles="$(PipelineComponentsAssemblyPath)" DestinationFolder=➥
"$(BtsInstallLocation)\Pipeline Components" />
  </Target>

  <Target Name="GetBizTalkInstallLocation">
<Registry.Get RegistryHive="LocalMachine" Key=➥
"Software\Microsoft\BizTalk Server\3.0\" Value="InstallPath">
      <Output TaskParameter="Data" PropertyName="BtsInstallLocation"/>
</Registry.Get>
<Message Text="BizTalk Install Location is $(BtsInstallLocation)" />
  </Target>

</Project>
```

This sample MSBuild deployment script, as well as the BtsAutomatedBuildSample solution, is available in the example download for this book on www.apress.com.

As you look over this script, you'll see a number of interesting items. The first is that the script will build the solution by invoking MSBuild inside an MSBuild script. The invocation is done with the MSBuild task. This task uses the same MSBuild process to execute the child build process. This approach is faster than using the Exec task since no new MSBuild process is created.

Next, the BuildBTSSolution target controls what other targets are called. It becomes very easy to see what steps the script will follow during execution.

Take a look at the RemoveApplication target. You can set conditions that will determine whether the target will get executed. A condition can also be set on the PropertyGroup node. In this sample, we could create additional PropertyGroup nodes with different conditions such as Release. The new node would contain the specific data required for that type of build.

Lastly, our example uses the SDC tasks to provide specific BizTalk deployment functions. The library currently differentiates between BizTalk 2004 and BizTalk 2006 functions. The BizTalk 2006 methods still apply to BizTalk 2009.

Moving Forward with MSBuild

Our intention has not been to provide a tutorial on MSBuild. We merely wanted to show how easy it is to create a fully functional build and deploy script. You can find more information on MSDN at http://msdn.microsoft.com/en-us/library/0k6kkbsd.aspx. One useful ability not shown here is being able to keep track of which targets were successful so that if an error occurred and you needed to restart the script, it would not rerun the successfully executed targets.

When looking at deployment technologies, a frequent question is, why use MSBuild instead of the MSI functionality built into BizTalk? There are a number of factors that may sway you to one side over the other.

If you are doing continuous builds or are going to use the Team Build functionality, then you are most likely already working with MSBuild. At this point you can continue to expand on the MSBuild script to include the deployment. This will automate the entire process including such things as stopping applications and uninstalling, installing, and restarting hosts.

MSBuild is also beneficial if you have more artifacts to your application than those contained in BizTalk. The MSI functionality is primarily focused on artifacts used by the BizTalk application. MSBuild allows you to script the deployment and configuration of all portions of the larger application including security settings, IIS functionality, custom .NET components, and other server functionality such as SQL Server, Commerce Server, and others.

PowerShell

Windows PowerShell is a command-line shell that includes a scripting language. The scripting language is integrated with the .NET Framework through specialized .NET classes called *cmdlets* (pronounced "commandlets"). These cmdlets, along with regular .NET classes, are the building blocks for creating scripts to perform administrative tasks.

Many Microsoft applications have started creating their interfaces on top of exposed PowerShell cmdlets. The stated direction is that management applications will be built on top of PowerShell. Examples of products currently following that direction are SQL Server and

Exchange Server. BizTalk, at this point, is not built on a set of cmdlets. However, that doesn't have to stop you from taking advantage of using PowerShell with BizTalk.

Interacting with BizTalk's WMI Model

BizTalk has an extensive WMI object model that you can use to manage your servers (as discussed earlier in the WMI section). WMI, however, can be rather difficult to work with. PowerShell makes working with WMI quite a bit easier, and you can interactively execute and test any WMI query or command.

A quick example of using PowerShell to query WMI can be as simple as listing all the BizTalk hosts. Here's how to do that:

```
$hosts = get-wmiobject MSBTS_HostInstance -namespace 'root\MicrosoftBizTalkServer'
$hosts | sort HostName | ft HostName, HostType
```

Earlier in this chapter, in Listings 10-3 and 10-4, we looked at creating hosts using WMI. Those examples utilized C# and VBScript. Let's take a look at the same functionality, but this time we'll utilize PowerShell. The following script creates the same hosts as in Listings 10-3 and 10-4:

```
function CreateHost
{
    param
     (
        [string] $HostName,
        [string] $HostType,
        [string] $NTGroupName,
        [bool] $Trust
    )

    $WMIBizTalkHostSettings = ([WmiClass]"root\MicrosoftBizTalkServer: ➥
MSBTS_HostSetting").PSBase.CreateInstance()


            #set the properties for the Managementobject
            $WMIBizTalkHostSettings["Name"] = $HostName
            $WMIBizTalkHostSettings["HostType"] = $HostType ➥
#1 - In process 2-Isolated
            $WMIBizTalkHostSettings["NTGroupName"] = $NTGroupName
            $WMIBizTalkHostSettings["AuthTrusted"] =$Trust # -1

            #create the Managementobject
            $WMIBizTalkHostSettings.PSBase.Putx(2) #2 = Create Host
}
```

You can also utilize PowerShell to interact with the ExplorerOM classes as well as executables such as BTSTask.exe, and you can create PowerShell scripts to do other administration tasks.

Starting and Stopping BizTalk Applications

The following code shows how you can use PowerShell to manage (starting or stopping) a BizTalk application:

```
function ManageApplication
{
    param
    (
        [string] $ApplicationName,
        [bool] $StartApplication,
        [int] $ApplicationOptions #6 - Stop All
    )
    $BizTalkExpObj.Refresh()
    [Microsoft.BizTalk.ExplorerOM.Application] $BizTalkApplication = ➥
$BizTalkExpObj.Applications[$ApplicationName]

    if($StartApplication -eq $TRUE)
    {

        foreach($RecPort in $BizTalkApplication.ReceivePorts)
        {
            foreach($RecLoc in $RecPort.ReceiveLocations)
            {
                $RecLoc.Enable = $TRUE
                Write-Output  $RecLoc.PSBase.Name " Starting Receive Location "
            }
        }

        foreach($SendPort in $BizTalkApplication.SendPorts)
        {
            $SendPort.Status =3
            Write-Output  $SendPort.PSBase.Name " Starting Send Port "
        }

        foreach($Orchestration in $BizTalkApplication.Orchestrations)
        {
            $Orchestration.Status = 3
                Write-Output  $Orchestration..PSBase.FullName ➥
" Starting Orchestration "
        }
    }
    else
```

```
    {
        foreach($RecPort in $BizTalkApplication.ReceivePorts)
        {
            foreach($RecLoc in $RecPort.ReceiveLocations)
            {
                $RecLoc.Enable = $FALSE
            }
        }

        foreach($SendPort in $BizTalkApplication.SendPorts)
        {
            $SendPort.Status =1
        }

        foreach($Orchestration in $BizTalkApplication.Orchestrations)
        {
            $Orchestration.Status = 1
        }
    }

    Write-Output "Commiting changes...."
    $BizTalkExpObj.SaveChanges()
    Write-Output "Done!"
}
```

Starting and Stopping Host Instances

Although the preceding script showed how to manage the application, you will definitely find the need to be able to start and stop host instances. The following script shows how you can do that:

```
param
    (
        [switch] $start,
        [switch] $stop
    )

function get-hosts
{
   get-wmiobject MSBTS_HostInstance `
      -namespace 'root\MicrosoftBizTalkServer' `
      -filter HostType=1
}
```

```
function stop-host($host)
{
   $hostname = $host.HostName
   if ( $host.ServiceState -ne 1 )
   {
      "Stopping Host $hostname"
      [void]$host.Stop()
   }
}

function start-host($host)
{
   $hostname = $host.HostName
   if ( $host.ServiceState -eq 1 )
   {
      "Starting Host $hostname"
      [void]$host.Start()
   }
}

if ( !($stop) -and !($start) )
{
   $stop = $true
   $start = $true
}

if ( $stop )
{
   get-hosts | %{ stop-host($_) }
}

if ( $start )
{
   get-hosts | %{ start-host($_) }
}
```

When working with the previous script, you can call it, and it will stop and start each host instance. If you call it and pass either `-start` or `-stop`, it will do only that task.

Deploying with PowerShell

Administration tasks aren't limited to managing an application once it has been deployed. PowerShell can also be used for deployment. The following code shows an example of interacting with BTSTask.exe to import a bindings file:

```
function ImportBindingFile
{
    param
    (
        [string] $BindingsFile,
        [string] $ApplicationName
    )

    BTSTask ImportBindings "/ApplicationName:$ApplicationName",➥
 "/Source:$BindingsFile"

    if($LASTEXITCODE -eq 0)
    {
        "Bindings file succesfully imported"
    }
    else
    {
        "Bindings file FAILED imported"
    }

}
```

Now let's take a look at a simple fully functional PowerShell deployment script. This script performs essentially the same tasks that were provided by the MSBuild script earlier. The following script will deploy the sample solution that is included in the download for this chapter:

```
set-psdebug -strict

[System.Reflection.Assembly]::LoadFrom( "C:\Program Files\Microsoft BizTalk ➥
Server 2009\Developer Tools  \Microsoft.BizTalk.ExplorerOM.dll" )

[Microsoft.BizTalk.ExplorerOM.BtsCatalogExplorer] $BizTalkExpObj = ➥
New-Object Microsoft.BizTalk.ExplorerOM.BtsCatalogExplorer

$BizTalkExpObj.ConnectionString = "SERVER=.;DATABASE=BizTalkMgmtDb;➥
Integrated Security=SSPI"

function DeployApplication
{
    #Set the deployment variables and locations
    $ApplicationName = "BtsAutomatedBuildSample"

    $ProjectDirectory = "C:\BtsAutomatedBuildSample"

    $BindingFilePath = $ProjectDirectory + "\BtsAutomatedBuildSample. ➥
BindingInfo.xml"
```

```
    $SchemaAssemblyPath = $ProjectDirectory + "\BtsAutomatedBuildSampleSchemas\➥
bin\Debug\BtsAutomatedBuildSampleSchemas.dll"
    $MapAssemblyPath = $ProjectDirectory + "\BtsAutomatedBuildSampleMaps\bin\➥
Debug\BtsAutomatedBuildSampleMaps.dll"
    $PipelineAssemblyPath = $ProjectDirectory + ➥
"\BtsAutomatedBuildSamplePipelines\bin\Debug\BtsAutomatedBuildSamplePipelines.dll"
    $PipelineComponentAssemblyPath = $ProjectDirectory + ➥
"\BtsAutomatedBuildSamplePipelineComponents\bin\Debug\➥
BtsAutomatedBuildSamplePipelineComponents.dll"
    $OrchestrationAssemblyPath = $ProjectDirectory + ➥
"\BtsAutomatedBuildSampleOrchestrations➥
\bin\Debug\BtsAutomatedBuildSampleOrchestrations.dll"

    $BizTalkInstallPath = "c:\Program Files\Microsoft BizTalk Server 2009\➥
Pipeline Components"

    $BizTalkExpObj.Refresh()
    "Refeshing the BizTalk Explorer Object"

    #Check to see if the application already exists
    if($BizTalkExpObj.Applications[$ApplicationName].Name -eq $ApplicationName)
    {
        RemoveApplication -BizTalkApplicationName:$ApplicationName
    }

    CreateApplication -BizTalkApplicationName:$ApplicationName -➥
BizTalkApplicationDescription:"Sample Build Application"

    "Loading Assemblies"
    LoadBizTalkAssembly -assemblyDLL:$SchemaAssemblyPath ➥
-BizTalkApplicationName:$ApplicationName
    LoadBizTalkAssembly -assemblyDLL:$MapAssemblyPath -BizTalkApplicationName:➥
$ApplicationName
    LoadBizTalkAssembly -assemblyDLL:$PipelineAssemblyPath ➥
-BizTalkApplicationName:$ApplicationName
    LoadBizTalkAssembly -assemblyDLL:$OrchestrationAssemblyPath -➥
BizTalkApplicationName:$ApplicationName

    #copy pipeline component
    Copy-Item $PipelineComponentAssemblyPath $BizTalkInstallPath

    ImportBindingFile -ApplicationName:$ApplicationName -BindingsFile:➥
$BindingFilePath

    ManageApplication -ApplicationName:$ApplicationName -ApplicationOptions:6 -➥
StartApplication:$TRUE
}
```

```
function RemoveApplication
{
    param
    (
        [string] $BizTalkApplicationName
    )

    #Backup the current configuraiton before we remove everything
    ExportApplication -ApplicationName:$BizTalkApplicationName  -ExportPath:➥
"C:\TEMP\"  -PolicyName:$PolicyName -MajorVersion:1 -MinorVersion:0

    "Shutting down any running instances...."
    #Shutdown the application and its send/receive ports
    ManageApplication -ApplicationName:$BizTalkApplicationName  ➥
-StartApplication:
$FALSE

    "Removing Application...."
    #Remove the application from the administrative database
    RemoveBizTalkApplication -Application:$BizTalkApplicationName

    "Commiting Removal Changes......"
    $BizTalkExpObj.SaveChanges()
    $BizTalkExpObj.Refresh()
}


function CreateApplication
{
    param
    (
        [string] $BizTalkApplicationName,
        [string] $BizTalkApplicationDescription
    )

    #$BizTalkExpObj.Refresh()
    $Application = $BizTalkExpObj.AddNewApplication();

    $Application.Name = $BizTalkApplicationName
    $Application.Description = $BizTalkApplicationDescription
    $BizTalkExpObj.SaveChanges()
}
```

```
function CreateHost
{
    param
    (
        [string] $HostName,
        [string] $HostType,
        [string] $NTGroupName,
        [bool]   $Trust
    )

    $WMIBizTalkHostSettings = ([WmiClass]"root\MicrosoftBizTalkServer:➥
MSBTS_HostSetting").PSBase.CreateInstance()

            #set the properties for the Managementobject
            $WMIBizTalkHostSettings["Name"] = 'TEST'
            $WMIBizTalkHostSettings["HostType"] = 1 #1 - In process 2-Isolated
            $WMIBizTalkHostSettings["NTGroupName"] = "BizTalk Application Users"
            $WMIBizTalkHostSettings["AuthTrusted"] = -1

            #create the Managementobject
            $WMIBizTalkHostSettings.PSBase.Putx(2) #2 = Create Host
}


function LoadBizTalkAssembly
{
    param
    (
        [string] $assemblyDLL,
        [string] $BizTalkApplicationName
    )

    # This is a demonstration of capturing output from a command line application
    $RC = (BTSTask AddResource "/ApplicationName:$BizTalkApplicationName" ➥
"/Type:System.BizTalk:BizTalkAssembly" "/Source:$assemblyDLL" ➥
"/Options:GacOnAdd" "/Overwrite")
}


function ImportBindingFile
{
    param
    (
        [string] $BindingsFile,
        [string] $ApplicationName
    )
```

```
    BTSTask ImportBindings "/ApplicationName:$ApplicationName", ➥
"/Source:$BindingsFile"

    if($LASTEXITCODE -eq 0)
    {
        "Bindings file succesfully imported"
    }
    else
    {
        "Bindings file FAILED imported"
    }
}

function RemoveBizTalkApplication
{
    param
    (
        [string] $Application
    )

    BTSTask RemoveApp "/ApplicationName:$Application"
}

function ManageApplication
{
    param
    (
        [string] $ApplicationName,
        [bool]   $StartApplication,
        [int]    $ApplicationOptions #6 - Stop All
    )

    $BizTalkExpObj.Refresh()
    [Microsoft.BizTalk.ExplorerOM.Application] $BizTalkApplication = ➥
$BizTalkExpObj.Applications[$ApplicationName]

    if($StartApplication -eq $TRUE)
    {
        foreach($RecPort in $BizTalkApplication.ReceivePorts)
        {
            foreach($RecLoc in $RecPort.ReceiveLocations)
            {
                $RecLoc.Enable = $TRUE
Write-Output  $RecLoc.PSBase.Name " Starting Receive Location "
            }sendmail
        }
```

```
        foreach($SendPort in $BizTalkApplication.SendPorts)
        {
            $SendPort.Status =3
            Write-Output  $SendPort.PSBase.Name " Starting Send Port "
        }

        foreach($Orchestration in $BizTalkApplication.Orchestrations)
        {
            $Orchestration.Status = 3
Write-Output  $Orchestration..PSBase.FullName " Starting Orchestration "
        }
    }
    else
    {
        foreach($RecPort in $BizTalkApplication.ReceivePorts)
        {
            foreach($RecLoc in $RecPort.ReceiveLocations)
            {
                $RecLoc.Enable = $FALSE
            }
        }

        foreach($SendPort in $BizTalkApplication.SendPorts)
        {
            $SendPort.Status =1
        }

        foreach($Orchestration in $BizTalkApplication.Orchestrations)
        {
            $Orchestration.Status = 1
        }
    }

    Write-Output "Commiting changes...."
    $BizTalkExpObj.SaveChanges()
    Write-Output "Deployment Finished!"
}


function ExportApplication
{
    param
```

```
    (
        [string] $ApplicationName,
        [string] $ExportPath,
        [string] $PolicyName,
        [string] $MajorVersion,
        [string] $MinorVersion
    )

    #Export file Names
    $MSIFileName = $ExportPath + $ApplicationName + ".msi"
    $BindingsFileName = $ExportPath + $ApplicationName + "Binding.xml"

    #Export the BizTalk Application to an MSI File
    BTSTask ExportApp "/ApplicationName:$ApplicationName" "/Package:$MSIFileName"
}

#Call Functions - Script Body

#Remember that PowerShell runs sequentially and we need to declare the functions
#before we can call them.

DeployApplication

#End of Script
```

As you look over this script, there are a number of interesting items to point out:

- The first is that all functions in PowerShell must be evaluated first before they can be called. As you look at the bottom of the script, you will see the `Script Body` section where the function we want to run first is called.
- Next, you can see examples of how to call and invoke external objects and how to interact with WMI.
- Take a look at the `LoadBizTalkAssembly` function. You can see how you can interact with the BTSTask.exe command-line tool as well as how to capture the output information.
- Lastly, PowerShell can call methods on .NET components, as well as COM components and script files, making it an extensible platform for both administering as well as deploying BizTalk solutions.

As you can see, using PowerShell is straightforward, and it is very powerful. The PowerShell online help is updated frequently; you can find it on TechNet at www.microsoft.com/technet/scriptcenter/topics/winpsh/manual/default.mspx.

CHAPTER 11

To Tune or Not to Tune? Nobody Should Ask That Question

Gathering metrics to serve as the baseline for your stress and performance tests should be part of your requirements gathering. They will help you identify the maximum load that the application and environment can handle before it breaks, as well as the maximum sustainable load that can be processed. Those will become the performance goals for your solution and constitute your performance release criteria.

Most architects and developers want to jump right in and start turning BizTalk's knobs and switches without really understanding what the performance characteristics of a particular solution really are or even whether it needs to be tuned at all. Another option would be to ignore tuning altogether and end up with an application that isn't living up to its potential or getting the most out of its host hardware. This chapter will walk you through a proper load/stress test approach and provide ways that you can optimize your system's performance based on the results of those tests.

In the previous version of the book, we did exactly what you should not do. We jumped into tuning without really explaining how to get there and have been reminded by several people of this fact—our bad. We will explain a proper performance testing approach along with what types of deliverables and work analysis will need to be completed before we ever start tuning BizTalk.

What to Do First

The solution is fully developed and ready; now what? Well, since you are about to go to production, the assumption is that the application went through rigorous functional and integration testing. So what is next? Performance testing and performance tuning! To ensure a successful deployment in production, you need to gather performance statistics and come up with the proper configuration to tune your production environment.

Gather Metrics on Expected Loads

Metrics should have been gathered as part of the requirements, but if this did not happen, now would be the right time for it. If this solution is replacing an existing application or set of applications in your production environment, gathering statistics should be an easy task, and you probably had them before you started. If this is a new business application, you have to base your numbers on the expected number of users and transactions to extrapolate the number of messages and concurrent requests going through your applications.

Those metrics will then serve as the baseline for your stress and performance tests. You have to identify the maximum load that the application and environment can handle before they break as well as the maximum sustainable load that can be processed. The **maximum sustainable load** is the maximum load that your application can handle indefinitely in the production environment. This is not only a function of your solution but also a function of the environment; and if that is a shared environment, your solution's performance is affected by other applications sharing resources with yours on the same servers. This means that your performance testing environment should be as close as possible to your production environment, including other applications and solutions running on the same servers as your solution.

Prepare the Proper Environment and Gather Performance Metrics

Before immersing yourself in a tuning exercise, make sure first that you have the proper environment set up. If your organization's IT governance policies include guidelines for deploying BizTalk solutions, there is not much to do here. You simply have to follow the guidelines and use the metrics gathered earlier to ensure the availability of the proper capacity in production.

On the other hand, if this is the first time BizTalk is being used in your enterprise environment and there are no IT standards, some capacity planning and server allocation is required. It is best if this is done early on in the development process, but this absolutely must be finalized after analyzing the results of preliminary performance tests. One of the major pitfalls that many BizTalk newbies fall into is lumping BizTalk and SQL Server on one big iron server, which is not a good investment to make. It is best to separate BizTalk Server and SQL Server on separate hardware. Depending on your High Availability requirements, you may want to look into a SQL Server cluster in the backend as well. Scaling out BizTalk into a multiserver group might be an option if High Availability is a requirement or if a single BizTalk server is not enough to handle the expected load.[1]

After allocating the proper servers for the platform, you should consider using BizTalk hosts to isolate and better manage your application. Separating the send, receive, and processing functionality in different hosts is a good idea, allowing for better memory and thread management. Leveraging BizTalk hosts to isolate Send or Receive Adapter instances expected to handle a high load or large messages, or orchestrations expected to consume a considerable amount of resources, is a good idea as well. It is also highly recommended to create a separate host to handle tracking in order not to overload a processing host with that functionality. Figure 11-1 illustrates basic solution partitioning across hosts.

1 For more information on High Availability and how to scale BizTalk Server, refer to the BizTalk planning and architecture resources at msdn.microsoft.com/en-us/library/dd938840.aspx.

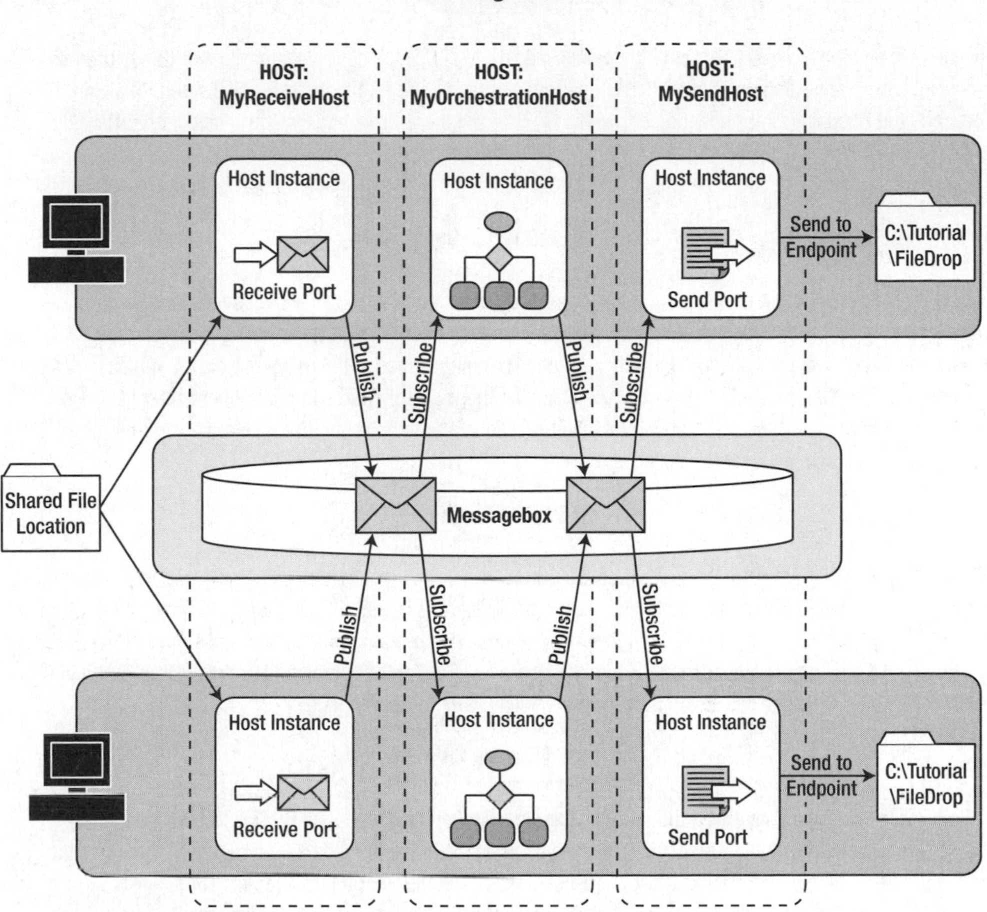

Figure 11-1. *Basic solution partitioning across hosts to optimize resource usage*

Now that the proper environment[2] is in place and your performance testing vertical is ready, you next start the load tests. In your test vertical, you need to simulate the production environment along with its relative load. This will allow for the collection of realistic performance metrics.[3] Stop the processing and sending hosts so that you gather timing metrics for message receives. Then start the processing hosts to gather timing metrics for message receives and orchestration processing. Last of all, start the sending hosts to gather metrics for the full process. Now you have the ability to estimate which part of the process is taking more time than it should and can start your tuning.

2 Make sure that you have the proper testing tools in place as well. BizUnit may be the right tool for unit testing, but you might want to look at LoadGen for stress testing. A link to the latest LoadGen version is available on MSDN.

3 Use the Performance Monitor or MOM to monitor and log performance counters, as well as the Performance tab in the Task Manager to monitor resource utilization.

WHAT HAPPENED OVER THE PAST 3 YEARS?

For those of us who have lived through the past 5 years of BizTalk's evolution, we have seen things progress to a point where analyzing and tuning BizTalk performance is no longer the art of warlocks and magicians. The tools and capabilities are now present within BizTalk and the BizTalk ecosystem to help you accurately understand what performance issues a BizTalk installation will have and accurately model the performance of that system as load increases. Let's start with BizTalk 2004 and see how the situation has progressed.

BTS 2004 Tuning

Tuning BizTalk 2004 applications is not a task for the fainthearted. The property pages for the different BizTalk artifacts in the management console had very limited capabilities, if any. Tuning the server was mainly about dabbling with obscure registry keys and changing values in the management DB tables in SQL Server—yes, the infamous adm_ServiceClass table with the magical entries to control host settings. These facts, coupled with the difficulty in understanding how the server is behaving in the first place, made BizTalk tuning closer to black magic than a science.

BTS 2006 Tuning

OK! Maybe not all the obscure registry keys have disappeared. Let's hope that will happen one day, though. For some HTTP and SOAP adapter tuning, you still have to use the registry. But, in BizTalk Server 2006, throttling is automatic. You can control it through a set of variables in property pages, or if you would like, you can still mess with config files and/or registry settings. The adm_ServiceClass table did not disappear, but it is being deprecated. You can set most of these values today using property pages.

BTS 2009 Tuning

BizTalk 2009 has essentially the same runtime engine, switches, and levers as BizTalk 2006. There is very little difference in the way that the engine behaves under load. There are new adapters that you will need to tune separately such as the WCF adapter, the SQL adapter, and the SharePoint adapter. The biggest change that has come in the past 3 years are the tools for generating load and measuring performance. We will talk about these new tools in the following sections.

Three Phases of Tuning

Whether you have been tuning BizTalk for an entire lifetime or this is your first attempt to do so, the process is not complicated and really is quite intuitive. We break performance testing up into three phases:

Phase 1—Plan your tests: Everyone makes the mistake of simply jumping into testing without really attempting to understand what the testing goals are and knowing exactly what system features you want to test. There is a potential to spend weeks of time analyzing the business requirements of a particular solution, deciding exactly how you can model a particular transaction or set of transactions. After being involved in countless BizTalk performance-tuning projects, planning is the phase that we find is always left out or marginalized. Be prepared to do a fair amount of grunt work, dummy data creation, and business analysis before you even start to think about pressing the "go" button.

Phase 2—Execute and monitor: This is the meat and potatoes of performance testing. Once you plan your tests, create your test data, and determine the set of transactions to test, this is where you run those tests and monitor the health of your system. Be prepared for many "false starts," load failures, general errors, and moments of "What is this thing doing now? Is it still working?"

Be prepared to run at least three sets of complete tests. The word *complete* means end to end with no failures. Often under load a system appears to be very busy, but in reality the tests are simply generating thousands of errors that go unnoticed. Be prepared to run several different types of tests, including steady state, floodgates, overdrive, and maximum sustainable throughput (MST).

Phase 3—Tune and retest: Tuning is where you take all the results of your hard work in phases 1 and 2 and start to see where you can improve the system's performance. Assuming everything isn't perfect the first time around, then you need to start by running a series of tests, make small incremental changes to the system, and finally retest those changes to see whether there is any improvement/degradation.

It may be surprising, but in some cases you can actually avoid phase 3. If the results of the load tests indicate that the system meets the requirements that were specified in phase 1, then stop. The following rule applies here:

If it ain't broke, don't fix it.

Don't try to tweak the performance of your solution if you met the goals—you are only setting yourself up for a headache. The ideal scenario is that BizTalk works perfectly, out of the box, with no changes from the default settings. This is by far the easiest type of solution to support should you need to call Microsoft Product Support.

Ready-to-Bake BizTalk Performance Plan

Now that you understand the three phases, we want to give you a ready-to-bake performance plan that has been proven to work over countless performance-tuning engagements. We do that in the following subsections. The expected deliverables or outputs of each phase are described so that you can have a good appreciation for the amount of work that should be invested into each phase.

Phase 1: Plan Your Tests

The first thing you need to do is write down how you will test BizTalk, the types and frequency of transactions you will model, and how you will measure and grade the performance of the system against the performance metric requirements. This plan and its associated deliverables will essentially be the performance acceptance criteria and sign-off for the solution owner. Luckily, this plan is spelled out in detail in this section for you.

These are the expected deliverables from this phase:

Performance test plan: This is a detailed plan for each type of performance test that will be executed.

A transaction set: This is a complete description of what transactions will be modeled for each type of performance test.

Required test data: This is an analysis of the type of data that will be required for each system.

Downstream system impact: This is the impact of any downstream systems that will be updated as a result of the tests.

Transaction volumes: This will be a number of quantifiable transactions per second that will represent the frequency of new messages being submitted to BizTalk.

One of the first steps that you'll want to perform in phase 1 is to model your transactions. The results from that step feed into several of the deliverables in the preceding list.

Modeling Your Transactions

Modeling transactions is by far the most important step in this phase. This step is to ensure that what you are modeling accurately represents the real-world usage of the system. Up until now, the majority of documents that you have created have been developer test data, or *dummy data*.

This also may be the first time that a system has been run end-to-end in an integrated manner under load. Often there is a series of integration tests that are done prior to this phase, but you can also use this phase to kick off the integrated system phase of your project since the deliverables and outputs will be very similar.

What you need to do is get a representation of the business transactions that will be performed once the system is put into production. Often there are "read-only" transactions and "update transactions." Following our examples from previous chapters, read-only transactions would be either product inventory data requests or product catalog data requests. In the banking sector, these would be account balance requests. Update transactions are exactly that—they update some other system based on the data sent in the document. These are typically purchase orders or account withdrawal type of transactions.

The goal here is to work with your business analysts and system owners to figure out what the most common types of transactions will be and what transactions have the biggest effect on the business. Most solutions have dozens of different transaction types, so you will have to pick an arbitrary number—say the top five transactions—and focus on them. Most projects do not have the time to accurately performance test all potential transactions types, so you will need to figure out what ones give you the biggest bang for your buck.

Determine Transaction Frequency

As part of modeling transactions, you need to determine the rate and frequency at which they occur. The terms *rate* and *frequency* may sound synonymous, but we really are referring to two different things. *Rate* refers to quantity, and *frequency* refers to how often.

For example, assume we are modeling two potential transaction types that can occur within our system within 1 hour of production. Our duration for the performance test will be 1 hour, and we need to figure out exactly how many times each of those transactions will show up within that 1-hour period. Let's assume that we have purchase order transactions and stock verification transactions; the first is an update, and the second is a read. When we receive purchase orders, we actually receive them in batches since the customers will wait until their "purchase order bucket" is full before submitting them. On average, each customer will send us 30 purchase orders at a time. Also on average, we receive orders from a customer every 2 minutes. In this case, the rate will be 30 documents, and the frequency will be 2 minutes. The stock verification requests come in as they are needed, and on average we receive three every second. In this case, we will be receiving three documents per second. It is very important to think about your transaction volumes like this because it will allow you to have a common language with the business owners who really have no idea about the intricacies of performance testing, but they do understand how many orders/stock requests they receive each day.

You also need to model the "bell curve" of your application. Almost every solution in the world has something called the 8 to 5 effect, in that they receive 95% of their usage during regular business hours. Knowing this is important because if you are unable to determine the frequency of your document submission and have only "orders per day" numbers, then you need to take that effect into account when extrapolating what your usage will look like. Often the usage bands are much smaller—more like 10 a.m. to 2 p.m. This type of load is very "bursty" and often lends itself to a system that is always in an overdrive state during regular hours.

You also need to account for the 4:30 effect. This is a pattern that sometimes occurs at the end of the day when users of the system attempt to jam in all the remaining data at the end of the day before they go home. This last-minute effort often leads to a floodgate scenario in which the load unexpectedly jumps to a point where the system is above its steady state. We will talk about this effect along with the types of performance tests you should plan to execute to account for this and several other "normal" usage spikes.

The other thing to be aware of is the "not so often but really big" transaction that occurs very infrequently but will have a major impact on the solution. These are often things like product updates or batch updates that can potentially have thousands of nested transactions within them. If your solution has this type of transaction, you need to determine whether it will be processed during the day and whether it will have a dramatic impact on performance. If it is possible, consider offloading these transactions to a receive location that is active only during nonpeak hours.

Understand the Background Noise

In most solutions, there will be a certain amount of operational work that will be happening in parallel to BizTalk. We refer to this work as "background noise." It's important to understand the types of noise that you might encounter and to account for the effects of background noise in your testing. Here are some things to watch for:

Traffic being serviced from a public web site: Often a web site that is taking customer orders, for example, will have its database physically located on the same database cluster as BizTalk. You will need to account for this load by having a web site load test running at the same time as your BizTalk performance test if this situation applies to you.

BizTalk background jobs: There are many BizTalk jobs that are executing on a scheduled basis that can affect the overall throughput of the system. It is important to make sure that the SQL Server Agent is started for the duration of your performance tests to ensure that these jobs are running while the performance test is taking place.

System scheduled tasks: Are there any operational scripts or scheduled tasks that run during the day that can affect performance such as backup jobs, log shipping jobs, cleanup scripts, and so on? In a perfect world, these should be running as well while the performance test is taking place.

Other BizTalk applications: Is this hardware that is to be used dedicated exclusively for this system, or are their other BizTalk applications running? If it is a shared environment, then performance characteristics, uptime requirements, and transaction volumes will need to be considered for all applications running in the environment.

Create Test Data

To properly load test a system, you need to have data that accurately represents what you will be expecting in production. This is where any old data from a solution that you are replacing becomes invaluable. If you don't have such data, then what teams often do is start creating spreadsheets of test data. Each sheet will represent one document type, and each column becomes a field in that message. This way, the data can easily be loaded into a database (you will see why that is important later). Be wary of repeating IDs such as OrderId or CustomerId, which can cause errors should you get a duplicate entry (don't worry, we will give you a solution to that in a bit). Try to give yourself enough data variety so that you are not repeating the same test data over and over again. You would be surprised to see how many performance problems are masked because every customer is named "Jon Doe" or every company is named "Contoso" and they are all ordering the same products.

Planning Your Test Types

There are several different types of performance tests that you will need to implement. The goals of each are different but equally important. The types of tests are as follows:

Steady state:[4] This is what you define as a "typical" usage scenario. This needs to model what you believe will be the real-world usage of your solution given the assumptions you made in phase 1. Based on this scenario, you will determine whether your solution is sustainable in that the regular operating state of your solution can adequately process the rate at which messages are published and subscribed with no backlog. This is usually where you figure out whether the hardware for your solution is adequate. Additionally, should you determine that your solution is not sustainable, you need to start identifying

4 There is an excellent article from Microsoft about what exactly sustainable throughput means. We don't want to simply rehash that information here, so see msdn.microsoft.com/en-us/library/aa560011.aspx for more information about sustainable throughput and how to define what that means for your solution.

bottlenecks or areas to tune in your solution to make it sustainable before proceeding with the other tests. In reality, if your solution is not sustainable under a steady-state condition, you have a serious problem that you need to fix by purchasing more hardware/software, tuning the application, or doing a combination of both.

Floodgate: Assuming your solution is in a steady state that is sustainable, this scenario accounts for spikes in message processing that can occur normally throughout the day. Part of the deliverables of performance testing is to make assumptions about what these spikes will look like based on past usage data, or SWAG (scientific wild-ass guess). The important factor here is to state your assumptions in your performance deliverable and have your business/system owners agree or disagree with your assumptions. These assumptions are what drives the modeling and are really the important tool to gain acceptance of the performance test approach.

Overdrive: This is a test that measures what the solution performance will look like given a constant message delivery rate that exceeds the anticipated load and creates a backlog of work. Overdrive load is load that is clearly not sustainable. The important take-away from this test is, can my solution continue to function and eventually clear the backlog assuming a constant and overwhelming flood of messages? You need to understand whether BizTalk will continue to process messages if it gets overloaded or whether the entire solution come to a grinding halt. Assuming the overdrive condition stops, how long does it take to clear the backlog, and is it linear and predictable? When the system is in overdrive, is the message processing rate constant, or does it degrade because of backups in correlating messages or related processes that also are not completing?

Determining Your Exit Criteria

Knowing when to stop is often overlooked but is very important. How do you know when you are done? Each performance test/tuning exercise needs to document what the exit criteria is for that test. The following are a few different options for exit criteria:

Pass—Performance criteria met immediately: The system was able to meet the performance criteria without any tuning required by the development team.

Pass—Performance criteria met after tuning: After tuning, the team was able to tune the solution enough to meet the performance criteria.

Fail—Performance was not met, significant redevelopment needed: This isn't necessarily a bad thing. What you are stating here is that the current code does not meet the requirements. You need to qualify that with what the current performance level is, along with an estimate to rework the solution to have it meet the requirements. If the estimate to redesign, develop, and test that piece of the application is quite big, the project management/business owner may decide that the current performance is acceptable and not worth the additional cost. This way, the decision is based on a dollar value vs. the benefit of the additional work and not on an emotional "but I need this" basis.

Fail—Performance was not met, additional hardware required: Again, this isn't necessarily a bad thing. What you are stating here is that the code cannot be optimized or changed in any way that will meet the current requirements, and all tuning options have been exhausted. The only solution is to go buy more hardware. This is often an easy decision to make because the costs associated with hardware are generally well known. Also, there is a potential to expropriate hardware that was destined for another purpose to retool a server for a dual purpose. In any case, this is a decision for the solution owner to make based on the options available at the time.

Phase 2: Create, Execute, and Analyze

Having done your planning, you can enter phase 2. Your goals in phase 2 are to create your tests, to execute them, and to analyze the results.

Your deliverables from this phase are as follows:

- The actual performance tests using your tool of choice (Visual Studio, LoadGen, and so on)
- The results of each performance test and whether the test passed the exit criteria
- An analysis of the performance counters that were captured during the tests

So, you have created your plan and you know exactly what you are going to test, how you are going to test it, and what the expected outcomes of each test are—now what? Well, you need to accurately create a series of tests that implement the goals outlined in phase 1. Additionally, you need to monitor the results of those tests to determine what exit criteria have been met. Luckily, one of the big improvements over the past 3 years has been in the tool set for this area. Each of the tools will be described as they are appropriate.

Creating Your Load Tests Using Visual Studio Team Suite

Depending on the type and complexity of the tests you want to run, you have a couple of different options for creating them. The simplest approach is to use Visual Studio Team Suite to create a set of unit tests that can be used to create messages and submit them into a queue or receive location. The easiest approach for this is to create a generic "message maker" component that reads a particular schema and gets values for new messages based on entries in a database table (this is why it is important to put your data in a database). The first thing you need to do is use the `xsd` command to generate a typed dataset for the XSD schema using the following syntax:

```
xsd /d /language:CS C:\BizTalkMessage.xsd /namespace:ProBizTalk2009
```

Figure 11-2 shows an example execution of the `xsd` command using the syntax that we've just shown. The result is a class file that we can use in our message maker component.

The message maker component will be responsible for loading the typed dataset and populating it with data from our database of test values. The class has intelligence in it to cycle through the rows in the table and mark that a row has been used in a test. If all rows are used, then it resets all usage marks and starts over. This is a very handy class because it is generic enough to be called from a Visual Studio unit test or from LoadGen, as you will see in the next section.

We then use Visual Studio to create a unit test for our message maker component, as shown in Figure 11-3. We navigate to Add and then select Unit Test.

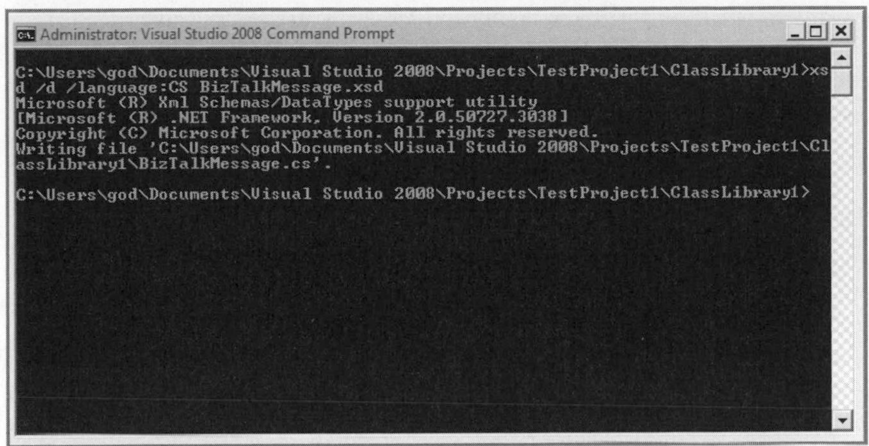

Figure 11-2. *Using xsd.exe to generate a new class from an xsd command*

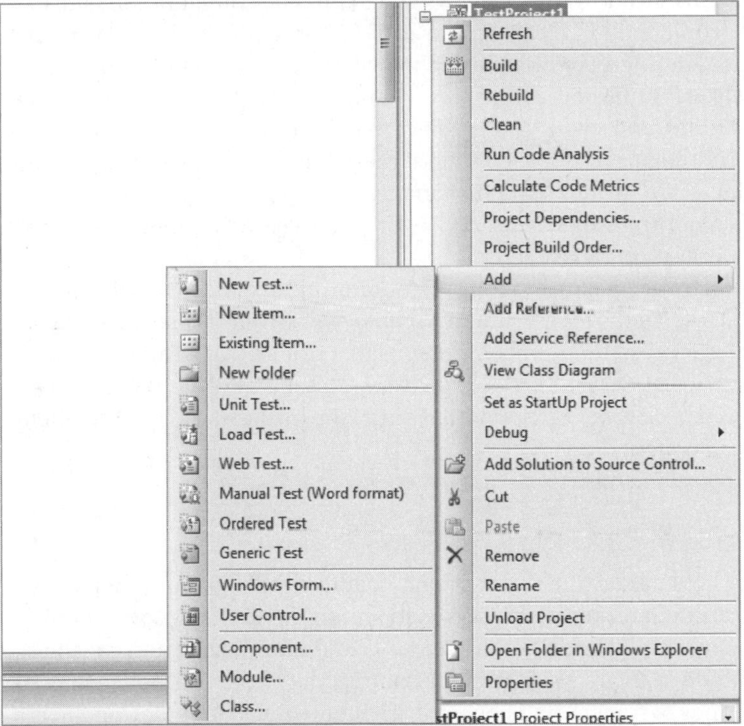

Figure 11-3. *Creating a unit test*

Once we create our unit test, all we need to do is create some simple iterative code that loops over our message creation a fixed number of times. This will, in effect, create a series of dynamic messages that can be used to test a single transaction. This is by far the easiest and most straightforward way to do performance testing in BizTalk. It also has the advantage of being tracked and can be reported against in Team Foundation Server. In reality, most performance tests can be modeled only so far using this technique before the amount of test harness code starts to become nontrivial to manage. In these cases, we need to move up to using LoadGen.

Creating Your Load Tests Using LoadGen 2007

The LoadGen 2007[5] tool is one of the big advances in tools for BizTalk performance testing. Although not officially part of BizTalk Server, it is one of the best tools available for properly modeling load within BizTalk Server. LoadGen comes with its own series of help files and documentation designed to support the tool, so we won't try to teach you the tool in great detail. What we will cover are the key things you will want to use LoadGen for and what sorts of customization you will want to do once you become comfortable with LoadGen.

LoadGen 101

LoadGen is essentially a command-line tool that allows you to provide configuration data to the tool itself through .NET configuration files. You can also customize the tool by providing your own code to be executed during a LoadGen test. There are mechanisms for submitting messages to BizTalk natively using one of the transport component interfaces such as MSMQ, File, WSE, WCF, SOAP, MQSeries, and so on. These transport components allow you to use the native adapters within BizTalk and have LoadGen submit messages using those adapters without having to write any "glue code." If your particular adapter transport isn't available, you have the option of writing your own using LoadGen's API or creating a WCF service that calls whatever underlying transport you may have.

LoadGen implements the concept of throttling and monitoring so that you can dynamically throttle back your load test should your solution become overdriven. These throttling behaviors are controlled by a series of monitor components that can look at a variety of things such as performance counters, SQL Server, files, and delivery rates. Like everything in LoadGen, if there is something you need that isn't supported out of the box, you can use the API to create your own monitor components.

You execute LoadGen by calling this:

```
$LoadGenInstallDir\Bins\LoadGenConsole <configurationfile>
```

The configuration file is essentially the run data that LoadGen will load for that particular execution. Sample configuration files are provided within the tool and cover many basic scenarios. The configuration file specifies the "stop" criteria for the test and specifies other important variables such as the retry interval for failures, the sleep time between message submission, and the types of transports to be used. The following configuration file is a sample that shows how you would do a simple file drop with a monitor:

5 LoadGen is available for download at www.microsoft.com/downloads/details.aspx?FamilyID=c8af583f-7044-48db-b7b9-969072df1689&DisplayLang=en.

```
<LoadGenFramework>
    <CommonSection>
        <LoadGenVersion>2</LoadGenVersion>
        <OptimizeLimitFileSize>204800</OptimizeLimitFileSize>
        <NumThreadsPerSection>5</NumThreadsPerSection>
        <SleepInterval>200</SleepInterval>
        <LotSizePerInterval>25</LotSizePerInterval>
        <RetryInterval>10000</RetryInterval>
        <StopMode Mode="Files">
            <NumFiles>5000</NumFiles>
            <TotalTime>3600</TotalTime>
        </StopMode>
        <Transport Name="FILE">
            <Assembly>FileTransport.dll/FileTransport.FileTransport</Assembly>
        </Transport>
        <ThrottleController Mode="Custom">
            <Monitor Name="File">
        <Assembly>FileMonitor.dll/DropLocationFileMonitor➥
.DropLocationFileMonitor</Assembly>
                <ThresholdRange>1000-2000</ThresholdRange>
                <SleepInterval>1000</SleepInterval>
                <Parameters>C:\Scenarios\FileToFile\Receive</Parameters>
            </Monitor>
            <ThrottleCondition>File</ThrottleCondition>
        </ThrottleController>
    </CommonSection>
    <Section Name="FileSection">
        <SrcFilePath>C:\LoadGen\ConfigFiles\ConsoleConfigFiles\➥
FileToFileLG.xml</SrcFilePath>
        <DstLocation>
            <Parameters>
                <DstFilePath>C:\Scenarios\FileToFile\Receive</DstFilePath>
            </Parameters>
        </DstLocation>
    </Section>
</LoadGenFramework>
```

Creating Messages Using Data Files

There are three ways to create messages with LoadGen. The first that we'll discuss is using data files as a source for creating messages.

By default LoadGen will use messages that are stored in an input file as specified in the LoadGen configuration file element `<SrcFilePath>`. Essentially, XML messages that are in this file are used as input for LoadGen when it needs to submit a new message. This is easy to configure, but it's too simplistic for most needs. If your data is static and able to be modeled in this way, then this option is a good choice.

Creating Messages Using the Custom Message Creator

LoadGen ships with a component called the CustomMC, or the Custom Message Creator component. This allows you to control the message creation behavior by using the `<MessageCreator>` tag in your configuration file and specifying a template for the CustomMC component to load. The following XML file shows how this is done:

```
<Section Name="FileSection">
      <Transport Name="FILE">
        <Assembly>FileTransport.dll/FileTransport.FileTransport</Assembly>
      </Transport>
      <SrcFilePath>C:\Scenarios\SourceData.xml</SrcFilePath>
      <DstLocation>
        <Parameters>
          <DstFilePath>C:\Scenrios\Receive</DstFilePath>
        </Parameters>
      </DstLocation>

          <MessageCreator Mode="Asynchronous">
          <SleepInterval>1</SleepInterval>
          <QueueLength>10</QueueLength>
          <Assembly>CustomMC.dll/CustomMC.CustomMC</Assembly>
          <TemplateFilePath>C:\Scenarios\TemplateFile_MC.xml</TemplateFilePath>
      </MessageCreator>
```

The template file will contain the following entries:

```
<MessageCreator SourceFilePath="SampleSource.xml"
NumDuplicates="1" OutEncoding="ascii">
    <Field>
        <InitialValue>IDField_0</InitialValue>
        <DataType>Guid</DataType>
        <InputFilePath></InputFilePath>
        <ContentMinSize>1</ContentMinSize>
        <ContentMaxSize>1024</ContentMaxSize>
        <AllowDuplictaes>False</AllowDuplictaes>
    </Field>
</MessageCreator>
```

This template is essentially the layout for the dynamic fields that LoadGen will populate based on the data specified in the file SampleSource.xml. Assume the sample file has the following data:

```
<PurchaseOrder>
    <CustomerID>IDField_0</CustomerID>
    <ContactInfo>IDField_0</ContactInfo>
    <OrderNumber>IDField_1<OrderNumber>
</PurchaseOrder>
```

All instances of `IDField_0` will be replaced with a new GUID value. Table 11-1 shows the possible types that can be replaced by CustomMC.

Table 11-1. *CustomMC Replaceable Datatypes*

Value	Description
Integer	The new value is randomly generated within the range given by the <ContentMaxSize> and <ContentMinSize> elements.
Guid	The new value is generated with a unique GUID.
RandomSelection	The new value is randomly chosen from the values in the file specified by the <InputFilePath> element.
Timestamp	The current date and time on this computer is used for the new value in the "ddd, dd MMM yyyy hh:mm:ss:ffffff" format.
IntegerSeries	An integer value greater than 100,000 is used for the new value. The value is increased by 1 whenever a new value is generated.

As you can see, there are a number of options to choose from, but in large performance test scenarios where data can potentially be related to other data elements and external factors, these options quickly become useless. The solution to this problem is to create your own custom message creator that can create data in any way you choose.

Creating Your OwnCustom Message Creator

Out of all of LoadGen's numerous customization features, the most useful by far is the ability to create your own message creators. A message creator is used to control the messages that LoadGen will submit during the executed test. The configuration section for the <Transport> tag within the configuration is modified so that your custom message creator can be invoked instead of the default one.

A custom message creator is a type that implements the IMessageCreator interface. This interface has one method called CreateNewMessage, which passes three properties:

OriginalMessage: The message object containing the content of the file that the <SrcFilePath> element indicates

TemplateFilePath: The file path that is in the <TemplateFilePath> element in the parent <MessageCreator> element

NewMessageUniqueFileSuffix: The number of messages that a LoadGen task thread has created

The method returns a new Message object, which will be submitted to BizTalk. The Message object is a LoadGen message type that has the following constructor:

```
Message constructor (byte[], long, string, string)
```

The constructor initializes a new instance of the Message class with the following parameters:

byte[] MessageData: The array of bytes containing the message data

long MessageLength: The size of the message data

string MessageExtension: The extension of a file that contains the message data

It has the following properties, which are traditionally passed on the constructor:

`MessageData` property: The array of bytes containing the message data

`MessagePath` property: The path of a file that contains the message data

`MessageExtension` property: The extension of a file that contains the message data

`MessageLength` property: The size of the message data

Using the `Message` class, you can create messages and message constructors that will behave in any way you want. The code to create these message types is actually quite trivial and will plug into the LoadGen framework using the configuration files, as you saw previously. The samples for this book show a custom message creator that will read values from a database and create messages based on an input schema.

Creating a Reset Button

A key script to create is one that "resets" your test environment to the original state so that you can rerun tests multiple times. Usually this involves resetting counters in your test data so that the records will be created again, removing any suspended instances and queued items from the BizTalk Messagebox and resetting any downstream systems such as an ERP or a custom database that may have been updated as a result of the tests. A number of cleanup scripts for BizTalk are included in the book samples that you can use. Resetting updated third-party applications can be tricky depending on the type of system, its age, and its accessibility.

Executing Your Load Tests

As you have seen, you can design load tests using LoadGen that can accurately model how you expect the solution to be used in production. You can have a LoadGen configuration file that specifies any number of different message types to be created, each of which can use a different transport and have different data created for each message. You can also control the data that is placed in the message by creating your own messages using the LoadGen API. Once you have created all tests, you need to run them.

Be prepared to run each test several times. The first few runs will be to simply prove that the tests are working properly. You should have a set of expected outcomes or expected record counts created to verify that the test ran properly. There are a few areas that you should keep a close watch on while your test is running:

Out-of-memory (OOM) exceptions: BizTalk is notorious for generating OOM exceptions. These will show up in the Event Log as a BizTalk critical error. We'll talk about OOM exceptions later in the chapter. If you are getting OOM exceptions, something is misconfigured with your solution, and your first priority is to identify what component is going OOM and troubleshoot it so that it is stable.

General errors: Checking the Event Log during the performance test will help you identify potential issues as they are occurring. BizTalk will throw any number of errors while under load, especially DBNetLib errors. If you see these types of errors, it is important to identify the root cause of the error before proceeding. Errors that indicate a serious problem with the environment generally invalidate the entire performance test.

Downstream system errors: It is very important to validate that any downstream systems that were affected by the performance tests were actually updated as expected. It is not uncommon to see BizTalk execute the performance tests as expected but the downstream system that was the target of the test failed to do any real updating because of being overwhelmed by the transaction volume.

PERFORMANCE MONITOR

The first tool people generally learn when they start performance testing is Performance Monitor, or Perfmon. Perfmon is by far the most useful tool that comes preinstalled on the Windows platform. It is a good idea to have the Performance Monitor console up and running while the performance test is executing so you can keep watch—in real time—what is happening with the system. It is also a good idea to have the Perfmon console running on another workstation and be remotely viewing the server's counters. This way, you will minimize the CPU usage of Perfmon that is taking cycles away from the application.

Analyzing the Results

In the old days, you would need to hire a set of incredibly bright consultants to come into your organization, run the performance tests for you, and analyze the test results to give you recommendations on what counters to change. Well, those days have been replaced by a tool called Performance Analyzer for Logs (PAL).[6] In the simplest terms, PAL is the bread-slicer of performance testing. PAL does the following for you:

- It will tell you what counters to monitor based on the Microsoft product you are testing.
- It will analyze the counters gathered from multiple machines.
- It will generate reports for you of what counters violated the acceptable thresholds as published by Microsoft.
- It will tell you what areas of your solution are currently not performing properly (CPU, memory, disk, and all well-known BizTalk counters)
- It will then give you some recommendations on what settings to change to increase performance.

It does all that, it's free, and the source code is available on www.codeplex.com. The best part is that not only does it work for BizTalk, but there are PAL analyzer sets for most Microsoft products including SharePoint, SQL Server, Windows Server, Exchange, and IIS. It truly is a wondrous tool. Figure 11-4 shows the servers that can be analyzed using PAL.

6 Download PAL at www.codeplex.com/PAL.

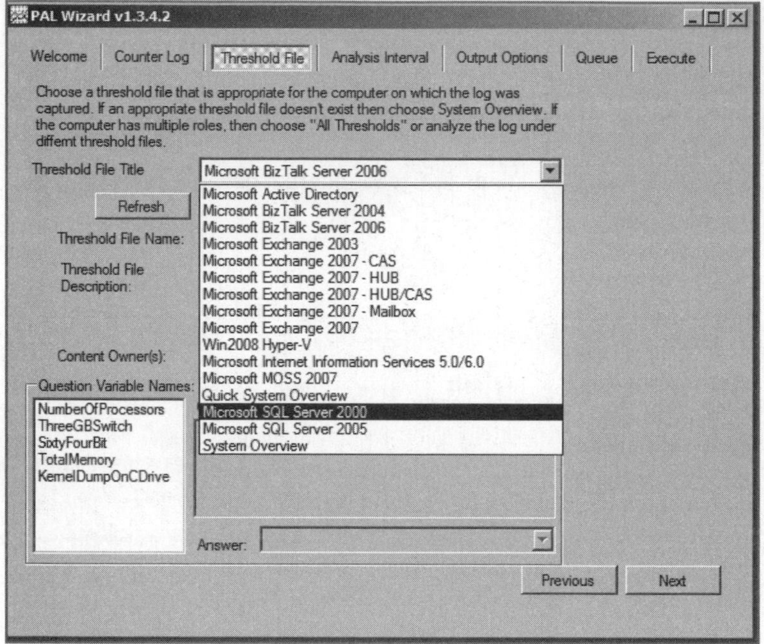

Figure 11-4. *PAL-supported servers*

The information that PAL gives you will help take the grunt work out of identifying what counters are worrisome and help get you pointed in the right direction so you don't start changing settings that won't help or that will make things worse.

To ensure that you are capturing the correct performance counters that PAL requires for a particular server, you need to check the counter file for that particular product. Just click the Edit button, and you will be shown what counters a particular product is requiring, as shown in Figures 11-5 and 11-6.

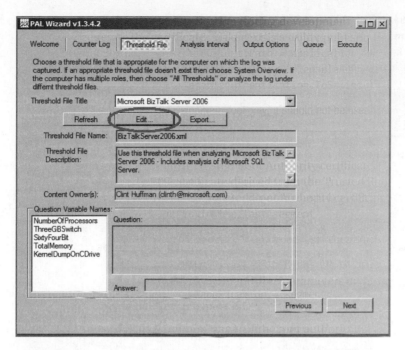

Figure 11-5. *Edit button for editing a particular counter file*

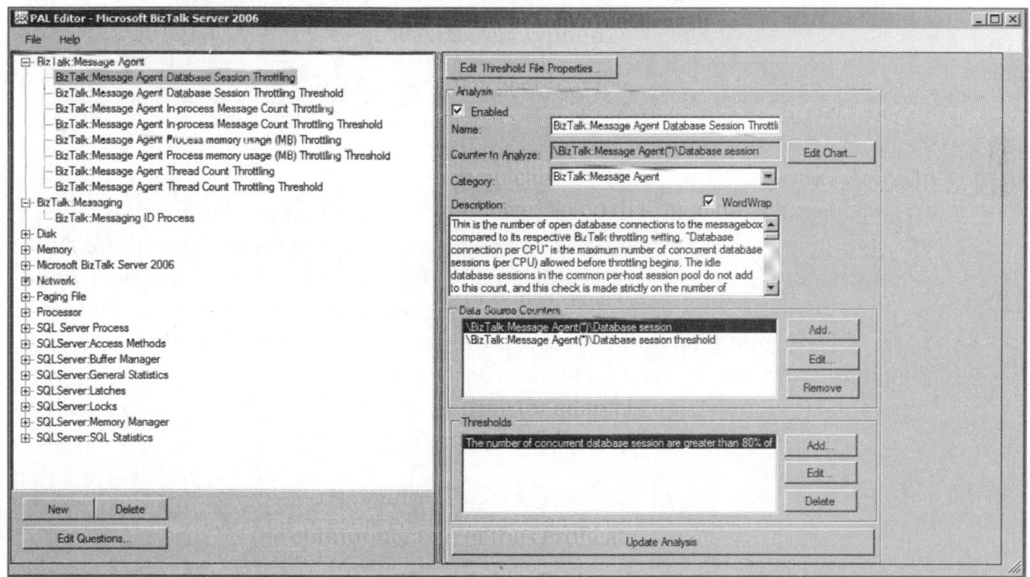

Figure 11-6. *The BizTalk Server 2006 counter file*

Once you have determined what counters you need to monitor, use a workstation to record the desired counters from each BizTalk server in your environment being tested. Simply add the required counters from each server and log them to a Performance Monitor Log the .blg file. It is also recommended that you create a set of logs from each of the IIS servers in your environment, along with a separate log file for the SQL Servers if they do not reside on the BizTalk servers. This way you can use PAL to analyze the logs from these environments as well and not limit the performance testing to solely BizTalk, as shown in Figure 11-7.

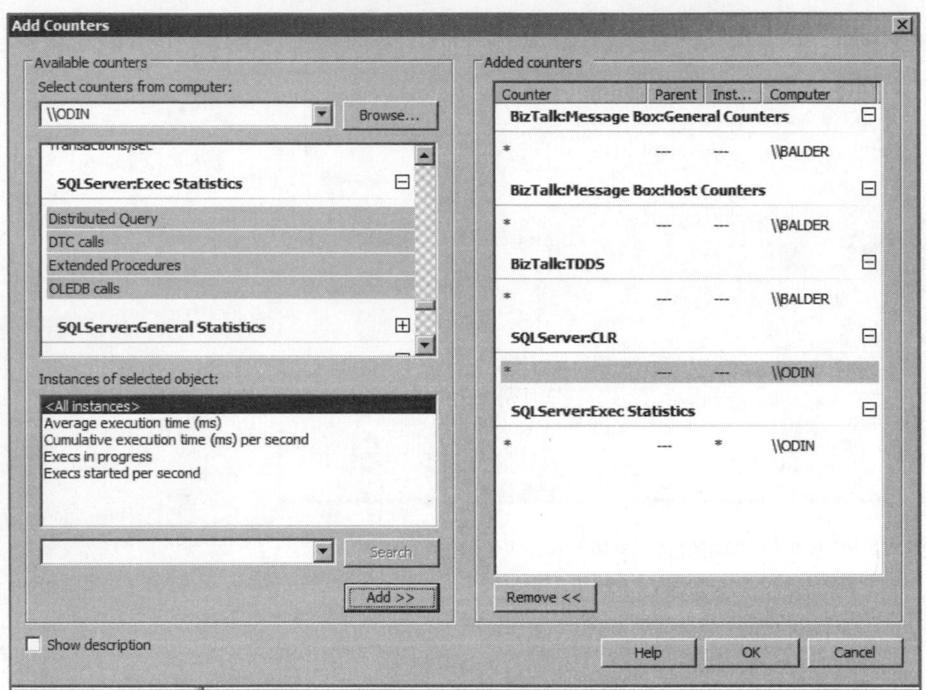

Figure 11-7. *Adding counters from multiple servers*

Once you have executed your tests, stop gathering the Performance Monitor counters, and save the .blg file to the server where you installed PAL. Once you execute the wizard and have PAL analyze your logs, you will get detailed HTML reports that look like Figures 11-8 and 11-9. The reports detail the analysis of each counter of interest and whether the threshold values are exceeded throughout the test. The reports even detail the source of the threshold and what documentation references that counter and its threshold values.

An alert is generated if any of the thresholds were broken during one of the time intervals analyzed. The background of each of the values represents the highest priority threshold that the value broke. See the each of the counter's respective analysis section for more details about what the threshold means. A white background indicates that the value was not analyzed by any of the thresholds.

Time	Condition	Counter	Min	Avg	Max	Hourly Trend
14/08/2007 3:40:00 PM	Condition	Counter	Min	Avg	Max	Hourly Trend
	Very low on available memory - less than 5% available	\\ZACH-PC\Memory\Available MBytes	79	79	79	0
14/08/2007 3:41:00 PM	Condition	Counter	Min	Avg	Max	Hourly Trend
	High processor utilization - more than 75% CPU utilization	\\ZACH-PC\Processor(_Total)\% Processor Time	82	82	82	4,929
	High processor utilization - more than 75% CPU utilization	\\ZACH-PC\Processor(0)\% Processor Time	82	82	82	4,929
	More than 30% CPU in Privileged Mode CPU - This may indicate a high I/O issue	\\ZACH-PC\Processor(0)\% Privileged Time	44	44	44	2,664
	Average disk responsiveness is slow - more than 15ms	\\ZACH-PC\PhysicalDisk(_Total)\Avg. Disk sec/Write	0.011	0.011	0.011	0.632
	Average disk responsiveness is slow - more than 15ms	\\ZACH-PC\PhysicalDisk(0 C:)\Avg. Disk sec/Write	0.011	0.011	0.011	0.632
	Very low on available memory - less than 5% available	\\ZACH-PC\Memory\Available MBytes	107	107	107	1,680
	More then 10 page file reads per second	\\ZACH-PC\Memory\Pages Input/sec	128	128	128	7,689
14/08/2007 3:42:00 PM	Condition	Counter	Min	Avg	Max	Hourly Trend
	High processor utilization - more than 75% CPU utilization	\\ZACH-PC\Processor(_Total)\% Processor Time	87	87	87	2,607
	High processor utilization - more than 75% CPU utilization	\\ZACH-PC\Processor(0)\% Processor Time	87	87	87	2,607
	More than 30% CPU in Privileged Mode CPU - This may indicate a high I/O issue	\\ZACH-PC\Processor(0)\% Privileged Time	46	46	46	1,391

Computer | Protected Mode: Off 100%

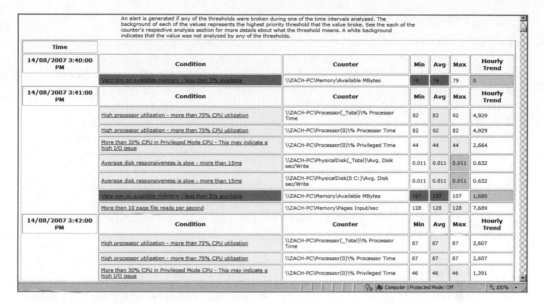

Figure 11-8. *PAL Executive Summary report*

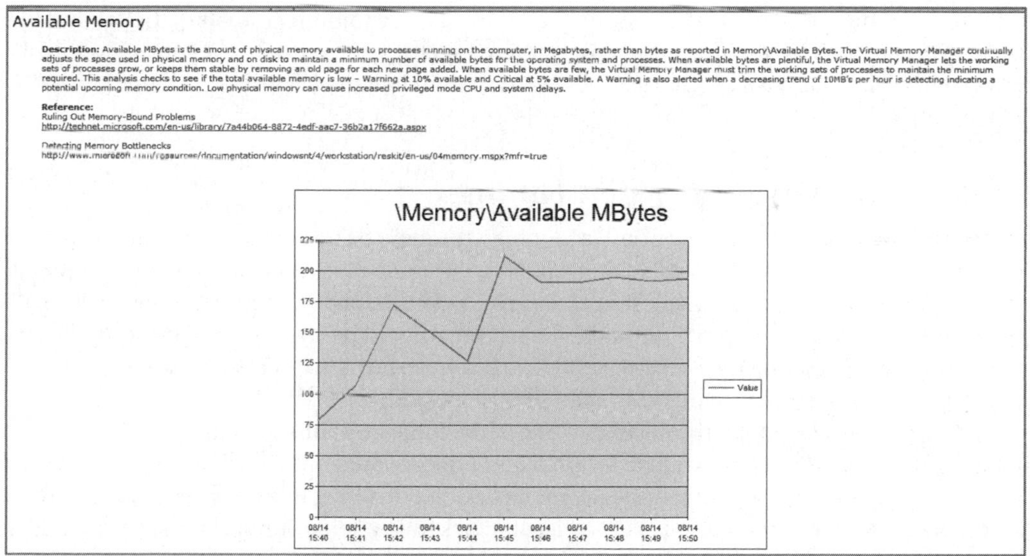

Figure 11-9. *PAL detailed counter report*

Checking for Errors and Validating Results

Even though PAL provides a great way to analyze the data that Perfmon can gather, you still need to be diligent to verify that the data PAL is analyzing is valid. Even though a performance test may run to completion, care should be taken to ensure that the outcomes of a performance test accurately match the expected outcomes. For example, let's assume that your performance test was geared around order creation. If you followed the process outlined earlier, then you have an accurate representation of the test data that was used during the performance test run. The last step of the test is to go back and verify that all records that were supposed to be created were in fact created or updated as per the expected outcomes of the test. If there are any variances, you need to start to investigate why. This will often lend itself to finding unknown instabilities in a particular solution. For example, a message may become suspended should a schema validation fail or should an adapter unexpectedly fail. Performing this last piece of analysis will validate your tests and provide your testing approach with a degree of credibility that it would not otherwise have.

Phase 3: Tuning

Now that you have your performance metrics and have used PAL to help you identify bottlenecks and potential areas of improvement, you are ready to do some tuning. You have to identify the different adapters and hosts used by the solution. This allows you to focus your attention on the components that require the tuning. Before jumping into that, though, you need to understand how to decipher those gathered metrics and ensure that your solution follows coding best practices and the guidelines that eliminate unnecessary extra configuration and tuning work.

What to Keep in Mind When Tuning

Out of the box, BizTalk Server is optimized for high throughput by adaptively managing its rate of polling received messages. This adaptive polling mechanism can cause a maximum latency of 0.5 seconds by default. If the solution at hand includes interactive scenarios where 0.5 seconds of latency is an issue, that internal polling interval could be changed to a value as low as 0.1 seconds by modifying the `MaxReceiveInterval` value in the adm_ServiceClass table, which is part of the BizTalk Management Database (BizTalkMgmtDb).

Managing the incoming throughput is one of the tuning options to handle bottlenecks whether they are internal or external. Internal bottlenecks could be caused by long execution times for a transform or a poorly designed orchestration, resulting in extra persistence points. External bottlenecks are usually caused by legacy backend systems or poorly designed services that cannot keep up with the load.

To properly tune the server, you need to know the expected throughput of the application, whether there are external bottlenecks or not, and what the expected peak input and its duration are. Knowing these, you need to analyze the gathered performance counters accordingly and identify which counters are showing problem areas. Table 11-2 highlights important performance counters and common causes for undesirable performance values for these counters as well as some troubleshooting options to rectify them.

Table 11-2. *Main Bottleneck Analysis*

Performance Counter	Analysis	Options
Low % CPU Idle on BizTalk Server	Too many hosts running on the server. Improper use of custom pipelines. Custom components requiring optimization.	Isolate the receive, process, and send functionality into different hosts and run host instances on different servers within the BizTalk Server Group. Move message transformation out of orchestrations to your ports to avoid the creation of new copies. Move message filters to your ports and receive locations. Optimize your schemas. Large schemas reduce performance. Use distinguished fields in orchestrations rather than properties or XPath. Use pass-through pipelines whenever possible.
Low % CPU Idle on SQL Server	Check whether the DBA changed any of the default database settings set by the BizTalk installation. Auto-Update Statistics and Max Degree of Parallelism are set to off and 1, respectively, on purpose.	Minimize the number persistence points* in your orchestrations. Use static methods instead of wrapping nonserializable components in atomic scopes. Avoid using Parallel shapes, except when needed.** In a multi-Messagebox scenario, ensure that you have at least three Messageboxes. The master Messagebox is doing all the routing to secondary Messageboxes, which is CPU intensive. Whenever you are using multiple Messageboxes, Microsoft's Distributed Transaction Coordinator (DTC) is involved; therefore, you need to jump from one Messagebox to three instead of only two to offset that overhead.
Low % Disk Idle on SQL Server High Avg. Disk Queue Length on SQL Server	Check whether the tracking database and Messagebox are on the same disks. Check whether the data and log files are on the same disks. Check the log sizes. Check the SQL Agents to ensure that the databases are being backed up. Check whether the tracked messages' bodies are being archived.	Use a SAN. Ensure that the tracking and Messagebox databases are on different servers. If they are on the same server, ensure that they are on different disks. Ensure that the data and log files are not sharing the same disks. Make sure the BizTalk agents are enabled on the server. The agents copy tracking data from the Messagebox to the tracking database. They also back up the databases and clean up the logs.

* *Persistence points also represent a performance metric that can be monitored using the BizTalk performance counter named Persistence Points.*

***Parallel shapes are usually used to allow for the execution of independent flows upon the arrival of different messages, when the order of delivery is unknown.*

If any of the scenarios outlined in Table 11-2 hold true, this means that the whole BizTalk platform is underperforming, not just your solution, because these counters influence the performance of the core BizTalk subsystems. Problems or inefficiencies in one BizTalk solution could affect all other solutions sharing the same environment with that problematic solution. It is therefore a good idea to look at the overall platform when troubleshooting performance issues in a BizTalk solution.

IMPORTANT MESSAGEBOX METRICS

Other important metrics that you can gather directly from your Messagebox are your spool table and queue length. This gives you a complete understanding of what is happening on the Messagebox level. The following is a set of code snippets that you can use in a SQL script to gather this information; another way to get this data is to create your SQL custom counters to gather it. It is a good idea when doing any server analysis or troubleshooting a problem to use a similar script to gather metrics on your production environment before you start going through endless logs.

```
-- -----------------------------------------------------
-- Get the number of rows in the spool table (backlog)
-- -----------------------------------------------------
SET NOCOUNT ON
SET TRANSACTION ISOLATION LEVEL READ COMMITTED
SET DEADLOCK_PRIORITY LOW
SELECT  COUNT(*) as Messages,
        'Spooled Messages' as State
FROM [BizTalkMsgboxDb]..[spool] WITH (NOLOCK)
-- -----------------------------------------------------


-- -----------------------------------------------------------
-- Get the number of orchestrations and their state per host
-- -----------------------------------------------------------
SET NOCOUNT ON
SET TRANSACTION ISOLATION LEVEL READ COMMITTED
SET DEADLOCK_PRIORITY LOW
SELECT  o.nvcName AS Orchestration, COUNT(*) as Count,
        CASE i.nState
                WHEN 1 THEN 'Ready To Run'
                WHEN 2 THEN 'Active'
                WHEN 4 THEN 'Suspended Resumable'
                WHEN 8 THEN 'Dehydrated'
                WHEN 16 THEN 'Completed With Discarded Messages'
                WHEN 32 THEN 'Suspended Non-Resumable'
        END as State
```

```
FROM [BizTalkMsgboxDb]..[Instances] AS i WITH (NOLOCK)
JOIN [BizTalkMgmtDb]..[bts_Orchestration] AS o
WITH (NOLOCK) ON i.uidServiceID = o.uidGUID
--WHERE dtCreated > '2004-08-24 00:00:00'
--AND dtCreated < '2004-08-24 13:30:00'
GROUP BY o.nvcName, i.nState
-- ---------------------------------------------------------


-- ---------------------------------------------------------
-- Get the number of Messages per host Q
-- IMPORTANT! Replace each instance of Q with the name of the
-- host that you are inspecting.
-- and the number of messages in the spool that are in that Q
-- ---------------------------------------------------------
SET NOCOUNT ON
SET TRANSACTION ISOLATION LEVEL READ COMMITTED
SET DEADLOCK_PRIORITY LOW

SELECT COUNT(*) as Messages, 'Suspended Non-Resumable' as State,
                'FROM [BizTalkMsgBoxDb]..[WITH (NOLOCK)
--WHERE dtCreated > '2004-08-24 00:00:00'
--AND dtCreated < '2004-08-24 13:30:00'
SELECT  COUNT(*) as Messages,
        'Spooled Suspended Non-Resumable' as State,
        'FROM [BizTalkMsgboxDb]..[spool] AS i WITH (NOLOCK)
JOIN [BizTalkMsgboxDb]..[WITH (NOLOCK) ON i.uidMessageID = o.uidMessageID
--WHERE dtCreated > '2004-08-24 00:00:00'
--AND dtCreated < '2004-08-24 13:30:00'

SELECT COUNT(*) as Messages, 'Scheduled' as State,
        'FROM [BizTalkMsgBoxDb]..[WITH (NOLOCK)
--WHERE dtCreated > '2004-08-24 00:00:00'
--AND dtCreated < '2004-08-24 13:30:00'

SELECT  COUNT(*) as Count, 'Spooled Scheduled' as State,
        'FROM [BizTalkMsgboxDb]..[spool] AS i WITH (NOLOCK)
JOIN [BizTalkMsgboxDb]..[AS o WITH (NOLOCK) ON i.uidMessageID = o.uidMessageID
--WHERE dtCreated > '2004-08-24 00:00:00'
--AND dtCreated < '2004-08-24 13:30:00'

SELECT COUNT(*) as Messages, 'Active' as State,
        'FROM [BizTalkMsgBoxDb]..[WITH (NOLOCK)
--WHERE dtCreated > '2004-08-24 00:00:00'
--AND dtCreated < '2004-08-24 13:30:00'
```

```
SELECT  COUNT(*) as Count, 'Spooled Active' as State,
        'FROM [BizTalkMsgboxDb]..[spool] AS i WITH (NOLOCK)
JOIN [BizTalkMsgboxDb]..[WITH (NOLOCK) ON i.uidMessageID = o.uidMessageID
--WHERE dtCreated > '2004-08-24 00:00:00'
--AND dtCreated < '2004-08-24 13:30:00'
-- ------------------------------------------------------------
```

What to Keep in Mind About Your Code

A few simple things to keep in mind before jumping into tuning your BizTalk solution as well are your current coding practices. Coding is a constant improvement process. While coding and performing code reviews, since the Assembly/C/C++ days, we have constantly written and seen comments like "// —TBD: refactor or rewrite in next rev." This is an obvious sign that no matter what stage you are in, there is always some code in your application or library that, given the time, you would revisit, rewrite, or repackage.

Some of the BizTalk coding caveats that tend to apply to most BizTalk developers, and that generally represent quick performance wins, are as follows:

- **Move your message transformations to the ports**: This minimizes the number of message copies created in your orchestration.
- **Avoid using `XmlDoc` objects in your orchestration and use distinguished fields on a message**: `XmlDoc` objects load the full message into a DOM and consume a considerable amount of memory resources. Each transformation from an `XmlDoc` to a message object and back results in copies of these objects being created in memory. Using distinguished fields simply references the existing message and minimizes memory churn.
- **Move data validation to the pipeline or schema**: If you are performing any data validation on your input messages, for example, validating that an order number is numeric and within a prespecified range, you are better off specifying this form of validation when defining the data types in the schema. If you require other forms of contextual validation, you are better off doing that in a pipeline. It is better to do this before persisting the message to the Messagebox, running the routing logic to find the proper schedule subscribed to the message instance, and then spawning an orchestration instance and allocating the required resources for it to run, only to realize that the data was not good enough to start with and issues an exception or sends back an error. You can save a lot of system resources and processing time by handling this in the pipeline and generating an error message there that you can then route back to the sender using content-based routing.

- **Avoid using orchestrations for routing**: If all your orchestration is doing is checking message fields to route the message to the proper handler or another worker orchestration to perform a particular task, strongly consider redesigning that piece of your application as a set of port filters. Leverage receive ports with multiple receive locations and send groups to route messages coming in from multiple sources and send messages to multiple destinations instead of relying on orchestrations to achieve that.
- **Avoid calls to external assemblies that perform extensive processing, especially if they call web services or make calls to a database**: Avoid calling slow external assemblies from within your orchestrations.[7] This holds the processing host resources and valuable host threads from servicing other orchestration instances while waiting for that external logic to terminate and return. If these calls stall or take a considerable amount of time, there is no way for the BizTalk engine to dehydrate that orchestration instance and use the resources assigned to it to service another one, because the engine sees the instance's state as running while in fact the external code that it called is idle. Leverage the messaging infrastructure to issue such calls that span multiple processes boundaries.
- **Do not wrap calls to .NET objects in atomic transactions because they are nonserializable**: Do not create transaction scopes around an expression to simply get around the shortcoming of an external object that you are using. If it makes sense, make this object serializable, or if it is simply a utility, use static methods instead of instantiating an object. Change the class's implementation or implement a façade that provides you with the required interface[8] if needed.
- **Use Parallel shapes carefully**: As illustrated in Figure 11-10, Parallel shapes should be used to parallelize receives if the order of incoming messages is unknown. The cost of persistence points associated with Parallel shapes is high.
- **Differentiate between scopes and transactions**: Transaction scopes affect persistence points. Atomic transactions batch state persistence points and write them to the database in a single call. Long-running transactions, on the other hand, persist state at different points along the process. If you are not really running a transaction, do not assign a transaction type to your scope.

---

7 Ensure that all external assemblies being called are not making calls to web services or communicating with external systems or backend databases that might hold the calling thread until they complete. Also, ensure that all external assemblies adhere to the .NET development guideline and best practices.

8 For more details on implementing a façade, refer to *Design Patterns: Elements of Reusable Object-Oriented Software* by Erich Gamma, Richard Helm, Ralph Johnson, and John Vlissides (Addison-Wesley, 1995). The definition of the Façade pattern can be found at Wikipedia: en.wikipedia.org/wiki/Facade_pattern.

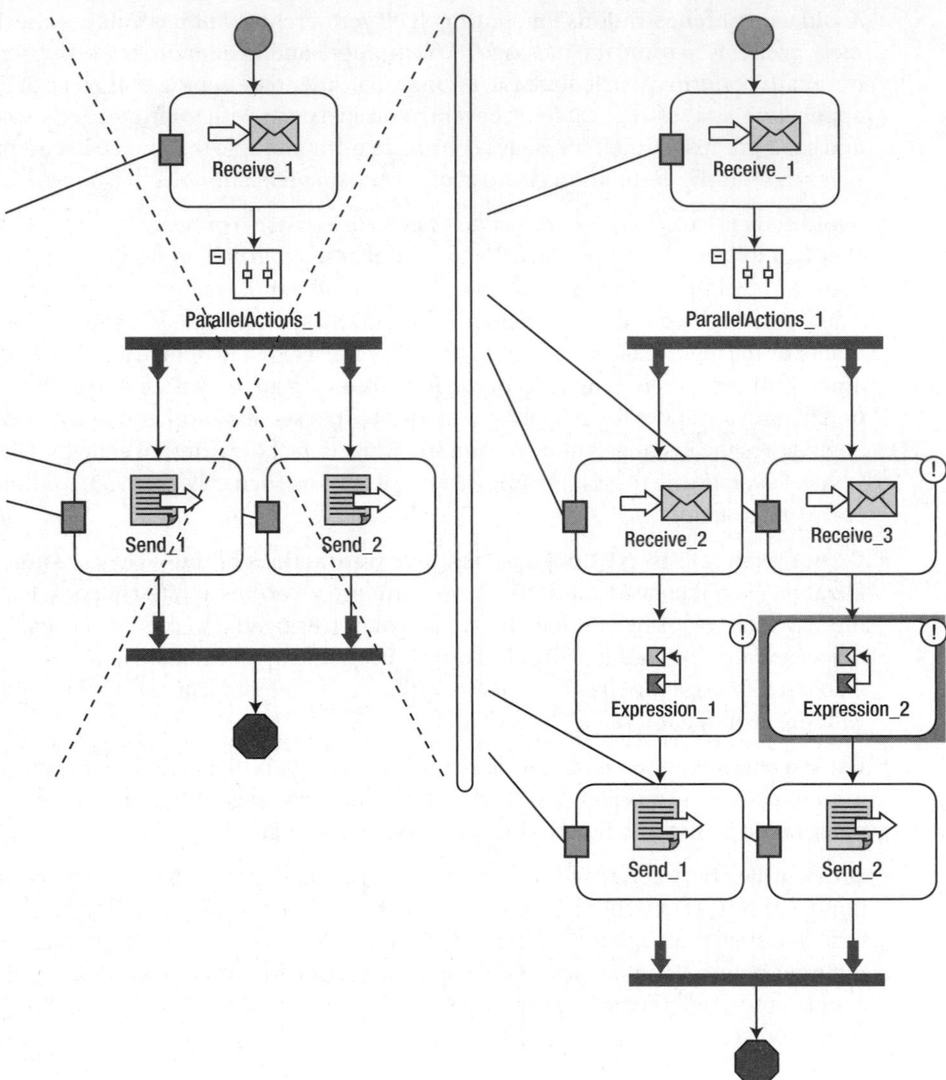

Figure 11-10. *The proper use of Parallel shapes in an orchestration*

- **Use pass-through pipelines where possible**: The XMLSend or XMLReceive pipelines do a fair amount of work to validate and assemble the data going through them. If you are sure that outgoing and incoming messages are in a valid XML form, use a pass-through pipeline to eliminate this unneeded overhead.

Note The pass-through pipeline does not promote any message properties. You might still want to use the XMLReceive pipeline if you want to access promoted properties.

- **Clean up suspended messages**: Suspended messages are held in the suspended queue and thus retain an entry in the Messagebox spool table. An unexpected growth in the spool table affects overall performance, because all instances added to, changed, or removed from the system touch the spool table. It is therefore wise to help maintain as small a size as possible for the spool table. Suspended-resumable instances have a worse impact on the system because they are considered by the engine to be dehydrated messages on a server recovery from an unexpected failure and are rehydrated back to memory, consuming valuable threads and resources. Leverage exception handlers in orchestrations and subscribe to negative acknowledgments or use a cleanup script to clear your system from suspended instances regularly only after verifying that the data is nonrepairable or unnecessary in the target system.[9]

Regular code reviews during the development cycle should ensure that these guidelines are being followed and save the development team valuable time spent in performance testing and bug fixing to meet performance requirements.

SUSPENDED INSTANCES CLEANUP SCRIPT

The following script can be used to periodically clean up suspended messages. Add it to your task scheduler on the server to run periodically—every day or couple of days—and clean up suspended messages. The script needs to be configured with the different hosts to inspect and clean up. The approved way of cleaning up suspended messages programmatically is using the WMI APIs exposed by BizTalk, which is unfortunately a resource-intensive way to perform this task. To avoid locking up the server, the script cleans up instances in batches. The number of instances in a batch—*nMaxInstancesToClean*—as well as the hosts—*aryHostNames*—to clean up suspended instances for and the log file location—*strDirectory* and *strFile*—can be easily modified. The script also generates and appends data to the same log file with each run for administrators to track its progress and keep track of cleaned-up messages. Enter your host names in order of priority, such that the one that needs to be cleaned first will run first.

```
dim objServices, objMsg, svcinsts, inst, msg, ndx, size, nHostCount

Dim aryClassIDs()
Dim aryTypeIDs()
Dim aryInstanceIDs()

Dim aryClassIDsTemp()
Dim aryTypeIDsTemp()
Dim aryInstanceIDsTemp()
```

9 Although you should not be seeing suspended instances in your system, because they are signs of an error and you should be handling all errors, sometimes the occurrence of suspended instances is out of your hands. For example, you may be making a request-response call to a web service that was unavailable or issuing a query to a database that was taken offline during a valid change window for maintenance. Such actions, though valid, will result in suspended instances on the host instance running those adapters. The recommended approach to handle these suspended instances is to handle error reports or to create a context-sensitive orchestration that subscribes to NACK, inspects the instances' details and archives them, and then cleans them up.

```
'-----------------------------------------------
Dim strKey2Instance
Dim strQuery2Msg
Dim objQueue

'-----------------------------------------------
'-- Creating and opening log file to append info
'-----------------------------------------------
Dim strDirectory, strFile, objFSO, objTextFile
'Create the File System Object
Set objFSO = CreateObject("Scripting.FileSystemObject")

'Check that the folder and file exists
If objFSO.FileExists(strDirectory & strFile) Then
    'OpenTextFile Method needs a Const value
    'ForAppending = 8 ForReading = 1, ForWriting = 2
    Const ForAppending = 8
    Set objTextFile = objFSO.OpenTextFile(strDirectory & strFile,
                                          ForAppending, True)
Else
    Set objTextFile = objFSO.CreateTextFile(strDirectory & strFile)
End If

'----------------------------
'-- Set the object reference
'----------------------------
set objServices = GetObject("winmgmts:\\.\root\MicrosoftBizTalkServer")

'---------------------------------------------------------------------
'-- Create array of hostnames to loop over hosts
'-- increase the array's size,
'-- add as many hostnames as required to the array,
'-- and initialize the corresponding aryHostSuspendedMessages entries
'---------------------------------------------------------------------
'---------------------------------------------------------------------------
'-- The maximum number of suspended instances to clean up in a single batch
'---------------------------------------------------------------------------

Dim strHost
nHostCount = 0

objTextFile.WriteLine("------- SCRIPT EXECUTION STARTED -------")
```

```
'----------------------------------------------------------------------
'-- Terminate instance in each suspended Queue for the selected hosts
'----------------------------------------------------------------------
for each strHost in aryHostNames

    'wscript.echo "Host: " & strHost
    objTextFile.WriteLine("----------------------------------------")
    objTextFile.WriteLine(Now() & " :    Host: " & strHost)

'--------------------------------
'-- Query for Suspended instances
'--------------------------------
    wbemFlagReturnImmediately = 16
    wbemFlagForwardOnly = 32
    IFlags = wbemFlagReturnImmediately + wbemFlagForwardOnly
    set svcinsts = objServices.ExecQuery(
             "select * from MSBTS_serviceinstance
              where (servicestatus=32 or servicestatus=4)
              and HostName="""&strHost&"""",, IFlags)

    'Using a semi-synchronous therefore the count property doesn't
    'work with wbemFlagForwardOnly
    'size = svcinsts.Count
    'wscript.echo "Suspended Message: " & size

    strKey2Instance = "MSBTS_HostQueue.HostName=""" & strHost & """"

    set objQueue = objServices.Get(strKey2Instance)

    If Err <> 0 Then

        wscript.echo Now() & " :    Failed to get MSBTS_HostQueue instance"
        wscript.echo Now() & " :    " & Err.Description & Err.Number
        objTextFile.WriteLine(Now() & " :
                                 Failed to get MSBTS_HostQueue instance")
        objTextFile.WriteLine(Now() & " :    " + Err.Description & Err.Number)

    Else

        ndx = 0
```

```
redim aryClassIDs(nMaxInstancesToClean)
redim aryTypeIDs(nMaxInstancesToClean)
redim aryInstanceIDs(nMaxInstancesToClean)

'Loop through all instances and terminate nMaxInstancesToClean at a
'time.
'This number was choosen for optimization, so it can be changed if
'desired.
for each inst in svcinsts

     If ndx > nMaxInstancesToClean Then
          'Currently 500 entries are ready to be terminated

          'wscript.echo "Attempting to terminate "
          '& ndx & " suspended instances in host"
          objTextFile.WriteLine(Now() &
                 " :    Attempting to terminate "
                 & ndx & " suspended instances in host")

          objQueue.TerminateServiceInstancesByID aryClassIDs,
                            aryTypeIDs, aryInstanceIDs

          If Err <> 0 Then
               wscript.echo Now() & " :    Terminate failed"
               wscript.echo Now() & " :    " & Err.Description
                                   & Err.Number
               objTextFile.WriteLine(Now() & " :    Terminate failed")
               objTextFile.WriteLine(Now() & " :    " + Err.Description
                                            & Err.Number)
          Else
               'wscript.echo "SUCCESS> " & ndx &
               '" Service instance terminated"
               objTextFile.WriteLine(Now() &
                  " :    SUCCESS> " & ndx &
                  " Service instance terminated")
          End If

          'Reinitialize the arrays and counter
          'to ensure we store non-terminated
          'Entries for the next round of termination
          ndx = 0
          redim aryClassIDs(nMaxInstancesToClean)
          redim aryTypeIDs(nMaxInstancesToClean)
          redim aryInstanceIDs(nMaxInstancesToClean)
```

```
            'Suspends script execution for 30 seconds,
            'then continues execution
            'wscript.echo "Suspending script execution for 30 seconds"
            objTextFile.WriteLine(Now() &
              " :    Suspending script execution for 30 seconds")
            Wscript.Sleep 30000

        End If

        aryClassIDs(ndx) = inst.Properties_("ServiceClassId")
        aryTypeIDs(ndx) = inst.Properties_("ServiceTypeId")
        aryInstanceIDs(ndx) = inst.Properties_("InstanceId")

        ndx = ndx + 1

next

'If count <> zero then the arrays are still populated
'and the messages need to be terminated one last time.
If ( ndx > 0 ) then

        redim aryClassIDsTemp(ndx-1)
        redim aryTypeIDsTemp(ndx-1)
        redim aryInstanceIDsTemp(ndx-1)

        for i=1 to ndx
            aryClassIDsTemp(i-1) = aryClassIDs(i-1)
            aryTypeIDsTemp(i-1) = aryTypeIDs(i-1)
            aryInstanceIDsTemp(i-1) = aryInstanceIDs(i-1)
            aryHostSuspsendedMessages(nHostCount) =
               aryHostSuspsendedMessages(nHostCount) + 1
        next

        'wscript.echo "Attempting to terminate " &
        'ndx & " suspended instances in host"
        objTextFile.WriteLine(Now() &
            " :    Attempting to terminate " & ndx &
            " suspended instances in host")

        objQueue.TerminateServiceInstancesByID aryClassIDsTemp,
                aryTypeIDsTemp, aryInstanceIDsTemp
```

```
            If Err <> 0 Then
                wscript.echo Now() & " :    Terminate failed"
                wscript.echo Now() & " :    " & Err.Description & Err.Number
                objTextFile.WriteLine(Now() & " :    Terminate failed")
                objTextFile.WriteLine(Now() &
                              " :    " + Err.Description & Err.Number)
            Else
                'wscript.echo "SUCCESS> " & ndx &
                '" Service instance terminated"
                objTextFile.WriteLine(Now() &
                   " :    SUCCESS> " & ndx & " Service instance terminated")
            End If
        Else
            'wscript.echo "No suspended instances in this host"
            objTextFile.WriteLine(Now() &
                    " :    No suspended instances in this host")
        End If
    End If

    nHostCount = nHostCount + 1

Next

objTextFile.WriteLine("")
objTextFile.WriteLine("-------       SUMMARY START      -------")

nHostCount = 0
for each strHost in aryHostNames
    wscript.echo Now() & " :    Total of " &
                aryHostSuspsendedMessages(nHostCount) &
                " suspended messages were terminated in " &
                strHost & " host"
    objTextFile.WriteLine(Now() & " :    Total of " &
                         aryHostSuspsendedMessages(nHostCount) &
                         " suspended messages were terminated in " &
                         strHost & " host")
    nHostCount = nHostCount + 1
Next
objTextFile.WriteLine("-------        SUMMARY END       -------")
objTextFile.WriteLine("")
```

```
wscript.echo Now() & " :    Script Execution Completed"
objTextFile.WriteLine(Now() & " :    Script Execution Completed")
objTextFile.WriteLine("-------  SCRIPT EXECUTION ENDED  -------")
objTextFile.Close
Set objTextFile = nothing
```

A sample log file output with multiple batch runs to clean the hosts:

```
 ------- SCRIPT EXECUTION STARTED -------
----------------------------------------
08/11/2009 3:42:31 PM :    Host: BizTalkServerApplication
08/11/2009 3:42:37 PM :    Attempting to terminate 500 suspended instances in
                           host
08/11/2009 3:42:43 PM :    SUCCESS> 500 Service instance terminated
08/11/2009 3:42:43 PM :    Suspending script execution for 30 seconds
08/11/2009 3:43:13 PM :    Attempting to terminate 162 suspended instances in
                           host
08/11/2009 3:43:14 PM :    SUCCESS> 162 Service instance terminated
----------------------------------------
08/11/2009 3:43:14 PM :    Host: BizTalkServerIsolatedHost
08/11/2009 3:43:15 PM :    No suspended instances in this host

-------       SUMMARY START       -------
08/11/2009 3:43:25 PM :    Total of 662 suspended messages were terminated in
                           BizTalkServerApplication host
08/11/2009 3:43:30 PM :    Total of 0 suspended messages were terminated in
                           BizTalkServerIsolatedHost host
-------        SUMMARY END        -------

08/11/2009 3:43:32 PM :    Script Execution Completed
-------  SCRIPT EXECUTION ENDED  -------
```

How to Tune Each Subsystem

A typical BizTalk solution includes adapters, pipelines, maps, message schemas, orchestrations, and ports. Figure 11-11 shows a logical illustration of a BizTalk solution detailing the different components that might be involved in it and dividing them into their logical containers, inbound Receive Adapters and receive pipelines, processing orchestrations and business rules, as well as outbound send pipelines and Send Adapters. The illustration highlights the constant reliance on the Messagebox and a typical message flow within the solution. The receive locations and send locations are implied as the **Inbound** and **Outbound** containers. The maps and filters are applied to the implied ports. To properly tune the environment and the solution, you need to identify the different components used by your solution.

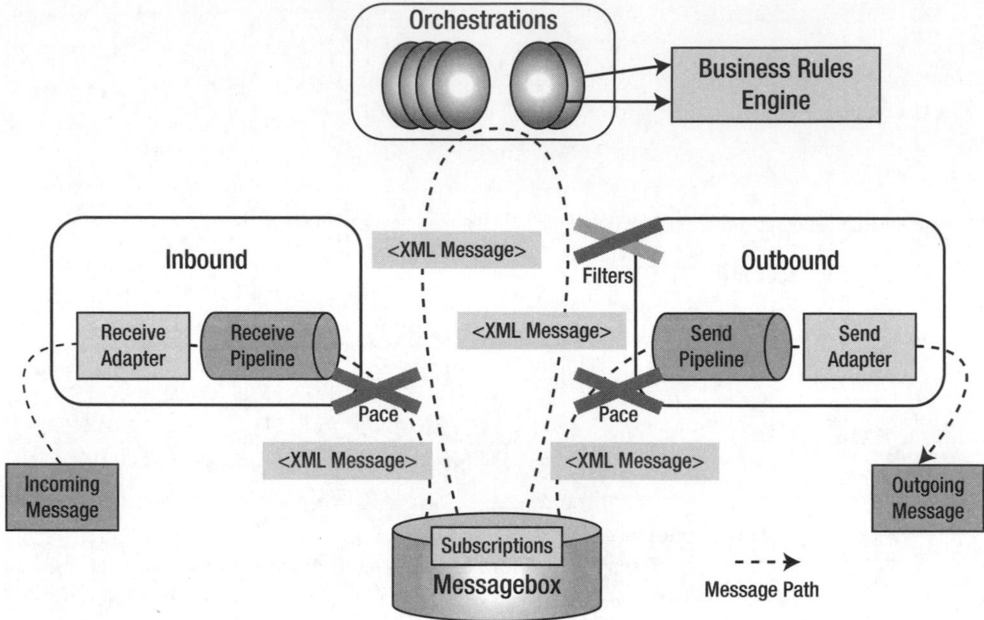

Figure 11-11. *The different components constituting a BizTalk solution*

ASP.NET, SOAP, and HTTP

To tune HTTP, as well as SOAP Send and Receive Adapters and WCF adapters, you have to fiddle around with ASP.NET web.config and machine.config files as well as BTSNTSvc.exe.config and the registry keys for the BTSNTSvc.exe service instance that is hosting the adapter.

Receive Adapter Tuning

Tuning the SOAP and WCF receive host is mostly about tuning web services, IIS, and the ASP.NET worker process. You can use LoadGen or the Microsoft Web Application Stress (WAS) Tool[10] to stress test the isolated host and gather performance metrics. Table 11-3 shows a set of performance metrics to monitor while load testing the web services. Web services use ASP.NET thread pooling to process requests. To ensure that your web services use the thread pool most effectively, consider the following guidelines (Meier, 2004):[11,12]

10 This is a free stress-testing application that can simulate loads of hundreds or thousands of users accessing your ASP.NET application or web service and generates a summary report with performance information. The tool is downloadable from www.microsoft.com/downloads/details.aspx?familyid=e2c0585a-062a-439e-a67d-75a89aa36495&displaylang=en.

11 The following settings' values should be used as guidelines and a starting point. They should be tuned either up or down based on the results of the load tests.

12 Copyright © 2004 by Microsoft Corporation. Reprinted with permission from Microsoft Corporation.

- Set the maximum thread-pool thresholds to reduce contention:
    - Set *maxIOThreads* and *maxWorkerThreads* in machine.config to 100. The *maxIOThreads* setting controls the maximum number of I/O threads in the common language runtime (CLR) thread pool. This number is then automatically multiplied by the number of available CPUs. The recommendation is to set this to 100. The *maxWorkerThreads* setting controls the maximum number of worker threads in the CLR thread pool. This number is then automatically multiplied by the number of available CPUs. The recommendation is to set this to 100.
    - Set *minFreeThreads* in machine.config to 88 × the number of CPUs. The worker process uses this setting to queue up all the incoming requests if the number of available threads in the thread pool falls below the value for this setting. This setting effectively limits the number of concurrently executing requests to *maxWorkerThreads* – *minFreeThreads*. The recommendation is to set this to 88 times the number of CPUs. This limits the number of concurrent requests to 12 (assuming *maxWorkerThreads* is 100).
    - Set *minLocalRequestFreeThreads* to 76 × the number of CPUs.[13] This worker process uses this setting to queue up requests from localhost (where a web application calls a web service on the same server) if the number of available threads in the thread pool falls below this number. This setting is similar to *minFreeThreads*, but it applies only to requests that use localhost. The recommendation is to set this to 76 times the number of CPUs.
- Set the minimum thread-pool thresholds to handle load bursts. Set *minIOThreads* and *minWorkerThreads* to prep the thread pool for incoming large loads instead of creating new threads as requests come in to fill up the pool.

Table 11-3. *Basic Counters to Monitor for ASP.NET (Northrup)*[14]

Object	Counter	Description
Processor	% CPU Utilization	The overall measure of total processor utilization on a web server. The processor is the most common bottleneck on ASP.NET web servers. If this counter peaks near 100% while the web server is under load, you should add the % Processor Time counter for the Process object to isolate which process is bogging down the server.

Continued

13 The difference between minFreeThreads and minLocalRequestFreeThreads is intentional to ensure that local requests have a higher priority than remote requests. This allows remote calls to web service A, which calls local web service B, to acquire the required resources to make the second web service call and complete successfully. Had both settings been the same, a sudden spike in concurrent calls to web service A would result in a timeout and eventually a process recycle, as the process would consume the available threads to service the calls to web service A and would not find enough resources to service the calls from web service A to web service B.

14 Copyright © 2004 by Microsoft Corporation. Reprinted with permission from Microsoft Corporation.

Table 11-3. *Continued*

Object	Counter	Description
Process	% Processor Time	This counter provides similar information to the % CPU Utilization counter but identifies which specific process is using the most CPU time. To be certain you gather all the information you need, you should select the All Instances radio button in the Add Counters dialog box when adding this counter. If the aspnet_wp process is consuming most of the processor, it is a good indication that rendering ASP.NET pages is the bottleneck. If the inetinfo process is to blame, IIS itself is the cause of the problem. These conditions can be remedied by upgrading the web server's processor, adding multiple processors, or adding more web servers. If your ASP.NET application is database-driven and you run a Microsoft SQL Server on the same system, you will very likely discover that the process named sqlservr is causing the CPU bottleneck. The best remedy for this situation is to move the SQL Server software to another physical server. Alternatively, upgrading the processor or adding more processors will help.
ASP.NET Applications	Requests/Sec	This counter measures the current rate of incoming ASP.NET requests and is a useful way to measure the peak capacity of your web application while under load. The counter will report on only the number of requests for files with extensions configured in IIS to be passed to ASP.NET—most commonly, .aspx and .asmx files. To view the total number of requests, including requests for images, add the Get Requests/Sec counter from the Web Service object instead.
ASP.NET Applications	Sessions Active	This counter measures the current number of active ASP.NET sessions. A session is created by an ASP.NET application when a new user makes the first request. The session lives until 1) the application explicitly abandons it when the user logs out, or 2) no requests are received from the user for the period of the session timeout. By default, ASP.NET sessions timeout after 20 minutes. This setting can be adjusted by modifying the `timeout` attribute of the `sessionState` element in the web.config or machine.config files.
ASP.NET	Requests Queued	Requests are queued when the time required to render a page is greater than the time between incoming client requests. In normal web traffic, request rates are very erratic, and queuing might occur for a few seconds during a busy moment. This will cause page load times to increase temporarily, but the queue is quickly eliminated during the next quiet moment. Traffic generated by a load-testing tool such as WAS might not have the same erratic patterns and might cause the ASP.NET Requests Queued counter to climb before it would do so under real traffic conditions. To simulate these random peaks and valleys in web traffic, enable the Use Random Delay check box on the script settings page of WAS. If this counter still increases with this setting enabled, the server is currently above its peak capacity, and a bottleneck should be identified and resolved before continuing testing. By default, ASP.NET is configured to queue a maximum of 100 requests. This limit is defined by the `appRequestQueueLimit` attribute of the `httpRunTime` element of the web.config or machine.config files.

Object	Counter	Description
ASP.NET	Requests Rejected	After the ASP.NET request queue is full, new requests are rejected. This process is generally a good way for ASP.NET to behave under extremely heavy load because it is better to return an error to the user immediately and remove the request from the web server's queue than to force users to wait for their browser to timeout. Monitoring this counter gives you a running total of the requests received while the queue length was at the maximum.

Send Adapter Tuning

The default number of maximum concurrent outgoing SOAP connections is two. This can cause outgoing SOAP requests to timeout and create a bottleneck in scenarios where a high volume of outgoing SOAP requests is expected. If not treated, this problem can cause a buildup of messages in the Messagebox and entries in the spool table resulting in overall performance degradation. It may also cause the host instances running the SOAP Send Adapter to recycle because eventually, if the load is high enough and the time taken for the called web method to complete is long enough, all threads in that host instance's thread pool will be exhausted, and the host instance will be unable to service new requests as it runs out of threads. Increasing the batch size in this scenario will only make the situation worse. Decreasing it might eliminate the errors, but it will not improve the performance of the solution.

To rectify this problem, you need to increase the maximum number of connections for the host instances hosting the SOAP Send Adapter. The recommended value is 25 connections × the number of CPUs on the server.[15] This is done by adding a `maxconnection` element to the ConnectionManagement node in the BTSNTSvc.exe.config file on each of the BizTalk Servers in the BizTalk Server Group. This file holds the common configuration for the BizTalk host services. If the solution needs to call web services with performance issues that cannot handle more than a specific number of concurrent transactions, the same setting can be used to specify a low number of maximum concurrent connections for that specific web service and ensure that you do not overdrive that service to failure. Per the config file fragment that follows, the `maxconnection` key could be defined multiple times with different `name` attributes identifying different endpoints, thus allowing for the customization of different maximum values for the concurrent number of connections for different endpoints. To specify the default value used for all web service endpoints not specifically called out by name, use * as the `name` attribute for the default key value.

15 The actual maximum number of connections entered to the configuration file should be a factor of the total number of CPUs on the server running the BizTalk host instance, because the thread-pool size in each host depends on the number of CPUs on the server.

```
<configuration>
...
   <system.net>
      <connectionManagement>
         <add name = "www.MyLowThroughputWebService.com" maxconnection = "4" />
         <add name = "*" maxconnection = "50" />
      </connectionManagement>
   </system.net>
</configuration>
```

Web services located on the same computer as your BizTalk solution share the same thread pool with web services exposed by the BizTalk solution if running within the same application pool. Therefore, the client-facing web services and the web service being called through the SOAP Send Adapter share the same threads and other related resources, such as CPU for request processing. Calling a local web service also means that your request travels through the entire processing pipeline and incurs overhead, including serialization, thread switching, request queuing, and deserialization.

In addition, the `maxconnection` attribute of machine.config has no effect on the connection limit for making calls to local web services. Therefore, local web services always tend to give preference to the requests that come from the local computer over requests that come from other machines. This degrades the throughput of the web service for remote clients (Meier, 2004). If the local web services are not making calls to any external systems and their web method processing time is considerably low, package them into a .NET library and call them from within your orchestrations. If those web services are calling external systems or take a considerable amount of processing time, move them off the BizTalk Server Group servers.

By default, the .NET thread pool used by BizTalk host instances is 100 threads per CPU. To configure the maximum number of threads allocated by the thread pool, set the *MaxWorkerThreadsPerProcessor* DWORD registry key under software\Microsoft\BizTalk Server\3.0\Administration.

HTTP-Specific Tuning

Several configuration and tuning parameters are accessible for the HTTP adapter through registry key entries and through the modification of the BTSNTSvc.exe.config file that is located in the root BizTalk installation directory. Table 11-4 describes the registry settings that affect the performance of the HTTP and WCF adapter. Note that by default there are no HTTP adapter keys in the registry, so the HTTP adapter uses the default settings. To change the default settings, you need to create the following registry keys under the following locations in the registry:

DisableChunkEncoding, *RequestQueueSize*, and *HttpReceiveThreadsPerCpu* must be defined in HKEY_LOCAL_MACHINE\SYSTEM\CurrentControlSet\Services\BTSSvc.3.0\HttpReceive.

HttpOutTimeoutInterval, *HttpOutInflightSize*, and *HttpOutCompleteSize* must be defined in HKEY_LOCAL_MACHINE\SYSTEM\CurrentControlSet\Services\BTSSvc{$HostName}.[16]

16 {$Host Name} is the actual host name. In BizTalk Server 2004 or a BizTalk Server 2009 upgrade from BizTalk 2004, the key may be HKEY_LOCAL_MACHINE\SYSTEM\CurrentControlSet\Services\BTSSvc{GUID}, where GUID is the ID of the host for the HTTP send handler.

Table 11-4. *HTTP Adapter Settings (Microsoft, "BizTalk Server 2009 Documentation," 2006)*[17]

Key Name	Type	Default Value	Description
DisableChunkEncoding	DWORD	0	Regulates whether or not the HTTP Receive Adapter uses chunked encoding when sending responses back to the client. Set to a nonzero value to turn off chunked encoding for HTTP Receive Adapter responses. Minimum value: 0 Maximum value: Any nonzero value
RequestQueueSize	DWORD	256	Defines the number of concurrent requests that the HTTP Receive Adapter processes at one time. Minimum value: 10 Maximum value: 2048
HttpReceive ThreadsPerCpu	DWORD	2	Defines the number of threads per CPU that are allocated to the HTTP Receive Adapter. Minimum value: 1 Maximum value: 10
HttpOutTimeoutInterval	DWORD	2,000	Defines the interval in seconds that the HTTP Send Adapter will wait before timing out. Minimum value: 500 Maximum value: 10,000,000
HttpOutInflightSize	DWORD	100	This is the maximum number of concurrent HTTP requests that a BizTalk Server HTTP Send Adapter instance will handle. The recommended value for latency is between three to five times that of the *maxconnection* configuration file entry. Minimum value: 1 Maximum value: 1024
HttpOutCompleteSize	DWORD	5	This is the size of the batch of messages that is returned from the HTTP Send Adapter. If the buffer is not full and there are outstanding responses, the adapter will wait for 1 second until it commits the batch. For low-latency scenarios, this should be set to 1, which will allow the adapter to send response messages immediately to the Messagebox for processing. This will have the greatest effect during times of low-throughput activity with varied response times from backend systems. Minimum value: 1 Maximum value: 1024

The number of concurrent connections that the HTTP or WCF adapter opens for a particular destination server is configured by modifying the *maxconnection* entry in the BTSNTSvc.exe.config file that is located in the root BizTalk installation directory.

17 Copyright © 2004 by Microsoft Corporation. Reprinted with permission from Microsoft Corporation.

Caution This property will be applied to both the HTTP and SOAP adapters if they send messages to the same destination HTTP server. By default the maximum connections for all URIs is 20.

This configuration file entry replaces the functionality of the *HttpOutMaxConnection* registry key that was used in BizTalk 2004. If you have upgraded from BizTalk Server 2004 to BizTalk Server 2009 and you were using this registry key, you will need to apply this configuration file entry instead (Microsoft, 2006).[18]

CLR Tuning

Bottlenecks caused by contention for resources, misuse of threads, inefficient resource cleanup, or resource leaks can be rectified by tuning the CLR thread pool or memory thresholds. The use of memory thresholds will be discussed later in the "Throttling" section.

In situations with low CPU utilization or the CPU is fully saturated and yet the solution is not meeting the required throughput, increasing the maximum number of threads in the .NET thread pool by modifying the *maxIOThreads* and *maxWorkerThreads* registry keys might improve performance. Tuning the maximum number of threads in the thread pool down might come in handy if the CPU utilization is pretty high, while the solution's overall throughput is still lower than expected. This could be because the system is spending more time context-switching between threads than processing.

If the solution is expected to handle load bursts, prepping the engine to maintain a minimum number of threads active to avoid the overhead of resources and thread allocation when those bursts occur is a good idea. This is done by setting the *minIOThreads* and *minWorkerThreads* registry keys to ensure that a minimum number of threads are always allocated in the thread pool. A value of the expected load during a spike + 10% is usually the recommended value for the *minIOThreads* and *minWorkerThreads* settings.

To modify the hosted CLR .NET thread pool for a particular BizTalk host, you have to create the following registry keys and set their values for that particular host:

- HKEY_LOCAL_MACHINE\SYSTEM\CurrentControlSet\Services\BTSSvc{$HostName}\CLR Hosting\MaxWorkerThreads (REG_DWORD)
- HKEY_LOCAL_MACHINE\SYSTEM\CurrentControlSet\Services\BTSSvc {$HostName}\CLR Hosting\MaxIOThreads (REG_DWORD)
- HKEY_LOCAL_MACHINE\SYSTEM\CurrentControlSet\Services\BTSSvc {$HostName}\CLR Hosting\MinWorkerThreads (REG_DWORD)
- HKEY_LOCAL_MACHINE\SYSTEM\CurrentControlSet\Services\BTSSvc {$HostName}\CLR Hosting\MinIOThreads (REG_DWORD)[19]

18 Copyright © 2004 by Microsoft Corporation. Reprinted with permission from Microsoft Corporation.

19 The {$HostName} in BTSSvc{$HostName} should be replaced by the actual host name. In BizTalk 2004 or BizTalk 2006 installations that are an upgrade from BizTalk 2004, the {$HostName} should be replaced with the GUID for that host. To get the GUID for a particular host, open the Services Console from the Administrative Tools, locate the host that requires the tuning, and get its ServiceName including the GUID.

File Tuning

Several issues can occur with the file adapter. File adapter–related issues are usually the result of NetBIOS limitations or the polling agent. Microsoft's support articles recommend to increase the *MaxMpxCt* and the *MaxCmds* registry keys at HKEY_LOCAL_MACHINE\SYSTEM\CurrentControlSet\Services\lanmanworkstation\parameters to 2048 on the BizTalk Server as well as the file server holding the file share.[20]

BizTalk Server 2009 can encounter problems when a polling notification and a file change notification occur at the same time. This problem can be avoided by disabling FRF (File Receive Functions) polling through the File Receive Location property pages.

File Tuning: Batch Files

When dealing with large flat files that generate thousands of subdocuments in an envelope, isolate the File Receive Adapter in a separate host. Set the batch size to 1 and the thread-pool size for that host to 1. This will reduce the number of files you are processing in one transaction from 20 to 1 and single thread the host. The batch size property could be set on the receive location property page. To set the thread-pool size to 1, set the *MessagingThreadsPerCpu* property, which defines the number of threads per CPU for the thread pool, on the host's property pages and create the *MessagingThreadPoolSize* registry key, which defines the number of threads per CPU in the thread pool, under HKEY_LOCAL_MACHINE\SYSTEM\CurrentControlSet\Services\BTSSvc {$HostName }. The respective default values for both properties are 2 and 10. Setting those two values to 1 and dedicating a single thread in the host's thread pool to message processing ensures that multiple large flat files will not be competing for system resources within that host and that all the host's memory resources will be dedicated to processing the large message.

■ **Note** If you have multiple receive locations receiving large flat files as well as smaller ones, group them under different receive handlers running on different hosts. This ensures that the tuning performed on the host instances running the File Receive handler for large-flat-file processing does not affect the rest of the file receive functions processing smaller files. It is recommended to partition those receive handlers on different servers within the BizTalk Server Group by interleaving host instances on the different servers to ensure they are not competing for the same system resources.

When supporting large interchanges in BizTalk Server 2009, multiple smaller interchanges utilize the CPU processor more efficiently than fewer large interchanges. As a general guideline, use the following formula to determine the maximum size of an interchange for any given deployment (number of CPU processors):

20 The support article "'The Network BIOS Command Limit Has Been Reached' Error Message in Windows Server 2003, in Windows XP, and in Windows 2000 Server" can be found at support.microsoft.com/?id=810886.

Maximum number of messages per interchange <= 200,000 / (Number of CPUs × BatchSize × MessagingThreadPoolSize)

So, for example, a BizTalk host running on a four-CPU server tuned for large-flat-file processing, having a batch size of 1 and a single thread in its messaging thread pool, would be able to process an infinite number of interchanges as long as each interchange contains a maximum of 50,000 messages (200,000 divided by 4).Thus, *MessagingThreadPoolSize* is set to 1.

Parsing and Persistence

Persistence affects the overall system performance. Message parsing affects performance due to the incurred persistence points in the process. To tune the BizTalk solution and minimize the number of persistence points, change the Large Message Threshold and Fragment Size property of the BizTalk Server Group. The default value for this property is 1MB, meaning that each 1MB read from the message will result in a fragment being persisted to the Messagebox. To further elaborate, as stated in the white paper "BizTalk Server 2006 Runtime Improvements" (Microsoft, 2005):[21]

In previous releases of BizTalk Server, mapping of documents always occurred in-memory. While in-memory mapping provides the best performance, it can quickly eat up resources when large documents are mapped. For this reason, BizTalk Server 2006 introduced support for large message transformations. A different transformation engine is used when transforming large messages so that memory is utilized in an efficient manner. When dealing with large messages, the message data is buffered to the file system instead of being loaded into memory using the DOM (Document Object Model). This way the memory consumption remains flat as memory is used only to store the cashed data and indexes for the buffer. However, as the file system is used, there is expected performance degradation when comparing with in-memory transformation. Because of the potential performance impact, the two transformation engines will coexist in BizTalk Server 2006.

When message size is smaller than a specified threshold, the in-memory transformation will be used. If message size exceeds the threshold then the large message transformation engine is used. The threshold is configurable using the registry

** DWORD 'TransformThreshold'*

** 'HKLM\\Software\\Microsoft\\BizTalk Server\\3.0\\Administration'.*

If the solution handles a low number of large messages, increase this value to a large value like 5MB. If the solution handles a high number of small/medium messages, set this value to 250K. You will need to experiment with this setting to find the optimum value for your solution and messages. Increasing the Large Message Threshold and Fragment Size property for the

21 Copyright © 2005 by Microsoft Corporation. Reprinted with permission from Microsoft Corporation.

BizTalk Server Group results in fewer persistence points, in turn causing fewer round-trips to the database and faster message processing. The drawback of this approach is higher memory utilization, as fragments kept in memory now are much larger in size. To compensate for the expected higher memory utilization by the large message fragments, control the number of large message buffers that are created by the BizTalk host. You can do so by creating a *MessagingLMBufferCacheSize* (DWORD) registry key under System\CurrentControlSet\Services\BTSSvc<HostName> and setting its value to 5.

By controlling the number of large message buffers, you are hedging the risk of having the host run into low memory situations due to large message processing without incurring the penalty of constant round-trips to the Messagebox (Wasznicky, 2006).[22]

Latency

The time taken to process a message is dependent on how often the different BizTalk Server components pick up work items from the Messagebox. This interval affects the rate at which received messages are being published to the Messagebox as well as the rate at which they are being picked up from the Messagebox for processing or delivery. To deliver enterprise capabilities such as fault tolerance and scalability, the distributed BizTalk Server agents have to communicate asynchronously through the Messagebox. This asynchronous communication scheme means that the agents have to check the Messagebox for state updates to pick up new items for processing and update the Messagebox at appropriate points in the process. This polling process contributes to the inherent latency of BizTalk solutions. If the end-to-end processing time per business transaction under low loads is unacceptable, you might want to look into tuning the interval at which the different agents check the Messagebox. By default, the *MaxReceiveInterval* is set to 500 msecs. You can reset this interval to a value as low as 100 msecs by modifying it in the adm_ServiceClass table for the XLANG/s, Messaging Isolated, and Messaging In-Process hosts. If the overall environment is experiencing high loads on the database while the overall end-to-end business transaction processing speed is acceptable, you can increase the *MaxReceiveInterval* and check whether that improves the overall environment's stability.

Throttling

Throttling is the mechanism by which the runtime engine prevents itself from thrashing and dropping dead when exposed to a high load. A properly throttled engine takes up only the amount of load that it can handle, and detects a stressed situation quickly and mitigates the situation accordingly.

Before BizTalk Server 2009

In BizTalk 2004, throttling BizTalk Server includes manipulating entries in the adm_ServiceClass table. Manipulating that table manually is now deprecated as it was troublesome and originally undocumented. Throttling BizTalk Server 2004 manually usually leads to more problems if inexperienced administrators start manipulating it, as it is mostly a trial-and-error exercise.

22 Copyright © 2006 by Microsoft Corporation. Reprinted with permission from Microsoft Corporation.

Manipulating the adm_ServiceClass table affects the entire BizTalk Server Group, not just a specific host instance. The configuration settings are not host specific and hence are not useful in any configuration with multiple hosts. If different servers in the BizTalk Server Group have different hardware configurations, having the same settings across different hardware is not the best approach. Other problem areas in BizTalk Server 2004 are as follows:

- The stress detection mechanism in BizTalk 2004 is grossly dependent on user input, namely the low and high watermark numbers in the adm_ServiceClass table.
- The configuration parameters are not exposed to the user through the UI.
- The inbound throttling heuristic (session count based) is not very effective because XLANG does not factor this at all, and all the sessions are shared across all the service classes.
- The agent's memory-based throttling policy has two major drawbacks:
  - First, it looks into the global memory and does not take into account the local memory usage. So if the server has more memory than 2GB, it might not be throttling properly, as the maximum amount of memory that a host instance can consume is 2GB on a Windows 32-bit platform. So, while the server could still have free memory that is not being consumed by other services, a particular host might be running out of the memory that it could consume without throttling.
  - Second, while enforcing throttling due to low memory condition, the agent does not do anything to improve the memory usage situation, other than elevating the stress level. Once it enters a stress mode due to high memory condition, no measure is taken for it to come out of this stage, and hence it remains in this state for a long time. As the system starts again, it reloads all dehydrated orchestrations, resulting in an elevated rate of resource consumption leading to the same situation that caused the throttle in the first place (Wasznicky, 2006).[23]

Throttling Goals for BizTalk Server

One of the Microsoft development team's objectives for BizTalk Server was to get around the nuances of throttling configuration. The target was a system that avoids using user-input parameters for detecting stress condition—a system with heuristics that include monitoring of resources (e.g., memory, threads, database sessions), utilization, and progress of work items against submitted work items. This would allow the system to function automatically without the administrator having to deal with the unknowns surrounding the various control knobs for the watermark numbers and other settings in the adm_ServiceClass table. Some parameters still have to be configured manually. The bright side is that they can be set and manipulated through the administration UI, and they have out-of-box valid settings. Those parameters are now at host level rather than group level.

The aim is to eventually communicate throttling actions to the system administrator through Event Logs and performance counters. Currently only the inbound throttling is communicated through the Event Log.

If the system is throttled due to lack of a particular resource, the engine proactively tries to mitigate the situation by releasing that particular resource so that it comes out of the stress

23 Copyright © 2006 by Microsoft Corporation. Reprinted with permission from Microsoft Corporation.

situation. For example, under low memory, cache should be shrunk and MSMQ instances should be dehydrated.

Unlike BizTalk Server 2004, BizTalk Server 2006 and BizTalk 2009 throttling takes into account process memory, in addition to global memory. All components follow uniform throttling policies to ensure a fair distribution of resources.

Auto-Throttling in 2009

BizTalk Server 2009 auto-throttling consists of a set of load detection algorithms and mitigation plans. Table 11-5 highlights those algorithms.

Table 11-5. *BizTalk Server 2006 Auto-Throttling Mechanisms (Wasznicky, 2006)*[24]

Detection	Mitigation	Affected Components	Monitors
Compare Message Delivery Rate with the Message Completion Rate. When the latter falls short, it is an indication of the fact that messages are being pushed at higher rate than the service can handle.	Throttle message delivery so that the delivery rate comes down and becomes at par with the completion rate.	XLANG All outbound transports	Need to monitor Message Delivery Rate and Message Completion Rate.
Compare the Publishing Request Rate with Publishing Completion Rate. When the latter falls short, it is an indication of the Messagebox being unable to cope with the load.	Block the publishing threads to slow down the publishing rate AND/OR indicate service class to slow down publishing.	XLANG All inbound transports	Need to monitor entry and exit of Commit Batch call.
Process memory exceeds a threshold.	Throttle publishing if batch has steep memory requirement. Throttle delivery. Indicate service to dehydrate/ shrink cache.	XLANG All transports	Monitor Private Bytes.
System memory exceeds a threshold.	Throttle publishing if batch has steep memory requirement. Throttle delivery.	XLANG All transports	Monitor physical memory.
Database sessions being used by the process exceed a threshold count.	Throttle publishing.	XLANG All inbound transports	Monitor average session usage per Messagebox.

Continued

24 Copyright © 2006 by Microsoft Corporation. Reprinted with permission from Microsoft Corporation.

Table 11-5. *Continued*

Detection	Mitigation	Affected Components	Monitors
Any host message queue size, the spool size, or the tracking data size exceeds a particular host-specific threshold in database.	Throttle publishing if batch is going to create more records in the database than delete.	XLANG All inbound transports	Monitor queue size against respective threshold.
Process thread count exceeds a particular threshold.	Throttle publishing. Throttle delivery. Indicate service to reduce thread-pool size.	XLANG All transports	Monitor threads per CPU.
Number of messages delivered to a service class exceeds a particular threshold count.	Throttle delivery.	XLANG All outbound transports	This is needed for send port throttling where the EPM expects only a limited number of messages at a time.

To perform this auto-throttling, the server uses the configurable parameters detailed in Table 11-6.

Table 11-6. *BizTalk Server 2006 Auto-Throttling Parameters (Wasznicky, 2006)*[25]

Name	Type	Description	Default Value	Min Value	Max Value
Message Delivery Throttling Configuration					
Sample-space size	Long	Number of samples that are used for determining the rate of the message delivery to all service classes of the host. This parameter is used to determine whether the samples collected for applying rate-based throttling are valid or not. If the number of samples collected is lower than the sample size, the samples are discarded because the system is running under a low load and hence no throttling may be required. Thus this value should be at par with a reasonable rate at which messages can be consumed under a medium load. For example, if the system is expected to process at 100 docs per second in a medium load, then this parameter should be set to (100 × sample window duration in seconds). If the value is set too low, the system may overthrottle on low load. If the value is too high, there may not be enough samples for this technique to be effective. **Zero indicates rate-based message delivery throttling is disabled.**	100	0	N/A
Sample-space window	Long	Duration of the sliding time window (in milliseconds) within which samples will be considered for calculation of rate. **Zero indicates rate-based message delivery throttling is disabled.**	15,000	1,000	N/A
Overdrive factor	Long	Percent factor by which the system will try to overdrive the input. That is, if the output rate is 200 per second and the overdrive factor is 125%, the system will allow up to 250 (200 × 125%) per second to be passed as input before applying rate-based throttling. A smaller value will cause a very conservative throttling and may lead to overthrottling when load is increased, whereas a higher value will try to adapt to the increase in load quickly, at the expense of slight underthrottling.		125	100

Continued

25 Copyright © 2006 by Microsoft Corporation. Reprinted with permission from Microsoft Corporation.

Table 11-6. *Continued*

Name	Type	Description	Default Value	Min Value	Max Value
Maximum delay	Long	Maximum delay (in milliseconds) imposed for message delivery throttling. The actual delay imposed is a factor of how long the throttling condition persists and the severity of the particular throttling trigger. **Zero indicates message delivery throttling is completely disabled.**		300,000	0
Message Publishing Throttling Configuration					
Sample-space size	Long	Number of samples that are used for determining the rate of the message publishing by the service classes. This parameter is used to determine whether the samples collected for applying rate-based throttling are valid or not. If the number of samples collected is lower than the sample size, the samples are discarded because the system is running under a low load, and hence no throttling may be required. Thus this value should be at par with a reasonable rate at which messages can be consumed under a medium load. For example, if the system is expected to publish 100 docs per second in a medium load, this parameter should be set to (100 × sample window duration in seconds). If the value is set too low, then the system may overthrottle on low load. If the value is too high, there may not be enough samples for this technique to be effective. **Zero indicates rate-based message publishing throttling is disabled.**	100	0	N/A
Sample-space window	Long	Duration of the sliding time window (in milliseconds) within which samples will be considered for calculation of rate. **Zero indicates rate-based message publishing throttling is disabled.**	15,000	1,000	N/A
Overdrive factor	Long	Percent factor by which the system will try to overdrive the input. That is, if the output rate is 200 per second and the overdrive factor is 125%, the system will allow up to 250 (200 × 125%) per second to be passed as input before applying rate-based throttling. A smaller value will cause a very conservative throttling and may lead to overthrottling when load is increased, whereas a higher value will try to adapt to the increase in load quickly, at the expense of slight underthrottling.	125	100	N/A

Name	Type	Description	Default Value	Min Value	Max Value
Maximum delay	Long	Maximum delay (in milliseconds) imposed for message publishing throttling. The actual delay imposed is a factor of how long the throttling condition persists and the severity of the particular throttling trigger. **Zero indicates message publishing throttling is completely disabled.**	300,000	0	N/A
Other Configuration and Thresholds					
Delivery queue size	Long	Size of the in-memory queue that the host maintains as a temporary place-holder for delivering messages. Messages for the host are dequeued and placed in this in-memory queue before finally delivering to the service classes. Setting a large value can improve low-latency scenarios since more messages will be proactively dequeued. However, if the messages are large, the messages in the delivery queue would consume memory and hence a low queue size would be desirable for large message scenarios to avoid excessive memory consumption. The host needs to be restarted for this change to take effect.	100	1	N/A
Database session threshold	Long	Maximum number of concurrent database sessions (per CPU) allowed before throttling begins. Note that the idle database sessions in the common per-host session pool do not add to this count, and this check is made strictly on the number of sessions actually being used by the host. This is disabled by default and may be enabled if the data-base server is low end compared to the host servers. **Zero indicates session-based throttling is disabled.**	0	0	N/A
System memory threshold	Long	Maximum system-wide physical memory usage allowed before throttling begins. This threshold can be presented either in absolute value in MB or in percent-available format. A value of less than 100 indicates a percent value. Throttling based on this factor is equivalent to yielding to other processes in the system that consume physical memory. **Zero indicates system memory-based throttling is disabled.**	0	0	N/A

Continued

Table 11-6. *Continued*

Name	Type	Description	Default Value	Min Value	Max Value
Process memory threshold	Long	Maximum process memory (in MB) allowed before throttling begins. This threshold can be presented either in absolute value in MB or in percent-available format. A value of less than 100 indicates a percent value, and when a percent value is specified, the actual MB limit is dynamically computed based on the total virtual memory that the host can grow to (limited by the amount of free physical memory and page file; and on 32-bit systems, this is further limited by the 2GB address space). The user-specified value is used as a guideline, and the host may dynamically self-tune this threshold value based on the memory usage pattern of the process.This value should be set to a low value for scenarios having large memory requirement per message. Setting a low value will kick in throttling early on and prevent a memory explosion within the process. **Zero indicates process-memory-based throttling is disabled.**	25%	0	N/A
Thread threshold	Long	Maximum number of threads in the process (per CPU) allowed before throttling begins. The user-specified value is used as a guideline, and the host may dynamically self-tune this threshold value based on the memory usage pattern of the process. The thread-based throttling is disabled by default. In scenarios where excessive load can cause an unbounded thread growth (e.g., custom adapter creates a thread for each message), this should be enabled. **Zero indicates thread-count-based throttling is disabled.**	0	0	N/A
Message count in database threshold	Long	Maximum number of unprocessed messages in the database (aggregated over all Messageboxes). This factor essentially controls how many records will be allowed in the destination queue(s) before throttling begins. In addition to watching the destination queues, the host also checks the size of the spool table and the tracking-data tables and ensures they do not exceed a certain record count (by default, 10 times the message-count threshold). **Zero indicates database-size-based throttling is disabled.**	50,000	0	N/A

Name	Type	Description	Default Value	Min Value	Max Value
In-process message threshold	Long	Maximum number of in-memory inflight messages (per CPU) allowed before message delivery is throttled. In-process messages are those that are handed off to the transport manager/XLANG engine, but not yet processed. The user-specified value is used as a guideline and the host may dynamically self-tune this threshold value based on the memory usage pattern of the process. In scenarios where the transport may work more efficiently with fewer messages at a time, this value should be set to a low value. **Zero indicates in-process message-count-based throttling is disabled**.	1,000	0	N/A

CHAPTER 12

WCF Adapters: Standardizing Your Integration Endpoints

When architecting an enterprise solution, providing standards-compliant access is a must in today's heterogeneous environments. Developers have enough to consider when designing an application's business purpose without having to consider how other applications will need to integrate with the service provided.

Gone are the days where developers know who and, more important, how other solutions will be consuming their applications. This is especially true for BizTalk developers. Our endpoints are purposely designed to be generic and interoperable in order to provide maximum reusability.

With the introduction of Windows Communication Foundation in .NET Framework 3.0 in November 2006, it has never been easier to provide a consistent, flexible, standards-compliant programming model as part of your solution. As such, WCF has become an integral part of many .NET-based enterprise applications.

WCF and BizTalk 2009

Web services support in BizTalk has been available natively since BizTalk 2004, but that version could exploit only the limited service capabilities included in ASP.NET web services (ASMX).

With the introduction of BizTalk Server 2006, and now 2009, Windows Communication Foundation is a first-class citizen in the BizTalk architecture with native support for WCF-based Send and Receive Adapters.

Leveraging the WCF adapter as your solution's integration endpoints automatically provides a highly configurable, standards-compliant, and interoperable option for other applications to communicate with your service.

WCF and the BizTalk adapter model fit nicely together. Table 12-1 compares how each of these technologies can work together to provide a seamless communication model.

Table 12-1. *WCF and BizTalk Feature Comparison*

WCF Feature	BizTalk Feature
Multiple transport bindings	Multiple adapters, each having their own transport
Configurable setup via application configuration files	Adapter configuration via the BizTalk Administration Console
Multiple endpoints for a single application	Multiple receive locations for a single application
Multiple security options	Each receive location can have different security configurations and/or pipelines

Exploring the Built-in WCF Adapter Transport Support

BizTalk 2009 has seven WCF adapters. Each of the adapters, with the exception of the WCF-CustomIsolated adapter, consists of Send and Receive Adapters.

The WCF Receive Adapters are provided as two types of adapters: isolated WCF adapters and in-process WCF adapters. Although in-process adapters are managed by BizTalk Server, isolated adapters are not instantiated by BizTalk Server. Rather, they are instantiated and hosted in another process. The isolated WCF adapters are hosted in web applications running in Internet Information Services (IIS).

You can find these adapters as part of the configuration of a receive location or send port. Figure 12-1 shows the list of WCF Receive Adapters.

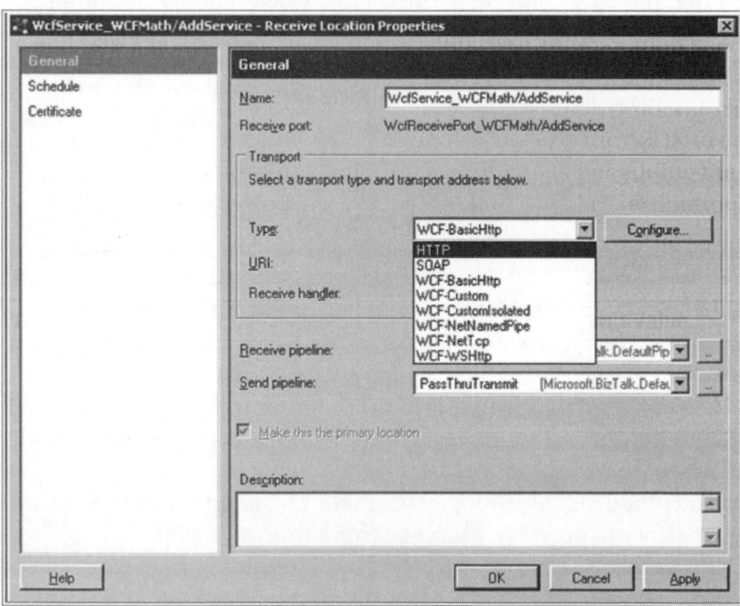

Figure 12-1. *BizTalk WCF Receive Adapters*

Table 12-2 describes each of the adapters natively supported by BizTalk and explains when each is best used or should be considered to meet your requirements.

Table 12-2. *BizTalk Receive Adapters*

Adapter	WCF Binding Name	Description
WCF-BasicHttp	basicHttpBinding	The WCF-BasicHttp adapter is commonly used as a default transport. It provides maximum backward compatibility with first-generation web services and leverages the HTTP and HTTPS protocols for enhanced security configuration. Since this binding relies on HTTP, it is limited to the features it supports. On the other hand, it is also one of the faster bindings that WCF supports. Consider using this binding if you need to communicate with ASMX web services, need support for communication through a firewall, or just want the fastest possible HTTP communication.
WCF-WSHttp	wsHttpBinding	The WCF-WSHttp adapter provides compatibility with the WS-* specifications including WS-Security, WS-AtomicTransactions, and WS-Addressing. Using this adapter provides enhanced security features, including the ability to apply security at the message level instead of the transport level. This allows the messages to be passed along multiple endpoints and transports without losing the security context of the original request. Using wsHttpBinding also provides maximum compatibility with other vendors. The WS-* specifications were jointly developed by Microsoft, IBM, Sun, BEA, and other major platform vendors.
WCF-NetNamedPipe	netNamedPipeBinding	Named Pipes is a fast, binary communication used for on-machine communication. The WCF-NetNamedPipe Receive Adapter is useful when you're preprocessing service requests before processing within BizTalk. For example, you may want to build your web service to prevalidate the message values to meet certain business rules with BRE prior to submitting the request to your orchestration.
WCF-NetTcp	netTcpBinding	The netTcpBinding is a fast communication protocol using binary encoding. It's targeted toward intranet communication and is intended for WCF-to-WCF use only. In its default configuration, netTcpBinding is faster than wsHttpBinding because its security behavior is an opt-in model, rather than opt-out.

Continued

Table 12-2. *Continued*

Adapter	WCF Binding Name	Description
WCF-Custom WCF-CustomIsolated	<various>	The WCF-Custom and WCF-CustomIsolated adapters are used to fully control how you want your endpoint to behave. With the other adapters, BizTalk provides a user interface to customize the common properties of the corresponding binding. With the WCF-Custom and WCF-CustomIsolated adapters, all WCF properties are customizable. This makes configuration more flexible but also assumes an increased level of knowledge of how the WCF platform works. Since this is an advanced-level book, this chapter will be focusing on the WCF-CustomIsolated adapter for the examples.
WCF-NetMsmq	netMsmqBinding	Microsoft Message Queuing (MSMQ) is a hidden gem in the Windows platform that is underused in today's enterprise environments. There are many uses for MSMQ, which fits very nicely with BizTalk. With many BizTalk services being asynchronous, MSMQ is a natural fit for guaranteed, transactional delivery across computers. Consider using the WCF-NetMsmq adapter if you need a fire-and-forget model of communication.

■ **Tip** MSMQ can even be leveraged over the Internet. MSMQ supports submission of messages via HTTP and supports routing and proxies for communications through a DMZ.

Using the WCF Service Publishing Wizard

After you've developed your orchestration, you must complete a series of steps before consumers can call your service:

1. Select a WCF transport.
2. Choose whether to publish orchestrations or schemas as a WCF service.
3. Specify the assembly containing your orchestrations and schemas.
4. Specify service names and schema types.
5. Specify a service namespace.
6. Specify an endpoint URI.

Performing all these steps would be time-consuming and error-prone manually. Instead, the BizTalk WCF Service Publishing Wizard will automate this entire process. This program, which you start by clicking its icon in your Start menu, steps you through a series of screens to gather all the information needed to generate your WCF service. Then the wizard generates the service as you have specified it.

Step 1: Select a WCF Transport

Figure 12-2 shows the first screen in the BizTalk WCF Service Publishing Wizard. This screen allows you to either create a new service endpoint or publish a MEX endpoint only. A metadata exchange endpoint provides consuming applications with the information needed to know how to call your service. When creating a new service endpoint, you must do the following:

1. Select a transport type of either WCF-WSBasicHttp, WCF-WSHttp, or WCF-CustomIsolated.
2. Optionally enable a MEX endpoint that describes your service.
3. Optionally create the required receive location and receive port in the selected BizTalk application.

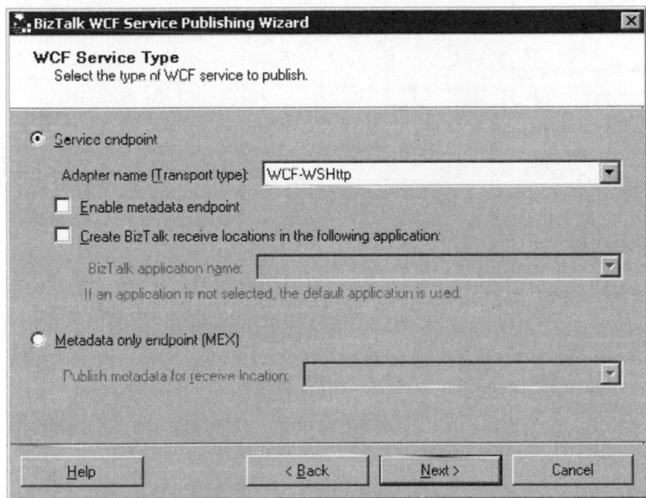

Figure 12-2. *BizTalk WCF Service Publishing Wizard's WCF Service Type screen*

Step 2: Choose Whether to Publish an Orchestration or a Schema

Once you've selected your transport type and optional choices, click Next to display the Create WCF Service page. On the Create WCF Service screen, you can choose from one of the following options:

- **Publish BizTalk Orchestrations As a WCF Service**: This will create your service based upon selected orchestrations and ports in a BizTalk assembly.
- **Publish Schemas As WCF Service**: This will publish WCF services by specifying operations and messages of WCF services using selected schemas from BizTalk assemblies as request or response message parts.

Step 3: Select Your Assembly

Once you've chosen your option, click Next to display the BizTalk Assembly page. This simple page provides a location for you to browse to and select your BizTalk assembly containing the orchestrations or schemas you want to publish. The wizard will use .NET reflection to load the types in this assembly.

Step 4: Customize Your WCF Service

At this point, the wizard has all it needs to generate a WCF endpoint except names for your service and your web methods. Figure 12-3 shows the default names given to a new service, which you can then customize.

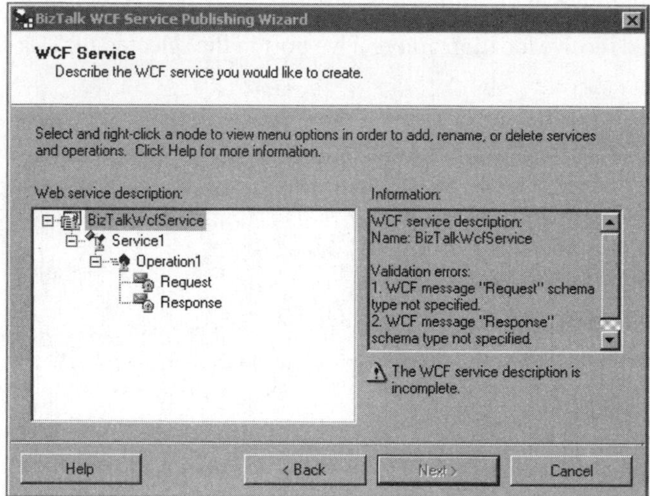

Figure 12-3. *Customizing your WCF service name and methods*

You will want to modify the default web service description to provide a more meaningful set of names to your consumers. To do this, simply right-click each root, service, operation, and method node within the tree and select the corresponding Rename option.

Additionally, for the Request and Response nodes, right-click, and choose the Select Schema Type option. Selecting this option displays a dialog box to browse to the assembly that contains the schemas to send or receive. Choose the appropriate schemas for your application.

Once you've customized each of the nodes, click Next to display the WCF Service Properties page.

Step 5: Set Your Service Namespace

This step is to provide a namespace for your service. On the WCF Service Properties page, simply provide your service a namespace, and click Next.

Step 6: Specify Your WCF Endpoint URI

Lastly, you need to provide the wizard where you would like it to create your endpoint. Figure 12-4 shows the options available when creating your endpoint location.

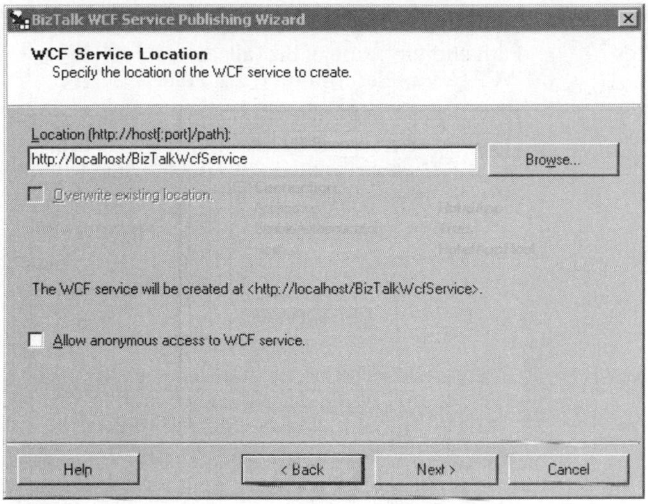

Figure 12-4. *Specifying your endpoint location*

Once you've selected your URL and optionally allowed anonymous access, the wizard will create your endpoint in IIS where it will be accessible to consuming applications.

Publishing Your WCF Service from the Command Line

The BizTalk WCF Service Publishing Wizard is convenient to use when deploying an endpoint within your development environment. For more advanced users or when automating your deployment, there is an additional downloadable command-line tool from Microsoft called the `BtsWcfServicePublishing`[1] tool.

The tool has the following syntax:

```
BtsWcfServicePublishing PathName [-AdapterName:value] [-EnableMetadata]
[-ReceiveLocation] [-ApplicationName:value] [-MetadataOnly]
[-MetadataReceiveLocationName:value] [-MergePorts]
[-TargetNamespace:value]
[-Location:value] [-Overwrite] [-Anonymous]
```

This is a basic sample invocation of this tool:

```
BtsWcfServicePublishing.exe "MyAssembly.dll" ➥
    -Location:http://localhost/MyVdir -Overwrite
```

This sample publishes the orchestration in MyAssembly.dll to http://localhost/MyVdir with the default values and overwrites any existing service at this location.

1 Download the BTSWCFServicePublishing tool from `http://go.microsoft.com/fwlink/?LinkId=92955`.

Of course, the default values are not very friendly; therefore, the tool supports many parameters to customize the output. Table 12-3 lists these parameters.

Table 12-3. *Command-Line Parameters for the BtsWcfServicePublishing Tool*

Parameter	Required	Description
PathName	Yes	Path and file name of BizTalk assembly (*.dll) or WCF service description (*.xml) file.
-AdapterName	No	Publishes a service endpoint. Specify which adapter will be used: WCF-BasicHttp, WCF-WSHttp, or WCF-CustomIsolated. This field is valid when publishing a service endpoint. The default is WCF-WSHttp.
-EnableMetadata	No	Enables metadata endpoint in addition to service endpoint. This field is valid when publishing a service endpoint. The default is False.
-ReceiveLocation	No	Creates receive locations in the specified BizTalk application. This field is valid when publishing a service endpoint with the BizTalk application name specified. The default is False.
-ApplicationName	No	Name of the BizTalk application in which to create receive locations. This field is valid when publishing a service endpoint with the receive location specified. The default is BizTalk Application 1.
-MetadataOnly	No	Publishes a metadata-only endpoint. This field is valid when publishing a service endpoint. The default is False.
-MetadataReceiveLocationName	No	Name of WCF-adapter receive location to expose at metadata-only endpoint. You can further edit it in Web.config after publishing. This field is valid when publishing a metadata endpoint. The default is Null.
-MergePorts	No	Merges all ports into a single WCF service if possible. The default is False.
-TargetNamespace	No	Target namespace of WCF service. The default is http://tempuri.org.
-Location	No	Location in which to publish. For example, http://host[:port]/path. This is automatically generated based on the project name.
-Overwrite	No	Overwrites (deletes contents of) specified location. The default is False.
-Anonymous	No	Allows anonymous access to WCF service. The default is False.

Consuming WCF Services

Just as there is a wizard to help you publish a WCF service, there is also a BizTalk WCF Service Consuming Wizard. You can launch this wizard from within the orchestration designer; it creates port types and message types necessary for consuming WCF services. The wizard also creates two binding files that can be imported by the development command-line tool or wizard to configure the send ports with the system-provided binding WCF adapters and the WCF-Custom adapter.

To add schemas and types for WCF services to your orchestration, follow the steps described in the following subsections.

Step 1: Start the BizTalk WCF Consuming Wizard

In the Solution Explorer, right-click your project, click Add, and select Add Generated Items. In the Add Generated Items dialog box, select Consume WCF Service, and click Add to launch the wizard.

Step 2: Import Metadata

Click Next on the welcome screen to display the Metadata Source screen, as shown in Figure 12-5.

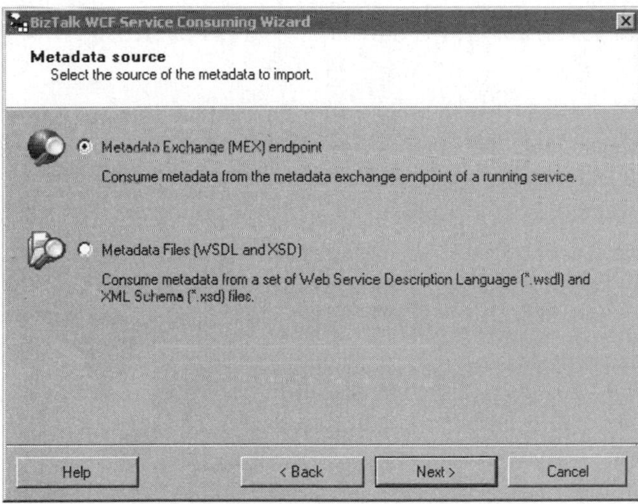

Figure 12-5. *Selecting a metadata source*

The easier option is to use a MEX endpoint, which will dynamically download the WSDL and supporting XSDs. If you have previously downloaded or been provided with these files, then choose the Metadata Files option. Leave the default option, and click Next.

Step 3: Supply a Metadata URL

On the Metadata Endpoint screen, enter the URI to the metadata endpoint you want to include, and click Next.

■ **Tip** The metadata endpoint doesn't have to be over HTTP or HTTPS. The wizard also supports net.tcp and net.pipe URIs.

Step 4: Complete the Wizard

After the WSDL has been downloaded, click Next to complete the wizard. The necessary port types and message types will be created and ready to use within your orchestration. Simply bind your message types to an orchestration port and connect to shapes.

Specifying Dynamic Port Properties

As with other adapters, the WCF adapters support dynamic send ports. These are useful for customizing parameters of WCF calls with runtime values that may be passed with incoming messages or as a result of a business rule.

The following code demonstrates how to modify the transport security option of a WCF-NetTcp adapter:

```
MessageOut=MessageIn;
MessageOut(WCF.Action)="http://tempuri.org/IReceiveMessage/ReceiveMessage";
MessageOut(WCF.SecurityMode)="Transport";
MessageOut(WCF.TransportClientCredentialType)="Windows";
DynamicSendPort(Microsoft.XLANGs.BaseTypes.Address)= ➥
    "net.tcp://localhost:8001/netTcp";
DynamicSendPort(Microsoft.XLANGs.BaseTypes.TransportType)="WCF-NetTcp";
```

Using the WCF context object, all properties of the WCF adapter can be dynamically changed if necessary to meet your requirements. The previous example tells the adapter to implement transport-level security leveraging the Windows identity as its credential token. The code also overrides the WCF endpoint address and sets the transport type to the WCF-NetTcp adapter.

Securing Your Endpoints

A well-written service has an appropriate level of security. Windows Communication Foundation makes it very easy to implement security at multiple levels of the communication stack by configuring endpoint behaviors and bindings.

A common mistake by developers, though, is to leave security to the last minute before an application is about to launch. Although WCF configuration makes security easier than ever, there are also lots of configuration settings that have performance and design impacts on the end solution. Leaving security to the last minute may result in a service not working as expected.

Later in this chapter, we'll walk through securing your endpoint in the BizTalk Server Administration tool. For now, let's look at the different configuration options available natively within Windows Communication Foundation.

Transport, Message, or Mixed?

Depending on the WCF binding, multiple security options and configurations are available. Typically, most developers will use either basicHttpBinding or wsHttpBinding as their binding because these are easily hosted in IIS. Others, such as netTcpBinding or netNamedPipeBinding, rely on a service host, such as a custom Windows service, to host the endpoint.

Tip Windows Server 2008 support Windows Activation Service (WAS). This will allow you to leverage IIS as a host for non-HTTP endpoints.

When determining how to publish your endpoint, there are multiple security modes that you'll want to consider. The BizTalk WCF Service Publishing Wizard typically publishes to an HTTP endpoint in IIS. Table 12-4 lists the different modes of security the HTTP bindings support.

Table 12-4. *Security Modes for HTTP Bindings*

Security Mode	Supported HTTP Binding(s)	Description
None	basicHttpBinding wsHttpBinding	No transport or message security. Anonymous access. All data is sent in clear-text format across the wire.
Transport	basicHttpBinding wsHttpBinding	Security occurs at the transport later. For example, basicHttpBinding and wsHttpBinding rely on SSL to encrypt the message contents. This type of security mode can encrypt data across only one communication channel. If the messages get routed to other services, each communication channel must ensure the contents are secured appropriately. When using transport security, there are multiple credential types supported including Basic, Digest, Ntlm, Windows, and Certificate.
Message	basicHttpBinding wsHttpBinding	Message-level security involves additional attributes added to the SOAP message to support encryption, identification, or both. Messages security can be implemented via x.509 certificates, username/password, and Windows or issued tokens. (Windows and issued tokens are supported by wsHttpBinding only.) When using message security, you can provide identification by either username or certificate. To secure the credentials, an optional algorithmSuite mode can be specified. The default algorithmSuite is Basic256 encryption. There are many supported encryption algorithms. Review the MSDN documentation for a full list.

Continued

Table 12-4. *Continued*

Security Mode	Supported HTTP Binding(s)	Description
TransportWith Message Credential	basicHttpBinding wsHttpBinding	Transport security is implemented via HTTPS, and the message is authenticated using x.509 or username/ password.
Transport CredentialOnly	basicHttpBinding	This security mode relies on the transport to authenticate the user. It does not provide message confidentiality or integrity. This should be used only when another form of transport encryption is used such as IPSec.

When deploying your endpoint, you need to consider who will be accessing your solution and by what transport(s). This is especially important for BizTalk endpoints. Most non-BizTalk services are typically point-to-point, meaning that when a client calls a service, the service processes the request by performing some business logic or accessing a database and returns the results to the client. BizTalk, on the other hand, being an integration tier, typically routes between many services.

There are three important aspects of security that need to be considered when choosing your security mode:

- **Integrity**: The message was delivered from a trustworthy source and has not been modified.
- **Confidentiality**: The message was delivered in an encrypted format.
- **Authentication**: The message has been authenticated, either via transport or message level.

Relying only on transport-level security to implement integrity, confidentiality, and authentication is not always the best way to expose services. Message-level security provides the ability to flow the message integrity, confidentiality, and authentication across many endpoints. If only transport security is used, then each communication channel must implement their own security, and the original requestor's credentials are lost.

The TransportWithMessageCredential security mode uses a good balance of both transport and message security options and is often a choice for many organizations. Offloading the confidentiality of the message to the transport via HTTPS is often faster than implementing encryption within the WCF message. But instead of relying on IIS to enforce authentication, leave IIS with Anonymous access enabled, and attach the source credentials as part of the SOAP message. This provides the benefit of being able to forward the message credentials onto the next endpoint if necessary. Although this can offer flexibility, it also introduces a performance hit because WCF needs to perform additional functionality. Consider your environment and performance needs when implementing this security mode.

Using makecert to Implement Message-Level Encryption

Using a certificate to implement confidentiality at the message level is a good way to be transport-agnostic. The encrypted message can travel over multiple endpoints without having to be decrypted by individual services.

To implement certificate encryption during development, you'll need to use a tool called makecert to generate the certificates. makecert is a utility published as part of the Windows SDK and Visual Studio.

Caution makecert.exe is a development tool only. It should not be used for production deployments.

First, you'll need to create a Trusted Root Authority certificate. Once created, you will be able to create a second x.509 certificate derived from the Trusted Root Authority certificate to encrypt the message. To create the Trusted Root Authority certificate, type the following at a command prompt:

```
makecert -pe -n "CN=My Root Authority" -ss root -sr LocalMachine -a sha1 ➥
    -sky signature -r
```

Here is an explanation of the command-line parameters in this example:

-pe marks the private key as exportable.

-n "CN=<name>" is the common name of the root authority.

-ss root stores the generated certificate in the Trusted Root Authorities container.

-sr LocalMachine specifies that the store is located on the local computer.

-a sha1 specifies SHA1 is to be used for encryption.

-sky signature specifies the key type.

-r makes a self-signed certificate.

Now that you have the root authority, you can create another certificate, signed by your root authority, to use for encrypting the message. To do this, type the following at a command prompt:

```
makecert -pe -n "CN=certsample" -ss my -sr LocalMachine -a sha1 ➥
    -sky exchange -eku 1.3.6.1.5.5.7.3.1 -in "My Root Authority" -is root ➥
    -ir localmachine ➥
    -sp "Microsoft RSA SChannel Cryptographic Provider" -sy 12
```

Again, the command-line parameters are as follows:

-pe marks the private key as exportable.

-n "CN=<name>" is the common name of the certificate.

-ss my stores the generated certificate in the Personal container.

-sr LocalMachine specifies that the store is located on the local computer.

-a sha1 specifies SHA1 is to be used for encryption.

-sky signature specifies the keytype.

-eku 1.3.6.1.5.5.7.3.1 specifies the certificate is used for server authentication.

`-in "My Root Authority"` specifies the root authority.

`-is root` specifies the root authority is located in the Trusted Root Authorities container.

`-ir localmachine` specifies the root authority is located on the local machine.

`-sp "Microsoft RSA SChannel Cryptographic Provider"` specifies who the certificated is encrypted by.

`-sy 12` specifies the provider type.

Now that both certificates have been created, they can be used to encrypt WCF messages. We'll do this as part of the end-to-end sample later in this chapter.

Using Metadata Exchange

A metadata exchange (MEX) endpoint is a special endpoint added to your service that will expose your WSDL and supporting schemas required to call your service. MEX conforms to the WS-MetadataExchange standard. Once a MEX endpoint has been added to your service, consumers can use the Add Service Reference feature of Visual Studio 2008 to automatically create the proxy object required to call your service.

Publishing MEX Metadata

Publishing metadata is easy through the BizTalk WCF Service Publishing Wizard. On the WCF Service Type screen (see Figure 12-2, earlier), there is a check box for enabling metadata endpoints. When you select this option, the wizard adds some information to the generated Web.config file. The following is an entire file, with the additional information highlighted in bold:

```
<system.serviceModel>
  <behaviors>
    <serviceBehaviors>
      <behavior name="ServiceBehaviorConfiguration">
        <serviceDebug httpHelpPageEnabled="true"
             httpsHelpPageEnabled="false"
             includeExceptionDetailInFaults="false" />
        <serviceMetadata httpGetEnabled="true" httpsGetEnabled="false" />
      </behavior>
    </serviceBehaviors>
  </behaviors>
  <services>
    <service name="Microsoft.BizTalk.Adapter.Wcf.Runtime. ➥
                BizTalkServiceInstance"
             behaviorConfiguration="ServiceBehaviorConfiguration">
      <endpoint name="HttpMexEndpoint" address="mex"
             binding="mexHttpBinding" bindingConfiguration=""
             contract="IMetadataExchange" />
    </service>
  </services>
</system.serviceModel>
```

There are three additional elements in this file:

- A `serviceMetadata` tag that allows HTTP GET access to your WSDL. This is the common way developers will access your metadata.
- A `behaviorConfiguration` tag in the `service` element that attaches the behavior to the service. This tag triggers the ability to use HTTP GET access to the specified service.
- A new `endpoint name="HttpMexEndpoint"` tag that provides standard WS-MetadataExchange access to the WSDL. Notice the MEX endpoint must conform to standard address, binding, and contracts (ABCs) of WCF, but the contract implemented is `IMetadataExchange` and not your custom service.

Customizing the SOAP Address Location

Adding the default MEX output is easy to do and works just fine. But sometimes it is necessary to modify the default output. This need to modify is quite common in scenarios where your service is located behind a network load balancer such as Windows Network Load Balancing because the autogenerated WSDL includes the computer name, as shown in Figure 12-6.

```
- <wsdl:service name="BizTalkServiceInstance">
  - <wsdl:port name="BasicHttpBinding_ITwoWayAsync" binding="tns:BasicHttpBinding_ITwoWayAsync">
      <soap:address location="http://bts2009rc/WCFMath/AddService.svc" />
    </wsdl:port>
  </wsdl:service>
```

2

Figure 12-6. *Autogenerated WSDL with local computer name*

In Figure 12-6, the computer name is bts2009rc. A server-specific name like that is fine if we're running on one server, but when running in a web farm, each server would render a different name. When the consumer uses the Add Service Reference feature of Visual Studio 2008, the service would default to the computer name that rendered the MEX and not the virtual server name of the web farm.

Even though the default endpoint address would be tied to the computer name, the default can be easily overwritten in the application's configuration file. But nevertheless, it's not good practice to expose your server names to an outside consumer, especially if your service is public-facing. Exposing your server names publicly provides environment configuration details that should be kept away from possible intruders.

WCF will automatically use the IIS metabase server bindings of the web site to dynamically render the address of the service. Therefore, in order to modify the default behavior, the metabase needs to be updated to include the DNS name you'd like to use. To do this, run the following at the command prompt:

```
cscript //nologo %systemdrive%\inetpub\adminscripts\adsutil.vbs set ➥
      W3SVC/1/ServerBindings ":80:www.myserverfarm.com"
```

Tip Alternatively, the `serviceMetadata` element of a WCF endpoint behavior can be modified to use an external WSDL file. Point the `externalMetadataLocation` attribute to an external file containing your service's WSDL. This allows you to have complete control of your WSDL but does require you to keep it in sync with the functionality of your service.

Once completed, run IISRESET, or recycle the application pool to allow the change to be in effect, as shown in Figure 12-7.

```
- <wsdl:service name="BizTalkServiceInstance">
  - <wsdl:port name="BasicHttpBinding_ITwoWayAsync" binding="tns:BasicHttpBinding_ITwoWayAsync">
      <soap:address location="http://www.myserverfarm.com/WCFMath/AddService.svc" />
    </wsdl:port>
  </wsdl:service>
```

Web Farm Name

Figure 12-7. *Autogenerated WSDL with web farm name*

Customizing MEX with a WCF Behavior

Adding content to the MEX output is easy thanks to WCF's highly extensible architecture. Most organizations don't customize the output, but they should. Public-facing services should add copyright information, and all services should add some level of summary help to their endpoints.

To customize the MEX output, you'll need to create a class that inherits from BehaviorExtensionElement and implements the IWsdlExportExtension and IEndpointBehavior interfaces. This work sounds complex, but it's not that bad. The following is a sample class that implements all these objects and interfaces and exposes a property called `CopyrightText` allowing for the text to be configurable in the application's configuration file:

```
public class WSDLDocumentor : BehaviorExtensionElement,
                              IWsdlExportExtension,
                              IEndpointBehavior
{
    public WSDLDocumentor() { }

    public WSDLDocumentor(string CopyrightText)
    {
        this.CopyrightText = CopyrightText;
    }

    #region IWsdlExportExtension Members

    public void ExportContract(WsdlExporter exporter,
              WsdlContractConversionContext context)
    {}
```

```
public void ExportEndpoint(WsdlExporter exporter,
            WsdlEndpointConversionContext context)
{
    // Must set documentation to empty string or XmlDocument
    // will be null.
    context.WsdlPort.Documentation = string.Empty;
    XmlDocument summary =
        context.WsdlPort.DocumentationElement.OwnerDocument;
    XmlElement copyright = summary.CreateElement("Copyright");
    copyright.InnerText = CopyrightText;
    context.WsdlPort.DocumentationElement.AppendChild(copyright);
}

#endregion

[ConfigurationProperty("copyrightText", DefaultValue = "",
                        IsRequired = true)]
public string CopyrightText
{
    get { return (string)base["copyrightText"]; }
    set { base["copyrightText"] = value; }
}

private ConfigurationPropertyCollection configurationProperties;
protected override ConfigurationPropertyCollection Properties
{
    get
    {
        if (configurationProperties == null)
        {
            configurationProperties =
               new ConfigurationPropertyCollection();
            configurationProperties.Add(
               new ConfigurationProperty("copyrightText",
                   typeof(string), string.Empty,
                   ConfigurationPropertyOptions.IsRequired));
        }
        return configurationProperties;
    }
}

public override System.Type BehaviorType
{
    get { return typeof(WSDLDocumentor); }
}
```

```
        protected override object CreateBehavior()
        {
            return new WSDLDocumentor(CopyrightText);
        }

        #region IEndpointBehavior Members

        public void AddBindingParameters(ServiceEndpoint endpoint,
                    BindingParameterCollection bindingParameters)
        {}

        public void ApplyClientBehavior(ServiceEndpoint endpoint,
                    ClientRuntime clientRuntime)
        {}

        public void ApplyDispatchBehavior(ServiceEndpoint endpoint,
                    EndpointDispatcher endpointDispatcher)
        {}

        public void Validate(ServiceEndpoint endpoint)
        {}

        #endregion
    }
```

After compiling this class, the next step is to add content to your Web.config file to hook in your custom behavior. For example, notice the bold lines in the following configuration file:

```
<?xml version="1.0" encoding="utf-8" ?>
<configuration>
    <system.serviceModel>
        <extensions>
            <behaviorExtensions>
                <add name="WSDLCopyright"
                     type="ProBizTalk.WSDLExtension.WSDLDocumentor,
                            ProBizTalk.WSDLExtension, Version=1.0.0.0,
                            Culture=neutral, PublicKeyToken=null" />
            </behaviorExtensions>
        </extensions>
        <bindings>
            <basicHttpBinding>
                <binding name="SayHelloBindingConfig">
                    <security mode="None" />
                </binding>
            </basicHttpBinding>
        </bindings>
```

```
        <behaviors>
            <endpointBehaviors>
                <behavior name="CopyrightBehavior">
                    <WSDLCopyright
                        copyrightText="Copyright Pro BizTalk 2009!" />
                </behavior>
            </endpointBehaviors>
        </behaviors>
        <services>
            <service name="CertService.SayHello">
                <endpoint address=""
                    behaviorConfiguration="CopyrightBehavior"
                    binding="basicHttpBinding"
                    bindingConfiguration="SayHelloBindingConfig"
                    contract="CertService.ISayHello" />
            </service>
        </services>
    </system.serviceModel>
</configuration>
```

■ **Tip** You can also use the WCF Configuration Editor as part of the Windows SDK to add the additional configuration settings.

Be sure to reference the custom behavior DLL in your solution and build! When viewing your WSDL, you should notice text similar to the bold code in the following example:

```
<wsdl:service name="SayHello">
   <wsdl:port name="BasicHttpBinding_ISayHello"
         binding="tns:BasicHttpBinding_ISayHello">
         <wsdl:documentation>
            <Copyright>Copyright Pro BizTalk 2009!</Copyright>
         </wsdl:documentation>
         <soap:address location="http://bts2009rc/SayHello" />
   </wsdl:port>
</wsdl:service>
```

Using the WCF-WSHttp Adapter

Now that we've covered a lot of the concepts with WCF, let's apply them to how BizTalk WCF adapters are configured. The BizTalk Administration tool provides a specific user interface to customize the WCF-BasicHttp, WCF-WSHttp, and WCF-NetTcp adapter properties. For all other bindings, the WCF-CustomAdapter adapter is used, which we will go through later in this chapter. For now, let's look at how the WCF-WsHttp adapter properties are configured.

Binding Configuration Options

The Binding configuration tab in Figure 12-8 shows the default configuration.

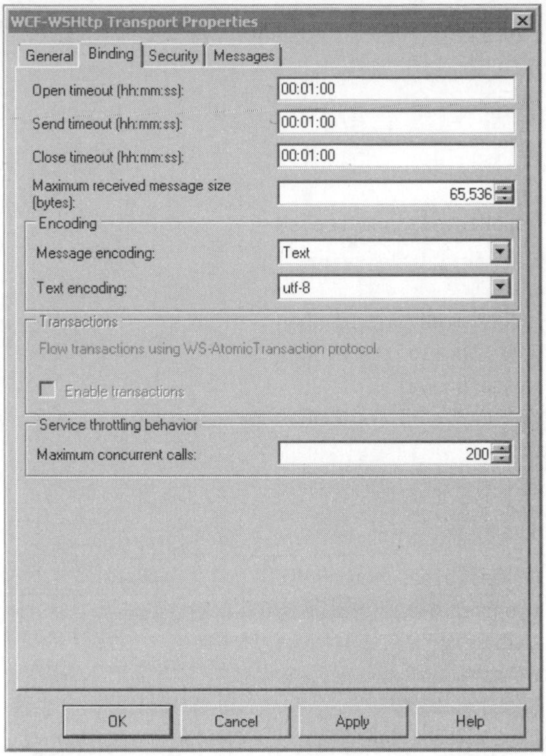

Figure 12-8. *WCF-WSHttp default binding configuration*

The open, close, and send timeouts default to one minute each. One minute may not be enough under certain circumstances. For example, you might have a synchronous service call that executes an orchestration that lasts longer than one minute.

■ **Caution** The timeouts in Figure 12-8 are not just for the orchestration time. The time starts once WCF has submitted a call to the Messagebox, which means you'll need to take into consideration your "warm-up" time as well. Depending on your hardware, that warm-up time alone may be longer than a minute.

Security Configuration

The Security configuration tab shown in Figure 12-9 allows you to modify how the endpoint will be secured for authentication.

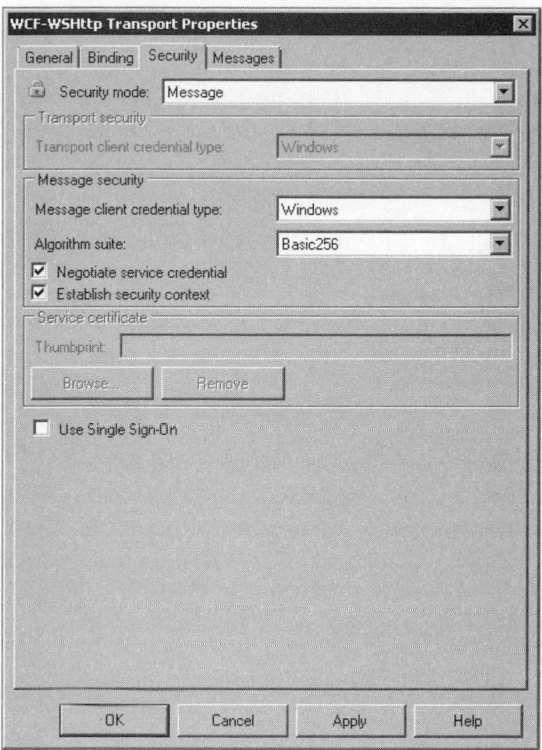

Figure 12-9. *WCF-WSHttp security configuration*

The default security mode is Message with a credential type of Windows, meaning WCF will require the consumer of the service to attach their Windows credential token as part of the message.

You can change the Security Mode drop-down to either None, Transport, Message, or TransportWithMessageCredential. Depending on the option you choose, either the Transport section or the Message section will be enabled. When choosing Message authentication, two additional check boxes are available that affect authentication: Negotiate Service Credential and Establish Security Context. The Negotiate Service Credential option tells BizTalk whether the service credential is negotiated automatically between the client and the service. The Establish Security Context option specifies whether a security context token is established through a WS-SecureConversation exchange between this send port and the service. If this check box is selected, then the destination service must support WS-SecureConversation.

Caution Depending on the message credential type, the Negotiate Service Credential option has different implementations. Check the MSDN documentation at `http://msdn.microsoft.com/en-us/library/bb226397.aspx` for more information.

Message Options

The Messages tab of the WCF adapter provides the ability to customize which components of a SOAP message get stored in the message box for processing. By default, the entire `<soap:body>` will be stored, but you can customize your adapter to extract only certain sections of a request.

Figure 12-10 shows the default properties for the Messages tab.

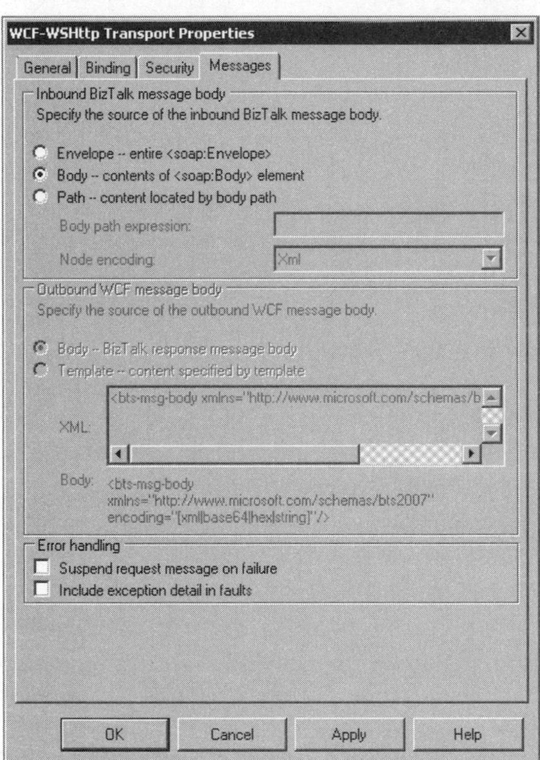

Figure 12-10. *WCF-WSHttp Receive Adapter default message properties*

Table 12-5 describes the options available in the Messages tab shown in the figure.

Table 12-5. *Message Tab Options*

Grouping	Option	Description
Inbound	Envelope	The entire SOAP envelope from the message is imported. The body is ignored.
	Body	This is the default option. The entire body of the message will be used as the message. If the body contains more than one element, then the first element is imported.
	Path	An XPath query will be used to identify the element to be imported.

Grouping	Option	Description
	Body Path Expression	The XPath query to the element to be imported. This expression is evaluated from the immediate child of the `<soap:body>`. If the result contains more than one element, then the first element is imported. If you plan on doing content-based routing, then this element must match an entire schema deployed to BizTalk
	Node Encoding	Specifies the type of encoding the adapter will use to decode the text. Options include Base64, Hex, String, or XML (default).
Outbound	Body	Specifies the output message will be used as the SOAP body. This option is available only on a request-response receive location.
	Template	Provides a template for the contents of the SOAP body message. This option is available only on a request-response receive location.
Error Handling	Suspend message on failure	When chosen, the message will be suspended if the request fails because of a pipeline or routing failure.
	Include exception in faults	When chosen and an exception occurs, the error details will be included as part of the SOAP fault message. This option is useful for debugging but should be turned off in production environments.

WS-AtomicTransaction Support

Support for transactional communication with an integration tier like BizTalk is an important feature in an enterprise application. BizTalk has had transaction support previously using other adapters such as MSMQ and SQL, but these are limited to Windows platforms. Now with Windows Communication Foundation and its support for the WS-AtomicTransaction protocol, heterogeneous platforms can enlist in BizTalk transactions.

WS-AtomicTransaction, or WS-AT for short, is an interoperable transaction protocol. It enables you to flow distributed transactions by using web service messages and to coordinate in an interoperable manner between heterogeneous transaction infrastructures. WS-AT uses the two-phase commit protocol to drive an atomic outcome between distributed applications, transaction managers, and resource managers. When using WS-AT, the service's transaction is enlisted up to and including the point where the message has been committed to the Messagebox.

BizTalk's WS-AtomicTransaction support is defined within a WCF receive location by simply clicking the Enable Transactions check box on the Binding tab. Figure 12-11 shows the receive location with the Enable Transactions check box.

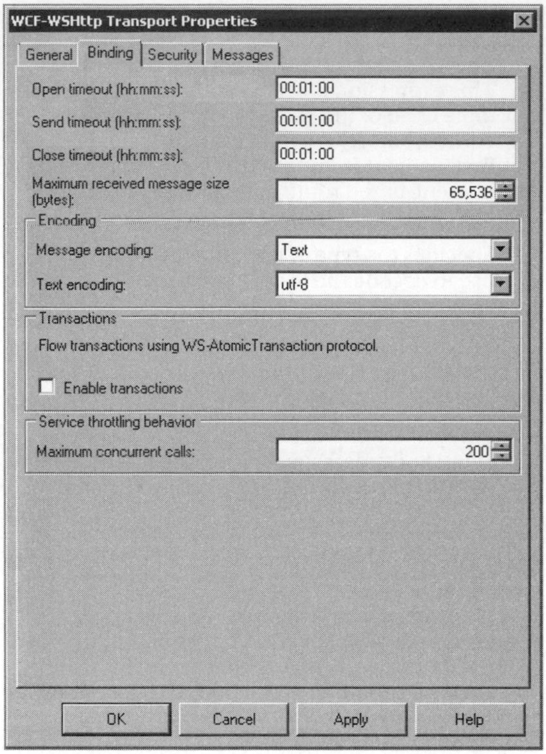

Figure 12-11. *WS-AtomicTransaction protocol configuration*

■ **Tip** The scope of the transaction is limited to a one-way receive port. When the receive location is bound to a request-response receive port, the Transactions section will be disabled. BizTalk will flow the WS-AtomicTransaction request until the message has been committed to the Messagebox for processing.

When the Enable Transactions check box is selected and a message is received that requires WS-AtomicTransactions, the WCF adapter will enlist the request using the Microsoft Distributed Transaction Coordinator (MSDTC) and transactionally commit the request to the Messagebox when the WS-AT request completes.

End-to-End Example: Exposing a WCF Service

Now that we've covered all the core topics of using WCF-based adapters with BizTalk, we'll put them all together to provide an end-to-end example.

In the example, we will do the following:

1. Create a simple math orchestration that adds two numbers together.
2. Expose the receive location using a WCF-CustomIsolated adapter.

3. Attach a certificate to support message-level encryption.
4. Attach a custom behavior that adds copyright information to the WSDL.
5. Create a test WCF client to call the service.

Creating an Addition Orchestration

Figure 12-12 shows the simple orchestration created to support our math service. It receives two numbers from a request-response port and uses a map with an addition functoid to sum the numbers into our response message.

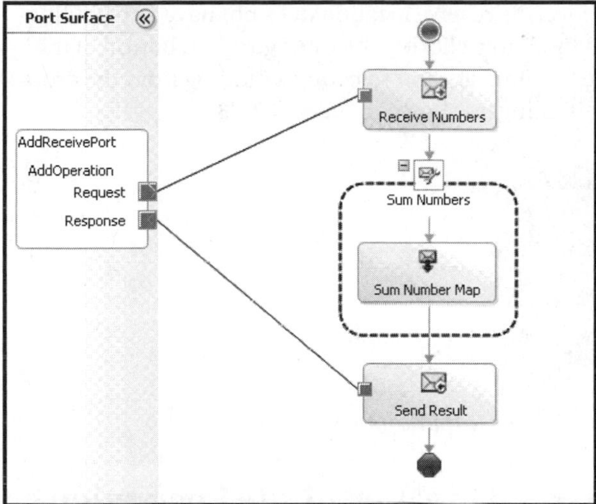

Figure 12-12. *Math orchestration*

Because the focus of this chapter is on WCF, we won't dig into the details of the orchestration or the map.

Exposing the Orchestration via the WCF-CustomIsolated Adapter

Once the orchestration has been signed, compiled, and deployed, we're ready to expose the orchestration using the WCF-CustomIsolated adapter. We're using this adapter because it provides a higher degree of customization than the other WCF adapters that we'll use in subsequent steps.

Using the BizTalk WCF Service Publishing Wizard, we've created a receive location for the service. During the wizard, we chose the following options:

- Selected Create a Service Endpoint
- Selected the WCF-CustomIsolated adapter
- Enabled the Metadata Endpoint option

- Created a BizTalk receive location in the WCFMath application
- Selected Publish BizTalk Orchestrations as WCF Service
- Selected the BizTalk orchestration assembly DLL
- Set the namespace to `http://probiztalk2009/mathservice/v1`
- Set the endpoint location to `http://localhost/math`
- Allowed anonymous access to the WCF service

After the orchestration is published with the wizard, we're left with a basic receive location that needs additional configuration before it can be used. During the wizard, we chose the WCF-CustomIsolated adapter. Therefore, the receive location does not have any binding associated with it. The binding can be set by simply clicking the Configuration button of the receive location's properties, going to the Binding tab, and selecting a binding from the drop-down. For the example, we chose wsHttpBinding, as shown in Figure 12-13.

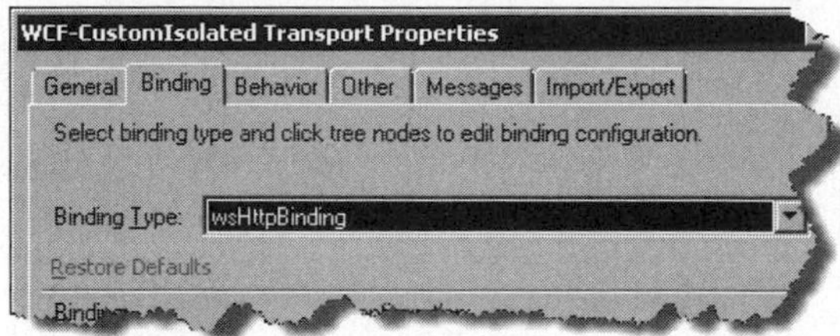

Figure 12-13. *Selecting the binding type for a WCF-CustomIsolated adapter*

Securing Requests with Message-Level Certificate Encryption

To encrypt the message, a development certificate is necessary. As described earlier in this chapter, we can use `makecert` to create nonproduction certificates.

Two certificates are necessary, a trusted root authority and an x.509 certificate issued by the trusted root. To create the trusted root, execute the following command from the Visual Studio command prompt:

```
makecert -pe -n "CN=My Root Authority" -ss root -sr LocalMachine -a sha1 ➥
    -sky signature -r
```

This command creates the root with a common name of My Root Authority in the Trusted Root Authorities container. Once this is done, we can create an x.509 certificate issued by the new trusted root by executing the following:

```
makecert -pe -n "CN=certsample" -ss my -sr LocalMachine -a sha1 ➥
    -sky exchange -eku 1.3.6.1.5.5.7.3.1 -in "My Root Authority" -is root ➥
    -ir localmachine ➥
    -sp "Microsoft RSA SChannel Cryptographic Provider" -sy 12
```

This command creates a certificate with a common name of "certsample" in the Personal container of the local computer.

Before the certificate can be used, though, the certificate also needs to be copied to the Trusted People container. We need to do that because we are using the same certificate for both the service and the client. WCF has the ability to support different certificates for each end of the communication, but for simplicity we are using the same certificate on both ends. To copy the certificate to the Trusted People container, follow these steps:

1. Load a Microsoft Management Console (MMC).
2. Click Add/Remove Snap-ins and Add Certificates.
3. Select Computer, click Next, and select Local Computer.
4. Open the Personal ➤ Certificates tree.
5. Right-click the certificate named "certsample," and select Copy.
6. Open the Trusted People ➤ Certificates tree node.
7. Right-click and select Paste.

Figure 12-14 shows the containers where the certificate needs to be installed.

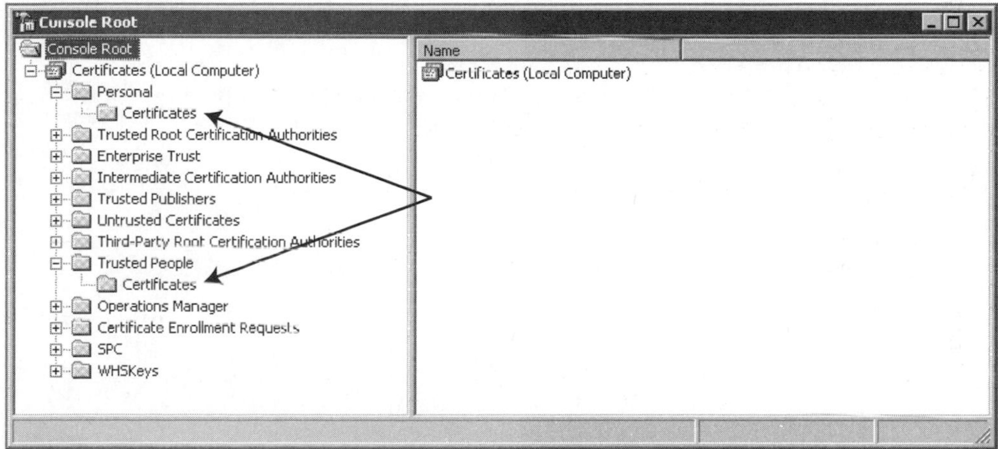

Figure 12-14. *Certificate store locations*

Now that the certificates are in place, we can customize the receive location with the required information to use these certificates. Using the Configuration screen of the WCF-CustomIsolated adapter, make the following changes:

- **Binding**: In the Binding tree, expand Security, and click Message. Change the clientCredentialType value from Windows to Certificate.
- **Behavior**: In the Behavior tree, right-click Service Behavior, and select Add Extension. Select serviceCredentials, and click OK. Expand the new serviceCredentials node, and click ServiceCertificate. Set the findValue property to "certsample," set x509FindType to FindBySubjectName Expand ClientCertificate, and select Authentication. Set revocationMode to NoCheck. This is required to stop WCF from checking the certificate revocation list (CRL) because we are using development certificates.

Creating the WCF Test Client

Now that the orchestration has been configured, we can focus on creating a client that uses the certificate to encrypt the data when calling the service. To do this, create a console application in Visual Studio 2008. After creating a console application, connect to the BizTalk WCF endpoint by doing the following:

1. Right-click the References node in Solution Explorer.
2. Select Add Service Reference.
3. Enter the URI to the WCF endpoint, and click GO.
4. Change the namespace to a meaningful name.
5. Click OK to add the reference.

■Tip For a MEX endpoint, the URI is entered as `http://<servername/<vdir>/<servicename>.svc/mex`.

Once the service has been added, your App.config file should look something like the following:

```
<?xml version="1.0" encoding="utf-8" ?>
<configuration>
    <system.serviceModel>
        <bindings>
            <wsHttpBinding>
                <binding name="WSHttpBinding_ITwoWayAsync">
                    <security mode="Message">
                        <transport clientCredentialType="Windows"/>
                        <message
                                       clientCredentialType="Certificate"
                                       negotiateServiceCredential="true"
                              ........algorithmSuite="Default"
                                       establishSecurityContext="true" />
                    </security>
                </binding>
            </wsHttpBinding>
        </bindings>
        <client>
            <endpoint address="http://bts2009rc/Math/ ➥
                BTS2009_WCFDemo_Math_AddOrchestration_AddReceivePort.svc"
                binding="wsHttpBinding"
                bindingConfiguration="WSHttpBinding_ITwoWayAsync"
```

```
contract="MathService.BTS2009_WCFDemo_Math_AddOrchestration_AddReceivePort"
                name="WSHttpBinding_ITwoWayAsync">
                <identity>
                    <certificate encodedValue="AwAAAAEAAAAUAAAAV....
" />
                </identity>
            </endpoint>
        </client>
    </system.serviceModel>
</configuration>
```

The Add Service Reference feature detected that a certificate is required, but there is still additional work necessary before the service can be called. The application needs to be told what certificate to use. To do this, there is additional configuration necessary. The following bold code shows the additional code added to the App.config file:

```
    <system.serviceModel>
        <behaviors>
            <endpointBehaviors>
                <behavior name="MathBehavior">
                    <clientCredentials>
                        <clientCertificate
                            findValue="certsample"
                            storeLocation="LocalMachine"
                            x509FindType="FindBySubjectName" />
                        <serviceCertificate>
                            <authentication revocationMode="NoCheck" />
                        </serviceCertificate>
                    </clientCredentials>
                </behavior>
            </endpointBehaviors>
        </behaviors>
        <bindings>
            <wsHttpBinding>
                <binding name="WSHttpBinding_ITwoWayAsync">
                    <security mode="Message">
                        <transport clientCredentialType="Windows"
                            proxyCredentialType="None"
                               realm="" />
                        <message clientCredentialType="Certificate"
                            negotiateServiceCredential="true"
                               algorithmSuite="Default"
                            establishSecurityContext="true" />
                    </security>
                </binding>
            </wsHttpBinding>
        </bindings>
```

```
        <client>
            <endpoint address="http://bts2009rc/Math/ ➥
                BTS2009_WCFDemo_Math_AddOrchestration_AddReceivePort.svc"
                behaviorConfiguration="MathBehavior"
                           binding="wsHttpBinding"
                bindingConfiguration="WSHttpBinding_ITwoWayAsync"
                          contract="MathService.BTS2009_ ➥
                          WCFDemo_Math_AddOrchestration_AddReceivePort"
                name="WSHttpBinding_ITwoWayAsync">
                <identity>
                    <certificate
encodedValue="AwAAAAEAAAAUAAAAVYAae3Zx..." />
                </identity>
            </endpoint>
        </client>
    </system.serviceModel>
```

The behavior named MathBehavior tells WCF two important items:

- The application client should use the certificate with a subject name of "certsample" that is stored LocalMachine.
- The application client should not check the server's certificate against a CRL.

Tip Instead of modifying the App.config file by hand, use the WCF Service Configuration Editor as part of the Windows SDK. To access this, select Tools ➤ WCF Service Configuration Editor within Visual Studio, or right-click the App.config file and select Edit WCF Configuration.

Once the application configuration has been set up, we can write the following few lines of code to call the service. The result is a working application that uses message-level certificate encryption.

```
static void Main(string[] args)
{
    MathService.AddOrchestrationPort client =
        new MathService. AddOrchestrationPort ();

    MathService.Add request = new MathService.Add();
    request.Number1 = 100;
    request.Number2 = 200;

    MathService.MathResult response = client.AddOperation(request);
    Console.WriteLine(response.Result.ToString());
    Console.ReadLine();
}
```

If we enable the diagnostics features of WCF to trace messages, the WCF Service Trace Viewer application will show that the data being sent over the wire from the BizTalk service is now encrypted. You can see this in Figure 12-15.


```
        </e:ReferenceList>
        <e:EncryptedData Id="_6" Type="http://www.w3.org/2001/04/xmlenc#Element" xmlns:e="http://www.w3.org/2001/04/xmlenc#">
          <e:EncryptionMethod Algorithm="http://www.w3.org/2001/04/xmlenc#aes256-cbc"></e:EncryptionMethod>
          <KeyInfo xmlns="http://www.w3.org/2000/09/xmldsig#">
            <o:SecurityTokenReference>
              <o:Reference URI="#_1"></o:Reference>
            </o:SecurityTokenReference>
          </KeyInfo>
          <e:CipherData>
            <e:CipherValue>+ySIvR5mBgOrwvGAOqedQGyDexm0mtbrGS+DGNE4yDG8cIX7HKj2OS/g89RAnDX2hQf1C83kVznwKuaZP94EIanEN
          </e:CipherData>
        </e:EncryptedData>
      </o:Security>
    </s:Header>
    <s:Body u:Id="_2">
      <e:EncryptedData Id="_3" Type="http://www.w3.org/2001/04/xmlenc#Content" xmlns:e="http://www.w3.org/2001/04/xmlenc#">
        <e:EncryptionMethod Algorithm="http://www.w3.org/2001/04/xmlenc#aes256-cbc"></e:EncryptionMethod>
        <KeyInfo xmlns="http://www.w3.org/2000/09/xmldsig#">
          <o:SecurityTokenReference xmlns:o="http://docs.oasis-open.org/wss/2004/01/oasis-200401-wss-wssecurity-secext-1.0.xsd">
            <o:Reference URI="#_1"></o:Reference>
          </o:SecurityTokenReference>
        </KeyInfo>
        <e:CipherData>
          <e:CipherValue>PZYoBMQpSAMvO/i9/vFayLhBk3Rn4VRiISaB/7AKHdn8d6ACepFQxq5TaZwBLf2yzzeXeR2SHpLgnXiyApG0se4yCsVWR
        </e:CipherData>
      </e:EncryptedData>
    </s:Body>
  </s:Envelope>
</MessageLogTraceRecord>
```


Figure 12-15. *Service Trace Viewer showing the encrypted traffic*

BizTalk Endpoint Management

In today's SOAs, there is now a need for a "service governance" tool to help manage SOA infrastructures. The Microsoft Managed Services Engine (MSE), which was built by Microsoft Services and is available on `http://www.codeplex.com`, helps address this need.

It is always easy to integrate the initial application consuming a service. That's because the service is typically built for that specific application. But as the 5th, 10th, or even 50th application wants to join in using the service, any slight change to the original service can have exponential impact on testing as the number of consuming applications grows.

Changes to services are just one of many problems that you'll encounter as service-oriented architectures continue to grow. Without a common infrastructure focused on manageability, most SOAs become an unwieldy mess of intertwined services. These out-of-control services can end up negating the entire benefit of a service-oriented architecture. That's where the Managed Services Engine comes into play. It helps you gain and keep control over services and manage their change over time.

The Problem with WSDL

In today's environment, WSDL is static. It describes a service in its current form. Any changes to the service require a new WSDL to be published. Depending on the change, it can break existing applications.

To address this, organizations typically don't change existing services but rather create a duplicate method or possibly even a completely duplicate service. For example, let's assume we have a math service that has the following data contract:

```
[ServiceContract]
public interface IMathService
{
    [OperationContract]
    int AddIntegers(int IntegerA, int IntegerB);
}
```

This contract works fine for the first application, but the next application may need to support adding an array of integers. The only way to do add that support without breaking the first application would be to add another version of the same method that supports an array of integers. For example:

```
[ServiceContract]
public interface IMathService
{
    [OperationContract]
    int AddIntegers(int IntegerA, int IntegerB);


    [OperationContract]
    int AddIntegersArray(int[] Integers);
}
```

Although this example of adding support for new requirements is overly simplified, the problem becomes very large for both development teams and operationally as the number of methods changes over time. Typically organizations won't even know which applications use which version(s) of methods, so determining what methods to deprecate can become overwhelming if not impossible due to risk.

Where Does the MSE Help?

The Managed Services Engine sits in front of all services and acts as governance tool for understanding the end-to-end communication dependencies of all applications and services. Quickly, administrators can easily see via the Windows Presentation Foundation–based interface how components of the SOA relate to each other. Figure 12-16 shows an example of the Managed Services Engine WPF interface.

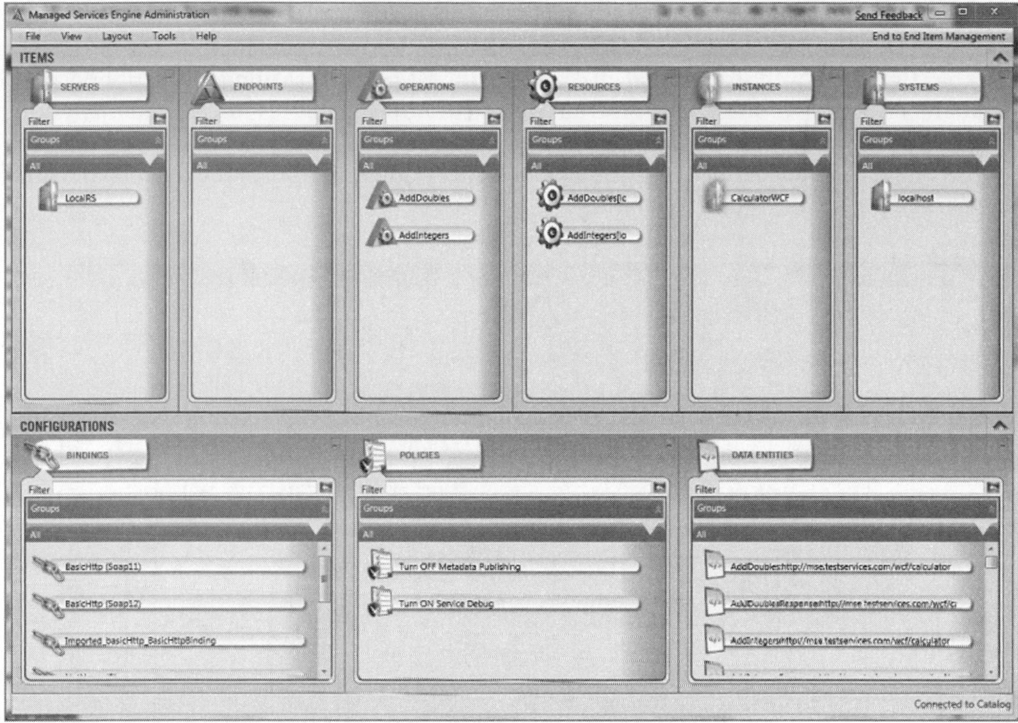

Figure 12-16. *MSE user interface*

The interface in Figure 12-16 is broken down into the groups described in Table 12-6.

Table 12-6. *MSE User Interface Groups*

Group	Description
Servers	A list of servers that are running the MSE software and can host WCF endpoints.
Endpoints	A list of endpoints that can be hosted on one or more servers.
Operations	A list of all operations that have been imported into the MSE.
Resources	A list of all operation resources that have been imported into the MSE.
Instances	A list of all service endpoints the MSE can communicate to.
Systems	A list of all servers that endpoints are hosted on.
Bindings	A list of all bindings used within the MSE, including default bindings.
Policies	Policies are a collection of assertions that define a behavior. For example, there are default policies for turning off metadata publishing and turning on service debugging. Policies contain XAML-based assertions that when associated to an endpoint are programmatically called to modify how an endpoint behaves. If we used MSE in the end-to-end example, a policy could have been added to add the message-level certificate requirements.
Data entities	A list of all composite objects.

Importing a WCF service into the MSE is as simple as running through a wizard. Start the wizard by selecting Tools ➤ Load Resources ➤ Web Service Metadata. Provide the wizard with the URL to the web service, and click Next to have MSE start reading the web service metadata. Figure 12-17 shows that MSE has detected the schemas, resources, and operations that are defined in the WSDL. The MSE will compare the schemas, resources, and operations against what is already defined in its catalog repository and import only the objects that are not yet defined.

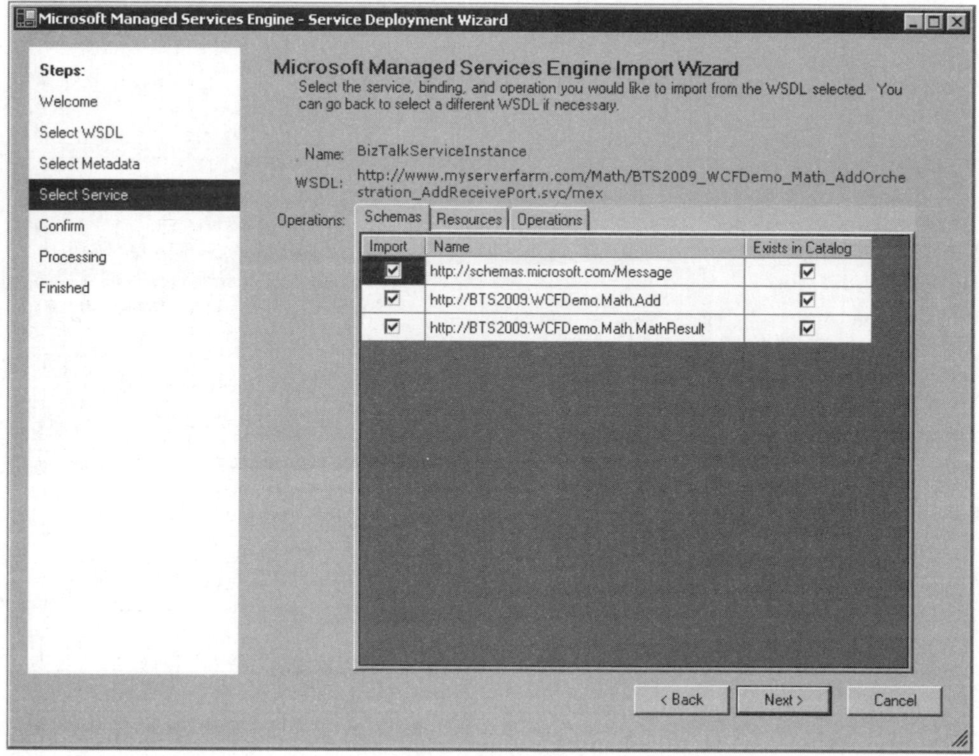

Figure 12-17. *MSE Web Service Metadata Import Wizard*

Once you've imported all your services, the MSE user interface will have filled all the groups with their respective types. Clicking any object within the UI will then filter all other groups to only the objects that are associated with the selected object. The result provides a quick end-to-end "service map" of how any single object is associated right from the service runtime servers all the way to the backend-hosted servers. The service map is all created with WPF animations to add extra visual effect.

Endpoint Virtualization

Now that you understand the basics of the MSE, let's take it one step further. Assume the MSE catalog repository has been filled with both your BizTalk-based WCF orchestrations as well as non-BizTalk services, or even non-Microsoft-based web services. All these operations need to be published to endpoint(s) to allow consumers to call them. Without the MSE, each application would need to have multiple service references to all required services, which would create a mess of intertwined endpoint configurations to manage.

Instead, MSE can help "virtualize" an endpoint. Endpoints in MSE are any combination of operation contracts (web methods) from one or more backend services dynamically created to expose a single view. For example, consider you had five backend services totaling 50 operations. Application A is being built that needs to use one operation from each of the five services. Instead of Application A adding five service references, a single virtual endpoint can be created in MSE to combine the five operations into a single MSE endpoint.

Figure 12-18 shows how individual methods can be virtualized into an application endpoint providing a simplified operational and development view into how services are used.

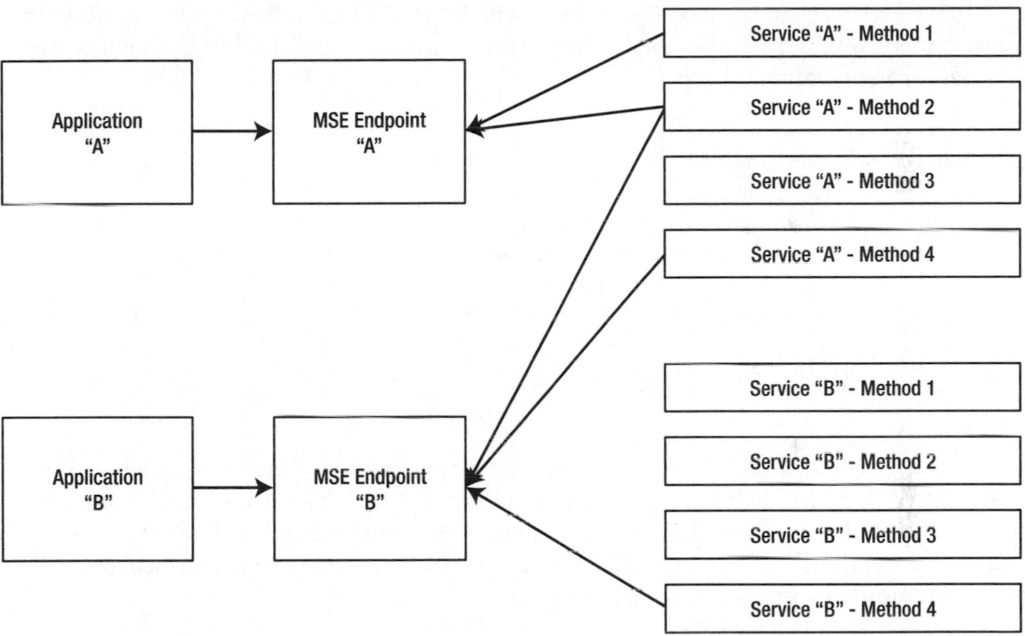

Figure 12-18. *MSE endpoint virtualization*

The design pattern from Figure 12-18 provides multiple benefits:

- Applications have to know only about their required operations and not be cluttered with operations that are not applicable to them.
- Virtual endpoints can have their own binding and policies allowing for application-level security.
- Messages can be routed through many tiers without requiring each application to have direct connectivity to all services.
- Backend service security can be defined once between the MSE and the service and not between each of the applications and the backend services.

For BizTalk orchestrations, this virtualization is very beneficial. Typically an orchestration contains one operation that is the only operation published in the WCF Service Publishing Wizard. Therefore, providing a mechanism to combine multiple WCF Service orchestrations into a single endpoint can simplify a large number of orchestrations URLs into a simple single view.

Operation Versioning

Another advantage to using MSE is the ability to support versioning of an operation. Instead of having multiple operations, each performing the same business logic but having different method contracts, the MSE can support transforming a request from one version to another and back again.

In the earlier section called "The Problem with WSDL," we described a problem whereby organizations would create methods similar to the following to support different method signatures for an operation:

```
[ServiceContract]
public interface IMathService
{
    [OperationContract]
    int AddIntegers(int IntegerA, int IntegerB);


    [OperationContract]
    int AddIntegersArray(int[] Integers);
}
```

Instead, wouldn't it be better to have a single `AddIntegers(...)` method that was always the "current" version and have the ability to transform between legacy operation contracts? This is where the power of MSE really shines. Whenever an operation is published, it is marked with two properties: Published and Active. Figure 12-19 shows the MSE screen displayed when you associate an operation to an endpoint.

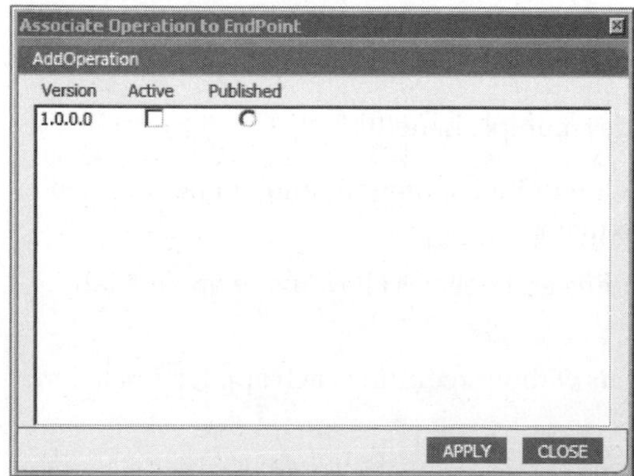

Figure 12-19. *Adding an operation to an endpoint*

At any point in time, only one version of an operation can be Published, meaning that when a new application downloads the application metadata, it will receive the Published version, which guarantees they always receive the most current version.

At the same time, multiple versions of the same operation can be Active. This way, any existing applications that have been previously bound to an older version of the WSDL can continue to work without breaking.

Take, for example, Figure 12-20, which describes how version 1 of a service was exposed via MSE to Application A. If a new version of the service is available and the old definition is still required to be Active, then an XSLT must be provided to transform between the old version to the new and back again. Figure 12-21 shows how MSE transforms the message to and from the new version.

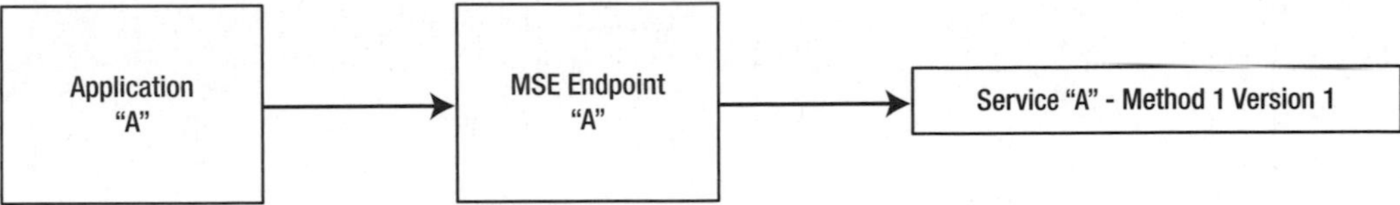

Figure 12-20. *Version 1 of a service*

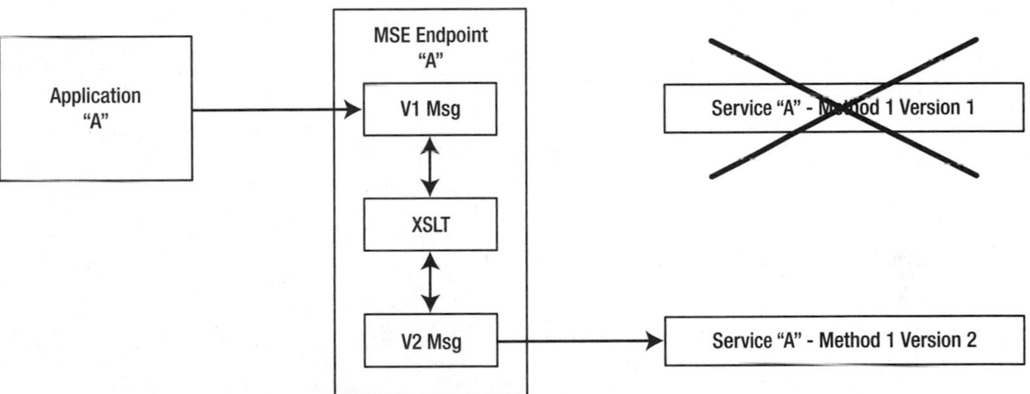

Figure 12-21. *Transforming the message*

This model also has significant benefits to BizTalk developers. Our maps can get very complicated, and supporting multiple versions of different schemas within an orchestration can get very complex and error-prone. Although this could be accomplished using multiple maps on a receive port, externalizing this functionality into a service governance tier can help simplify the BizTalk deployment, and the pattern can also be leveraged for non-BizTalk services.

Tip With MSE's Policy model, a logging policy could be added to feed BAM with who is calling which versions of methods. This data can then be used to quantify operational impacts of supporting older versions of methods, forcing legacy applications to update to new versions of the contract.

CHAPTER 13

WCF LOB Adapter SDK

The WCF LOB Adapter SDK (ASDK) is a set of runtime components and design-time UI tools providing a consistent framework for the development, management, and runtime execution of adapters for line-of-business (LOB) systems. (Systems such as SAP, Siebel, relational database management systems, and others are collectively known as the *LOB applications*.) Although the old COM-based framework for BizTalk adapter development is still available and fully supported by Microsoft, adapters built with the WCF LOB Adapter SDK offer significant advantage over adapters built on the old framework because they can be consumed not only from BizTalk but also from any .NET WCF-enabled application using familiar WCF semantics. As a complete development framework, the WCF LOB Adapter SDK offers tools to facilitate the development process for both adapter developers and adapter consumers.

If you are an adapter developer, the SDK offers you the following tools and features:

- A code generation wizard
- Runtime metadata management
- Runtime connection pooling
- Tracing/performance counters

If you are an adapter consumer, you are offered two Visual Studio add-ins with nearly identical UIs for browsing and selecting metadata, but they generate different artifacts depending on what the consuming application is. Here's what you get:

- **Add Adapter Service Reference plug-in for regular .NET applications**: This tool generates proxy files and also updates application configuration files for adding adapter configuration settings.
- **Consume Adapter Service add-in for BizTalk applications**: This tool generates schema definition files for the selected operations and the binding file to create and configure physical ports with the WCF-custom transport.

We'll discuss these tools and features in greater detail later in the chapter. We will also review the core use cases of the WCF LOB Adapter SDK and do a full walk-through of a custom adapter.

The WCF LOB Adapter SDK is a wide topic, and unfortunately it is hardly possible to cover all the nuances within one chapter. Besides the product documentation, you should be aware of two other sources of the in-depth information. Sonu Arora, a former WCF LOB Adapter SDK product manager, provides lots of invaluable information in her blog (`http://blogs.msdn.com/sonuarora/`). The product team's blog (`http://blogs.msdn.com/adapters/`)

is another great source offering very practical recommendations on using adapters from the BizTalk Adapter Pack.

■ **Note** Please note that Visual Studio and BizTalk Administration Console are 32-bit applications. This means that even if your computer is running under a 64-bit operating system and you therefore installed the 64-bit BizTalk runtime environment, you still must install both 32-bit and 64-bit adapter packs on your computer. Otherwise, you'll be spending many happy hours trying to figure out why installation went smoothly with no error messages but no adapters are available in BTS Administration Console.

Understanding the WCF LOB Adapter

Most people ask whether a WCF LOB Adapter is in fact a WCF service. The answer is no, it is not. WCF LOB Adapters are built on top of the WCF channel model and exposed as custom WCF bindings. This enables a client application to communicate with WCF LOB Adapters as if they are classic WCF services, but such similarity also confuses many developers. To understand this better, let's take a very brief excursion into WCF fundamentals.

WCF Endpoints

To establish a communication process with clients, a service must expose at least one endpoint. The WCF endpoints consist of three parts known as the "A, B, and C" of the WCF. The three parts are as follows:

- **Address**: This takes the form of the URI that specifies the address where the service listening for incoming messages can be reached.
- **Binding**: Bindings specify a communication protocol when the message is sent to a particular address.
- **Contract**: Contracts specify what operations and data types are supported by the service.

Communication between client and service is conducted through a so-called communication channel. When you instantiate the `ServiceHost` class, it builds a channel listener, which in turn builds a communication channel for the service. On the client side, the proxy creates a channel factory that is responsible for building an equivalent communication channel for the client. The channels have a layered structure where each layer or binding element in stricter terms performs its own part of message processing as the message goes from one layer to another, as shown in Figure 13-1. As you can notice, the bottom layer in the communication channel is a transport layer, and that's exactly where WCF LOB Adapter fits within the channel stack.

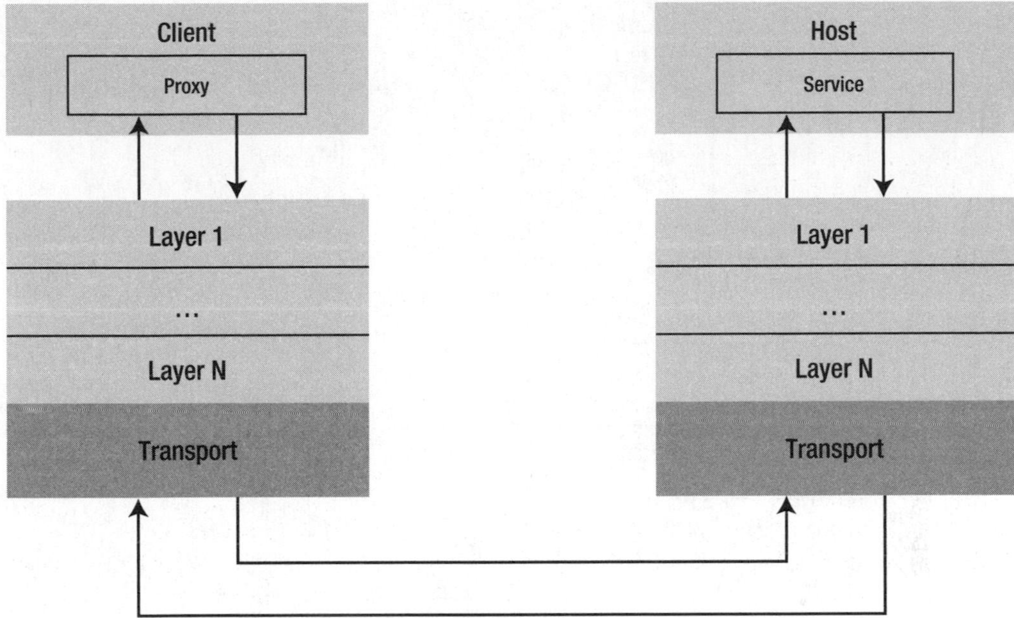

Figure 13-1. *The layered structure of the WCF*

WCF Transports

Out of the box, WCF supports a few predefined transports such as TCP, Named Pipes, HTTP, and MSMQ, but being designed with extensibility in mind, WCF allows you to use your own custom transport components tailored to your specific needs. If you take a look at the sample adapter code provided for this chapter, you will see that the core adapter class is derived from the `System.ServiceModel.Channels.TransportBindingElement` class. Figures 13-2 and 13-3 show the message flow for the WCF LOB Adapters in inbound and outbound exchanges.

As you can see in the outbound scenario, the WCF LOB Adapter, instead of sending the message over the network, just communicates with the LOB system and sends a response to the client application.

In the inbound scenario, the WCF LOB Adapter monitors the target LOB system for particular events and generates a notification message containing event-specific data for the hosting application.

■ **Note** If you are interested in taking a deeper look at WCF channels, you can find detailed information at `http://go.microsoft.com/fwlink/?LinkId=82614`.

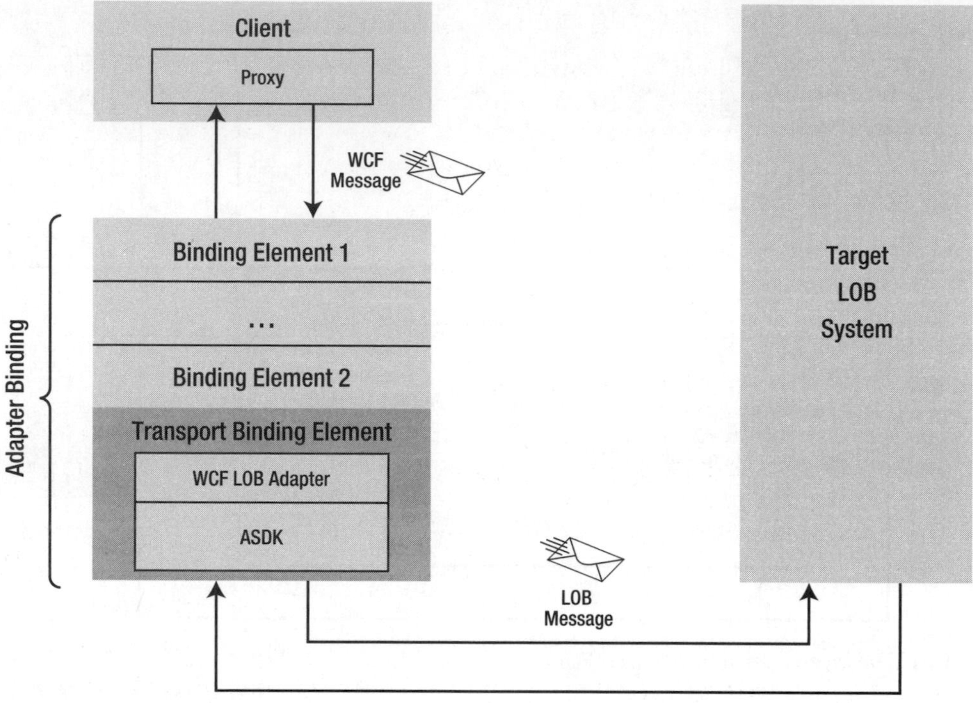

Figure 13-2. *WCF LOB Adapter outbound exchange*

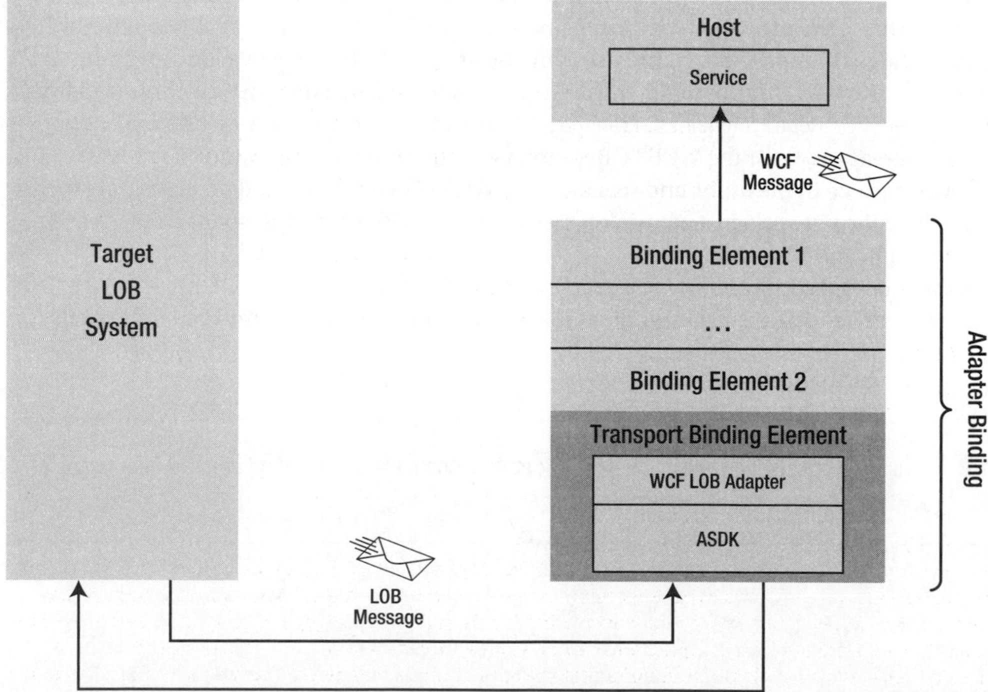

Figure 13-3. *WCF LOB Adapter inbound exchange*

WCF LOB Adapters vs. WCF Services

You may now be asking yourself the following, quite logical, question: if WCF LOB Adapters are built on top of the WCF channel model, and if for consuming applications they even look like the WCF services, what advantage then do WCF LOB Adapters offer over classic WCF services? To answer this question, let's consider a typical development cycle with WCF services. In a nutshell, the steps are as follows:

1. Define the service contract.
2. Implement the contract.
3. Configure and host the service.
4. Build and configure client applications to consume the service.

Now imagine a situation when your LOB application is, for example, DBMS-based. Further imagine that as your application evolves, the number of stored procedures (or metadata[1] in terms of ASDK) keeps growing. To expose the new operations to external clients through WCF services, the service provider will either have to update existing contracts or implement new ones by essentially starting the cycle again.

Dynamic Metadata Discovery and Resolution

The issue is that WCF contracts are static by its nature. If the underlying LOB application changes and you want to make the new functionality available to external clients, the existing contracts also have to change. In contrast, WCF LOB Adapters offer dynamic metadata discovery and resolution at design time. All changes in the underlying LOB system will be available automatically.

Let's look at a concrete example. As you likely know, BizTalk Server 2009 ships with a BizTalk Adapter Pack containing adapters for major LOB systems built using ASDK. Assume you are using the SQL Server Adapter from the pack to communicate with your SQL Server–based LOB application. To generate a proxy file for your .NET application, you will use the Add Adapter Service Reference plug-in, as shown in Figure 13-4. This plug-in functionally is similar to the Add Service Reference dialog box that you use to generate a proxy for WCF services.

When new stored procedures become available, adapter consumers who want to use those procedures will of course have to regenerate proxies using the Add Adapter Service Reference plug-in. The most important thing is that the new stored procedures will be discovered by the adapter and show up in the plug-in automatically, with no action required from the adapter developers.

1 Although *metadata* is a very broad term and it is hardly possible to give a one-size-fits-all definition, in the context of the WCF LOB Adapter SDK, *metadata* can be defined as a set of data, operations, and other artifacts determining and constituting functionality of the target LOB system. For example, metadata for a DBMS-based application can be stored procedures and data tables, or it can be assemblies containing classes implementing the application's business objects. It is up to the adapter designer to decide what constitutes metadata for a particular application and how to expose it to the adapter consumers.

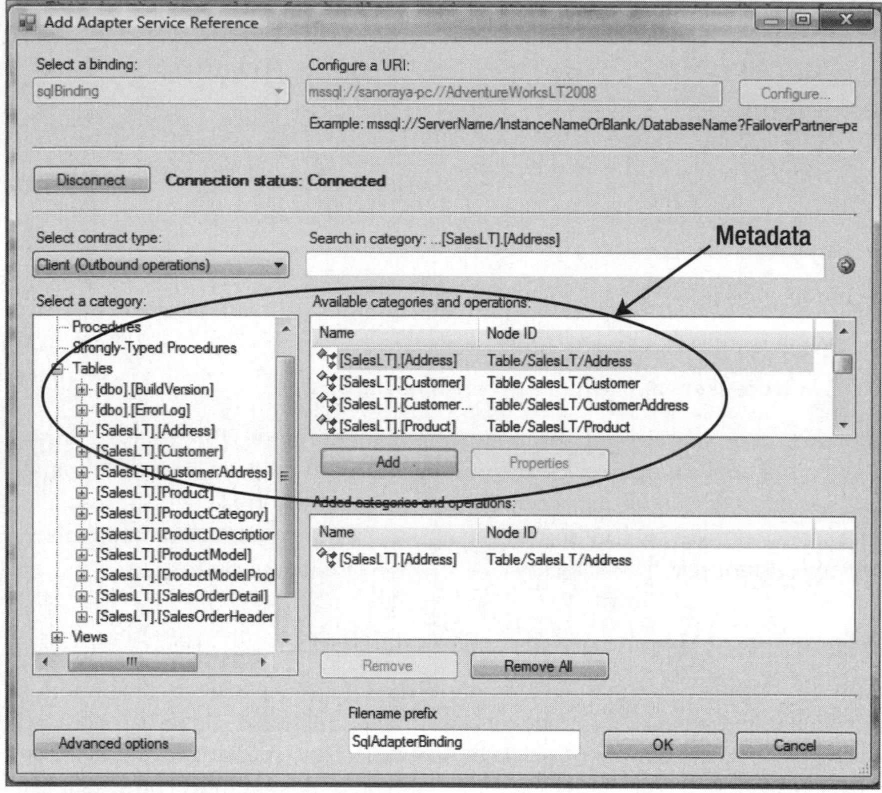

Figure 13-4. *Add Adapter Service Reference plug-in*

Although the process we've described sounds like magic, of course it is not. It is the sole responsibility of the adapter developer to implement the interfaces to enable adapter metadata capabilities. If that seems confusing, please read on. After completing the walk-through later in the chapter, you'll have a much clearer idea of how this "magic" actually happens.

As a general rule, Microsoft suggests[2] the following guidelines for evaluating whether your organization will benefit from using ASDK.

You should consider writing adapter when:

- the target system is an existing system that is not enabled for web services;
- the target system is dynamic and can be enhanced with new operations;
- the target system has a large amount of metadata;
- there is a large, diverse number of users for the target system's data; or
- consuming applications need rich application metadata discovery functionality.

2 http://msdn.microsoft.com/en-us/library/bb798089.aspx

You should use the WCF service or channel model to create a service when:

- the target system is static and has a fixed set of operations;
- the target system has little or no metadata;
- service developers have detailed knowledge of the application to be exposed; or
- a new application is being exposed.

WCF LOB Adapter Vivisected

Now that you are becoming familiar with the adapter fundamentals and you've learned where the WCF LOB Adapter fits into WCF model, it is time to take a look inside the WCF LOB Adapter in detail. Figure 13-5 shows the major components and how they interact with each other.

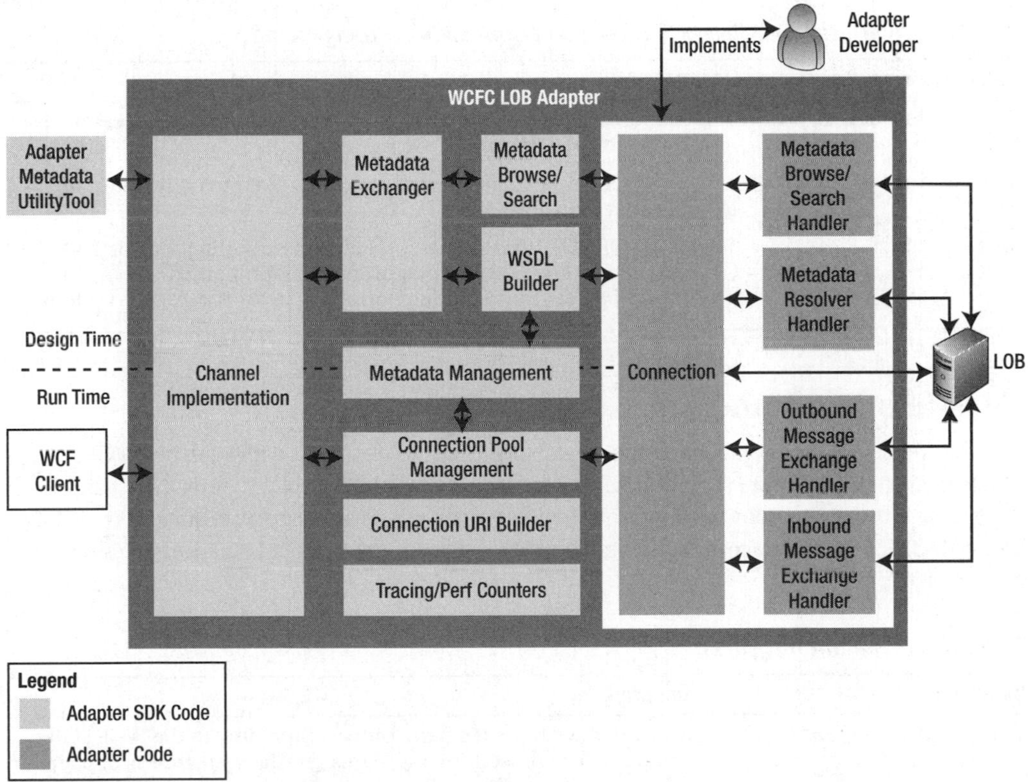

Figure 13-5. *WCF LOB Adapter's internal structure*

As you can see, the WCF LOB Adapter as a code entity can be split into two big parts; one part is provided by the ASDK, and the other part has to be implemented by the adapter developer. Essentially, a developer—that's you—has to provide the implementation for three blocks of functionality: the connection, metadata handlers, and inbound/outbound handlers. The WCF LOB Adapter Development Wizard generates skeleton classes supporting the required methods and interfaces; you as the adapter developer need to provide an implementation specific to the target LOB system.

The Connection

Creating and opening a connection to a LOB system is in many cases an expensive procedure in terms of machine resources. One of the key features provided by the WCF LOB Adapter SDK is connection management, which takes the form of *connection pooling*.

When a connection is required to perform a metadata or inbound/outbound operation, the WCF LOB runtime component either creates a new connection or gets an existing one from a connection pool. When the operation completes, the WCF LOB SDK runtime component returns a connection to the connection pool.

To enable connection management, you have to provide the implementation of three interfaces and classes defined in the `Microsoft.ServiceModel.Channels.Common` namespace. We've listed them for you in Table 13-1.

Table 13-1. *Interfaces and Classes to Implement Connection Management*

Class/Interface	Description
`IConnectionFactory`	This interface is used by the WCF LOB SDK when it needs to create a new connection to the target LOB system.
`IConnection`	This interface encapsulates the methods required to connect to the target LOB system.
`ConnectionUri`	The WCF LOB SDK Wizard generates a class extending the abstract `ConnectionUri` class. You have to provide the implementation of the properties representing a connection string to the target LOB system.

The Metadata Handlers

As we have discussed, metadata support is an important feature that distinguishes WCF LOB Adapters from WCF services. To enable an adapter's metadata capability, you as the adapter developer must implement two mandatory interfaces; there is also one optional interface (see Table 13-2). These interfaces are defined in the `Microsoft.ServiceModel.Channels.Common` namespace.

Table 13-2. *Metadata Interfaces*

Interface	Description
`IMetadataBrowseHandler`	This interface represents the browse capability of the WCF LOB Adapters. You must implement this interface regardless of your adapter functionality.
`IMetadataSearchHandler`	Optional. This interface represents the search capability of the WCF LOB Adapters.
`IMetadataResolverHandler`	This interface is used when the WCF LOB Adapter SDK needs to generate the proxy files in case of .NET applications or XSD specifications in case of BizTalk applications. You must implement this interface regardless of your adapter functionality.

The Message Exchange Handlers

Message exchange handlers are represented by four interfaces from the `Microsoft.ServiceModel.Channels.Common` namespace. We've listed them for you in Table 13-3.

Table 13-3. *Message Exchange Handlers*

Interface	Description
`IOutboundHandler`	Supports one-way send or request-response pattern.
`IAsyncOutboundHandler`	Optional. Supports asynchronous one-way send or request-response pattern.
`IInboundHandler`	Optional. Supports one-way receive or reply pattern.
`IAsyncInboundHandler`	Optional. Supports asynchronous one way receive or reply pattern.

Walk-Through

Now that you are familiar with the major classes and interfaces that the WCF LOB Adapters have to support, let's put all the pieces together and implement a simple adapter for a mythical hotel reservation system. In the inbound scenario, an adapter monitors the system and sends notification if new guests arrive. In the outbound scenario, an adapter accepts requests and returns the number of available rooms for the specified hotel.

Step 1: Generating Adapter Skeleton Code

First, you have to create WCF LOB Adapter project. Begin by using Visual Studio's WCF LOB Adapter Development Wizard to generate some skeleton code. Here is the process to follow:

1. To create a WCF LOB Adapter project, open Visual Studio 2008. Select File ➤ New Project. The New Project dialog box will open. Select a Visual C# project for the project type, and select WCF LOB Adapter from the Templates pane. Specify the project name and location, as shown in Figure 13-6.
2. Click OK. The WCF LOB Adapter Development Wizard, shown in Figure 13-7, will open.
3. Click Next.

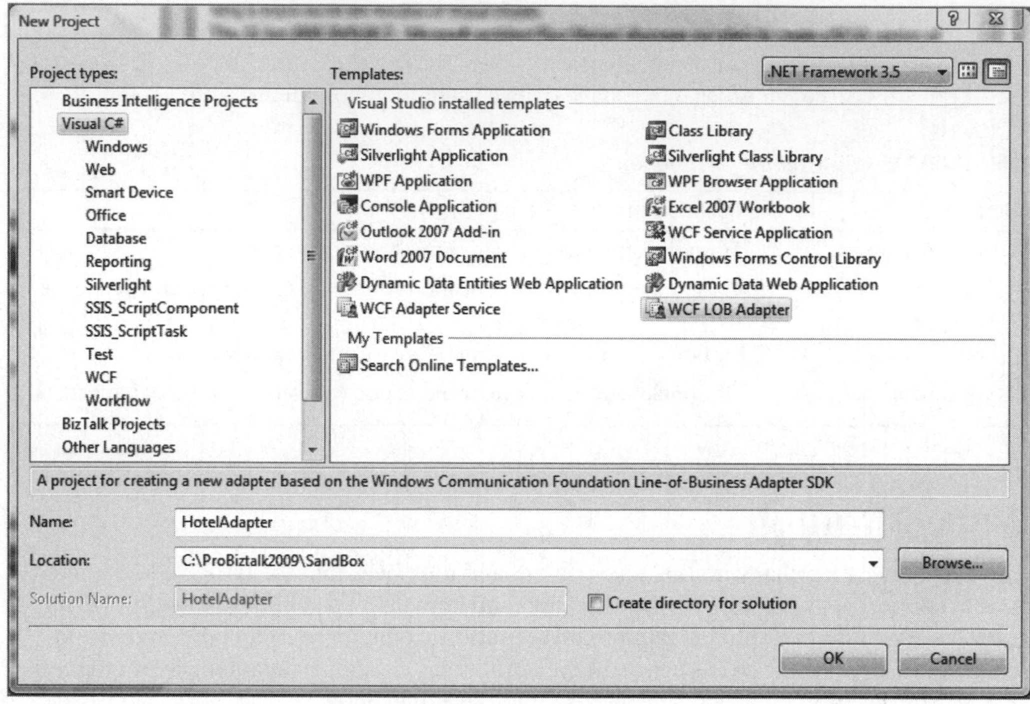

Figure 13-6. *Creating a WCF LOB Adapter project*

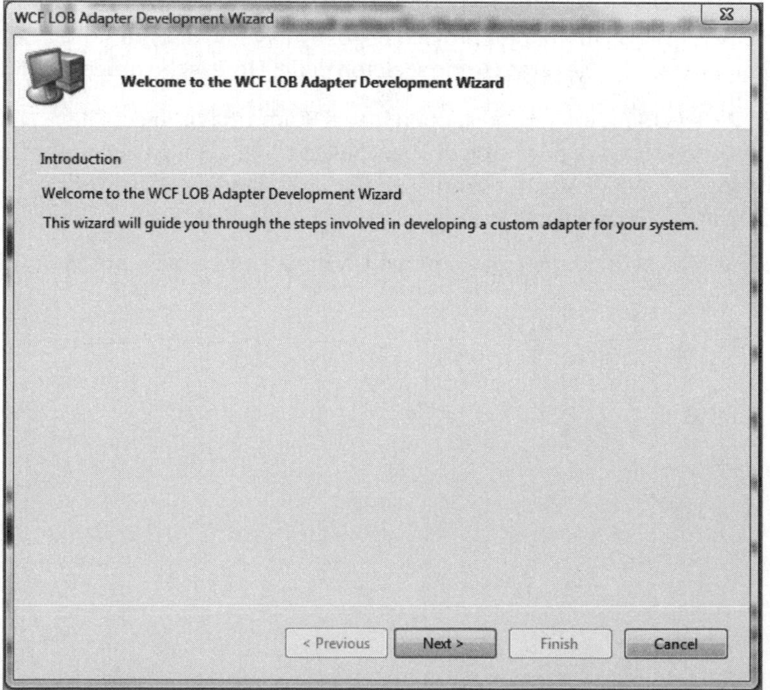

Figure 13-7. *The WCF LOB Adapter Wizard*

4. On the Scheme, Namespace and URI Information page, specify the parameters shown in Figure 13-8. If you want to override the default namespace, select the "Override default namespace" check box, and type the desired namespace in the "Service namespace" field.

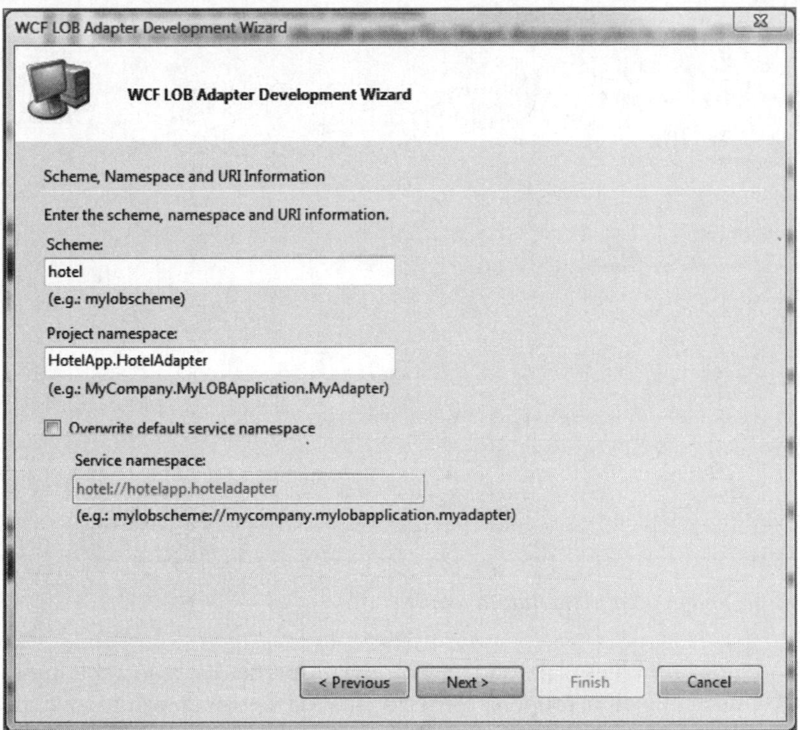

Figure 13-8. *Scheme, Namespace, and URI Information page*

5. Click the Next button.

6. Specify the parameters shown in Figure 13-9, and click the Next button.

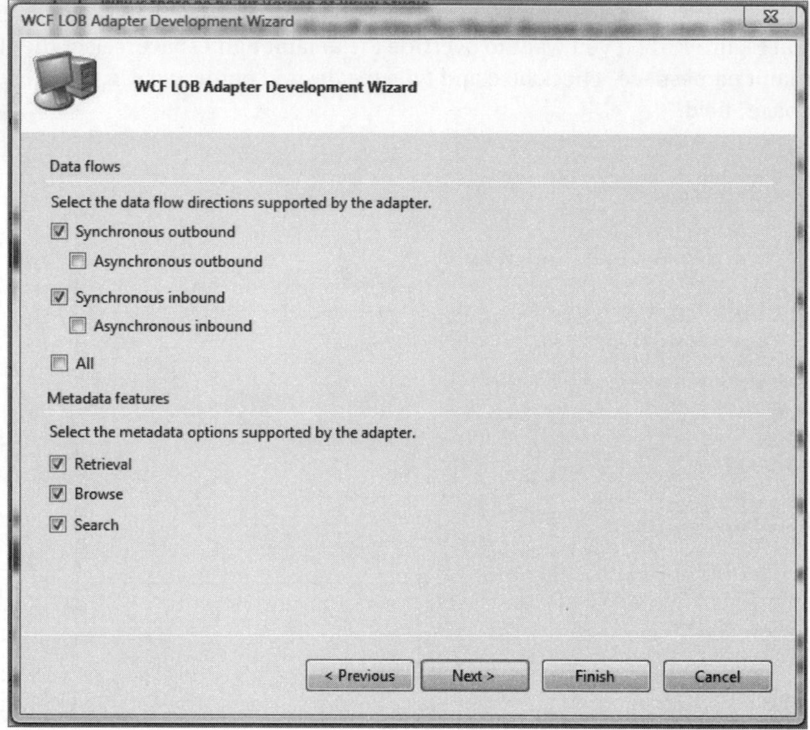

Figure 13-9. *Data flows and metadata features*

7. On the Adapter Properties page, add the binding properties listed in Table 13-4. The EnableConnectionPooling property is used by the ASDK to enable or disable the runtime connection pooling. Make sure that after adding the properties, the Adapter Properties page looks like Figure 13-10. Click the Next button.

Table 13-4. *Adapter Binding Properties*

Property Name	Data Type	Default Value
EnableConnectionPooling	System.Boolean	True
PollingPeriod	System.Integer	10

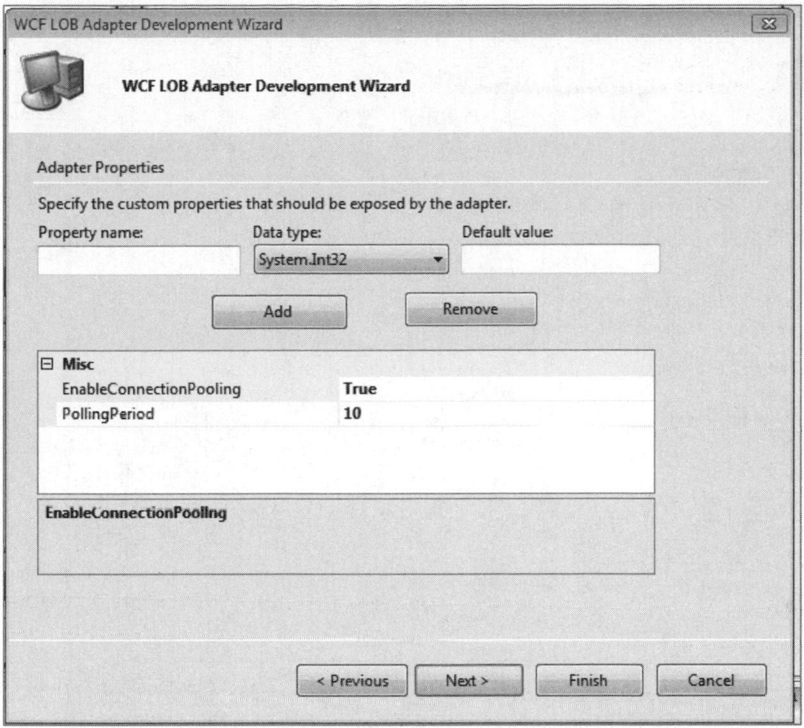

Figure 13-10. *Adapter Properties page*

8. On the Connection Properties page, add the connection properties listed in Table 13-5. After adding the properties, the Connection Properties page should look like Figure 13-11.

Table 13-5. *Adapter Connection Properties*

Property Name	Data Type	Default Value
Application	System.String	HotelApp
EnableAuthentication	System.Boolean	True
Host	System.String	HotelAppHost

9. Click the Next button. On the Summary page, click the Finish button. Figure 13-12 shows the Solution Explorer with the files generated by the WCF LOB Adapter Development Wizard.

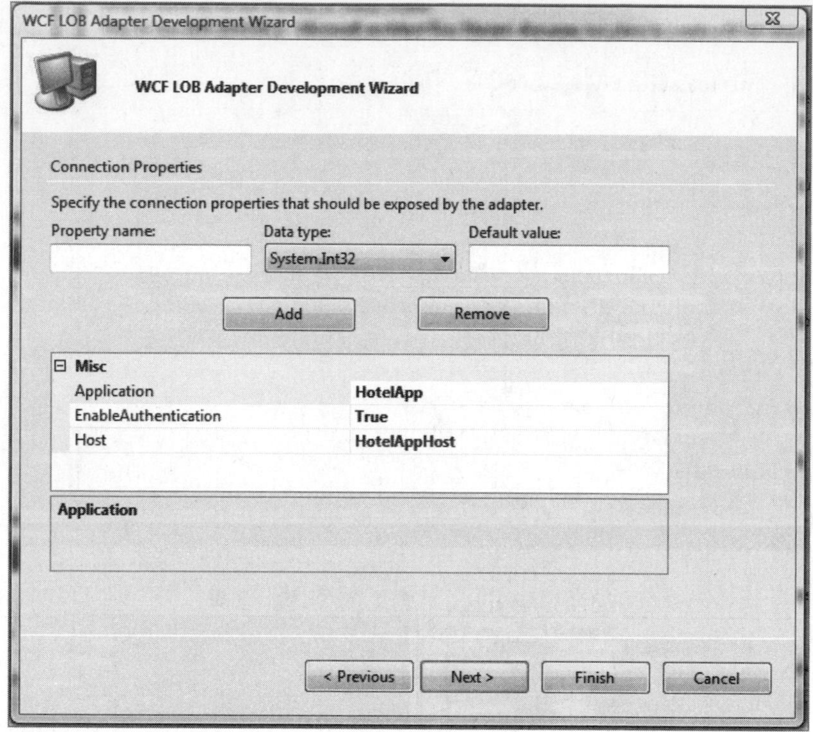

Figure 13-11. *Connection Properties page*

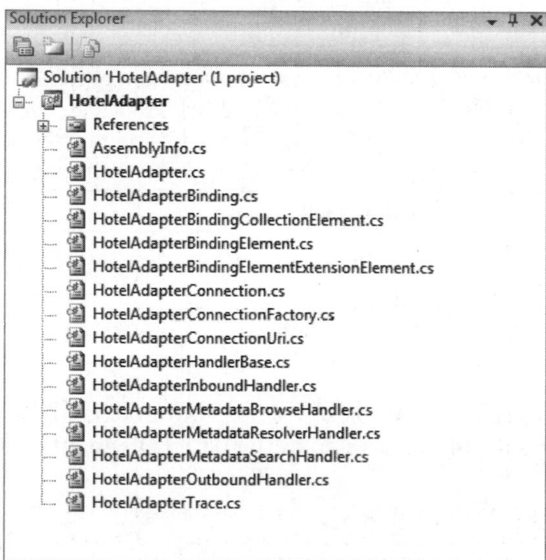

Figure 13-12. *HotelAdapter generated project*

Tables 13-6 to 13-10 give a brief description of the files generated by the wizard.

Table 13-6. *Connection Group*

File	Description
HotelAdapterConnection.cs	Contains the definition of the class implementing the `IConnection` interface. This class is responsible for a single connection to the target LOB system.
HotelAdapterConnectionFactory.cs	Contains the definition of the class implementing the `IConnectionFactory` interface. This class creates an instance of the class implementing the `IConnection` interface, that is, `HotelAdapterConnection`.
HotelAdapterConnectionUri.cs	Contains the definition of the class representing connection string to the target LOB system.

Table 13-7. *Metadata Handlers Group*

File	Description
HotelAdapterMetadataBrowseHandler.cs	Contains the definition of the class implementing the `IMetadataBrowseHandler` interface. This class is responsible for the metadata browse capabilities of the adapter.
HotelAdapterMetadataResolverHandler.cs	Contains the definition of the class implementing the `IMetadataResolverHandler` interface. This interface is used by ASDK to get the information about supported operations and data types. This information is used to generate proxy files or message type specifications.
HotelAdapterMetadataSearchHandler.cs	Contains the definition of the class implementing the `IMetadataSearchHandler` interface. This class is responsible for the search metadata capabilities of the adapter.

Table 13-8. *Inbound/Outbound Handlers Group*

File	Description
HotelAdapterHandlerBase.cs	Contains the definition of the base class for adapter handlers.
HotelAdapterInboundHandler.cs	Contains the definition of the class implementing the `IOutboundHandler` interface. This class is responsible for listening to events or polling for data on the target LOB system.
HotelAdapterOutboundHandler.cs	Contains the definition of the class implementing the `IInboundHandler` interface. This class is responsible for sending data to the target system.

Table 13-9. *Custom Binding Group*[3]

File	Description
HotelAdapterBinding.cs	Contains the definition of the class representing a binding for the WCF LOB Adapter. This class hosts a collection of the `BindingElements`, which the WCF channel is built upon.
HotelAdapterBindingCollection Element.cs	Contains the definition of the class used to register the adapter with WCF.
HotelAdapterBindingElement.cs	This class is used to apply configuration properties to the adapter binding.
HotelAdapterBindingElement ExtensionElement.cs	Contains the definition of the class used to expose the adapter as a custom adapter binding. This class is used to configure the adapter using the WCF-custom adapter.

Table 13-10. *Core Files*

File	Description
HotelAdapter.cs	Contains the definition of the main adapter class derived from `Microsoft.ServiceModel.Channels.Common.Adapter`.
HotelAdapterTrace.cs	Contains the definition of a supplementary class that can be used in the code for debugging purposes and tracing in particular.

After completing this step, you have WCF LOB Adapter skeleton classes that you will fill with functionality in the subsequent steps. In the next step, you will categorize the properties that you created using the wizard.

Step 2: UI Logical Grouping

In this step, you will modify the `HotelAdapterBindingElement` and `HotelAdapterUri` classes to logically group the binding and connection properties that you created in step 1. You will create three categories and arrange the properties within these categories, as shown in Table 13-11.

Table 13-11. *Adapter Property Categories*

Property Name	Category
`EnableConnectionPooling`	Misc
`Application`	Connection
`EnableAuthentication`	Connection
`Host`	Connection
`PollingPeriod`	Inbound

3 We recommend the following readings for in-depth coverage of the custom bindings: extending bindings (http://msdn.microsoft.com/en-us/library/ms731751.aspx), custom bindings applied to WCF LOB Adapters (http://blogs.msdn.com/sonuarora/archive/2007/03/26/how-to-use-an-adapter-built-using-wcf-lob-adapter-sdk-within-a-wcf-custom-binding.aspx), and how to configure WCF extensibility points to use with WCF adapters (http://msdn.microsoft.com/en-us/library/bb743310.aspx).

When you complete this step and build the project, the binding and connection properties will be grouped and presented in the Add Adapter Service Reference plug-in and Consume Adapter Service add-in, as shown in Figures 13-13 and 13-14.

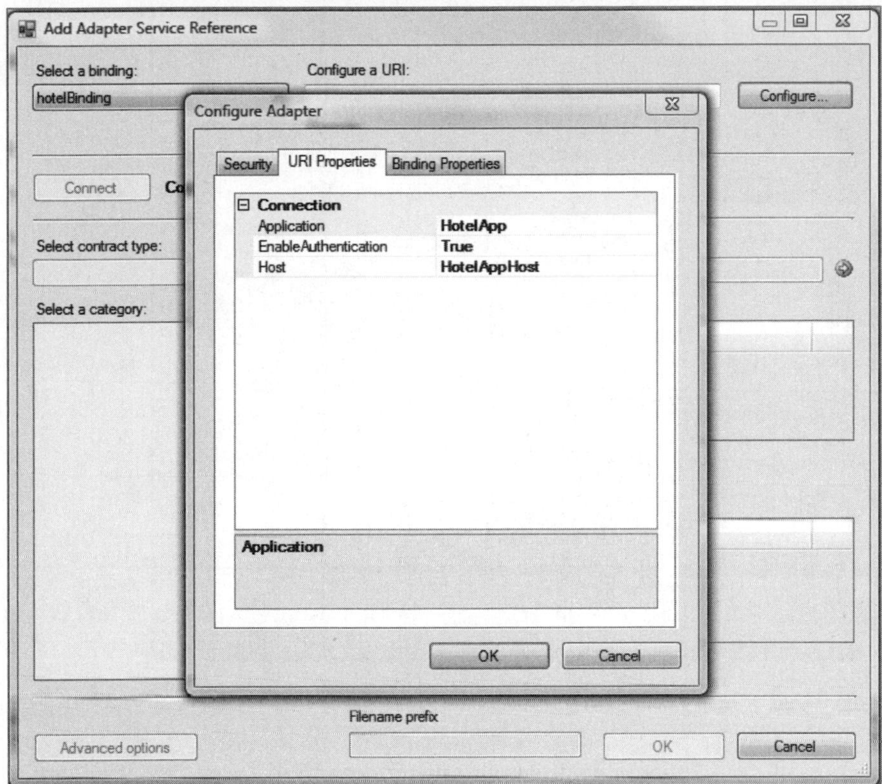

Figure 13-13. *Categorized connection properties*

Although categorizing properties is optional, we recommend that you don't ignore this step. The reasoning is simple—categorizing improves user experience, since in many if not most cases adapter consumers will configure adapters using the UI tools.

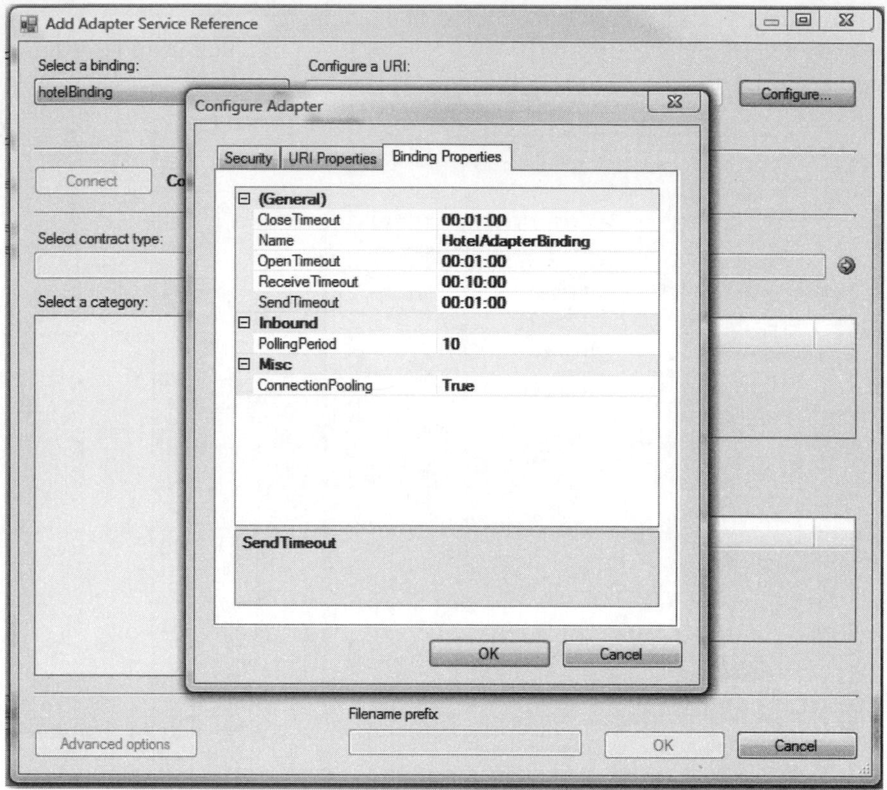

Figure 13-14. *Categorized binding properties*

As you can guess, the implementation is fairly straightforward and doesn't require more than applying the `System.ComponentModel.Category` attribute to the custom properties. Let's start with the `HotelAdapterBindingElement` class:

1. In Visual Studio, open the HotelAdapterBindingElement.cs file.
2. To assign the Misc category to the `EnableConnectionPooling` property, place the `[System.ComponentModel.Category("")]` line of code at the beginning of the `EnableConnectionPooling` implementation, as shown here:

```
[System.Configuration.ConfigurationProperty("enableConnectionPooling",
                                            DefaultValue = true)]

public bool EnableConnectionPooling
{
    get
    {
        return ((bool)(base["EnableConnectionPooling"]));
    }
    set
```

```
        {
            base["EnableConnectionPooling"] = value;
        }
    }
```

3. Specify the Inbound category for the PollingPeriod property by placing the [System.ComponentModel.Category("Inbound")] line of code at the beginning of the PollingPeriod property, as shown in the following code snippet:

```
    [System.ComponentModel.Category("Inbound")]
    [System.Configuration.ConfigurationProperty("pollingPeriod",
        DefaultValue = 10)]

    public int PollingPeriod
    {
        get
        {
            return ((string)(base["pollingPeriod"]));
        }
        set
        {
            base["pollingPeriod"] = value;
        }
    }
```

Follow a similar procedure for the HotelAdapterConnectionUri class:

1. In Visual Studio, open the HotelAdapterConnectionUri.cs file.
2. Expand the Custom Generated Properties region, and apply the [System.ComponentMode.Category("Connection")] attribute to each of the properties in the region. When you finish, the Custom Generated Properties region should match the following code snippet:

```
    #region Custom Generated Properties

    [System.ComponentModel.Category("Connection")]
    public string Application
    {
        get
        {
            return this.application;
        }
        set
        {
            this.application = value;
        }
    }
```

```
[System.ComponentModel.Category("Connection")]
public bool EnableAuthentication
{
    get
    {
        return this.enableAuthentication;
    }
    set
    {
        this.enableAuthentication = value;
    }
}

[System.ComponentModel.Category("Connection")]
public string Host
{
    get
    {
        return this.host;
    }
    set
    {
        this.host = value;
    }
}

#endregion Custom Generated Properties
```

3. Save and build the project.

In the next step, you will work with the classes and interfaces responsible for establishing and managing connection to the LOB systems.

Step 3: Implementing the Connection

As we mentioned earlier, the runtime connection management is one of the features that makes the WCF LOB Adapters stand apart from their closest competitors: WCF services. Implementing a connection is a mandatory step, even if your LOB system doesn't require a connection, as in the case of our mythical hotel application. Most, if not all, real-life LOB applications do require establishing a connection before granting access to their features.

To enable runtime connection management, you have to implement three classes generated by the WCF LOB Development Wizard, each performing its specific task:

- `HotelAdapterConnectionUri`
- `HotelAdapterConnectionFactory`
- `HotelAdapterConnection`

Implementing the HotelAdapterConnectionUri Class

The `HotelConnectionUri` class inherits the abstract `ConnectionUri`[4] class from the `Microsoft.ServiceMode.Channels.Common` namespace. The `ConnectionUri` class represents a connection string to a target LOB system. Table 13-12 shows the methods and properties that you have to implement in the `HotelAdapterConnectionUri` class.

Table 13-12. *The HotelAdapterConnectionUri Cass's Methods and Properties*

Method/Property	Description
`public override Uri Uri`	Contains the connection URI.
`public HotelAdapterConnectionUri`	Instantiates the `HotelAdapterConnectionUri` class.
`public override string SampleUriString`	Gets the sample URI string to present in the Add Adapter Service Reference plug-in and Consume Adapter Service add-in, as shown in Figure 13-15.

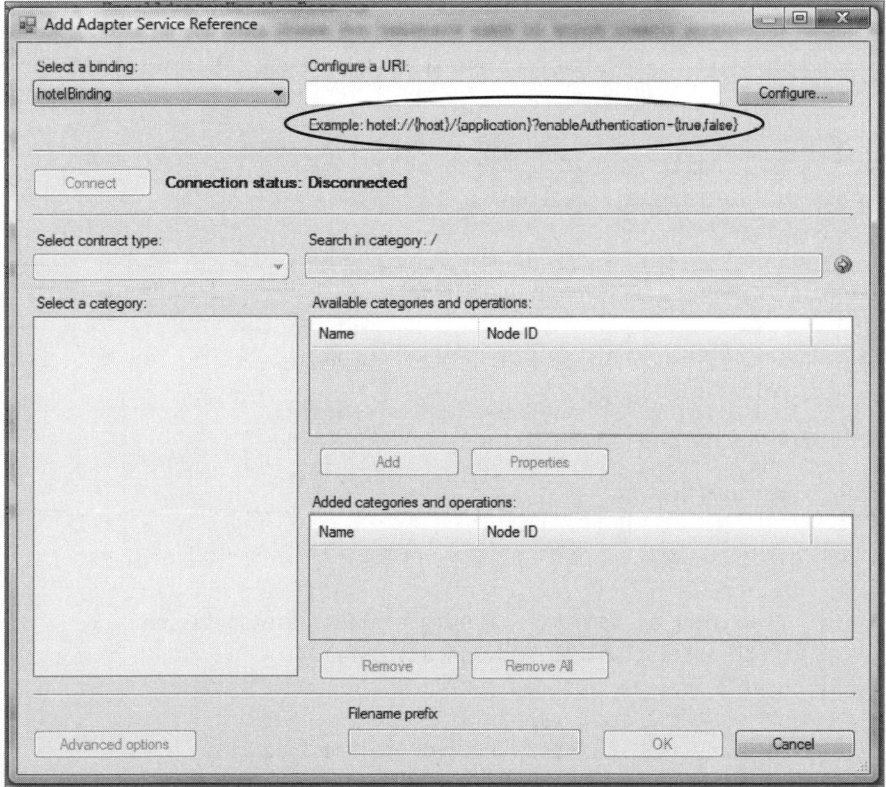

Figure 13-15. *Sample Uri string*

4 http://msdn.microsoft.com/en-us/library/microsoft.servicemodel.channels.common.connectionuri.aspx

Here is the process to follow:

1. In Visual Studio, open the HotelAdapterConnectionUri.cs file.
2. Add a new private variable `UriBuilder` type to the class definition:

```
private UriBuilder uriBuilder;
```

3. Update the class constructor as follows:

```
#region Constructors

        /// <summary>
        /// Initializes a new instance of the ConnectionUri class
        /// </summary>
        public HotelAdapterConnectionUri()
        {
            uriBuilder = new UriBuilder();
        }

        /// <summary>
        /// Initializes a new instance of the ConnectionUri
        /// class with a Uri object
        /// </summary>

        public HotelAdapterConnectionUri(Uri uri)
            : base()
        {
            uriBuilder = new UriBuilder(uri);
        }

        #endregion Constructors
```

4. Locate the `Uri` property, and replace it with the following code:

```
    public override Uri Uri
        {
            get
            {
                //check if connection string elements are specified
                if (String.IsNullOrEmpty(this.host))
                {
                    throw new InvalidUriException(
                              "Host name must be specified.");
                }
                if (String.IsNullOrEmpty(this.application))
                {
                   throw new InvalidUriException(
                        "Application name must be specified.");
                }
                // the connection uri object
```

```
                this.uriBuilder.Scheme = HotelAdapter.SCHEME;
                this.uriBuilder.Host = host;
                this.uriBuilder.Path = application;
                this.uriBuilder.Query = "enableAuthentication="
                    + enableAuthentication.ToString();

                return uriBuilder.Uri;
            }
            set
            {
                this.host = value.Host;
                //walk through connection string segments and get app name
                //it is in the last segment
                if (value.Segments != null && value.Segments.Length > 1)
                {
                    foreach (string segment in value.Segments)
                    {
                        application = segment;
                    }
                }
                this.enableAuthentication = false;
                string[] enableAuthenticationValue =
                    GetQueryStringValue(value, "enableAuthentication");
                if (enableAuthenticationValue.Length == 1)
                {
                    this.enableAuthentication =
                        Boolean.Parse(enableAuthenticationValue[0]);
                }

            }
        }
```

Please note the use of the `UriBuilder`[5] class. This class simplifies building and parsing connection strings.

5. Specify a sample string as shown in the following code snippet. Although this is not a requirement, providing a sample string for adapter consumers is a good practice.

```
/// <summary>
        /// Returns the sample connection string
        /// to be presented in UI design-time tools
        /// </summary>
        public override string SampleUriString
        {
            get
```

5 http://msdn.microsoft.com/en-us/library/system.uribuilder_members.aspx

```
            {
                return HotelAdapter.SCHEME +
                   "://{host}/{application}?enableAuthentication={true,fals
e}";

            }
        }
```

In the next subsection, you will implement the HotelAdapterConnectionFactory class.

Implementing the HotelAdapterConnectionFactory Class

The HotelAdapterConnectionFactory class implements the IConnectionFactory interface from the Microsoft.ServiceModel.Channels.Common namespace. This interface is located in the Microsoft.ServiceModel.Channels assembly. The WCF LOB Development Wizard provides the implementation for the CreateConnection method, which is the only public method exposed by the IConnectionFactory interface. The purpose of this method is to instantiate the HotelAdapterConnection class, which represents a single connection to the target LOB system.

Here is the process to follow to implement the HotelAdapterConnectionFactory:

1. In Visual Studio, open the HotelAdapterConnectionFactory.cs file.
2. Locate the Private Fields region, and add a new variable:

```
private HotelAdapterConnectionUri uri;
```

3. Update the HotelAdapterConnectionFactory constructor so that it looks like the following:

```
/// <summary>
/// Initializes a new instance of the
///HotelAdapterConnectionFactory class
/// </summary>
public HotelAdapterConnectionFactory(ConnectionUri connectionUri
    , ClientCredentials clientCredentials
    , HotelAdapter adapter)
{
    this.uri = (HotelAdapterConnectionUri)connectionUri;
    this.clientCredentials = clientCredentials;
    this.adapter = adapter;
}
```

4. Locate the Public Properties region, and add the ConnectionUri and ClientCredentials properties, as shown here:

```
public ClientCredentials ClientCredentials
{
    get
```

```
            {
                return this.clientCredentials;
            }
        }
        /// <summary>
        /// Returns the connectionuri
        /// </summary>
        public HotelAdapterConnectionUri Uri
        {
            get
            {
                return this.uri;
            }
        }
```

In the next section, you will implement the `HotelAdapterConnection` class, the last of the three required to enable the WCF LOB SDK connection management.

Implementing the HotelAdapterConnection Class

The `HotelAdapterConnection` class represents a single connection to the target LOB system and implements the `IConnection`[6] interface from the `Microsoft.ServiceModel.Channels.Common` namespace. This interface is located in the Microsoft.ServiceModel.Channels.dll assembly. Table 13-13 shows the public methods and properties exposed by the `IConnection` interface.

Table 13-13. *IConnection Interface Methods and Properties*

Method/Property	Description
`Abort`	Aborts the connection to the external system/application.
`BuildHandler`	Builds a new instance of the class that implements the `IConnectionHandler` interface.
`ClearContext`	Clears the context of the connection. This method is called when a connection is returned to the connection pool.
`IsValid`	Returns a value indicating whether the connection is valid.
`Close`	Closes the connection to the target LOB system.
`Open`	Opens the connection to the target LOB system.
`ConnectionId`	Property. Returns the ID of the connection.

Although `HotelAdapter` doesn't require a connection to the target system as we mentioned earlier, we nevertheless will show you how to handle user credentials. Most LOB systems require client applications to provide valid credentials before authorizing access to their data and functionality. To set user credentials, you can use the Add Adapter Service Reference plug-in or Consume Adapter Service add-in, as shown in Figure 13-16.

6 http://msdn.microsoft.com/en-us/library/microsoft.servicemodel.channels.common.iconnection_members.aspx

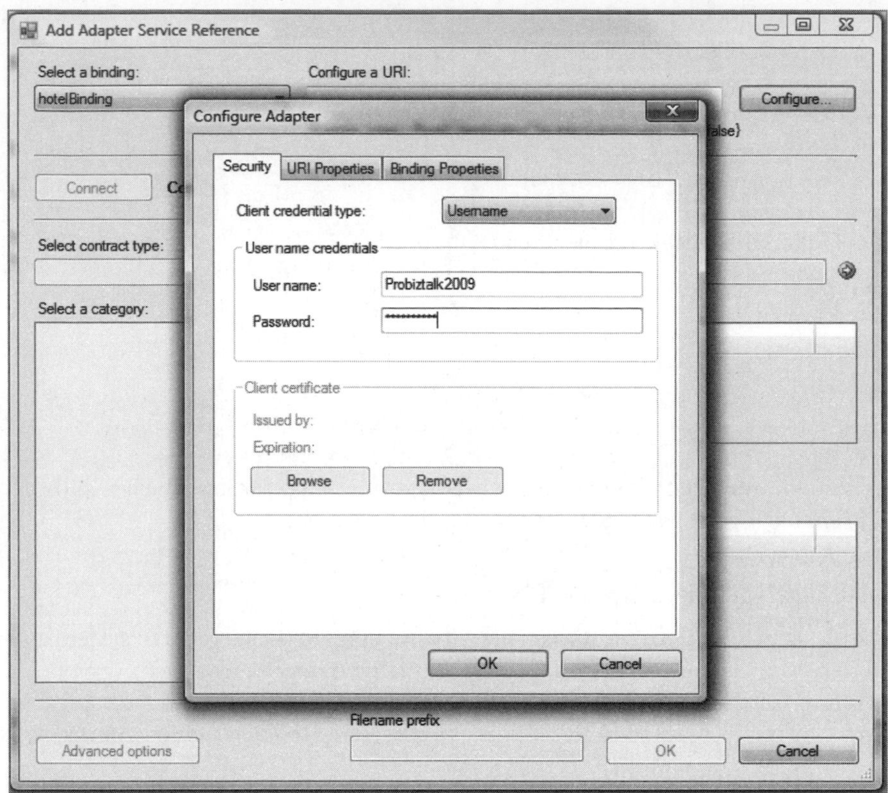

Figure 13-16. *Security configuration page*

When you close the Configure Adapter dialog box and click the Connect button, the WCF LOB SDK runtime component will call the Open method of the `HotelAdapterConnection` class, which handles the user credentials.

Here is the process you have to follow to implement the `IConnect` interface and user credentials handling:

1. In Visual Studio, open the HotelAdapterConnection.cs file.
2. Comment out all the `NotImplemented` exceptions. Modify the `IsValid` method so that it returns `true`.
3. In the `IConnection Members` region, locate the `Open` method, and replace it with the following code:

```
if (this.ConnectionFactory.Uri.EnableAuthentication == true)
{
    if (this.connectionFactory.ClientCredentials != null &&
        string.IsNullOrEmpty(
        this.connectionFactory.
        ClientCredentials.UserName.UserName))
```

```
                {
                    throw
                      new CredentialsException("Username is expected.");
                }
            }
```

4. Build and deploy the project.

Now that you are familiar with the key classes and interfaces that define connection functionality, we will show you how to implement the connection-based metadata handlers.

Step 4: Implementing the Metadata Handlers

The metadata support is probably the most distinguishing feature of the adapters written using the WCF LOB Adapter SDK. In thc "WCF LOB Adapters vs. WCF Services" section, we mentioned the magic of the automatic metadata discovery and resolution. In this step, you will implement the interfaces that turn that magic into realty. Table 13-14 lists the interfaces.

Table 13-14. *Metadata Interfaces*

Interface	Description
`IMetadataBrowseHandler`	This interface represents the browse capability of the WCF LOB Adapters. You must implement this interface regardless of your adapter functionality.
`IMetadataSearchHandler`	Optional. This interface represents the search capability of the WCF LOB Adapters.
`IMetadataResolverHandler`	This interface is used when the WCF LOB Adapter SDK needs to generate the proxy files in case of .NET applications or XSD specifications in case of BizTalk applications.

Implementing the IMetadataBrowseHandler Interface

To enable the browse capability of the adapter, you have to implement the `IMetadataBrowseHandler`[7] interface from the `Microsoft.ServiceModel.Channels.Common` namespace. The WCF LOB Adapter Development Wizard generated the derived `HotelAdapterMetadataBrowseHandler` skeleton class for you.

The `IMetadataBrowseHandler` interface is located in the Microsoft.ServiceModel.Channels.dll assembly and is defined as follows:

```
public interface IMetadataBrowseHandler : IConnectionHandler, IDisposable
    {
        MetadataRetrievalNode[] Browse(string nodeId,
                                                          int childStartIndex,
                                                          int maxChildNodes,
                                                          TimeSpan timeout);
    }
```

We've put a description of the parameters accepted by the `Browse` method in Table 13-15.

7 http://msdn.microsoft.com/en-us/library/microsoft.servicemodel.channels.common.imetadatabrowsehandler_methods.aspx

Table 13-15. *IMetadataBrowseHandler.Browse Method Parameters*

Parameter	Description
nodeId	The node identifier. Browse method evaluates the nodeId and returns either a collection of child nodes, if any, or a collection of operations associated with the given nodeId.
childStartIndex	The index of the first child to return.
maxChildNodes	The maximum number of child nodes to return.
Timeout	The maximum time to wait to complete the operation.

The Browse method returns an array of the MetadataRetrievalNode[8] objects representing either the operation or category type. Table 13-16 lists the public properties of the MetadataRetrievalNode class.

Table 13-16. *MetadataRetrievalNode Public Properties*

Property	Description
Description	Gets or sets the node description.
Direction	Gets or sets the direction (inbound or outbound) in which the node is being retrieved.
DisplayName	Gets or sets the node name to be displayed by UI.
IsOperation	Gets or sets the value indicating that the node is operation.
NodeId	Gets or sets the NodeId, which uniquely identifies the node. The NodeId is usually a concatenation of the node path and node name. The node name is not necessarily the same as the DisplayName.
Root	Read-only. Gets the root node.

When you finish implementation and deploy the project, you will be able to explore the operations supported by the adapter using the Add Adapter Service Reference or Consume Adapter Server reference tools, as shown in Figure 13-17.

8 http://msdn.microsoft.com/en-us/library/microsoft.servicemodel.channels.metadataretrievalnode.aspx

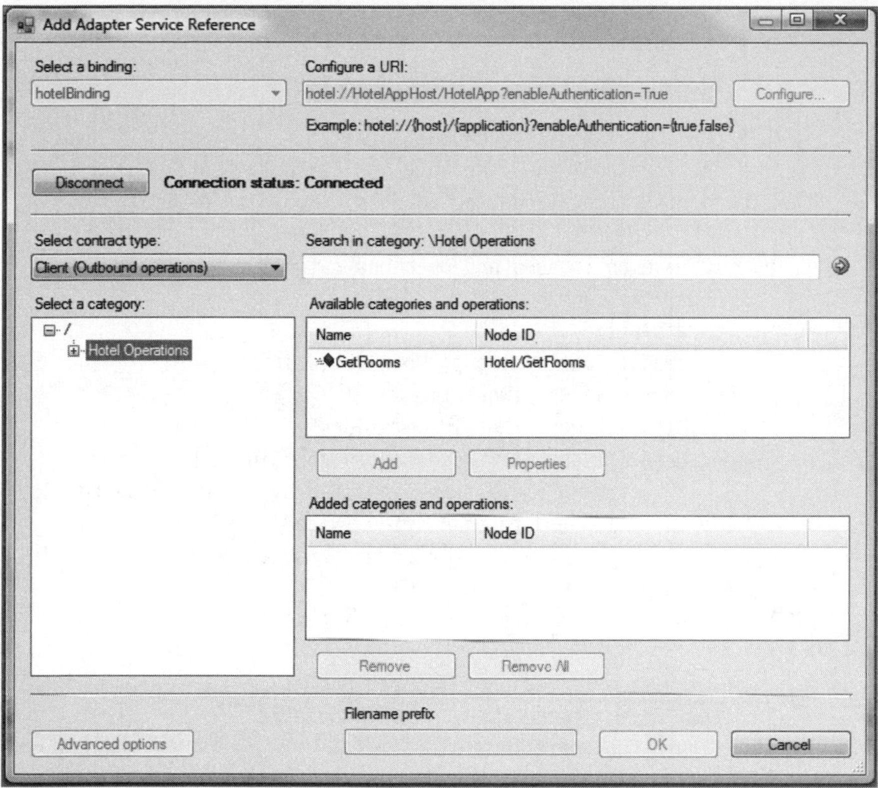

Figure 13-17. *`HotelAdapter` metadata*

Now let's get to the code and implement the `IMetadataBrowseHandler` interface. Here is the process to follow:

1. In Visual Studio, open the HotelAdapterMetadataBrowserHandler.cs file.
2. Find the `IMetadataBrowseHandler` region, and replace it with the following code:

```
/// <summary>
/// Retrieves an array of MetadataRetrievalNodes from the target
/// system. The browse will return nodes starting from the
/// childStartIndex in the path provided in absoluteName, and
/// the number of nodes returned is limited by maxChildNodes.
/// The method should complete within the specified timespan or
/// throw a timeout exception.
/// If absoluteName is null or an empty string, return nodes starting
/// from the root + childStartIndex.
/// If childStartIndex is zero, then return starting at the node
/// indicated by absoluteName (or the root node if
///absoluteName is null or empty).
/// </summary>
```

```
public MetadataRetrievalNode[] Browse(string nodeId
    , int childStartIndex
    , int maxChildNodes, TimeSpan timeout)
{
    //WCF LOB SDK UI tools by deafult start with the root "\" node.
    //for the root node there is only one category "Hotel Operations"
    if (MetadataRetrievalNode.Root.NodeId.CompareTo(nodeId) == 0)
    {
        // Create an inbound and outbound category
        //under the root node
        MetadataRetrievalNode node = new
            MetadataRetrievalNode("HotelOperations");
        node.NodeId = "HotelOperations";
        node.DisplayName = "Hotel Operations";
        node.Description = @"This category contains inbound and
                outbound operations supported by the HotelAdapter.";
        node.Direction = MetadataRetrievalNodeDirections.Inbound |
                           MetadataRetrievalNodeDirections.Outbound;
        node.IsOperation = false;
        return new MetadataRetrievalNode[] { node };
    }
        // if user selected "HotelOperations" in
        //the "Select Category" control populated
        //return two operations
        //OnGuestArrived in Inbound scenario
        //GetRooms in outbound
     else if ("HotelOperations".CompareTo(nodeId) == 0)
    {
        // Create outbound operation
        MetadataRetrievalNode nodeOutbound =
                   new MetadataRetrievalNode("Hotel/GetRooms");
        nodeOutbound.NodeId = "Hotel/GetRooms";
        nodeOutbound.DisplayName = "GetRooms";
        nodeOutbound.Description =
             "This operation returns the number of available rooms.";
        nodeOutbound.Direction =
            MetadataRetrievalNodeDirections.Outbound;
        nodeOutbound.IsOperation = true;
        // Create inbound operation
        MetadataRetrievalNode nodeInbound =
            new MetadataRetrievalNode("Hotel/OnGuestArrived");
        nodeInbound.NodeId = "Hotel/OnGuestArrived";
        nodeInbound.DisplayName = "OnGuestArrived";
        nodeInbound.Description =
                  "This operation notifies of client arrival.";
```

```
                nodeInbound.Direction =
                    MetadataRetrievalNodeDirections.Inbound;
                nodeInbound.IsOperation = true;
                return new MetadataRetrievalNode[]
                          { nodeOutbound, nodeInbound };
            }
            return null;
        }
        #endregion IMetadataBrowseHandler Members
```

3. In Visual Studio, open the HotelAdapterHandlerBase.cs file.
4. Find the `Dispose` method, and comment out the `NotImplementedException` exception.
5. Save and build the project.

As you can see, the code is not complicated, but it indeed requires accuracy. Although the sample adapter deals with only two operations, adapters for the real-life LOB systems will likely have to provide dozens if not hundreds or even thousands of operations. Imagine if you as an adapter developer had to add an `if-else` block every time you wanted to expose a new operation. If this is the case, then the very idea of "automatic metadata discovery" turns into "manual metadata discovery" with very little advantages over classic WCF services if at all.

To decide whether your LOB system is a good candidate for being front-ended by the WCF LOB Adapters, you have to take into account how the metadata is organized and whether new operations will be accessible by the previously written code, ideally with no changes (the "write-code-once" concept). If getting to new metadata requires serious modifications of the existing code, this should probably be taken as an alarm bell, because it indicates that the system is not optimally designed. Please note that the "write-code-once" concept applies not only to the browse handler but also to the search and resolve handlers that we will discuss in the next two sections. All three metadata interfaces constitute the metadata capabilities of the WCF LOB Adapters and have to be written according to the concept. To see the "write-code-once" concept in action, we recommend you take a close look at the Contoso Adapter supplied with the WCF LOB Adapter SDK. This adapter is a good example of how metadata in the form of SQL Server stored procedures can be accessed in a unified manner.

Implementing the IMetadataSearchHandler interface

To enable the optional "search" capability of the adapter, you have to implement the `IMetadataSearchHandler`[9] interface from the `Microsoft.ServiceModel.Channels.Common` namespace. The WCF LOB Adapter Development Wizard generated the derived `HotelAdapterMetadataSearchHandler` skeleton class for you.

The `IMetadataSearchHandler` interface is located in the Microsoft.ServiceModel.Channels.dll and is defined as follows:

9 http://msdn.microsoft.com/en-us/library/microsoft.servicemodel.channels.common.imetadatasearchhandler_members.aspx

```
public interface IMetadataSearchHandler : IConnectionHandler, IDisposable
    {
        MetadataRetrievalNode[] Search(string nodeId, string searchCriteria,
                                       int maxChildNodes, TimeSpan timeout);
    }
```

The Search method returns an array of the MetadataRetrievelNode objects that satisfy specified search criteria. We introduced this class earlier in the "Implementing IMetadataBrowseHandler" section.

We've listed the parameters accepted by the Search method in Table 13-17.

Table 13-17. *IMetadataSearchHandler.Search Method Parameters*

Parameter	Description
nodeId	The node identifier to start the search from. If nodeId is null or an empty string, then the adapter will start evaluating nodes from the root node (/).
searchCriteria	Search criteria. If not specified, the adapter should return all nodes.
maxChildNodes	Maximum number of the child elements to return. To return all matching nodes, use the Int.Max32 value.
Timeout	Maximum time to wait to complete the operation.

Here is the process to implement the IMetadataSearchHandler interface:

1. In Visual Studio, open the HotelAdapterMetadataSearchHandler.cs file.
2. Find the IMetadataSearchHandler Members region, and replace it with the following code:

```
#region IMetadataSearchHandler Members
        /// <summary>
        /// Retrieves an array of MetadataRetrievalNodes
        /// (see Microsoft.ServiceModel.Channels) from the target system.
        /// The search will begin at the path provided in absoluteName,
        /// which points to a location in the tree of metadata nodes.
        /// The contents of the array are filtered by SearchCriteria and the
        /// number of nodes returned is limited by maxChildNodes.
        /// The method should complete within the specified timespan or
        /// throw a timeout exception.  If absoluteName is null or an
        /// empty string, return nodes starting from the root.
        /// If SearchCriteria is null or an empty string, return all nodes.
        /// </summary>
        public MetadataRetrievalNode[] Search(string nodeId
            , string searchCriteria
            , int maxChildNodes, TimeSpan timeout)
        {
            List<MetadataRetrievalNode> searchResult =
                               new List<MetadataRetrievalNode>();
```

```
            searchCriteria = searchCriteria.ToLower();
            //we have only two operations
            // check them one by one
            if ("OnClientArrived".ToLower().Contains(searchCriteria))
            {
                MetadataRetrievalNode nodeInbound =
                    new MetadataRetrievalNode("Hotel/OnClientArrived");
                nodeInbound.DisplayName = "OnClientArrived";
                nodeInbound.Description = @"This operation notifies
                                    external clients of client arrival.";
                nodeInbound.Direction =
                    MetadataRetrievalNodeDirections.Inbound;
                nodeInbound.IsOperation = true;
                searchResult.Add(nodeInbound);
            }
            if ("GetRooms".ToLower().Contains(searchCriteria))
            {
                MetadataRetrievalNode nodeOutbound =
                    new MetadataRetrievalNode("Hotel/GetRooms");
                nodeOutbound.DisplayName = "GetRooms";
                nodeOutbound.Description = @"This operation returns the
                                         number of available rooms.";
                nodeOutbound.Direction =
                    MetadataRetrievalNodeDirections.Outbound;
                nodeOutbound.IsOperation = true;
                searchResult.Add(nodeOutbound);
            }
            return searchResult.ToArray();
        }
        #endregion IMetadataSearchHandler Members
```

3. Save and build the project.

Implementing the IMetadataResolverHandler Interface

To provide ASDK with information on the operations and data types supported by the HotelAdapter, you have to implement the IMetadataResolverHandler[10] interface from the Microsoft.ServiceModel.Channels.Common namespace. As we mentioned earlier, the IMetadataResolverHandler interface is used by ASDK when it generates proxy files or message type specifications.

The WCF LOB Adapter Development Wizard generated the derived HotelAdapterMetadataResolverHandler skeleton class for you.

The IMetadataResolverHandler interface is located in the Microsoft.ServiceModel.Channels.dll and is defined as follows:

10 http://msdn.microsoft.com/en-us/library/microsoft.servicemodel.channels.common.imetadataresolverhandler_members.aspx

```
public interface IMetadataResolverHandler :
                                IConnectionHandler, IDisposable
{
    bool IsOperationMetadataValid(string operationId,
        DateTime lastUpdatedTimestamp, TimeSpan timeout);
    bool IsTypeMetadataValid(string typeId,
        DateTime lastUpdatedTimestamp, TimeSpan timeout);
    OperationMetadata ResolveOperationMetadata(string operationId,
        TimeSpan timeout,
        out TypeMetadataCollection extraTypeMetadataResolved);
    TypeMetadata ResolveTypeMetadata(string typeId, TimeSpan timeout,
        out TypeMetadataCollection extraTypeMetadataResolved);
}
```

Table 13-18 describes what each method does.

Table 13-18. *IMetadataResolverHandler Methods*

Method	Description
IsOperationMetadataValid	Returns a Boolean value indicating whether operation metadata is valid. For the HotelAdapter, we assume that operation metadata is always valid.
IsTypeMetadataValid	Returns a Boolean value indicating whether type metadata is valid. For the HotelAdapter, we assume that type metadata is always valid.
ResolveOperationMetadata	Maps supplied operationId to corresponding Microsoft.ServiceModel.Channels.Common.OperationMetadata.
ResolveTypeMetadata	Maps supplied typeId to corresponding Microsoft.ServiceModel.Channels.Common.TypeMetadata.

Here is the process to implement the IMetadataResolverHandler interface:

1. In Visual Studio, open the HotelAdapterMetadataResolverHandler.cs file.
2. Find the IsOperationMetadataValid method, and modify it to return true.
3. Find the IsTypeMetadataValid method, and modify it to return true.
4. Find the ResolveOperationMetaData method, and replace it with the following code:

```
/// <summary>
/// Returns an OperationMetadata object resolved from absolute
/// name of the operation metadata object.
/// The method should complete within the specified time
/// span or throw a timeout exception.
/// </summary>
public OperationMetadata ResolveOperationMetadata(string operationId,
                TimeSpan timeout,
                out TypeMetadataCollection extraTypeMetadataResolved)
```

```
{
    extraTypeMetadataResolved = null;
    ParameterizedOperationMetadata om =
        new ParameterizedOperationMetadata(operationId, operationId);
    // set this if you want this operation to belong
    // to this interface name
    // in the generated proxy, the interface name
    // will be HotelService and the client implementation name
    // will be HotelServiceClient.
    om.OperationGroup = "HotelService";
    // set the operation namespace to be same as service namespace
    om.OperationNamespace = HotelAdapter.SERVICENAMESPACE;
    switch (operationId)
    {
        case "Hotel/GetRooms":
            om.DisplayName = "GetRooms";
            om.OriginalName = "originalGetRooms";
            OperationParameter parm1 =
                new OperationParameter("hotelName",
                    OperationParameterDirection.In,
                    QualifiedType.StringType, false);
            parm1.Description = @"This string will
                contain hotel name for which
                number of rooms is being requested";
            OperationResult result =
                new OperationResult(new
                    SimpleQualifiedType(XmlTypeCode.String), false);
            om.Parameters.Add(parm1);
            om.OperationResult = result;
            return om;
        case "Hotel/OnClientArrived":
            om.DisplayName = "OnClientArrived";
            om.OriginalName = "originalOnClientArrived";
            OperationParameter pName =
                new OperationParameter("FirstName",
                    OperationParameterDirection.In,
                    QualifiedType.StringType, false);
            pName.Description = "Client's first name.";
            OperationParameter pLastName=
                new OperationParameter("LastName",
                    OperationParameterDirection.In,
                    QualifiedType.StringType, false);
```

```
                    pLastName.Description = "Client's last name.";
                    om.Parameters.Add(pName);
                    om.Parameters.Add(pLastName);
                    om.OperationResult = null;
                    return om;

        return null;
    }
```

Step 5: Implementing the Message Exchange Handlers

Now that you have learned how to implement the metadata handlers, it's time to get to the meat and potatoes of any WCF LOB Adapter—communicating with the target LOB system. In this step, you will learn how to implement the synchronous inbound and outbound handlers. In the outbound scenario, the WCF LOB Adapters communicate with the target LOB systems by sending the request and receiving the response that will be returned to the client. In the inbound scenario, the WCF LOB Adapters monitor the target system for a particular event or data and notify the client. These message exchange patterns are represented by two interfaces: `IOutboundHandler` and `IInboundHandler`.

Implementing the IOutboundHandler Interface

To enable the outbound capabilities of the adapter, you have to implement the `IOutboundHandler`[11] interface from the `Microsoft.ServiceModel.Channels.Common` namespace. The `IOutboundHandler` interface is located in the Microsoft.ServiceMode.Channels.dll assembly and is defined as follows:

```
public interface IOutboundHandler : IConnectionHandler, IDisposable
    {
        Message Execute(Message message, TimeSpan timeout);
    }
```

The `Execute` method extracts data from the incoming WCF message, invokes the corresponding method on the target LOB system passing the extracted data as parameters, and returns a WCF response message to the client application. Implementing the `Execute` method, you have to follow two rules:

- If your adapter participates in one-way operations and doesn't expect to receive any outgoing message, the `Execute` method has to return null.
- If your adapter participates in two-way operations with `Microsoft.ServiceModel.Channels.Common.OperationResult` equal to nothing, the `Execute` method has to return the WCF message with an empty body. Otherwise, the outgoing message has to contain the operation result. To be consumable by BizTalk applications, your adapter must support two-way operations because of the restrictions imposed by the BizTalk WCF-adapter.

11 http://msdn.microsoft.com/en-us/library/microsoft.servicemodel.channels.common.ioutboundhandler.aspx

As the product documentation[12] states, the WCF LOB Adapter SDK forms incoming and outgoing messages according to the following rules.

For the incoming WCF request messages:

- Message action = operation's `nodeID`
- Message body is formed according to the following pattern:

```
<displayname><parametername>[value]</parametername></displayname>
```

For the outgoing WCF response messages:

- Message action = operation's `nodeID` + `\response`
- Message body takes the following form:

```
<displayName + "Response"><displayName + "Result">
<datatype>[value]</datatype>
</displayName + "Result"></displayName + "Response">
```

For example, for the `string GetRooms (string)` operation supported by the hotel adapter with `nodeId = "Hotel\GetRooms" and displayName="GetRooms"`, the incoming and outgoing messages will look as follows.

For the incoming message:

```
<GetRooms>
    <string>{data}
    </string>
</GetRooms>
```

For the outgoing message:

```
<GetRoomsResponse>
    <GetRoomsResult>
        <string>{data}</string>
    </GetRoomsResult>
</GetRoomsResponse>
```

Now let's get to the code:

1. In Visual Studio, open the HotelAdapterOutboundHandler.cs file.
2. Add the `using System.Xml` and `using System.IO` directives.
3. Find the `Execute` method, and replace it with the following code:

```
/// <summary>
/// Executes the request message on the target system
/// and returns a response message.
/// If there isn't a response, this method should return null
/// </summary>
public Message Execute(Message message, TimeSpan timeout)
```

12 http://msdn.microsoft.com/en-us/library/bb798099.aspx

```
            {
                OperationMetadata om = this.MetadataLookup.
                                     GetOperationDefinitionFromInputMessageAction(
                                                   message.Headers.Action, tim-
eout);
                if (om == null)
                {
                    throw new AdapterException("Invalid action " +
                                                    message.Headers.Action);
                }
                //actions are specified in the proxy files
                //or can be configured in WCF-custom adapter
                switch (message.Headers.Action)
                {
                    case "Hotel/GetRooms":
                        XmlDictionaryReader inputReader =
                            message.GetReaderAtBodyContents();
                        // move to the content
                        while (inputReader.Read())
                        {
                            if ((String.IsNullOrEmpty(inputReader.Prefix) &&
                                           inputReader.Name.Equals("hotelName"))
                                || inputReader.Name.Equals(
                                        inputReader.Prefix + ":" + "hotelName"))
                                break;
                        }
                        inputReader.Read();
                        //assume there are 10 rooms available.
                        string responseValue = inputReader.Value + ":10 rooms";
                        StringBuilder outputString = new StringBuilder();
                        XmlWriterSettings settings = new XmlWriterSettings();
                        settings.OmitXmlDeclaration = true;
                        // Create response message
                        XmlWriter replywriter =
                                 XmlWriter.Create(outputString, settings);
                        replywriter.WriteStartElement("GetRoomsResponse",
                            HotelAdapter.SERVICENAMESPACE);
                        replywriter.WriteElementString("GetRoomsResponseResult",
                            responseValue);
                        replywriter.WriteEndElement();
                        replywriter.Close();

                        XmlReader replyReader =
                            XmlReader.Create(
                                    new StringReader(outputString.ToString()));
```

```
                    // Output Message Format
                    // <GetRoomsResponse><GetRoomsResult>{rooms}
                    //</GetRoomsResult></GetRoomsResponse>
                    // create output message
                    return Message.CreateMessage(
                            MessageVersion.Default,
                            "Hotel/GetRooms/response",
                            replyReader);
                default: throw new AdapterException("Invalid action " +
                    message.Headers.Action);
            }
        }
        #endregion IOutboundHandler Members
}
```

Implementing the IInboundHandler Interface

To enable the inbound capabilities of the adapter, you have to implement the `IInboundHandler`[13] interface from the `Microsoft.ServiceModel.Channels.Common` namespace. The `IInboundHandler` interface is located in the Microsoft.ServiceMode.Channels.dll assembly and is defined as follows:

```
public interface IInboundHandler : IConnectionHandler, IDisposable
{
    void StartListener(string[] actions, TimeSpan timeout);
    void StopListener(TimeSpan timeout);
    bool TryReceive(TimeSpan timeout, out Message message,
                                      out IInboundReply reply);
    bool WaitForMessage(TimeSpan timeout);
}
```

Table 13-19 describes what each method does.

Table 13-19. *`IInboundHandler` Public Methods*

Method	Description
`StartListener`	Starts listening to messages with the provided WS-Addressing actions. If none is specified, it listens to all or the default actions.
`StopListener`	Stops listening.
`TryReceive`	Tries to receive an inbound message from the target system.
`WaitForMessage`	Waits for the inbound WCF-message from the LOB system.

13 http://msdn.microsoft.com/en-us/library/microsoft.servicemodel.channels.common.ioutboundhandler.aspx

Here is the process you have to follow:

1. In Visual Studio, open the HotelAdapter.cs file.
2. Add new `ServiceName` property, as shown here:

```
public string ServiceNamespace
  {
      get
      {
          return SERVICENAMESPACE;
      }
  }
```

3. In Visual Studio, open the HotelInboundHandler.cs file.
4. Expand the `Using Directives` region, and make sure it matches the following code snippet:

```
using System;
using System.Collections.Generic;
using System.Text;
using System.Xml;
using System.IO;
using System.ServiceModel.Channels;
using System.Timers;
using Microsoft.ServiceModel.Channels.Common;
```

5. Add the following class member variables to the class:

```
private Queue<Message> inboundMessages;
private int pollingPeriod;
private Timer pollingTimer;
private Object syncLock;
```

6. Replace the `HotelInboundHandler` constructor with the following code snippet:

```
public HotelAdapterInboundHandler(HotelAdapterConnection connection
    , MetadataLookup metadataLookup)
    : base(connection, metadataLookup)
{
    pollingPeriod =
        connection.ConnectionFactory.Adapter.PollingPeriod;
    syncLock = new Object();
}
```

7. Add the implementation for the `StartListener` and `StopListener` methods, as shown here:

```
/// <summary>
/// Start the listener
/// </summary>
```

```
public void StartListener(string[] actions, TimeSpan timeout)
{
    //listen for all actions
    //create a Queue to hold inbound messages;
    inboundMessages = new Queue<Message>();
    //set up a timer to pool for guest arrivals

    pollingTimer = new System.Timers.Timer(pollingPeriod * 1000);
    pollingTimer.Elapsed +=
        new System.Timers.ElapsedEventHandler(CheckArrivals);
}


/// <summary>
/// Stop the listener
/// </summary>
public void StopListener(TimeSpan timeout)
{
    if (pollingTimer != null)
    {
        pollingTimer.Stop();
        pollingTimer = null;
    }
    lock (syncLock)
    {
        inboundMessages.Clear();
        inboundMessages = null;
    }
}
```

8. Now add the implementation for the `TryReceive` and `WaitForMessage` methods:

```
/// <summary>
/// Tries to receive a message within a specified interval of time.
/// </summary>
public bool TryReceive(TimeSpan timeout,
                out System.ServiceModel.Channels.Message message,
                out IInboundReply reply)
{
    reply = new HotelAdapterInboundReply();
    message = null;

    //assume timeout is infinite
    while (true)
    {
        lock (syncLock)
```

```
                {
                    if (inboundMessages == null)
                    {
                        //listener has been closed
                        return false;
                    }
                    if (inboundMessages.Count != 0)
                    {
                        message = inboundMessages.Dequeue();
                        if (message != null)
                        {
                            return true;
                        }
                    }
                }
                System.Threading.Thread.Sleep(500);
            }
        }

        /// <summary>
        /// Returns a value that indicates whether a message
        /// has arrived within a specified interval of time.
        /// </summary>
        public bool WaitForMessage(TimeSpan timeout)
        {
            //wait for message to appear in the queue
            while (inboundMessages.Count == 0) { };
            //check if message is there but don't remove it
            Message msg = inboundMessages.Peek();
            if (msg != null)
            {
                return true;
            }
            return false;
        }
```

9. Add the implementation for the ElapsedEventHandler callback, as shown in the following code snippet:

```
        private void CheckArrivals(object sender, ElapsedEventArgs args)
        {
            //poll for example a database
            //if new guest found create inbound message
```

```
            HotelAdapter adapter = this.Connection.ConnectionFactory.Adapter;
            String xmlData = String.Format(@"<OnGuestArrived xmlns=""{0}"">
                                 <FirstName>{1}</FirstName>
                                 <LastName>{2}</LastName></OnGuestArrived>",
                                 adapter.ServiceNamespace,
                                 "John",
                                 "Smith");
            XmlReader reader = XmlReader.Create(new StringReader(xmlData));
            // create WCF message
            Message requestMessage =
                Message.CreateMessage(MessageVersion.Default
                        , "Hotel/OnGuestArrived"
                        , reader);
            // add it to inbound queue
            inboundMessages.Enqueue(requestMessage);
        }
```

10. Save and build the project.

You have finished the development stage of the `HotelAdapter`.

■ Note In the "scale-out" architecture, your adapters may be deployed on more than one server. If this is the case, then in the inbound scenario, there is a potential danger of sending duplicate messages to the client application when different instances of your adapter react on the same event on the target LOB system. Unfortunately, this issue doesn't have a generic solution, and therefore you, an adapter developer, have to provide the implementation specific to your target LOB system to prevent duplicate messages from occurring.

Step 6: Deployment

To make the `HotelAdapter` available for consumption by the client applications, you have to deploy it. The deployment procedure is not complicated. First you have to GAC the adapter by signing the adapter's assembly with a strong name key and calling the gacutil.exe utility with the `/if` switch. Second, you have to register the adapter with WCF by making a few entries in the machine.config file. Here is the process to follow to register the `HotelAdapter` with WCF:

1. Go to the `<%WINDIR%>\Microsoft.NET\Framework\Config` folder, locate the machine.config file, and open it in Visual Studio.
2. Update the `<system.serviceModel>` configuration section to include the `HotelAdapter` entries as follows:

```
<system.serviceModel>
<system.serviceModel>
  <client>
    <endpoint binding="hotelBinding" contract="IMetadataExchange"
      name="hotel" />
  </client>
  <extensions>
    <bindingElementExtensions>
      <add name="HotelAdapter"
           type="HotelApp.HotelAdapter.HotelAdapterBindingElementExtension,
            HotelApp.HotelAdapter.HotelAdapter,Version=1.0.0.0,
            Culture=neutral, PublicKeyToken=XXXXXXXXXXXXX" />
    </bindingElementExtensions>
    <bindingExtensions>
      <add name="hotelBinding"
           type="HotelApp.HotelAdapter.HotelAdapterBindingCollectionElement,
           HotelApp.HotelAdapter.HotelAdapter,Version=1.0.0.0,
           Culture=neutral, PublicKeyToken=XXXXXXXXXXXXX" />/>
    </bindingExtensions>
  </extensions>
</system.serviceModel>
```

Step 7: Consuming from an .NET Application

Now that you have finished the deployment, the `HotelAdapter` can be consumed from the WCF-enabled client applications. You have to generate a proxy and update the app.config file to include the adapter configuration. The Add Adapter Service Reference plug-in is your main tool to do the job.

Here is the process to follow:

1. Open Visual Studio, and create new project called ConsumeAdapterApplication.
2. In the Solution Explorer, right-click the ConsumeAdapterApplication project, and select the Add Adapter Service Reference menu item.
3. In the Select Binding combo box, select hotelBinding. Click the Configure button. The Configure Adapter dialog box will open.
4. Specify the username and password, as shown in Figure 13-16. Click the OK button to return to the Add Adapter Service Reference plug-in.
5. Click the Connect button. Make sure that the connection status has changed to "connected."
6. In the "Select a category" list, select "Hotel operations."
7. In the "Available categories and operations" list, select Get Rooms, and click the Add button. The Add Adapter Service Reference window now should look like Figure 13-18.

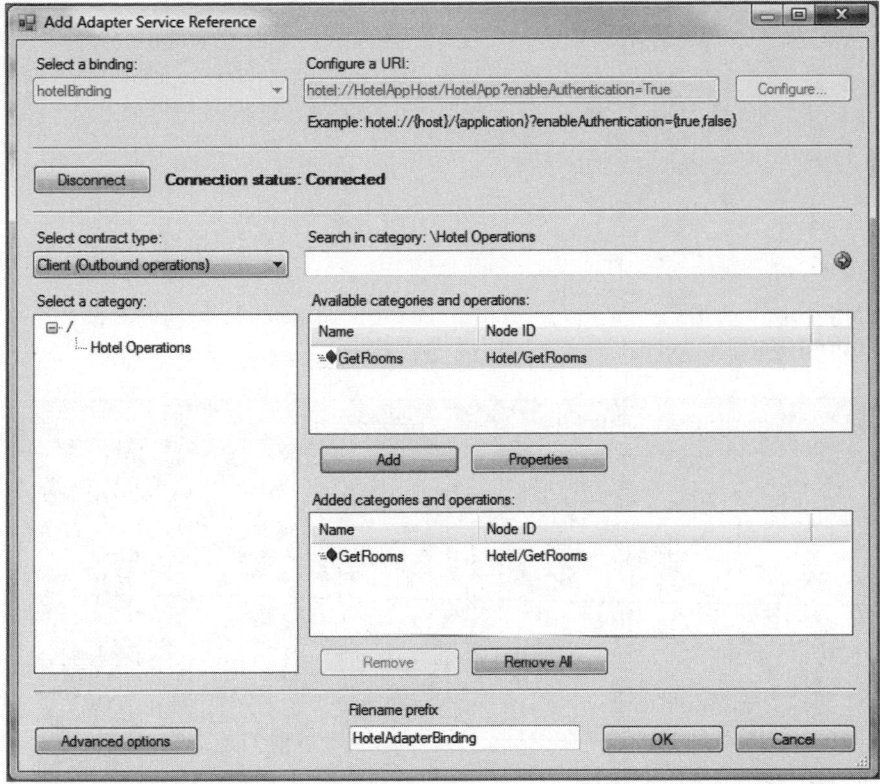

Figure 13-18. *Add Adapter Service Reference window*

8. Click the OK button to generate a proxy file. The app.config file will also be updated. Note that the proxy file named HotelAdapterBindingClient.cs is now part of the solution.

9. Open the Program.cs file, and replace content with the following code:

```
using System;
using System.Collections.Generic;
using System.Linq;
using System.Text;

namespace ConsumeAdapterApplication
{
    class Program
    {
        static void Main(string[] args)
```

```
            {
                HotelServiceClient client = new HotelServiceClient();
                client.ClientCredentials.UserName.UserName = "Probiztalk2009";
                string response = client.GetRooms("Indigo hotel");
                Console.WriteLine(response);
                Console.Read();
            }
        }
    }
```

10. Build and run the application. You will see the HotelAdapter response, as shown in Figure 13-19.

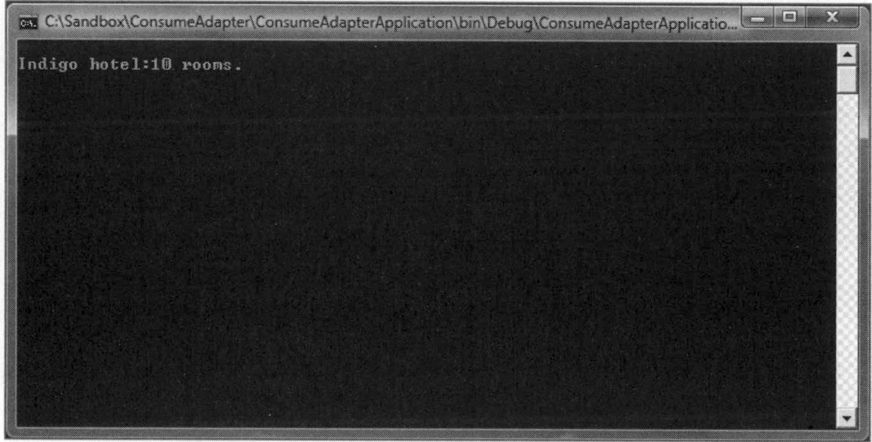

Figure 13-19. *The HotelAdapter response*

Step 8: Consuming from BizTalk Application

To consume the HotelAdapter from a BizTalk application, you have to generate the schemas for the operations supported by the adapter and the binding file to create physical ports. In case of a BizTalk application, the tool to do the job is the Consume Adapter Service add-in. This tool has the same UI as the Add Adapter Service Reference plug-in, but it generates different artifacts.

Here is the process to follow:

1. In Visual Studio, open your BizTalk project.
2. In Solution Explorer, right-click the project, and select Add ➤ Add Generated Items ➤ Consume Adapter Service.
3. In the Select Binding box, select hotelBinding. Click the Configure button. The Configure Adapter dialog box will open.
4. Specify the username and password. Click the OK button to return to the Add Adapter Service Reference window.

5. Click the Connect button. Make sure that the connection status has changed to "connected."

6. In the "Select a category" list, select "Hotel operations."

7. In the "Available categories and operations" list, select Get Rooms, and click the Add button.

8. Click OK to generate the schemas and the binding file. The schema file named HotelAdapterBindings.xsd contains message definitions for the `HotelAdapter` request and response messages, as shown in Figure 13-20.

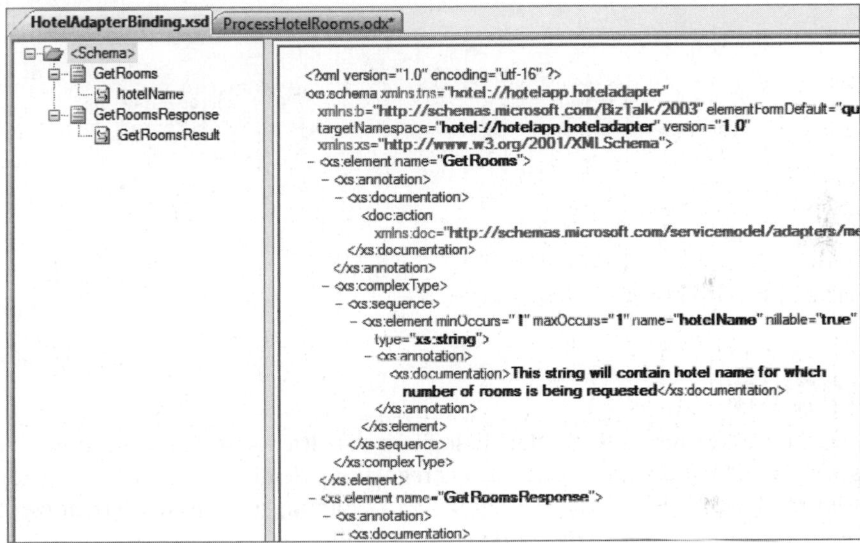

Figure 13-20. *Generated schema definitions*

9. Implement your project orchestration to communicate with the `HotelAdapter` through a request-response port. Your orchestration should look like Figure 13-21.

10. Build and deploy the project.

11. Open the BizTalk Administration Console.

12. Import the binding file to create physical ports. Right-click your application under the Applications group, select Import ➤ Bindings, navigate to your binding file, and click the Open button.

13. Map the orchestration logical ports to the newly created physical ports.

14. Enlist and start your orchestration.

15. Start your application.

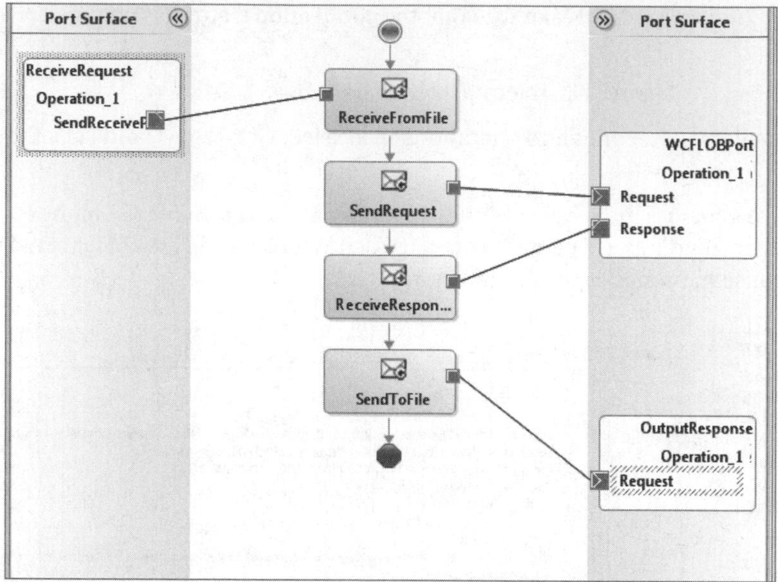

Figure 13-21. *`HotelAdapter` orchestration*

Debugging

The best way to explore new APIs and technologies is to use a debugger. Debugging WCF LOB Adapters is not as straightforward as debugging regular applications since adapters cannot be instantiated and launched from Visual Studio. Before wrapping up the chapter, though, we'll introduce a debugging technique that you may find handy.

Here are the instructions:

1. Open Visual Studio, and create a client console application.
2. Open a second instance of Visual Studio, and load your adapter project. Set breakpoints.
3. In the second instance that contains your adapter, select Debug ➤ Attach to Process. The Attach to Process dialog box shown in Figure 13-22 will open. In the Available Processes control, select the Visual Studio instance with your client application, and click the Attach button.
4. Switch to Visual Studio instance containing your client application, open the Add Adapter Service Reference window, and perform the desired actions. The breakpoints that you set in your adapter code will be hit.

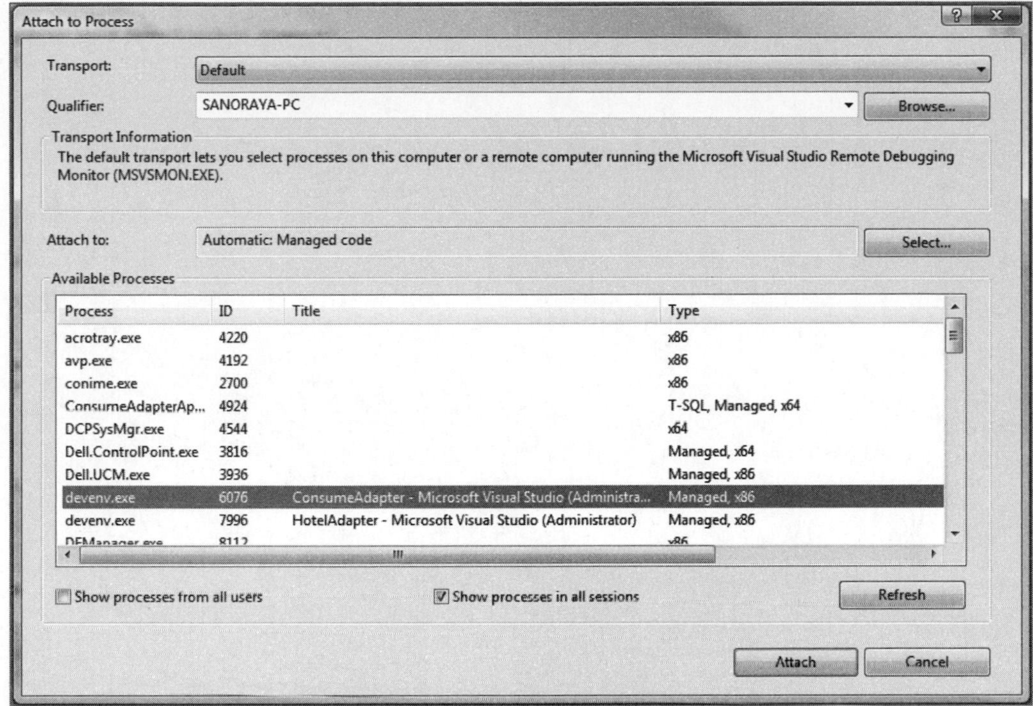

Figure 13-22. *Attach to Process dialog box*

CHAPTER 14

Host Integration Server 2009

We've had the opportunity to work with a wide variety of customers across the world who use mainframe platforms to store critical data and to run critical applications. Most of those customers have needed to present their mainframe data on (or access their legacy applications from) a web browser, console, or mobile device application. Their frequently asked questions include the following:

- "How is our application going to get connected to the host?"
- "What is the communication protocol that we are going to use?"
- "Is it possible for us to use two-phase commit?"
- "Can we execute Windows programs from inside our mainframe programs?
- "What do we need to enable screen scraping?"

Sometimes the answers to these questions are quite straightforward. However, oftentimes getting the answers requires that customers share technical and business plans, along with their specific integration needs.

Many of the customers we've met have no plans to migrate their mainframes to Microsoft .NET. Yet they still need to access mainframe data from more modern platforms. Microsoft BizTalk Server 2009 provides a solution that allows those customers to reach all the ends of their enterprise architectures and in many cases answer the common questions just mentioned.

BizTalk Server 2009 provides the following components to interact with legacy platforms:

- **Microsoft BizTalk Adapter for Host Applications**: Allows BizTalk Server to interact with IBM mainframes or midrange Report Program Generator (RPG) server programs.
- **Microsoft BizTalk Adapter for Host Files**: Allows BizTalk Server to access host files that run on IBM mainframes and AS/400 platforms.
- **Microsoft BizTalk Adapter for DB2**: Allows BizTalk Server to access DB2 databases running on IBM mainframes, AS/400, and Universal Database (UDB) platforms.
- **Microsoft BizTalk Adapter for WebSphere MQ**: Allows BizTalk Server to interact with IBM WebSphere MQ.

- **Host Integration Server**: Allows the following:
  - Provides system network architecture (SNA) services and APIs to interact with SNA networks and others
  - Provides Session Integrator technologies for screen scraping
  - Provides Transaction Integrator technologies for application-level integration
  - Provides MSMQ-MQSeries Bridge deployment capabilities
  - Provides data providers for DB2 and host files
  - Provides the Enterprise Single Sign-On services to manage a centralized repository of credentials

Before starting with the technical content, we'll address a few questions you may have about this chapter:

- **What is the difference between Host Integration Server and the BizTalk Adapter for Host Systems?** The answer to this question is that although the product names are different, the bits are the same. From a licensing perspective, Host Integration Server, formerly known as SNA Server, is part of the BizTalk Server product and has been since the BizTalk Server 2006 R2 release. Depending on the type of Host Integration Server deployment, you may need to license the BizTalk Adapter for Host Systems 2.0. Please consult the BizTalk Server 2009 licensing terms at www.microsoftvolumelicensing.com/userights/PUR.aspx.
- **Which Host Integration Server features are not addressed in this chapter?** There are excellent product features that we will not be addressing in this chapter. For example, Host Integration Server 2009 provides excellent connectivity for DB2 systems. Host Integration Server (HIS) 2009 DB2 integration capabilities are widely used from .NET applications and from BizTalk Server. HIS 2009 targets DB2 systems running on both AS/400 and mainframe platforms.

  Other great features we will not target are the BizTalk Adapter for Host Files and the BizTalk Adapter for WebSphere MQ. We recommend visiting www.microsoft.com/hiserver to review the information available about these features.
- **What is the main objective of this chapter?** Technically speaking, HIS allows the Microsoft Windows world to interact with IBM mainframes and AS/400 platforms. One objective in this chapter is to present guidance and recommended practices for deploying Host Integration Server in customer environments using the SNA protocol and Transaction Integrator. It is also a collateral objective to stress the importance of a thorough planning process whenever you have the requirement of integrating legacy platforms (mainframe or AS/400 platforms) with .NET applications. Without planning, it is easy for the customer or even a consultant to misunderstand the real dimension and scope of a legacy integration solution.

Planning Your Host Integration Server Topology

In this section, we will discuss some Host Integration Server topologies based on different application integration scenarios. *Topologies* are component arrangements that help you model and organize your solutions. Figure 14-1 shows a sample architecture of a legacy integration solution at a high level.

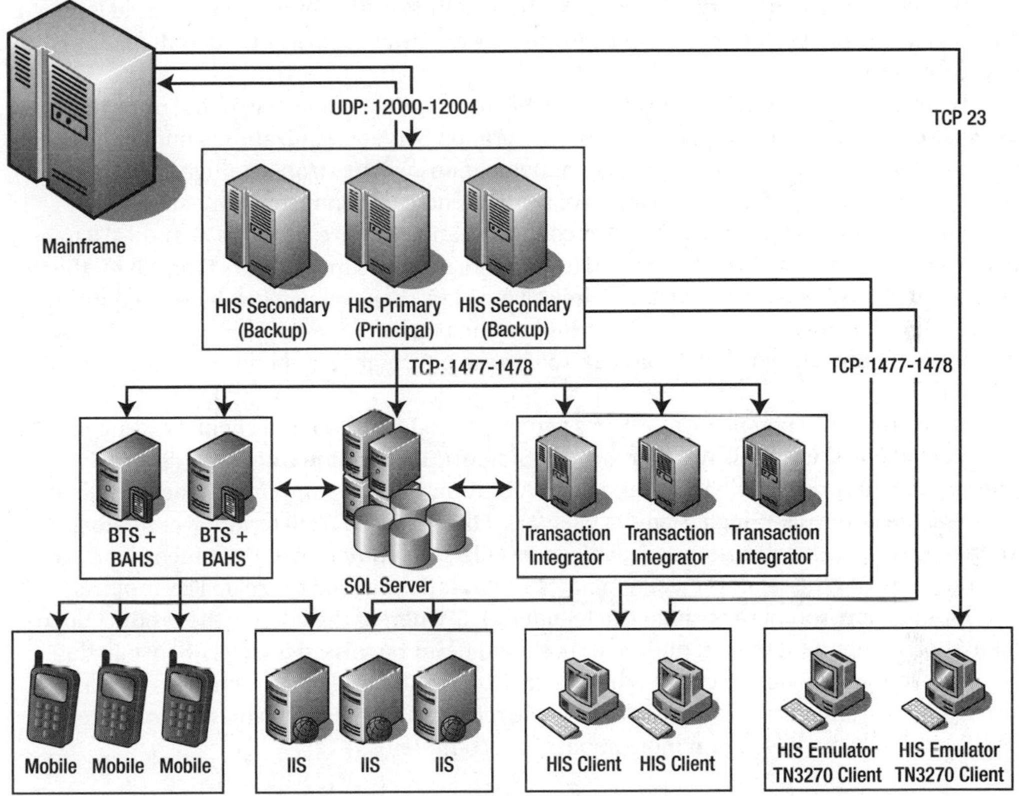

Figure 14-1. *Legacy integration solution architecture*

Setup Considerations

Host Integration Server is organized into subdomains. That gives the capacity of sharing resources between nodes. Actually, when HIS clients try to connect to an HIS server (a sponsor server), they are contacting the entire Host Integration Server subdomain.

Host Integration Server SNA Gateway services store configuration information in a file called COM.cfg. This file is shared across all the servers in the Host Integration Server subdomain. Although we will address service accounts later in the chapter, our first recommendation is to make sure the service account that Host Integration Server will use is a valid Windows domain account and member of the Host Integration Server runtime users group of every HIS server.

Host Integration Server provides host connectivity by centralizing the responsibility for the node and physical connectivity at the server level, while still allowing the client to access the full SNA protocol stack. This configuration releases resources from the client by not having the client accessing the host but instead having the client connected to the Host Integration Server. The connection from the client to the Host Integration Server uses standard LAN protocols and uses one of two modes: sponsor connections or Active Directory. With sponsor connections, the connection is direct from the Host Integration Server client to the server, whereas with Active Directory connections, the Host Integration Server client should locate an Active Directory server first to run LDAP queries to retrieve the information that needs to populate its service table.

To decide on either one discovery mechanism or another, you have to find out whether the customer is interested in having a Host Integration Server organizational unit and also verify that its Active Directory network communications will be strong enough to handle the additional load successfully. Otherwise, we recommend using sponsor connections.

Host Integration Server client-server communication requires ports 1477 and 1478 to be open between the client and the server. HIS 2009 creates rules in Windows Firewall for those ports, so if your servers have Windows Firewall enabled, then you will just have to enable the Host Integration Server exception. Keep this in mind when setting up your solution. During the HIS setup process, you will be asked to complete information depending on the topology selected.

From a software perspective, HIS has two setup modes: server and client. Server components include the BizTalk Adapter for Host Systems, Transaction Integrator, Session Integrator, Enterprise Single Sign-On, and SNA Gateway. Client components include client libraries, the Enterprise Single Sign-On client, and the 3270 and 5250 terminal emulators. There are a couple more options available to install: Development and Documentation. The first one provides the set of project templates and libraries needed to create HIS projects in development environments using Visual Studio 2008, whereas the latter is the product documentation component that, in our opinion, should never be missed in any HIS installation.

Host Integration Server can also be installed and configured in unattended mode using the Setup and Configuration commands. Please refer to the readme file on the Host Integration Server 2009 media to learn more about these commands.

Host Integration Server Topologies

From a topology perspective, now that you are familiar with the HIS client-server concept, we'll cover the server topologies. The determining factors of the server topologies in HIS are the SNA Gateway services. If they are available in the server, then it means that they can provide mainframe connectivity services and also can act as sponsor servers of other HIS servers. A *sponsor server* is a server that provides the HIS clients with information about the resources available in the HIS subdomain. Nevertheless, if an HIS server does not provide SNA Gateway services, then the HIS server will require an additional server that does. The type of server that does not include SNA Gateway services is called a *nodeless* server, because it will route its SNA application requests to a sponsor server.

In distributed environments, like the one I will present shortly, Transaction Integrator—a key HIS component for application integration that will be addressed later in this chapter—is usually installed as a nodeless server. This configuration allows the creation of isolated layers for the application servers and the SNA Gateway servers. It is of the utmost importance to have the SNA Gateway servers isolated in a dedicated layer, because the SNA Gateway servers will likely provide many legacy integration services for the entire organization such as application integration, host printing sessions, and terminal emulation.

Figure 14-2 shows the configuration screen under the Network Integration option for a SNA Gateway mode install. In the Role drop-down list, you can change the role to Secondary Configuration Server, if you want the server to be one of the allowable backup servers in the Host Integration Server subdomain. Remember that the Host Integration Server subdomain is not a Windows domain but requires a Windows domain to exist.

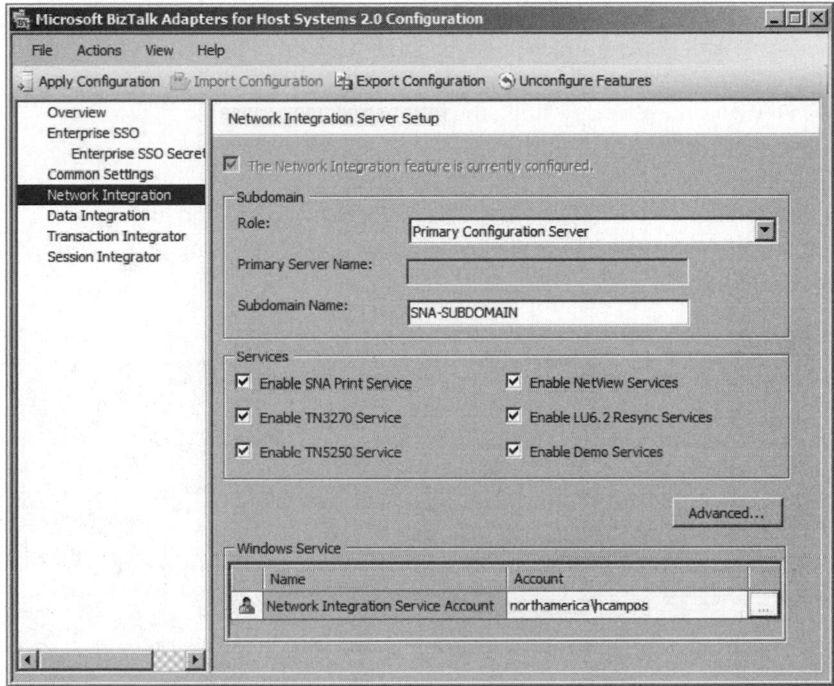

Figure 14-2. *Network integration server setup configuration*

Mainframe Access

A few years back, constraints such as network bandwidth and hardware resources defined the topology design for customer legacy systems access. Today, living in a different technological and financial landscape, customers need to have their old systems integrated to their new ones more than ever. Customers still using protocols that are being phased out face the challenge of legacy modernization. For instance, the Distributed Link Control (DLC) protocol is being phased out by IBM and will not likely offer support for 64-bit platforms. If customers use DLC, they may have to decide whether to adapt their architecture to interact with it or move forward and leverage the IP network.

Using TCP/IP

Host Integration Server can use two protocols to access a mainframe. It can use SNA or TCP/IP. The choice depends on many factors. Availability is one of them. Sometimes the mainframe does not expose Customer Information Control System (CICS) transactions using TCP/IP because the mainframe doesn't have the TCP/IP listener installed. Consequently, you will have to use IP-DLC or even SNA over DLC. Other times you may need to run two-phase commit (2PC) transactions, which are supported only using SNA (unless you use DB2, which supports 2PC over TCP/IP).

From a configuration perspective, configuring TCP/IP access to the mainframe is very straightforward. To do that, you must deploy the IBM listener program EZACIC02 in CICS. This program is used by the CSKL transaction.[1] CSKL is the CICS transaction ID of the IBM distributed listener that provides CICS terminal management for CICS TCP/IP.

Next you will need to ask the mainframe team to provide you with information about the ports and the IP address on the mainframe, as well as the TCP/IP port number of the listener. You can verify the TCP/IP port number by issuing the following CICS command:

```
EZAC DISPLAY LISTENER.
```

Figure 14-3 shows the output of the `EZAC DISPLAY LISTENER` command and highlights the `APPLID`, `TRANID`, and `PORT` values. The `PORT` value will be required when using Transaction Integrator.

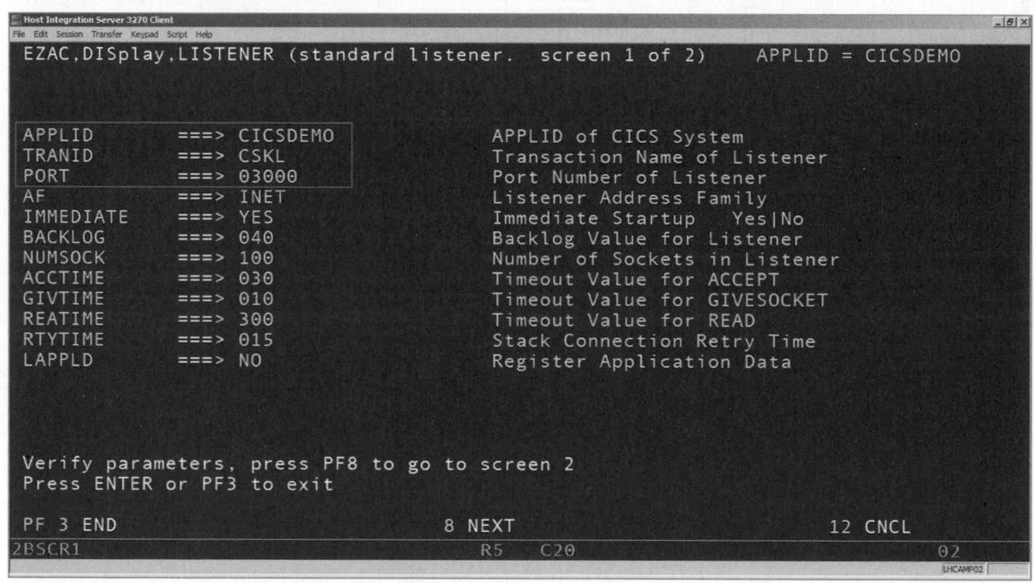

Figure 14-3. *EZAC DISPLAY LISTENER output*

Once you have the mainframe information available, enter the IP address and TCP port number in the Transaction Integrator (TI) CICS TCP/IP Remote Environment (RE) definition. Figure 14-4 shows a TCP/IP Enhanced Listener Message (ELM) link remote environment definition.

1 For more details on how to configure the listener, you can read the "z/OS V1R10.0 Communications Server IP CICS Sockets Guide" IBM Redbook.

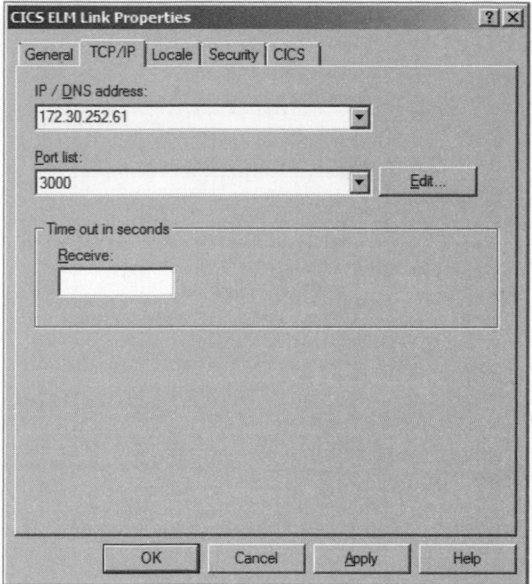

Figure 14-4. *CICS ELM remote environment definition*

Using SNA

The other protocol supported by Host Integration Server 2009 is SNA, which is widely used in mainframe environments. Hence, we'll focus much of this chapter on its use.

Host Integration Server offers the IP-DLC Link Service that provides SNA connectivity over native IP networks. It requires that the mainframe or AS/400 has deployed the IBM Enterprise Extender. The IP-DLC configuration process is addressed in the technical white paper "Configuring IP-DLC Link Service for IBM Enterprise Extender," which you can download from the Microsoft web site.

Before setting up the IP-DLC Link Service in Host Integration Server, we recommend that your Host Integration Server administrator ensures that the IBM Enterprise Extender has been set up properly in the mainframe and that the required UDP ports have been opened in the firewall. Table 14-1 shows the required ports to be opened between the network node server and the Host Integration Server.

Table 14-1. *Enterprise Extender Port Priorities*

Priority	UDP Port	Common Use
LDLC priority	Signaling	12000 Enterprise Extender only
Network priority	12001	Advanced Peer-to-Peer Networking (APPN) environment
High priority	12002	Interactive traffic
Medium priority	12003	Client-server traffic
Low priority	12004	Batch traffic

The Microsoft Host Integration Server product group provides a tool available with the Host Integration Server product media called Microsoft EEDiag. This tool issues an LDLC probe "ping" against a network node server (NNS). A successful EEDiag call will return a sense code of 0x00000000. We recommend stopping the IP-DLC Link Service before running this test; otherwise, the Results tab will display a "No response" message. Figure 14-5 shows an execution of the EEDiag tool.

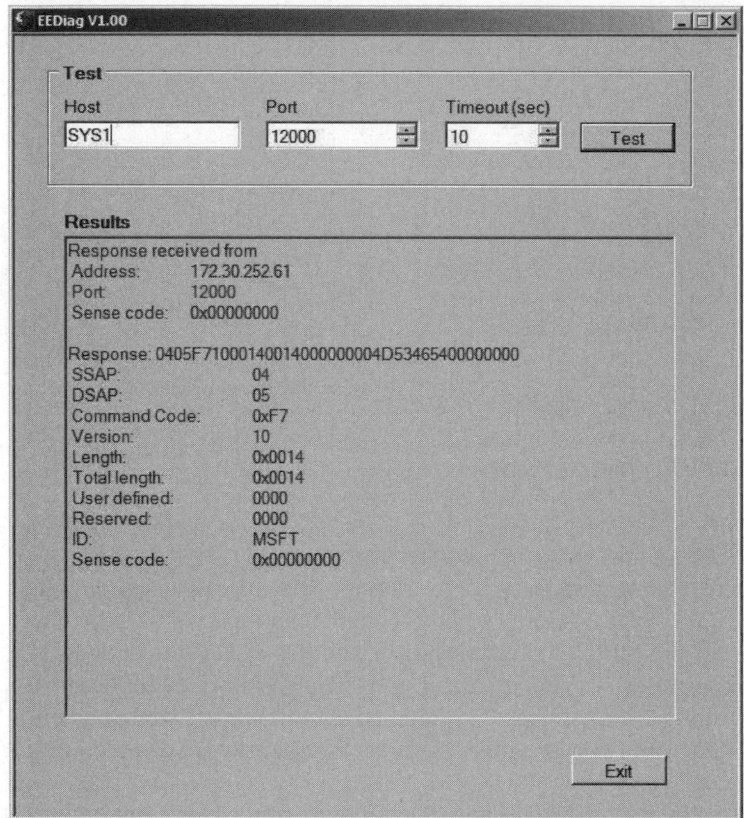

Figure 14-5. *Microsoft EEDiag output*

You can also run either ISPF or SDSF and issue the command `/D NET, EE` to display the current status of the IBM Enterprise Extender configuration. If you are deploying Enterprise Extender for the first time, our recommendation at this stage is to ask the mainframe team to enable the Virtual Telecommunications Access Method (VTAM) logs. Figure 14-6 shows the output of the `/D NET, EE` command as executed from SDSF.

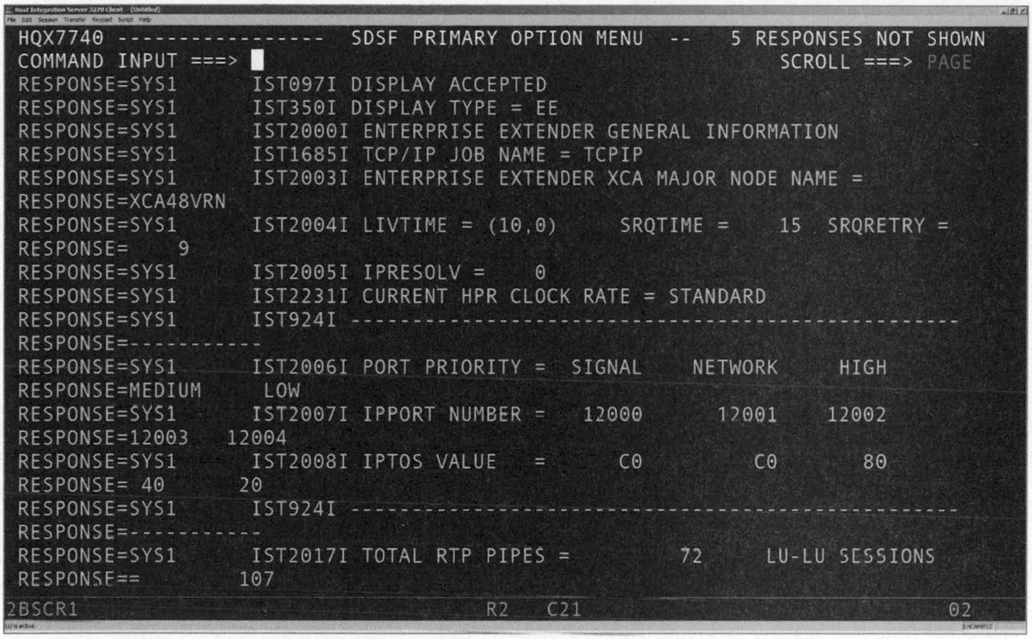

```
HQX7740 -----------------  SDSF PRIMARY OPTION MENU  --    5 RESPONSES NOT SHOWN
COMMAND INPUT ===>                                        SCROLL ===> PAGE
RESPONSE=SYS1        IST097I DISPLAY ACCEPTED
RESPONSE=SYS1        IST350I DISPLAY TYPE = EE
RESPONSE=SYS1        IST2000I ENTERPRISE EXTENDER GENERAL INFORMATION
RESPONSE=SYS1        IST1685I TCP/IP JOB NAME = TCPIP
RESPONSE=SYS1        IST2003I ENTERPRISE EXTENDER XCA MAJOR NODE NAME =
RESPONSE=XCA48VRN
RESPONSE=SYS1        IST2004I LIVTIME = (10,0)     SRQTIME =    15  SRQRETRY =
RESPONSE=     9
RESPONSE=SYS1        IST2005I IPRESOLV =     0
RESPONSE=SYS1        IST2231I CURRENT HPR CLOCK RATE = STANDARD
RESPONSE=SYS1        IST924I -------------------------------------------------
RESPONSE=-----------
RESPONSE=SYS1        IST2006I PORT PRIORITY =  SIGNAL     NETWORK      HIGH
RESPONSE=MEDIUM       LOW
RESPONSE=SYS1        IST2007I IPPORT NUMBER =   12000       12001     12002
RESPONSE=12003    12004
RESPONSE=SYS1        IST2008I IPTOS VALUE    =      C0          C0        80
RESPONSE= 40        20
RESPONSE=SYS1        IST924I -------------------------------------------------
RESPONSE=-----------
RESPONSE=SYS1        IST2017I TOTAL RTP PIPES =          72      LU-LU SESSIONS
RESPONSE==          107
2BSCR1                                R2   C21                               02
```

Figure 14-6. *Execution of /D NET, EE from SDSF*

Configuring the IP-DLC Link Service

Once the Enterprise Extender configuration is in place, the Host Integration Server administrator should create and configure the IP-DLC Link Service in the Host Integration Server. As we mentioned earlier, the IP-DLC Link Service requires the Enterprise Extender to be deployed in the mainframe.

Among the steps you will have to complete to configure the IP-DLC in Host Integration Server is creating an IP-DLC Link Service definition from SNA Manager, as shown in Figure 14-7. Once you have created the definition, you will have to create a connection to target the remote system (mainframe). This connection can be either a host connection or a peer connection.

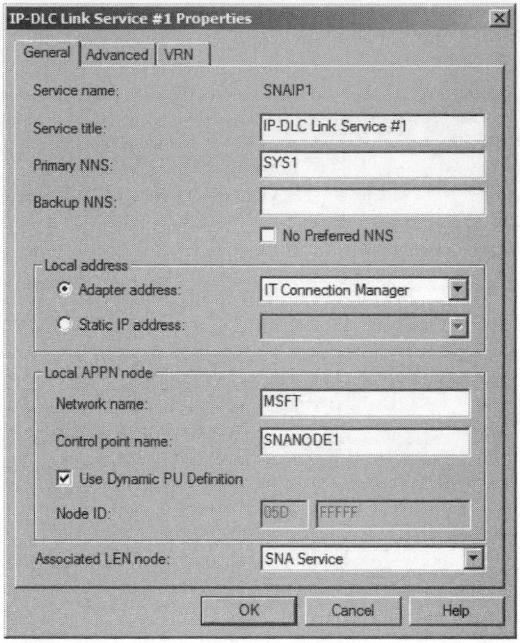

Figure 14-7. *Host Integration Server IP-DLC Link Service*

From the moment the Host Integration Server connects to an APPN network, it becomes an additional node in that network. Therefore, Host Integration Server will be an active member in the network that can create either independent sessions or mainframe-controlled sessions. For instance, if you want to have your Host Integration Server connected in an "independent" way to the mainframe, you have to define your connection's remote end as a "peer system." Nevertheless, if you plan to have your Host Integration Server node sessions depending on the mainframe (like 3270 sessions), then you will need to define your connection's remote end as a "host system." In the case of 3270 sessions, they will depend on the system services control points (SSCPs).

In an APPN network, which is an evolved SNA network, every node has a role. Terms such as *physical units* (PUs) and *logical units* (LUs) identify hardware, software, and protocols needed to control and send data across the network. APPN networks typically use type 6.2 LUs, also known as Advanced Program-to-Program Communications (APPC) LUs. Microsoft Host Integration Server supports the APPC API and also includes libraries that allow the developers to create APPC applications using Host Integration Server.

In an APPN network, there are three types of nodes: network nodes, end nodes, and low-entry networking (LEN) nodes. Basically, network nodes provide directory services, LU sessions control, and routing services. End nodes have limited capabilities for routing because they need a network node to work, and LEN nodes don't have any routing capability. LEN nodes are members of an APPN network that can participate in LU 6.2 sessions in both independent and dependent ways. Independent APPC LUs provide the ability to run multiple, concurrent, parallel sessions between a single pair of LUs. The SNA server service of Host Integration Server is a LEN node in an APPN network. The IP-DLC Link Service is a branch network node (BrNN). Host Integration Server is also a PU 2.1 device. The mainframe is a PU5 device. Figure 14-8 shows how Host Integration Server interacts in an APPN network.

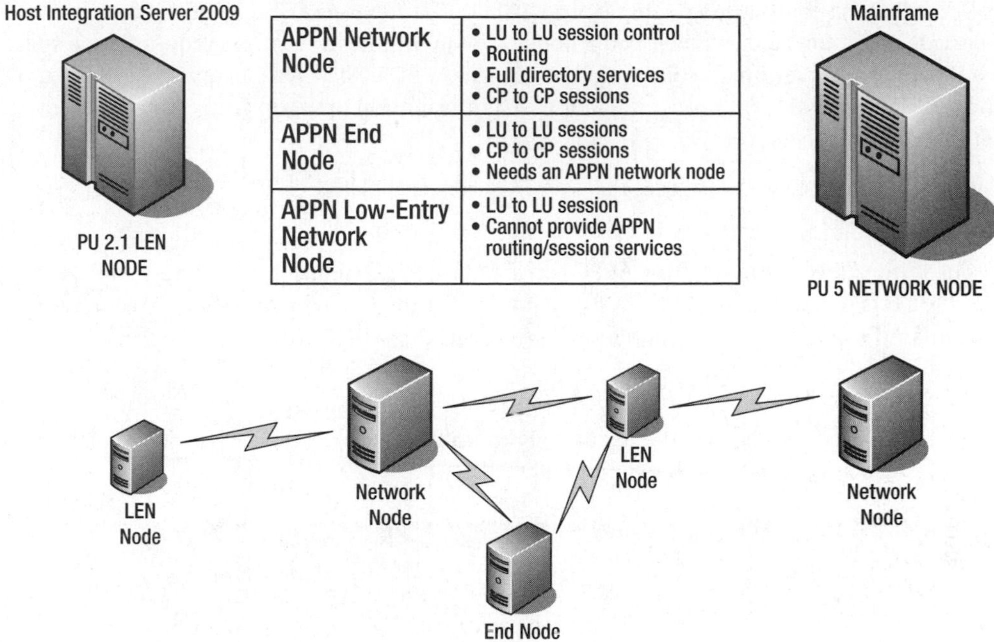

Figure 14-8. *Host Integration Server in the APPN network*

For an APPC LU-LU conversation to take place, it is necessary to have three elements: the local LU, the remote LU, and the mode. The local APPC LU should match with the independent LU 6.2 configured on the VTAM PU definition for the Host Integration Server 2009 connection. The remote APPC LU should match to the APPLID as configured on the VTAM APPL definition for the CICS region. Finally, the APPC mode definition must correspond to the mode configured on the VTAM LU definition for the local APPC LU and on the mode used by the APPL definition in VTAM. The combination of these three elements together will define an APPC conversation between the Host Integration Server PU and the mainframe PU. Technically, the information of names and values of these objects should be provided by the mainframe team since they will have to create/define them in VTAM and CICS.

Remember that for Host Integration Server to work with BizTalk Server using independent LU 6.2 sessions, your local APPC LU should have coded an `LOCADDR` entry with the value of zero. If you are not familiar with the requirements in the mainframe for Host Integration Server, you will find excellent guidance in the folder Support\Worksheets\EN\ in the Host Integration Server media. There you will find two directories: the PU and Environment directories. In the PU directory, there are a few text files with sample definitions for every PU and link service available. For independent sessions over IP-DLC, you will find the indipdlc.txt file with the title "Worksheet for Independent LU6.2 over IP-DLC." In the Environment directory, you will find worksheets for configuring environments such as CICS, DB2, IMS, and so on. For instance, for CICS, there is a file called indcics.txt with the title "Worksheet for Independent LU6.2 for CICS." These worksheets should be handed to the mainframe team to complete the required values. It definitely will help you in accelerating the configuration process in Host Integration Server.

The following code shows a sample of a VTAM definition for a Local APPC LU for Independent Sessions (LOCADDR=0). You'll notice two out of the three values required for a successful APPC conversation. The first value is the local APPC LU (LHCAMP00), and the second one is the APPC mode (PA62TKNU). You should use that information to set up your SNA aliases in Host Integration Server.

```
LHCAMP00 LU     LOCADDR=0, RESSCB=10,                         X
DLOGMOD= PA62TKNU
```

The third value required for the APPC conversation to take place is the remote APPC LU (CICSDEMO). It is defined in the VTAM APPL definition for the CICS region. The following code shows a sample of a VTAM definition for the remote APPC LU CICSDEMO:

```
APPLID= CICSDEMO
```

Figure 14-9 shows the SNA Manager configuration for the local APPC LU LHCAMP00, the remote APPC LU CICSDEMO, and the mode PA62TKNU.

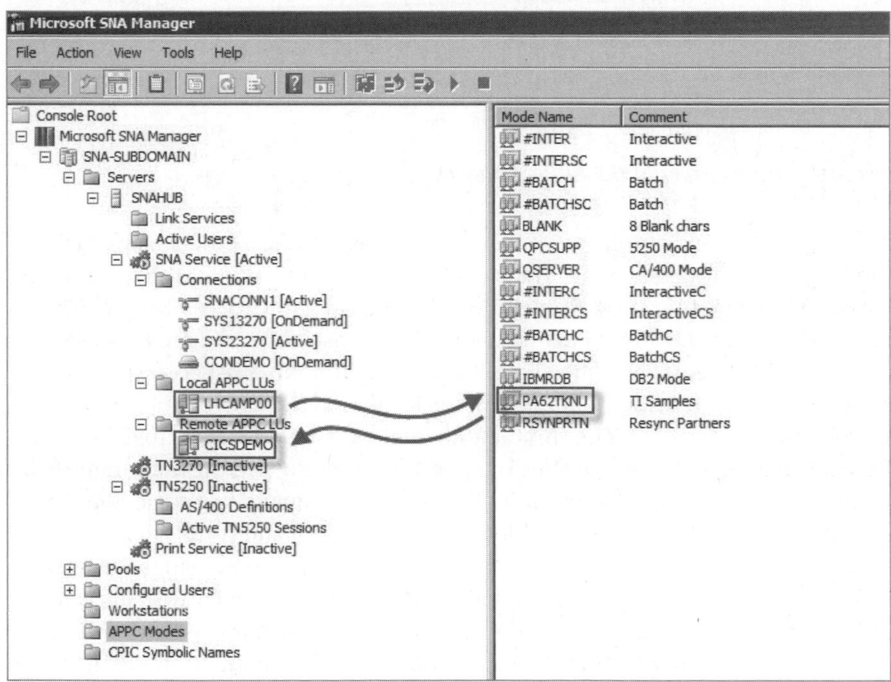

Figure 14-9. *SNA aliases known as SNA triplet*

The following code shows the CICS definitions (session, connection, and transaction) that correlate with the previous SNA aliases for the local APPC LU LHCAMP00, the remote APPC LU CICSDEMO, and the mode PA62TKNU.

```
OBJECT CHARACTERISTICS                         CICS RELEASE = 0650
CEDA   View   CONnection(  SC02  )
Group                     :  GINFGROUP
DEscription   :
CONNECTION IDENTIFIERS
Netname                  :     LHCAMP00
INDsys                          :
REMOTE ATTRIBUTES
REMOTESYSTem          :
REMOTEName             :
REMOTESYSNet           :
CONNECTION PROPERTIES
ACcessmethod             :     Vtam     Vtam       | IRc     | Ndirect | Xm
Protocol                    :       Appc    Appc      |      Lu61     |    Exci
Conntype                      :       Generic         |        Specific
SInglesess                  :       No                           No       |         Yes
DAtastream                :     User      User     | 3270  |SCs     | STrfield | Lms
RECordformat               :        U                  U           |          Vb
SECURITY
SEcurityname                :
ATtachsec                   :    Local    Local       |    Identify | Veri    | Mixidpe
BINDPassword              :                PASSWORD NOT SPECIFIED
BINDSecurity                 :    No                   No            |         Yes
Usedfltuser                    :      No                 No             |        Yes

                SYSID=CICS      APPLID=CICSDEMO


OBJECT CHARACTERISTICS                                   CICS RELEASE = 0650
CEDA   View   Sessions(           SC02SESS         )
Group                          :       GINFGROUP
DEscription    :
SESSION IDENTIFIERS
Connection                  :        SC02
SESSName                     :
NETnameq                    :
MOdename                  :        PA62TKNU
SESSION PROPERTIES
Protocol                       :       Appc      Appc     |  Lu61          |  Exci
MAximum                     :       005     ,        005                     0-999
RECEIVEPfx                  :
RECEIVECount             :                                         1-999
SENDPfx                        :
SENDCount                   :                                          1-999
SENDSize                       :       04096                             1-30720
RECEIVESize                 :       04096                            1-30720
```

```
              SYSID=CICS      APPLID=CICSDEMO

OBJECT CHARACTERISTICS          CICS RELEASE = 0650
CEDA  View    TRANSaction( GINF )
TRANSaction :           GINF
Group:                GINFGROUP
DEscription:
PROGram:                 GTEMPINF
TWasize:                     00000                    0-32767
PROFile:                 DFHCICST
PArtitionset:
STAtus:                Enabled           Enabled            |          Disabled
PRIMedsize      :    00000            0-65520
TASKDATALoc     :  Below            Below |          Any
TASKDATAKey     :  User              User     |          Cics
STOrageclear    :    No              No        |          Yes
RUnaway         :    System          System | 0 | 500 2700000
SHutdown        :    Disabled        Disabled           |          Enabled
ISolate         :    Yes                          Yes      |          No
Brexit          :
+          REMOTE ATTRIBUTES
           SYSID=CICS                      APPLID=CICSDEMO
```

SNA Load Balancing

SNA load balancing is a feature that requires configuration in Host Integration Server and in the mainframe environment as well. SNA load balancing provides both failover and redundancy. It relies on the Host Integration Server subdomain concept. When a SNA request is sent from any of the Host Integration Server clients or Transaction Integrator servers, it is redirected to one of their corresponding SNA Gateway servers available for their subdomain. The SNA Gateway servers are the ones actually responsible for handling the APPC conversations with the mainframe.

The redirection process is performed with the help of the sponsor servers, which provide information about where the requested resources (LUs) are defined. The HIS client or Transaction Integrator server then searches through its service table to find the SNA Server services that were in the returned list. It then opens a connection to the SNA Server service (over port 1477) to request a session. If the request is not granted, it will try one of the other servers that were in the returned list. It continues this process until it gets a session or until it is determined that a session cannot be obtained.

The HIS subdomain makes it possible for all the servers of a subdomain to have the same priority for session allocation. Except for the fact that the primary server keeps the read/write copy of the COM.cfg file, all the HIS servers of the subdomain work identically. It is by configuring the local APPC LUs available in every load-balanced server as members of a common local LU APPC pool that the solution achieves redundancy. Figure 14-10 shows the "Member of default outgoing Local APPC LU pool" configuration setting.

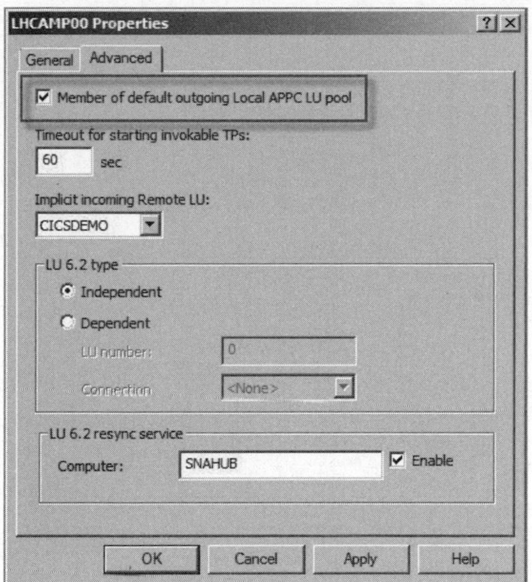

Figure 14-10. *Default local APPC LU pool configuration*

By choosing the setting "Member of default outgoing local APPC LU pool" option shown in Figure 14-10, you enable the requests sent from the Host Integration Server clients to hit any of the LUs members in the default pool. Something you will need to take into account when configuring the local APPC LUs as members of the default APPC LU pool across the HIS subdomain is that each of those LUs should have a unique LU name, although they can share the same LU alias. Creating unique names will help you identify where the requests are being sent and also will help you manage the SNA aliases better.

In special configurations, sometimes you may require extending the scope of the SNA load balancing. Although the limit of HIS systems per subdomain is 15 (including the principal configuration server) and every HIS system can have up to 4 nodes installed (and therefore the maximum numbers of node for a subdomain is 60), Host Integration Server will always try to use only its own resources to achieve mainframe connectivity. If you want to avoid the default behavior and extend the scope of your requests to other servers in the Host Integration Server subdomain, you can add the `reslocflags` `DWORD` entry with the `Data` value of `0x8001` under the following registry key: HKEY_LOCAL_MACHINE\System\CurrentControlSet\Services\SnaBase\Parameters\Client\.

To prepare the mainframe to work with the SNA load balancing, there should be as many local APPC LU entries as nodes in the SNA load-balanced servers. The local LUs should have the `LOCADDR` set to zero (when working with peer connections) and should be members of the default local APPC pool. Every LU should have defined a CEDA connection to the corresponding CICS region they target. Failing to create the right connections or LU definitions means the Host Integration Server will not be allowed to create APPC conversations.

Figure 14-11 shows how SNA Manager looks in an SNA load-balancing scenario. The local APPC LU `LHCAMP00` is defined as a member of the APPC LU pool. The local APPC LU `LHCAMP00` in the SNABACKUP server has the name of `HCAM200`.

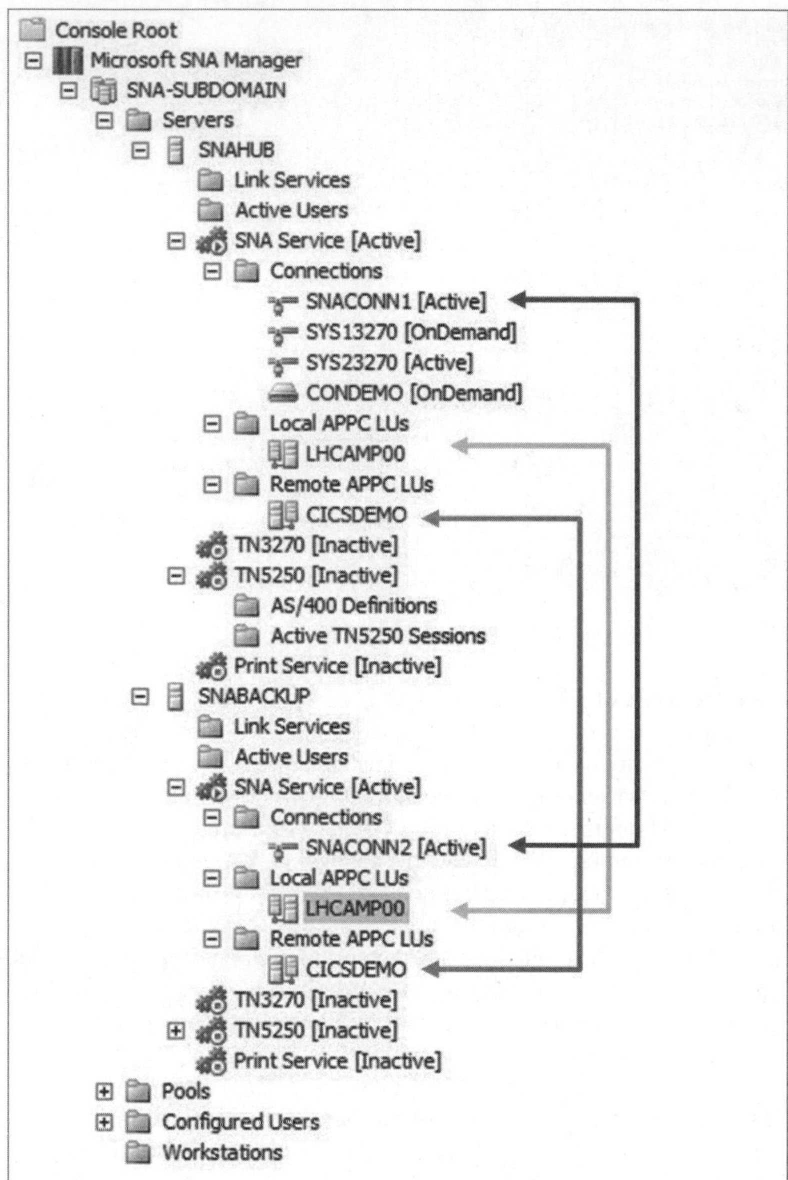

Figure 14-11. *SNA load balancing*

Once you have finalized the creation of your SNA aliases, you should go to the top menu in the SNA Manager and select Diagnostics. On the APPC Test tab, you should select the server whose SNA aliases you are trying to test and click the Test button. We recommend selecting the Report All Return Codes check box. Doing so will give you a better idea of the APPC commands executed and the values returned from the mainframe. A successful test will return sessions using the SNA Service Manager mode also known as SNASVCMG and the APPC mode you are using. Figure 14-12 shows the Microsoft Host Integrator Server Diagnostics tool.

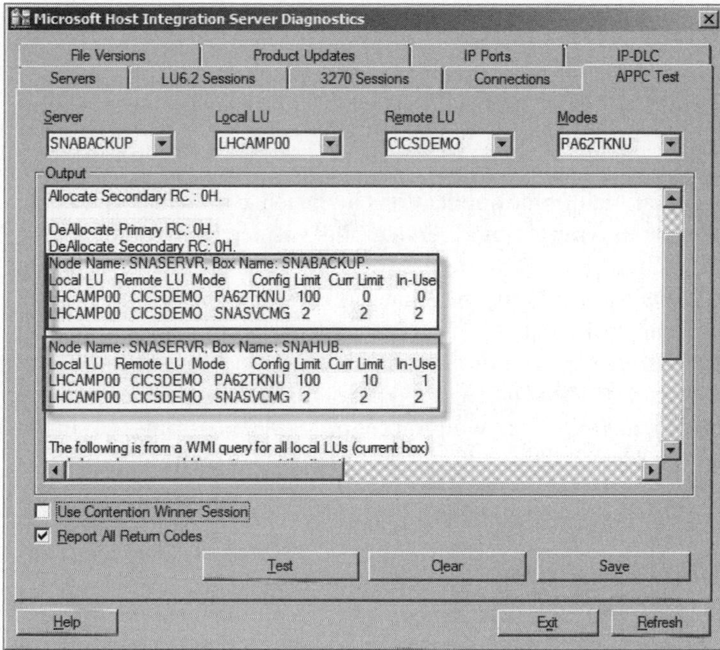

Figure 14-12. *Diagnostics APPC test screen*

You can use the Diagnostics tool from the TI nodeless servers as well. Just go to the %SNA-ROOT% folder, and double-click display.exe. Remember to run the tool under the context of a user with permissions in the actual server that hosts the LUs.

Figure 14-13 shows an arrangement of three Host Integration Server systems configured as an SNA Gateway using the IP-DLC Link Service and the IBM Enterprise Extender.

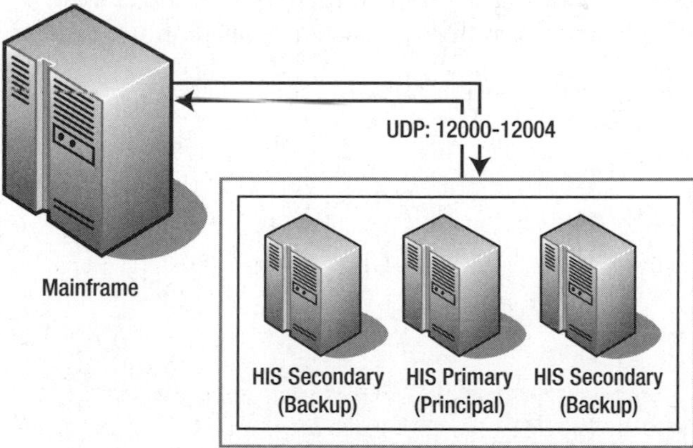

Figure 14-13. *SNA Gateway arrangement*

Transaction Integrator

Let's move to the Application layer. Now that you have your environment ready to handle SNA sessions, you can start thinking of adding the Application layer, which will allow you to expose mainframe applications to the .NET environment.

Transaction Integrator is the Host Integration Server feature that allows you to create and configure objects that will act as mainframe applications in the .NET context. It provides libraries, tools, and assistants to create wrappers and services that will access mainframe program by using SNA, TCP, or HTTP transports.

Transaction Integrator offers two mechanisms for legacy integration. The first one is called *Windows-initiated processing* (WIP). With WIP, you can create and manage .NET object definitions that will be used when triggering mainframe calls synchronously from the .NET clients. The second one is called *host-initiated processing* (HIP). With HIP, you can create listeners that will be able to receive requests from mainframes or AS/400 platforms. To summarize, both mechanisms were designed to close the loop between legacy platforms and the Windows world.

Enabling Transaction Integrator

To use Transaction Integrator, first you will need to enable it. During the setup configuration process, you will be asked to enable it and to provide a database server where the HIP database will reside. The HIP database is a SQL Server database whose main purpose is to store HIP configuration information. An important note here is that in a multiserver installation, you can share the same HIP database between multiple Transaction Integrator server instances. Bear in mind that even though all your Transaction Integrator servers will be using the same HIP database, Transaction Integrator WIP objects will not be shared across multiple servers or stored in the HIP database; consequently, you will have to use the export/import definitions wizard to deploy your Transaction Integrator objects. One of the benefits of using a shared HIP database for WIP is that whenever a user tries to manage the tracing, regions, or Transaction Integrator objects (including import/export features) for one Transaction Integrator server, the other ones will be automatically locked for performing those activities. Figure 14-14 shows the actions menu for the WIP feature.

Figure 14-14. *WIP actions menu locked by user accessing remote TI server*

For HIP applications, though, the HIP database allows remote administration. In a multiserver TI HIP installation, every TI HIP server can be managed from the other TI HIP servers that use the same TI HIP database.

Deploying Transaction Integrator Servers

The Transaction Integrator deployment options totally depend on your architecture. There is a base premise here. Transaction Integrator should be deployed on application servers. The reason for this is that if you deploy Transaction Integrator with the SNA Gateway services, Transaction Integrator will always try to use the local SNA Gateway services. Although having both Transaction Integrator and SNA Gateway services on the same box is a supported configuration, we don't recommend it for multilayer architectures. In multilayer architectures, scalability is a critical factor. So, unless you plan to scale out both roles (SNA and Transaction Integrator) always at the same time, you wouldn't want to have the servers with total dependency upon each other.

We recommend using Transaction Integrator nodeless servers. Basically, a Transaction Integrator nodeless server is a Transaction Integrator server that does not run the SNA Server service (it does still run the SnaBase service). In this configuration, requests can be routed to remote sponsor servers that provide SNA services and that make possible the execution of remote requests using Host Integration Server client-server connectivity. The effect is similar to installing an HIS client, which will implicitly be part of its sponsor Host Integration Server subdomain. Figure 14-15 shows the configuration screen you will need to populate with information about the sponsor servers.

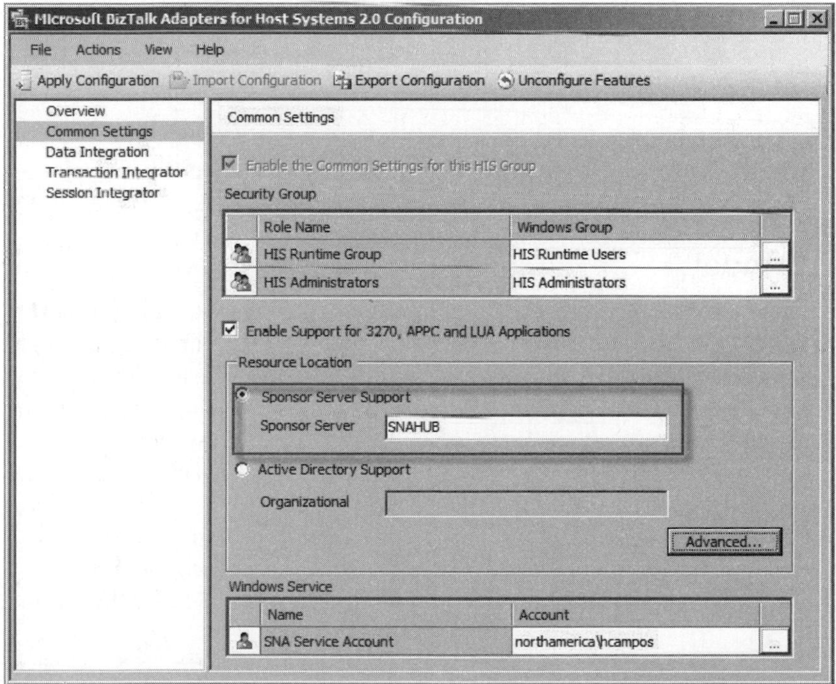

Figure 14-15. *Transaction Integrator nodeless server using sponsor server SNAHUB*

Figure 14-16 shows three Transaction Integrator nodeless servers connected to an enterprise SNA Gateway. They use the 1477 and 1478 ports to access the SNA Gateway. A SQL

Server is required to work with Transaction Integrator, so the port 1433 should be opened, and remote access should be enabled.

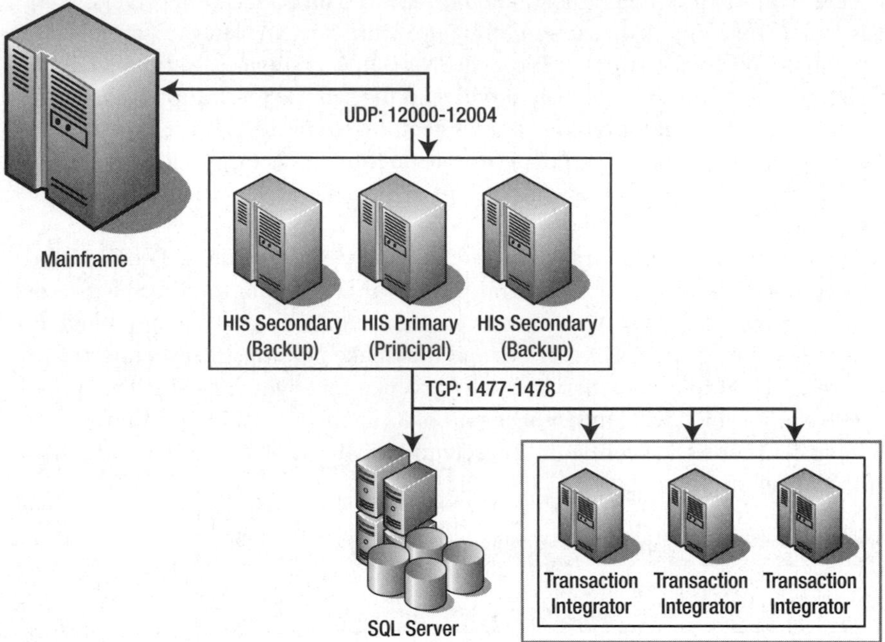

Figure 14-16. *Transaction Integrator multiserver architecture*

Programming Model

Transaction Integrator requires you to choose a programming model before creating your TI projects. A *programming model* is the definition of how Transaction Integrator will interact with the mainframe at the transaction level. Although the SNA Gateway is the low-level layer, now you will need to make sure that your application structure and data will be handled in an expected way for the mainframe application. There is a chart available in the product documentation that we strongly recommend you review, understand, and use; it's called "Choosing the Appropriate Programming Model," and you can find it at http://msdn.microsoft.com/en-us/library/aa770990.aspx. It is extremely important to bring this information to your customer and discuss with them the requirements and characteristics of every programming model. The following are the programming model requirements for the CICS LU 6.2 link programming model:

- IBM MVS operating system version 4.3 or later
- IBM CICS version 3.3 or later
- The CICS mirror transaction, which is included in CICS version 3.3 or later
- VTAM

- One or more CICS regions defined in an application (APPL) statement in VTAM with transaction programs configured
- The VTAM PU, LU, and mode definitions necessary to establish SNA connectivity

Once you have decided which programming model you will use, then you can design your Transaction Integrator solution. For this chapter, we will use the CICS LU 6.2 link programming model. This model is based on the LU 6.2 APPC independent sessions discussed earlier. With this model, the transaction is transferred from Transaction Integrator to the mainframe using Distributed Program Link (DPL) to a CICS transaction called CSMI. CSMI is known as a *mirror* transaction, because it is used to access mainframe transaction programs (TPs) on behalf of other TPs. It also issues the `EXEC CICS` link command in CICS and transfers the DFHCOMMAREA[2] with all the values populated in the Windows application. After the TP is executed, it returns the data to Transaction Integrator by issuing an `EXEC CICS RETURN` command.

In a nutshell, managing Transaction Integrator is about managing libraries. Therefore, before creating the Transaction Integrator object, you should plan ahead for the COBOL program you will need to invoke. Some things you should have handy are the program ID and the transaction ID. Your mainframe team should be able to provide you with these values, and each combination of these two values should represent a unique program in the CICS environment. But the most important resources will be the Host Definition-COBOL copybook when working with mainframes and the RPG copybook when working with AS/400. With Transaction Integrator, you can either create one host definition or import one. Transaction Integrator gives you the possibility of creating one from scratch by using legacy data types or importing one from a COBOL copybook definition. We prefer the second approach.

When working with the CICS link programming model, you are accepting that the size of each block of data that you send will be less than or equal to 32KB. This limitation has nothing to do with Host Integration Server; it is actually a restriction imposed by IBM on the size of the DFHCOMMAREAS.

Host Integration Server uses the CICS intersystem communication (ISC) concept to execute CICS transactions. SNA and APPC provide the needed network and APIs, and it is finally the DPL, which allows the execution of CICS link commands to transfer Transaction Integrator requests to the DFHCOMMAREA in the remote system.

There is an option in Transaction Integrator called Enable 32KB, which allows you to send 32KB and receive 32KB as the DFHCOMMAREA. We recommend you select it so you are using 100 percent of the DFHCOMMAREA size. There are also other important considerations when working with DFHCOMMAREAS. First, DFHCOMMAREAS can include an extraordinary number of fields. When the DFHCOMMAREA is imported using Transaction Integrator, your object definition will expose all the fields of the DFHCOMMAREA. Sometimes this number of fields can be a little overwhelming for .NET developers not used to manipulating more than five or six parameters per method. We recall once that we had to invoke a Transaction Integrator object whose definition had more than 45 parameters. Our advice here is to work with your COBOL programmer to totally understand the copybook she is preparing for you, and try to limit the number of fields when possible.

---

2 DFHCOMMAREA is the name of the data area, known also as the *communication area,* that is specified in the LINKAGE SECTION and is used by the COBOL programs to receive data.

You should also review the data types that your program will receive and the data types that the program will have to send. They have to be compatible with the mainframe data types. For the complete list of the TI-supported data types, please visit http://msdn.microsoft.com/en-us/library/aa754292.aspx. Also review the COBOL UNIONS that you will need to populate and its corresponding discriminator, if available. Fortunately, Transaction Integrator can handle COBOL UNIONS and render dynamic content depending on the discriminator value. For example, you might have a valid EBCDIC array "redefined" as a set of COMP-3 values. Although a COBOL programmer can handle this situation easily, Transaction Integrator may fail if you don't specify a valid discriminator. Again, take the time to review and validate such things before taking the COBOL copybooks as input.

Another issue with copybooks is that you need to ensure that they follow basic COBOL coding rules. Sometimes we have received copybooks that break the rules. Table 14-2 presents the basic rules that a COBOL program should follow.

Table 14-2. *COBOL Coding Rules*

Columns	Type	Observations
1–6	Sequence number	The programmer doesn't have to enter anything in these positions.
7	Indicator	This can be used to code a comment (*). A slash (/) is also accepted.
8–11	A margin (area A)	77 level numbers and 01 level numbers.
12–72	B margin (area B)	These are reserved for 02 levels and upper.
73–80	Identification	No definitions are allowed here.

Transaction Integrator does evaluate some of the rules, but not all of them. The following are additional recommendations you may want to take into account when working with COBOL copybooks:

- Remember that COBOL is not case sensitive.
- Don't forget to add the dots at the end of every line. Although with the COBOL latest versions this is not required, be prepared.
- If there are REDEFINES in the copybook, talk to the mainframe team to verify the definition that you will actually use if there is no "discriminant" available.
- Remove any character other than the ones stated in the previous chart. Make sure you have the right count of characters.

One of the most important recommendations that we have for you when working with Transaction Integrator WIP is to include the Metadata Error Control Block. The Metadata Error Control Block is a Transaction Integrator feature that, once enabled, provides a COBOL program with an additional mechanism to report errors to Transaction Integrator. Instead of having a mainframe transaction "abending" because of a critical error, you can have the COBOL program write to one of the fields in the Metadata Error Control Block section to report to Transaction Integrator without even reaching the point in the code that triggers the abend. The Metadata Error Control block is shown here:

```
 01  GETEMPINFO-META-DATA.
* META-DATA GENERATED BY TRANSACTION INTEGRATOR.
  02  LMETADATALEN                        PIC 9(9) COMP-4.      INOUT
  02  BSTRRUNTIMEVERSION                  PIC X(32).            INOUT
  02  BSTRMETHODNAME                      PIC X(32).            INOUT
  02  BSTRPROGID                          PIC X(40).            INOUT
  02  BSTRCLSID                           PIC X(40).            INOUT
  02  USMAJORVERSION                      PIC 9(4) COMP-4.      INOUT
  02  USMINORVERSION                      PIC 9(4) COMP-4.      INOUT
  02  SREADYTOCOMMIT                      PIC 9(4) COMP-4.      INOUT
  02  SWILLINGTODOMORE                    PIC 9(4) COMP-4.      INOUT
  02  SRETURNERRORTOCLIENT                PIC 9(4) COMP-4.      INOUT
  02  SERRORCODE                          PIC 9(4) COMP-4.      INOUT
  02  LHELPCONTEXT                        PIC 9(9) COMP-4.      INOUT
  02  BSTRHELPSTRING                      PIC X(256).           INOUT
```

To use the Metadata Error Control Block, you should select the Include All Metadata option in the Metadata field for the Transaction Integrator object. Bear in mind that there is no need to include the metadata COBOL definition in the copybook that you will import, but the mainframe team should include the metadata COBOL definition in the DFHCOMMAREA of the program that you are planning to call using Transaction Integrator.

■Note For a detailed explanation of every field in the Metadata Error Control Block, please visit `http://support.microsoft.com/kb/220967`.

Importing the Copybook

Once your COBOL copybook is sanitized and completely defined, you can start thinking about the import procedure. Other than COBOL coding rules, you should take some additional considerations from an application integration perspective into account when importing COBOL copybooks. During the import process, you will be required to enter information about transaction IDs, program names, and of course the programming model. Remember that the same naming conventions rules that are followed on the mainframe for transaction programs also apply to the Transaction Integrator. Program names should have a length of eight characters, while the CICS transaction IDs should have a length of four characters.

For the LU 6.2 CICS link programming model, you will have to specify a mirror transaction. A *mirror transaction* is a transaction provided by CICS to execute CICS transactions on behalf of other transaction programs. By default, the transaction CSMI is specified. You will also have to locate your DFHCOMMAREA in the copybook definition. You will have to enter the direction of the parameters (whether they are input, output, or input/output).

Let's take a look at a COBOL copybook. The following shows a simple COBOL program that returns static data. We have put the DFHCOMMAREA definition in bold, because it will be used in the import process.

```
IDENTIFICATION DIVISION.
PROGRAM-ID. GTEMPINF.
ENVIRONMENT DIVISION.
DATA DIVISION.
WORKING-STORAGE SECTION.
LINKAGE SECTION.
01  DFHCOMMAREA.
    05 CODEMP                         PIC X(5).
    05 EMPLOYEE-INFO.
        10 LO-HR-DATA.
           15 LO-HR-FNAME             PIC X(30).
           15 LO-HR-LNAME             PIC X(30).
           15 LO-HR-FULLNAME          PIC X(71).
           15 LO-HR-DNI               PIC X(08).
           15 LO-HR-STAT              PIC X(01).
           15 LO-HR-REQ               PIC 9(10).
           15 LO-HR-CONTRIB-LAST2     PIC 9(10).
           15 LO-GRADE OCCURS 2 TIMES PIC X(02).
           15 FILLER                  PIC X(90).
        10 LO-PRJ-MGMT.
           15 LO-PRJ-DPT OCCURS 2 TIMES.
              20 LO-PRJ-ID            PIC X(05).
              20 LO-PRJ-NAME          PIC X(40).
              20 LO-DIR-REP           PIC X(10).
              20 LO-PRJ-DES           PIC X(10).
              20 LO-PRJ-VERT          PIC X(65).
*
* THIS PROGRAM READS THE CODEMP VALUE AND FILLS IN THE
* HR DATA AND PROJECT DATA FOR THAT PARTICULAR EMPLOYEE
* DATA IS RETURNED TO THE CALLING PGM VIA THE DFHCOMMAREA
*
 PROCEDURE DIVISION.
     IF CODEMP = 'HVCUN' THEN
        MOVE SPACES TO EMPLOYEE-INFO
        MOVE 'Harold' TO LO-HR-FNAME
        MOVE 'Campos' TO LO-HR-LNAME
        MOVE 'Harold Campos Urquiza' TO LO-HR-FULLNAME
        MOVE '99999999' TO LO-HR-DNI
        MOVE '1' TO LO-HR-STAT
        MOVE '1234567890' TO LO-HR-REQ
        MOVE 'A+' TO LO-GRADE(1)
        MOVE 'A+' TO LO-GRADE(2)
        MOVE '00010' TO LO-PRJ-ID(1)
        MOVE 'Legacy Integration with .NET' TO LO-PRJ-NAME(1)
        MOVE '10' TO LO-DIR-REP(1)
        MOVE 'Legacy Integration' TO LO-PRJ-DES(1)
        MOVE 'RETAIL'TO LO-PRJ-VERT(1)
```

```
        MOVE '00011' TO LO-PRJ-ID(2)
        MOVE 'Legacy MIgration to .NET' TO LO-PRJ-NAME(2)
        MOVE '45' TO LO-DIR-REP(2)
        MOVE 'Legacy Migration'  TO LO-PRJ-DES(2)
        MOVE 'BANKING' TO LO-PRJ-VERT(2)
    END-IF.
    EXEC CICS RETURN END-EXEC.
```

Figure 14-17 presents the outcome of the Transaction Integrator import process for the copybook. The Visual Studio template for the Host Applications project required to create Transaction Integrator objects is available only when you select the development support option during the product installation. Visual Studio 2005 and Visual Studio 2008 are supported.

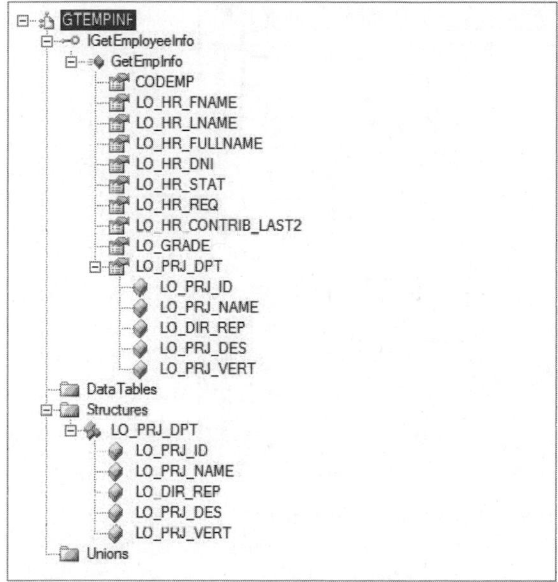

Figure 14-17. *Transaction Integrator object definition after the import process*

Host application projects support .NET and COM libraries. For .NET, in WIP scenarios, a .NET Client Library template should be selected. The other option is use the .NET Server library template, which is used in host-initiated processing scenarios. One of the additions to Host Integration Server 2009 is the support of WCF. In previous editions, there was support for web services and BizTalk Server templates. Now, with the addition of the WCF support, the TCP and HTTP bindings are available as are behaviors for metadata with exceptions.

Security

Host Integration Server provides security at many levels required to support the split stack architecture and connectivity against the legacy system. From a user-level access standpoint, it is through the common settings, shown in Figure 14-18, where you have to define the groups named HIS Runtime Group and Host Integration Server Administrators. The

HIS Administrators group should be used for the operations team, whereas the HIS Runtime Group should contain the client application users (including Host Integration Server service accounts). If you have a client application like a .NET web application, you have to add your web application pool identity user as a member of the Host Integration Server runtime users group.

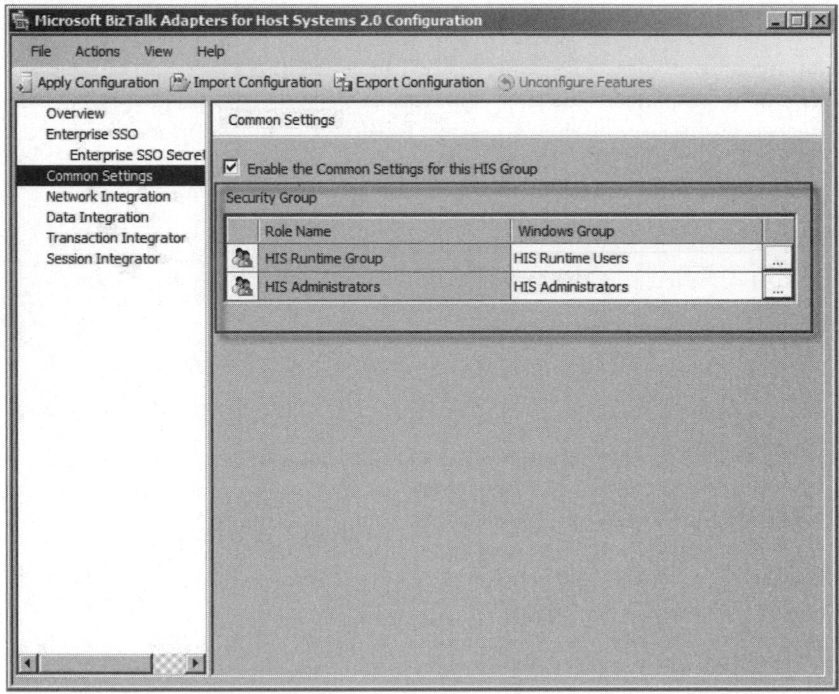

Figure 14-18. *Host Integration Server 2009 Common Settings configuration*

Once you have created the user groups, you have to define service accounts for every Host Integration Server service. If you are wondering how to manage password expirations with the Host Integration Server service accounts, you can use the Host Integration Server configuration tool to do an unattended update of the service account password.

From an SNA configuration perspective, the COM.cfg file, which contains all the configuration information for the gateway, is located in a locked-down directory, and only a service account or an account belonging to one of the Host Integration Server groups can perform changes onto it. It is also shared as COMCFG$.

From a network perspective, the discussion is different. The ports required by a Host Integration Server client, or a Transaction Integrator nodeless server to get connected against a Host Integration Server, are 1477 (SnaServerPort) and 1478 (SnaBase-Datagram). Port 1477 is used for application connectivity (SNA application), and port 1478 is used for the sponsor and broadcast connections. Remember that when using Named Pipes, port 139 is also used. To change the default port from 1478 to something else, you can add the SnaBasePort and TargetServerSnaBasePort entries to the registry key System\CurrentControlSet\Services\SnaBase\Parameters\SnaTcp\ in the server and client, respectively, with the new value.

To change the default SnaServerPort port 1477 to a different number, you can add the SnaServerPort entry with the new value in the same registry key.

Now, for the IP-DLC Link Service, we strongly recommend using IPSec in cases where connectivity implies external components. Although there are customers who use SNA session-level encryption, Host Integration Server doesn't support SNA session-level encryption.

The mainframe handles security in different ways. The most common security schema provided by the mainframe is the IBM Resource Access Control Facility (RACF). RACF provides access control for the z/OS. One important consideration when working with mainframes is that when using the CICS link programming model, IBM DPL doesn't transfer the Windows credentials to the CICS application. On top of this, the CICS application assumes that the validation has taken place already and will use the default CICS application's account. If you want to change this behavior, you will need to change the `ATtachsec` parameter in the CEDA `CONNECTION` definition to reflect any of the following values:

`LOCAL`: This setting does not require SSO, and it provides no authentication. You can use `LOCAL` if you do not want to use authentication. Your client may consider that the authority of the link is enough for the Transaction Integrator system.

`Non-LOCAL`: This setting should be used if you require the users to be authenticated by requiring a user ID, or a user ID and a password, to be sent. `Non-LOCAL` includes the following types of validations:

- `IDENTIFY`: A user ID must be sent, but no password is requested.
- `VERIFY`: A password must be sent.
- `PERSISTENT VERIFICATION`: A password is sent on the first attach request for a specific user.
- `MIXIDPE`: It represents either identify or persistent verification.

From an application standpoint, Enterprise Single Sign-On (Enterprise SSO) should be deployed in the Windows environment to allow credentials mapping between the mainframe and Host Integration Server. To deploy it, you need to install Enterprise SSO from the Host Integration Server or BizTalk Server's Setup program. Once you have installed Enterprise SSO, you will need to create an affiliate application that will represent the mainframe application and that will store Windows and mainframe credentials for the applications you are targeting to use. We recommend you deploy the Enterprise SSO in a clustered environment, if possible, so you add high availability to the solution.

Once Enterprise SSO is deployed and the mainframe security mechanism has been defined and/or the security credentials are known, you need to assign an Enterprise Single Sign-On "Affiliated Application" in the SNA Manager and Transaction Integrator. In the SNA Manager, you can do this inside your IP-DLC connection properties window. There is a drop-down list where you can select Affiliated Application so the security will be applied at the connectivity level. In the Transaction Integrator, you can set an affiliate application on the Security tab of the remote environment properties window.

When selecting the Enable Single Sign-On option, shown in Figure 14-19, there are also a few more options available: User Credentials and the COM+ Application Credentials. You should select the first if the user credentials can be captured from the Transaction Integrator runtime. You should select the latter whenever you will allow Transaction Integrator to capture the credentials information as defined for a COM+ application. If you plan to control the pass of credentials from code, even though you are using Enterprise SSO, then you should select the "Allow application to override selected authentication" option.

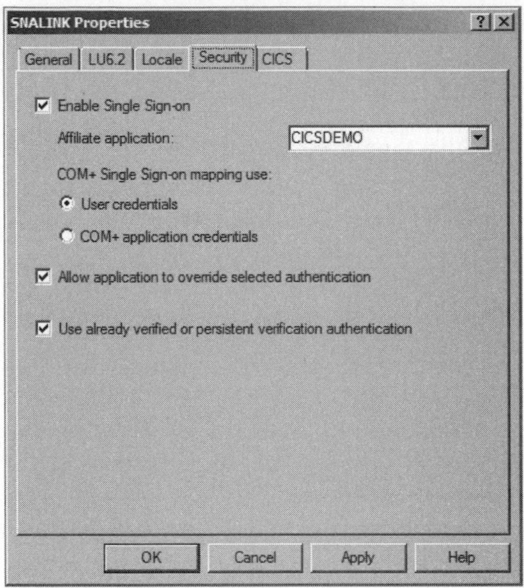

Figure 14-19. *Security properties window in Transaction Integrator remote environment definition*

To be in line with the `Attachsec` parameter of the CICS `CONNECTION` definition, you should select the "Use already verified or persistent verification authentication" option. So, what if you are not using Enterprise SSO at all? Then you can still pass credentials from your Transaction Integrator client application using the "Require client provided security" option and using the `ClientContext` object from your custom code. You will have to pass the credentials using the `USERID` and `PASSWORD` properties of the referred object. The client context has been updated in Host Integration Server 2009 to support dynamic remote environments while maintaining backward compatibility. With Host Integration Server 2009, a user no longer needs to specify Include Context Parameter on a method in the Transaction Integrator library. The user still has the ability to not allow the client context; it's just included by default now.

Session Integrator

Session Integrator is Microsoft's offering for screen scraping. Among the many benefits provided by it, we can say that simplicity is where its more powerful capability resides. With a few API objects, you can achieve complex screen scraping scenarios by using SNA or the TN3270 transport. To set it up, you should select the Session Integrator option during the product install process. Then you configure it by selecting the Enable the Session Integrator Feature option in the configuration panel and adding a Windows service account.

The Session Integrator feature targets LU0 and LU2 (3270) applications. The LU0 capabilities of Session Integrator are richer than the LU2-provided ones since the interface of the first makes available low-level access to the session data stream. In the case of LU2, the Host Integration Server product group has taken care of the complexities around the data stream manipulation, allowing developers to build applications that interface directly with the 3270 data stream. Table 14-3 shows the interfaces available for the developers to program with Session Integrator using LU2.

Table 14-3. *Interfaces Available for the Developers to Program with Session Integrator Using LU2*

.NET Interface	Remarks
`SessionDisplay`	Provides the connection interface for the `SessionDisplay` class
`ScreenPosition`	Provides access to a position on the LU2 screen
`ScreenCursor`	Provides access to the cursor on the screen
`ScreenPartialField`	Provides access to a part of a screen field
`ScreenField`	Provides access to a particular area of the LU2 screen including the data and attributes
`ScreenFieldCollection`	Contains a collection of `ScreenField` classes
`ScreenPartialFieldCollection`	Contains a collection of `ScreenPartialField` classes
`ScreenFieldAttributeData`	Provides all of the attributes about the `ScreenField` data

Here we will give a sample of how to use Session Integrator with a Display LU (LU2). Because we already have an IP-DLC Link Service configured for the example in this chapter, we will just need to add a new connection that will point to the mainframe environment we need to access, which is under the control of the SSCP (VTAM). The sessions used in these types of connections are known as *dependent sessions*, because they need the VTAM to arbitrate the LU-LU session startup. Once you have the information available, then you will need to create the objects in the SNA Manager. HIS 2009 Session Integrator does not support 5250/TN5250 screen scraping on IBM AS/400 systems.

From a development perspective, you should add a reference to the microsoft.hostintegration.sna.session.dll library available in the %snaroot% directory from your .NET code to be able to use Session Integrator. From a coding perspective, to create either an SNA session or a TN3270 session, you should use the `SessionDisplay` class. Once your application has opened a session, you can use the `WaitForContent` method to wait for any string you need to read or capture to appear on the screen. Remember to call your method to render the screen as many times as you need to reflect your latest 3270 session data. As the session data arrives to the terminal in the EBCDIC format, you should use the `ConvertEbcdicToUnicode` method to convert the EBCDIC strings to the Unicode format. In the Host Integration Server SDK, you will find examples for LU0 and LU2.

For instance, in our configuration, we have a connection called SYS13270, with a few display LUs. All of our LUs are grouped in the LU pool called SYS1LU. The following code example belongs to our Session Integrator application and is used to create a 3270 session using the SNA and TN3270 transports. In this case, we will use the SNA transport with a local

LOGICALUNITNAME set to SYS1LU, and for the TN3270 transport we will use the name of the TN3270 server.

```
try
{
m_Handler = new SessionDisplay();
if (strTransport=="SNA")
{
m_Handler.Connect("TRANSPORT=SNA;LOGICALUNITNAME=" + LUSession);
}
else
{
SessionConnectionDisplay TNDisplay = new SessionConnectionDisplay();
TNDisplay.DeviceType = SDeviceType;
TNDisplay.Transport = SessionDisplayTransport.TN3270;
TNDisplay.TN3270Port = Convert.ToInt32(TN3270Port);
TNDisplay.TN3270Server = TN3270Server;
m_Handler.Connect(TNDisplay);
}
m_Handler.Connection.HostCodePage = 37;
FontFamily fontFamily = new FontFamily("Courier New");
m_FixedFont = new Font(fontFamily, 18, FontStyle.Regular, GraphicsUnit.Pixel);
ScreenText.Font = m_FixedFont;
DrawScreen();
m_Handler.WaitForContent("TERM NAME", 20000);
DrawScreen();
SessionStatusLabel.Text = "Currently in Session";
}
catch (Exception ex)
{
MessageBox.Show(ex.Message);
}
```

The following code example uses ConvertEbcdicToUnicode to convert the EBCDIC session data to the Unicode format recognized by Windows:

```
public String CurrentScreen()
{
…
ScreenData screenData = m_Handler.GetScreenData(1, 1, -1);
screen = HostStringConverter.ConvertEbcdicToUnicode(screenData.Data);
return screen;
}
```

The following code applies when using the TN3270 transport and is used to present all the TN3270 devices supported by Host Integration Server:

```
foreach(string item in Enum.GetNames(typeof(TNDeviceType)) )
{
cboDeviceTypes.DropDownStyle = ComboBoxStyle.DropDownList;
cboDeviceTypes.Items.Add(item);
cboDeviceTypes.SelectedItem = "IBM3278Model2E";
}}
```

The following code applies when using the TN3270 transport and is used to capture the TN3270 device that the Session Integrator application will represent:

```
SIDemo.SDeviceType = (TNDeviceType)Enum.Parse(typeof(TNDeviceType),
cboDeviceTypes.SelectedItem.ToString(), true);
```

Figure 14-20 shows the list of TN3270 devices available for a TN3270 session.

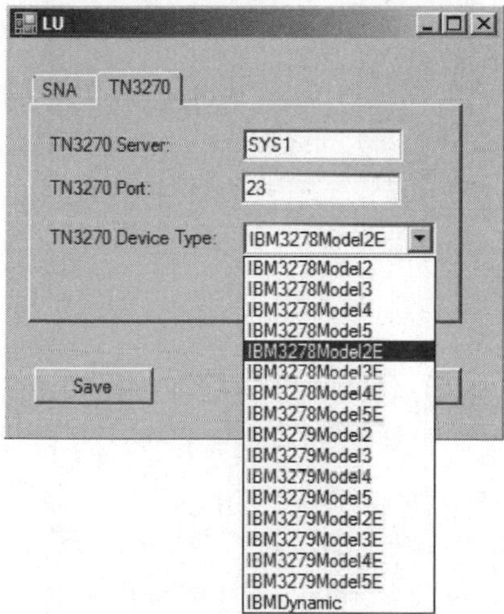

Figure 14-20. *TN3270 devices available for a TN3270 session*

Once the 3270 session is established (SNA or TN3270), to start working with the session stream, you have to use the SendKey method to send commands to the 3270 stream. It is like working with a 3270 emulator. The only difference is that the keyboard commands are performed by the Session Integrator application and not by the end user. Figure 14-21 shows the main screen of the Session Integrator Demo application.

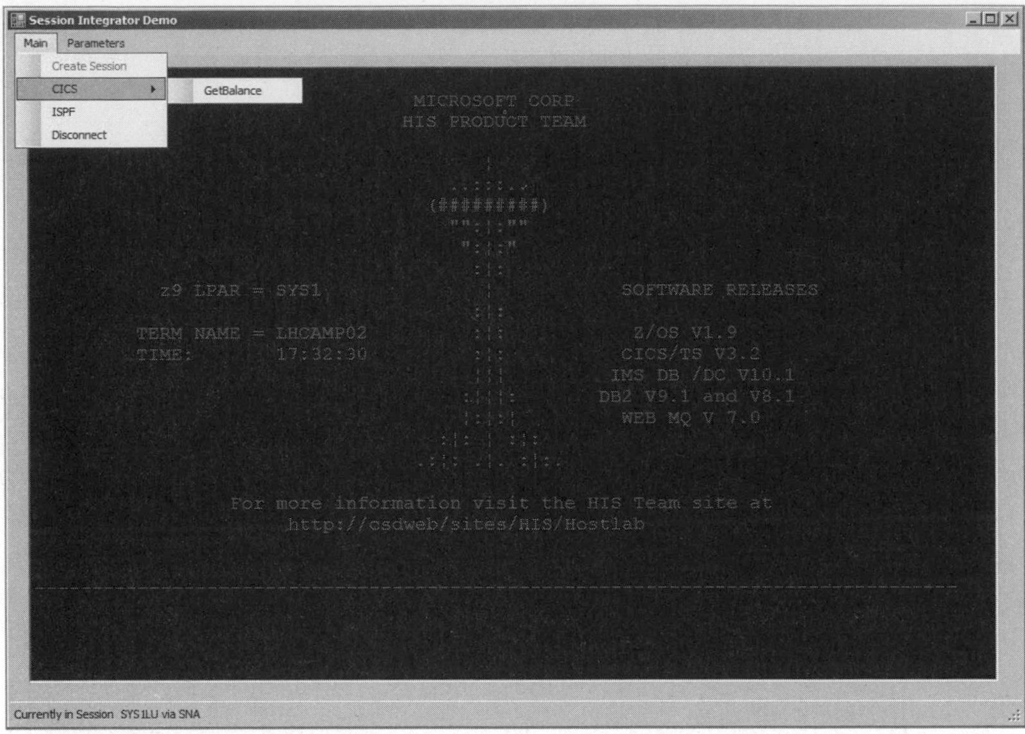

Figure 14-21. *Session Integrator Demo application*

The following code example shows how to call a CICS region (CICSDEMO) from the current screen. The example also shows how to execute a CICS transaction (WBGB-GetBalance):

```
private void getBalanceToolStripMenuItem1_Click(object sender, EventArgs e)
{
createSessionToolStripMenuItem.Enabled = false;
m_Handler.SendKey("CICSDEMO@E");
DrawScreen();
m_Handler.WaitForSession(SessionDisplayWaitType.PLUSLU, 5000);
DrawScreen();
m_Handler.WaitForContent(@"CICS", 5000);
DrawScreen();
try
{
ClearScreenAndWait();
m_Handler.SendKey("WBGB@E");
DrawScreen();
m_Handler.WaitForContent("F6=Get Cust", 5000);
DrawScreen();
GetBalance GBAL = new GetBalance();
GBAL.ShowDialog();
```

Figure 14-22 shows how the screen for the transaction `WBGB-GetBalance` looks. It also shows the Windows form that is displayed to capture the name and account number required for the application session to return the actual balance.

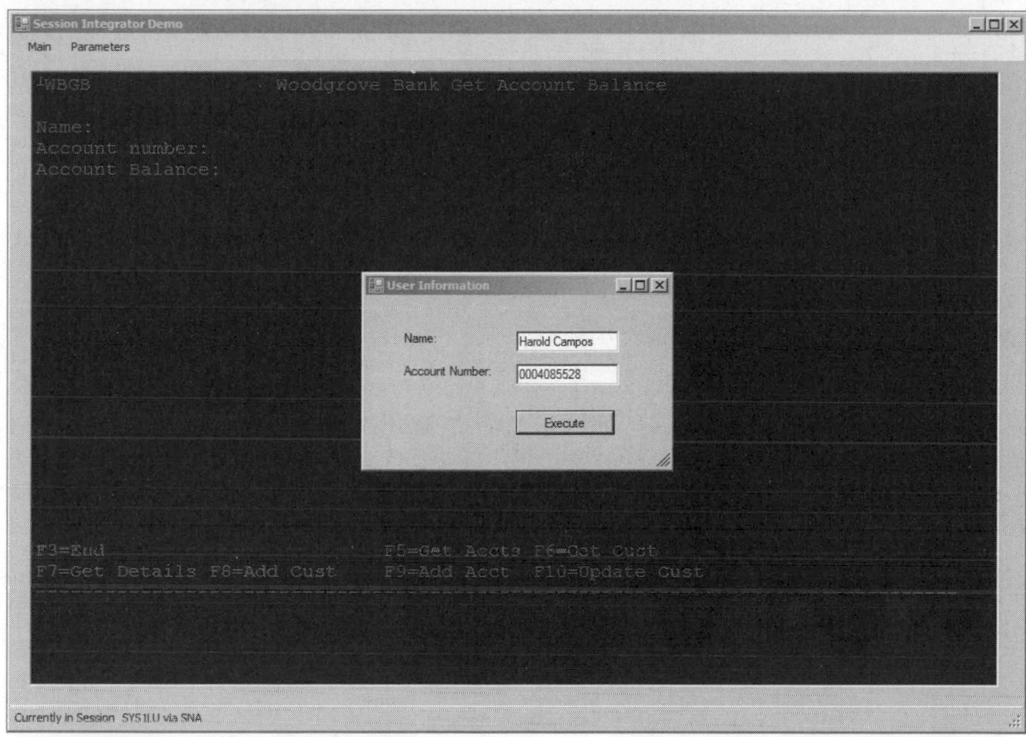

Figure 14-22. *Get account balance transaction*

Right after the capture takes place, an Enter is issued by the application to capture the response, as shown in the following example:

```
m_Handler.CurrentField.Data = GBAL.txtName.Text;
m_Handler.MoveNextField(new
ScreenFieldAttributeData(ScreenFieldAttribute.Normal)).Data =
GBAL.txtAccountNumber.Text;
m_Handler.SendKey("@E");
DrawScreen();
```

The following code example shows how to capture the response from the 3270 stream. The example uses the `ScreenPartialField` method to access parts of the screen fields:

```
ScreenPartialFieldCollection fields = new ScreenPartialFieldCollection(3);
fields.Add(new ScreenPartialField("Customer name not found", 21, 2));
fields.Add(new ScreenPartialField("Name / account could not be found", 21, 2));
fields.Add(new ScreenPartialField(".", 5, 31));
int indexOfField = m_Handler.WaitForContent(fields, 5000); DrawScreen();
```

```
if (indexOfField == 0)
throw new ArgumentException("Customer Name incorrect", GBAL.txtName.Text);
if (indexOfField == 1)
throw new ArgumentException("Account Name incorrect", GBAL.txtAccountNumber.Text);
string amountString = m_Handler.GetField(5, 20)[2].Data;
MessageBox.Show("Account Balance: " + amountString.ToString(), "Balance");
DrawScreen();
}catch (Exception ex)
{
MessageBox.Show(ex.Message);
}}
```

Figure 14-23 shows that the response for the GetBalance transaction is presented in the screen and through the message box window.

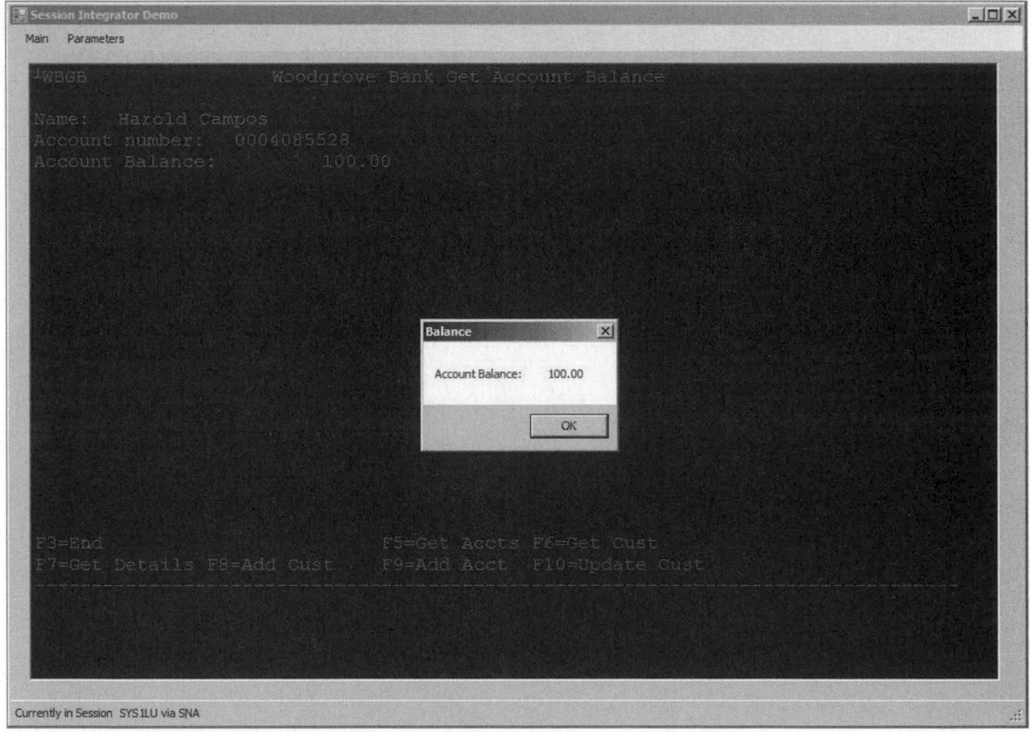

Figure 14-23. *Get account balance transaction response*

BizTalk Adapter for Host Applications

BizTalk Adapter for Host Applications (BAHA) is a subset of the BizTalk Adapter for Host Systems. BAHA provides BizTalk Server with the extensibility needed to access legacy systems. It leverages the Transaction Integrator capabilities by supporting Windows-initiated processing scenarios and therefore supports all the programming models for mainframe and AS/400 access. From a BizTalk configuration perspective, it provides a solicit-response adapter that targets remote environments defined in the TI Manager. Every time the BAHA receives an XML instance to be sent to a mainframe, the BAHA Runtime compares the received instance against its corresponding BizTalk schema and transfers the data to Transaction Integrator. From there, Transaction Integrator is responsible for sending the data to the mainframe, receiving the response, and then returning the data to the BAHA.

The BAHA Runtime maps the mainframe datatypes and data back to .NET datatypes, creates the XML response document, and passes the data back to the Messagebox through its corresponding port. From a send port configuration perspective, the Host Type property allows you to select a TI remote environment—your mainframe region. The Allow Advanced Override and Allow Security Overrides properties allow you to manipulate the TI Client Context object. The Persistent Connections property allows you to create persistent connections when working with batches of messages. We recommend the use of persistent connections to improve the performance and also to maintain the state in the server. The SSO Affiliate Application property allows you to use either a specific SSO Affiliate Application or the settings of the TI remote environment selected in the Host Type property. Figure 14-24 shows the available properties for the BAHA solicit-response port.

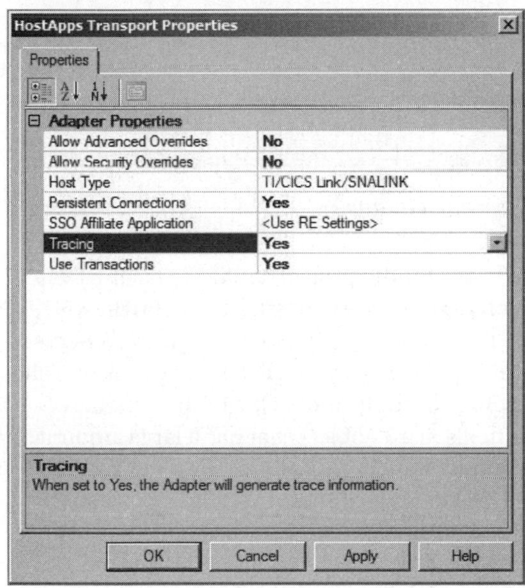

Figure 14-24. *BizTalk Adapter for HostApps Transport Properties window*

As we pointed out earlier, BAHA relies on the Transaction Integrator to access legacy systems. The setting that you need to set up in the Transaction Integrator object to generate a BizTalk schema is its Type Restrictions property. You have to set its value to BizTalk Adapter for Host Applications. The purpose of this Type Restriction is to prevent the TI client application from using conventions unsupported by BizTalk Server. However, it doesn't stop the client application from calling the assembly directly from any other Windows application. Figure 14-25 shows the TI Assembly Properties window highlighting the type restrictions available.

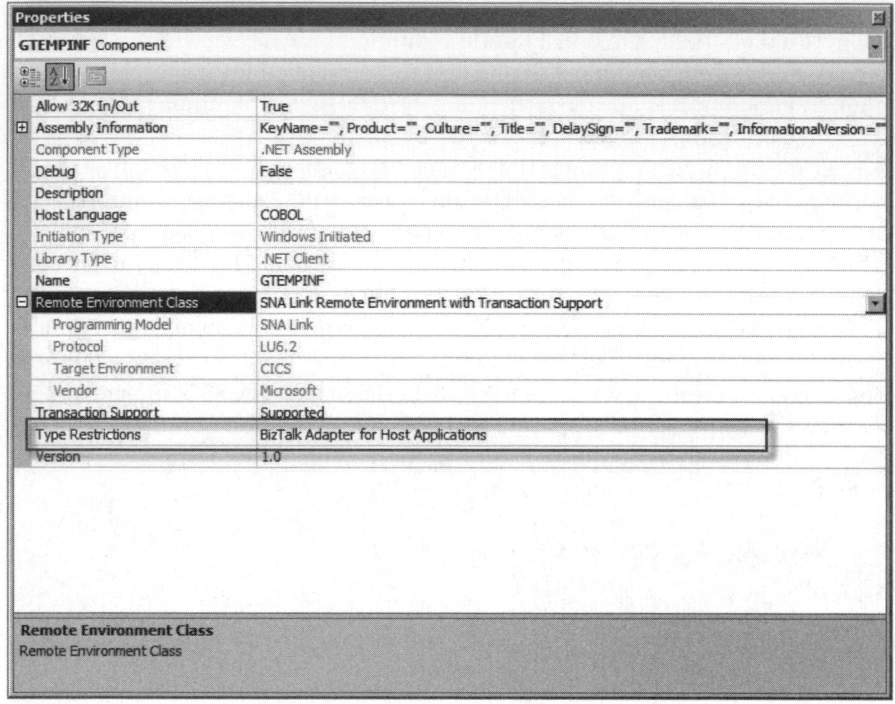

Figure 14-25. *Transaction Integrator Assembly properties window*

Once you have saved your TI changes in the Visual Studio project, an XML Schema Definition (XSD) file with the definitions for the request and response messages that BAHA will use will be generated. Afterward, you will need to import the XSD file into your BizTalk Server project. By doing so, when you deploy your BizTalk application, you will have the new BizTalk schema available in the schemas directory in the BizTalk application. One of the benefits of this approach is that you if you need to populate fields in a TI object that has a large amount of fields, you can use a BizTalk Server map and populate the input fields easily from an orchestration. Nonetheless, I recommend you ensure that you handle the TI object versions properly, so the XSD definitions you use in your BizTalk Server project always reflects the latest changes/updates you may have performed to your TI object definition and deployed to TI Manager. Figure 14-26 shows a sample TI XSD file imported in a BizTalk Server project.

Figure 14-27 shows two BAHA nodes connected to an enterprise SNA Gateway. Remember that every BAHA node should have installed and configured Transaction Integrator to access the SNA Gateway. A SQL Server is required to work with Transaction Integrator, so port 1433 should be opened, and remote access should be enabled as well.

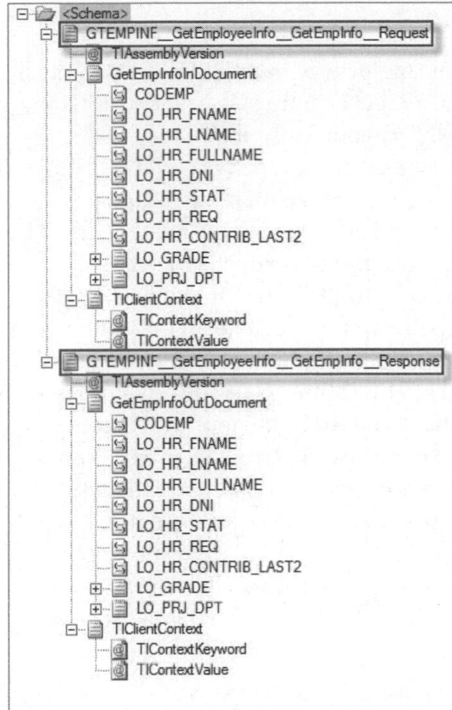

Figure 14-26. *BizTalk schema definition for a TI object*

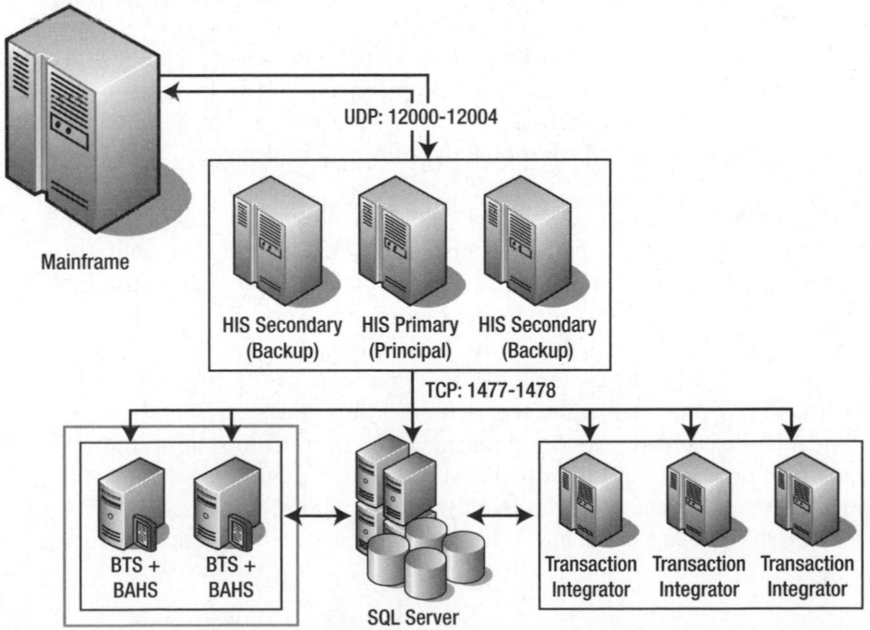

Figure 14-27. *BAHA systems providing mainframe transactional access*

Two-Phase Commit

Transactional processing is a critical requirement for the majority of institutions. In fact, most of the financial institutions require transactional support for every one of its transactions. Mainframe and AS/400 platforms have been provided this capability for many years. Host Integration Server, formerly SNA Server, incorporated support for two-phase commit (2PC) transactions in its version SNA Server 4.0 SP2 (many years ago). Since then, many improvements have been made in it, such as the support of 2PC running with SNA load balancing.

From a design perspective, you have to use a programming model that supports 2PC. When using the CICS link programming model, which supports 2PC, Host Integration Server uses the Distributed Program Link. The DPL is a mainframe mechanism that allows a CICS application to call another CICS application using a `LINK` command. DPL will be the mechanism that will control any 2PC transaction triggered by TI objects using the CICS link programming model. Hence, the COBOL developers should not have to modify their code to manage the entire transaction. However, if your application uses the user data programming model, the mainframe program will have to control the transaction commit and rollback from its code. Although this may require changes in COBOL programs that do not support transactions already, when using this programming model, you do not face the 32KB restriction on the DFHCOMMAREAS size. That's because the user data programming model doesn't use DFHCOMMAREAS. We strongly recommend reviewing the following IBM Redbooks to learn about the mainframe requirements for 2PC:

- "Systems Programmer's Guide to Resource Recovery Services (RRS)"
- "SC31-8134-00: SNA Sync Point Services Architecture Reference"

2PC needs to be enabled and configured in the mainframe and the Host Integration Server. Host Integration Server includes the Resynchronization service that works with MS DTC to support 2PC transactions. This service is installed when you select the Enable LU 6.2 Resync Services option under the Network Integration option of the Host Integration Server initial configuration. The option is not available for TI nodeless servers. For TI nodeless servers, you have to enable 2PC support in the remote environment configuration by using the TI Manager.

The Resynchronization service is also known as SNA LU 6.2 Resync TP. The SNA LU 6.2 Resync TP service implements the Exchange Log Names and Compare States functions of a SNA transaction manager. The Resynchronization service allows the Microsoft Distributed Transaction Coordinator (DTC) and IBM CICS to coordinate a recovery process as required during system startup or after a system or communication failure.

The Exchange of Logs (XLN) is the shared indicator of the state of 2PC transactions in the environment. The XLN reflects the local status of the Resynchronization service and the remote status of the mainframe readiness for establishing 2PC transactions. Both statuses should have the same value. If the statuses have different values, it might represent the existence of 2PC issues between the mainframe and the Host Integration Server that need to be analyzed. Figure 14-28 shows a successful log exchange between Host Integration Server and the mainframe.

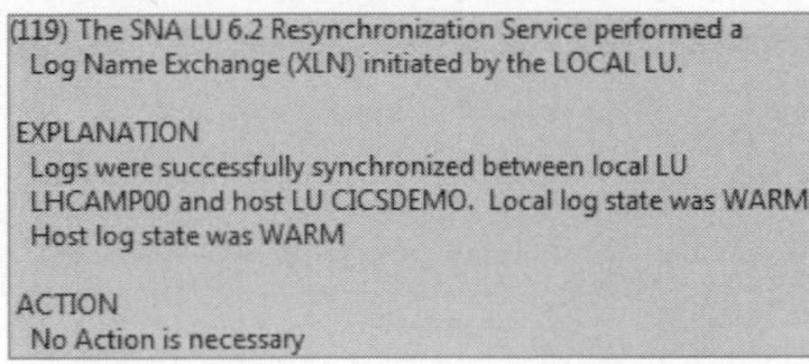

Figure 14-28. *Successful log exchange*

The Host Integration Server 2009 requirements for 2PC are the following:

- The local and remote LUs must each have SyncPoint support enabled in the Host Integration Server node, as shown in Figures 14-29 and 14-30.
- The local and remote LUs should each point to the computer that is running Resynchronization services, as shown in Figures 14-29 and 14-30.

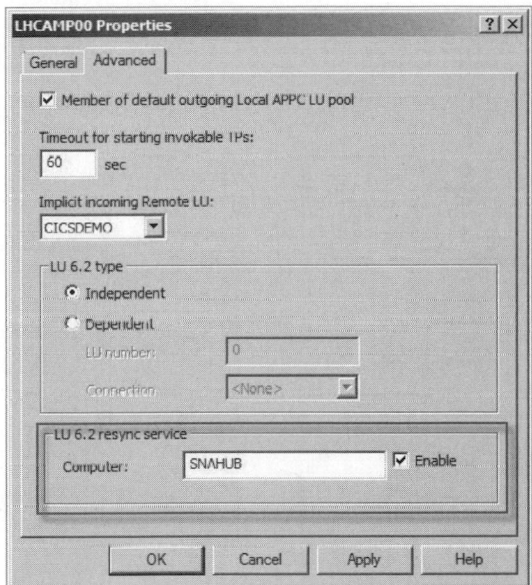

Figure 14-29. *LU 6.2 Resync service enabled and pointing to SNAHUB in the Local APPC LU LHCAMP00*

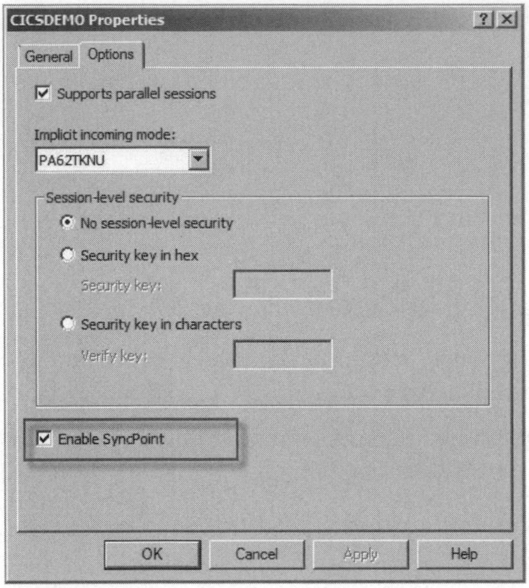

Figure 14-30. *Remote APPC LU CICSDEMO with SyncPoint enabled*

The mainframe must be configured for Sync Level 2 support. The TI remote environment (RE) must have Sync Level 2 support enabled as well. To check these items, right-click the RE in TI Manager, click Properties, and then click the LU 6.2 tab, as shown in Figure 14-31.

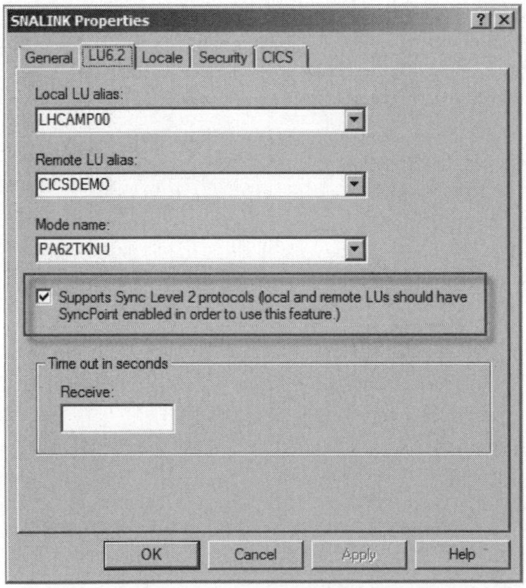

Figure 14-31. *TI remote environment with Sync Level 2 protocols enabled*

The Transaction Integrator object must have transaction support set to Supported, Required, or Requires New. If working with BAHA, you will have to set its Use Transactions property to Yes. Bear in mind that transactions will take place between the BizTalk Messagebox and the mainframe resource manager.

Performance Testing and Tuning

Performance has never been as critical as it is today. The compelling need to get the most out of our resources has led Microsoft to improve the mechanisms available to conduct performance testing and also performance tuning.

The concept of measuring performance is very much like that of addressing security. Performance has to be addressed in several layers. In mainframe integration scenarios, you should start from the mainframe layer, and then you can move to the Network layer, the Services layer, and finally to the Application layer. The fact that every layer has its own characteristics and constraints makes planning for thorough and successful performance testing and tuning a required activity.

Performance Testing

When working with Transaction Integrator, we recommend using the Microsoft Visual Studio Test Edition. Although many tools are available for performance testing, Microsoft Visual Studio Test Edition is the one tool that integrates best with .NET servers. By using it, you can create test scripts to stress your application. You can stress test TI objects published as web services and as WCF services, and you can also test their web consumer applications. To target BizTalk applications that consume TI objects or that use the BizTalk Adapter for Host Applications, you can also use LoadGen. Remember that the BAHA runtime captures the data sent from the BizTalk Messagebox database and sends it to the Transaction Integrator runtime. From there you can create your own custom message creator implementing the `IMessageCreator` interface and generate as many input instances as you need.

Performance Counters

Once you decide which approach you will follow to stress Transaction Integrator, then you have to define which performance counters you will collect. Yes, you are right; we're skipping the part of the service-level agreement (SLA) definition because that will entirely depend on your architecture. Host Integration Server includes numerous counters for the different roles that can be deployed. The use of the Host Integrator performance counters will allow you to capture critical data about multiple elements of your solution, including variables such as the time that it takes a transaction to go to the mainframe and back to the client application or the time that applications like BizTalk Server take to call TI objects.

For instance, for the CICS link programming model, we recommend the following counters for the SNA Gateway server role:

- SNA Connections: Throughput Bytes/Sec
- SNA Logical Unit Sessions: Throughput Bytes/Sec
- SNA Logical Unit Sessions: Data Bytes Received/Sec

- SNA Logical Unit Sessions: Data Bytes Transmitted/Sec
- SNA Adapter *adaptername*: Throughput Frames/Sec
- SNA Adapter *adaptername*: Connection Failures
- SNA Adapter *adaptername*: Successful Connects

And for the Transaction Integrator server role, we recommend the following:

- App Integration WIP\Average method call time
- App Integration WIP\Cumulative calls
- App Integration WIP\Host resp time CICS link
- App Integration WIP\Link calls/sec
- App Integration WIP\Total errors/sec
- App Integration WIP\Bytes received from an SNA host/sec
- App Integration WIP\Bytes sent to an SNA host/sec

Ultimately, the selection of the performance counters will depend on your specific needs. The list of counters provided here is suggested for an architecture using TI nodeless servers and SNA Gateway servers.

■ **Note** You can find detailed information about the performance counters available for Host Integration Server at `http://msdn.microsoft.com/en-us/library/aa771453.aspx`.

IBM RMF Monitor

One way to monitor mainframe performance is through the use of the IBM RMF Monitor. It performs post-processing and online monitoring functions. It is accessible from TSO and among other things can monitor the VTAM address space and performance relevant data in a z/OS environment.

Figure 14-32 shows the main options for RMF Monitor. For details on how to use it, you can read the IBM Redbook entitled "SG24-7110-00 z/OS Diagnostic Data Collection and Analysis."

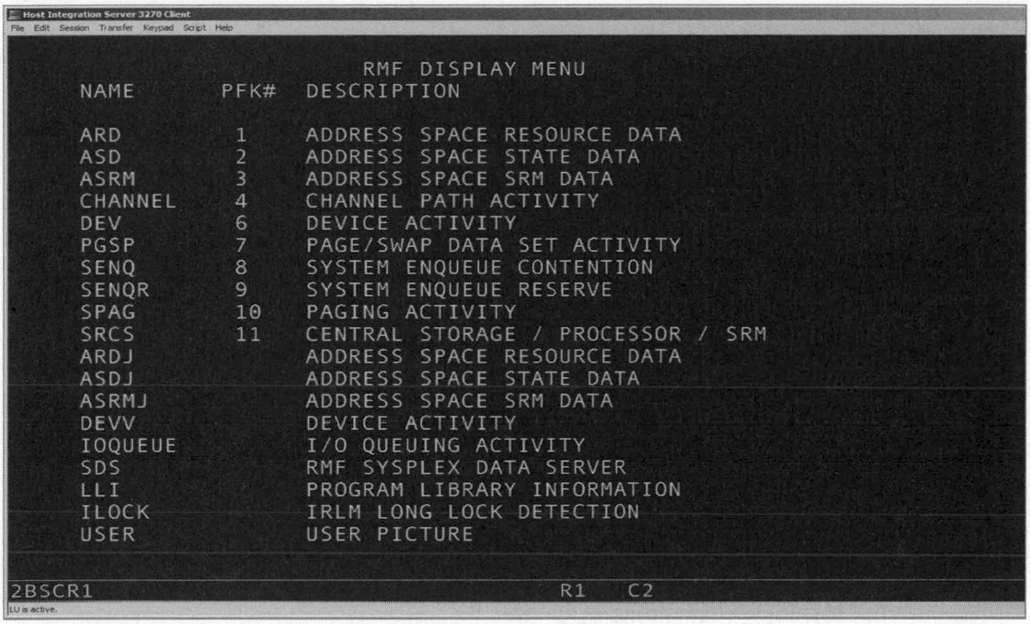
Host Integration Server 3270 Client
File Edit Session Transfer Keypad Script Help
RMF DISPLAY MENU
NAME PFK# DESCRIPTION
ARD 1 ADDRESS SPACE RESOURCE DATA
ASD 2 ADDRESS SPACE STATE DATA
ASRM 3 ADDRESS SPACE SRM DATA
CHANNEL 4 CHANNEL PATH ACTIVITY
DEV 6 DEVICE ACTIVITY
PGSP 7 PAGE/SWAP DATA SET ACTIVITY
SENQ 8 SYSTEM ENQUEUE CONTENTION
SENQR 9 SYSTEM ENQUEUE RESERVE
SPAG 10 PAGING ACTIVITY
SRCS 11 CENTRAL STORAGE / PROCESSOR / SRM
ARDJ ADDRESS SPACE RESOURCE DATA
ASDJ ADDRESS SPACE STATE DATA
ASRMJ ADDRESS SPACE SRM DATA
DEVV DEVICE ACTIVITY
IOQUEUE I/O QUEUING ACTIVITY
SDS RMF SYSPLEX DATA SERVER
LLI PROGRAM LIBRARY INFORMATION
ILOCK IRLM LONG LOCK DETECTION
USER USER PICTURE
2BSCR1 R1 C2
LU is active.

Figure 14-32. *RMFMON available from ISPF*

Performance Tuning

There are a few recommendations from a performance standpoint that we would like to highlight. Some of them are also available at `http://msdn.microsoft.com/en-us/library/aa745251.aspx`.

APPC

The following recommendations apply when working with the APPC API and/or SNA aliases:

- **Pre-activate the LU 6.2 sessions**: This will prevent a short delay in establishing new LU 6.2 sessions. Sometimes the mainframe preactivates the sessions, which may cause a short delay in the Host Integration because the mainframe is actually deciding when to serve the request.
- **Perform SNA link tuning**: This should be performed depending on the type of network used. For IP-DLC, we recommend validating the advanced settings in the IP-DLC Link Service with the mainframe team.
- **SNA load balancing**: Although this is not a tuning activity, we recommend the use of APPC load balancing for fault tolerance and redundancy.

Transaction Integrator

The following performance improvement recommendations apply when working with Transaction Integrator:

- **Tune the Remote Application (Mainframe TP)**: This should be performed by the mainframe team.
- **If you are not using 2PC, configure the TI component as Does Not Support Transactions so that 2PC is not attempted**: The same applies for the BAHA configuration. Verify that the Use Transactions property is set to No if you are not using transactions.
- **It is very important to tune the network**: Host Integration Server performance is very impacted by the number of hops between the mainframe and it. If you cannot have the Host Integration Server located in the same switch where the mainframe is connected to, then try to minimize the number of hops between them. Something additional you will have to analyze is whether the network switches are set up to half-duplex or full-duplex. Work with the network engineers to analyze Netmon traces and to troubleshoot any possible bottleneck.

Session Integrator

For Session Integrator transport, we recommend the use of the SNA transport (DLC or IP-DLC) over TN3270 to maintain 100% reliability of the 3270 conversation.

BizTalk Adapter for Host Applications

From a performance standpoint, we recommend you create a new send handler and configure the HostApps adapter to use it. By doing this, you can set up the HostApps adapter to run in a host instance other than the default BizTalkServerApplication one. By doing that, you avoid having the HostApps adapter in competition with resources designated for orchestrations and other in-process resources. Likewise, if you have more than one server available, you can create more host instances for the HostApps adapter. Doing so will improve the BAHA throughput and also will provide redundancy for your solution. Figure 14-33 shows a BizTalk Server solution with two BizTalk Servers hosting two BAHA host instances.

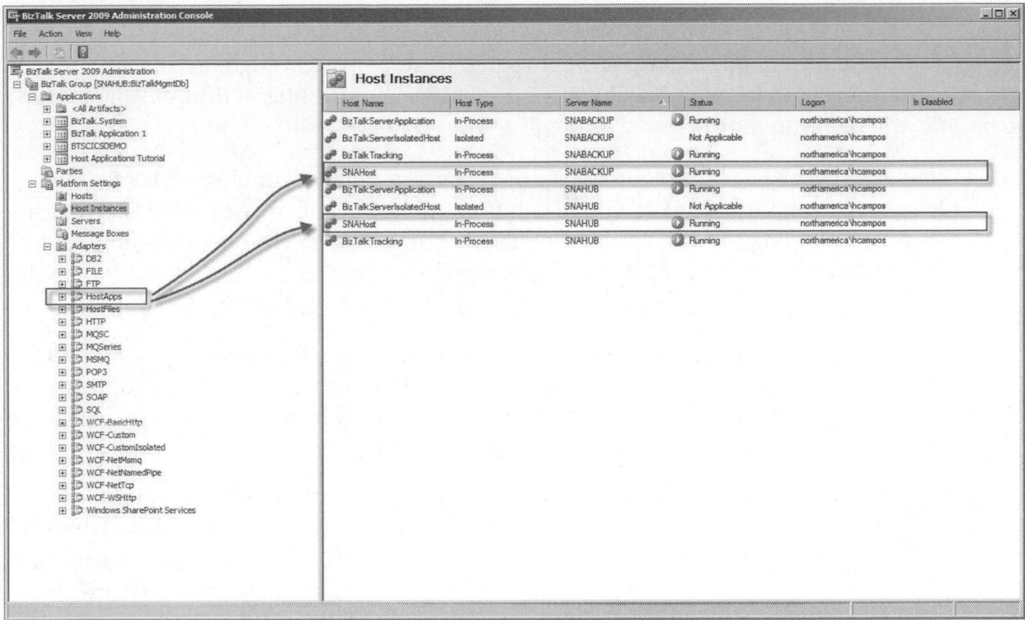

Figure 14-33. *SNAHost hosts for SNANODE and SNABACKUP servers in SNAHUB BizTalk Server group*

Troubleshooting and Diagnostics

Host Integration Server offers two tracing mechanisms: tracing for the Application layer and tracing for the SNA and connectivity services layer. Although the information provided by the Windows Event Log is very useful, sometimes it is not enough to determine the root causes of a problem. Alternatively, the traces provided by Host Integration Server cover pretty much all the areas where you can potentially run into issues. Something you should consider is that you will likely need additional expertise to be able to understand the traces. In some cases, you will have to request help from the Microsoft Premier Support Services (PSS) team to analyze traces and help you to define action plans.

The fact of the matter is that Host Integration Server is a very easy-to-configure product. It is perhaps the easiest mainframe integration solution currently available in the market. That said, the difficulties that IT professionals experience when trying to troubleshoot issues are in great part because of the lack of protocols and mainframe-related skills. Nowadays, IT professionals are not skilled in APPC, Logical Unit Application (LUA), Common Programming Interface for Communication (CPI-C), Link Services, or SNA formats. Although Host Integration Server doesn't require that the Host Integration Server administrators or operators have experience in the matters mentioned, it assumes that the specialists have a certain level of understanding of those concepts so they can troubleshoot issues successfully.

As problem resolution goes, we recommend you follow a phased approach. When troubleshooting, put the solution in context, and analyze all of the elements that participate in it. Do it in a structured way. Start with the elements that you can control in the solution before moving to layers that will require another team's involvement. Just be sure to give them a heads-up about the problem so they can start thinking about the problem with you.

Troubleshooting Plan

The following are some steps that we've put together to guide you through the general process of troubleshooting a performance problem. Consider the steps as rules of thumb. Adapt them to best fit your own situation.

1. Prepare a checklist of the requirements of the implemented technology. What we mean here is that you should create a list of points to validate your choice of whatever HIS features or technologies you are using. For instance, the connectivity checklist component for Session Integrator will likely include configuration verification for LU0 or LU2. On the other hand, for Transaction Integrator, you will likely deal with LU 6.2 or TCP/IP.

2. Reproduce the problem. Most of the time, there are quite a few ways to reproduce a problem. The challenge here is to coordinate the right resources to reproduce it. Mainframe environments and Windows environments should be in sync, so the problem can be tracked in both environments at the same time.

3. Create a list of the possible points of failure involved. Once you are able to reproduce the problem and have the checklist, you are off to a good start. Prepare a list of the possible points of failure, and move to the next step. The IBM sense codes available at `http://publibfp.boulder.ibm.com/cgi-bin/bookmgr/library` may come in handy for this step. Look for them by typing **sense data** in the search text box.

4. Capture logs and traces. This is where you will need to learn how to capture and use the SNA and WIP traces. You'll also need to know a little bit about what you should ask the mainframe team. To analyze the network traffic, we recommend using the Microsoft Network Monitor.

5. Analyze the traces. Escalate to Microsoft PSS if needed. Once you have the traces, you can start analyzing them using the Host Integration Server product documentation and, depending of the implemented technology, any of the following IBM Redbooks:

    - SC33-1695-02: "CICS Intercommunication Guide"
    - GA27-3136-20: "Systems Network Architecture Formats"
    - SC33-1701-02: "CICS RACF Security Guide"
    - GG24-4485-00: "Multiplatform APPC Configuration Guide"
    - SC09-4471-02: "Using Microsoft SNA Server with CICS"
    - SC31-8134-00: "SNA Sync Point Services Architecture Reference"
    - "Enterprise Extender Implementation Guide"

6. Apply corrective measures. Before applying corrective measures, you must prepare a plan to safely roll out those changes. Our recommendation here is the same that applies for every change rollout. Deploy first in your development environment, then in your quality assurance environment, and finally in your production environment.

Host Integration Server Tracing and Log Analysis

Capturing logs and traces is something that you need to address at different levels. The first level of tracing is provided by the Windows Event Log. If you go to the SNA Manager and right-click Properties in the subdomain node, you will find the Error/Audit Logging tab. You can route the messages to any server of the subdomain and also set up the level of logging according your troubleshooting needs. From a problem resolution perspective, we recommend you enable the detailed problem analysis. Bear in mind that after applying this setting, you will have numerous entries in the Event Log, so we advise you to use this setting only when you have a need for troubleshooting. We recommend this setting neither for performance testing nor for production environments. Use it only for problem resolution purposes. Figure 14-34 shows the Error/Audit Logging tab options.

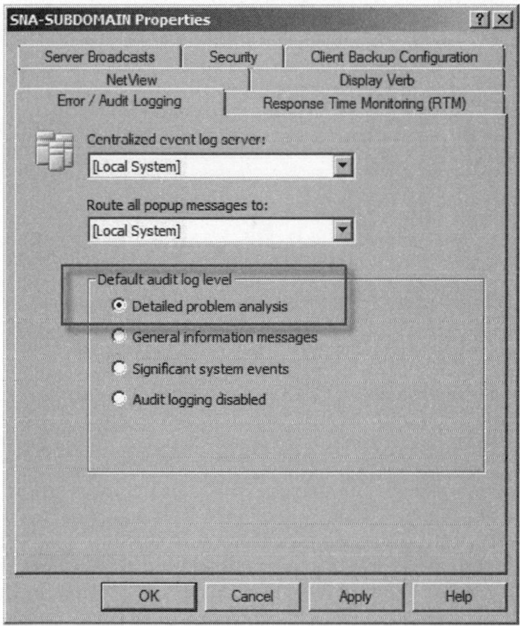

Figure 14-34. *Error/Audit logging options at SNA subdomain level*

Network Tracing

For Network Information collection, we recommend the use of the Microsoft Netmon. It captures information about the network traffic. You can download Netmon from the Microsoft Download Center: `http://download.microsoft.com`.

When monitoring Host Integration Server Link Services network traffic, you have to look for the `snalink.exe` process name in the capture file. If you are monitoring the SNA Gateway servers and you are using IP-DLC, you will see traffic to the mainframe and from it using ports 12000 to 12004. If you are monitoring Host Integration Server clients or Transaction Integrator nodeless servers, you will see traffic to the sponsor servers using ports 1477 to 1478—unless you have changed them as pointed out earlier. Netmon can group frames into conversations and also create filters so it will be easier for you to find traffic related to Host Integration Server.

SNA Trace Utility

The SNA Trace Utility is a tool that allows you to enable settings in HIS to capture SNA traces. The traces will be stored at the %SNAROOT%\traces location. Figure 14-35 shows the SNA Trace Utility.

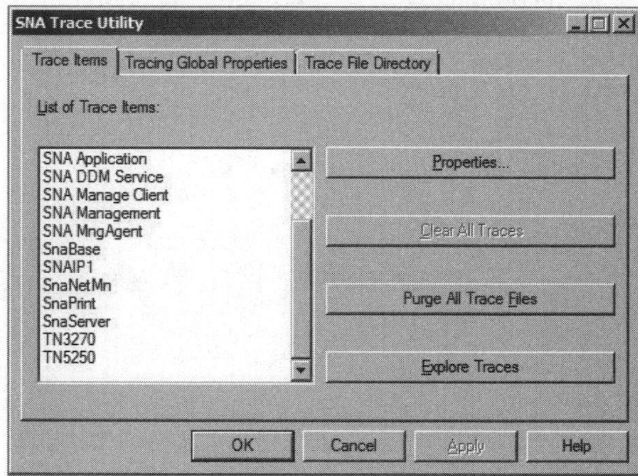

Figure 14-35. *SNA Trace Utility*

To enable a particular trace item, you have to select it and click Properties to access the tracing options. Once there, you should select the type of tracing you are interested in and then click OK to leave the tracing running.

Please remember that sometimes tracing can generate hundreds of megabytes of data. As soon as you finish capturing trace data, go to the SNA Trace Utility, and click Clear All Traces. If you want to delete the captured files, click Purge All Trace Files. By doing that, you will erase all the SNA trace files from the tracing location.

Required Skills

As we said before, additional expertise may be necessary to understand the traces and troubleshoot your SNA application. Table 14-4 provides you with an idea of the skills necessary to analyze the traces.

Table 14-4. *Skills Necessary to Analyze Traces*

Type of Tracing	Software Component Traced	Area of Expertise Required
APPC API	SNA applications	APPC programming
CPI-C API	SNA applications	CPI-C programming
LUA API	SNA applications	LUA programming
SNA Formats	SNA Server (PU 2.1 Node)	SNA formats
Data Link Control (messages)		SNA Server (PU 2.1 node) or Link Service DLC interface
Level 2 Messages	Link Service	Link Service interface

Type of Tracing	Software Component Traced	Area of Expertise Required
3270 Messages	SNA applications, SNA Server (PU 2.1 Node), or SnaBase	3270 emulator interface
Internal Messages	All software components for Host Integration Server 2009	Intended for Premier Support Services
APPC Messages	SNA applications, SNA Server (PU 2.1 Node), or SnaBase	Intended for Premier Support Services
Internal	All software components for Host Integration Server 2009	Intended for Premier Support Services

Tip Internal tracing is intended for use by product support technicians. Interpreting internal traces and certain types of message traces requires a specialized knowledge base.

SNA tracing can be customized. On the Tracing Global Properties tab, there is a field called the Trace File Flip Length, which is used to limit the size of the trace files. By default it has a size value of 20MB. In most cases, the flip length value needs to be increased (and often when you are doing performance testing or troubleshooting) to a value of around 200MB. Specify the flip length from the SNA Trace Utility's Tracing Global Properties tab, as shown in Figure 14-36.

If you are looking for a specific event ID in the Windows Event Log to occur, you can use the Monitor Event Log option to stop the SNA tracing when the event you are looking for occurs. Figure 14-36 also shows the Event ID field that allows you to specify the event of interest.

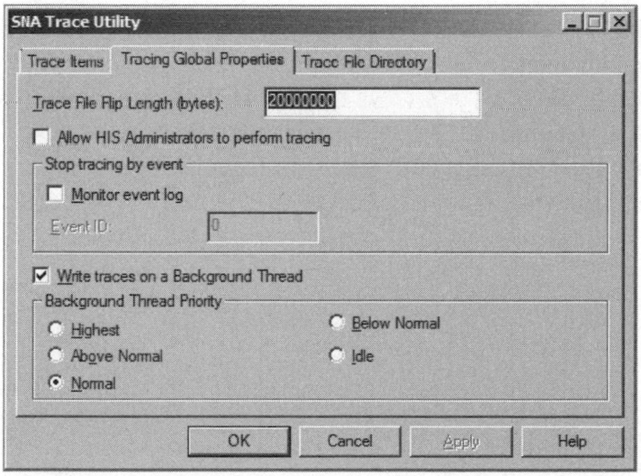

Figure 14-36. *SNA Trace Utility tracing global properties*

Windows-Initiated Processing Trace Utility

The WIP Trace Utility is a component of Transaction Integrator. It targets the execution of WIP transactions calls and provides real-time tracing information about the packing, unpacking, and specifics to the programming model used. Figure 14-37 shows the WIP Trace Utility, which is available by right-clicking the WIP node in TI Manager.

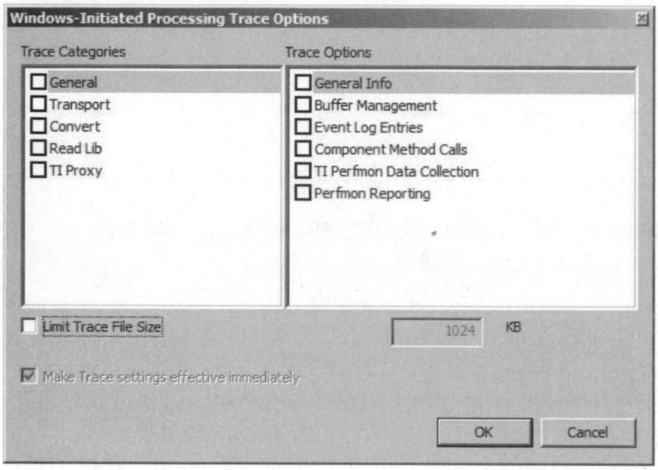

Figure 14-37. *WIP Trace Utility available from TI Manager*

From a mainframe perspective, there are two facilities with critical information relevant for diagnostics and troubleshooting: VTAM and CICS. For protocol tracing, you can use the GTF – Generalized Tracing Facility and the SNA – VTAM Trace (Buffer and IO). For collecting diagnostics information, you can use the VTAM System Logs, and for CICS, you can use the CEDF for SNA and the job logs.

It is unlikely that you or any other single person will have all the expertise and resource access required to handle all the elements involved in the development and deployment of a legacy integration solution. Therefore, you might have to involve teams with different expertise to successfully deploy a legacy integration solution. The key of any solution of this type is to plan first and then involve the right resources. When it comes to mainframe integration, you will need to involve the network administrator; the mainframe VTAM administrator; the CICS, IMS, or DB2 specialist; and the COBOL developers. All of them are key participants in any solution. In addition, the business team needs to be aware of the implications of developing and deploying a solution. So plan. Involve the right resources. Implement. Good luck in your journey.

CHAPTER 15

The Enterprise Service Bus Toolkit 2.0

As organizations continue to adopt the principles of service-oriented architecture (SOA), many new usage scenarios have arisen. Development teams throughout organizations are rapidly creating mountains of new web services. Off-the-shelf software packages are shipping with prebuilt web services to enable easier integration with other applications. Developers are using portals, mash-ups, and composite application frameworks to rapidly consume these services in order to create incredibly creative, rich, flexible, and powerful user-facing applications.

Architects working in this SOA world have quickly realized that they likely do not want applications to just consume services whenever and however they want in a willy-nilly, unstructured way. They realize that they need to implement a layer within their overall SOA that can provide order to the chaos. This is what Enterprise Services Buses (ESBs) have been designed to provide, and in the last few years, many organizations have begun to implement them.

For many people, ESBs have become the technology of choice for connecting service consumers to service providers, and this has left BizTalk developers with a very valid concern: where does BizTalk fit in with all of this? BizTalk has traditionally been positioned as an enterprise application integration (EAI) server, and many people see EAI as a very outdated pattern for integrating systems and services. Therefore, they often think that BizTalk as an EAI server cannot offer the same benefits as an ESB. These people tend to ask questions such as these: Has BizTalk's role as an EAI engine been made obsolete by ESBs and web services? Will Microsoft release a new ESB server that will deprecate BizTalk? Will BizTalk be relegated to some small corner of the office to handle minor and insignificant integration needs? *Is BizTalk dead?*

BizTalk and the ESB Concept

Fortunately, if you love the product like you do, you can be assured that BizTalk has *not* been relegated to the graveyard by these sexy new ESBs. In fact, BizTalk forms the very heart of Microsoft's ESB solution. BizTalk is so important that Microsoft has issued a collection of documents and components to help you get the most from BizTalk in an ESB environment. That collection is termed the *Enterprise Service Bus Toolkit*.

Functional Capabilities

The question that you should be asking yourself at this point is, how can BizTalk, which has always been positioned as a hub-and-spoke EAI engine, now act as an ESB? Some people might suspect that Microsoft is simply trying to take an existing product and squeeze a little more life out of it by rebranding it to align with the architectural flavor of the day.

Well, in order to answer this question, you need to take a look at the capabilities that most ESBs typically need to provide:

- Service invocation
  - Dispatch of service after mediation
  - Support for synchronous and asynchronous protocols
- Routing
  - Endpoint resolution and routing
  - Support for content-based and rules-based routing
- Mediation and messaging
  - Support for multiple transport protocols
  - Mapping between transport protocols
  - Message enrichment
  - Message transformation and mapping
  - Composite calls across multiple services
  - Integration with external service registries and repositories
- Process orchestration
- Management
  - Monitoring
  - Logging
  - Business activity monitoring
  - Auditing
- Mediation policies (or itineraries), which define how the ESB components work together

This is not meant to be an exhaustive list of all ESB requirements or a formal definition of an ESB. The focus of this chapter is Microsoft's ESB Toolkit and not the concept of ESBs in general. We've just included this list to give a general baseline with which to compare the core functions that an ESB provides against the native capabilities that BizTalk provides. Any experienced BizTalk developer will quickly see that a large number of these ESB requirements align nicely with the capabilities that BizTalk already provides.

Aligning the ESB with Your Core SOA Goals

Now, if you were to look at these functional requirements only, you might easily arrive at the conclusion that BizTalk can act as an ESB for you. This would not be a bad conclusion per se; however, before settling on this conclusion, you need to stop and look beyond these core functional requirements. ESBs are simply one layer within an overall SOA. Therefore, you need to remember some of the core principles that are driving the decision to adopt SOA in the first place. Flexibility, agility, and reuse are three key goals of SOA, and since the ESB is just a layer within the SOA, then it too needs to be aligned with these goals.

You probably design services with the goal of having them be reusable building blocks that can be easily composed or assembled into new business processes. As business requirements change, you expect that you will be able to quickly modify these services and the processes they are a part of. The hope is that SOA will provide you with an application platform that is quicker to adapt to change and that can be modified with less effort than the older monolithic applications can. To achieve this, developers are designing services to be loosely coupled, highly reusable, and generic. Since an ESB is a core building block within an overall SOA, it needs to strive to achieve these same goals. An ESB should make it easy for applications to quickly locate and consume remote services and allow developers to quickly compose base services into larger processes. An ESB must not, under any circumstances, become a bottleneck to the overall speed at which services, processes, and applications can be developed or modified. It really needs to be a lightweight, flexible, and generic layer that sits between service consumers and service providers.

BizTalk as an ESB?

It is this need for reusability, flexibility, and agility that makes some people question BizTalk's ability to function as an ESB. In the past, BizTalk was positioned as an EAI engine that functioned as a hub-and-spoke solution. Within its role as the hub, BizTalk had to know everything and define everything. For example, it required a schema for every message it would ever process. Its send ports had to be configured to point to specific locations. Receive ports were configured to pick up specific messages from only one exact location. It was not unusual for BizTalk solutions to be very large, complex, and tightly coupled. They rarely resembled the flexible, agile, and reusable type of solution required for an ESB.

However, just because BizTalk solutions have traditionally been implemented this way does not mean that they need to be. In fact, BizTalk has many dynamic tools and components that can be used in a highly reusable and dynamic manner to build very flexible solutions. So, the issue is not that BizTalk is inherently inflexible but rather that people have not been designing their projects to take advantage of the flexibility that it does provide.

One example of this is the way in which most developers use maps inside BizTalk. Most developers use a map either by linking it directly to a port or by using a Transform shape in an orchestration. Both of these approaches require that you specify the map name while developing and configuring the project. By specifying the map during development, you are essentially hard-coding the map name into the project. That map and only that map will run when a message is processed. This results in an incredibly tightly coupled solution.

To support the goals of the ESB, what you really need is a mapping engine that will allow you to specify a map name at runtime instead of at design time. This way, you can determine the name of the map that you need just as a message is received, and then you can dynamically execute that one map. The next time you receive a message, you might decide that you need to run an entirely different map.

What many BizTalk developers do not know is that BizTalk already has this functionality built in. BizTalk's mapping engine can be invoked directly via .NET APIs. These APIs allow you to pass in the name of the map you want to run at runtime. Therefore, if you spend a bit of time writing code, you can implement a very dynamic, generic, and reusable mapping service using BizTalk.

Getting Developers on Board

There are many other examples showing how BizTalk can be used in a more flexible and generic way. So, a valid question to ask is, if BizTalk has these dynamic abilities, why are developers and architects not using them? The quick answer to this question is fairly simple; many developers either do not know about these features or do not understand how to use them. Or they find them difficult to design, troubleshoot, and maintain. Now, if this were the only problem, then it could easily be solved through simple education. However, there is a second reason that it is much more problematic. To use a lot of these dynamic capabilities, developers have to write a significant amount of code on their own. They have to build a bunch of "plumbing" to hook together all of these BizTalk components in order to implement an effective ESB. Most developers have neither the time nor the mandate to work on this type of plumbing and instead need to focus on the core needs of the business.

Therefore, it is simply not practical to tell someone that BizTalk can function as an ESB as long as they're willing to invest a fair amount of time to develop all of this required plumbing. You are faced with a significant gap between what BizTalk can do in theory and what is practical to do in reality.

It was this gap that drove the initial development of Microsoft's Enterprise Service Bus Toolkit. The ESB Toolkit has a number of key goals:

- Providing an architectural toolkit on how to use BizTalk as an ESB
- Reducing the amount of plumbing that developers need to build in order to implement the prescribed architecture
- Providing ready-to-use components and tools that reduce the amount of time and effort that organizations need to invest in order to deploy an ESB
- Providing detailed samples and a toolkit on how to use the ESB Toolkit components to implement common integration patterns

In this toolkit (or, as we'll often refer to it, the ESB Toolkit or ESBT), Microsoft has built a number of new components and frameworks that allow you to use BizTalk in a much different way than you have in the past. This toolkit really represents a new way of thinking about BizTalk and a new way of using it. Essentially, you can think of the ESB Toolkit as an accelerator that sits on top of BizTalk in order to implement a highly reusable, flexible, and generic ESB.

Version 1.0 of the ESB Toolkit was first released to run on top of BizTalk 2006-R2. Version 2.0 was released shortly after BizTalk 2009 was released. In this chapter, we will do the following:

- Review the architecture and concepts that make up version 2.0 of the ESB Toolkit
- Review the components and frameworks that are used to implement the ESB Toolkit architecture
- Show how to use these tools and components to implement common ESB requirements

---

■ **Note** The ESB Toolkit was initially developed by Microsoft's Patterns & Practices team, and it was released through Microsoft's open source project-hosting site CodePlex. With version 2.0 of the toolkit, Microsoft no longer includes the source code for the core components as part of the default installation, and it is no longer available via CodePlex. The toolkit is now available at www.microsoft.com/downloads/.

The Architecture

Conceptually, the ESB Toolkit consists of five layers, as outlined in Figure 15-1. The ESB requires BizTalk's mapping engine, adapters, ports, pipelines, orchestrations, rules engine, and host environment in order to function. Therefore, BizTalk Server and its capabilities form the foundation layer upon which everything else is built.

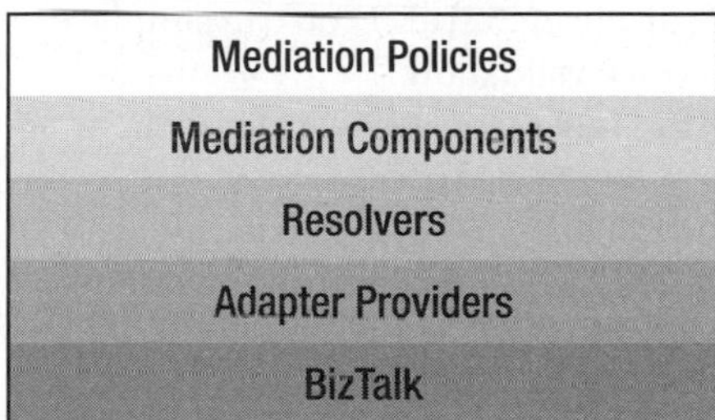

Figure 15-1. *The architectural concepts that comprise the ESB Toolkit*

Since the ESB Toolkit is built on top of BizTalk, it obviously forms the foundational layer. The other four layers consist of .NET components, web services, and prebuilt BizTalk components (such as pipelines and orchestrations) that ship exclusively as part the ESB Toolkit. It is these four layers that we will focus on in the following sections.

■ **Note** One question we are often asked is whether the ESB Toolkit can be used without BizTalk. The answer is no! The ESB Toolkit is made specifically to extend BizTalk and cannot function without it.

Mediation Components

Even though the Mediation Components layer falls right in the middle of the overall architecture, we are going to start by looking at it first. The reason for this is that the mediation components perform all the functions that you will want your ESB to do. They provide dynamic transformations, give you the ability to dynamically route your messages to remote services, manage any required adaptation between transport protocols, and so on.

To get started with the ESB Toolkit mediation components, you will need to understand four core components. The first two components are the generic Routing Service and the generic Transformation Service. These are often referred to as the *ESB services* or *ESB agents*. The other two mediation components are the on-ramps and off-ramps.

Before you dig into these components, you should know that although all four of them perform very different functions, there is one common design pattern to all of them. They are all designed to work with untyped messages. This may seem strange to you if you are an experienced BizTalk developer, since you likely start all of your BizTalk projects by defining very structured XSD schemas for every message you will ever receive, send, or work with. However, as we said in the introduction to this chapter, the ESB needs to be much more generic, reusable, and flexible than a traditional BizTalk solution. In order to ensure that these mediation components are as flexible as possible, you really should avoid locking them down to specific schemas. Every schema you deploy into the architecture can potentially reduce the reusability of the overall system. You should also remember that in a web services world, developers are already defining a very specific schema for each service they develop (in other words, the WSDL). The service they develop is already going to validate incoming messages against this schema. Why then do you need to duplicate this schema inside of BizTalk? You can simply let the end service be responsible for its own schema and its own validation.

Let's look at a scenario where you are using BizTalk to route messages between a client application and a web service and you are told that the web service's WSDL has just been changed. You realize that you will now need to modify the schema inside of BizTalk before it will be able to successfully route messages to this updated web service. This involves opening up the BizTalk project in Visual Studio, importing the updated WSDL into the project, recompiling the project, redeploying it, and finally restarting the host so that BizTalk will use the new version of the schema. You would have to do all of this before the client application could even begin to test the updated web service. Once testing is done, you would have to deploy this new schema from your development environment all the way back out to your production environment. This is a crazy amount of work to have to do just to make a simple change to a web service's WSDL. In this scenario, BizTalk would really be a bottleneck to the agility of the overall development team.

To avoid this crazy scenario, it makes much more sense to have an ESB that does not require a schema for every message that is going to flow through it. Instead, the ESB should treat every message simply as a black box. The only requirement that the ESB should have on the message is that it be well-structured XML. Following this design principle, you could avoid having to update BizTalk whenever web services needed to change their schema or add a new message type.

This is the pattern that all of the ESB mediation components follow (that is, generic, reusable components that are not tightly bound to any one schema). They have all been built to support generic XML messages so that they do not need to be modified when you introduce a new schema within your organization.

■Note There are certain cases where you would want the ESB to validate the structure of a message before processing it. An example of this would be a case where the ESB needs to execute a mapping. In this scenario, the map is dependent on the message having an exact structure. Therefore, it would make sense to have the ESB validate the message schema before executing the map. What you are saying here is that there are some cases where it does not make sense to validate the structure of the message, such as when the ESB only needs to provide routing capabilities for you. The issue with a traditional BizTalk project is that you had to pretty much deploy a message schema no matter what you wanted to do. What the ESB Toolkit provides is an *option*. You can decide whether it makes sense to have the ESB validate the message structure or whether it makes sense to treat the message as a black box. That is an important concept to understand. The ESB Toolkit does not represent the best or only way of architecting new BizTalk solutions. Instead, what it does is to provide you with new options for creating new types of solutions that were not easily achieved before. Ultimately, the project architects will need to look at the new tools as well as the traditional ones and determine what the best fit is.

On-Ramps and Off-Ramps

Although the ESB agents are really the heart of the ESB (since they provide the key capabilities of dynamic routing and dynamic transformation), we'll talk about the concepts of on-ramps and off-ramps first. The ESB agents have been developed as BizTalk components and thus have to reside on a BizTalk server. Since your service consumers and service providers will most likely reside on different machines than BizTalk, you need to provide some way of getting information into and out of the BizTalk server so that you can use the ESB agents. In the world of the ESB Toolkit, these entry points are *on-ramps*, and the exit points are *off-ramps*. On-ramps are responsible for the following:

- Providing a common and reusable entry point for applications to use when they want to leverage the ESB agents
- Initializing several properties associated with message that the other mediation components depend on

Now, these on-ramps and off-ramps probably will not seem like all that new of a concept to you as a BizTalk developer. You are probably thinking that you could just use BizTalk's Windows Communication Foundation (WCF) Publishing Wizard to expose a BizTalk schema as a web service. You could then configure a new BizTalk receive port to wrap this service using the WCF adapter, and, *voila*, you would now have a mechanism that most systems could use to send a message into BizTalk and thereby access ESB agents. What's the big deal? Well, we just finished saying in the previous section that the ESB components have been built to be highly reusable and loosely coupled. This means they cannot be tied directly to a specific schema. However, in the approach we just outlined, you would have exposed a web service using a schema that was already defined within BizTalk. Using this approach, you would need to expose one web service and one receive port for each message that you would ever want your ESB to receive. Imagine if your ESB needed to route messages to hundreds of different services. You would need hundreds of different web services and ports just to get the messages into BizTalk for processing. Every time you added a new service within your organization, a developer would need to build a new web service and receive port. You would quickly end up with a bloated and slow-moving environment.

When working in an SOA world, this traditional approach to exposing a typed web service is just not practical. You need a different approach that does not require you to deploy all of these distinct web services and receive ports.

What you need is a *generic* web service that would be able to accept any valid XML. This means that it will not define a detailed schema for the incoming data but rather will accept any and all XML as long as it is well formed.

Using this approach, the ESB will be able to easily accept new messages as needed without a developer having to make any change to the BizTalk environment. This also means that BizTalk administrators will have an easier job since they will have fewer ports to configure and manage.

Note that on-ramps do not represent a new component or feature within BizTalk. They are still comprosed of web services, ports, adapters, and pipelines that developers have always used. We simply use the term *on-ramp* to refer to a generic and reusable entry point into the ESB. In a later section, you will look at the actual BizTalk components that comprise these on-ramps.

Now, in a utopian and purely theoretical world, we can talk about the possibility of having just a single receive port to accept all of our messages. However, in reality, this is not going to be possible. In the most basic scenario, you are going to need to support at least two web services: one that handles one-way messages and one that provides two-way request-response messages. You also have to remember that as ubiquitous as web services are, they will never be able to handle all of your messaging needs. Many systems will need to access the ESB using MQ Series, FTP, flat files, or any number of other transport mechanisms. Therefore, in reality, ESB will need multiple on-ramps. However, as long as your on-ramps are capable of accepting generic messages without requiring a set schema, you can still dramatically reduce the number of ports that your BizTalk environment will need to support.

ESB Services

The generic Routing Service and generic Transformation Service represent the core functions that you will want to leverage right out of the box.

The generic Transformation Service does just what its name implies. It allows you to run any map that has been deployed into the BizTalk environment against your message. What makes this different from traditional BizTalk projects is that this service does not require you to specify, at design time, the name of the exact map that you want to run. Traditionally, a BizTalk developer has used a map by adding a map shape to their orchestration. Or they have specified the name of the map directly in the configuration properties for a send or receive port. The problem with both of these approaches is that only one map will ever be able to run. This is not a very dynamic or reusable solution and certainly does not fit into the overall goal of your ESB. To change this, the generic Transformation Service does not require a developer to lock in the exact name of a map at design time. Instead, it can dynamically run any map that exists within BizTalk, removing the need to specify the map name prior to runtime. This is accomplished by relying on the BizTalk APIs; doing this allows you to execute a map using code. By using these APIs, you can build a more intelligent and reusable service that is able to specify the name of the map as a parameter. This allows you to set up a single service that can be reused to handle any transformation that you need. Inside the ESB Toolkit, the Transformation Service is formally named Microsoft.Practices.ESB.Services.Transform.

■ **Note** It is important to note here that the BizTalk mapping engine does require you to have a schema deployed that defines both the incoming message structure and the outgoing message structure. The ESB Toolkit components cannot change this requirement. Therefore, although the other mediation components are built so that you do not have schemas in order to work, the generic Transformation Service still does.

Based on its name, you might think that it would be pretty easy to figure out what the generic Routing Service does. You might assume that this service handles the routing of message to remote services. However, what this service does is not quite as straightforward as that.

You have to remember that the actual transmission of a message is handled by off-ramps. What the generic Routing Service does is prepare a message so that it contains all the information required by an off-ramp. Off-ramps rely on dynamic ports to handle the actual transmission of messages. These dynamic ports work by reading a series of context properties that are attached to the message. The job of the generic Routing Service is to assign these context properties to the message so that the off-ramp can function. To do this, the generic Routing Service service must do the following:

1. Figure out which service you actually need to call.
2. Figure out where that service lives, that is, its endpoint.
3. Figure out any additional configuration information for that service. This might include the transport protocol you need to use (File, SOAP, MQ, and so on) or any IDs/passwords that need to be included.
4. Write all of this information into the context properties of the message.

Conceptually, you present the ESB services as single isolated services within the ESB. However, they are actually implemented in two different places. Both of these services exist as messaging-level services and orchestration-level services. Messaging-level services are implemented within BizTalk pipelines. Orchestration-level services are implemented as orchestrations. Both messaging and orchestration services perform exactly the same function for you. They simply give you an option of where you want the service to execute. Messaging-level services have much better performance than orchestration services. However, orchestration services can be chained together with other orchestrations. This allows you to build your own custom business processes within orchestrations while still leveraging the ESB services.

So, to summarize, the mediation components in the ESB Toolkit are composed of on-ramps, off-ramps, and the ESB services. Figure 15-2 illustrates how complex a BizTalk project can get if you use traditional BizTalk practices to integrate services.

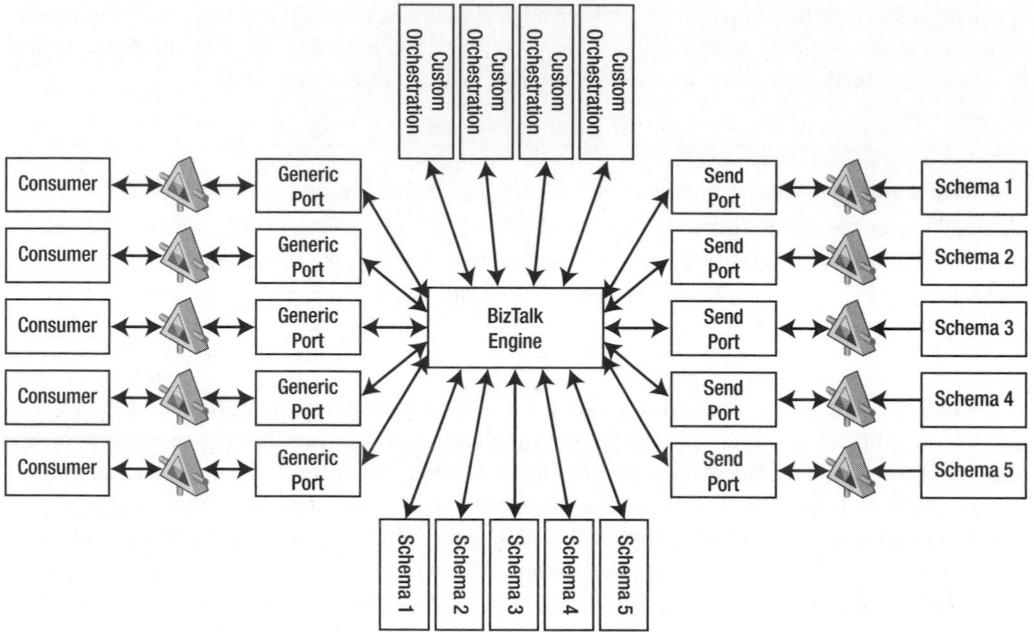

Figure 15-2. *A complex solution that can result from traditional BizTalk design patterns*

Figure 15-3 illustrates the much more generic and elegant pattern that the ESB Toolkit implements through the use of its mediation components.

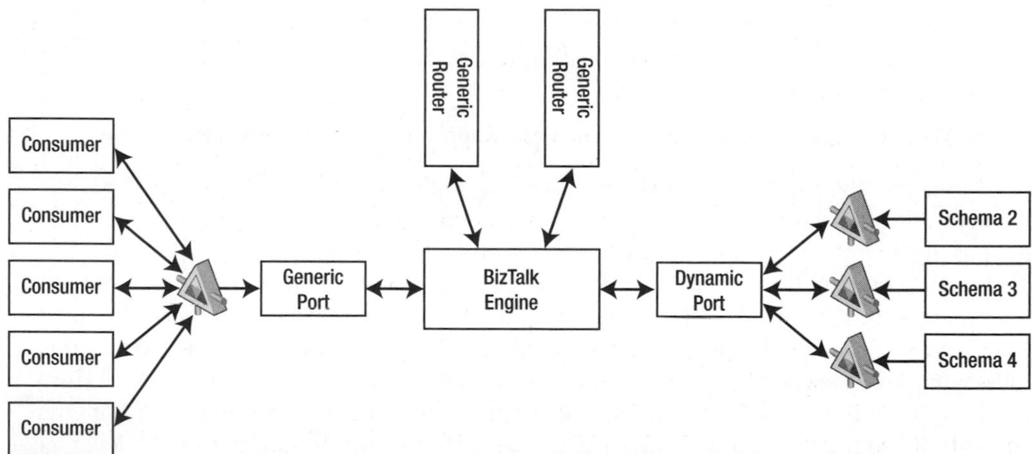

Figure 15-3. *The dramatically simplified architecture using the ESB pattern*

Note We have referred to the generic Transformation Service and generic Routing Service as *ESB services*. Some people refer to these as *ESB agents*. The terms can be used interchangeably.

Resolvers

When ESB components execute, they need to be provided with some data on how they should run. For example, the mapping service needs to know which map it should execute. Likewise, the Routing Service needs to know how it should route a particular message. Off-ramps need to know what BizTalk adapter they should use.

To build truly generic and reusable mediation components, you need to avoid hard-coding configuration parameters into these components. In an SOA, these parameters might be stored in a number of different locations (all outside of BizTalk). Service endpoint information might be stored in a centralized UDDI server or some other kind of service repository. It might be stored in a database, a rules engine, or any number of different locations. Therefore, the ESB needs to be able to interact with all of these diverse data stores at runtime in order to retrieve runtime parameters.

This is where resolvers enter the picture. The resolver mechanism can be used to retrieve runtime data from a number of different data sources using a number of different transport mechanisms. The ESB Toolkit ships with resolvers that have been prebuilt to retrieve configuration data from a specific source. An example of these prebuilt resolvers is the UDDI resolver. Many people want to use a UDDI server to store information about where their services are currently located. The UDDI resolver allows the ESB to call out the UDDI server and inquire about where a current service is currently located. The ESB can then use the information returned from the UDDI server to route the message to the service's current endpoint.

The Resolver Mechanism

As you begin to examine the resolver mechanism, you will see that it is a fairly elegant solution that is quite flexible and very extensible. As mediation components execute, they call the Resolver Manager and provide it with a resolver connection string. This connection string specifies the resolver that you want to use, and it also includes parameters that the resolver will need to use when trying to retrieve your data. The ESB Toolkit contains a number of different resolvers that all implement the `IResolveProvider` interface. Since they all implement the same interface, the Resolver Manager can instantiate any of them at any time and know that they will behave the same way. Each resolver has been built to know how to retrieve information from one specific location while still implementing the same interface as every other resolver. Figure 15-4 shows this Resolver Manager and outlines the different resolvers that the ESB Toolkit 2.0 provides.

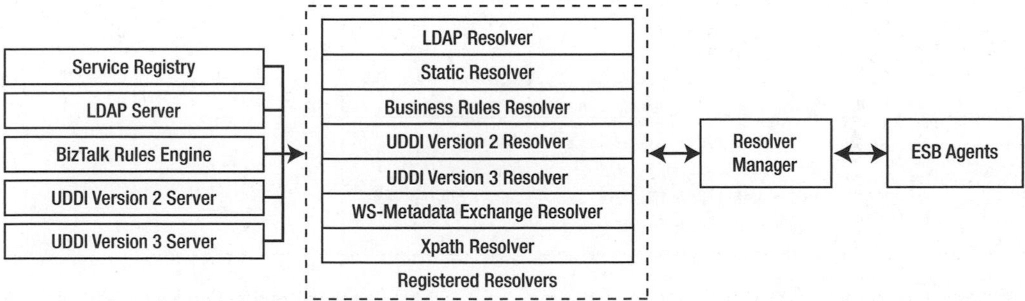

Figure 15-4. *The resolver mechanism*

When the generic Routing Service executes, you might want it to route your message to a service that is defined in a UDDI 2 server. To do this, you would need to provide the generic Routing Service with the following resolver connection string:

```
UDDI:\\ServerUrl=http://localhost/uddi;ServiceKey=;ServiceName=MySampleService;
ServiceProvider=MyServiceProvider.
```

The UDDI part of the string that proceeds the `:\\` is referred to as the *moniker*. It is this moniker that the Resolver Manager will use to determine which resolver you want to use. The remaining part of the string consists of the parameters that the UDDI resolver will need to have in order to connect to the UDDI server and retrieve information for the desired service.

The Out-of-the-Box Resolvers

The UDDI 2, UDDI 3, and WS-Metadata Exchange resolvers can be used to retrieve service information from service registries. The Business Rules resolver can be used to invoke a policy in the BizTalk Business Rule Engine. The XPath resolver can be used to retrieve information that is stored in the body of the message itself. The Static resolver is used when you want to hard-code configuration information into a mediation policy (you will learn about these shortly). The LDAP resolver is useful if you have a message that needs to be routed to a human via e-mail since you can use it to query an LDAP directory to find their current e-mail address.

The resolver framework has been designed to be incredibly reusable and extensible. Each resolver returns the data that it collects using a .NET dictionary object. This object is not tightly bound, which means you can add or remove data to/from your external data store without having to modify the resolver. To help you understand this concept, Figure 15-5 shows a screenshot from a UDDI server.

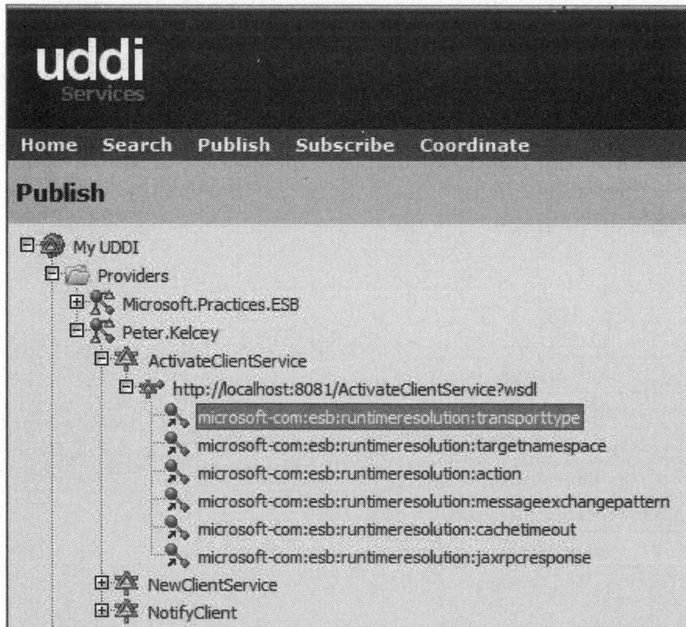

Figure 15-5. *Services registered in a UDDI server that the ESB will use*

In Figure 15-5, you can see that a number of services are registered within the Microsoft. Practices.ESB provider. You can also see that the ActivateService has nine bindings defined, whereas the OrderFileServiceWBindings service has only five bindings defined. The UDDI resolver is set up so that it will return whatever binding information it finds, no matter what the structure is of those bindings. This means that it can be used to retrieve information for both of these services. Whatever data it does find is returned in a .NET dictionary object that uses a key/value pair configuration. The resolver is not going to validate the structure of the data it retrieves; it simply retrieves it. This makes the resolver mechanism very flexible.

If you are wondering where you define these resolver connection strings, be patient just a bit longer. We'll discuss how to define resolver connection strings in the "Mediation Policies (Itineraries)" section later in this chapter.

Adapter Providers

Dynamic ports are the key component of ESB off-ramps; however, on their own they do not give you everything you need to achieve the highly reusable, generic pattern that the off-ramps should be providing. Dynamic ports read context properties from the messages that they are sending and then use the settings in these properties to configure themselves as needed.

In a traditional BizTalk project, a developer would figure out what properties needed to be set and would then assign values to them from within an orchestration or pipeline component. However, this does not work in the ESB Toolkit since a developer is not going to know what properties need to be set. This information is going to be available only at runtime after the resolver framework has executed.

You'll run into a problem when you realize that the resolver mechanism returns data using a dictionary object that send ports are not able to understand. For the send port to route your message for you, the information contained in the dictionary object must be extracted and placed into BizTalk context properties. That is what the adapter provider framework is for—to extract the data contained in the resolver's dictionary object and write it into the message's context properties so that the dynamic port can read it. Figure 15-6 shows this process.

Just like the resolver framework, the adapter provider framework follows a factory pattern. When configuration information is received from a resolver, the adapter manager reads it and determines which adapter needs to be used. Once the adapter manager figures this out, it instantiates the adapter provider associated with that adapter. If you refer to Figure 15-5, you will recall that the ActivateService service has a binding called `TransportType://WCF-BasicHTTP`. This binding is what the adapter manager uses to determine which adapter needs to be used. In this case, it is the WCF-BasicHTTP adapter.

Once the adapter manager loads the required adapter, it passes in the dictionary object and the message that needs to be sent out. Each adapter provider knows which context properties need to be set in order for a dynamic send port to use a specific adapter. The adapter provider works by extracting data from the dictionary object and writing it into the required context properties. Once it is finished, the adapter provider returns the BizTalk message, which can now be handed over to an off-ramp to be sent out.

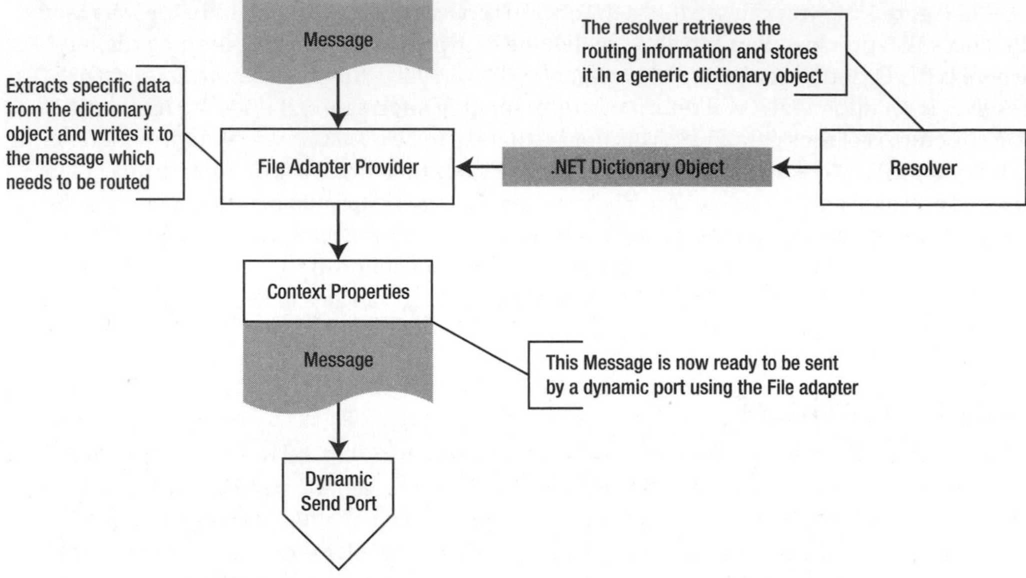

Figure 15-6. *The file adapter provider updating a message with data provided by a resolver*

Currently, the ESB Toolkit provides seven adapter providers, listed in Table 15-1.

Table 15-1. *Out-of-the-Box Adapter Providers*

Adapter Provider	Purpose
File provider	Used when you have specified a file folder as your service endpoint
Ftp provider	Used when your endpoint is an FTP site
WCF-BasicHTTP provider	Used when your endpoint is a basic web service (SOAP)
WCF-WSHTTP provider	Used when your endpoint is a web service that requires support for WS* standards
WCF-Custom provider	Used when you need to be able to modify any of the available WCF settings.
MQ provider	Used when you want to route your message to an MQSeries queue
SMTP provider	Used when your service endpoint is an e-mail address

---

■ **Note** The WCF-Custom provider can be used to connect to any of the adapters that ship as part of the BizTalk WCF LOB adapter pack. Therefore, by using the WCF-Custom provider, you can actually set up an off-ramp that uses the Oracle Database adapter, SQL Server adapter, SAP adapter, and so on.

One thing to keep in mind is that although BizTalk server ships with a large number of adapters out of the box, you will not be able to use every adapter as a dynamic ESB off-ramp. You will be able to use only those adapters that have an adapter provider available. However, you can continue to use any adapter as long as you are setting up a static or dynamic port that does not need to retrieve its configuration information using the resolver framework. In this manner, you'll see a number of developers creating hybrid solutions that use elements of the ESB Toolkit alongside traditional BizTalk practices. Of course, the ESB Toolkit consists of a very extensible framework that allows you to extend almost every feature of it. Therefore, you can easily create your own custom adapter provider if needed.

Mediation Policies (Itineraries)

So, you have seen that the ESB gives you on-ramps, off-ramps, reusable services, and resolvers to use. The next thing you need to know is how to use them. How do you hook them all together and use them to process your message?

This is where the concept of *mediation policies* comes in. Mediation policies allow you to define how your message should be processed by all of the mediation components. They also allow you to specify which resolvers should be used by each of those mediation components.

To avoid too much confusion, there is one thing that we should clear up before you proceed any further. *Mediation policy* is a conceptual term that we use when explaining the high-level architectural components within the ESB. Once we get down into the details of the ESB Toolkit, you will see that we change terminology and refer to these policies as *itineraries*. For the rest of this chapter, we will use the term *mediation policy* and *itinerary* interchangeably. Do not panic—they mean exactly the same thing. *Mediation policy* is simply the conceptual term, whereas *itinerary* is the lower-level technical term.

We have found that the best way to understand the itinerary concept is to start with a real-world scenario, so let's define one. You have a basic web application that needs to route a message to a back-end web service. This service is defined in a UDDI 3 server, and all of the details about the service's endpoint are stored in this server. Now, the data structure that the web application uses is slightly different from the structure that the web service uses.

Fortunately, the ESB already has several maps in place to handle the kind of transformation just described. However, you do not know which map is needed, so you need the ESB to use the Business Rule Engine to figure that out. Essentially, you need the ESB to transform the message and route it to the back-end service. Let's assume for this sample that this is a one-way, fire-and-forget service.

Looking at the mediation components that are in the ESB, you know that this should be straightforward to do. All you need to do is follow these steps:

1. Submit the message into the ESB by invoking the generic one-way WCF-based on-ramp.
2. Once the message is received, the ESB should automatically invoke the dynamic Transformation Service. This service will invoke the resolver mechanism that will call a policy in the Business Rule Engine in order to figure out which map should be run. The service will then invoke the resolved map.
3. Once the Transformation Service has completed, the ESB will launch the Routing Service. This service will need to invoke the resolver mechanism to call into the UDDI server to determine what the endpoint is for the web service and what its configuration is.
4. Once the Routing Service is complete, the generic one-way off-ramp should automatically pick up the message and transmit it to the web service.

What you have just defined here at a high level is a mediation policy. It defines how your message should be processed by the various mediation components and where those components should retrieve their configuration information from.

How Mediation Policies Are Implemented

In a traditional BizTalk environment, you might use an orchestration to implement the process just described. It would be fairly easy to use an orchestration to hook all of the receive and send ports together. You could add the Business Rule Engine shape to access the rules engine, drop in a map shape to execute the map, drop in an expression shape, and write .NET code to call the UDDI server. However, as we have said multiple times already, the ESB is designed to be generic and reusable. Therefore, you do not want to create a heavy custom orchestration that would be able to handle only one specific process. You also want to avoid having to modify the BizTalk environment at all if possible. This is why you are going to use a mediation policy instead of an orchestration to configure this process.

What makes a mediation policy fundamentally different from an orchestration is that it is nothing more than XML data that travels along with the message as it passes through the ESB instead of being a static artifact that is deployed into the ESB. Unlike orchestrations, mediation policies do not need to be compiled into a DLL, and they don't need to be registered in the global assembly cache or even in BizTalk. The XML is stored in the message's context properties and can be accessed by any component as the message flows through the ESB.

Before digging too far into the implementation of mediation policies, let's take a look at an actual itinerary for the scenario we just put forth. The itinerary is in the following code example. Please note that the line numbers are not part of the itinerary. We have simply added them to make it easier to refer to specific lines.

```
 1. <?xml version="1.0" encoding="utf-8"?>
 2. <Itinerary xmlns:xsi="http://www.w3.org/2001/XMLSchema-instance"
xmlns:xsd="http://www.w3.org/2001/XMLSchema" uuid="" beginTime="" completeTime=""
state="Pending" isRequestResponse="false" servicecount="0"
xmlns="http://schemas.microsoft.biztalk.practices.esb.com/itinerary">
 3. <BizTalkSegment interchangeId="" epmRRCorrelationToken="" receiveInstanceId=""
 messageId="" xmlns="" />
 4. <ServiceInstance name="Microsoft.Practices.ESB.Services.Transform"
type="Messaging"  state="Pending" position="0" isRequestResponse="false"
 xmlns="" />
 5. <Services xmlns="">
 6. <Service uuid="cfbe36c5-d85c-44e9-9549-4a7abf2106c5" beginTime=""
completeTime="" name="Microsoft.Practices.ESB.Services.Transform"
type="Messaging" state="Pending" isRequestResponse="false"
position="0" serviceInstanceId="" />
 7. </Services>
 8. <Services xmlns="">
 9. <Service uuid="6a594d80-91f7-4e10-a203-b3c999b0f55e" beginTime=""
completeTime="" name="Microsoft.Practices.ESB.Services.Routing"
type="Messaging" state="Pending" isRequestResponse="false"
position="1" serviceInstanceId="" />
```

```
10. </Services>
11. <Services xmlns="">
12. <Service uuid="0e1d2b42c9564352b6878accc290fe52" beginTime=""
completeTime="" name="DynamicOffRamp" type="Messaging"
state="Pending" isRequestResponse="false" position="2" serviceInstanceId="" />
13. </Services>
14. <ResolverGroups xmlns="">
15. <Resolvers serviceId="Microsoft.Practices.ESB.Services.Transform0">&lt;![
CDATA[BRE:\\Policy=ResolveMap;Version=1.0;UseMsg=False;]]&gt;
</Resolvers>
16. <Resolvers serviceId="Microsoft.Practices.ESB.Services.Routing1">&lt;![
CDATA[UDDI3:\\ServerUrl=http://localhost/uddi;SearchQualifiers=andAllKeys;
CategorySearch=;BindingKey=uddi:esb:orderfileservicev3.1;]]&gt;
</Resolvers>
17. <Resolvers serviceId=" DynamicOffRamp " />
18. </ResolverGroups>
19. </Itinerary>
```

Interpreting Itineraries

The XML that comprises this previous sample itinerary can look fairly scary the first time you see it. Fortunately, with version 2.0 of the ESB Toolkit, you will not need to work directly with this XML. Later in this chapter, you'll look at the tools that you can use to visually design these itineraries and avoid having to write the raw XML. We're showing you only the raw itinerary because it is important that you understand its basic structure and its basic function.

The first lines you should look at are lines 5 through 13. In these lines, you can see that we have a repeating node called `<Services>` that has a child node called `<Service>`. This `<Services>` node is where you define which services need to run and where you also define the order in which they need to run. For this example, we required three services: the Transformation Service, the Routing Service, and an off-ramp to transmit the message. This `<Service>` node requires the following structure:

```
<Services xmlns="">
<Service uuid="" beginTime="" completeTime="" name="" type="" state = ""
isRequestResponse="" position="" serviceInstanceId=""
</Services>
```

The key attributes to be aware of are `name`, `type`, `isRequestResponse`, `state`, and `position`. The `name` field is used to specify which service you want to run, that is, the map service, the Routing Service, an off-ramp, and so on. The `type` field is used to specify whether this service is a messaging-level service (meaning a pipeline will execute it) or an orchestration-level service. The `isRequestResponse` field is used to specify whether this is a one-way, fire-and-forget service or a two-way, request-response service. The `state` attribute is a marker that indicates whether this service has been processed yet by the ESB components. Its value is either `Pending` or `Complete`. Finally, the `position` field is used to define the order in which the services should run.

■ **Note** The position the services are defined in the XML has nothing to do with the order in which they are run. The itinerary mechanism uses the `position` value to determine the processing order.

On line 6 in the sample itinerary, you can see that we have specified that the dynamic mapping service should execute first. We have also said this is a one-way service and that it should be executed by the ESB at the messaging level.

On line 9, we have declared that the dynamic Routing Service should be executed by ESB next. Again, this is a one-way service that is to be implemented at the messaging level.

Finally on line 12, we have said that the one-way dynamic off-ramp name `DynamicOffRamp` should be used by the ESB to transmit the message to the remote service.

Now, the ESB components are not set up to parse through these repeating `<Services>` nodes to find out which services need to be processed. Such parsing would represent too much overhead and would certainly be a slow process.

What we really need is some kind of pointer that would contain the information for the current service that needs to be implemented. All of the ESB components could then look to this one pointer to quickly figure out what work needed to be done next. The `<ServiceInstance>` node (which is on line 4) acts as this pointer. It contains the same information that the repeating `<Service>` nodes have. The only difference is that the `<ServiceInstance>` node holds only the information for the service that currently needs to be executed. When a message is first submitted into the ESB, the `<ServiceInstance>` node will have the same values as the first `<Service>` node. Each ESB component is designed so that once it completes its unit of work (whatever it is), it calls into the itinerary mechanism and asks that the itinerary be updated. This means that the XML is updated, and the current service has its `state` attribute set to `Complete` and its `completeTime` attribute set to the current time. The attributes in the `<ServiceInstance>` node are all updated to contain the values for the next service that needs to be run. At this point, the message is essentially thrown back into the ESB infrastructure, and whatever ESB agent is required to run next will execute.

The final lines that you should look at are 14 through 18. In these lines you can see where we are actually defining the resolver connection string that we talked about in the "Resolvers" section of this chapter. These are the connection strings that the resolver framework will use for each of the ESB services that we have defined. You can identify which resolver goes with which service by looking at the `serviceId` attribute in the `<Resolvers>` node. For example, look at line 15. You will see that this `<Resolver>` node has a `serviceId` equal to `Microsoft.Practices.ESB.Services.Transform0`. This value is a concatenation of the `name` and `position` attributes from the service defined on line 6. When each ESB service runs, it looks for a resolver that has a `serviceId` matching the `name` and `position` of the currently executing service. One line 15, you can see that we have said that the mapping service should use the Business Rule Engine to determine which map to run. You can determine this since a "BRE" connection string is defined for this resolver. For each service defined in the itinerary, there is a corresponding resolver defined for it.

Based on this itinerary, the ESB components would function as follows:

1. When the message is initially received, the `<ServiceInstance>` node specifies that the ESB should run the Transformation Service first. Based on this, the Transformation Service starts up, uses the resolver to call into the rules engine, and dynamically executes a map.
2. The Transformation Service updates the itinerary and releases the message.
3. Based on the new settings in the `<ServiceInstance>` node, the Routing Service picks up the message. It uses the Resolver services to call into the UDDI server. It then uses the information from the UDDI server to enrich the message so that it contains all the information that an off-ramp would need to route this message.
4. The Routing Service updates the itinerary and releases the message.
5. Based on the new settings in the `<ServiceInstance>` node, the off-ramp picks up the message and transmits it according to the configuration that the Routing Service assigned to the message.

Figure 15-7 shows a visual representation of how this process would execute. From this example, you can see how an itinerary can link the various mediation components together for you.

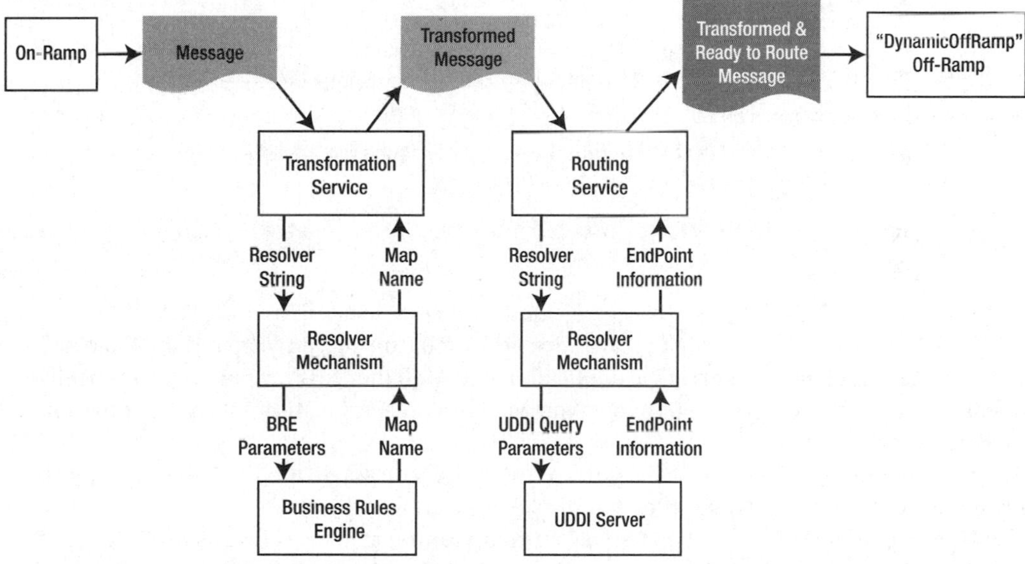

Figure 15-7. *Shows how process flows for an itinerary*

To reiterate, the great thing about this approach is that we did not need to generate any new code to do this. We did not need to modify BizTalk and did not create a static, tightly coupled orchestration. This means that if we needed to make a change to this itinerary in the future (or add a new one), we could just edit the XML, and we would not need to make any change to BizTalk or recompile any low-level code.

The Functional Components

In the previous section, you looked at the core concepts and architecture that makes up the ESB Toolkit. You have learned about mediation components, itineraries, resolvers, and adapter providers. Now we are going to start digging into the actual components that implement these concepts.

Web Services

The ESB Toolkit ships with a number of ASMX and WCF web services. We'll review the most important of those services in the following subsections.

On-Ramp Services

The ESB Toolkit has been designed so that you can use any adapter as part of your on-ramps. However, when you install the toolkit, a number of on-ramps are installed by default for you. These on-ramps are web services and rely on WCF and ASMX services that have been deployed into Internet Information Services (either version 6.0 of 7.0). These services and their default install locations are as follows:

- *A one-way ASMX web service*: Installed into `http://localhost/ESB.ItineraryServices/ProcessItinerary.asmx`
- *A two-way ASMX web service*: Installed into `http://localhost//ESB.ItineraryServices.Response/ProcessItinerary.asmx`
- *A one-way WCF web service*: Installed into `http://localhost//ESB.ItineraryServices.WCF/ProcessItinerary.svc`
- *A two-way WCF web service*: Installed into `http://localhost/ESB.ItineraryServices.Response.WCF/ProcessItinerary.svc`

Each of these four services has a corresponding receive location in BizTalk. To find these receive locations, open the BizTalk Administration Console, and expand the Microsoft.Practices.ESB application. This is the application where all the ESB components have been installed. In the Receive Locations folder, you will see a receive location set up around each of these web services.

You use one-way services if you simply want to fire a message into the ESB without waiting for a response. Two-way services are for request-response scenarios.

If you open the WSDL for the one-way on-ramp (found at `http://localhost/ESB.ItineraryServices/ProcessItinerary.asmx`), you should notice two things. First, you should look at the `SubmitRequest` operation that is defined. A section of the WSDL that defines this operation is shown here:

```
<SubmitRequest xmlns="http://microsoft.practices.esb">
    <Root xmlns="http://schemas.microsoft.com/BizTalk/2003/Any">xml</Root>
</SubmitRequest>
```

`SubmitRequest` is the method you will use to submit a one-way message into the ESB, and it is expecting a single parameter (defined by the `Root` node). As you can see, the `Root` node is defined using the Any type. The Any type allows you to submit any valid XML. This aligns with our goal of setting up a generic on-ramp that will receive multiple messages.

The second thing that you should notice within the WSDL is the <soap:Header> node. This node has a number of elements that are designed to contain an itinerary for the message that you are submitting. To submit a message to this web service, you need to include the message itself and also include itinerary information into the SOAP headers.

The Transformation Web Service

Throughout this chapter, we have presented the ESB Toolkit somewhat as a "whole"—a fully functional solution that has multiple parts that all work together to achieve the ESB vision. However, many of the components within the ESB Toolkit can be used completely on their own. One of these components is the Transformation Service, which exposes BizTalk's underlying mapping engine.

There are many times and situations where someone might want to use BizTalk's mapping engine only without having to worry about the rest of the BizTalk or ESB components. If all you want to do is transform some data, then why would you care about on-ramps, resolvers, itineraries, and so on? In fact, it would be really nice to be able to invoke the mapping engine directly, and it would be really nice to avoid having to post a message into BizTalk's Messagebox.

Interestingly enough, it is entirely possible to invoke the mapping engine directly. BizTalk's mapping engine can be called directly via its APIs, so there is no reason why you cannot expose a web service that exposes these APIs to other applications. The Transformation Service that ships with the ESB Toolkit does precisely that. You can use this web service to access the BizTalk mapping engine directly in memory without having to submit a message into BizTalk at all. There is then no need for a receive port and no need for the message to be submitted into the Messagebox.

The Transformation Service is exposed as a basic ASMX web service and as a WCF service. On a default install of the ESB Toolkit, these services will be located at http://localhost/ESB.TransformServices/TransformationService.asmx and http://localhost/ESB.ResolverServices.WCF/ResolverService.svc, respectively.

The ASMX version of the service exposes the following WSDL:

```
<soap:Envelope xmlns:xsi=http://www.w3.org/2001/XMLSchema-instance
 xmlns:xsd="http://www.w3.org/2001/XMLSchema"
xmlns:soap="http://schemas.xmlsoap.org/soap/envelope/">
  <soap:Body>
    <Transform xmlns="http://Microsoft.Practices.ESB.TransformServices/">
      <message>string</message>
      <mapName>string</mapName>
    </Transform>
  </soap:Body>
</soap:Envelope>
```

You can see from this WSDL that the service accepts two parameters, message and mapName. To execute a map, you simply pass in your message as a string in the first parameter while including the fully qualified name of the BizTalk map in the other. The transformed message will be returned as a string.

You also have the option of invoking a WCF service, which does the same thing as the ASMX-based service. The following code outlines how you can call the WCF-based service to perform a simple transformation. In this example you pass in a string (containing the data you want transformed) and the name of the BizTalk map that you want to execute to the `client.Transform()` function. The transformed message is returned as a string.

```
private string  CallTransformService(string inputText)
{
   try
      {
         string sOutput;

         //Create a new instance of the service client
         TransformationServiceClient client = new TransformationServiceClient();

         //Use a fully qualified map name as defined in BizTalk
         string sMap = "GlobalBank.ESB.TransformServices.Maps.
         CanonicalOrder_To_OrderConfirmation,GlobalBank.ESB.
         TransformServices.Maps, Version=1.0.0.0, Culture=neutral,
          PublicKeyToken=c2c8b2b87f54180a";

         sOutput = client.Transform(inputText, sMap);

         client.Close();

         return sOutput;
      }
      catch (Exception ex)
      {
            // Handle Exception
      }
}
```

The Resolver Service

When we introduced the resolver concept earlier in the chapter, we said that resolvers are invoked by ESB services when they need to retrieve their configuration information. However, ESB services are not the only components that can access the resolver mechanism. Any application can access the resolver mechanism using the Resolver service. Like most of the ESB web services, there are ASMX and WCF versions of this service.

In a default installation, the ASMX version is located at http://localhost/ESB.ResolverServices/Resolverservice.asmx, and the WCF version is located at http://localhost/ESB.ResolverServices.WCF/ResolverService.svc.

We are not going to dive too deeply into the Resolver service other than to say that it exists and the ESB Toolkit contains a detailed example on how to use it if you are interested in learning more. You can find this example at C:\Projects\Microsoft.Practices.ESB\Source\Samples\ResolverService if you have installed the toolkit to the default location.

The one thing that you should be aware of is that the Itinerary Designer (which you will be introduced to later in the chapter) relies on this service. The designer uses it to test resolvers that you have configured in your itineraries, and it allows you to see the data that one of your resolver will return once it is put into the live ESB environment. This is an incredibly handy tool for you to have as you are designing and debugging itineraries.

Schemas

We have mentioned several times that the ESB components do not rely on schemas to define the structure of the messages they are processing. However, there are in fact some schemas used in the ESB Toolkit for other reasons. System-Properties.xsd is a property schema that defines a list of context properties that are used extensively through the ESB. For sake of simplicity, we will refer to all of these properties collectively as the ESB *context properties*, and Table 15-2 describes each of them. The properties are critical to understand because they form the backbone for how messages are passed between the ESB components inside of BizTalk.

Table 15-2. *ESB-Specific Context Properties*

Property	Description
`ServiceName`	This is a string that holds the name of the current service that needs to process the message next.
`ServiceState`	This is a string that holds the state of the current service. It is either `Pending` or `Complete`.
`IsRequestResponse`	This is a Boolean that indicates whether the current service is a two-way or one-way service. `True` indicates a two-way service.
`ServiceType`	This is a string that indicates whether the current service should be processed by a messaging component or an orchestration.
`ItineraryHeader`	This is a string that holds a copy of the entire itinerary.
`CurrentServicePosition`	This is an integer that indicates which position the current service holds within the overall itinerary (this is, is it the first service, second service, and so on).

The first property to look at is `ItineraryHeader`. This property will hold the itinerary that is associated with this message for the entire time that the message is inside of BizTalk.

If you remember back to the "Mediation Policies (Itineraries)" section of this chapter where you looked at an actual itinerary, you'll remember that you saw an XML node named `<Service>`. This node has a number of attributes that we said you should be aware of: `name`, `type`, `isRequestResponse`, `state`, and `position`. Looking at these, you can see that they line up fairly closely to the context properties defined in System-Properties.xsd. This is no coincidence. The `ItineraryHeader` property is used to hold the entire raw XML of the itinerary. However, BizTalk components are not really set up to work with raw XML. Therefore, key data from the itinerary is extracted and placed into the other ESB context properties so that the BizTalk components can easily access it. By moving this information into context properties, it allows you to route your message between the various ESB services using BizTalk's publish and subscribe mechanism.

In the "Mediation Policies (Itineraries)" section, we also mentioned that when each ESB Service completes its unit of work, it asks the `ItineraryHelper` component to *update* the itinerary and to identify the next service that needed to be executed. What we did not mention is that when this next service is found, its corresponding XML data is written to the message's ESB context properties, and the old values are overwritten.

This idea that pieces of the larger itinerary are continually being extracted and stored within the message's context properties is important to grasp if you are going to understand how the overall itinerary processing mechanism works. The raw itinerary is always stored in the message's `ItineraryHeader` property and can be accessed at any time if needed. As a message flows into the ESB, data from this XML-based itinerary is extracted and inserted into specific context properties. BizTalk's publish and subscribe mechanism then routes the message to whichever ESB component has a subscription that matches the values contained in the context properties. As each ESB component completes, it updates the itinerary. Updating the itinerary involves retrieving the next service from the overall itinerary and writing its information into the context properties (thereby overwriting the old values). Once the context properties are updated, the newly modified message is dropped back into the BizTalk Messagebox, and the publish and subscribe mechanism runs and again routes the message to an ESB service. This process continues until all of the services in the itinerary have been completed.

The process we've just described is how messages are routed through the ESB and across the ESB services. This process provides you with a mechanism for loosely coupling together ESB services and ESB components at runtime.

One point to note is that components inside the ESB define subscriptions to messages based on these properties and *only* these properties. As you begin to use the ESB Toolkit, you are going to want to create your own orchestrations or send port to extend it, and you must make sure that you follow this principle so that your new components will play nicely with the out-of-the-box ones.

The Itinerary Database

Not long after a developer creates their first itinerary, they will likely start to wonder about how they can version, store, and manage it. If you have a large ESB environment, it might potentially have to process thousands of messages and use hundreds of different itineraries. In this scenario, you will obviously need a proper mechanism for managing itineraries. To address this need, the ESB Toolkit ships with an Itinerary Database that runs within SQL Server (both SQL Server 2005 and 2008 are supported). This database is named EsbItineraryDb and has one key table named Itinerary. It allows you to version your itineraries (both major and minor versions) as well as to define a name and description for the itinerary.

The Itinerary Database serves two purposes:

- It gives developers a managed repository to store their itineraries in.
- It acts as a runtime repository that the on-ramps can use to retrieve itineraries as messages flow into the ESB.

The first purpose will be examined in more detail in the "Working with Itineraries" section later in this chapter, where you will see how you can export itineraries from Visual Studio 2008 directly into this database. The second purpose will become clearer when you review the ESB Itinerary Selector pipeline component. For now, it is enough for you to know that the ESB provides a database for you to store and access itineraries as needed at both design time and runtime.

With regard to high availability and disaster recovery of this database, you can simply use SQL Server's built-in capabilities. This is not a BizTalk database. It is a stand-alone basic SQL Server database. You can use standard clustering to provide high availability for this database, and you can use SQL Server's built-in backup features within your disaster recovery plans.

ItineraryHelper

ESB *itineraries* are simply raw XML. Working with raw XML can be a pain, but ESB components need to interact with itineraries routinely in order to function. They need to retrieve information from them, update them, and validate them. Therefore, in order to avoid the pain of having to access this XML directly, the ESB Toolkit contains a component called ItineraryHelper. This component acts as a .NET wrapper to the underlying XML and prevents you from having to touch it directly. Although you might never need to call this component directly, it is used by most of the core ESB components. Therefore, we have included this brief section about it so that you have some concept of it when it is mentioned. Also, if you plan to develop your own components to extend the ESB Toolkit or if you want to build a new orchestration to perform some custom business logic, then you will need to understand how to use this component.

The ItineraryHelper component provides the following methods:

`AdvanceItinerary`: This method takes a single parameter that is a reference to a message, and it advances the itinerary by one step. It populates the service instance with the properties of the service for the next step, marks the current service as completed, sets the time stamp, and updates other relevant ESB context properties.

`CurrentStep`: This method takes a reference to a message, and it returns an instance of the `ItineraryStep` class for the current step. It also changes the state of the current service instance from `Pending` to `Active` and sets the `BeginTime` property.

`GetItineraryHeader`: This method retrieves the value of the itinerary property from the BizTalk message context. It gives you back the entire raw XML representing the itinerary.

`GetResolvers`: This method returns a typed collection of resolvers as a `ResolverCollection` instance, populated by parsing the itinerary.

`GetServiceResolversXML`: This method returns an XML string that represents the resolvers associated with a specific service located at specific position within the itinerary.

`ProcessItinerary`: This method takes a single parameter (a reference to a message), reads the itinerary, and writes it to a custom BizTalk context property in the message for future retrieval.

`ValidateItinerary`: This method takes as its single parameter a reference to a message, sets the default values of the `Itinerary` context property within the message, removes any values that should not be set, and updates the Itinerary property.

In an orchestration, you can use this component to retrieve the current service for a message by using the following code:

```
// Retrieve the current itinerary step
itineraryStep = Microsoft.Practices.ESB.Itinerary.ItineraryHelper.CurrentStep(➥
InMessage);
```

You could also update a message's itinerary by using the following code:

```
// Call the Itinerary helper to advance to the next step
Microsoft.Practices.ESB.Itinerary.ItineraryHelper.AdvanceItinerary(OutMessage, ➥
itineraryStep);
```

■ **Note** This code is assuming that your incoming message and outgoing message are named `InMessage` and `OutMessage`, respectively. If you have different message names, you will need to use them instead.

Pipeline Components

Pipelines play an incredibly important role in the ESB. Beyond the standard BizTalk pipeline components, eight new components come with the ESB Toolkit. It is critical to understand what they do and how they work.

ESB Itinerary Component

Some of the web services used within the default ESB on-ramps allow you to submit both a message and its itinerary at the same time. For these services, you are able pass in the itinerary within the SOAP headers (if you are using the ASMX web service) or the WCF headers (if you are using the WCF-based service). What the ESB Itinerary component does is extract the itinerary information from these SOAP or WCF headers and convert it into the format that BizTalk requires. Essentially, it reads the incoming itinerary, validates that it is in the proper format, and then writes it as raw XML into the message's `ItineraryHeader` context property.

You should note that this component is needed only if the web service within your on-ramp allows you to submit an itinerary along with the message. If you want the ESB to determine what itinerary your message should have, then you will need to use the ESB Itinerary Selector pipeline component.

In the default installation of the ESB Toolkit, there are four on-ramps that use this component, and these can all be found in the Receive Locations folder within the Microsoft.Practices.ESB BizTalk application. In this folder you will find the OnRamp.Itinerary.WCF, OnRamp.Itinerary.SOAP, OnRamp.Itinerary.Response.WCF, and OnRamp.Itinerary.SOAP receive locations. All four of these locations use the ItineraryReceiveXML receive pipeline, which contains the ESB Itinerary component. This is because all four of these receive locations are tied to an ASMX or WCF service that allows the itinerary to be submitted along with the message.

ESB Itinerary Selector Component

In version 1.0 of the toolkit (or *Toolkit* as it was referred to in that version), on-ramps required you to pass in a valid itinerary along with the message that the ESB needed to process. This was a problem for many people since they thought that the ESB should be responsible for figuring out which itineraries needed to be used for incoming messages. They also thought that they did not want the end user to have to worry about itineraries and that the ESB should abstract this entire concept from the client application.

In version 2.0, you no longer have this issue because the on-ramp no longer requires you to submit an itinerary along with your message. You can simply submit your message into the ESB without any knowledge of itineraries at all.

However, the ESB components are still designed to process messages based on itineraries. So, you need some way to attach an itinerary to a message after it has been submitted into the ESB. The ESB Itinerary Selector component gives you this capability. It is a receive pipeline that allows you to do the following:

- Use the resolver framework to figure out what itinerary an incoming message should have
- Load that itinerary from the itinerary database
- Attach the itinerary to the incoming message
- Initialize all of the ESB context properties based on the data inside the itinerary so that the ESB components can begin processing the message

Figure 15-8 shows this process and the components involved. You can see in this image that the ESB Itinerary Selector component starts by passing a resolver connection string to the Resolver Manager. This in turn executes either the Static or Business Rules resolver, which provides an itinerary name (and version number). The ESB Itinerary Selector component then uses this name and version information to load the requested itinerary from the Itinerary Database.

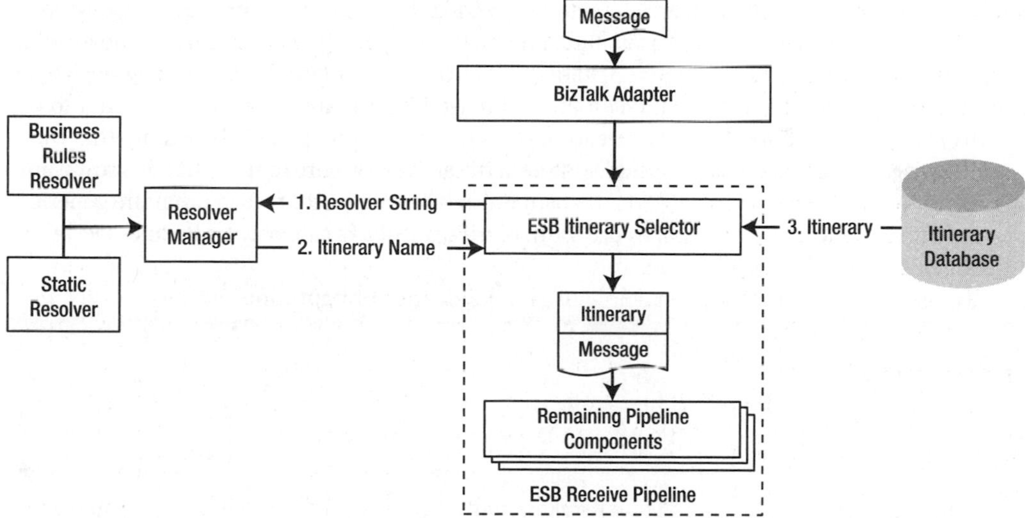

Figure 15-8. *The mechanism behind the ESB Itinerary Selector component*

With the ESB Itinerary Selector, two resolvers are available to determine the name of the itinerary you need to load: the Static resolver and Business Rules resolver. Both of these resolvers work the same way that the mapping and endpoint resolvers do. You provide a resolver connection string that the Resolver Manager uses to figure out what resolver you want. This resolver is then called, and it returns an itinerary name based on the parameters you provided in the connection string.

As you can see in Figure 15-9, the properties for ESB Itinerary Selector component can be set using the Configure Pipeline dialog box in the BizTalk Administration Console.

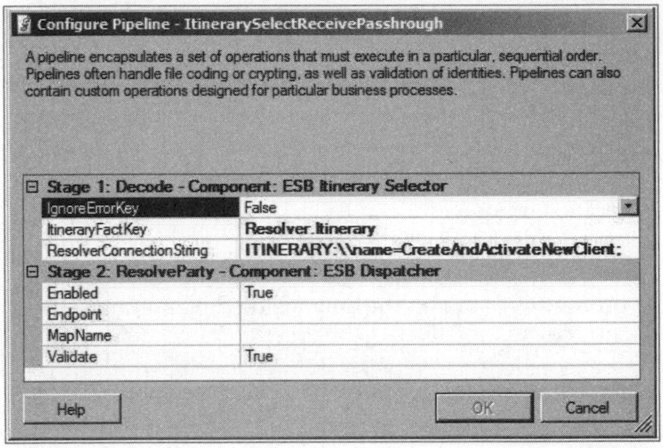

Figure 15-9. *The configure screen for a pipeline using the ESB Itinerary Selector component*

The Static resolver is very basic and simply allows you to hard-code the name of the itinerary that you want. The need to hard-code the name does not give you a very flexible solution since it means that you would need to create a separate receive port for every itinerary that you need to resolve. Therefore, the Business Rule Engine Itinerary (BRI) resolver is by far the more useful and valuable one for you to use. It allows you to invoke a policy in the rules engine, which is able to dynamically figure out which itinerary you need. This pattern aligns much better to the overall design goals for the ESB and allows you to create a truly "generic" on-ramp that can handle multiple messages using multiple different itineraries. Be sure to note that this resolver is referred to as the *BRI resolver* in order to distinguish it from the BRE resolver that the generic routing and generic mapping services use. Both of these resolvers call into the Business Rule Engine, but for very different reasons.

To use the Static resolver, you would use the following configuration settings:

```
IgnoreErrorKey = False
ItineraryKeyFact = Resolver.Itinerary
ResolverConnectionString = ITINERARY:\\name=YourItineraryName;
```

You will need to replace `YourItineraryName` with the name of the itinerary that you want to load from the database.

To use the BRI resolver, you can use the following configuration settings:

```
IgnoreErrorKey = False
ItineraryKeyFact = Resolver.Itinerary
ResolverConnectionString = BRI:\\policy=MyPolicy;version=1.1;useMsg=True;
```

You will need to replace the `MyPolicy` and `1.1` values with ones that match the policy you have deployed in your rules engine. Optionally, you can leave the version parameter empty so that you do not have to update this configuration string every time you deploy a new version of the policy.

Using the ResolverConnectingString we provided earlier, the BRI resolver passes only the message's context properties into the rules engine. This means that your policy will be able to determine only which itinerary to use based on these properties. If you want to use content from the body of the message to make these decisions, then you would need to set the `useMsg` property to `True`. Doing that instructs the BRI resolver to submit the message body as well as the context properties into the invoked policy.

If you want to see an example of an on-ramp that uses this component, you can find one in the Microsoft.Practices.ESB BizTalk application. If you expand the Receive Locations folder, you will find a receive location named OnRamp.Itinerary.Generic.WCF. If you open this receive location, you will see that it uses the ItinerarySelectReceive pipeline. One of the components within this pipeline is the ESB Itinerary Selector component.

Note The ESB Itinerary Selector component will try to use the name that the resolver returns to load an itinerary from the itinerary database. Therefore, you need to ensure that the itinerary the resolver returns actually exists in the database.

ESB Dispatcher Component

The Dispatcher is a critical component to understand in order to use the ESB. In itineraries, you can specify a number of services that you want to execute and specify whether they should be processed by the ESB at the messaging level or at the orchestration level. Messaging-level services are executed in pipelines, and it is the Dispatcher component that executes them. The Dispatcher component can be used in any stage of both receive and send pipelines.

In the default ESB pipelines, the Dispatcher runs after the ESB Itinerary or the ESB Itinerary Selector component has executed. By the time one of these two components has run, the message will have a valid itinerary that needs to be processed. It is at this point that the Dispatcher takes over. It starts by examining the message's itinerary to find out what current itinerary service is. If the service is a messaging-level service and it is either the Transformation Service or Routing Service, then the Dispatcher will execute it. If the Transformation Service is specified, the Dispatcher will call the resolver mechanism to figure out what map needs to be run, and then it will execute it. If the Routing Service is specified, then the Dispatcher also calls the resolver mechanism, but this time it asks it to figure out where the service needs to be routed to. The resolver will return a list of data that can be used to configure a dynamic send port.

When the Dispatcher has finished executing this initial service, it calls into the Itinerary-Helper component and asks it to update the message's itinerary. This component updates the itinerary XML, marks the current service as complete, and then updates the other ESB context properties to indicate that the next service in the itinerary is now the current one.

Once this update is complete, the Dispatcher will "loop" and begin this process all over again. It will check to see what the new "current" service is, and if it is a messaging-level service, it will attempt to execute it. This loop continues until all of the services in the itinerary have been completed or until a service is found that the Dispatcher cannot process. This could be because a service has been requested that the Dispatcher does not understand, or an orchestration-level service has been requested. Once the Dispatcher is finished, the message is passed into any remaining pipeline components and finally published into the BizTalk Messagebox. When you use the Dispatcher component, you will see that it has six properties that can be set using the BizTalk management console. Table 15-3 describes each of them.

Table 15-3. *Dispatcher Pipeline Properties*

Property	Description
`Enabled`	You can enable or disable the Dispatcher by using this component. It accepts either `True` or `False`.
`Endpoint`	You can specify a resolver connection string here to resolve an endpoint service to route the message to. You would use this property if your message does not have an itinerary.
`Validate`	You use this to indicate whether you want the Dispatcher to validate the incoming message against a schema before executing a map. This accepts either `True` or `False`. By default this is set to `True`.
`RoutingServiceName`	This property holds the name of the messaging-level Routing Service so that the dispatcher can call it. The default value for this is Microsoft.Practices.ESB.Services.Routing, and you should not change it unless you plan to override the default behavior of the dispatcher by providing your own version of the Routing Service.
`TransformationServiceName`	This property holds the name of the messaging-level Transformation Service so that the dispatcher can call it. The default value for this is Microsoft.Practices.ESB.Services.Transform, and you should not change it unless you plan to override the default behavior of the dispatcher by providing your own version of the Transformation Service.
`MapName`	You can specify a resolver connection string here to resolve a map to run in the Dispatcher. You would use this property if your message does not have an itinerary.

The `Endpoint` and `MapName` properties might be confusing since this information is already defined in the message's itinerary. Why then would you need to enter this into the pipeline component as well?

The key thing to remember is that all of the ESB Toolkit components have been designed to be as flexible and reusable as possible. The design team realized that you might want to be able to use the Dispatcher without having to add the extra overhead associated with itineraries. Therefore, they designed the Dispatcher so that it could handle some basic routing and mapping capabilities entirely on its own without the need for any itinerary. That is why the `Endpoint` and `MapName` properties have been added. You can place resolver strings into these properties and use the resolver mechanism to determine which map to run or service to route to. The Dispatcher can use this information to run the dynamic mapping service and/or Routing Service once per incoming message. If you want to do anything more complex than this, then you will need an itinerary. The ESB Toolkit ships with a sample named

DynamicResolution that shows you how to implement this scenario. This sample project also includes a pipeline named ESBReceiveXML that contains only the ESB Dispatcher component and not the ESB Itinerary or ESB Itinerary Selector components.

ESB Dispatcher Disassembler Component

The ESB Dispatcher Disassembler Component works the same way that the ESB Dispatcher component does. It is designed to execute messaging-level services. The only difference between it and the ESB Dispatcher is that it combines the BizTalk message debatching functionality. This component inherits from the XSML disassembler class `XmlDasmComp`. You would use this component if you wanted to debatch an incoming XML message before dispatching the individual messages.

ESB Itinerary Cache Component

The difference between on-ramps and off-ramps seems fairly easy to grasp. On-ramps are used to receive message into the ESB, and off-ramps are used to send messages out of the ESB. However, these nice clean lines get blurred when you start using two-way solicit/response send ports in our off-ramps. When a two-way send port receives the response message back from the remote service, it is actually acting as an on-ramp. This presents an interesting design challenge. A message's itinerary is stored in the message's own context properties for the entire time that it is in BizTalk. However, when a message is sent out through a send port, the context properties are dropped, and the message no longer has any concept of the overall itinerary that it is part of. When a response message comes back into the ESB via the solicit-response port, it will not have any concept of the original itinerary either. If the original itinerary contained more services that needed to be executed after this one, then you need some way to associate this response message back to the original itinerary. This issue is solved by the ESB Itinerary Cache component.

The Itinerary Cache component can be used in both receive and send pipelines. However, as shown in Figure 15-10, it performs a very different function based on which one it is used in. When the ESB Itinerary Cache component is used in a send pipeline, it stores a copy of the outgoing message's itinerary into the itinerary cache. When the component is used in a receive pipeline, it extracts the itinerary out of the cache and adds it back to the incoming message.

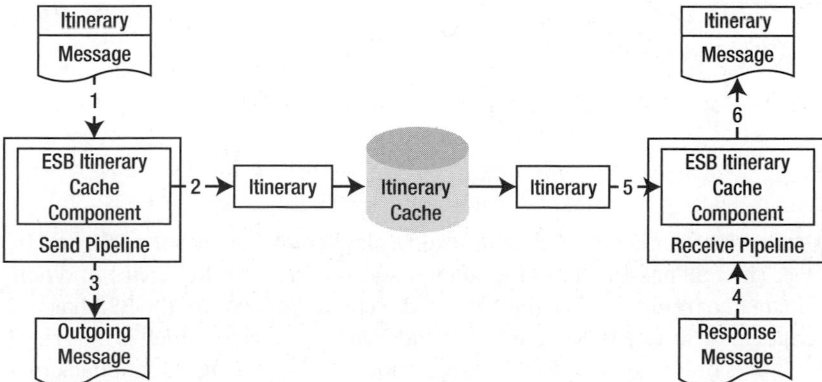

Figure 15-10. *A logical view of how the Itinerary Cache component functions*

If the component is part of a send pipeline, then its job is to save a copy of the outgoing message's itinerary into the itinerary cache. If the component is part of a receive pipeline, then its job is to check and see whether the message has an associated itinerary stored in the cache. If an itinerary does exist, it is stored back in the message's context properties. Once this is done, the other ESB components can continue to process the message and complete any remaining services defined in the itinerary. You might be thinking that this looks an awful lot like correlation. However, be aware that this does not use BizTalk's built-in correlation capabilities. This entire mechanism is implemented in .NET components that were created new for the ESB Toolkit.

One of the most common questions that we get from BizTalk developers when it comes to the ESB Toolkit is about the Itinerary Cache mechanism. Many people are worried about its impact on performance and high availability for the underlying BizTalk environment. In Figure 15-10 the itinerary cache is represented as a database. However, the Itinerary Cache is actually built using the Enterprise Library's caching block. This means that you can implement this cache using any of the library's built-in options. These options include (but are not limited to) the following:

- In-memory (the fastest option, but it's prone to data loss in the case of a system failure)
- IsolatedStorage (disaster tolerant, but it's slower than In-memory)
- Database (slower than In-memory, but it's the most robust)

To set up high availability for the itinerary cache, you will need to familiarize yourself with the Enterprise Library and its capabilities.

Forwarder Component

A key capability for an ESB is the ability to enable service composition and service chaining. In the world of web services, you might want to take the output of one service and forward it into another service. Figure 15-11 outlines a scenario where the ESB is composing messages across three different web services.

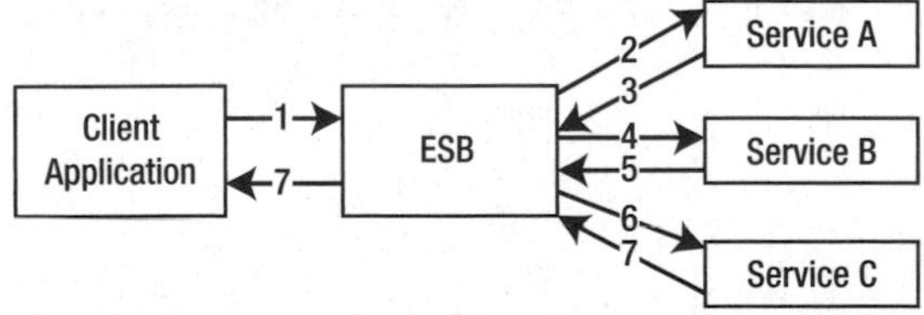

Figure 15-11. *A simple scenario for service composition*

In this scenario, the client application has submitted a single message into the ESB and is waiting for a response. The ESB has taken this initial message and routed it to Service A. When Service A responds, instead of returning this message to the client application, the ESB has forwarded this message on to Service B. Service B responds with a message, which is in turn forwarded to Service C. It is only after Service C has responded that a message is sent back to the original client.

In BizTalk, this type of scenario has always been implemented using orchestrations. However, now that we have the concept of itineraries, it would be highly preferable to use them to implement this process. Itineraries do not carry the same performance overhead as orchestrations often do, and as we have already discussed, they are easier to change if necessary.

BizTalk has always been able to support the first part of this process by requiring an orchestration (that is, steps 1, 2, 3, and 7 where the client application calls Service A, which responds to the client). This can be done using a two-way receive port, a two-way send port, and dynamic subscriptions. When a message enters BizTalk through the two-way receive port, it is routed to the two-way send port. At this point, BizTalk creates a dynamic subscription for the message that will eventually return from the send port and be routed to the original receive port. It is this functionality that causes a problem for the ESB components. If you allow this default functionality to occur, the client application will receive a response back after step 3 (as shown in the diagram) instead of after step 7.

The Forwarder component solves this problem for you. It functions by intercepting the response message that is coming back from the first web service, and it allows you to redirect it to another ESB service or another off-ramp. With this component, you can now compose multiple external services together without the need for an orchestration, and it allows you to create much more complex and useful itineraries.

So, look again at Figure 15-11; messages 3 and 5 would need to be processed by a receive pipeline that contained the Forwarder component. Message 7 would need to be processed by a send port that did not contain the Forwarder component. So when configuring your ESB environment, you will need to set up multiple off-ramps to support these two scenarios.

The Forwarder component can be added to the Decode, Validate, or PartyResolver stages in a pipeline, and it does not contain any configurable properties. To use the component, you simply need to add it to your pipeline (or use a pipeline that already contains it).

ESB Add and Remove Namespace Components

It is not uncommon in many organizations to have XML documents without namespaces. Since traditional BizTalk components require namespaces in order to process XML documents, you have a disconnect. Because most organizations will not want to modify their XML documents just to appease BizTalk, the ESB Add Namespace and Remove Namespace components were developed. These components allow you to add root namespaces to incoming documents and remove a namespace as the document leaves BizTalk. They can be added to any stage of a receive or send pipeline.

The Add Namespace and Remove Namespace components are not fundamentally tied to any other component in the ESB Toolkit. In fact, they are not really even related to the ESB concepts that you have been looking at. They simply solve a logistical problem for you. They have great value even to traditional non-ESB BizTalk projects, and you can extract them from the toolkit and use them completely on their own.

Since these components are not really critical in order to implement the ESB pattern that you are looking at in this chapter, this chapter will go any deeper into them. If you are interested in using them, then you should reference the Namespace sample that ships with the ESB Toolkit. You can find it in the Samples folder.

Component Summary

In this section, you have looked at the new pipeline components that are included in the ESB Toolkit. Table 15-4 reviews these components and their uses.

Table 15-4. *Pipeline Components and Their Purposes*

Pipeline	Purpose
ESB Itinerary Selector	Used to resolve an itinerary for an incoming message, load that itinerary from the itinerary database, and store the itinerary in the `ItineraryHeader` context property.
ESB Dispatcher	Processes messaging-level services specified in the itinerary including the Transformation Service and Routing Service.
ESB Dispatcher Disassembler	Implements the same functionality as the Dispatcher component but includes support for XML disassembly and debatching of incoming messages.
ESB Itinerary	Used to initialize an incoming message that was received from an on-ramp that also accepted the message itinerary.
ESB Forwarder	Used when a receive port needs to intercept the incoming message are resend it back out to another external service.
ESB Itinerary Cache	In a send pipeline, it stores a message's itinerary to the cache. In a receive pipeline, it retrieves a message's itinerary from the cache.
ESB Add Namespace	Used to add a namespace to a message entering BizTalk.
ESB Remove Namespace	Used to remove a namespace from a message leaving BizTalk.

Pipelines

You can use any and all of the ESB pipeline components to build your own custom pipelines. However, the ESB Toolkit comes with 12 preconfigured pipelines already (well, 13 if you count the ESB Fault Processor pipeline, but you are not going to count that one as part of the core ESB Toolkit since it really is part of the Exception Management Framework, which is covered in another chapter).

The Receive Pipelines

ItineraryReceive, ItineraryReceivePassthrough, and ItineraryReceiveXML are receive pipelines first shipped with version 1.0. They are designed to be used when you are using a SOAP-based on-ramp (that is, the ASPX web service or WCF service) that allows the external application to send in an itinerary along with their message. In these scenarios, the itinerary is added into the SOAP headers or WCF headers as part of the service call. These three pipelines look into these headers to extract the itinerary. They also all contain the ESB Dispatcher component to process the itinerary once it is extracted. You should decide which one to use based on the type of message you are submitting. The ItineraryReceive pipeline is used if you are going to be receiving XML that needs to be disassembled. The ItineraryReceivePassthrough pipeline can be used if your message is not XML or you do not want to disassemble the XML. You should use the ItineraryReceiveXml pipeline if you are receiving XML and you want to use the ESB Dispatcher Disassembler.

When creating two-way solicit-response ports, you need to be careful that you do not accidentally use one of these three pipelines as your receive pipeline. These pipelines will show up in the drop-down list of available pipelines, but they are not designed to work as part of a send port. They are to be used only as part of a receive port.

ItinerarySelectReceive, ItineraryReceivePassthrough, and ItinerarySelectReceiveXml perform pretty much similar functions as the last three pipelines except that they all include the ESB Itinerary Selector component. Therefore, you should use these pipelines if you need to resolve an itinerary for your incoming message.

ItinerarySendReceive and ItinerarySelectSendReceive are receive pipelines, but they are designed to be used only within a dynamic two-way solicit-response send port. You should not try to use them as part of a receive port. The ItinerarySendReceive pipeline functions much the same way as the ItineraryReceive, except that it contains the ESB Itinerary Cache component. Likewise, the ItinerarySelectSendReceive pipeline functions in much the same way as the ItinerarySelectReceive pipeline does except with the addition of the ESB Itinerary Cache component.

ItineraryForwarderSendReceive and ItineraryForwarderSendReceiveXml are designed to be used as receive pipelines in two-way solicit response ports. They contain the Forwarder component, so they are intended for ports that will be used as part of an itinerary that requires service composition.

■ **Note** Many of the receive pipelines make use of the Xml Disassembler component. This component has a property named `AllowUnrecognizedMessage`, which is set to `True` by default. When set to `True`, this tells the component to validate the incoming message against a schema deployed in the BizTalk environment. This default behavior will break the "generic" design of on-ramps since it forces you to have a schema deployed for each and every message. If you are planning to use generic on-ramps, be sure to set this property to `False`.

The Send Pipelines

ItinerarySend and ItinerarySendPassthrough are the two send pipelines that are included in the ESB Toolkit. Both of these pipelines are designed to be used within a two-way solicit-response dynamic. Both of these components contain the ESB Dispatcher component and the ESB Itinerary Cache component. The key function of these pipelines is to store a copy of the outgoing message's itinerary into thc itincrary cache.

Orchestrations

There are two default orchestrations in the ESB Toolkit, and they are designed to implement the orchestration-level version of the Dynamic Mapper and Dynamic Routing Service. If you look into the ESB Toolkit course code, you will find these orchestrations in the ESB.Agents project that is in the Core ➤ Orchestrations solution folder. Orchestrations used to implement ESB services follow the same design:

- They subscribe to messages using the ESB context properties.
- They use the resolver framework to retrieve their runtime information.
- They implement their business function.

- They update the itinerary once they are done processing the message.
- They republish the message back to the Messagebox if there are more services defined in the itinerary.

Delivery Orchestration

The orchestration-level Routing Service is implemented in the Delivery.odx orchestration file. As per ESB orchestration design guidelines, this orchestration subscribes to messages using the ESB context properties (as shown in Figure 15-12).

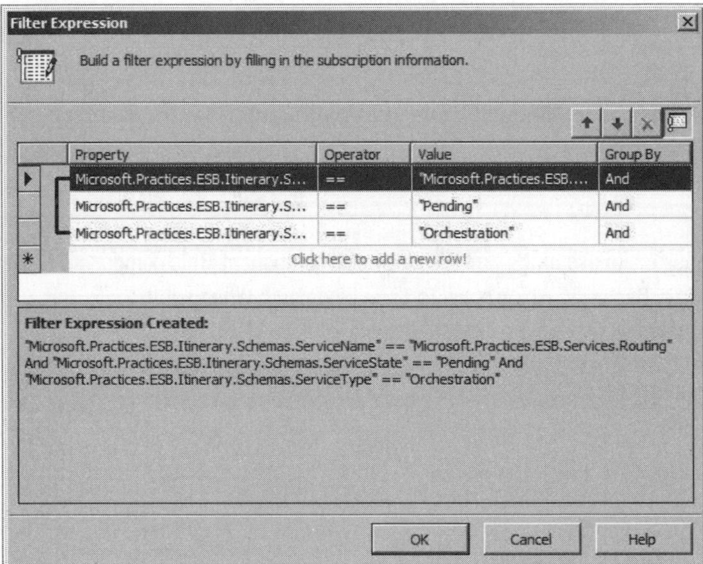

Figure 15-12. *The filter expression used by the first receive shape in the Delivery.odx orchestration*

Transform

The orchestration-level mapping service is implemented in the Transform.odx orchestration file. As per ESB orchestration design guidelines, this orchestration subscribes to messages using the ESB context properties (as shown in Figure 15-13).

If you open this orchestration, you will see that it has three core sections. The first section is in the Get Itinerary and Resolve scope shape. This is where the orchestration calls into the resolver mechanism to retrieve the name of the map it needs to execute.

The second section is in the Execute Map and Advance Itinerary scope shape. In this section, the orchestration performs its actual business function, which is to actually execute the map. It also calls into the `ItineraryHelper` component and asks it to update the message's itinerary. You can see these two steps in Figure 15-14.

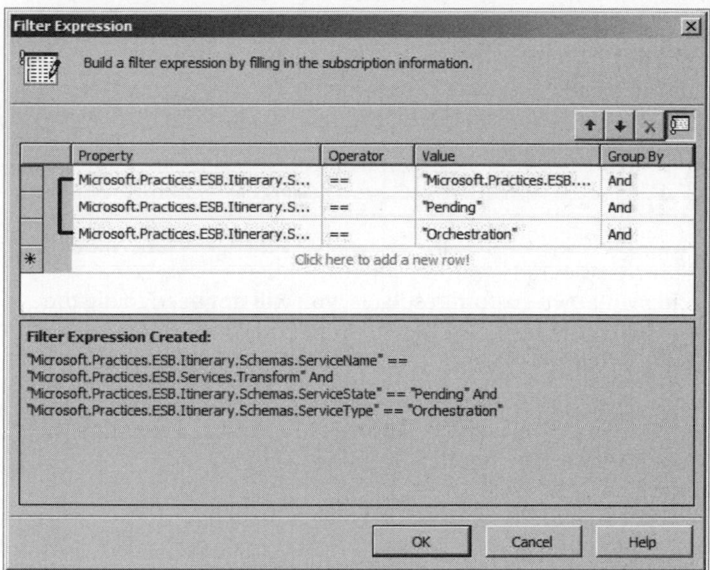

Figure 15-13. *The filter expression used by the first receive shape in the Transform.odx orchestration*

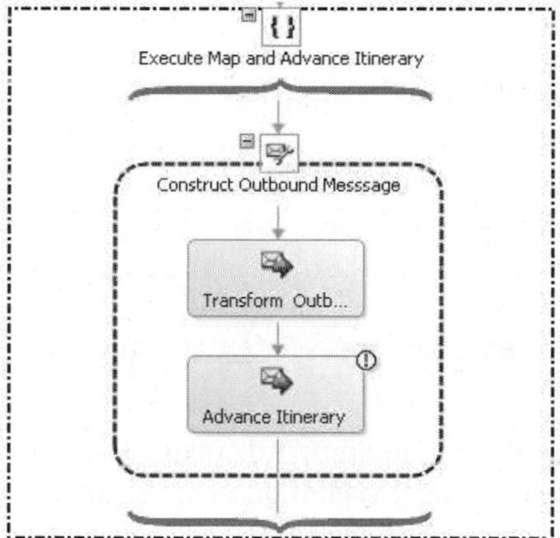

Figure 15-14. *Advancing the itinerary in an orchestration*

In the More Itinerary Steps section, the orchestration is checking to see whether the message has any further ESB services that need to be executed. If it does, then the orchestration uses a direct bound port to publish the message back into the Messagebox.

Caution The orchestration-level Routing Service can be used only for the one-way routing of services. It is not designed to handle two-way request-response message routing. For that, you must use the messaging-level Routing Service.

Resolver Components

Unless you are planning to develop your own custom resolvers, you will not need to dig too deep into the components that are part of the resolver mechanism. The key things to understand is what resolvers are available to you and how you can define connection strings to properly use them.

At runtime, a mediation component provides the Resolver Manager with a connection string that it parses, populates, and validates. It does this by doing the following:

- It parses the connection string to determine which resolver type to load.
- It matches this type to a moniker defined in the ESB's configuration file (the key is the root moniker, such as UDDI or WSMEX).
- It reads the assembly name of the resolver for this moniker.

The following is the connection string to use for the Static resolver:

```
STATIC:\\TransportType=WCF-BasicHttp;
TransportLocation=http://localhost:8081/NewClientService?wsdl;
Action=INewClientService/AddClient;EndpointConfig=;
JaxRpcResponse=False;MessageExchangePattern=;
TargetNamespace=http://tempuri.org/;TransformType=;
```

The following is the connection string to use a string for the UDDI version 2.0 resolver:

```
UDDI:\\ServerUrl=http://localhost/uddi;ServiceKey=;ServiceName=NewClientService;
ServiceProvider=Microsoft.Practices.ESB;
```

Since all these connection strings are already clearly defined in the ESB Toolkit documentation, we will spare you the pain of repeating each of them here. It is enough to understand that a connection string consists of a moniker and a series of parameters.

Beyond simply providing resolvers out of the box for you to use, the resolver framework has also been designed so that you can develop and add your own resolvers without having to recompile any of the existing ESB Toolkit components. The Resolver Manager uses late binding to instantiate resolvers. When it parses an incoming connection string, it compares the string's moniker against its list of registered resolvers to find a match. Resolvers are registered in the BTSNTSvc.exe.config and Machine.config files. When resolvers are registered in these config files, they include the fully qualified name of the .NET assembly that they are implemented by. When the Resolver Manager finds the appropriate resolver in the configuration file, it instantiates a new instance of the requested assembly.

In version 1.0 of the toolkit, you had to know how to create these connections strings manually. Fortunately, in version 2.0 you have great tool in Visual Studio 2008 that can help you build and validate these. (This tool is covered in the "Working with Itineraries" section.) However, it is still a good idea to understand how they work in case you want to extend the toolkit by creating your own resolvers.

Adapter Provider Components

Much like the resolver mechanism, you will not need to dig too deeply into the components that comprise the adapter provider mechanism unless you are interested in creating your own adapter provider.

Business Rule Engine

Once you begin using the ESB Toolkit, the Business Rule Engine takes on significantly more importance than in the past. If you want to perform any kind of "intelligent" resolution of endpoints, maps, or itineraries, you are going to need to use the BRE.

You can think of all the other resolvers as simple "lookup" resolvers. You give them some parameters or keys, and they use this to retrieve corresponding data. They always look up the same data, however. They are not able to make any type of decision for you about what data is needed. You have to make this decision ahead of time and define it in the resolver connection string within your itinerary. This works fine if you know exactly what service you need to route a message to. However, if you need to make a decision at runtime about which service you need, then you need to use the rules engine. An experienced BizTalk developer will know how to perform context-based routing and content-based routing. However, the ESB Toolkit introduces significant changes, and you are going to need to understand how to leverage the Business Rule Engine.

To make it quicker and easier to work with ESB messages in the BRE, the ESB Toolkit includes several new vocabularies that you can use to access ESB-specific information about a message as well as to set ESB-specific properties. In the following section, we will show you how to use these to perform some common tasks.

Resolving an Itinerary Dynamically

One thing that most developers will need to know how to do is to dynamically resolve an itinerary using the Business Rule Engine Itinerary (BRI) resolver. The BRI resolver allows you to pass an incoming message and its context properties into a BRE policy. It then expects that the policy will provide it with the name and version number of the itinerary that needs to be assigned to the message. A developer will need to know how to create the rules that can provide this.

You will need to use the new ESB.Itinerary vocabulary, which allows you to set the name and version of the itinerary that you want to use. This vocabulary provides two core functions called Set Itinerary Name and Set Itinerary Version. You use these functions in the Actions section of a rule to define which itinerary you want to use. Figure 15-15 shows these functions in use.

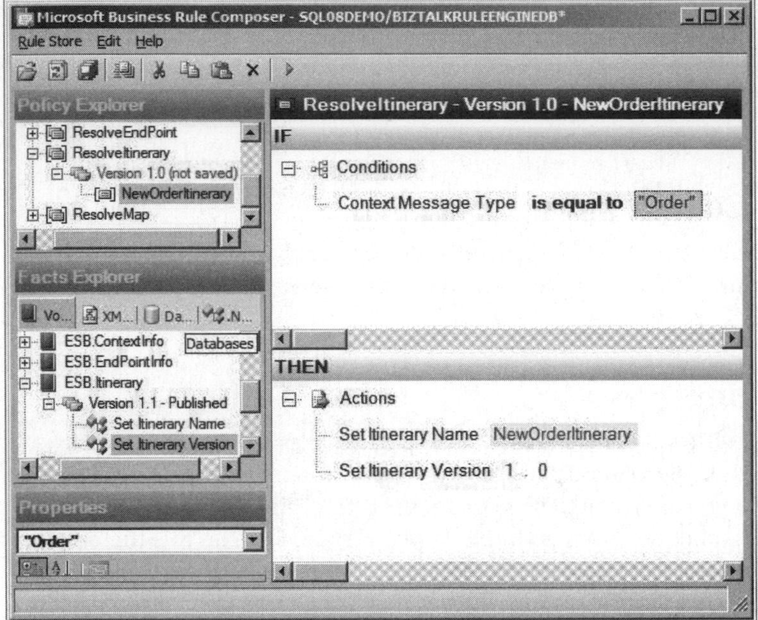

Figure 15-15. *A rule resolving an itinerary that the ESB Itinerary Selector pipeline component will load*

In the previous figure, you can see a rule that has been set up to assign itinerary NewOrderItinerary to a message. In the Conditions section of this rule, you can see that this itinerary will be assigned to a message only if it has a message type of Order. The Context Message Type argument comes from the ESB.ContextInfo vocabulary, which ships with the ESB Toolkit. You can use this vocabulary to access a number of read-only properties associated with the incoming message. Figure 15-16 shows which properties can be accessed.

■ **Note** To invoke the ResolveItinerary policy shown in the Figure 15-15, you would need to use the ESB Itinerary Selector component in one of your on-ramps, and you would provide its ResolverConnectionString parameter with the following: `BRI:\\policy=ResolveItinerary;version=1.0;useMsg=false;`.

The rule shown in Figure 15-15 is a very basic rule, and you can obviously create much more complex conditions that do more than just check the message's type. However, the basic pattern for resolving an itinerary will always be similar to this. You specify a rule condition (likely using definitions from the ESB.ContextInfo vocabulary or by checking data in the message itself), and then you specify the itinerary name and version that you want to load from the Itinerary Database.

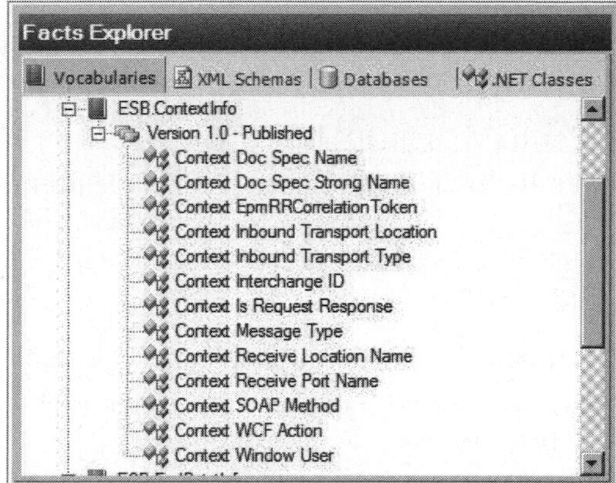

Figure 15-16. *All of the context properties that you can access from the ESB.ContextInfo vocabulary*

Resolving a Map Name Dynamically

Another common task that developers will have to do is to use the rules engine to tell the ESB Transformation Service which map it should run. For this task, you will need to use the ESB.TransformInfo vocabulary. This vocabulary has a function called Set Transform Transform Type where you can set the name of the map that you want to execute. Figure 15-17 shows how you can create a rule that looks at the values of two context properties and then assigns a specific map to run if that rule is two.

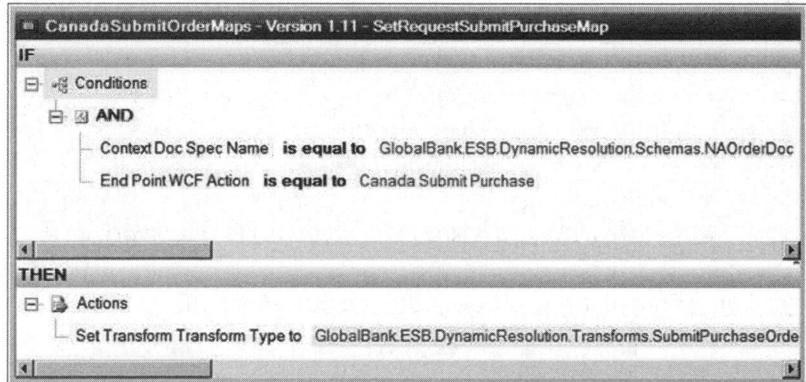

Figure 15-17. *A rule that tells the Transformation Service which map to execute*

In the previous image, the full name of the map is not shown because of its length. The full value that was used is as follows:

```
GlobalBank.ESB.DynamicResolution.Transforms.
SubmitPurchaseOrderResponseCN_To_SubmitOrder
ResponseNA, GlobalBank.ESB.DynamicResolution.Transforms, Version=2.0.0.0,
Culture=neutral,PublicKeyToken=c2c8b2b87f54180a
```

This is a fully qualified name for a BizTalk map, and this is what you have to provide the Set Transform Transform Type function.

Resolving a Service Endpoint Dynamically

The Business Rule Engine can also be used to dynamically resolve the endpoint where a message needs to be routed to. To do this, you will need to use the ESB.EndPointInfo vocabulary. The ESB.EndPointInfo vocabulary gives you the ability to read and write all of the properties that the ESB requires in order to route a message. Figure 15-18 shows the ESB.EndPointInfo vocabulary.

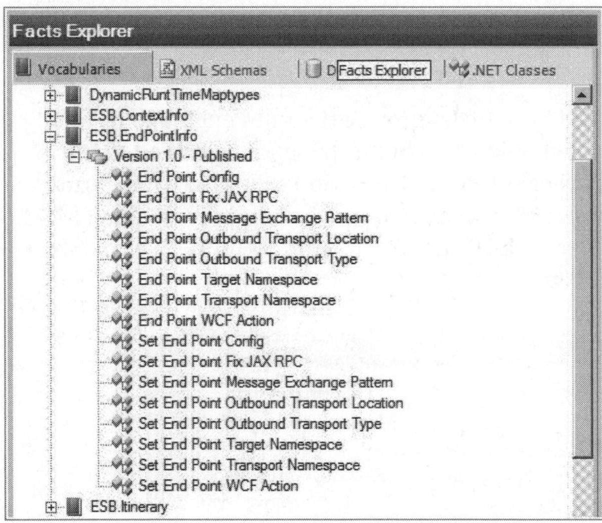

Figure 15-18. *All of the read/write functions exposed by the ESB.EndPointInfo vocabulary*

Depending on what type of endpoint you want to route your message to (that is, FTP, SOAP, WCF, File, and so on), you will need to assign values to different context properties. Figure 15-19 shows how you can create a rule to route a message to a basic SOAP-based web service. You can see that four properties need to be set in order for the ESB to route the message. The Set End Point Outbound Transport Location is used to tell the ESB what the web service's URL is. The Set End Point Outbound Transport Type tells the ESB which adapter provider to use. The Set End Point Target Namespace is where you tell the ESB what namespace the remote web service uses. Finally, the Set End WCF Action is where you can put in which method you need to invoke in the service.

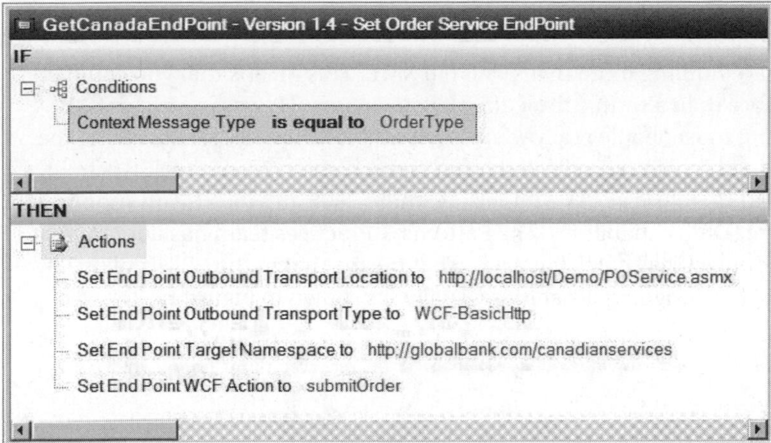

Figure 15-19. *The structure for a rule if you want to route a message to a remote web service*

One last vocabulary that you need to be familiar with is ESB.TransportTypes. In Figure 15-19 you can see that the Transport Type is set to WCF-BasicHttp. The value assigned to the Transport Type must match up with one of the adapter providers that are included in the ESB Toolkit. To make it easier for to assign this valid properly, the ESB.TransportTypes contains a list of all the valid adapter providers. To use this list, expand the ESB.TransportTypes vocabulary, and you will see a vocabulary definition called Adapter Providers. You can drag this Adapter Providers definition and drop it into the argument field for the Set End Point Outbound Transport Type function. Once you do this, you can click the argument, and a drop-down list will appear showing all the default adapter providers. Figure 15-20 shows what this looks like.

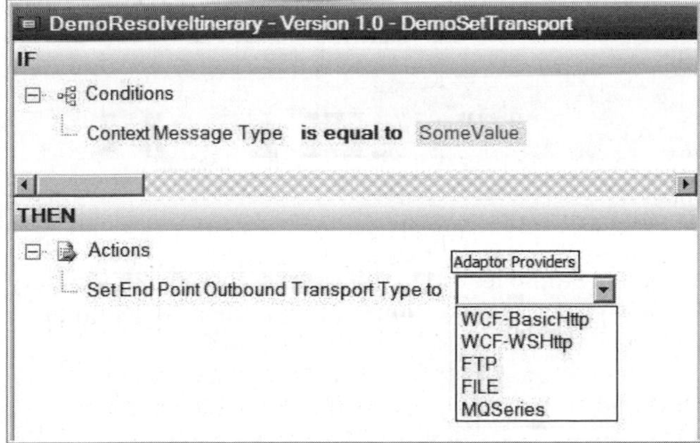

Figure 15-20. *The Adapter Providers list*

Working with Itineraries

At their core, itineraries are nothing more than plain old XML. This means that you could create one using nothing more than a simple text editor if you wanted. However, writing XML manually is not something most people really want to do, and fortunately, version 2.0 of the ESB Toolkit gives you a great tool for visually designing them. Version 2.0 of the ESB is built on top of BizTalk 2009 and therefore works with Visual Studio 2008 and its built-in support for domain-specific language (DSL) capabilities. The Patterns & Practices team has done a great job of defining a new DSL specifically for itineraries. That means that in the ESB Toolkit 2.0 you have a great new tool for designing itineraries visually (as shown in Figure 15-21).

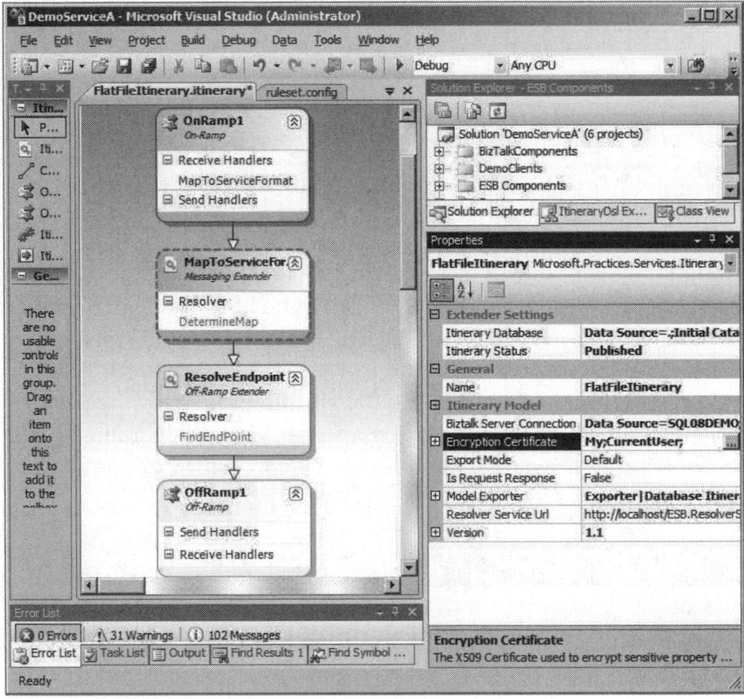

Figure 15-21. *The visual Itinerary Designer*

This design makes use of the usual Visual Studio features, such as the Toolbox for itinerary shapes, the Properties window for configuring itinerary elements, and the Itinerary Explorer for navigating all of the components in your itinerary.

Setting Up a New Itinerary

Start by creating a new project in Visual Studio. You can use any project type (we typically use a class library), and you can use either C# or Visual Basic. You are not going to be compiling this project or writing any code, and you will never need to compile this project, so it does not matter what you select. You are just using the project to hold the itinerary while you have it in Visual Studio. Eventually, you will export this itinerary out of Visual Studio in order to use it.

A new itinerary is be created by right-clicking a project and selecting Add ➤ New ItineraryDSL. Once you have a new itinerary, you will need to set up some basic configuration information for it. Figure 15-22 shows the properties that you can set for your overall itinerary.

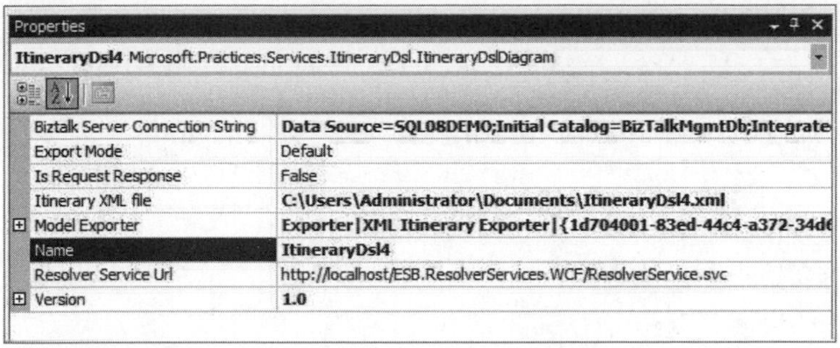

Properties

ItineraryDsl4 Microsoft.Practices.Services.ItineraryDsl.ItineraryDslDiagram

Property	Value
Biztalk Server Connection String	**Data Source=SQL08DEMO;Initial Catalog=BizTalkMgmtDb;Integrate**
Export Mode	Default
Is Request Response	False
Itinerary XML file	**C:\Users\Administrator\Documents\ItineraryDsl4.xml**
⊞ Model Exporter	**Exporter | XML Itinerary Exporter | {1d704001-83ed-44c4-a372-34d**
Name	**ItineraryDsl4**
Resolver Service Url	http://localhost/ESB.ResolverServices.WCF/ResolverService.svc
⊞ Version	**1.0**

Figure 15-22. *The property window for an itinerary*

Beyond setting the initial version and name for this itinerary, you are going to need to set up the BizTalk Server Connection String. The Itinerary Designer is able to connect directly into a BizTalk environment, which will ultimately make the job of designing itineraries much easier.

One example of this is when you want to use an off-ramp in your itinerary. Doing so means that your itinerary will have an XML structure like the following.

```
<Service uuid="0e1d2b42c9564352b6878accc290fe52" beginTime=""completeTime=""
  name="DynamicOffRamp" type="Messaging"
state="Pending" isRequestResponse="false" position="2"
serviceInstanceId="" />
```

For this to work, the values for the `name`, `type`, `state`, and `isRequestRequest` attributes need to have the exact same values as the ones set up in the off-ramps filters. Figure 15-23 shows these filters.

Since the XML values match the values in the send ports, then this itinerary will be able to route a message to this off-ramp.

Now, manually having to set up these values in the itinerary can be slow and painful. However, since the designer can connect directly into the BizTalk environment, it is capable of pulling down these values directly from the send port. All you need to do is to say which send port you want to use, and this data is extracted for you and added to your itinerary.

There are a number of other areas where the designer can connect to BizTalk as well as other remote servers to make your design-time experience much nicer. These are some other examples:

- When building a Static resolver for the mapping service, the tool will provide you with a list of all the maps that have been deployed into BizTalk.
- The tool can connect into remote UDDI servers and allow you to select a web service when you are defining a UDDI resolver.
- When building a BRE resolver, the tool will provide you with a list of all the available policies.

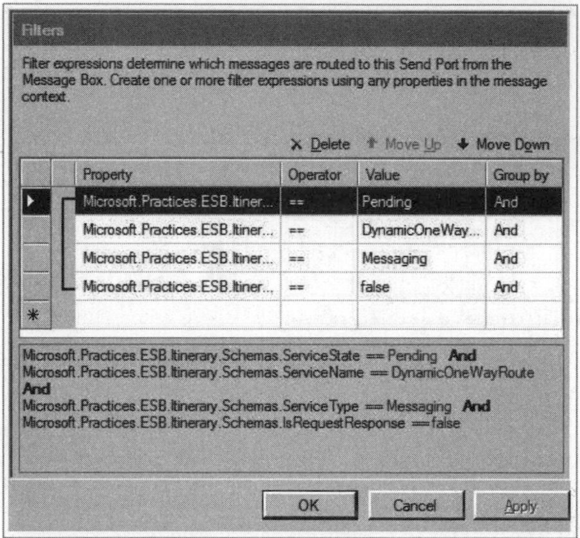

Figure 15-23. *The filter expression used by a send port*

In addition to setting up this BizTalk Service Connection String, you will also need to specify an export model for your itinerary. Itineraries can be exported automatically via an XML file or the Itinerary Database. If you select the database option, then you will need to provide a connection string for the ItineraryDb database. Once you have set this property, you can export an itinerary by right-clicking anywhere on the design surface and selecting Export Model.

Since the itineraries you design using this tool are eventually going to be exported and converted into plain old XML, you may face a security issue. These itineraries may contain sensitive data or processes that should not be easily readable by just anyone. To address this issue, the Itinerary Designer allows you to assign a certificate to your itinerary that will be used to encrypt it during the export process. In the Properties window for your itinerary, you will see a property named Encryption Certificate. This property allows you to select a specific certificate from a specific certificate store to use for the encryption process.

When setting up your itinerary, one last step you will want to take is to check the Resolver service Url property. This should contain the URL of the ESB Resolver service. This will be very important later when you want to be able to test your resolvers from within Visual Studio.

Defining Your Itinerary

The Itinerary Designer is a relatively complex tool, and it can't be covered adequately in a few pages. Fortunately, the ESB Toolkit ships with a number of prebuilt itinerary models that you can use to fully understand this tool. Assuming you have installed the toolkit source to `C:\projects` as per the default installation instructions, you can find these samples at C:\Projects\Microsoft.Practices.ESB\Source\Samples\Itinerary\Source\ESB.Itinerary.Library. This section will cover the high-level basics concepts of the tool.

Defining an itinerary is composed of two core activities:

- Adding and configuring the on-ramps, off-ramps, and Itinerary Services that you want your itinerary to have
- Defining resolves for each of the Itinerary Services

To add an on-ramp, off-ramp, or Itinerary Service, you simply drag the require shape from the toolbox onto the design surface. As you click each shape that you have added, the Properties window will show you a list of all the properties you need to configure for that component. For on-ramps, you need to start by setting the Extender property equal to `on-ramp ESB Service Extension`. Once you do this, the Properties window will change, and the designer will retrieve a list of all available applications from the BizTalk environment. Once you select an application, you will be given a list of all available on-ramps that have been configured in that application. To use the default ESB on-ramps, you would need to select the Microsoft.Practices.ESB application, at which point you will be able to select one of the default on-ramps.

Adding an off-ramp follows pretty much the same process. You add the shape to the design surface, you select a BizTalk application, and then you select a send port that exists in that application. Once you do that, the designer will retrieve a bunch of data about that port, and the designer will include it in your itinerary. Figure 15-24 shows the data that the designer retrieved from BizTalk, once a specific send port is selected.

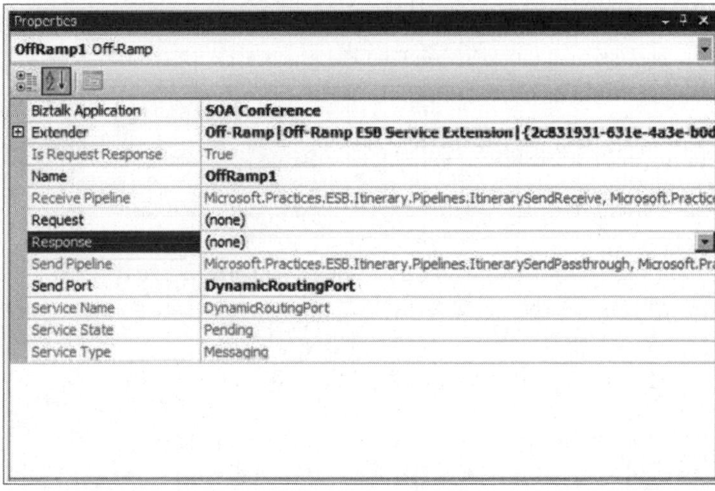
Properties

OffRamp1 Off-Ramp

Biztalk Application	SOA Conference
Extender	Off-Ramp|Off-Ramp ESB Service Extension|{2c831931-631e-4a3e-b0d
Is Request Response	True
Name	OffRamp1
Receive Pipeline	Microsoft.Practices.ESB.Itinerary.Pipelines.ItinerarySendReceive, Microsoft.Practic
Request	(none)
Response	(none)
Send Pipeline	Microsoft.Practices.ESB.Itinerary.Pipelines.ItinerarySendPassthrough, Microsoft.Pr
Send Port	DynamicRoutingPort
Service Name	DynamicRoutingPort
Service State	Pending
Service Type	Messaging

Figure 15-24. *The Properties window for an off-ramp that has been added to an itinerary*

In this case, we selected the DynamicRoutingPort that we had already set up in the BizTalk environment. You can see that the designer pulled down information about the values that this port is looking for with regard to the ESB context properties.

The Itinerary Service shape, as you might expect, allows you to add a new service to your itinerary. When you add this shape, you need to specify whether it a messaging-level service, orchestration-level service, or off-ramp service. If you define the service is an off-ramp service, then you need to define where this service should run. This is done setting the Itinerary Service's Container property, and you will need to select an off-ramp that has already been added to the itinerary. If this is a messaging- or orchestration-level service, then you will need to specify which service should be run. Using the Service Name property, you can select either the Routing Service or the Transform Service. If this is a messaging-level service, you will again need to specify where this service will run. You can select a send or receive pipeline for either an on-ramp or off-ramp for this.

You can add as many different Itinerary Services to the design surface as you require. To connect all of these on-ramps, off-ramps, and Itinerary Services, you need to use the Connector component. The connectors show the flow of the messages across your various services. Figure 15-25 shows how an on-ramp, an Itinerary Service (which implements the Transformation Service), another Itinerary Service (which implements the Routing Service), and an off-ramp have been connected together to create an itinerary that dynamically maps and routes a message. (Note that this is a one-way itinerary, but you can use the Itinerary Designer to create a synchronous request/response message flow.)

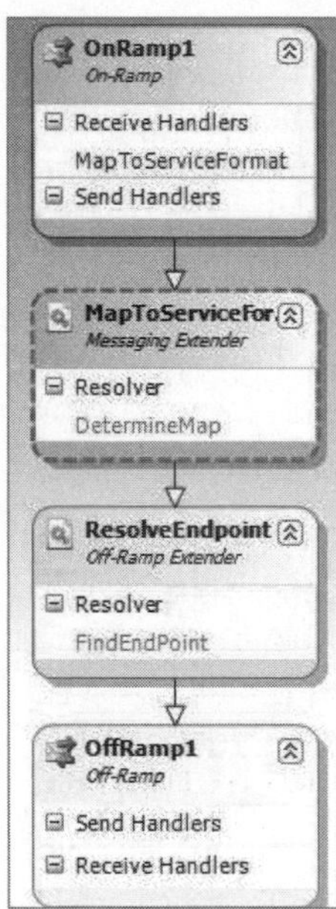

Figure 15-25. *A sample itinerary model*

Once you have defined and connected all your on-ramps, off-ramps, and services, you will need to start adding in your resolvers. To add a resolver, right-click an itinerary service, and select Add New Resolver from the context window that appears. This resolver will appear in your service. When you click this service, its properties will appear in the Properties window. If you click the Resolver Implement property, you will be given a drop-down list containing all of the registered resolvers. After you pick the one that you want, the Properties window will update and will now contain the properties for the resolver that you selected. You need to assign all of these properties to properly configure your resolver.

Once you have done this, then a properly structure resolver connection string will have been added to your itinerary.

Validating and Testing

You can also use the designer to validate your itineraries and test your resolvers. To validate an entire itinerary, you can right-click anywhere on the design service and select Validate All from the context window. Any errors with your itinerary will be output to the usual Visual Studio Error List window. If you want to validate a single service, on-ramp, or off-ramp, you can simply right-click it and select Validate. Any errors with this one component will be shown in the Error List window. Both of these validation processes are simply checking the overall structure of your itinerary.

When it comes to resolvers, you very likely want to be able to see the data that these resolvers are returning before you deploy your itinerary out to the ESB. Fortunately, because the designer is able to connect the live resolver mechanism by way of the Resolver Web Service, you can do this. To test a resolver, simply right-click it, and select Test Resolver Configuration. If an error occurs, it will be shown in the Error List window. If the resolver runs successfully, then the data is collected will be shown in the output window.

Now, testing the BRE resolver is slightly more complex than this since it allows you to pass in a message as part of the resolver process. Fortunately, the designer allows you to test this behavior as well by assigning a test message to use when the resolver is tested. You can assign this message by setting the Message File property of the resolver. To assign this property, you provide it with the path to an XML file that contains the message you want to use.

Using the Toolkit

This chapter is obviously very heavy on the theory and mechanisms that make up the ESB Toolkit 2.0. When writing this chapter, we had a difficult decision to make on what we wanted to focus on. We could either focus on the theory and design of the toolkit take more of a "how-to" focus where we walked you through common use cases. We made the decision to focus on the theory since we decided the toolkit introduced enough new concepts that if you did not understand the theory, then you would not be able to fully appreciate or take advantage of the toolkit. We also knew that the toolkit already ships with a number of detailed how-tos. Our hope is that once you have read this chapter, those how-tos will make more sense to you, and you will better understand the ultimate engine that the toolkit provides. To find these how-tos, you will need to download the ESB Toolkit 2.0 documentation and browse to the "Development Activities" topic under the "Creating Itineraries Using Itinerary Designer" section. These how-tos walk you through the most common use-case scenarios that you will run into and are a great next step to take once you have finished this chapter.

Summary

This chapter explored the concepts that the ESB Toolkit for BizTalk server introduces. You looked at four architectural concepts that the toolkit uses to extend BizTalk into the ESB world. These were mediation services, mediation policies, resolvers, and adapter providers.

The goal of these components is to deliver a BizTalk environment that makes use of reusable, generic components to create flexibly and agile environments well suited to web service–focused integration.

You then examined the different components that implement these four concepts, and you looked at how each of these components worked and contributed to processing an itinerary.

You also reviewed the new designer tool that the ESB Toolkit exposes in Visual Studio 2008 and showed how it can be used to visual design and validate new itineraries.

A key thought to take away after this chapter is that ESB Toolkit is not a new self-contained product. It is a series of components that can be used together to form a comprehensive Enterprise Service Bus. But it is also a series of individual reusable components that implement a series of best practices when it comes to designing BizTalk components. You can choose to use some of the pieces or all of them. The ESB Toolkit is about providing you with a flexible framework for implementing ESB functionality in whatever form you might require.

Index

B

D

E

■F

G

O

P

T

U

X

Y

Z